The Idea of the University
Volume 1

GLOBAL STUDIES IN EDUCATION

A.C. (Tina) Besley, Michael A. Peters,
Cameron McCarthy, Fazal Rizvi
General Editors

Vol. 17

The Global Studies in Education series is part of the Peter Lang Education list.
Every volume is peer reviewed and meets
the highest quality standards for content and production.

PETER LANG
New York • Bern • Frankfurt • Berlin
Brussels • Vienna • Oxford • Warsaw

The Idea of the University

A Reader

Volume 1

Edited by
Michael A. Peters and Ronald Barnett

With the assistance of
Richard Heraud

PETER LANG
New York • Bern • Frankfurt • Berlin
Brussels • Vienna • Oxford • Warsaw

Library of Congress Cataloging-in-Publication Data

Names: Peters, Michael (Michael A.), editor. | Barnett, Ronald, editor.
Title: The idea of the university: a reader, vol. 1 / edited by
Michael A. Peters, Ronald Barnett.
Description: New York: Peter Lang, 2018.
Series: Global studies in education; vol. 17 | ISSN 2153-330X
Includes bibliographical references and index.
Identifiers: LCCN 2016023379 | ISBN 978-1-4331-2191-3 (hardcover: alk. paper) |
ISBN 978-1-4331-2190-6 (pbk.: alk. paper) | ISBN 978-1-4539-1888-3 (ebook pdf)
ISBN 978-1-4331-3646-7 (epub) | ISBN 978-1-4331-3647-4 (mobi)
Subjects: LCSH: Education, Higher—Aims and objectives.
Classification: LCC LB2322.2.I33 | DDC 378—dc23
LC record available at https://lccn.loc.gov/2016023379
DOI 10.3726/978-1-4539-1888-3

Bibliographic information published by **Die Deutsche Nationalbibliothek.**
Die Deutsche Nationalbibliothek lists this publication in the "Deutsche Nationalbibliografie"; detailed bibliographic data are available on the Internet at http://dnb.d-nb.de/.

29 Broadway, 18th floor, New York, NY 10006
www.peterlang.com

Table of Contents

Preface

This volume of *The Idea of the University* has gone through many iterations. It began when I co-taught a course with Prof Fazal Rizvi at the University of Illinois Urbana-Champaign in the mid-2000s that became a class that everyone enjoyed. It was based on excerpts from some of the greatest Western philosophers going back to Kant and Humboldt on the idea of the modern research university. At that point I tried to get the project started and conceived of it as a class and then group project started but other things got in the way. Over the intervening years I built up an archive of selected texts and a bibliography. It became clear that there was a need for such a book and that there was not a collection like the one I had envisaged. I mentioned the project to Ron Barnett at the London Institute and to Chris Myers at Peter Lang and both were enthusiastic about the project. Ron brought to the project his customary discipline and insight. Chris saw in the idea a workable project and provided his support and guidance. Later, Farideh Koohi, Sarah Bode and Timothy Swenarton at Peter Lang took over and expressed confidence in the project to see it through to final production.

The resulting volume has taken us a great deal longer than we expected. The project as grown in different ways with what seemed like interminable discussions over the selections and exact excerpts. Procuring the texts, locating the copyright holders and procuring the permissions also was a time-consuming business.

Professor Roger Moltzen the, then, Dean Faculty of Education generously provided funds to pay for half the copyright permissions. I used my personal research funds to pay for the others. I wish to personally thank him and the Faculty for his generosity. Also I would like to thank Professor Bronwen Cowie, Director of the Wilf Malcolm Institute of Educational Research (WMIER) for her support and encouragement. Finally, I would like to thank both Ronald Barnett my co-editor for his expertise and Richard Heraud for his research assistance on a project that was much larger and more complex than any of us ever imagined.

MP
21 March 2017

Introduction

The Very Idea of the University

MICHAEL A. PETERS AND RONALD BARNETT

An evolving canon

Higher education is a global phenomenon. It is found in almost every country of the world, some two hundred million people are directly involved in it, it consumes billions of dollars in some countries alone, it is engaged with economic and social institutions and is a matter of public and political debate both nationally and internationally. Under neoliberalism it has recently become central to debates concerning the engine of innovation and its contribution to the economy. Disputes over higher education have even played a significant part in leading to the overthrow of governments. Every major town looks, it seems, to have its own university. *As an institution*, therefore, higher education is a major force. Separately, the university as an idea—the very *idea of the university*—has spawned a literature which began its modern development around two hundred years ago, a literature that has steadily evolved over time, although we can point to the medieval university dating from the establishment of Bologne in 1088 and ancient centres of learning that go back to the origins of classical civilizations. However, that literature on the idea of the university is seldom a point of reference in the contemporary debates over higher education. University systems have mushroomed and universities have been established and developed with very little in the way of a consciousness that there is a long-standing literature that might inform the debate. There is a blankness towards that literature. The university qua institution takes little heed of the university qua idea.

We wish, therefore, with this present volume, to help in addressing this situation. We have assembled here extracts from many of the seminal writings on the idea of the university over the past two centuries. In doing so, we are trying to achieve a number of purposes. *Firstly*, to our knowledge, there has never been an attempt to bring together the leading contributions to the debate, revealing its history to the present time. At one level, therefore, we wish as stated simply to redress a gap in the literature.

Secondly, and by extension, we want to bring into view a literature that is seldom recognized in the policy and practical spheres, even though it is relevant to the development the university. It is certainly the case that references to, say, von Humboldt and Newman are to be seen in the contemporary debate. But (i) while those contemporary references are characteristically made to one or the other—there is seldom if ever an attempt made to place together von Humboldt and Newman and the different (Germanic and English) traditions that serve as their textual context; (ii) there are many other writings in the literature that are unfairly lost from view; and (iii) the writings of von Humboldt and of Newman can properly only be appreciated when placed in the larger debates of which they are part and which continued to evolve after their work (in the early and mid-nineteenth centuries).

Thirdly, we want to show that the literature on the idea of the university has an integrity of its own. Many works over the last two hundred years have had 'The idea of the university' as their title—or some variant on that theme. But much more than that, the works present in this volume are characteristically engaging with a common set of themes, such as knowledge, reason and human and social development, and so have come to constitute a canon. A 'canon', after all, depicts a musical form precisely in which subjects are picked up and developed in successive waves of interpretation and variation. So here too.

Fourthly, we wish to draw attention to the contribution of philosophy to contemporary debates given that the discourse concerning the idea of the university is philosophical in nature concerned not only with questions of knowledge, purposes and moral ideals but also with specific concepts such as *Bildung* that concern the transformation of subjectivity of students, the use of public reason and question of citizenship within an emerging global society.

Fifthly, this volume emphasizes that while the discourse of the Idea of the university is a tradition some two hundred years old, it is an *open and living tradition* with contributions from the leading scholars of the age such as Habermas, Derrida, Lyotard, Said and Readings. We mention this aspect because the Idea of the university has the power to transform ideals even within the contemporary policy environment when the options seem to be effectively closed off and solidified around the form of the neoliberal university.

The idea of a canon

The Idea of the University has been represented in a range of edited texts, seminal essays and a critical tradition dating from Kant who with Descartes inaugurates the tradition of modern philosophy. Sometimes, borrowing the concept from Biblical and literary studies, this critical tradition is referred to as a 'canon'—indeed the idea of the philosophical canon is associated with the Western tradition in general. Inevitably perhaps, and especially since the 1960s, the notion of the canon and canon-formation has led to questions concerning *authority*—who should have the power to determine what works are worth reading and teaching? This is a question above all about the university, about the taken for granted assumptions concerning the seemingly mundane and ritualistic practices of readings lists, of courses, of curricula in general. The canon is seen as a unitary tradition and yet increasingly the politics and ethics of anthologization, and of the selection of texts, writers and philosophers, have been questioned by those who belong to the critical tradition defined in the widest sense—feminists, critical theorists, deconstructionists, postcolonialists and others. This process and tradition of questioning also has its own canon but part of the effect of the criticism has been to recognize that there are different kinds of canon and canon-formation. Canons are formed for very different reasons: for controlling and transmitting a cultural heritage, for legitimating a particular worldview, for creating a common frame of reference or unconsciously in terms of a formation of preference. While canons change and it is a critical educational and philosophical task to inquire how the canon was created, who created it and by what authority. The canon also implicitly can be seen in terms of the aesthetic and philosophical criteria used for the selection of texts deemed worthy of study within a culture.

The book of readings presented here follows this heuristic model: it does not deny the ideological effects of the canon, nor its theological values such as the norming of the importance of a literary culture for the education of the young but it does provide within the context of a book a number of chapters based on those expressions of the Idea of the University within the national (and nationalistic) traditions of Germany, the United Kingdom, America and France. There are many gaps, holes, omissions, and exclusions both within these national traditions as we have represented them. There are many European cultures and languages that have strong university traditions not mentioned here. In one sense we cannot dispense without the notion of the canon even although under the force of criticism we are driven to acknowledge its cultural production, reception, and its role in the formation of the disciplines (Fishelov, 2010; Damrosch & D'haen, 2011; Gorak, 2013).

While the question of the canon is in part a question of who is privileged, and invoked and thereby, through the logic of exclusion who is silenced and marginalised, it is also an evaluation of what texts are important and which have become recognized as providing the measuring stick for an idea or philosophy. Canon (κανών, όνος, ὁ; *kanṓn*) in the Greek means measuring standard, a rule, norm, principle or law, that in the early Church quickly became its 'consensual theology.' We can say that our selections are according to the national traditions we have arranged are strategic texts based on consensual agreement, often implicit and deeply philosophical and expressive of certain universal ideals of the university as an institution that transcends its age.

All collections of readings constituted by the selection of 'strategic texts' are implicitly involved in periodizations of history and constructions of historical narratives. The anthology of the modern university is no different. All systems of periodization are more or less arbitrary: some are defined by the magical decimal systems of decades as though history is episodic and naturally divided into handy decades—the 1960s, the 1970s etc.—reflecting our cultural predilections for the seemingly inherited 'natural' divisions of the Gregorian Christian calendar. Other periods are named after kings and queens—'the Victorian era'—or influential individuals—'the Kantian university', 'the Humboldtian University' or 'Newman's Idea of the University'. Some follow numerical conventions of carving off the modern age from the medieval and the classical, and then categorizing it as early, middle and late. Again, other have taken a more normative stance to talk of stages in a Marxist or literary sense—premodern, modern, late modern of postmodern—as though there is some implicit historical unfolding of an idea or practice.

We have decided to proceed pragmatically. Given that this is a selection of texts about the Idea of the modern university—that is a philosophical discourse, rather than a historical one—we have been guided by the canon that has become established over the years, beginning with the founding texts and discourse of the university in different national traditions, passing through the Enlightenment and scientific revolution, to the establishment and spread of modern university institutions during the nineteenth and twentieth centuries, leading to the contemporary period of global forms of the entrepreneurial, enterprise, and innovation forms of university under the sway of neoliberalism.

The Idea of the University establishes the founding discourses of the modern university not in its early modern form but rather in relation to 'reason' and 'enlightenment.' The idea of a university in which teaching and research were first combined in the search for impartial truth reached classic form in nineteenth-century Germany, and eventually became the dominant model that became influential in a global sense. Intellectual freedom in research and teaching, university autonomy, the growth of independent disciplines with their own standards and priorities, and a kind of cosmopolitanism established the parameters of the university as a liberal institution comprised the basic features that came to characterize the university institution.

The notion of a canon has led to questions concerning *authority*—who should have the power to determine which works are worth reading and teaching? It has also led to questions about legitimation—by which criteria are works being picked out as constitutive of a canon? These questions are especially apt in relation to the university, where taken for granted assumptions have permanently to be held under review. Increasingly, any selection of texts can be questioned by those who belong to critical traditions defined in the widest sense—feminists, critical theorists, deconstructionists, postcolonialists and others from non-Western traditions. Further, canons change, and it is a legitimate educational and philosophical task to inquire how a canon has been created, who created it and by what authority. These questions about the construction of the canon also indicate how we can proceed or how the canon itself can accommodate differences from outside it.

The selection of readings presented here is proffered against the background of such considerations. It does not deny the ideological aspects of the selection (with its undoubted partialities), nor its theological linkages (after all, many universities have had faith and church origins), nor the question-begging character of any such selection. We readily admit, therefore, to there being many gaps, holes, omissions, and exclusions both within this selection. There are many cultures and languages that have strong university traditions not included here. We acknowledge, accordingly, the questionable nature of the canon, as we present it here, including its cultural production, reception, role in the formation of the disciplines (Fishelov, 2010; Damrosch & D'haen, 2011; Gorak, 2013). Nevertheless, we consider that the texts included here could be said to constitute prima facie membership of a canon devoted to the idea of the university. Each offers a particular articulation of the idea of the university—so revealing that, over time, the canon has provided a multiplicity of idea*s* of the university.

We have proceeded pragmatically. Given that this is a selection of texts about the Idea of the University—really, the idea of the modern university—we have been guided by the thread of debates over the last two hundred years, beginning with the founding texts in different national traditions, passing through the Enlightenment and scientific revolution, to the establishment and spread of modern university institutions during the nineteenth and twentieth centuries. We bring the story up-to-date with texts that reflect the contemporary global forms of mass, multi-faculty, entrepreneurial and digital forms of the university under the sway of neoliberalism.

Within these readings, there is a story or, rather, an integrated set of stories, therefore. The Idea of the University was initially elaborated as a self-conscious idea of the university at the beginning of the nineteenth century. If there was a central concern in this founding set of discourses of the modern university, it was perhaps that of 'reason.' This concern took institutional form in Germany in the early nineteenth century, in which teaching and research were first combined in the search for impartial truth. Subsequently, this institutional form became the dominant model that remained influential in a global sense until well into the twentieth century. Intellectual freedom in research and teaching, university autonomy, the growth of independent disciplines with their own standards and priorities, and a kind of cosmopolitanism established the parameters of the university as a liberal institution comprised the basic features that came to characterize the university institution.

While there are significant differences across the texts represented here, more striking is the overlap between them across time and across national traditions. Themes characteristically present in the writings here include those of knowledge, truth and the mind and their relationships, intellectual freedom, human and social development, culture, reason and the relationship between universities and the wider society. Crucial sub-themes are those of teaching, understanding, students and research, inquiry and disciplines. This has been more than a loose assembly of themes for, in their pursuit of these themes, these writings sought to advance a particular conception of the university, namely—and as implied—a university imbued with the spirit of reason. Through its association with reason, it was considered that the university could play a major role in the elevation of humanity and, indeed, the world. (A favourite metaphor of Newman in England was that of 'ascent'.) However, especially in the last fifty years (towards the end of the twentieth century and the advance into the twenty-first century), the attachment to the university of reason has loosened as other ideas—and forms—of the university have made their appearance. The university of utility, markedly in the entrepreneurial university and the performative university, have appeared as ideas.

This volume is the first of two volumes. As indicated, this first volume contains extracts from historically important writings—and writers—on the idea of the university. The second volume contains specially commissioned chapters from some of the most influential contemporary writers who have been wrestling with the nature of the university in the twenty-first century. This volume (volume one of the two volumes), accordingly, is in a way deliberately situated in the past. Is this collection, therefore, as it might pejoratively be felt, merely of historical interest? Worse still, only of 'academic' interest? We believe to the contrary. The canon of writings on the idea of the university constitutes even a great tradition in that it contains reflections and concerns that are pertinent to the considerations about the evolution of the university in the twenty-first century. Issues of the purposes of universities are matters of public debate today: what kind of knowledge might be central to universities? How might its connection with the development of students be construed? Does the concept of culture carry any weight today? What is the point of research? How, if at all, might or should universities engage with the wider society? On all these matters—and many others—the writings here have things to say and which speak to us, even across two centuries.

Of course, at the limit, the selection here could have been otherwise. But many, if not most of the texts, presented themselves without challenge. A volume such as this would have been manifestly incomplete without inclusions from Kant's *The Conflict of the Faculties*, von Humboldt's statement about *University Reform in Germany*, Newman's *The Idea of the University*, Heidegger's inaugural lecture on *The Self-Assertion of the German Universities*, Jaspers' *The Idea of the University*, and Ortega and Gasset's *Mission of the University*. Whatever one's view of these individual texts, they have undeniably been influential in shaping the ideational landscape of the university over the past two hundred years.

Thereafter, certainly, choices have come into play. A key influence here lay in our sense that the major writings on the university have not only helped to shape but have also been shaped by their unfolding context social and institutional context. Accordingly, the great tradition—of writings on the idea of the university turns out to constitute several lines of thought. Four such sub-traditions stand out for us, those of Germany, England, the United States and the French postmodern perspective.

The German idea of the university

The University of Berlin was founded in 1810 by the Prussian linguist and philosopher Wilhelm von Humboldt, whose humanist version of the university served as a model for the rest of Europe and for the West more generally.[1] As a philosopher

1 For a list of modern universities in Europe (1801–1845) see the webpage http://en.wikipedia.org/wiki/List_of_modern_universities_in_Europe_(1801%E2%80%931945 that indicates that after the establishment of Bologne at the end of the twelfth century

Humboldt had written a treatise on the limits of State action and defended the principles of public education in 1792 as an extension of the liberties of the Enlightenment, asserting 'the ultimate task of our existence is to give the fullest possible content to the concept of humanity in our own person [...] through the impact of actions in our own lives' (*Gesammelte Schriften*, I, p. 283).

By the time that Humboldt founded the University of Berlin in 1810 there were already some 125 universities established in Europe. What distinguished the model of the University of Berlin was the 'Universitas litterarum' that was intended to achieve a *unity* of teaching and research and provide students with an all-round humanist education. Humboldt was influenced by Johann Gottlieb Fichte, the first vice chancellor of the University, Friedrich Schleiermacher, Schiller and Goethe.

> At the outset, Berlin University had the four classical faculties of Law, Medicine, Philosophy and Theology. The first academic term began with 256 students and 52 academic staff. Professors such as Georg Friedrich Wilhelm Hegel (Philosophy), Karl Friedrich von Savigny (Law), August Boeckh (Classical Philology), Christoph Wilhelm Hufeland (Medicine) and Albrecht Daniel Thaer (Agriculture) shaped the profile of the individual faculties in accordance with Humboldt's concept.[2]

Against the bloody background and mass executions of the aftermath of the French Revolution Friedrich von Schiller (1794) writes *Letters on the Aesthetic Education of Man* where he provides a theory on the moral development of mankind that springs from the aesthetic state.[3] Schiller attacks 'Kant's belief that morality can only be achieved by negating man's negative sensuous impulses and proposed instead that we should educate the emotions of man, in order to bring them into harmony with reason.' As William Wertz (2005) points out 'For Schiller, a human being who has achieved such harmony, by transforming his selfish, infantile erotic

---

there were some 13 established in the thirteenth century (France, English, Italy, Spain & Portugal), 17 in the fourteenth century (same countries and in addition Germany, Austria, Czech Republic, Hungary, and Poland), 27 in the fifteenth century (in addition, Scotland, Belgium, Slovakia, Switzerland & Denmark), 31 in the sixteenth century (in addition, Russia, Netherlands, Ukraine, Lithuania, Ireland and Malta), 20 in the seventeenth century (in addition, Estonia, Finland, Sweden, and Croatia), 9 in the eighteenth century, 60 in the nineteenth century (in addition, Serbia, Slovenia, Norway, Wales, Greece, Belgium, Northern Ireland, Romania, and Bulgaria), 60 in the twentieth century (in addition, Iceland, Belarus, Georgia, Latvia, Armenia, Finland, and Moldova).

2 See https://www.hu-berlin.de/ueberblick-en/history/huben_html

3 See Modern History Sourcebook at http://legacy.fordham.edu/halsall/mod/schiller-education.asp

emotions into *agape* of truth, justice, and beauty, is a "beautiful soul"' (p. 81). Philosophy is thus recast as aesthetics and proceeds from considerations of beauty as a means of reaching a truly aesthetic state of mind (Wertz, 2005, p. 82). There is no doubt that this vision exercised a strong influence over Humboldt who twenty five years after Schiller's death publishes 'On Schiller and the Course of His Spiritual Development,' as an introduction to a book of their correspondence:

> concerning the concept of beauty, concerning the aesthetic in creation and action, and thus the foundations of art, as well as art itself, these works contain everything essential in a manner which can never possibly be excelled. (p. 537, cited in Wertz, 2005, p. 82)

The German idea of the university was born in the new research-centered university known as the 'Humboldtian' university that emerged from German idealist and Romantic philosophy. As Marek Kwiek (2006) argues:

> There are three main principles of the modern university to be found in the founding fathers of the University of Berlin. The first principle is the unity of research and teaching (*die Einheit von Forschung und Lehre*); the second is the protection of academic freedom: the freedom to teach (*Lehrfreiheit*) and the freedom to learn (*Lernfreiheit*); and the third is the central importance of the faculty of philosophy (the faculty of Arts and Sciences in modern terminology) ... The three principles are developed, to varying degrees, in Schelling, Fichte, Schleiermacher and Wilhelm von Humboldt. Together, the three principles have guided the modern institution of the university through the 19th century to the 20th century. (p. 5)

In this configuration the University is granted autonomy from the State as an essential premise of its development: culture, freedom and learning trumps the State. *Bildung* is the basis for a national self-knowledge rooted in the search for truth and a kind of virtue or spiritual vocation. The German 'Humboldtian' research-university recovers the idea of the university from its medieval closed mind and rescued the institution that was perilously close to the prospect of its demise. Thus Timothy Bahti in his 'Histories of the University: Kant and Humboldt' describes the situation of the German universities of the period in the following way:

> the eighteenth [century] had been a lowpoint for German universities: unruly students, dropping enrollments, little apparent correlation between subjects taught and post-university positions available, financial marginality, etc. At this very time, the last decade of the eighteenth century, there was talk of abolishing the university; its place could be taken by the already existing academies of science and by new, practical vocational schools (*Hochschulen*). And yet in 1810, the University of Berlin was founded. (Bahti, 1987, p. 438)

Timothy Bahti discusses the historiography of the modern university in terms which not only emphasize its historical break with the medieval university but also echo the theme of the posthistorical:

> Standard histories of the university distinguish the 'older' and modern versions according to a chronology that is familiar from other such histories as the history of literature, the history of industrialization and modernization (urbanization, rationalization, etc.), and the history of warfare. Somewhere between the eighteenth and the early nineteenth centuries, the model at hand changes: whether the opposition is (neo)classical/romantic, early capitalist/high capitalist, or manual/mechanized, the switch is made, the revolution occurs, and we are all henceforth *post—postromantic,* postrevolutionary, postfeudal—which is to say *modern.* With respect to the university, the opposition is medieval/modern, the place is Germany and the time is the end of the eighteenth century. (Bahti, 1987, p. 438)

Bahti indicates that whereas the seventeenth century had been heyday for the European academies of sciences, the eighteenth had been the lowpoint for German universities, with student rioting and drunkenness, dropping enrolments and little relationship between subjects taught and vocations. In the last decade of the eighteenth century there was talk of abolishing the university altogether, allowing the academies of sciences and the new practical vocational schools to take its place. And then in 1810, the University of Berlin was founded. In the intervening years following the defeat of Prussia by Napoleon, the reorganization of the Prussian bureaucracy occurred and, as Bahti (1987, p. 439) points out, also the discourse of German idealism becomes established with 'the philosophical writings on and for the university, from Kant and Schelling and then from Fichte, Schleiermacher, and Humboldt.'

For Kant, it was the idea of reason that provided an organizing principle for the disciplines, with 'philosophy' as its home. Reason is the founding principle of the Kantian university: it confers universality upon the institution and, thereby, ushers in modernity. As the immanent unifying principle of the Kantian university, reason displaces the Aristotelian order of disciplines of the medieval university based on the seven liberal arts, and substitutes a quasi-industrial arrangement of the faculties. In *The Conflict of the Faculties* Kant writes:

> It was not a bad idea, whoever first conceived and proposed a public means for treating the sum of knowledge (and properly the heads who devote themselves to it), in a quasi-industrial manner, with a division of labour where, for so many fields as there may be of knowledge, so many public teachers would be allotted, professors being trustees, forming together a kind of common scientific inquiry, called a university (or high school) and having autonomy (for only scholars can pass judgement on scholars

> as such); and, thanks to its faculties (various small societies where university teachers are ranged, in keeping with the variety of the main branches of knowledge), the university would be authorized to admit, on the one hand, student-apprentices from the lower schools aspiring to its level, and to grant, on the other hand—after prior examination, and on its own authority—to teachers who are 'free' (not drawn from members themselves) called 'Doctors,' a universally recognized rank (conferring upon them a degree)—in short *creating* them. (Kant [1789], 1979, p. 23)

The free exercise of a self-critical and self-legislating reason controls the higher faculties of theology, law, and medicine, establishing autonomy for the university as a whole. Readings (1996, p. 59) argues that there is, in Kant, a problem or paradox that haunts the constitution of the modern university: how to institutionalize reason's autonomy, or how to unify reason and the state, institution, and autonomy? Kant attempts to reconcile this conflict through the republican subject, the universal subject of humanity, who incarnates this conflict. Thus, while it is one of the functions of the university to produce technicians or men of affairs for the state, the state must protect the university to ensure the rule of reason in public life. Philosophy, as the tribunal of reason, must protect the university from the abuse of power from the state and must act to distinguish legitimate from illegitimate conflict, that is, the arbitrary exercise of authority.

Humboldt's project for the foundation of the University of Berlin in 1810 is decisive for the modern university up until the present day. Once the Kantian idea of reason is replaced with the Humboldtian idea of a national culture, the university becomes pressed into service of the state. For the German idealists the unity of knowledge and culture has been lost and needs to be reintegrated into a unified cultural science (*Bildung*). The university is assigned the task of producing and inculcating national self-knowledge and as such becomes the institution charged with watching over the life-world of the people. In other words, the notoriously difficult concept of *Bildung* has to be understood within a broader German interest in inquiry as such. Inquiry benefitted the mind but the mind was itself understood not just as a property of individuals, but had also wider societal connotations. This perspective on mind, and on *Bildung*, was connected with large themes in German idealist philosophy about the development of reason and indeed the spirit of reason.

The English idea

The German line of thought was soon followed by an English school of thought. John Henry Newman is the most well-known figure here but he was part of a large conversation that went on for decades in the middle of the nineteenth century; and the writers included here from that time (Sedgwick, Whelwell, Stuart Mill and Arnold) are only representative. Others—such as Haldane, Huxley and Playfair—could equally have been chosen here.

The debates in Germany and England had much in common and, from one perspective, might have been felt to have resembled each other. Both had a concern with the development of mind, both saw reason as central to that endeavour, and both considered it crucial that the university had a measure of autonomy from the state. On one reading, at least, there seemed to be little difference between the German idea of *Bildung* and the English idea of liberal education and its association with the cultivation of the mind. But there were, as implied, major differences between the two intellectual traditions. In England, the themes of liberal education, of knowledge 'as its own end' and of a 'philosophical outlook' (as Newman put it) had their place in an intellectual war on two fronts. On the one hand, Newman was contending with German idealism: not for him, a metaphysical sense of the onward march of reason. On the other hand, Newman was fighting against a spreading instrumentalism, or the advance of a belief in utility—pressed in particular by English philosophers (such as Bentham and Mill). Given this stance, Newman's objection to research was understandable, for his concern lay precisely in the cultivation of the individual person.

The English, from John Henry Newman and Matthew Arnold, substitute literature for philosophy as the central discipline of the university, and, therefore, also of national culture. The possibility of a unified national culture is defined explicitly in terms of the study of a tradition of national literature. In England, the idea of culture came to gain its purchase in opposition to science and technology, partly as a result of the threat posed by industrialization and mass civilization. Newman gives us a 'liberal education' as the proper function of the university, which educates its charges to be gentlemen through the study of literature. Readings argues that 'For Arnold, as for Eliot and Leavis after him, Shakespeare occupies the position that the German Idealists ascribed to the Greeks: that of immediately representing an organic community to itself in a living language' (Readings, 1996, p. 78). In 'The Idea of a University,' F. R. Leavis proposes that all study should be centred in the study of literature, centred in the seventeenth century, and based on Shakespeare as the natural origin of culture. Leavis believes that the University of Culture can provide the lost center and heal the split between organic culture and mass civilization.

In 'Literature: A Lecture in the School of Philosophy and Letters,' delivered in 1858, Newman (1968, pp. 201–221) 'explicitly positions as the site of the development both an idea of the nation and the study of literature as the means of training national subjects' (Readings, 1996, p. 76). Newman suggests that 'a literature, when it is formed, is a national and historical fact; it is a matter of the past and present, and can be as little ignored as the present, as little undone as the past' (Newman, 1968, p. 230). National language and literature defines the character of 'every great people,' and Newman speaks of the classics of a national literature by which he means 'those authors who have had the foremost place in exemplifying the powers and conducting the development of its language' (p. 240).

The American tradition

The American tradition was concerned neither with the growth of a world spirit and the life of reason in that regard (the German outlook) nor in the cultivation of persons and in immediate utility (the English stance) but in the birth and development of a multi-cultural society. Service to society, a 'general education', an active learning orientation, and universities supporting economic and social development became key early themes. But these themes were quickly accompanied by a democratic interest in access, such that America witnessed the first truly mass higher education system. Unsurprisingly, perhaps, arose a plea—espoused especially by Robert Maynard Hutchins at Chicago, for a 'general education' that would help to supply a common foundation for participation in civic life. In turn, as the American universities grew in size and function, emerged concerns that they no longer possessed a unifying function, either within or across institutions. Famously, as Clark Kerr put it, the American university was a 'multiversity', held together only by 'a common grievance over car-parking'.

That view, however, was quickly overtaken as America saw, in Burton Clark's telling phrase, the birth of 'the entrepreneurial university'. This development has surely to be seen as a shorthand for a mix of movements, which have not been with their critics from various quarters. Bloom famously pointed to what he saw as 'the closing of the American mind', as universities were invaded by a popular culture with its relativism and a sense that 'anything goes'. Rather more gently, a leading university leader, Derek Bok voiced concern over 'the commercialization of higher education' in America as the universities were required to secure their positions 'in the marketplace'. For Readings, however, the universities were 'in ruins'. As such, their relationship to culture in any serious sense was lost: all that might be eked out was to work towards a space of 'dissensus', in which competing views might have their day.

The French tradition

The French tradition, as we are placing it here, takes the form of a critical commentary on what has befallen the university over recent decades. We term it a 'postmodern tradition': after all, its most prominent writings have come from French philosophers who self-consciously proffered their ideas of the university in a context in which the large themes for which the university stood—reason, truth and knowledge—were all in the dock as having no secure foundations. Indeed, Jean-Francois Lyotard, in his book on *The Postmodern Condition: A Report on Knowledge*, not only inaugurated the postmodern movement but explicitly linked postmodernism with the university. Originally published in Paris in 1979, the book became an instant cause célèbre because Lyotard analyzed the status of knowledge, science, and the university in way that many critics believed signaled an epochal break not only with the so called modern era but also with various traditionally 'modern' ways of viewing the world. It was written, Lyotard asserts, 'at this very Postmodern moment that finds the University nearing what may be its end' (p. xxv).

In *The Postmodern Condition,* Jean-François Lyotard was concerned with grand narratives which had grown out of the Enlightenment and had come to mark modernity. Grand narratives are the stories that cultures tell themselves about their own practices and beliefs in order to legitimate them. They function as a unified single story that purport to legitimate or found a set of practices, a cultural self-image, discourse, or institution. For Lyotard, such narratives were irredeemably suspect. The university could not be immune from such a development. After all, it had its own grand narratives, marked out in the previous one and a half centuries, with knowledge as its central and now apparently shaky concept.

Lyotard writes in a now famous formulation: 'I will use the term modern to designate any science that legitimates itself with reference to a metadiscourse … making explicit appeal to some grand narrative, such as the dialectics of the Spirit, the hermeneutics of meaning, the emancipation of the rational or working subject, or the creation of wealth' (1984, p. xxii). By contrast, he defines post-modern simply as 'incredulity toward metanarratives' (p. xxiv). Lyotard holds that capitalist renewal after the 1930s and the postwar upsurge of technology has led to a 'crisis' of scientific knowledge and to the internal erosion of the very prospect of legitimation. He locates the seeds of such 'delegitimation' in the decline of the legitimating power of the grand narratives of the nineteenth century.

The speculative narrative of the unity of all knowledge held that knowledge is worthy of its name only if it can generate a second-order discourse that functions to legitimate it, otherwise such 'knowledge' would amount to mere ideology. Lyotard claims that the process of 'delegitimation' has revealed that not only does science play its own language game (and consequently is both on a par with and incapable of legitimating other language games) but also it is incapable of legitimating itself as speculation assumed it could. In particular, the process of European cultural disintegration is symbolized most clearly by the end of philosophy as the universal metalanguage able to underwrite all claims to knowledge and, thereby, to unify the rest of culture. By European cultural disintegration Lyotard is referring, first, to the collapse of the European monarchies and the two world wars, and, second, what Nietzsche calls the question of European nihilism (see Shapiro, 1991).

Given this postmodern condition, the university no longer had secure conceptual foundations available to it but only rival sets of ideas. The university could perforce secure its legitimacy through being seen to perform efficiently in the world. If, therefore, there was a watchword for this university, it was that of 'performativity'. Efforts to outflank the limitations of this knowledge condition—whether through interdisciplinarity or through 'teamwork'—were themselves manifestations of 'the performative criterion' (p. 52). Consequently, 'the question ... now asked by the professionalist student, the State, or institutions of higher education is no longer "Is it true?" but "What use is it?"' (p. 51).

The coming of neoliberalism

Since the late 1970s neoliberalism has become the dominant global narrative. (The publication of Lyotard's *The Postmodern Condition* coincided with the election to power of Margaret Thatcher's Conservative government in Britain). The discourse of neoliberalism revitalizes the master discourse of economic liberalism and advances it as a basis for a global reconstruction of society. A form of economic reason encapsulated in the notion of *homo economicus*, with its abstract and universalistic assumptions of individuality, rationality, and self-interest, has captured the policy agendas of Western countries and of university development. Part of its innovation has been the way in which the neoliberal global narrative has successfully extended the principle of self-interest into the status of a paradigm for understanding politics itself, and, purportedly, all behavior and human action. In the realm of higher education policy at every opportunity the market has been substituted for the state: students are now 'customers' and teachers are 'providers.' The notion of vouchers is suggested as a universal panacea to problems of funding and quality. The teaching/learning relation has been reduced to an implicit contract between buyer and seller. As Lyotard argued prophetically in *The Postmodern Condition*, 'Knowledge is and will be produced in order to be sold, it is and will be consumed in order to be valorized in a new production: in both cases, the goal is exchange' (1984, p. 4).

A key text in its analysis of this story of the modern university—extracts from which we reproduce here—is that of Bill Readings *The University in Ruins*. As Readings argues: 'The University … no longer participates in the historical project for humanity that was the legacy of the Enlightenment: the historical project of culture' (Readings, 1995, p. 5). Accordingly, the grand narrative of the university, centered on the cultural production of a liberal, reasoning, citizen subject, in the wake of not just this neoliberalism but also globalization, is no longer credible. Excellence has become the last unifying principle of the modern university, yet the discourse of excellence brackets out the question of value in favor of measurement and substitutes accounting solutions for questions of accountability. As an integrating principle excellence is entirely meaningless: it has no real referent. Under corporatization universities have become sites for the development of 'human resources.' As Readings remarks: 'University mission statements, like their publicity brochures, share two distinctive features nowadays. On the one hand, they all claim that theirs is a unique educational institution. On the other hand, they all go on to describe this uniqueness in exactly the same way' (Readings, 1996, p. 12).

Readings goes on to tell the true story about of how Cornell University Parking services received an award recently for 'excellence in parking.' The discourse of excellence is contentless: it does not enable us to make judgments of value or purpose and it does not help us to answer questions of what, how, or why we should teach or research. We may also observe that this story about Cornell's carparking arrangements has a particular irony. Famously, in his book on *The Uses of the University* (extracted here), Clark Kerr observes that the modern university might be understood as 'a series of individual faculty entrepreneurs held together by a common grievance over parking'. (… 15) Cornell, it seems, had clearly attended to its new core purpose.

Taking stock

It could be felt that this volume leads to a dismal conclusion, namely that the great tradition of writings on the idea of the university is at an end. The justifications for this point of view are as intimated. The university is variously a 'multiversity' without direction being all things to all people, is 'entrepreneurial' and is without direction save that of money, is 'digital' and is therefore yet again directionless given the fluidity of the world of digital and social media, is an institution located only by vacuous terms such as 'excellent' and 'world-class' having become merely the creature of world rankings. On all these counts, serious consideration of the idea of the university is at an end; or so it may be suggested, and some do suggest just this (Rothblatt, 1977).

We believe to the contrary. The idea of the university cannot yet be judged to be at an end. Rather, we suggest that the idea of the university is on a cusp. A number of reasons can be advanced in support of this contention.

First, when one delves beneath the surface of the writings on the idea of the university over the past two centuries, one can see that they had their place amid fierce debates. There was considerable argument and disagreement, over reason and utility, over science and the humanities (including theology) and over the life of the mind and the value that lay in its development. In that latter debate, views differed as to whether value lay in the personal development of the individual or contributed more significantly to the wider society or even to the state. All of these issues remain with us today: they may be hidden from view but they are all present in current debates over skills, the value of research, the merits of humanities in relation to the STEM (science, technology, engineering and mathematics) disciplines, and the extent to which higher education is of private or public benefit.

Second, as the twenty-first century moves on, there is to be found a proliferation of ideas of the university. We are witnessing a new age, a rebirth indeed, of the idea of the university. In the contemporary literature, one finds ideas around the university of wisdom, the public university, the open university (in a digital age), the civic university (anew), the creative university and the ecological university. Characteristically, these are set out in explicit opposition to the idea of the entrepreneurial university, the digital university and the university of excellence (or the world-class university). The contemporary landscape of the idea of the university is not just awash with ideas but is a site of conflicting ideas. Further, the current oppositional ideas of the university enlist in support concepts such as those of wellbeing, care, otherness (or alterity), the public sphere and global community. And so the conceptual base of the idea of the university is being widened.

Our second volume is intended to help in opening this widening conceptual landscape. The point here, for this volume, is that the historical debate around and evolution of the idea of the university matters today, precisely because the idea of the university is not at an end but has potential 'lines of flight' in front of it and that historical set of perspectives may offer shrewd insights that may just help to open vistas even today. This is in no way to want to return to some kind of glorious past. The university of reason, undisturbed by matters of calculated impact and income generation, cannot be recovered as such. But yet, it may harbour nuances that can help to prompt new and imaginative ideas for the twenty-first century.

Sources for reconstruction

For us, therefore, this volume presents past texts that are far more than mere 'historic' or 'academic' interest. We see this book as nothing less than a set of resources that can help to inform the contemporary debate over the university. And, thereby, it can help in reconstructing the university so that it might fulfil its potential and realize the opportunities that present in the twenty-first century.

For example, the Kantian idea of reason, with its sense of it assisting an onward development of the world, may yet have meaning today, precisely in a digital age, as the prospect opens of a genuinely cross-society and cross-nation public sphere. Even the somewhat hazy ideas of a worldly spirit of reason ('geist') may be helpful here, in speaking to the fluidity of the age and the near-instantaneous ways in which understandings can be transported across continents. With the coming of a 'university without walls' (Finnegan,) or a 'borderless university' ( )—as universities open their knowledge to the gaze and engagement of the wider society—surely universities have to sensitive to such dimensions of their possibilities.

As another example, the English liberal idea of the university may also yet have resonance today. Surely, in a world of strife, of non-comprehension of communities between each other, and of societal problems of many kinds (of loneliness, inter-generational difficulties, consideration for the elderly, widening gulfs across social strata and so on), life capacities—as we may term them—are going to become more important. And so beckons a reconsideration of the current imbalance, in which STEM disciplines are given preferential treatment, and the humanities are not just threatened but are already being reduced. Hutchins' plea—in this volume—for a general education are still timely here. Surely, too, Newman's ideas about a philosophical outlook, generously re-interpreted for a modern age, and even 'knowledge as its own end', could come into play. Here, in Newman's non-utilitarian outlook, encouraging a large understanding of the world, lies resources to help in recasting 'the student experience' beyond that of a set of performative skills. And with it, too, Oakeshott's insight and pregnant phrase about the university as 'the gift of an interval'—also in this volume—has weight today, and not only for younger students but for mature students (perhaps attending post-graduate courses in the evenings, for whom the university offers a place of respite from the world of work).

And as a last example, Habermas' idea of the university assisting the formation of society-wide 'learning processes'—again, reproduced here—is a crucially important idea, yet to be fully mined. Certainly, again, it needs to be interpreted with care. Even though offered only thirty years ago, it has to be reworked for an age in which there are multiple publics, split by age and education, characteristically using (and enjoying) different media. But the need for worldwide—not just societal—learning processes is surely now more pressing than ever before. And, at the same time, the university as a global institution, is so placed that it has the resources and wherewithal to begin to respond to this call. Here, surely, if there is a responsibility upon the university—which Derrida was reaching for in vain—this is it.

Conclusion: continuing tasks

As indicated, to see the writings included here—and the debates of which they are part—as resources that may be garnered to speak to the present age only opens up large tasks. There are scholarly tasks, practical tasks and imaginative tasks.

The scholarly tasks involve a serious delving into the oeuvres of the writers within the canon (of work on the idea of the university) and of getting on the inside of their form of thought and its own intellectual location. This would be a hermeneutic inquiry, concerned with unravelling the meanings of key concepts. Just what might have been commonly understood by terms such as spirit, science, knowledge, mind, and liberal education two hundred years ago? But it would also be a socio-politico-economic inquiry. Just what did higher education look like in previous generations? How extensive was it? To what extent did it constitute a system? What were the relationships between universities and the state? What were their functions and their role in the formation of social and cultural capital? Without such inquiries and such insights, writings in the canon on the idea of the university will be open to grave misinterpretations (as contemporary understandings are unwittingly poured in) or to manipulation (as may sometimes be seen today, as the names—if not the actual writings—of those such as von Humboldt and Newman are prayed in aid).

The practical tasks and the imaginative tasks dovetail each other. For example, Newman's idea of liberal education was intimately involved in freeing the mind. But what might that mean in the twenty-first century? This is an age, after all, in which large and complex institutions, such as the university, are subject to profound global forces and binding national policies. Academics, both individually and in their intellectual fields, are subject to swirls of knowledge, with new formations emerging with their own impulsion, constituting 'ethno-epistemic assemblages' as it has been termed (Irwin & Michael,). Students, too, are subject to a welter of images and messages bombarding them as the digital revolution gathers evermore speed. Under such conditions, the idea of 'liberal education' has be radically reinterpreted if it is to do work in the future. It may even need to be widened so as to encompass a sense of what it is to be 'free' in a world of such extraneous forces. The personal autonomy that 'liberal education' appears to promise seems to be in jeopardy in an age of such heteronomy.

Hutchins urged the institution of 'general education' and that could be felt to have a part to play here, in working out a new idea of liberal education. But, again, the heavy lifting has to be done. It could be said that that heavy lifting has already been done, in the world-wide reframing of curricula around 'transferable skills'. Justifiably in our view, that agenda has been critiqued extensively over the past two decades or more. However, despite much contemporary recourse (in the literature) to talk of virtue (or virtues), references to practical wisdom ('phronesis'), 'Bildung', 'citizenship' and human 'qualities', we still lack a practical way forward that can seriously be implemented by universities. Both more practical endeavour and a heightened imagination are called for, jointly, if the idea of liberal education is to have salience today.

Perhaps a totally new front needs to be opened here, and perhaps debates about citizenship and cosmopolitanism on the one hand, and the universities pursing strategies variously of civic or community engagement could be pertinent. The central claim here would be that the development of students in a space imbued with concepts of citizenship, human rights, social responsibility, 'otherness', 'alterity', hospitality (towards 'strangers'), civic responsibility and, indeed, community itself, would help to open up lines of travel towards forms of bounded freedom. These are matters for another day. The point here is that the writings of previous generations on the idea of the university can remind us of a conceptual hinterland in which universities have long been located but that any recuperation of the key concepts of those eras calls for considerable intellectual, practical and imaginative work. The ideas of those writers cannot be simply transposed into the current age. But those processes of uncovering and translation and re-imagining, difficult as they are, are necessary tasks if the current ideas and practices in the modern age are not to fall foul of contemporary ideologies on the one hand, and undue pessimism on the other hand.

Recommended Reading

Bahti, Timothy (1987). Histories of the university: Kant and Humboldt. *MLN* 102 (3): 437–60.

Clark, Timothy and Nicholas Royle (Eds.) (1995). The university in ruins: Essays on the crisis in the concept of the modern university. Special issue, *Oxford Literary Review* 15.

Damrosch, David and Theo D'haen (Eds.) (2011). *The Canonical Debate Today: Crossing Disciplinary and Cultural Boundaries.* Amsterdam, the Netherlands: Rodopi.

Delanty, Gerard (1998). The idea of the university in the global era: From knowledge as an end to the end of knowledge. *Social Epistemology* 12 (1): 3–26.

Derrida, Jacques (1983). The principle of reason: The university in the eyes of its pupils. *Diacritics* (Fall): 3–20.

Fallon, D. (1980). *The German University: A Heroic Ideal in Conflict with the Modern World.* Boulder, Colo: Colorado UP.

Foucault, Michel (1996). What is enlightenment? In *Michel Foucault: Ethics. The Essential Works*, ed. Paul Rabinow, 303–320. London: Allen Lane and Penguin.

Gorak, Jan (2013). *The Making of the Modern Canon: Genesis and Crisis of a Literary Idea.* London: Bloomsbury Academic.

Habermas, Jürgen (1987). The idea of the university—learning processes. *New German Critique* 41 (Spring–Summer): 3–22.

Humboldt, Wilhelm von (1903–36). *Gesammelte Schriften: Ausgabe Der Preussischen Akademie Der Wissenschaften.* Bd. I–XVII, Berlin.

Humboldt, Wilhelm von (1970). On the spirit and the organisational framework of intellectual institutions in Berlin. *Minerva* 8 (2): 242–250.

Kant, Immanuel [1789] (1979). *The conflict of the faculties.* Trans. M. Gregor. New York: Abaris Books.

Kwiek, Marek (2006). The Classical German Idea of the University Revisited, or on the Nationalization of the Modern Institution, The Center for Public Policy Studies, RPS Volume 1, http://www.cpp.amu.edu.pl/pdf/CPP_RPS_vol.1_Kwiek.pdf

Lyotard, Jean-François (1984). *The Postmodern Condition: A Report on Knowledge.* Trans. G. Bennington and B. Massumi. Minneapolis: University of Minnesota Press.

Mueller-Vollmer, Kurt (2014). 'Wilhelm von Humboldt', *The Stanford Encyclopedia of Philosophy* (Winter 2014 Edition), Edward N. Zalta (ed.), URL = http://plato.stanford.edu/archives/win2014/entries/wilhelm-humboldt/

Readings, Bill (1995). From emancipation to obligation: Sketch for a heteronomous politics of education. In *Education and the Postmodern Condition*, ed. Michael A. Peters, 193–208. Westport, Conn.: Bergin & Garvey.

Readings, Bill (1996). *The University in Ruins.* Cambridge, Mass.: Harvard University Press.

Rothblatt, Sheldon (1997). 'The Idea of the University and its Antithesis', in his *The Modern University and its Discontents: The fate of Newman's legacies in Britain and America.* Cambridge: Cambridge University Press.

Schiller, Friedrich (1983). *On the Aesthetic Education of Man In a Series of Letters, English and German Facing*, ed. and trans. with intro., commentary and glossary by Elizabeth M. Wilkinson and L. A. Willoughby [1967]. Oxford: Clarendon Press.

Shapiro, Gary (1991). Nietzsche and the future of the university. *Journal of Nietzsche Studies* 1: 15–28.

Smith, Anthony and Frank Webster (1997). *The postmodern university? Contested visions of higher education in society.* Buckingham, England: SRHE and Open University Press.

Wertz, William F. (2005). A reader's guide to letters on the aesthetical. *Fidelio* 14 (1–2), Spring–Summer, http://schillerinstitute.org/fidelio_archive/2005/fidv14n01-02-2005SpSu/fidv14n01-02-2005SpSu_080-a_readers_guide_to_schillers_let.pdf

PART ONE

The German (*Bildung*) Tradition

CHAPTER ONE

The Conflict of the Philosophy Faculty with the Theology Faculty

From *The Conflict of the Faculties* (1789/1992)

IMMANUEL KANT

Translated and Introduction by Mary J. Gregor, The Introduction to First Part: The Conflict of the Philosophy Faculty versus the Theology Faculty is a selection taken from *The Conflict of the Faculties*, by Immanuel Kant. Lincoln and London: University of Nebraska Press 1979, paperback 1992. Originally Published in English, by Abaris Books, Inc., New York, 1979. First published by Nicolovius in autumn 1798. Originally published 1789.

Editors' Note

The Conflict of the Faculties is a compilation of three essays written at different times during the mid-1790s although not published until 1798 for reasons to do with possible censorship. The conflict of the faculties that Kant refers to the relationship between the 'higher' faculties of Theology, Law and Medicine and the 'lower' faculty of Philosophy (today we would include other disciplines of the humanities, social and natural sciences). These are the faculties that reflected the structure of Kant's own University of Königsberg under Frederick William I who insisted that students enrol in one of the three 'higher' faculties as training for the Prussian bureaucracy. Kant addresses the general problem of the relationship between knowledge and power and the specific problem of the relationship between the university and the state arguing that a State is concerned with the welfare of its citizens under health, security and salvation that corresponds to bodies of knowledge generated in the 'higher' faculties by the use of reason. Philosophy carries no such responsibility for the administration of government but is rather devoted entirely to the pursuit of rational enquiry and the disinterested knowledge. In this way Kant examines the functions of the State and the Universities role within it linking the empirical facts of university and knowledge organisation with concepts and the public use of reason. This is a work dedicated to the cause of academic freedom in what Kant called "the age of criticism" to sustain the public use of reason through free and open discourse evident in Philosophy which because of its lack of vocational application became the most inclusive curriculum and most innovative subject in the university during the eighteenth century.

MP

Recommended Reading

Caygill, Howard (2015). Kant and the "Age of Criticism". In Howard Caygill (ed.) *A Kant Dictionary*. Blackwell Publishing, 1995. Blackwell Reference Online. 04 November 2015, http://www.blackwellreference.com/subscriber/tocnode.html?id=g9780631175353_chunk_g97806311753534

Derrida, Jacques (1992). Mochlos; or, The Conflict of the Faculties, Translated by Richard Rand and Amy Wygant. In Richard Rand (ed.) *Logomachia: The Conflict of Faculties*. Lincoln: University of Nebraska Press, pp. 1–34.

Evans, David (2008). The Conflict of the Faculties and the Knowledge Industry: Kant's Diagnosis, in His Time and Ours. *Philosophy*, 83, pp. 483–495. doi: 10.1017/S0031819108000843

* * * * *

Introduction

Whoever it was that first hit on the notion of a university and proposed that a public institution of this kind be established, it was not a bad idea to handle the entire content of learning (really, the thinkers devoted to it) by mass production, so to speak—by a division of labor, so that for every branch of the sciences there would be a public teacher or professor appointed as its trustee, and all of these together would form a kind of learned community called a university (or higher school). The university would have a certain autonomy (since only scholars can pass judgment on scholars as such), and accordingly it would be authorized to perform certain functions through its faculties[1] (smaller societies, each comprising the university specialists in one main branch of learning): to admit to the university students seeking entrance from the lower schools and, having conducted examinations, by its own authority to grant degrees or confer the universally recognized status of "doctor" on free teachers (that is, teachers who are not members of the university)—in other words, to create doctors.

In addition to these incorporated scholars, there can also be scholars at large, who do not belong to the university but simply work on part of the great content of learning, either forming independent organizations, like various workshops (called academies or scientific societies), or living, so to speak, in a state of nature so far as learning is concerned, each working by himself, as an amateur and without public precepts or rules, at extending and propagating [his field of] learning.

We must distinguish, further, between scholars proper and those members of the intelligentsia (university graduates) who are instruments of the government, invested with an office for its own purpose (which is not exactly the progress of the sciences). As such, they must indeed have been educated at the university; but they may well have forgotten much of what they learned (about theory), so long as they retain enough to fill a civil office. While only the scholar can provide the principles underlying their functions, it is enough if they retain empirical knowledge of the statutes relevant to their office (hence what has to do with practice). Accordingly they can be called the businessmen or technicians of learning. As tools of the government (clergymen, magistrates, and physicians), they have legal influence on the public and form a special class of the intelligentsia, who are not free to make public use of their learning as they see fit, but are subject to the censorship of the faculties. So the government must keep them under strict control, to prevent them from trying to exercise judicial power, which belongs to the faculties; for they deal directly with the people, who are incompetent (like the clergyman in relation to the layman), and share in the executive, though certainly not the legislative, power in their field.

---

1 Each of which has its Dean, who is the head of the faculty. This title, taken from astrology, originally meant one of the three astral spirits that preside over a sign of the zodiac (of 30 degrees), each governing 10 degrees. From the stars it was transferred to the military camp (*ab astris ad castra;* see *Salmasius de annis Climacteriis*, page 561), and finally to the university, where, however, the number 10 (of professors) was not taken into account. Since it was the scholars who first thought up most of the honorific titles with which state officials now adorn themselves, they can hardly be blamed for not having forgotten themselves.

General Division of the Faculties

The faculties are traditionally divided into two ranks: three higher faculties and one lower faculty. It is clear that this division is made and this nomenclature adopted with reference to the government rather than the learned professions; for a faculty is considered higher only if its teachings—both as to their content and the way they are expounded to the public—interest the government itself, while the faculty whose function is only to look after the interests of science is called lower because it may use its own judgment about what it teaches. Now the government is interested primarily in means for securing the strongest and most lasting influence on the people, and the subjects which the higher faculties teach are just such means. Accordingly, the government reserves the right itself to sanction the teachings of the higher faculties, but those of the lower faculty it leaves up to the scholars' reason. But even when the government sanctions teachings, it does not itself teach; it requires only that the respective faculties, in expounding a subject publicly, adopt certain teachings and exclude their contraries. For the government does not teach, but it commands those who, in accepting its offices,[2] have contracted to teach what it wants (whether this be true or not). If a government were to concern itself with [the truth of] these teachings, and so with the growth or progress of the sciences, then it would, in the highest person, be trying to play the role of scholar, and its pedantry would only undermine the respect due it. It is beneath the government's dignity to mingle with the people (in this case, the people in the learned professions), who cannot take a joke and deal impartially with everyone who meddles in the sciences.

It is absolutely essential that the learned community at the university also contain a faculty that is independent of the government's command with regard to its teachings;[3] one that, having no commands to give, is free to evaluate everything,

---

2 It is a principle in the British Parliament that the monarch's speech from the throne is to be considered the work of his ministers (since the House must be entitled to judge, examine, and attack the content of the speech and it would be beneath the monarch's dignity to let himself be charged with error, ignorance, or untruth). And this principle is quite acute and correct. It is in the same way that the choice of certain teachings which the government expressly sanctions for public exposition must remain subject to scholarly criticism; for this choice must not be ascribed to the monarch but to a state official whom he appoints to do it—an official who, it is supposed, could have misunderstood or misrepresented his ruler's will.

3 A minister of the French government summoned a few of the most eminent merchants and asked them for suggestions on how to stimulate trade—as if he would know how to choose the best of these. After one had suggested this and another that, an old merchant who had

and concerns itself with the interests of the sciences, that is, with truth: one in which reason is authorized to speak out publicly. For without a faculty of this kind, the truth would not come to light (and this would be to the government's own detriment); but reason is by its nature free and admits of no command to hold something as true (no imperative "Believe!" but only a free "I believe"). The reason why this faculty, despite its great prerogative (freedom), is called the lower faculty lies in human nature; for a man who can give commands, even though he is someone else's humble servant, is considered more distinguished than a free man who has no one under his command.

On the Relation of the Faculties

First Section
The Concept and Division of the Higher Faculties

Whenever a man-made institution is based on an Idea of reason (such as that of a government) which is to prove itself practical in an object of experience (such as the entire field of learning at the time), we can take it for granted that the experiment was made according to some principle contained in reason, even if only obscurely, and some plan based on it-not by merely contingent collections and arbitrary combinations of cases that have occurred. And a plan of this sort makes a certain kind of division necessary.

We can therefore assume that the organization of a university into ranks and classes did not depend entirely on chance. Without attributing premature wisdom and learning to the government, we can say that by its own felt need (to influence the people by certain teachings) it managed to arrive a priori at a principle of division which seems otherwise to be of empirical origin, so that the a priori principle happily coincides with the one now in use. But this does not mean that I shall advocate [the present system] as if it had no faults.

According to reason (that is, objectively), the following order exists among the incentives that the government can use to achieve its end (of influencing the people): first comes the *eternal* well-being of each, then his *civil* well-being as a member of society, and finally his *physical* well-being (a long life and health). By public teachings about the *first* of these, the government can exercise very great

---

kept quiet so far said: "Build good roads, mint sound money, give us laws for exchanging money readily, etc.; but as for the rest, leave us alone!" If the government were to consult the Philosophy Faculty about what teachings to prescribe for scholars in general, it would get a similar reply: just don't interfere with the progress of understanding and science.

influence to uncover the inmost thoughts and guide the most secret intentions of its subjects. By teachings regarding the *second*, it helps to keep their external conduct under the reins of public laws, and by its teachings regarding the *third*, to make sure that it will have a strong and numerous people to serve its purposes. So the ranks customarily assigned to the higher faculties—*theology* first, *law* second, and *medicine* third—are in accordance with reason. According to *natural instinct*, however, men consider the physician most important, because he prolongs their *life*. Next to him comes the jurist, who promises to secure their contingent *possessions*. And only last (almost at the point of death) do they send for the clergyman, though it is their salvation that is in question; for even the clergyman, no matter how highly he commends the happiness of the world to come, actually perceives nothing of it and hopes fervently that the doctor can keep him in this vale of tears a while longer.

All three higher faculties base the teachings which the government entrusts to them on *writings*, as is necessary for a people governed by learning, since otherwise there would be no fixed and universally accessible norm for their guidance. It is self-evident that such a text (or book) must comprise *statutes*, that is, teachings that proceed from an act of choice on the part of an authority (that do not issue directly from reason); for otherwise it could not demand obedience simply, as something the government has sanctioned. And this holds true of the entire code of laws, even those of its teachings, to be expounded to the public, which could also be derived from *reason*: the code takes no notice of their rational ground, but bases itself on the command of an external legislator. The code of laws is the canon, and as such it is quite distinct from those books which the faculties write as (supposedly) complete summaries of the spirit of the code, so that the community (of the learned and the ignorant) may grasp its concepts more easily and use them more safely—the *symbolic books*, for example. These can claim only the respect due to the organon, which gives easier access to the canon, and have no authority whatsoever. Even if the most eminent scholars in a certain field should agree to give such a book the weight of norm for their faculty, it would derive no authority from this: for the scholars are not entitled to do this, but only to establish the book as a pedagogical method for the time being—a method that can always be changed to suit the times and, in any case, concerns only the way they lecture [on the code], without in any way affecting the content of the legislation.

So the biblical theologian (as a member of a higher faculty) draws his teachings not from reason but from the *Bible*; the professor of law gets his, not from natural law, but from the *law of the land*; and the professor of medicine does not draw his *method of therapy as practiced on the public* from the physiology of the human body but from *medical regulations*. As soon as one of these faculties presumes to mix with its teachings something it treats as derived from reason, it offends against the authority of the government that issues orders through it and encroaches on the territory of the philosophy faculty, which mercilessly strips from it all the shining plumes that were protected by the government and deals with it on a footing of equality and freedom. The higher faculties must, therefore, take great care not to enter into a misalliance with the lower faculty, but must keep it at a respectful distance, so that the dignity of their statutes will not be damaged by the free play of reason.

A
The Distinctive Characteristic of the Theology Faculty

The biblical theologian proves the existence of God on the grounds that He spoke in the Bible, which also discusses His nature (and even goes so far into it that reason cannot keep up with the text, as when, for example, it speaks of the incomprehensible mystery of His threefold personality). But the biblical theologian as such cannot and need not prove that God Himself spoke through the Bible, since that is a matter of history and belongs to the philosophy faculty. [Treating it] as a matter of faith, he will therefore base it—even for the scholar—on a certain (indemonstrable and inexplicable) *feeling* that the Bible is divine. But the question of the divine origin of the Bible (in the literal sense) must not be raised at all in public discourses directed to the people; since this is a scholarly matter, they would fail completely to understand it and, as a result, would only get entangled in impertinent speculations and doubts. In such matters it is much safer to rely on the people's confidence in their teachers. The biblical theologian can also have no authority to ascribe a nonliteral—for example, a moral—meaning to statements in the text. And since there is no human interpreter of the Scriptures authorized by God, he must rather count on a supernatural opening of his understanding by a spirit that guides to all truth than allow reason to intervene and (without any higher authority) maintain its own interpretation. Finally, as far as our will and its fulfilment of God's commands is concerned, the biblical theologian must not rely on nature-that is, on man's own moral power (virtue)—but on grace (a supernatural but, at the same time, moral influence), which man can obtain only by, an ardent faith that transforms his heart-a faith that itself, in turn, he can expect only through grace. If the biblical theologian meddles with his reason in any of these tenets, then, even granting that reason strives most sincerely and earnestly for that same objective, he leaps (like Romulus's' brother) over the wall of ecclesiastical faith, the only thing that assures his salvation, and strays into the free and open fields of private judgment and philosophy. And there, having run away from the Church's government, he is exposed to all the dangers of anarchy. But note well that I am here speaking only of the *pure* (*purus*, *putus*) biblical theologian, who is not yet contaminated by the ill-reputed spirit of freedom that belongs to reason and philosophy. For as soon as we allow two different callings to combine and run together, we can form no clear notion of the characteristic that distinguishes each by itself.

B
The Distinctive Characteristic of the Faculty of Law

The jurist, as an authority on the text, does not look to his reason for the laws that secure the *Mine* and *Thine*, but to the code of laws that has been publicly promulgated and sanctioned by the highest authority (if, as he should, he acts as a civil servant). To require him to prove the truth of these laws and their conformity with right, or to defend them against reason's objections, would be unfair. For these decrees first determine what is right, and the jurist must straightaway dismiss as nonsense the further question of whether the decrees themselves are right. To refuse to obey an external and supreme will on the grounds that it allegedly does not conform with reason would be absurd; for the dignity of the government consists precisely in this: that it does not leave its subjects free to judge what is right-or wrong according to their own notions, but [determines right and wrong] for them by precepts of the legislative power.

In one respect, however, the faculty of law is better off in practice than the theology faculty: it has a visible interpreter of the law—namely, a judge or, if his decision is appealed, a legal commission, and (as the highest appeal) the legislator himself., The theological faculty is not so well provided for, when the sayings of its sacred book have to be interpreted. But this advantage is offset by a disadvantage at least equal to it: namely, that any secular code of laws always remains subject to change, as experience brings more or better insight, whereas the sacred code decrees that there will be no change (either by subtraction or addition), and maintains that it is closed forever. Furthermore, biblical theologians do not join in the jurist's complaint that it is all but vain to hope for a precisely determined norm for the administration of justice (*ius certus*); for they reject the claim that their dogma lacks a norm that is clear and determined for every case. Moreover, if the practicing lawyer (counsel or attorney-at-law) has harmed a client by giving him bad advice, he refuses to be held responsible for it (*ob consilium nemo tenetur* ["no one is bound by the advice he receives"]); but the practicing theologian (preacher or spiritual adviser) does not hesitate to take the responsibility on himself and to guarantee-at least to hear him talk-that any decision passed in the next world will correspond exactly with his decisions in this one. But he will probably decline if he is invited to declare formally that he will stake his soul on the truth of everything he would have us believe on the Bible's authority. And yet, the nature of the principles maintained by these public teachers permits no doubt whatsoever that their assurances are correct—assurances they can give all the more safely because they need not fear that experience will refute them in this life.

C
The Distinctive Characteristic of the Faculty of Medicine

Although medicine is an art, it is an art that is drawn directly from nature and must therefore be derived from a science of nature. So the physician, as a man of learning, must come under some faculty by which he must have been trained and to whose judgment he must remain subject. But since the way physicians deal with the people's health must be of great interest to the government, it is entitled to supervise their dealings with the public through an assembly chosen from the businessmen of this faculty (practicing doctors)—*a board of public health*—and through medical regulations. Unlike the other higher faculties, however, the faculty of medicine must derive its rules of procedure not from orders of the authorities but from the nature of things themselves, so that its teachings must have also belonged originally to the philosophy faculty, taken in its widest sense. And because of this special characteristic of the medical faculty, medical regulations deal not so much with what doctors should do as with what they should not do: they ensure, *first*, that there will be doctors for the public and, secondly, that there will be no spurious doctors (no *ius impune occidendi* ["law of killing with impunity"], according to the principle: *fiat experimentum in corpori vili* ["let experiments be made on worthless bodies"]). By the first of these principles, the government watches over the public's *convenience*, and by the second, over the public's *safety* (in the matter of the people's health). And since these two services are the function of a *police force*, all medical regulations really have to do only with *policing the medical profession*.

The medical faculty is, therefore, much freer than the other two higher faculties and closely akin to the Philosophy Faculty. Indeed, it is altogether free with regard to the teachings by which it *trains* doctors, since its texts cannot be sanctioned by the highest authorities but can be drawn only from nature. It can also have no laws strictly speaking (if by laws we mean the unalterable will of the legislator), but only regulations (edicts); and since learning requires [as its object] a systematic content of teachings, knowledge of these regulations does not constitute the learning [of the medical faculty]. This faculty does indeed possess such learning; but since the government does not have the authority to sanction it (because it is not contained in any *code of laws*), it must leave this to the faculty's discretion and concern itself only with helping medical practitioners to be of service to the public, by establishing dispensaries and hospitals. These practitioners (physicians), however, remain subject to the judgment of their faculty in matters which concern the medical police and so interest the government.

Second Section
The Concept and Division of the Lower Faculty

The lower faculty is the rank in the university that occupies itself with teachings which are not adopted as directives by order of a superior, or in so far as they are not so adopted. Now we may well comply with a practical teaching out of obedience, but we can never accept it as true simply because we are ordered to (*de par le Roi*). This is not only objectively impossible (a judgment that *ought not* to be made), but also subjectively quite impossible (a judgment that no one can make). For the man who, as he says, wants to err does not really err and, in fact, accept the false judgment as true; he merely declares, falsely, an assent that is not to be found in him. So when it is a question of the *truth* of a certain teaching to be expounded in public, the teacher cannot appeal to a supreme command nor the pupil pretend that he believed it by order. This can happen only when it is a question of *action*, and even then the pupil must recognize by a *free* judgment that such a command was really issued and that he is obligated or at least entitled to obey it; otherwise, his acceptance of it would be an empty pretence and a lie. Now the power to judge autonomously—that is, freely (according to principles of thought in general)—is called reason. So the philosophy faculty, because it must answer for the truth of the teachings it is to adopt or even allow, must be conceived as free and subject only to laws given by reason, not by the government.

But a department of this kind, too, must be established at a university; in other words, a university must have a faculty of philosophy. Its function in relation to the three higher faculties is to control them and, in this way, be useful to them, since *truth* (the essential and first condition of learning in general) is the main thing, whereas the *utility* the higher faculties promise the government is of secondary importance. We can also grant the theology faculty's proud claim that the philosophy faculty is its handmaid (though the question remains, whether the servant is the mistress's *torchbearer* or *trainbearer*), provided it is not driven away or silenced. For the very *modesty* [of its claim]—merely to be free, as it leaves others free, to discover the truth for the benefit of all the sciences and to set it before the higher faculties to use as they will—must commend it to the government as above suspicion and, indeed, indispensable.

Now the philosophy faculty consists of two departments: a department of *historical knowledge* (including history, geography, philology and the humanities, along with all the empirical knowledge contained in the natural sciences), and a department of *pure rational knowledge* (pure mathematics and pure philosophy, the metaphysics of nature and of morals). And it also studies the relation of these two divisions of learning to each other. It therefore extends to all parts of human knowledge (including, from a historical viewpoint, the teachings of the higher faculties), though there are some parts (namely, the distinctive teachings and precepts of the higher faculties) which it does not treat as its own content, but as objects it will examine and criticize for the benefit of the sciences.

The philosophy faculty can, therefore, lay claim to any teaching, in order to test its truth. The government cannot forbid it to do this without acting against its own proper and essential purpose; and the higher faculties must put up with the objections and doubts it brings forward in public, though they may well find this irksome, since, were it not for such critics, they could rest undisturbed in possession of what they have once occupied, by whatever title, and rule over it despotically. Only the businessmen of the higher faculties (clergymen, legal officials, and doctors) can be prevented from contradicting in public the teachings that the government has entrusted to them to expound in fulfilling their respective offices, and from venturing to play the philosopher's role; for the faculties alone, not the officials appointed by the government, can be allowed to do this, since these officials get their knowledge from the faculties. If, that is to say, these officials—for example, clergymen and legal officials—should want to put before the public their objections and doubts about ecclesiastical and civil laws that have been given, they would be inciting the people to rebel against the government. The faculties, on the other hand, put their objections and doubts only to one another, as scholars, and the people pay no attention to such matters in a practical way, even if they should hear of them; for, agreeing that these subtleties are not their affair, they feel obliged to be content with what the government officials, appointed for this purpose, announce to them. But the result of this freedom, which the philosophy faculty must enjoy unimpaired, is that the higher faculties (themselves better instructed) will lead these officials more and more onto the way of truth. And the officials, for their own part, also more enlightened about their duty, will not be repelled at changing their exposition, since the new way involves nothing more than a clearer insight into means for achieving the same end. And such a change can well come about without polemics and attacks, that only stir up unrest, on the traditional way of teaching, when [it is seen that] the content to be taught is preserved in its entirety.

Third Section
On the Illegal Conflict of the Higher Faculties with the Lower Faculty

A public conflict of views, hence a scholarly debate, can be illegal by reason of its matter or its form. It would be illegal by reason of its *matter* if it were not permissible to *debate*, in this way, about a public proposition because it was not permissible to *judge* publicly this proposition and its opposite. It would be illegal by reason of its *form*, or the way in which the debate is carried on, if one of the parties relied, not on objective grounds directed to his adversary's reason, but on subjective grounds, trying to determine his judgment through his *inclinations* and so to gain his assent by fraud (including bribery) or force (threats).

Now the faculties engage in public conflict in order to influence the people, and each can acquire this influence only by convincing the people that it knows best how to promote their welfare. But as for the way they propose to accomplish this, the lower faculty is diametrically opposed to the higher faculties.

The people conceive of their welfare, not primarily as freedom, but as [the realization of] their natural ends and so as these three things: being *happy* after death, having their *possessions* guaranteed by public laws during their life in society, and finally, looking forward to the physical enjoyment of *life* itself (that is, health and a long life).

But the philosophy faculty can deal with all these wishes only by precepts it derives from reason. It depends, accordingly, on the principle of freedom and limits itself to saying what man himself can and should do toward fulfilling these wishes—live *righteously*, commit no *injustice*, and, by being *moderate* in his pleasures and patient in his illnesses, rely primarily on the self-help of nature. None of this, indeed, requires great learning; but in these matters we can, for the most part, dispense with learning if we would only restrain our inclinations and be ruled by our reason. But since this requires self-exertion, it does not suit the people.

So the people (who find the philosophy faculty's teaching a poor substitute for their inclination to *enjoyment* and their aversion from *working* for it) invite the higher faculties to make them more acceptable proposals. And the demands they make on these scholars run like this. "As for the *philosophers'* twaddle, I've known that all along. What I want you, as men of learning, to tell me is this: if I've been a *scoundrel* all my life, how can I get an eleventh-hour ticket to heaven? If I've *broken* the law, how can I still win my case? And even if I've used and *abused* my physical powers as I've pleased, how can I stay healthy and live a long time? Surely this is why you have studied—so that you would know more than someone like ourselves (you call us laymen), who can claim nothing more than sound understanding." But now the people are approaching these scholars as if they were soothsayers and magicians, with knowledge of supernatural things; for if an ignorant man expects something from a scholar, he readily forms exaggerated notions of him. So we can naturally expect that if someone has the effrontery to give himself out as such a miracle-worker, the people will flock to him and contemptuously desert the philosophy faculty.

But the businessmen of the three higher faculties will always be such miracle-workers, unless the philosophy faculty is allowed to counteract them publicly-not in order to overthrow their teachings but only to deny the magic power that the public superstitiously attributes to these teachings and the rites connected with them—as if, by passively surrendering themselves to such skilful guides, the people would be excused from any activity of their own and led, in ease and comfort, to achieve the ends they desire.

If the higher faculties adopt such principles (and it is certainly not their function to do this), then they are and always will be in conflict with the lower faculty. But this conflict is also *illegal*; for the higher faculties, instead of viewing transgressions of the law as hindrances, welcome them as occasions for showing their great art and skill in making everything as good as ever, and, indeed, better than it would otherwise have been.

The people want to be *led*, that is (as demagogues say), they want to be *duped*. But they want to be led not by the scholars of the faculties (whose wisdom is too high for them), but by the businessmen of the faculties—clergymen, legal officials, and doctors—who understand a botched job (*savoir faire*) and have the people's confidence. And so the government, which can work on the people only through these practitioners, will itself be *led* to obtrude on the faculties a theory that arises, not from the pure insight of their scholars, but from calculations of the influence their practitioners can exert on the people by it. For the people naturally adhere most to doctrines which demand the least self-exertion and the least use of their own reason, and which can best accommodate their duties to their inclinations-in theology, for example, the doctrine that they can be saved merely by an implicit faith, without having to examine (or even really know) what they are supposed to believe, or that their performance of certain prescribed rites will itself wash away their transgressions; or in law, the doctrine that compliance with the letter of the law exempts them from examining the legislator's intentions.

[If the higher faculties adopt such principles], they are involved in an essential and irreconcilable conflict with the lower faculty. And this conflict is illegal because, if the government legislated for the higher faculties according to the principle attributed to it [in the preceding paragraph], its own principle would authorize anarchy itself. *Inclination* and, in general, what someone finds useful for his *private purposes* can never qualify as a law, and so cannot be set forth as a law by the higher faculties. A government that sanctioned such principles would offend against reason itself and, by this, bring the higher faculties into conflict with the lower faculty—a conflict that cannot be tolerated because it would completely destroy the philosophy faculty. This, admittedly, is the quickest way of ending a conflict; but it is also (in medical terms) a *heroic* means—one that endangers life.

Fourth Section
On the Legal Conflict of the Higher Faculties with the Lower Faculty

Regardless of their content, any teachings that the government may be entitled to sanction for public exposition by the higher faculties can be accepted and respected only as statutes proceeding from [the government's] choice and as human wisdom, which is not infallible. But the government cannot be completely indifferent to the truth of these teachings, and in this respect they must remain subject to reason (whose interests the philosophy faculty has to safeguard). Now this is possible only if complete freedom to examine these teachings in public is permitted. So, since arbitrary propositions, though sanctioned by the supreme authority, may not always harmonize with the teachings reason maintains as necessary, there will be a conflict between the higher and lower faculties which is, first, *inevitable*, but second, *legal* as well; for the lower faculty has not only the title but also the duty, if not to state the *whole* truth in public, at least to see to it that *everything* put forward in public as a principle is true.

If the source of a sanctioned teaching is *historical*, then—no matter how highly it may be commended as sacred to the unhesitating obedience of faith—the philosophy faculty is entitled and indeed obligated to investigate its origin with critical scrupulosity. If the teaching, though presented in the manner of historical knowledge (as revelation), has a rational origin, the lower faculty cannot be prevented from investigating, in the historical narrative, the rational basis of this legislation and also evaluating it as either technically or morally practical. Finally, the source of a teaching proclaimed as law may be only *aesthetic*: in other words, the teaching may be based on a feeling connected with it (for example, a pious feeling of supernatural influence—although, since feeling yields no objective principle, it is only subjectively valid and cannot provide the basis for a universal law). In this case the philosophy faculty must be free to examine in public and to evaluate with cold reason the source and content of this alleged basis of doctrine, unintimidated by the sacredness of the object which has supposedly been experienced and determined to bring this alleged feeling to concepts. The following paragraphs contain the formal principles of procedure for such a conflict and the consequences resulting from it.

1) This conflict cannot and should not be settled by an amicable accommodation (*amicabilis compositio*), but (as a lawsuit) calls for a verdict, that is, the decision of a judge (reason) which has the force of law. For the dispute could be settled only through dishonesty, by [the lower faculty's] concealing the cause of the dissension and letting itself be persuaded; but a maxim of this kind is directly opposed to the spirit of a *philosophy* faculty, which has the public presentation of truth as its function.
2) This conflict can never end, and it is the philosophy faculty that must always be prepared to keep it going. For there must always be statutory precepts of

the government regarding teachings to be set forth in public, since unlimited freedom to proclaim any sort of opinion publicly is bound to be dangerous both to the government and to the public itself. But because all the government's statutes proceed from men, or are at least sanctioned by them, there is always the danger that they may be erroneous or unsuitable; and this applies also to the statutes that the government's sanction supplies to the higher faculties. Consequently, the philosophy faculty can never lay aside its arms in the face of the danger that threatens the truth entrusted to its protection, because the higher faculties will never give up their desire to rule.

3) This conflict can never detract from the dignity of the government. The conflict is not between the faculties and the government but between one faculty and another, and the government can look on unmoved. Though it has indeed taken certain tenets of the higher faculties under its own protection, by directing the businessmen of these faculties to expound them to the public, it is not protecting the higher faculties, as learned societies, on account of the truth of these teachings, views and opinions they are to expound publicly, but only for the sake of its (the government's) own advantage; for it would be beneath the government's dignity to decide about the intrinsic truth of these tenets and so to play the role of scholar. The higher faculties, in other words, must answer to the government only for the instruction and information they give their businessmen to expound to the public; for these circulate among the people as a *civil* community and, because they could impair the government's influence over it, are subject to its sanction. On the other hand, the teachings and views that the faculties, as theorists, have to settle with one another are directed to a different kind of public—a learned community devoted to the sciences; and since the people are resigned to understanding nothing about this, the government does not see fit to intervene in scholarly discussions.[4] The rank of

4 On the other hand, if the businessmen of the faculties (in their role of practitioners) bring the conflict before the civil community (publicly—from the pulpits, for example), as they are prone to do, they drag it illegitimately before the judgment seat of the people (who are not competent to judge in scholarly matters), and it ceases to be a scholarly debate. And then begins the state of illegal conflict mentioned above, in which doctrines in keeping with the people's inclinations are set forth, the seeds of insurrection and factions are sown, and the government is thereby endangered. These self-appointed tribunes of the people, in doing this, renounce the learned professions, encroach on the rights of the civil constitution (stir up political struggles), and really deserve to be called neologists. This justly hated name is badly misused when it is applied indiscriminately to every author of innovations in doctrine and pedagogical method (for why should the old always be better than the new?). But those who introduce a completely different form of government, or rather a lack of any government (anarchy), by handing over scholarly questions to the decision of the people,

the higher faculties (as the right side of the parliament of learning) supports the government's statutes; but in as free a system of government as must exist when it is a question of truth, there must also be an opposition party (the left side), and this is the philosophy faculty's bench. For without its rigorous examinations and objections, the government would not be adequately informed about what could be to its own advantage or detriment. But if the businessmen of the faculties should want, on their own initiative, to make changes in the decrees given for them to expound publicly, then the government in its vigilance could lay claim to [jurisdiction over] them as *innovators* who could be dangerous to it. It could not, however, pass judgment on them directly, but only in accordance with the most loyal verdict drawn from the higher faculties, since it is only through the faculty that the government can direct these businessmen to expound certain teachings.

4) This conflict is quite compatible with an agreement of the learned and civil community in maxims which, if observed, must bring about a constant progress of both ranks of the faculties toward greater perfection, and finally prepare the way for the government to remove all restrictions that its choice has put on freedom of public judgment.

In this way, it could well happen that the last would some day be first (the lower faculty would be the higher)—not, indeed, in authority, but in counselling the authority (the government). For the government may find the freedom of the philosophy faculty, and the increased insight gained from this freedom, a better means for achieving its ends than its own absolute authority.

Outcome

So this antagonism, that is, this *conflict* of two parties united in [their striving toward] one and the same final end (*concordia discors, discordia concors*), is not a war, that is, not a dispute arising from conflicting final aims regarding the *Mine* and *Thine* of learning. And since, like the political Mine and Thine, this consists in freedom and property, with freedom necessarily preceding property as its condition, any right granted to the higher faculty entails permission for the lower faculty to bring its scruples about this right before the learned public.

---

really deserve to be branded neologists; for they can steer the judgment of the people in whatever direction they please, by working on their habits, feelings, and inclinations, and so win them away from the influence of a legitimate government.

CHAPTER TWO

A Closer Look at the University in General Terms

From *Occasional Thoughts on Universities in the German Sense, with an Appendix Regarding a University Soon to Be Established* (1808/1991)

FRIEDRICH D. E. SCHLEIERMACHER

This selection is taken from *Occasional Thoughts on Universities in the German Sense, with an Appendix Regarding a University Soon to Be Established* (1808/1991). The German original text was translated by G. Reimer in 1808, Berlin. This text is introduced and translated by Terrance N. Tice and Edwina Lawler, University of Michigan, Drew University, April, 1991. Published by EMText, San Francisco.

Editors' Note

Schleiermacher's *Occasional Thoughts* (1808) helped to provide the impetus for Humboldt's reform ideas based on the close relation of research and teaching, knowledge for its own sake and the notion of *Bildung*. He envisioned a 'Universitas litterarum' as the basis for a humanistic education and four pillars of Law, Medicine, Philosophy and Theology. He developed the philosophical system called the *Wissenschaftslehre* or 'science of knowledge' which sought new foundations for

Kant's Critical philosophy in the self-reproducing nature of the 'I' as the ground of all experience facilitated by a new form of national education that would enable the German nation. He was a member of a four member commission set up by Humboldt to draft provisional statues for the university in June 1810. The vocation of humankind was thus built into the concept of the modern university, the learned scholar and the student who is responsible for developing herself for her own sake as the highest goal of society that leads to complete unity, unanimity and equality of all its members. For Schleiermacher, Kant's abstract moral universalism goes against the ethics of individuality and the free development of a unique personality. Both Schleiermacher and Humboldt reflect a preference for individuality and originality that characterized early German Romanticism. This preference can be seen in accounts of academic freedom—both freedom from the external world and freedom granted within the institution. They agreed that while the institution was to be supported by the State it must remain free of any government interference. Academics also were allowed to choose topics for their teaching according to their research interests. Students were typically seen as 'getting to know themselves' before embarking on a professional career. Freedom—of the institution, of the professors, of the students—became the governing principle for the greater evolution of society. Schleiermacher's contribution to *Pedagogik* is legendary in Germany and his Occasional Thoughts became a standard text and a pivotal document in his intellectual biography.

MP

*****

Comparison of the university with the schools and academies has shown us its essential character, by virtue of which it necessarily fits in the middle between the two. Accordingly, through it the scientific spirit is to be awakened in young people and raised to clarity of consciousness. We have added—almost without proof, for the proposition is quite intuitively evident in itself—that for this purpose formal speculation alone does not suffice but must be embodied at the same time in "real" knowing.[1] Nor does just any selection of information one likes, such as is used for gymnastic exercise in schools, suffice.[2] The reason is that the scientific spirit is, by its very nature, systematic, and so it cannot possibly attain clarity of consciousness in an individual if that individual has not also gained perspective on the entire domain of knowledge, at least in its basic features. Still less can the general sensibility and special talent of individuals be cultivated to form a unique

1 Ed. note: See note 20 on "real" knowing.

2 Ed. note: See notes 10 and 12 on what is "gymnastic."

intellectual life if each does not find at the university that which can arouse one's special talent. The university thus has to embrace all knowing and, in the way it looks after each individual branch, it must express its natural internal relation to knowing as a whole, its degree of proximity or distance from the common center. Only one exception, it would appear, can be admitted: that one branch would be given a most prominent place because overall the talent of the nation surpassingly inclines to it. This exception could only show up where the arrangements of the university approach those of an academy.

This is how it would have to be if the scientific impulse alone were to found and organize the universities. Yet, if we look at how they are, we find everything quite different. From a scientific point of view, most of what we see appears quite disproportionate: what is insignificant is granted great indulgence; much that does not appear to belong together at all is externally joined; in reverse, what is important is minimized or is viewed entirely afresh as if it had only just now come into the picture; much is also treated as if designed not for those in whom the scientific spirit is to develop but for those in whom it can only remain forever alien.

Clearly this spirit does not arise in everyone, not even in all those who are indeed ready and inclined to collect a fine body of information and in a certain sense to work it over. For this reason, traditionally the scholarly school is supposed to comprise only a select number of young people, and, in turn, to send only a select number of these to the university. Still, since its role is preparatory and is not defined as bringing the scientific disposition to light, it cannot decide reliably or definitively as to the degree of scientific aptitude. It forms conclusions about the desire and ease with which the information offered by the school is grasped, also about any degree of budding predilection for the scientific content in such information. Yet, all this evidence is rather deceptive; precisely what is surest in it, moreover, admits least of being put into an externally valid form. How often one finds both remarkable diligence and great desire and love—such as stand out for the expert observer only through their sheer unconscious animality—paired with very little mental acumen[3] or talent.

Indeed, precisely in this decisive period of life a barren blossom opens in many students which is only too readily taken to be fertile, and, conversely, if the school were resolved to adjudge extreme strictness to be its law, many students who would only have developed later on would be rashly deprived of further support. In short, unavoidably many come to the university who are really unsuited for science in the highest sense-in fact, they make up the greater portion, since actually this

3 Geist. Ed. note: The word means literally "spirit," in this context specifically suggesting the scientific spirit, again paired with talent. See note 18.

situation can be far less damaging than one where a large, singular and decided talent would have to do totally without the salutary influences of this institution. For anyone who takes an active part in the formation of youth, it is a dreadful, a terrible thought to suppose that already at school, or as they leave it, a split is to be made between those who are capable of the highest scientific culture and those who are allotted to a subordinate echelon, and that for the second group special institutions are to be established where they would be further cultivated for their particular area of knowledge in a more mechanical, traditional manner and without the philosophical guidance of the university. This thought does not arise in an age when, by the nature of the case, every aristocratic feature must become extinct but in an age when people want to nurture and extend the formation of youth more than ever before. Or is it intended that these budding youth, who have been formed at the scholarly schools only with limited success, should implicate themselves in a judgment to downgrade themselves so, at a time when they cannot possibly know themselves well enough, instead of wanting to reach out for all the majesty of science? Truly, such students would deserve to be totally expelled and dishonored.

No, first let the more excellent and the lesser minds together go through the decisive efforts that the university makes to engender a scientific life in each young person. Only when they have all fallen short of their highest aims will the majority naturally place themselves on the subordinate echelon of good and faithful workers. The latter very much need the scientific association, for the few truly outstanding, formative minds can set a great many organs of that body into motion. This is why the universities have to be so composed that they are higher schools at the same time: so as to give further support to those whose talents can very well serve the supreme dignity of science, even if they disclaim it for themselves. Moreover, this arrangement certainly must not be externally distinguishable as a special one, since the two sets of learners are not externally differentiated but are to be separated from each other only by virtue of their actions.

The state needs even more members of the second set. It can very easily perceive that in each branch the principal duties are entrusted to good effect only to those permeated with the scientific spirit, but it must also make an effort to draw in the major portion of those lesser talents. Even without owning this higher spirit, such talents are useful to the state because they are scientifically cultured and possess a body of information. For the same reason, then, the state must see to it that the universities are at the same time advanced schools for specialists, dealing with all that information useful in its service which above all else coheres with actual scientific culture. Even if in this area it is not so necessary, moreover, it is nevertheless natural enough to avoid the external distinction among learners here too.

So far, so good. Even this latter arrangement is not to be viewed as an abuse or defilement of purely scientific institutions. Rather, it is admirable, and for three reasons. First, precisely in this way at least a sense for true knowledge can be aroused within the greater number of cultured people, so far as is possible for each one. Second, those who have constituted such a school must at least remain impressed with a feeling for the dependence of information they gathered there upon higher scientific endeavors. Third, through their connection with purely scientific institutions, cultural institutions for service of the state must remain more vital in themselves and more receptive to improvement. All this, furthermore, is indisputably the essence of the German universities, as they have been for a long while.

However, a very pernicious misunderstanding is involved when governments here and there begin to view the political aspect of these institutions as the main thing and, whenever there is conflict, to force the genuinely scientific element to wait. Moreover, when they actually intend to be completely spared of the form of the university and to join the special schools for the various departments of state service directly to the general scholarly schools, this is a tragic sign that the value of highest culture for the state is being denied and that mere mechanism is being preferred to life.

Yes, there are places where the state has ravaged the universities—the very center, the nursery of all knowledge—and has then sought, as it were, only to dismember scientific endeavors and to tear them away from their vital interconnection. There, it must not be doubted, the design, or the unconscious effect of such an operation at least, is to stifle the highest and freest culture and all scientific spirit; and the unfailing result in all departments is that a mechanistic way of being and a deplorable narrow-mindedness get the upper hand. Those who propose to us that the universities be dispersed and turned into specialized schools are acting thoughtlessly or are infected by a ruinous, non-German spirit. Likewise, in every land where the form of the university would die out on its own or where a true university would never come into being, even if the government did not stand in the way, but everything would always remain on the order of the school,[4] science must decline and its spirit slumber.

Now, how university instruction must be formed can easily be recognized in any university, even if it is only moderately established, so long as the state does not overstep the boundaries of legitimate influence allowable by science. That is, the most general subject matter is common to all; all begin with this, and only later

---

4 Schulmäßig. Ed. note: Here the word also carries echoes of its usual meaning "scholastic."

do they divide themselves within the domain of the particular, as in each person one's distinctive talent is awakened and along with this one's love for that occupation wherein one can especially exercise it. Everything begins, therefore, with philosophy, with pure speculation, and whatever belongs propadeutically to that as a transition from school to university. The life of the entire university, however, the prospering of its entire enterprise, rests on its not being the empty form of speculation wherewith its young charges are alone satisfied. It rests, rather, on the fact that from the immediate perspective available in reason and its activity, insight develops in terms of the necessity and compass of all real knowing, so that from the very outset any presumed opposition between reason and experience, speculation and an empirical base is abolished. In this way, not only is true knowing made possible but, clothed at least according to its nature, it is also immediately generated. Such is the case because, without deciding here about the comparative worth of different philosophical systems, it is clear that otherwise there would be no bond at all between philosophical instruction and the rest, that nothing whatsoever would come of such instruction than the knowledge of logical rules and an apparatus of concepts and formulas not understood as to its meaning and derivation. Already through philosophy, then, there must be opened up a prospect into the two great domains of nature and history, and the most general subject matter in each must be a common possession to no less a degree.

In each person must dwell the main ideas from higher philology, insofar as all the treasures of knowing are formulated in language and its forms are stamped upon it, and from ethics,[5] insofar as it presents the nature of all human being and doing, even if one seeks one's special training more on the side of natural science. Likewise, no scientific life is thinkable for the person in whom the idea of nature would remain alien, the knowledge of its most general processes and most essential forms -contrast and connection in the areas of organic and of the inorganic. Consequently, each must get a good grasp on the essence of mathematics, of geography, and of natural philosophy and natural history.[6]

Yet, the more one gets into the details of historical research, of the arts of cultural development in the state and among human beings,[7] of geology and physiology, the more one is restricted to the particulars of one's calling. Subsequently, then, the state applies to this restriction with its special institutes for those who are to work on the continuing political and religious advancement of the citizenry or

5 Sittenlehre. Ed. note: This term regularly refers to ethics, as representing the human Side versus the external, broadly natural side of science.

6 Der Erdkenntnis, der Naturlehre Dod Naturbeschreibung.

7 Staats- und Menschenbildungskunst.

on their physical sustenance and improvement. These institutes, if they are not to be entirely inimical and pernicious excrescences upon the university, must declare themselves dependent on and must subsist on the scientific treatment of nature and history, and along with that, on philosophy.

Even here, however, and despite the fact that many participate in such instruction for whom philosophical instruction has not provided a true initiation, the external difference between institute and university is still avoided as much as possible, so as not to disturb the unity of the whole even from this perspective. Moreover, in every area of instruction that to some extent remains true to the character of the university, scientific presentation is the main thing and the details have value only as an add-on, as a device, as raw material for individual attempts at combination and representation. Accordingly, with slight degrees of difference the mode of teaching is everywhere the same.

Few understand the significance of using lectures; but, oddly enough, this practice has always persevered despite its constantly being very poorly done by the majority of teachers. This continuance is clear proof of how very much lecturing belongs to the essence of the university and of how greatly it is worth the trouble to reserve this form of instruction always for those few who, from time to time, know how to handle it correctly. Indeed, one could say that the true and peculiar benefit a university teacher confers is always in exact relation to the person's proficiency in this art.

Every disposition, scientific as well as religious, is shaped and improved only in life, in community shared by a number of people. Issuing forth from more cultured persons, from those who are more accomplished, it is first aroused and awakened from its slumbers in the novices; through mutual communication it grows and is strengthened in those who bear likeness to one another. Now, since the whole university is such a shared scientific life, lectures in particular are its sanctuary. It has been supposed that dialogue can best awaken life from slumber and draw forth its first stirrings, as in this genre the marvellous art of antiquity still manifests the same results today. This may well occur between two persons or where one person out of a whole company can with surety be put forward as their representative, or if individuals enjoy exemplary written works of this sort and, as it were, revive what is presented repeatedly in themselves. However, among many persons and in modern times it need not be this way. This is so because, despite many renewed efforts, dialogue has never arisen as the general form for teaching in the scientific domain; rather, systematic discourse has continually been maintained. It is also easy to see why. Our culture is far more individual than ancient culture was. Thus, dialogue has become far more personal, so that no individual can be put forward as interlocutor in the name of all, and in that case dialogue would be a much too external, merely confusing and disruptive form. Still, because its first aim is to bring ideas to consciousness, university lecturing must in any case adhere in this respect to the nature of ancient dialogue, if not to its external form. Accordingly, it -must attempt to bring two things quite clearly to light: on the one hand, the shared inner features of the listeners, their not having what they are to acquire as well as their unconscious possession of this; on the other hand, the inner features of the teacher, the teacher's possession of the given idea and its activity within.

Hence, two elements are indispensable in this kind of discourse and comprise its distinct nature. The one I choose to call the popular kind: the exposition of whatever condition in which the listeners are surmised to find themselves, the art of pointing out to them what is problematic in it and the ultimate basis of all that is to be declared null and void in the state of ignorance.[8] This is the true dialectical art, and the more strictly dialectical it is the more popular. The other I would call the productive kind. Here the teacher must have all that is to be said emerge in front of the listeners, not simply recounting what one knows but reproducing one's own corning to know, the act itself, so that the listeners are not constantly gathering mere information but are directly perceiving the activity of reason in bringing forth knowledge and are perspicaciously continuing that activity.[9]

Assuredly, the chief place in which this art of lecturing resides is philosophy, the intrinsically speculative field; but all teaching at the university ought to be imbued with it, thus it is the proper art of the university teacher overall. Two virtues must be conjoined in it. On the one side, there are vitality and enthusiasm. The reproducing that occurs must be veracious, not a mere game. In the lecturing, whenever one truly looks upon knowledge in its origination, in its existence and having come into existence, whenever the lecturer traces the way from the center to the circumference of science, the lecturer must also make this real. In no true master of science does the situation ever become different from this. For such a scholar, no repetition is possible without some new combination enlivening oneself, without some new discovery drawing one to it. In teaching, one will continually learn, and will always stand before one's audience, in a vital and truly productive fashion.

Just as necessary to the lecturer, on the other hand, are reflectiveness and clarity. These must be present in order to make the inspired discourse understandable and effectual, to keep alive the consciousness of one's existence in common[10] with

---

8 Alles Nichtigen in Nichtwissen.

9 Sondern die Tatigkeit der Vernunft in Hervorbringen der Erkenntnis unmittelbar anschauen und anschauend nachbilden.

10 Seines Zusammenseins. Ed. note: Literally, this word means being together with.

the novices so that one speaks not simply for oneself but really for the listeners, bringing one's ideas and combinations really to the point of understanding in them and strengthening these ideas and combinations in their understanding so that merely dim presentiments of the glory of knowing do not arise in them instead of knowing itself.

No university teacher can be truly effective if entirely destitute of these excellences; and the genuinely healthy abundance of the institution consists in the fact that when one teacher surpassingly excels in one of these directions but is lacking, as is human, in the other, another teacher will compensate for it. These two virtues of discourse are its true basis, not an accumulation of literature, which is of no help to the beginner and which of necessity is rather formulated in writings than communicated orally. Out of these virtues flows genuine clarity, which does not consist in unflagging repetition or in marketable dilution and leanness of speech. Out of them flows true vitality, not out of a wealth of synonymous examples or out of incidental conceits and polemical attacks, good or bad. Amazingly enough, the erudition of a professor has become proverbial. To be sure, the more of it a professor has the better, but the greatest learning is useless without the art of lecturing.

Insofar as a teacher fittingly practices this art on students, it can be of little harm if they occasionally detect a lack of knowledge somewhere in the teacher's area of science; they will nevertheless know that the teacher is in full possession of the science as such. Indeed, one can always hope that erudition will yet come to a young faculty member. If, however, the teacher does not have that talent for communication in the years when one stands closest in age to one's listeners, that teacher will hardly attain it later on. What good does erudition do if instead of a real lecture what is presented is only false appearance, the empty form of it? One can think of nothing more lamentable than this. A professor who repeatedly reads from a notebook written down once and for all and for students to take down, quite inopportunely reminds us of that period when there was as yet no publishing and much value already attached to a learned man's dictating his manuscript to many people at once, a time when oral discourse also had to serve in place of books. Today, however, no one can see why the state should subsidize certain men so that they may enjoy the privilege of being allowed to ignore the benefit of publication, or indeed why such a man otherwise troubles people to come to him and does not rather sell his wisdom set down in permanent writings, in the usual way, black on white. Surely, to speak of such a work and way in terms of the marvellous impression the living voice makes would be laughable indeed.

However, if this mode of discourse is to have the character recommended, then certainly the actual lectures must not be the teacher's only contact with students. To be stiffly reserved and unable to be something for one's youthful students beyond the lectern ordinarily accompanies the vices of lecturing already faulted. If the teacher is to connect with the listeners' level of knowledge effectively, is to help them overcome the divergences to which they incline, and is to work successfully through the weak powers of comprehension that prevail among them, other modes and levels of living with them must come to the teacher's aid. This practice will enable the teacher to keep in touch with the everchanging generation of students, as is required. It would be wrong to say that this practice is impossible because of the number of students. Attached to the lectures is a chain of relationships, in which naturally the more intimate they become the fewer participate. These extend from discussion periods[11] and hours for review and testing, times in which works by different individuals are communicated and considered, to private association with students where actual dialogue predominates. There, if the teacher knows how to build trust, one can, by listening to what the best-read and most cultured youth convey, gain information about what may work especially well to impress and stimulate the larger group. Only by gradually forming and making use of these relationships can the teacher unite the splendid surety of the ancients, who would always hit just the right note in their conversations, with the noble modesty of the moderns, who must always presuppose an individual cultivation in each person, already begun and progressing independently.[12]

One can see that this gift of communication admits of the most varied differences. For one person it works better to undercut the mere semblance of knowledge and arouse the need for true science, for another to present the basic features of science so that they can be clearly perceived. One teacher will initiate more students to science by inspiring them; the other will secure it in them more through a process of reflection. One teacher will be more skilled in that one simply appears to be dealing with diverse details, yet always leads reflection back to the highest, innermost unity. Possessing a different talent, another will adhere to the particular, letting it predominate even where one appears to be fastened upon the highest and most general. Every person, however, will be an excellent teacher in whom all that is necessary, even if one of these elements outweighs the other, is vitally conjoined. The university, moreover, must also be literally the university in that it strives to unite all these differences within itself. In this way every young scholar would be in a position to find such a teacher as may be desired under the given circumstances and with whatever progress has been made.

---

11 Konversatorien. Ed. note: These periods comprise an early form of recitation or seminar session.

12 Eine schon angefangene und selbständig fortgehende individuelle Bildung jedes einzelnen.

However, no matter how vitalizing and fortunate this effort may be, a complete balance, wherein every need is provided for in a way equally complete, will probably never be attained in one such institution alone. In any period, each institution will lean to one side or another. One will distinguish itself through more lively arousal of the scientific spirit in general, while in most subject areas perhaps falling behind in the thoroughgoing exposition of particular aspects. Another will take the reverse course. The one will be more prominent in the purely philosophical respect; the other will excel as a pre-academy or as an aggregate of specialized schools. One university will emphasize preparing its students for further work, in turn leaving the free, higher tasks of combination to them. Another will emphasize leading students to these combinatory tasks but expect them to accomplish on their own whatever may be a matter requiring industrious effort. Indeed, for a rather long time, universities have often maintained the same character: one emphasizing the forming of speculative minds, which will however benefit from seeking the "real" sciences elsewhere, another for a long time almost exclusively educating technical experts,[13] because a decided talent for developing a higher scientific spirit there is already presupposed. The two types, then, are already dangerous extremes of one-sidedness between which the rest are arrayed and to their credit.

All this goes to show that, of necessity, a plurality of universities must be found within the sphere of one and the same national culture and that the freest possible concourse with and the most unrestricted use of each institution, according to the needs of each person, is indispensable. This truth is obvious, as can already be seen, no doubt, from the fact that universities stand in the middle between scholarly schools and the academy. To possess thirty-eight universities, as the German nation has so far tolerated having, may indeed be a great misfortune and may be the reason why so few have attained much stature. Yet, how is the right number to be found? First the right number of scholarly schools should be found, then more of a united spirit would be achieved among the Germans, so that not every district would want to have something special for itself. Then the matter would be left to settle itself, with no artificiality and with no wish to resurrect what is already dead. In this way, gradually the right policy will be found. Still, here it would always be better to exceed the right number than to let either the notion of a central German university or that of totally recasting the old form come into fashion. These are two extremes, either of which would 'be the greatest disaster of all that could still confront the Germans, after all those that have already befallen them.

---

13 Routiniers. Ed. note: Compare Schleiermacher's *Brief Outline of Theology as a Field of Study* §128.

Bibliographical Note (Terrance T. Tice with Edwina Lawler)

The chief immediate response to Schleiermacher's 1808 essay was conversational and organizational, among the university's planners themselves, though four notable but then anonymous reviews appeared in 1808–1809: by one of the prominent participants, law professor Friedrich Carl von Savigny and three others, two of whom remained anonymous. Savigny's appeared in *Heidelbergische Jahrbücher der Literatur* 1 (1808), 297–305; also in his *Vermischte Schriften*, Bd. 4 (Berlin, 1850), 255–269. Two others appeared in *Allgemeine Literatur-Zeitung* 1801, Bd. 1, Nr. 28 (30. Jan. 1809), 225–232, and *Das Morgenblatt für gebildete Stände* 2 (2. Juni 1808), 132ff, 525ff. A fourth, established in Karl Bulling's index as by a Pfarrer Schwarz in Münster, was contributed to the *Jenaische Allgemeine Literatur-Zeitung* 1809, Nr. 115 (17. Mai 1809), 305–312; Nr. 116 (18. Mai 1809), 313–316.

Over most of the past 183 years, when the founding of the University was mentioned by scholars, Schleiermacher's essay was usually noted as among pertinent essays by others, such as Friedrich Wilhelm Schelling (1803), Johann Gottlieb Fichte (1807, published in 1817), Schleiermacher's friend Heinrich Steffens (1809) and Wilhelm von Humboldt (1810, published in 1899), essays that best articulate the cultural vision underlying this effort. All five scholars' essays were collected in Ernst Anrich's book, *Die Idee der deutschen Universität: Die fünf Grundschriften aus der Zeit ihrer Neubegründung durch klassischen Idealismus und romantischen Realismus* (Darmstadt: Hermann Gentner, 1956), xvi, 386 S, a work often cited. Ordinarily, Schleiermacher's essay has been singled out as the most prominent and influential. For example, see Peter Berglar, *Wilhelm von Humboldt* (Reinbek bei Hamburg: Rowohlt Taschenbuch, 1970), S. 91. Reasons for this reputation will be indicated in the forthcoming edition of Schleiermacher's Writings on Academia (see iv. above), as will documentation supporting claims made in the Dedicatory Preface here.

Among contemporaries, not the least value of the essay would have lain in his refutation of the prevailing French norms in educational organization, particularly the preference for special technical schools over universities. He said nothing directly of this in his work, but, as he wrote to his friend Karl Gustav von Brinkmann on March 1, 1808: "My chief aim was simply to make the contrast between the German universities and the French special schools quite evident and to illuminate the worth of our native form without directly entering into polemic against it" (*Aus Schleiermachers Leben in Briefen*, Bd IV, Berlin: G. Reimer, 1863, S. 149). This contrast has not been thoroughly explored in the literature; nor have his other substantial contributions to the notion of the university as the sanctuary of "scientific culture" and to derived organizational principles been analyzed in detail. Both features are treated in the forthcoming edition just mentioned.

Generally, treatments of philosophical outlooks fueling the University of Berlin's early development are vaguely amalgamative rather than analytic. A prime, influential example is the attempt to outline an overarching neohumanist-idealist viewpoint among the founders by Helmut Schelsky in his treatise *Einsamkeit und Freiheit: Idee und Gestalt der deutschen Universität und ihrer Reformen* (Reinbek bei Hamburg: Rowohlt, 1963), 342 S. (especially 60–64; 2. urn einen Nachtrag 1970 erweiterte A., Düsseldorf: Bertelsmann, 1971, 288 S.). There can be no doubt that an array of views, very roughly summarized in this way—and to a significant extent misleadingly inaccurate with respect to Schleiermacher's historically oriented, critical realist perspective -did exist at the time, pitted especially against strong rationalist and utilitarian currents. It was far from being of one piece, however. At the present juncture it would seem more useful to sort these various views out so as to be able to consider which took hold, which did not, and why. Principles that might be reaffirmed by university advocates and reformers today but that were not fulfilled at the University of Berlin or through its considerable influence on other modern universities over the next two centuries must be assessed in the light of failures to reform in its own earliest years. See Walter M. Simon, *The Failure of the Prussian Reform Movement*, 1807–1819 (New York: Howard Fertig, 1971), xii, 272 p. As Schleiermacher insisted, however, the primary ground for any such assessment must be philosophical, and that was the main concern of his essay.

The basic documentation on the University of Berlin's founding is presented in four main sources: (1) Rudolf Köpke, *Die Gründung der königlichen Friedrich-Wilhelms-Universität zu Berlin* (Berlin: Gustav Schade, 1806), viii, 300 S.; (2) Max Lenz, *Geschichte der königlichen Friedrich-Wilhelms-Universität zu Berlin*, 1. Bd: *Gründung und Ausbau* (Halle: Verlag der Buchhandlung des Waisenhauses, 1910), with some material from other volumes; (3) Gustav Abb, *Schleiermachers Reglement für die königliche Bibliothek zu Berlin vom Jahre 1813 und seine Vorgeschichte* (Berlin: Martin Breslauer, 1926), viii, 119 S.; and (4) Wilhelm Weischedel, hg.v., *Idee und Wirklichkeit einer Universität: Dokumente zur Gesehichte der Friedrieh-Wilhelms-Universität zu Berlin* (Berlin: de Gruyter, 1960), xxxiv, 540 S. Much organizational and contextual material that might be desired is either lacking altogether or must be sought elsewhere.

Only a sparse literature has formed on Schleiermacher's role. The chief pieces are these seven: (1) In terms of general influence, a few pages in Friedrich Paulsen's, *The German Universities and University Study*, tr. by Frank Thilly and William W. Elwang (New York: Scribner, 1906), xvi, 451 p. (German ed., 1902); Johannes Bauer, "Schleiermacher über die Aufgabe der Universitäten 1808,"

Deutsch-Evangelisch, Monatsblätter für den gesamten deutsehen Protestantismus 1 (1910), 593–599; (3) Eduard Spragner, *Fichte, Sehleiermacher, Steffens über das Wesen der Universität, in Philosophische Bibliothek*, Bd 120 (Leipzig, 1910), xliii, 291 S.; (4) Otto Piper, "Schleiermacher und die neue Universität," *Zeitschrift für Theologie und Kirche* NF 14 (1933), 350–369; (5) *Die Humboldt-Universität: Gestem-Heute-Morgen-Zum einhundertfünfzig jährigen Bestehen der Humboldt-Universität zu Berlin und zum zweihundertfünfzig* jährigen *Bestehen der Charité, Berlin* (Berlin: Deutscher Verlag der Wissenschaft, 1960), 260 S.; (6) Luc Ferry et Alain Renaut, "Université et systeme: Réflexions sur les theories de l'université dans l'idéalisme allemand," Archives de philosophie 42, cah. 1 (1979), 59–90; and (7) Daniel Fallon, "Friedrich Schleiermacher and the Idea of the University: Berlin, 1810–1817," in his *The German University: A Heroic Ideal in Conflict with the Modern World* (Boulder: Colorado Associated University Press, 1980), 32–36.

Among the few more specialized accounts, particularly noteworthy is a set of eighteen essays by Heinrich Fink, et al., *Beiträge zur Gesehichte der Theologischen Fakultät Berlins: Zum 175. Jahrestag der Gründung der Berliner Universität, in Wissenschaftliche Zeitsehrift der Humboldt-Universität zu Berlin: Gesellsehafts und Sprachwissenschaftliche Reihe* 34 (1985), 517–628.

The principal editions of the work in German are as follows: (1) *Gelegentlicihe Gedanken über Universitäten in deutschem Sinn: Nebst einem Anhang über eine neu zu errichtende* (Berlin: G. Reimer, 1808), viii, 176 S.; (2) inclusion in Schleiermacher's *Sämmtliche Werke* III.1 (Berlin: G. Reimer, 1846), 535–644; (3) neu hg.v. Otto Braun (Leipzig: Fritz Eckardt, 1911), 110 S., also in *Schleiermacher's Werke in Auswahl*, hg.v. Otto Braun und Johannes Bauer, Bd 4 (Leipzig: Fritz Eckhardt, 1911); and (4) Anrich's volume cited above.

Translations have appeared in three languages: (1) Anders Siidermark, öfversatta af, *Af tillfället föranledda tankar om universiteter i tysk bemärkelse; Jämte ett tilltägg om inrättandet af ett nylt universitet* (Stockholm: A Gadelius, 1839), 138 sid.; (2) Luc Ferry, "Pensées de circonstance sur les universités de conception allemande," in Luc Ferry, Jean-Pierre Pesron et Allain Renaut, *Philosophies de l'Université: L'idealisme allemand et la question de l'Université* (Paris: Payot, 1970), 253–318 (the "Anhang" is excluded; the other texts are by Schelling, Fichte, von Humboldt and Hegel; introduction, 9–40); (3) the present English translation. An earlier English translation of part of the essay, by Gerhard E. Spiegler, "Reflections Concerning the Nature and Function of Universities," appeared in *The Christian Scholar* 48, no. 1 (Spring 1968), 139–157. Lucio D'Alesandro's essay, *Stato e Università nel pensiero di Sehleiermacher: Introduzione a: F.D.E. Schleiermacher "Pensieri occasionali sulla concezione tedesca dell'Università"* (Napoli: Istituto Universitario suor Orsola Bennincasa, 1984), 34 p., does not appear to have been followed by an Italian translation.

CHAPTER THREE

The Scientific and Moral Functions of Universities

From *On University Studies* (1802/1966)

F. W. J. SCHELLING

Translated by E. S. Morgan, this excerpt from Lectures delivered in 1802, is taken from *On University Studies*, by F. W. J. Schelling, 1966, Edited with Introduction by Norbert Guterman. Original English translation from University of California; digitalised 2007. Published by Ohio University Press, Athens, Ohio.

Editors' Note

Friedrich Wilhelm Joseph Schelling (1775–1854) was a German 'Idealist' philosopher whose major work is *Ideas for a Philosophy of Nature*. Andrew Bowie (2010) claims 'along with J. G. Fichte and G. W. F. Hegel, one of the three most influential thinkers in the tradition of "German Idealism."' *On University Studies* contains lectures given by Schelling at the University of Jena in 1802–1803 when he was 27 years old. In both texts he is concerned to search for and uncover 'primordial knowledge' as the basis for science and to apply this to an understanding of the actual structure of the university so that 'the unity of the whole may re-emerge amid widespread specialization'. Schelling went to Tubingen to study theology with fellow students Hegel and Holderlin. He replaced Fichte at Jena in 1799 when he was dismissed for 'atheism' and held professorships at Wurzburg. Munich and Erlangen, before becoming Hegel's successor at Berlin in 1841. Schelling's philosophical romanticism lay in his conception of art as yielding the highest kind of philosophical insight. In *Philosophical Investigations into the Essence of Human Freedom* Schelling (1809) explores traditional answers to the question of human nature to find freedom in nature in the ongoing struggle of cosmogenesis that is constitutive of nature herself.

MP

Recommended Reading

Bowie, Andrew (2010). “Friedrich Wilhelm Joseph von Schelling”, *The Stanford Encyclopedia of Philosophy* (Winter 2010 Edition), Edward N. Zalta (ed.), http://plato.stanford.edu/archives/win2010/entries/schelling

* * * * *

The concept of university studies led us to the higher concept of an existing body of scientific knowledge and thence to the highest Idea, namely, primordial knowledge. We shall now discuss the actual conditions under which the various sciences are taught in our universities.

It might seem that a philosopher should confine himself to drawing a picture of the body of scientific knowledge and formulating general methodological principles, without going into organizational matters or the temporal forms of our institution. However. I hope to show that these forms are not arbitrary, that they reflect the spirit of the modern world, and that they make it possible for the disparate elements of modern culture to interpenetrate. This process of interpenetration will eventually do away with the present confusion and give rise to superior institutions.

The reason why knowledge has a temporal aspect will be clear from the previous lecture. Just as the unity of the ideal and the real in its finite reflection expresses itself in space as a self-contained whole, as nature, so this unity, viewed in the infinite, expresses itself in the universal form of endless time. However, time does not exclude eternity, and science, though it manifests itself at the phenomenal level as a product of time, introduces an element of eternity. The true, like the good and the beautiful, is by nature eternal, and in the midst of time is independent of time. Science is temporal only insofar as it is expressed by individuals; in itself, knowledge is no more a matter of individuality than action is. Just as a true action is one that might take place in the name of the whole race, so in true knowledge it is not the individual but reason that knows. Science is essentially independent of time; it belongs to mankind, which is itself eternal. Therefore, like life itself, science must be passed on from individual to individual, from generation to generation—this process is an expression of its eternal character. This is not the place to prove in detail that all sciences and arts of the present generation of man have been bequeathed to us. It is inconceivable that man as he is today raised himself by his own efforts from instinct to consciousness, from animality to rationality: we must assume there existed before us a race which ancient legend celebrated as gods and the first benefactors of mankind. The hypothesis of a primordial people [i.e., the modern version of this ancient legend] can do no more than account for the already deformed traces of a high prehistoric culture which preceded the first separation of peoples and—if we refuse to assume the existence of an inborn carth spirit common to all men—it might also account for the similarities in the myths of the oldest peoples; but it does not account for the beginnings of culture, and, like any empirical hypothesis, merely pushes the explanation further back in time.

However that may be, it is well known that the earliest vehicles for transmitting higher ideas were actions, ways Of life, and symbols; even dogmas of the earliest religions were not stated explicitly but merely implied in prescriptions for religious practices. The states, laws, and institutions which were created to secure the preponderance of the divine principle in mankind were essentially expressions of speculative ideas. The invention of writing at first served only to stabilize tradition; the idea of using the spiritual medium of language to record artistic expression and thus give it enduring form could not arise until later. Even morality in the finest period of mankind was not an individual characteristic but reflected the spirit of the collectivity which was its source and its goal; similarly, science thrived in the light and air of public life as part of the collective organism. Subsequent ages were marked by a retreat from external reality and an internalization of life, which also affected science. The modern world is in every way, especially in science, a divided world which lives both in the past and in the present. The history of our sciences shows that the modern era took the past as its point of departure. The modern world had behind it a vanished world of the most magnificent scientific and artistic achievements. Separated from this ancient world by an unbridgeable gulf, it was linked to it only by the external bond of historical tradition, not by internal bonds of continuous organic growth. When the sciences revived in our part of the-world, the reawakened urge to knowledge could not first aim at original productions, but at understanding, admiring, and explaining the glories of the past. Rediscovery of forgotten ancient knowledge became the object of an additional new science. For this reason, and because good minds are needed even to gain insight into knowledge achieved by others, the terms scholar, artist, and philosopher came to be regarded as equal in dignity, and men who had not enriched previously existing knowledge by a single original insight were honored as men of science. Whereas the Greeks, as an Egyptian priest told Solon, were eternally young, the modern world was already old and experienced in its youth.

To study the history of the arts and sciences has become a kind of religion. In it philosophers discern more clearly the intentions, so to speak, of the world spirit. The profoundest minds, the greatest talents, have devoted themselves exclusively to this branch of knowledge.[1]

It is one thing to make the past an object of scientific investigation, another to put acquaintance with the past in the place of knowledge itself. Historical erudition in this sense becomes an obstacle to true knowledge; what it asks is no longer whether a thing is true, but whether it is in conformity with some derivative of the original insight, some imperfect copy of it. Aristotle in his writings on natural science interrogated Nature directly; in later times this direct approach was so completely forgotten that Aristotle took the place of Nature, and his authority was invoked against Descartes, Kepler, and others who clearly spoke in the name of Nature herself. Even today the majority of so-called scholars hold no idea important until it has passed through other brains and become historical, a thing of the past.

Our universities were organized more or less in the spirit of this historical knowledge, not so much perhaps in the early Renaissance as in later times. The whole of their organization could be inferred from the divorce which historical learning brought about between knowledge and its original object. Knowledge was divided into as many different branches as possible and the living whole was fragmented primarily because there was a great mass of already existing material still to be assimilated. Since all isolated parts of knowledge, i.e., the special sciences,

---

1 Changes in the external world correspond to quieter but no less profound changes in the minds of men, in accordance with a necessary law. To believe that intellectual changes—scientific revolutions and the ideas they produce, as well as works expressing a specific scientific or artistic spirit—reflect no necessity and are produced not in accordance with law but by chance, is utter barbarism. Classical antiquity must forever remain sacred to us; it is no less piety to make pilgrimages to surviving ancient remains than religion to search for a saint's alleged relics in devout simple-mindedness. As Goethe said:

Eagerly the pilgrim trudges: will he find his saint?
Will he hear and see the man who worked the miracles?
No, Time has carried him off; only bits are left;
A skull, a few bones have been preserved.
We are all pilgrims, who go in search of the past;
What we honor with such joy and piety is but scattered bones.
(Venetian Epigrams, No. 21)

can serve only as means to the attainment of absolute knowledge once the universal spirit has left them, this fragmentation eventually brought about a situation in which knowledge itself was almost lost sight of in an ever narrower concern for means and institutions. While a host of busywork scholars were mistaking the means for the end and trying to impose this view, knowledge, which is one and entire—and absolute in its oneness—withdrew to the higher disciplines and even there rarely exhibited much independence.

In the face of this situation, we have first of all to answer the question: What should be done within the accepted limitations, the actual structure of our universities today, in order that the unity of the whole may re-emerge amid the widespread specialization? I shall not be able to answer this question without mentioning a requirement that has to be met by the university teachers themselves. I shall not hesitate to speak frankly of such things to you. The young student, as he starts his academic career, is getting his first experience of emancipation from blind faith; for the first time he is acquiring and exercising his own judgment. No teacher worthy of his vocation will demand respect on any other grounds than the superiority of his intelligence, the breadth of his learning, and the zeal with which he seeks to communicate them. It would be an ignorant, incapable teacher who could wish to be respected on any other grounds. The reason I am speaking out on this matter is the following. How far a student's expectations of the university faculties will be rewarded depends in part on the character of those expectations. The scientific spirit once awakened among students reacts favorably on the whole body of the university, because the higher their expectations, the more the unfit teachers will be frightened away and the fit encouraged to greater efforts.

Since our demand—namely, that all sciences should be treated in the spirit of universal absolute knowledge—is inherently right, the question, Where are capable teachers to be found? is easily answered. The teachers themselves have had the experience of a university education; were they but given intellectual freedom, not shackled by scientifically irrelevant considerations, they would be able to rise to the occasion and be in a position to form other capable teachers.

It may be asked whether it is proper to make philosophical demands on the universities when everyone knows that they are instruments of the state and must be what the state intended them to be. If the intention were to impose on science a certain caution and moderation, to limit it to ordinary practical matters, we could hardly ask teachers to be progressive and to cultivate their disciplines in a philosophical spirit.

Surely, all of us assume—as we must—that the state intends the universities to be real scientific institutions and that whatever we say about them is valid only on this condition. Incontestably, the state has the authority to suppress the universities or to transform them into industrial training schools; however, it cannot intend the universities to be real scientific institutions without desiring to further the life of ideas and the freest scientific development. If the latter objective were abandoned for petty reasons, the incapable teachers would certainly be protected, but genius would be blocked and talent crippled.[2]

The fact that all the sciences are represented is not sufficient in itself to assure the true organic life of knowledge, which is supposedly the goal of universities (as their very name indicates). For this is required a spirit of co-operation which can come only from absolute science, the special sciences its willing instruments in supplying the objective, real aspect to complement it. I cannot dwell longer upon this view; however, it is clear that we are not here dealing with some "application" of philosophy such as has been attempted from time to time in every profession, even in connection with the most trivial subjects (trivial with respect to philosophy)—even agriculture, obstetrics, and the theory of first aid have not escaped this kind of "philosophical" treatment. Nothing is sillier than efforts by lawyers and physicians to give a "philosophical" cast to their professions, when they are ignorant of the first principles of philosophy. It is as though someone who did not

---

2 The usual view of the universities is that they should produce servants of the state, perfect instruments for its purposes. But surely, such instruments should be formed by *science*. Thus, to achieve such an aim through education, science is required. But science ceases to be science the moment it is degraded to a *mere* means, rather than furthered for its own sake. It is certainly not furthered for its own sake when, for instance, Ideas are rejected on the grounds that they arc of no use in ordinary life, have no practical application, are unrelated to experience. Such may very well be the case, as far as experience at a given moment is concerned, experience that has become what it is precisely because the Ideas have been neglected and for this reason cannot be in harmony with them. What is true, real experience, must be determined by the Ideas in the first place. Experience is doubtless a good thing if it is *genuine* experience, but whether and to what extent it is genuine, and what is really experienced in experience, that is the great question. For instance, Newtonian optics is allegedly based on experience, and yet its fundamental conception, as well as its consequences are recognizably false to anyone who has conceived the Idea of light. Similarly the alleged experience of physicians may often contradict true theory derived from the Ideas; but if, for instance, the physician himself produces morbid symptoms and then attributes them to spontaneous effects of nature. we are not dealing with genuine experience: rather, had the physician treated the disease on the basis of a correct conception derived from Ideas, the symptoms in question would not have been produced, and he would not attribute them to his "experience:" or at least would not see in them a contradiction to true theory. What Kant says of practical ideas is applicable to theoretical ideas: namely, that nothing is more harmful or un· worthy than appeal to experience, which after all would not exist in the first place, had it not been guided by crude notions.—But I digress.

know Euclid's first proposition were to try to measure a globe, cylinder, or other solid.

What I am referring to is the formlessness prevalent in most practical disciplines today, the total absence of art or logic, the kind of obtuseness which is incapable of rising above the particular, the inability even to imagine that every branch of knowledge, even one dealing with practical, empirical matters, must aim at the universal.

Only the universal as such is the source of Ideas, and Ideas are the life of science. He who knows his particular profession only as a specialty, who is unable to see what is universal in it or to express it in terms of universal scientific culture, is unworthy to be a teacher and custodian of science. He may be useful in various ways—as a physicist in the erection of lightning rods, as an astronomer in composing almanacs, as a physician in utilizing galvanism for therapeutic purposes, etc.—but the vocation of teacher requires more than mechanical skills. As Lichtenberg[3] observed, "Drawing boundary lines to fence off scientific fields may be very useful for farmers, but Reason, looking for unity, warns the philosopher at every step to take no notice of the fences, which are often matters of convenience or a sign of narrow-mindedness." Undoubtedly it was not just special skill in his profession but ability to inform it with a universally cultivated mind that made Lichtenberg the most intelligent physicist of his time and the best teacher in his field.

The demand that a particular profession be treated in the spirit of the whole is often interpreted in the sense that it should be only a means. Actually, the very opposite is the case: a scientist is faithful to the spirit of the whole only to the extent that he considers his field an end in itself, an absolute. Nothing can be conceived of as part of a true totality if it functions merely as a means. A state is perfect if every citizen, while a means in relation to the whole, is also an end in himself. Precisely because the particular is absolute in itself, it is within the absolute and an integral part of it, and vice versa.

The more a scholar conceives of his particular domain as an end in itself, even making it, as far as he is concerned, the central point of all knowledge—hoping to expand it into an all-embracing totality[4]—the more he is striving to express universal and absolute ideas in it. Conversely, the less able he is to conceive of it as universal, the more will he-consciously or unconsciously—comprehend it only as a means, for that which is not an end in itself can only be a means. This would

---

3 EDITOR: Lichtenberg, Georg Christoph (1742–1799) was a physist by profession. His occasional writings (among them, Letters from England and Aphorisms) are celebrated for their wit and humour.

4 So that it might reflect the whole universe.

be intolerable to a man who respects himself; hence, such narrowness is usually associated with pettiness and want of genuine interest in science-science is looked upon merely as a means to very tangible ends.

I am fully aware that in the eyes of very many, particularly those who appreciate science only for its practical uses, universities are no more than institutions for the transmitting of knowledge, places where a young man learns all that has been accomplished in science down to his own day; in this view, it might seem sheer accident if the teachers, besides communicating knowledge, were also to enrich science with discoveries of their own. But even granting that this alone is or ought to be the purpose of a university, we still demand that the transmitting of knowledge be intelligently effected. Otherwise, why should lectures by living men be at all necessary in a university? The student could as well be referred to popular textbooks expressly written for him or to voluminous compilations which exist in every branch of knowledge. But there can be no doubt that to transmit knowledge intelligently one must be able to understand the discoveries made by others, to understand them correctly, clearly, in all their implications. Many of them are of a kind whose inner essence can be grasped only by a kindred genius through a rediscovery in the literal sense of the word. A teacher who merely transmits will often give a radically false version of what he learned. Do we possess an exposition of ancient philosophy, even of a single philosopher of the ancient or modern world, which we can point to confidently as a successful exposition, at once true and adequate? A man who lives within his science as though on another's property, who is not himself in possession, who has never acquired a sure and living feeling for it, who is incapable of sitting down and reconstructing it for himself, is an unworthy teacher even when he attempts no more than to expound ideas of others. He is out of his depth, struggling at a task beyond his powers. Intelligent transmitting of knowledge certainly involves good judgment. But if a correct and comprehensive understanding of the discoveries of others is impossible without capacity for original thought, how much more impossible, then, is accurate judgment of them. To be sure, in Germany many self-styled "critics" from whom no original thought would drop if they were held upside down, pass judgment on everything. But such judgments are of no use whatever to knowledge.

A man incapable of reconstructing the totality of his science for himself, of reformulating it from his own inner, living vision, will never go beyond mere historical exposition of the science. This is the sort of thing we get in a well-known introduction to philosophy: "When we direct our attention to ourselves, we become aware of various manifestations of a something we call the soul. These various activities we refer to as different faculties; we call them faculties according to the different ways in which they manifest themselves—as sensation, understanding, imagination, etc."

What could be more stultifying, more senseless, more mind-killing than such a statement? Furthermore, we must remember that the university lecturer is supposed to explain his subject genetically. This is the real advantage of live instruction: the lecturer does not merely give results, as the writer does, but shows—in the higher sciences at least—how these results were reached, and at every point builds up the whole science, as it were, before the student's eyes.[5] How can a man who has not reconstructed his science for himself teach it in such a way that it appears not as something ready-made, but as something the student must rediscover for himself?

Mere transmitting of knowledge without personal creative understanding is not enough if the teacher is to obtain the results he should. At the same time, no one can teach a science unless he has previously mastered it as completely as possible. In every craft, even the lowliest, proofs of completed apprenticeship are demanded before one is allowed to practice it as a master. But considering

---

5 (the student's eyes) Schelling's portrait of the ideal teacher is suspiciously like himself. His tendency in the early period to present his ideas before they had fully matured has the saving grace of making him an exciting lecturer. Various contemporary sources confirm his popularity as a teacher. In his diaries, Henry Crabb Robinson, after describing the dullness of other professors, notes:

> "I shall at the close of this lecture instantly proceed to Schelling and purify my fancy polluted by the inspection of rotten carcasses and smoked skeletons, by hearing the modern Plato read for a whole hour his new metaphysical theory of Aesthetics of the Philosophy of Arts: I shall in spite of the obscurity of the philosophy compounded of the most profound abstraction and enthusiastic mysticism, be interested by particular ingenious remarks and amused by extravagant novelties … I shall be a little touched perhaps by the contemptuous treatment of our English critics and hear something like his abuse of [Erasmus] Darwin last Wednesday … I shall hear again Burke and Horne and the 'thick-skinned' Johnson and the 'shallow' Priestley briefly dispatched and hear it intimated that it is absurd to expect the science of beauty in a country that values the mathematics only as it helps to spinning jennies and stock-weaving machines and beauty only as it recommends their manufactories abroad. I shall sigh and say too true! … At 4 I shall again return to Schelling and hear his grand lecture on speculative philosophy. I shall be animated if I happen to be in an enthusiastic frame, at the sight of more than 130 enquiring young men listening with attentive ears to the exposition of a philosophy in its pretensions more glorious than any publicly maintained since the days of Plato and his commentators: a philosophy equally inimical to Locke's empiricism, Hume's scepticism and Kant's criticism, which has been but the ladder of the new and rising sect." (Crabb Robinson in Germany, 1801–1805, Oxford University press, 1929, pp. 117 f.)

how easy it is to attain a professorship in many universities, it would seem as though no vocation makes fewer demands than that of teaching. Under the circumstances, creative minds that expect to obtain a professorship speedily on the grounds that capacity for original work goes hand in hand with learning are likely to be disappointed.

We have so far examined how much universities could do to achieve—were it only the original purpose for which they were founded—the furthering of knowledge. But it would seem that they could do more than that, and that their original purpose was too narrow. We do not grant the validity of the antithesis between knowledge and action; we have seen that the antithesis vanishes as each of the opposing terms approaches its perfection, its absoluteness. If our universities have not yet begun to further culture in the universal sense, in addition to serving as nurseries of knowledge, it is because, even with respect to knowledge, they remain at a low level.

Here we must also consider the constitution of our universities in so far as it influences their ethical function in the community.

Civil society for the most part shows a decided want of harmony between the ideal and the actual. This is because for the time being its aims cannot be ideal and because the means have taken on so much importance that they defeat the ends. As universities are simply associations for the cultivation of the sciences, they need, apart from voluntary support from the state in its own interest, no further regulations than those rooted in the Idea itself. Wisdom and prudence here agree: it is necessary only to do what the Idea of a scientific institution prescribes in order to make the constitution of a university perfect.

Civil society, so long as it is obliged to pursue empirical ends to the detriment of absolute ends, can have only an apparent and forced identity, not a true inner identity. Universities can have only an absolute purpose—beyond that they have none.

To accomplish its aims the state must impose divisions—not such as arise out of inequalities of rank, but far more essential—by isolating and setting in opposition individual talents, by repressing many individualities and directing energies into various channels where they will serve more effectively.

All the members of a scientific association share a single purpose, namely, to give no weight to any other consideration but science and to permit no other distinctions save those of talent and culture. Men who are there only to assert themselves in other ways—by extravagance, by wasting their time in frivolous amusements, in short, the same sort of privileged idlers as are found in civil society (and they are chiefly responsible for rowdiness at universities)—ought not to be tolerated. Whoever cannot prove his diligence and readiness to work should be expelled.

If science were the paramount concern of all minds, there could be no misdirection of the noble impulses of youth. After all, the young are primarily interested in ideas. In this view, whenever misconduct did occur (or should it occur again), the fault lies with the teacher or the supervising personnel whose duty it is to foster the proper spirit.

Were teachers communicating nothing but the genuine scientific spirit to those around them, giving consideration to nothing but the advancement of science, and were not outbreaks of vulgarity which disgrace the vocation of teaching tolerated by the low standard of the community itself, those who are capable of distinguishing themselves only by their savagery would soon quit the student ranks of their own accord.

The realm of the sciences is not a democracy, still less an ochlocracy, but an aristocracy in the best sense of the word. The incapables whom nothing but some convenience or other recommends, the ambitious chatterboxes who dishonor the scientific estate with their petty pursuits, should be kept down. Left to their own devices and in no way encouraged, they would receive the contempt that ignorance and intellectual incapacity deserve; indeed, since these are usually associated with ridiculousness and meanness, they would serve as the sport of youth, whose natural aversion to such as they too often is blunted by the conditions prevailing today.

Talent needs no special protection so long as its opposite is not fostered; intellectual capacity naturally creates for itself the highest and most decided influence.

This is the only policy we need in order to make institutions of knowledge flourish, to give them all possible dignity within their walls and earn them respect outside. To make the university a model of organization, nothing is necessary beyond realizing what is in any case desirable and doing so consistently. Inasmuch as I do not concede the existence of a gulf between knowledge and action, I cannot allow it in reference to the university.

Training for rational thinking, by which I understand no superficial habit but a cultivation that goes deep into the innermost essence of man—the only really scientific culture—is also the only training for rational action. Ends that lie beyond this absolute sphere of scientific culture automatically fall outside the concern of universities by the very nature of their function.

A man who has mastered his particular science has thereby come close to absolute knowledge, has entered the realm of clarity and rationality. The most dangerous thing that can happen to a man is to be under the sway of muddy thinking. It is a great gain when such sway has been cut down to a minimum, and the process is complete when he has pressed on to the attainment of absolute consciousness and walks wholly in the light.

Science guides the mind directly to the vision which in a continuous self-creating process leads us to identity with ourselves and thereby to a truly blessed life. The experience of life educates slowly, not without loss of time and strength. To him who dedicates himself to knowledge it is granted to anticipate experience, to recognize directly and in himself that which after all is the only fruit of the most cultivated, most richly experienced life.

CHAPTER FOUR

On the Spirit and the Organisational Framework of Intellectual Institutions in Berlin (1809/1970)

WILHELM VON HUMBOLDT

This selection Wilhelm von Humboldt is taken from Reports and Documents, University Reform in Germany, from *Minerva: A Review of Science, Learning and Policy*, 1970—April, Volume 8, Number 2. Published by Macmillan (Journals) Ltd, London, United Kingdom. Originally written between autumn of 1809 and autumn of 1810.

Editors' Note

Wilhelm von Humboldt (1767–1835) was a Prussian philosopher, linguist and minister of education in the Prussian civil service who was responsible for reforming the university and school system according to humanist principles. In 1810 he founded the University of Berlin that was named after him (and his naturalist brother, Alexander) in 1949. Humboldt wrote *On the Limits of State Action* in 1791–1792 that was a passionate defense of liberty and the philosophical basis of his view that the university should be neutral and free from ideological influences, state interference and private interests providing both institutional autonomy and a notion of academic freedom. In his 'Theory of Education' written about 1793 he indicated that education was to assist the individual to give the fullest possible development of the concept of humanity and to establish personal autonomy in an environment of academic freedom. Humboldt studied Kant's and Hegel's works, read Leibniz, Hume, Locke, and Rousseau, and was close friends with Schlegel, Friedrich Jacobi and the poets Goethe and Schiller. As minister he appointed Schleiermacher, Fichte and Neibuhr among other scholars to the committee to found the University of Berlin. The University of Berlin became the model institution of the 19th century based on a set of unique characteristics that included the unity of teaching and research, the pursuit of higher learning in the philosophy faculty, freedom of study for students (*Lernfreiheit*), and the educational ideal of *Bildung* based on the revival of ancient Greece ideals, corporate autonomy for universities despite their funding by the state, and the notion of academic freedom. The University of Berlin became the basis of national cultural revival and the Humboldtian model had a strong influence throughout central, eastern, and northern Europe, before impacting on American universities that were quick to adopt the educational and scientifica principles underlying Humboldt's thinking. The Humboldtian model and its conflict with market-driven and neoliberal approaches to higher education is part of current debates in Germany with Jürgen Habermas, among others, arguing for a return to a neo-Humboldtian approach to the university.

MP

* * * * *

The idea of disciplined intellectual activity, embodied in institutions, is the most valuable element of the moral culture of the nation. These intellectual institutions[1] have as their task the cultivation of science and scholarship (*WissenSchaft*) in the deepest and broadest sense. It is me calling of these intellectual institutions to devote themselves to the elaboration of the uncontrived substance of intellectual and moral culture, growing from an uncontrived inner necessity.

Their essence, manifested in the individual, consists of the combination of objective scientific and scholarly knowledge with the development of the person; in institutional terms, this essence lies in the articulation of the mastery of

1 Von Humboldt uses the term *wissenschaftliche Anstalten* to cover both academies and universities. I have used "intellectual institutions" as the English equivalent. For *Wissenschaft*, I preferred to use "science and scholarship" which I think is more correct than the more usual alternatives of "science" or "higher learning". Here and there I have interpreted rather than translated. On the whole, however, I have adhered closely to the German text while trying to produce a translation which is closer to the intellectual idiom of early nineteenth century learned German than the twentieth century idiom of university discussion. [Editor.]

transmitted knowledge at the school stage with the first stages of independent inquiry. In other words, the task of these intellectual institutions is to effect the transition from the former to the latter. The main consideration is the cultivation of science and scholarship. Insofar as science and scholarship are kept free of corruption, they will be correctly apprehended in their essential nature and as a whole, whatever the variations in particular instances.

Since these institutions can only fulfil their purpose when each of them bears continuously in mind the pure idea of science and scholarship, their dominant principles must be freedom and the absence of distraction (*Einsamkeit*). The intellectual exertions of men, however, only prosper through a process of collaboration. This does not mean merely that one individual supplies what another lacks. Collaboration operates through a process in which the successful intellectual achievements of one person arouse the intellectual passions and enthusiasms of others, and through the fact that what was at first expressed only by one individual becomes a common intellectual possession instead of fading away in isolation. Given this collective character of individual accomplishment, the inner life of these higher intellectual institutions must be such as to call forth and sustain a continuously self-renewing, wholly uncoerced and disinterested collaboration.

One unique feature of higher intellectual institutions is that they conceive of science and scholarship as dealing with ultimately inexhaustible tasks: this means that they are engaged in an unceasing process of inquiry. The lower levels of education present closed and settled bodies of knowledge. The relation between teacher and pupil at the higher level is a different one from what it was at the lower levels. At the higher level, the teacher does not exist for the sake of the student; both teacher and student have their justification in the common pursuit of knowledge: The teacher's performance depends on the students' presence and interest—without this science and scholarship could not grow. If the students who are to form his audience did not come before him of their own free will, he, in his quest for knowledge, would have to seek them out. The goals of science and scholarship are worked towards most effectively through the synthesis of the teacher's and the students' dispositions. The teacher's mind is more mature but it is also somewhat one-sided in its development and more dispassionate; the student's mind is less able and less committed but it is nonetheless open and responsive to every possibility. The two together are a fruitful combination.

Higher intellectual institutions are, if we disregard their formal position in the state, nothing other than man's intellectual life which external opportunity and deeper motivation have led towards scientific and scholarly research. Thus, one person might burrow and collect information on his own, another might pursue learning through associating himself with men of his own age, while a third will do so by assembling around himself a circle of disciples. Even the state must respect these motives and dispositions to cultivate science and scholarship, when it seeks to give a more consolidated structure to what are by their nature ungovernable and, in a certain sense, contingent intellectual activities. It must therefore seek to maintain intellectual activity at its liveliest and most productive level; in order to prevent it from declining in its standards, it must maintain a sharply and firmly defined distinction between the higher intellectual institutions and the schools. (This applies both to general theoretical as well as to the most varied practical educational institutions.)

The state must always remain conscious of the fact that it never has and in principle never can, by its own action, bring about the fruitfulness of intellectual activity. It must indeed be aware that it can only have a prejudicial influence if it intervenes. The state must understand that intellectual work will go on infinitely better if it does not intrude. The state's legitimate sphere of action must be adapted to the following circumstances: in view of the fact that in the real world an organisational framework and resources are needed for any widely practised activity, the state must supply the organisational framework and the resources necessary for the practice of science and scholarship. The manner in which the state provides the organisational framework and resources can be damaging to the essence of science and scholarship; the very fact that it provides such organisational structures and resources, which are quite alien to the nature of the activity which they are to serve, can result in the degradation to a basely material level of what should be intellectual and lofty. Finally, that it must bear in mind, above all else, the essential nature of science and scholarship in order to foster what it might have, even quite innocently, sullied or obstructed.

Even if this is only another view of the same procedure, it has the substantial advantage that the state, if it considers this aspect of the matter, will exercise more self-restraint in whatever intervention it undertakes. In the practical sphere of state action, a theoretically incorrect view, whatever is said to the contrary, always does damage, since nothing the state does is a merely mechanical or superficial action without repercussions.

Once this is clear, it is easy to see that in matters of the spirit, i.e., of the intellectual and moral component of higher intellectual institutions, effective accomplishment depends on strict adherence to· the principle that science and scholarship do not consist of closed bodies of permanently settled truths; effective intellectual accomplishment is to be sought in ceaseless effort.

As soon as one ceases to pursue scientific and scholarly knowledge or imagines that it need not be pursued from the utmost depths of the mind and when one comes to believe that it can be cultivated simply by piling up unconnected facts, then the cause of learning is irremediably and permanently lost. If such an attitude is held for a long time, science and scholarship become dissipated; when this happens only their language survives as an empty shell. The state also has to suffer their loss in such circumstances. Only science and scholarship which come from the inner depths of the mind and which are cultivated only at those depths can contribute to the transformation of character. The state gains as little as mankind from mere facts and discussion. They are both more concerned with character and conduct.

Now, in order to avoid this wrong path, there must be a lively and spirited exertion of the intellect in three directions: first, all understanding in the wider sense must be sought by the application of a fundamental principle to explanations of natural events which penetrate from mechanical to dynamic, organic and ultimately psychological levels; all efforts at understanding should be directed towards an ideal; and ultimately, the principle and the ideals should be fused into a coherent idea.

Of course, this cannot be brought about simply by a contrived promotional scheme, nor will it occur to anyone that Germans would seek to do so by such superficial methods. It is an inherent tendency of the German intellectual tradition not to have recourse to such superficial procedures. We need only make sure that the right tendencies are not suppressed either by force or by hostility, which it must be admitted, does in fact exist.

Since every form of one-sidedness must be excluded from higher intellectual institutions, there will naturally be many who are active in them to whom this tendency towards depth and breadth is alien and there will be some to whom it is repugnant. In its pure and unqualified form, this tendency will, in any case, be found only in a handful of persons. It need, however, find expression only occasionally, here and there, to have a widespread and enduring impact. What is, however, very necessary is that this tendency towards depth and breadth should be respected by those who have an appreciation of it and that those who would damage it should be restrained.

This tendency towards depth and breadth is found mostly and in its most pronounced form in philosophy and art. Quite apart from their inherent inclination to decay, little is to be expected of them if their essential spirit is not appropriately expressed in other branches of knowledge and categories of research, or if it is applied there only in a logically or mathematically formalised manner.

If, however, the principle of cultivating science and scholarship for their own sake is placed in a dominant position in higher intellectual institutions, other matters may be disregarded. Neither unity nor full-roundedness will then be lacking; each naturally fosters the other and a proper balance will thereby be maintained. This is the secret of good research method.

With this, all of the requirements are satisfied as far as the spirit of things is concerned.

Now as regards the organisational and material side of the relationship of the institution to the state, the only concerns of the latter must be the profusion (in the sense of mental power and variety) of intellectual talents to be brought together in the institution. This can be achieved through care in the selection of persons and the assurance of freedom in their intellectual activities. This intellectual freedom can be threatened not only by the state, but also by the intellectual institutions themselves which tend to develop, at their birth, a certain outlook and which will therefore readily resist the emergence of another outlook. The state must seek to avert the harm which can possibly arise from this source.

The heart of the matter is the appointment of the persons who are to do the intellectual work. When we come to discuss the differentiation of the total system of intellectual institutions we will propose a method for avoiding certain dangers in the process of selection. Once appointment policy is taken care of, the next thing is the drawing up of organisational statutes, which should in general be few and simple but more effectively articulated than is usually the case. As in the previous case, organisational statutes can be dealt with only when the subdivisions are discussed.

Equipment must of course be considered and, in this respect, it must be remembered that the accumulation of dead collections is not the main thing. It should not be forgotten that it is quite easy for them to deaden and degrade the mind. After all, the richest academies and universities are by no means always those in which science and scholarship have grown most deeply and most imaginatively. The relationships of the higher intellectual institutions to the secondary level of education, on the one hand, and the relationships of scientific and scholarly activity to practical affairs, on the other, are of primary concern in any discussion of the role of the state in the total system of intellectual institutions.

The state must not deal with its universities as *Gymnasia* or as specialised technical schools; it must not use its academy as if it were a technical or scientific commission. It must in general—with certain exceptions among the universities which will be considered later—demand nothing from them simply for the satisfaction of its own needs. It should instead adhere to a deep conviction that if the universities attain their highest ends, they will also realise the state's ends too, and these on a far higher plane. On this higher plane, more is comprehended and forces and mechanisms are brought into action which are quite different from those which the state can command.

On the other side, it is above all the state's obligation to organise the lower levels of its educational system so that they are harmonious with the higher intellectual system. Success in doing this rests on a correct understanding of the relationship of the schools to higher intellectual life and the increasingly fruitful conviction that the schools are not expected to anticipate the instruction offered by the university. The state must understand that the universities are neither a mere complement to the schools within the same category, nor merely a further stage in school. This conviction requires that the transition from school to university constitute a stage in the life of a young person which—when it is successful—brings him to a point where physically, morally and intellectually he can be entrusted with freedom and with the right to act autonomously. The young person, on entry into university, should be released from the compulsion to enter either into a state of idleness or into practical life, and should be enabled to aspire to and elevate himself to the cultivation of science or scholarship which hitherto have only been pointed out to him from afar.

The way thereto is simple and sure. The aim of the schools must be the harmonious development of all the capacities of their pupils. Their powers must be focused on the smallest possible number of subject matters but every aspect of these must be dealt with to as great an extent as possible. Knowledge should be so implanted in the mind of the pupil that understanding, knowledge and creativity excite it, not through any external features, but through their inner precision, harmony and beauty. To this end, and for the preliminary training of the intellect for pure science and scholarship, mathematics above all should be employed, and what is more, from the first moment that the mental powers are capable of it.

A mind which has been trained in this way will spontaneously aspire to science and scholarship. Others with the same diligence and the same talent but with different training will immerse themselves in practical affairs—either immediately or before their education has been completed. They will therewith render themselves useless for science and scholarship, or, lacking the diligence to attain the higher plane of science and scholarship, they will disperse their abilities over unrelated fields of knowledge.

On the Criteria of Classification of Higher Intellectual Institutions; Types of Higher Intellectual Institutions

Ordinarily, when one speaks of higher intellectual institutions, one refers to universities and to academies of the sciences and arts. It is not difficult to derive these institutions which developed in a haphazard way as if they were the manifestations of an idea. But such derivations, which have been much favoured ever since Kant, are partly wrongheaded and partly useless.

It is more important to consider whether an academy should be created or maintained alongside a university, what tasks and jurisdiction should be assigned to each separately and to both together in order to aid each to accomplish what is possible for it alone to accomplish.

If one assigns to the university the tasks of teaching and dissemination of the results of science and scholarship and assigns to the academy the task of its extension and advancement, an injustice is obviously done to the university. Science and scholarship have been advanced as much and in Germany, even more—by university teachers as by members of academies. University teachers have made these contributions to the progress of their disciplines by virtue of their teaching appointments. For unconstrained oral communication to an audience, which includes a significant number of intelligences thinking in unison with the lecturer, inspires those who have become used to this mode of study just as surely as does the peaceful solitude of a writer or the less institutionalised activities of the members of an academy. The progress of science and scholarship is obviously more rapid and more lively in a university where their problems are discussed back and forth by a large number of forceful, vigorous, youthful intelligences. Science and scholarship cannot be presented in a genuinely scientific or scholarly manner without constantly generating independent thought and stimulation; it is inconceivable that discoveries should not be frequently made in such a situation. University teaching is moreover not such a strenuous affair that it should be regarded as a distraction from the calm needed for research and study; it is, rather, a help to it. At every large university, there are always some men who teach little or not at all and who devote themselves entirely to solitary study and research. It would be entirely safe to entrust the growth of scientific and scholarly knowledge to the universities as long as they are properly conducted; this is why the academies can be dispensed with.

The organised societies (*gesellschaftliche Vereine*) in which university teachers do not necessarily participate to the same extent everywhere, are scarcely on this account justified, in view of the fact of the costliness of their establishment. For one thing, these types of society are very loosely organised even in the academies; furthermore their usefulness is found mainly in those observational and experimental disciplines where the rapid communication of particular facts is important. Furthermore, in such disciplines, private scientific societies are formed readily and quite without the supplementary assistance of the state.

If one looks at the matter more closely, one sees that academies have flourished primarily in foreign countries where the universities are not as effective as the German universities or are not as well recognised. In Germany itself, academies have flourished in places where there have been no universities and in periods when universities did not exist in any liberal, many-sided form. In more recent times, the academies have not distinguished themselves especially and have played little or no part in the real rise of German science, scholarship and art.

In order to keep both of these types of institution functioning in a fruitful way, they should be linked with each other in such a way that, although their activities remain distinct, their individual members do not belong exclusively to the one or to the other. Linked in this way, their distinctive and separate existences can assume a new and superior form.

The utility of such a separation rests much less on the characteristic activities of each of the institutions than on the distinctiveness of their form and on their relations with the state. In fact, university teachers, quite without the establishment of their own academy, can achieve all the purposes assigned to an academy; they can form, as they did in Gottingen, their own learned society which is different from a genuine academy.

The university always stands in a close relationship to practical life and to the needs of the state, since it is always concerned with the practical affair of training the younger generation. Academies concern themselves only with science and scholarship. University teachers are generally integrated with each other simply through the internal culture and the organisational framework of their disciplines. But regarding their proper business of science and scholarship, they communicate with each other only insofar as they are inclined to do so. The academy is in contrast a society constituted for the purpose of subjecting the work of each member to the assessment of all the others.

In this way, the idea of an academy must be maintained as the highest and ultimate sanctuary[2] of science and scholarship and as that corporation which is freest of the control of the state. The risk must be run that such a corporation, through feebleness or one-sidedness, will show that what is right and desirable does not always occur even under the most favourable external circumstances. Nonetheless one must run this risk because the idea in itself is lofty and beneficent and because it might be realised at any time in a really worthy manner.

Through this relationship, the university and the academy can compete with and be critical of each other. The process of interaction between them will be such that any excesses or deficiencies which might give reason for apprehension will automatically balance themselves.

The disagreements between universities and academies arise in the first instance in connection with the selection of members of the two bodies. Every

2 Humboldt originally wrote "refuge" (*Zufluchtsort*), and it was subsequently replaced by "sanctuary" (*Freistätte*). [Editor.]

member of an academy must have the right to give lectures without having "habilitated" and without becoming, by virtue of that qualification, a member of the university. It is perfectly reasonable that many learned men should be both university teachers and academicians, but each of the institutions will have other members who belong to it exclusively.

The right of appointment of university teachers must be reserved exclusively to the state; it is certainly not a good arrangement to grant more influence to the faculties than a prudent and fair-minded body of trustees (*Curatorium*) would allow. Although disagreements and disputes within a university are wholesome and necessary, conflicts which might arise between teachers because of their specialised intellectual interests might unwittingly affect their viewpoints. The condition of the university is too closely bound up with the direct interest of the state to permit any other arrangement.

The choice of members of the academy, on the other hand, must be left to the academy itself, subject only to royal confirmation which will not lightly be withheld. The academy is a corporation in which the principle of unity is of the highest importance and, because of its purely scientific and scholarly concerns, what happens in it is not of immediate interest to the state as such.

It is at this point that it is relevant to discuss the previous corrective which will operate in elections to higher intellectual institutions. For insofar as the state and the academy have about the same share in the decision, the spirit in which each acts will soon become evident; where they go astray, public opinion will impartially set them back on the right path. But since it is not likely that both at the same time will go astray, at least not in the same way, not all decisions regarding appointments will run the same risks and the system as a whole will be safe from one-sidedness.

The diversity of talents and interests is further guaranteed by the fact that in addition to those who are appointed by the state and those who are elected by the academy, there will be the *Privatdozenten*, who at the beginning, at least, are dependent on the approbation of their audience.

The academy can, in addition to the performance of its regular duties, play a distinctive role in the systematic conduct of observation and experiments. Of these, some should be decided on entirely by the academy acting on its own free choice, others should be proposed to it and the university should have some influence in the making of these proposals. This will provide another occasion for reciprocal influence among the various intellectual institutions.

In addition to the academy and the university, the category of intellectual institutions includes the institutes which have no life of their own.

These latter must remain separate from the other two and should be directly under the supervision of the state. But both the academy and the university should have the use, with certain qualifications, of these institutes, and they should also have some supervisory powers over them.

They can exercise these supervisory powers over the institutes only if they present memoranda and proposals for their improvement, not directly to the institutes, but to the state.

Through the university, the academy will obtain the right to use such facilities of the institutes as the anatomical and comparative anatomical theatres. These have not been connected with the academy because hitherto the subjects which have fallen within their terms of reference have been dealt with from a narrow medical point· of view rather than from the broader standpoint of natural science.

The academy, the university, and the auxiliary institutes constitute three autonomous, integral units of the total system of intellectual institutions. All of them, particularly the latter two and to a lesser degree the academy, are under the supervision and guidance of the state.

Academy and university are equally independent. They are linked through having common members, through the university's power to grant the right of delivering lectures to all the members of the academy and through the academy's carrying out the observational and experimental projects proposed by the university.

The university and academy both utilise and supervise the auxiliary institutes, although the supervisory function has to be exercised through the state.

Regarding the Academy

Here the manuscript ends.

CHAPTER FIVE

Preface, Introduction and Lecture One

From *On the Future of Our Educational Institutions* (1872/2009)

FRIEDRICH NIETZSCHE

Translated, with Introduction, By J. M. Kennedy *The Complete Works Of Friedrich Nietzsche*, The First Complete And Authorised English Translation, Volume Three, Edited By Dr. Oscar Levy. This selection taken from The Project Gutenberg EBook of On the Future of our Educational Institutions, by Friedrich Nietzsche, February 20, 2009 [EBook #28146] at http://www.gutenberg.org/files/28146/28146-h/28146-h.htm.

Editors' Note

This selection from Nietzsche's early work 'On the Future of Our Educational Institutions' includes the Preface, Introduction and First Lecture delivered in 1872 of a work that comprises five lectures in total. This was to be Nietzsche's second book before he abandoned it to use parts of it in *Untimely Meditations*. Together with 'Schopeanhauer as Educator' this work expresses a deep cultural crisis that Nietzsche senses as German culture shifts from its classicist orientation based on the works of Goethe, Schiller, Humboldt and others, to a nationalist, industrial, and statist vision—in short, to a modernist view. 'Nietzsche criticized the educational and cultural institutions of his time for abandoning their perennial responsibilities in order to tailor these institutions to the interests of the political state' (Canis, 2000: iii). By contrast, he argues for an 'effective culture' [*wirkliche Bildung*] that engages in a continuous process of 'selfovercoming,' a process he calls 'untimeliness' wherein the radical sense of self is formed. Nietzsche has little faith in mass schooling and institutional pedagogy in forming human beings who are truly cultured and he does not believe they can foster democratic habits. In these early writings on *Bildung* written during the decade at Basel University (1869–1879), years before he mounts of critique of Western morality and forms a new cultural ideal of *der Ubermensch*, Nietzsche unfolds an 'untimeliness' as a new pedagogy for cultural healing, health, renewal and rebirth based on the creative energies of the age and the continuous process of cultural 'self-overcoming.'

MP

Recommended Reading

Canis, Laura Anders (2000). Untimely Education: Nietzsche's Early Experiments in Revaluing and Self-Overcoming Dissertation, The Pennsylvania State University (2000), https://philpapers.org/rec/CANUEN

* * * * *

Preface
(To be read before the lectures, although it in no way relates to them.)

The reader from whom I expect something must possess three qualities: he must be calm and must read without haste; he must not be ever interposing his own personality and his own special "culture"; and he must not expect as the ultimate results of his study of these pages that he will be presented with a set of new formulae. I do not propose to furnish formulae or new plans of study for *Gymnasia* or other schools; and I am much more inclined to admire the extraordinary power of those who are able to cover the whole distance between the depths of empiricism and the heights of special culture-problems, and who again descend to the level of the driest rules and the most neatly expressed formulae. I shall be content if only I can ascend a tolerably lofty mountain, from the summit of which, after having recovered my breath, I may obtain a general survey of the ground; for I shall never be able, in this book, to satisfy the votaries of tabulated rules. Indeed, I see a time coming when serious men, working together in the service of a completely rejuvenated and purified culture, may again become the directors of a system of everyday instruction, calculated to promote that culture; and they will probably be compelled once more to draw up sets of rules: but how remote this time now seems! And what may not happen meanwhile! It is just possible that between now and then all *Gymnasia*—yea, and perhaps all universities, may be destroyed, or have become so utterly transformed that their very regulations may, in the eyes of future generations, seem to be but the relics of the cave-dwellers' age.

This book is intended for calm readers,—for men who have not yet been drawn into the mad headlong rush of our hurry-skurrying age, and who do not experience any idolatrous delight in throwing themselves beneath its chariot-wheels. It is for men, therefore, who are not accustomed to estimate the value of everything according to the amount of time it either saves or wastes. In short, it is for the few. These, we believe, "still have time." Without any qualms of conscience they may improve the most fruitful and vigorous hours of their day in meditating on the future of our education; they may even believe when the evening has come that they have used their day in the most dignified and useful way, namely, in the *meditatio generis futuri*. No one among them has yet forgotten to think while reading a book; he still understands the secret of reading between the lines, and is indeed so generous in what he himself brings to his study, that he continues to reflect upon what he has read, perhaps long after he has laid the book aside. And he does this, not because he wishes to write a criticism about it or even another book; but simply because reflection is a pleasant pastime to him. Frivolous spendthrift! Thou art a reader after my own heart; for thou wilt be patient enough to accompany an author any distance, even though he himself cannot yet see the goal at which he is aiming,—even though he himself feels only that he must at all events honestly believe in a goal, in order that a future and possibly very remote generation may come face to face with that towards which we are now blindly and instinctively groping. Should any reader demur and suggest that all that is required is prompt and bold reform; should he imagine that a new "organisation" introduced by the State, were all that is necessary, then we fear he would have misunderstood not only the author but the very nature of the problem under consideration.

The third and most important stipulation is, that he should in no case be constantly bringing himself and his own "culture" forward, after the style of most modern men, as the correct standard and measure of all things. We would have him so highly educated that he could even think meanly of his education or despise it altogether. Only thus would he be able to trust entirely to the author's guidance; for it is only by virtue of ignorance and his consciousness of ignorance, that the latter can dare to make himself heard. Finally, the author would wish his reader to be fully alive to the specific character of our present barbarism and of that which distinguishes us, as the barbarians of the nineteenth century, from other barbarians.

Now, with this book in his hand, the writer seeks all those who may happen to be wandering, hither and thither, impelled by feelings similar to his own. Allow yourselves to be discovered—ye lonely ones in whose existence I believe! Ye unselfish ones, suffering in yourselves from the corruption of the German spirit! Ye contemplative ones who cannot, with hasty glances, turn your eyes swiftly from one surface to another! Ye lofty thinkers, of whom Aristotle said that ye wander through life vacillating and inactive so long as no great honour or glorious Cause calleth you to deeds! It is you I summon! Refrain this once from seeking refuge in your lairs of solitude and dark misgivings. Bethink you that this book was framed to be your herald. When ye shall go forth to battle in your full panoply, who among you will not rejoice in looking back upon the herald who rallied you?

Introduction

The title I gave to these lectures ought, like all titles, to have been as definite, as plain, and as significant as possible; now, however, I observe that owing to a certain excess of precision, in its present form it is too short and consequently misleading. My first duty therefore will be to explain the title, together with the object of these lectures, to you, and to apologise for being obliged to do this. When I promised to speak to you concerning the future of our educational institutions, I was not thinking especially of the evolution of our particular institutions in Bâle. However frequently my general observations may seem to bear particular application to our own conditions here, I personally have no desire to draw these inferences, and do not wish to be held responsible if they should be drawn, for the simple reason that I consider myself still far too much an inexperienced stranger among you, and much too superficially acquainted with your methods, to pretend to pass judgment upon any such special order of scholastic establishments, or to predict the probable course their development will follow. On the other hand, I know full well under what distinguished auspices I have to deliver these lectures—namely, in a city which is striving to educate and enlighten its inhabitants on a scale so magnificently out of proportion to its size, that it must put all larger cities to shame. This being so, I presume I am justified in assuming that in a quarter where so much is *done* for the things of which I wish to speak, people must also *think* a good deal about them. My desire—yea, my very first condition, therefore, would be to become united in spirit with those who have not only thought very deeply upon educational problems, but have also the will to promote what they think to be right by all the means in their power. And, in view of the difficulties of my task and the limited time at my disposal, to such listeners, alone, in my audience, shall I be able to make myself understood—and even then, it will be on condition that they shall guess what I can do no more than suggest, that they shall supply what I am compelled to omit; in brief, that they shall need but to be reminded and not to be taught. Thus, while I disclaim all desire of being taken for an uninvited adviser on questions relating to the schools and the University of Bâle, I repudiate even more emphatically still the rôle of a prophet standing on the horizon of civilisation and pretending to predict the future of education and of scholastic organisation. I can no more project my vision through such vast periods of time than I can rely upon its accuracy when it is brought too close to an object under examination. With my title: *Our* Educational Institutions, I wish to refer neither to the establishments in Bâle nor to the incalculably vast number of other scholastic institutions which exist throughout the nations of the world to-day; but I wish to refer to *German institutions* of the kind which we rejoice in here. It is their future that will now engage our attention, *i.e.* the future of German elementary, secondary, and public schools (Gymnasien) and universities. While pursuing our discussion, however, we shall for once avoid all comparisons and valuations, and guard more especially against that flattering illusion that our conditions should be regarded as the standard for all others and as surpassing them. Let it suffice that they are our institutions, that they have not become a part of ourselves by mere accident, and were not laid upon us like a garment; but that they are living monuments of important steps in the progress of civilisation, in some respects even the furniture of a bygone age, and as such link us with the past of our people, and are such a sacred and venerable legacy that I can only undertake to speak of the future of our educational institutions in the sense of their being a most probable approximation to the ideal spirit which gave them birth. I am, moreover, convinced that the numerous alterations which have been introduced into these institutions within recent years, with the view of bringing them up-to-date, are for the most part but distortions and aberrations of the originally sublime tendencies given to them at their foundation. And what we dare to hope from the future, in this behalf, partakes so much of the nature of a rejuvenation, a reviviscence, and a refining of the spirit of Germany that, as a result of this very process, our educational institutions may also be indirectly remoulded and born again, so as to appear at once old and new, whereas now they only profess to be "modern" or "up-to-date."

Now it is only in the spirit of the hope above mentioned that I wish to speak of the future of our educational institutions: and this is the second point in regard to which I must tender an apology from the outset. The "prophet" pose is such a presumptuous one that it seems almost ridiculous to deny that I have the intention of adopting it. No one should attempt to describe the future of our education, and the means and methods of instruction relating thereto, in a prophetic spirit, unless he can prove that the picture he draws already exists in germ to-day, and that all that is required is the extension and development of this embryo if the necessary modifications are to be produced in schools and other educational institutions. All I ask, is, like a Roman haruspex, to be allowed to steal glimpses of the future out of the very entrails of existing conditions, which, in this case, means no more than to hand the laurels of victory to any one of the many forces tending to make itself felt in our present educational system, despite the fact that the force in question may be neither a favourite, an esteemed, nor a very extensive one. I confidently assert that it will be victorious, however, because it has the strongest and mightiest of all allies in nature herself; and in this respect it were well did we not forget that scores of the very first principles of our modern educational methods are thoroughly artificial, and that the most fatal weaknesses of the present day are to be ascribed to this artificiality. He who feels in complete harmony with the present state of affairs and who acquiesces in it *as something* "*selbstverständliches*,"[1] excites our envy neither in regard to his faith nor in regard to that egregious word "*selbstverständlich*," so frequently heard in fashionable circles.

He, however, who holds the opposite view and is therefore in despair, does not need to fight any longer: all he requires is to give himself up to solitude in order soon to be alone. Albeit, between those who take everything for granted and these anchorites, there stand the *fighters*—that is to say, those who still have hope, and as the noblest and sublimest example of this class, we recognise Schiller as he is described by Goethe in his "Epilogue to the Bell."

> "Brighter now glow'd his cheek, and still more bright
> With that unchanging, ever youthful glow:—
> That courage which o'ercomes, in hard-fought fight,
> Sooner or later ev'ry earthly foe,—
> That faith which soaring to the realms of light,
> Now boldly presseth on, now bendeth low,
> So that the good may work, wax, thrive amain,
> So that the day the noble may attain."[2]

I should like you to regard all I have just said as a kind of preface, the object of which is to illustrate the title of my lectures and to guard me against any possible misunderstanding and unjustified criticisms. And now, in order to give you a rough outline of the range of ideas from which I shall attempt to form a judgment concerning our educational institutions, before proceeding to disclose my views and turning from the title to the main theme, I shall lay a scheme before you which, like a coat of arms, will serve to warn all strangers who come to my door, as to the nature of the house they are about to enter, in case they may feel inclined,

---

1 Selbstverständlich = "granted or self-understood."

2 *The Poems of Goethe.* Edgar Alfred Bowring's Translation. (Ed. 1853.)

after having examined the device, to turn their backs on the premises that bear it. My scheme is as follows:—

Two seemingly antagonistic forces, equally deleterious in their actions and ultimately combining to produce their results, are at present ruling over our educational institutions, although these were based originally upon very different principles. These forces are: a striving to achieve the greatest possible *extension of education* on the one hand, and a tendency *to minimise and to weaken it* on the other. The first-named would fain spread learning among the greatest possible number of people, the second would compel education to renounce its highest and most independent claims in order to subordinate itself to the service of the State. In the face of these two antagonistic tendencies, we could but give ourselves up to despair, did we not see the possibility of promoting the cause of two other contending factors which are fortunately as completely German as they are rich in promises for the future; I refer to the present movement towards *limiting and concentrating* education as the antithesis of the first of the forces above mentioned, and that other movement towards the *strengthening and the independence* of education as the antithesis of the second force. If we should seek a warrant for our belief in the ultimate victory of the two last-named movements, we could find it in the fact that both of the forces which we hold to be deleterious are so opposed to the eternal purpose of nature as the concentration of education for the few is in harmony with it, and is true, whereas the first two forces could succeed only in founding a culture false to the root.

First Lecture
(Delivered on the 16th of January 1872.)

Ladies and Gentlemen,—The subject I now propose to consider with you is such a serious and important one, and is in a sense so disquieting, that, like you, I would gladly turn to anyone who could proffer some information concerning it,—were he ever so young, were his ideas ever so improbable—provided that he were able, by the exercise of his own faculties, to furnish some satisfactory and sufficient explanation. It is just possible that he may have had the opportunity of *hearing* sound views expressed in reference to the vexed question of the future of our educational institutions, and that he may wish to repeat them to you; he may even have had distinguished teachers, fully qualified to foretell what is to come, and, like the *haruspices* of Rome, able to do so after an inspection of the entrails of the Present.

Indeed, you yourselves may expect something of this kind from me. I happened once, in strange but perfectly harmless circumstances, to overhear a conversation on this subject between two remarkable men, and the more striking points of the discussion, together with their manner of handling the theme, are so indelibly imprinted on my memory that, whenever I reflect on these matters, I invariably find myself falling into their grooves of thought. I cannot, however, profess to have the same courageous confidence which they displayed, both in their daring utterance of forbidden truths, and in the still more daring conception of the hopes with which they astonished me. It therefore seemed to me to be in the highest degree important that a record of this conversation should be made, so that others might be incited to form a judgment concerning the striking views and conclusions it contains: and, to this end, I had special grounds for believing that I should do well to avail myself of the opportunity afforded by this course of lectures.

I am well aware of the nature of the community to whose serious consideration I now wish to commend that conversation—I know it to be a community which is striving to educate and enlighten its members on a scale so magnificently out of proportion to its size that it must put all larger cities to shame. This being so, I presume I may take it for granted that in a quarter where so much is *done* for the things of which I wish to speak, people must also *think* a good deal about them. In my account of the conversation already mentioned, I shall be able to make myself completely understood only to those among my audience who will be able to guess what I can do no more than suggest, who will supply what I am compelled to omit, and who, above all, need but to be reminded and not taught.

Listen, therefore, ladies and gentlemen, while I recount my harmless experience and the less harmless conversation between the two gentlemen whom, so far, I have not named.

Let us now imagine ourselves in the position of a young student—that is to say, in a position which, in our present age of bewildering movement and feverish excitability, has become an almost impossible one. It is necessary to have lived through it in order to believe that such careless self-lulling and comfortable indifference to the moment, or to time in general, are possible. In this condition I, and a friend about my own age, spent a year at the University of Bonn on the Rhine,—it was a year which, in its complete lack of plans and projects for the future, seems almost like a dream to me now—a dream framed, as it were, by two periods of growth. We two remained quiet and peaceful, although we were surrounded by fellows who in the main were very differently disposed, and from time to time we experienced considerable difficulty in meeting and resisting the somewhat too pressing advances of the young men of our own age. Now, however, that I can look upon the stand we had to take against these opposing forces, I cannot help associating them in my mind with those checks we are wont to receive in our dreams, as, for instance, when we imagine we are able to fly and yet feel ourselves held back by some incomprehensible power.

I and my friend had many reminiscences in common, and these dated from the period of our boyhood upwards. One of these I must relate to you, since it forms a sort of prelude to the harmless experience already mentioned. On the occasion of a certain journey up the Rhine, which we had made together one summer, it happened that he and I independently conceived the very same plan at the same hour and on the same spot, and we were so struck by this unwonted coincidence that we determined to carry the plan out forthwith. We resolved to found a kind of small club which would consist of ourselves and a few friends, and the object of which would be to provide us with a stable and binding organisation directing and adding interest to our creative impulses in art and literature; or, to put it more plainly: each of us would be pledged to present an original piece of work to the club once a month,—either a poem, a treatise, an architectural design, or a musical composition, upon which each of the others, in a friendly spirit, would have to pass free and unrestrained criticism.

We thus hoped, by means of mutual correction, to be able both to stimulate and to chasten our creative impulses and, as a matter of fact, the success of the scheme was such that we have both always felt a sort of respectful attachment for the hour and the place at which it first took shape in our minds.

This attachment was very soon transformed into a rite; for we all agreed to go, whenever it was possible to do so, once a year to that lonely spot near Rolandseck, where on that summer's day, while sitting together, lost in meditation, we were suddenly inspired by the same thought. Frankly speaking, the rules which were drawn up on the formation of the club were never very strictly observed; but owing to the very fact that we had many sins of omission on our conscience during our student-year in Bonn, when we were once more on the banks of the Rhine, we firmly resolved not only to observe our rule, but also to gratify our feelings and our sense of gratitude by reverently visiting that spot near Rolandseck on the day appointed.

It was, however, with some difficulty that we were able to carry our plans into execution; for, on the very day we had selected for our excursion, the large and lively students' association, which always hindered us in our flights, did their utmost to put obstacles in our way and to hold us back. Our association had organised a general holiday excursion to Rolandseck on the very day my friend and I had fixed upon, the object of the outing being to assemble all its members for the last time at the close of the half-year and to send them home with pleasant recollections of their last hours together.

The day was a glorious one; the weather was of the kind which, in our climate at least, only falls to our lot in late summer: heaven and earth merged harmoniously with one another, and, glowing wondrously in the sunshine, autumn freshness blended with the blue expanse above. Arrayed in the bright fantastic garb in which, amid the gloomy fashions now reigning, students alone may indulge, we boarded a steamer which was gaily decorated in our honour, and hoisted our flag on its mast. From both banks of the river there came at intervals the sound of signal-guns, fired according to our orders, with the view of acquainting both our host in Rolandseck and the inhabitants in the neighbourhood with our approach. I shall not speak of the noisy journey from the landing-stage, through the excited and expectant little place, nor shall I refer to the esoteric jokes exchanged between ourselves; I also make no mention of a feast which became both wild and noisy, or of an extraordinary musical production in the execution of which, whether as soloists or as chorus, we all ultimately had to share, and which I, as musical adviser of our club, had not only had to rehearse, but was then forced to conduct. Towards the end of this piece, which grew ever wilder and which was sung to ever quicker time, I made a sign to my friend, and just as the last chord rang like a yell through the building, he and I vanished, leaving behind us a raging pandemonium.

In a moment we were in the refreshing and breathless stillness of nature. The shadows were already lengthening, the sun still shone steadily, though it had sunk a good deal in the heavens, and from the green and glittering waves of the Rhine a cool breeze was wafted over our hot faces. Our solemn rite bound us only in so far as the latest hours of the day were concerned, and we therefore determined to employ the last moments of clear daylight by giving ourselves up to one of our many hobbies.

At that time we were passionately fond of pistol-shooting, and both of us in later years found the skill we had acquired as amateurs of great use in our military career. Our club servant happened to know the somewhat distant and elevated spot which we used as a range, and had carried our pistols there in advance. The spot lay near the upper border of the wood which covered the lesser heights behind Rolandseck: it was a small uneven plateau, close to the place we had consecrated in memory of its associations. On a wooded slope alongside of our shooting-range there was a small piece of ground which had been cleared of wood, and which made an ideal halting-place; from it one could get a view of the Rhine over the tops of the trees and the brushwood, so that the beautiful, undulating lines of the Seven Mountains and above all of the Drachenfels bounded the horizon against the group of trees, while in the centre of the bow formed by the glistening Rhine itself the island of Nonnenwörth stood out as if suspended in the river's arms. This was the place which had become sacred to us through the dreams and plans we had had in common, and to which we intended to withdraw, later in the evening,—nay, to which we should be obliged to withdraw, if we wished to close the day in accordance with the law we had imposed on ourselves.

At one end of the little uneven plateau, and not very far away, there stood the mighty trunk of an oak-tree, prominently visible against a background quite bare of trees and consisting merely of low undulating hills in the distance. Working together, we had once carved a pentagram in the side of this tree-trunk. Years of exposure to rain and storm had slightly deepened the channels we had cut, and the figure seemed a welcome target for our pistol-practice. It was already late in the afternoon when we reached our improvised range, and our oak-stump cast a long and attenuated shadow across the barren heath. All was still: thanks to the lofty trees at our feet, we were unable to catch a glimpse of the valley of the Rhine below. The peacefulness of the spot seemed only to intensify the loudness of our pistol-shots—and I had scarcely fired my second barrel at the pentagram when I felt some one lay hold of my arm and noticed that my friend had also someone beside him who had interrupted his loading.

Turning sharply on my heels I found myself face to face with an astonished old gentleman, and felt what must have been a very powerful dog make a lunge at my back. My friend had been approached by a somewhat younger man than I had; but before we could give expression to our surprise the older of the two interlopers burst forth in the following threatening and heated strain: "No! no!" he called to us, "no duels must be fought here, but least of all must you young students fight one. Away with these pistols and compose yourselves. Be reconciled, shake hands! What?—and are you the salt of the earth, the intelligence of the future, the seed of our hopes—and are you not even able to emancipate yourselves from the insane code of honour and its violent regulations? I will not cast any aspersions on your hearts, but your heads certainly do you no credit. You, whose youth is watched over by the wisdom of Greece and Rome, and whose youthful spirits, at the cost of enormous pains, have been flooded with the light of the sages and heroes of antiquity,—can you not refrain from making the code of knightly honour—that is to say, the code of folly and brutality—the guiding principle of your conduct?—Examine it rationally once and for all, and reduce it to plain terms; lay its pitiable narrowness bare, and let it be the touchstone, not of your hearts but of your minds. If you do not regret it then, it will merely show that your head is not fitted for work in a sphere where great gifts of discrimination are needful in order to burst the bonds of prejudice, and where a well-balanced understanding is necessary for the purpose of distinguishing right from wrong, even when the difference between them lies deeply hidden and is not, as in this case, so ridiculously obvious. In that case, therefore, my lads, try to go through life in some other honourable manner; join the army or learn a handicraft that pays its way."

To this rough, though admittedly just, flood of eloquence, we replied with some irritation, interrupting each other continually in so doing: "In the first place, you are mistaken concerning the main point; for we are not here to fight a duel at all; but rather to practise pistol-shooting. Secondly, you do not appear to know how a real duel is conducted;—do you suppose that we should have faced each other in this lonely spot, like two highwaymen, without seconds or doctors, etc. etc.? Thirdly, with regard to the question of duelling, we each have our own opinions, and do not require to be waylaid and surprised by the sort of instruction you may feel disposed to give us."

This reply, which was certainly not polite, made a bad impression upon the old man. At first, when he heard that we were not about to fight a duel, he surveyed us more kindly: but when we reached the last passage of our speech, he seemed so vexed that he growled. When, however, we began to speak of our point of view, he quickly caught hold of his companion, turned sharply round, and cried to us in bitter tones: "People should not have points of view, but thoughts!" And then his companion added: "Be respectful when a man such as this even makes mistakes!"

Meanwhile, my friend, who had reloaded, fired a shot at the pentagram, after having cried: "Look out!" This sudden report behind his back made the old man savage; once more he turned round and looked sourly at my friend, after which he said to his companion in a feeble voice: "What shall we do? These young men will be the death of me with their firing."—"You should know," said the younger man, turning to us, "that your noisy pastimes amount, as it happens on this occasion, to an attempt upon the life of philosophy. You observe this venerable man,—he is in a position to beg you to desist from firing here. And when such a man begs—" "Well, his request is generally granted," the old man interjected, surveying us sternly.

As a matter of fact, we did not know what to make of the whole matter; we could not understand what our noisy pastimes could have in common with philosophy; nor could we see why, out of regard for polite scruples, we should abandon our shooting-range, and at this moment we may have appeared somewhat undecided and perturbed. The companion noticing our momentary discomfiture, proceeded to explain the matter to us.

"We are compelled," he said, "to linger in this immediate neighbourhood for an hour or so; we have a rendezvous here. An eminent friend of this eminent man is to meet us here this evening; and we had actually selected this peaceful spot, with its few benches in the midst of the wood, for the meeting. It would really be most unpleasant if, owing to your continual pistol-practice, we were to be subjected to an unending series of shocks; surely your own feelings will tell you that it is impossible for you to continue your firing when you hear that he who has selected this quiet and isolated place for a meeting with a friend is one of our most eminent philosophers."

This explanation only succeeded in perturbing us the more; for we saw a danger threatening us which was even greater than the loss of our shooting-range, and we asked eagerly, "Where is this quiet spot? Surely not to the left here, in the wood?"

"That is the very place."

"But this evening that place belongs to us," my friend interposed. "We must have it," we cried together.

Our long-projected celebration seemed at that moment more important than all the philosophies of the world, and we gave such vehement and animated utterance to our sentiments that in view of the incomprehensible nature of our claims we must have cut a somewhat ridiculous figure. At any rate, our philosophical interlopers regarded us with expressions of amused inquiry, as if they expected us to proffer some sort of apology. But we were silent, for we wished above all to keep our secret.

Thus we stood facing one another in silence, while the sunset dyed the tree-tops a ruddy gold. The philosopher contemplated the sun, his companion contemplated him, and we turned our eyes towards our nook in the woods which to-day we seemed in such great danger of losing. A feeling of sullen anger took possession of us. What is philosophy, we asked ourselves, if it prevents a man from being by himself or from enjoying the select company of a friend,—in sooth, if it prevents him from becoming a philosopher? For we regarded the celebration of our rite as a thoroughly philosophical performance. In celebrating it we wished to form plans and resolutions for the future, by means of quiet reflections we hoped to light upon an idea which would once again help us to form and gratify our spirit in the future, just as that former idea had done during our boyhood. The solemn act derived its very significance from this resolution, that nothing definite was to be done, we were only to be alone, and to sit still and meditate, as we had done five years before when we had each been inspired with the same thought. It was to be a silent solemnisation, all reminiscence and all future; the present was to be as a hyphen between the two. And fate, now unfriendly, had just stepped into our magic circle—and we knew not how to dismiss her;—the very unusual character of the circumstances filled us with mysterious excitement.

Whilst we stood thus in silence for some time, divided into two hostile groups, the clouds above waxed ever redder and the evening seemed to grow more peaceful and mild; we could almost fancy we heard the regular breathing of nature as she put the final touches to her work of art—the glorious day we had just enjoyed; when, suddenly, the calm evening air was rent by a confused and boisterous cry of joy which seemed to come from the Rhine. A number of voices could be heard in the distance—they were those of our fellow-students who by that time must have taken to the Rhine in small boats. It occurred to us that we should be missed and that we should also miss something: almost simultaneously my friend and I raised our pistols: our shots were echoed back to us, and with their echo there came from the valley the sound of a well-known cry intended as a signal of identification. For our passion for shooting had brought us both repute and ill-repute in our club.

At the same time we were conscious that our behaviour towards the silent philosophical couple had been exceptionally ungentlemanly; they had been quietly contemplating us for some time, and when we fired the shock made them draw close up to each other. We hurried up to them, and each in our turn cried out: "Forgive us. That was our last shot, and it was intended for our friends on the Rhine. They have understood us, do you hear? If you insist upon having that place among the trees, grant us at least the permission to recline there also. You will find a number of benches on the spot: we shall not disturb you; we shall sit quite still and shall not utter a word: but it is now past seven o'clock and we *must* go there at once."

"That sounds more mysterious than it is," I added after a pause; "we have made a solemn vow to spend this coming hour on that ground, and there were reasons for the vow. The spot is sacred to us, owing to some pleasant associations, it must also inaugurate a good future for us. We shall therefore endeavour to leave you with no disagreeable recollections of our meeting—even though we have done much to perturb and frighten you."

The philosopher was silent; his companion, however, said: "Our promises and plans unfortunately compel us not only to remain, but also to spend the same hour on the spot you have selected. It is left for us to decide whether fate or perhaps a spirit has been responsible for this extraordinary coincidence."

"Besides, my friend," said the philosopher, "I am not half so displeased with these warlike youngsters as I was. Did you observe how quiet they were a moment ago, when we were contemplating the sun? They neither spoke nor smoked, they stood stone still, I even believe they meditated."

Turning suddenly in our direction, he said: "*Were* you meditating? Just tell me about it as we proceed in the direction of our common trysting-place." We took a few steps together and went down the slope into the warm balmy air of the woods where it was already much darker. On the way my friend openly revealed his thoughts to the philosopher, he confessed how much he had feared that perhaps to-day for the first time a philosopher was about to stand in the way of his philosophising.

The sage laughed. "What? You were afraid a philosopher would prevent your philosophising? This might easily happen: and you have not yet experienced such a thing? Has your university life been free from experience? You surely attend lectures on philosophy?"

This question discomfited us; for, as a matter of fact, there had been no element of philosophy in our education up to that time. In those days, moreover, we fondly imagined that everybody who held the post and possessed the dignity of a philosopher must perforce be one: we were inexperienced and badly informed. We frankly admitted that we had not yet belonged to any philosophical college, but that we would certainly make up for lost time.

"Then what," he asked, "did you mean when you spoke of philosophising?" Said I, "We are at a loss for a definition. But to all intents and purposes we meant this, that we wished to make earnest endeavours to consider the best possible means of becoming men of culture." "That is a good deal and at the same time very little," growled the philosopher; "just you think the matter over. Here are our benches, let us discuss the question exhaustively: I shall not disturb your meditations with regard to how you are to become men of culture. I wish you success and—points of view, as in your duelling questions; brand-new, original, and enlightened points of view. The philosopher does not wish to prevent your philosophising: but refrain at least from disconcerting him with your pistol-shots. Try to imitate the Pythagoreans to-day: they, as servants of a true philosophy, had to remain silent for five years—possibly you may also be able to remain silent for five times fifteen minutes, as servants of your own future culture, about which you seem so concerned."

We had reached our destination: the solemnisation of our rite began. As on the previous occasion, five years ago, the Rhine was once more flowing beneath a light mist, the sky seemed bright and the woods exhaled the same fragrance. We took our places on the farthest corner of the most distant bench; sitting there we were almost concealed, and neither the philosopher nor his companion could see our faces. We were alone: when the sound of the philosopher's voice reached us, it had become so blended with the rustling leaves and with the buzzing murmur of the myriads of living things inhabiting the wooded height, that it almost seemed like the music of nature; as a sound it resembled nothing more than a distant monotonous plaint. We were indeed undisturbed.

Some time elapsed in this way, and while the glow of sunset grew steadily paler the recollection of our youthful undertaking in the cause of culture waxed ever more vivid. It seemed to us as if we owed the greatest debt of gratitude to that little society we had founded; for it had done more than merely supplement our public school training; it had actually been the only fruitful society we had had, and within its frame we even placed our public school life, as a purely isolated factor helping us in our general efforts to attain to culture.

We knew this, that, thanks to our little society, no thought of embracing any particular career had ever entered our minds in those days. The all too frequent exploitation of youth by the State, for its own purposes—that is to say, so that it may rear useful officials as quickly as possible and guarantee their unconditional obedience to it by means of excessively severe examinations—had remained quite foreign to our education. And to show how little we had been actuated by thoughts of utility or by the prospect of speedy advancement and rapid success, on that day we were struck by the comforting consideration that, even then, we had not yet decided what we should be—we had not even troubled ourselves at all on this head. Our little society had sown the seeds of this happy indifference in our souls and for it alone we were prepared to celebrate the anniversary of its foundation with hearty gratitude. I have already pointed out, I think, that in the eyes of the present age, which is so intolerant of anything that is not useful, such purposeless enjoyment of the moment, such a lulling of one's self in the cradle of the present, must seem almost incredible and at all events blameworthy. How useless we were! And how proud we were of being useless! We used even to quarrel with each other as to which of us should have the glory of being the more useless. We wished to attach no importance to anything, to have strong views about nothing, to aim at nothing; we wanted to take no thought for the morrow, and desired no more than to recline comfortably like good-for-nothings on the threshold of the present; and we did—bless us!

—That, ladies and gentlemen, was our standpoint then!—

Absorbed in these reflections, I was just about to give an answer to the question of the future of *our* Educational Institutions in the same self-sufficient way, when it gradually dawned upon me that the "natural music," coming from the philosopher's bench had lost its original character and travelled to us in much more piercing and distinct tones than before. Suddenly I became aware that I was listening, that I was eavesdropping, and was passionately interested, with both ears keenly alive to every sound. I nudged my friend who was evidently somewhat tired, and I whispered: "Don't fall asleep! There is something for us to learn over there. It applies to us, even though it be not meant for us."

For instance, I heard the younger of the two men defending himself with great animation while the philosopher rebuked him with ever increasing vehemence. "You are unchanged," he cried to him, "unfortunately unchanged. It is quite incomprehensible to me how you can still be the same as you were seven years ago, when I saw you for the last time and left you with so much misgiving. I fear I must once again divest you, however reluctantly, of the skin of modern culture which you have donned meanwhile;—and what do I find beneath it? The same immutable 'intelligible' character forsooth, according to Kant; but unfortunately the same unchanged 'intellectual' character, too—which may also be a necessity, though not a comforting one. I ask myself to what purpose have I lived as a philosopher, if, possessed as you are of no mean intelligence and a genuine thirst for knowledge, all the years you have spent in my company have left no deeper impression upon you. At present you are behaving as if you had not even heard the cardinal principle of all culture, which I went to such pains to inculcate upon you during our former intimacy. Tell me,—what was that principle?"

"I remember," replied the scolded pupil, "you used to say no one would strive to attain to culture if he knew how incredibly small the number of really cultured people actually is, and can ever be. And even this number of really cultured people would not be possible if a prodigious multitude, from reasons opposed to their nature and only led on by an alluring delusion, did not devote themselves to education. It were therefore a mistake publicly to reveal the ridiculous disproportion between the number of really cultured people and the enormous magnitude of the educational apparatus. Here lies the whole secret of culture—namely, that an innumerable host of men struggle to achieve it and work hard to that end, ostensibly in their own interests, whereas at bottom it is only in order that it may be possible for the few to attain to it."

"That is the principle," said the philosopher,—"and yet you could so far forget yourself as to believe that you are one of the few? This thought has occurred to you—I can see. That, however, is the result of the worthless character of modern education. The rights of genius are being democratised in order that people may be relieved of the labour of acquiring culture, and their need of it. Everyone wants if possible to recline in the shade of the tree planted by genius, and to escape the dreadful necessity of working for him, so that his procreation may be made possible. What? Are you too proud to be a teacher? Do you despise the thronging multitude of learners? Do you speak contemptuously of the teacher's calling? And, aping my mode of life, would you fain live in solitary seclusion, hostilely isolated from that multitude? Do you suppose that you can reach at one bound what I ultimately had to win for myself only after long and determined struggles, in order even to be able to live like a philosopher? And do you not fear that solitude will wreak its vengeance upon you? Just try living the life of a hermit of culture. One must be blessed with overflowing wealth in order to live for the good of all on one's own resources! Extraordinary youngsters! They felt it incumbent upon them to imitate what is precisely most difficult and most high,—what is possible only to the master, when they, above all, should know how difficult and dangerous this is, and how many excellent gifts may be ruined by attempting it!"

"I will conceal nothing from you, sir," the companion replied. "I have heard too much from your lips at odd times and have been too long in your company to be able to surrender myself entirely to our present system of education and instruction. I am too painfully conscious of the disastrous errors and abuses to which you used to call my attention—though I very well know that I am not strong enough to hope for any success were I to struggle ever so valiantly against them. I was overcome by a feeling of general discouragement; my recourse to solitude was the result neither of pride nor arrogance. I would fain describe to you what I take to be the nature of the educational questions now attracting such enormous and pressing attention. It seemed to me that I must recognise two main directions in the forces at work—two seemingly antagonistic tendencies, equally deleterious in their action, and ultimately combining to produce their results: a striving to achieve the greatest possible *expansion* of education on the one hand, and a tendency to *minimise and weaken* it on the other. The first-named would, for various reasons, spread learning among the greatest number of people; the second would compel education to renounce its highest, noblest and sublimest claims in order to subordinate itself to some other department of life—such as the service of the State.

"I believe I have already hinted at the quarter in which the cry for the greatest possible expansion of education is most loudly raised. This expansion belongs to the most beloved of the dogmas of modern political economy. As much knowledge and education as possible; therefore the greatest possible supply and demand—hence as much happiness as possible:—that is the formula. In this case utility is made the object and goal of education,—utility in the sense of gain—the greatest possible pecuniary gain. In the quarter now under consideration culture would be defined as that point of vantage which enables one to 'keep in the van of one's age,' from which one can see all the easiest and best roads to wealth, and with which one controls all the means of communication between men and nations. The purpose of education, according to this scheme, would be to rear the most 'current' men possible,—'current' being used here in the sense in which it is applied to the coins of the realm. The greater the number of such men, the happier a nation will be; and this precisely is the purpose of our modern educational institutions: to help everyone, as far as his nature will allow, to become 'current'; to develop him so that his particular degree of knowledge and science may yield him the greatest possible amount of happiness and pecuniary gain. Everyone must be able to form some sort of estimate of himself; he must know how much he may reasonably expect from life. The 'bond between intelligence and property' which this point of view postulates has almost the force of a moral principle. In this quarter all culture is loathed which isolates, which sets goals beyond gold and gain, and which requires time: it is customary to dispose of such eccentric tendencies in education as systems of 'Higher Egotism,' or of 'Immoral Culture—Epicureanism.' According to the morality reigning here, the demands are quite different; what is required above all is 'rapid education,' so that a money-earning creature may be produced with all speed; there is even a desire to make this education so thorough that a creature may be reared that will be able to earn a *great deal* of money. Men are allowed only the precise amount of culture which is compatible with the interests of gain; but that amount, at least, is expected from them. In short: mankind has a necessary right to happiness on earth—that is why culture is necessary—but on that account alone!"

"I must just say something here," said the philosopher. "In the case of the view you have described so clearly, there arises the great and awful danger that at some time or other the great masses may overleap the middle classes and spring headlong into this earthly bliss. That is what is now called 'the social question.' It might seem to these masses that education for the greatest number of men was only a means to the earthly bliss of the few: the 'greatest possible expansion of education' so enfeebles education that it can no longer confer privileges or inspire respect. The most general form of culture is simply barbarism. But I do not wish to interrupt your discussion."

The companion continued: "There are yet other reasons, besides this beloved economical dogma, for the expansion of education that is being striven after so valiantly everywhere. In some countries the fear of religious oppression is so general, and the dread of its results so marked, that people in all classes of society long for culture and eagerly absorb those elements of it which are supposed to scatter the religious instincts. Elsewhere the State, in its turn, strives here and there for its own preservation, after the greatest possible expansion of education, because it always feels strong enough to bring the most determined emancipation, resulting from culture, under its yoke, and readily approves of everything which tends to extend culture, provided that it be of service to its officials or soldiers, but in the main to itself, in its competition with other nations. In this case, the foundations of a State must be sufficiently broad and firm to constitute a fitting counterpart to the complicated arches of culture which it supports, just as in the first case the traces of some former religious tyranny must still be felt for a people to be driven to such desperate remedies. Thus, wherever I hear the masses raise the cry for an expansion of education, I am wont to ask myself whether it is stimulated by a greedy lust of gain and property, by the memory of a former religious persecution, or by the prudent egotism of the State itself."

"On the other hand, it seemed to me that there was yet another tendency, not so clamorous, perhaps, but quite as forcible, which, hailing from various quarters, was animated by a different desire,—the desire to minimise and weaken education."

"In all cultivated circles people are in the habit of whispering to one another words something after this style: that it is a general fact that, owing to the present frantic exploitation of the scholar in the service of his science, his *education* becomes every day more accidental and more uncertain. For the study of science has been extended to such interminable lengths that he who, though not exceptionally gifted, yet possesses fair abilities, will need to devote himself exclusively to one branch and ignore all others if he ever wish to achieve anything in his work. Should he then elevate himself above the herd by means of his speciality, he still remains one of them in regard to all else,—that is to say, in regard to all the most important things in life. Thus, a specialist in science gets to resemble nothing so much as a factory workman who spends his whole life in turning one particular screw or handle on a certain instrument or machine, at which occupation he acquires the most consummate skill. In Germany, where we know how to drape such painful facts with the glorious garments of fancy, this narrow specialisation on the part of our learned men is even admired, and their ever greater deviation from the path of true culture is regarded as a moral phenomenon. 'Fidelity in small things,' 'dogged faithfulness,' become expressions of highest eulogy, and the lack of culture outside the speciality is flaunted abroad as a sign of noble sufficiency."

"For centuries it has been an understood thing that one alluded to scholars alone when one spoke of cultured men; but experience tells us that it would be difficult to find any necessary relation between the two classes to-day. For at present the exploitation of a man for the purpose of science is accepted everywhere without the slightest scruple. Who still ventures to ask, What may be the value of a science which consumes its minions in this vampire fashion? The division of labour in science is practically struggling towards the same goal which religions in certain parts of the world are consciously striving after,—that is to say, towards the decrease and even the destruction of learning. That, however, which, in the case of certain religions, is a perfectly justifiable aim, both in regard to their origin and their history, can only amount to self-immolation when transferred to the realm of science. In all matters of a general and serious nature, and above all, in regard to the highest philosophical problems, we have now already reached a point at which the scientific man, as such, is no longer allowed to speak. On the other hand, that adhesive and tenacious stratum which has now filled up the interstices between the sciences—Journalism—believes it has a mission to fulfil here, and this it does, according to its own particular lights—that is to say, as its name implies, after the fashion of a day-labourer."

"It is precisely in journalism that the two tendencies combine and become one. The expansion and the diminution of education here join hands. The newspaper actually steps into the place of culture, and he who, even as a scholar, wishes to voice any claim for education, must avail himself of this viscous stratum of communication which cements the seams between all forms of life, all classes, all arts, and all sciences, and which is as firm and reliable as news paper is, as a rule. In the newspaper the peculiar educational aims of the present culminate, just as the journalist, the servant of the moment, has stepped into the place of the genius, of the leader for all time, of the deliverer from the tyranny of the moment. Now, tell me, distinguished master, what hopes could I still have in a struggle against the general topsy-turvification of all genuine aims for education; with what courage can I, a single teacher, step forward, when I know that the moment any seeds of real culture are sown, they will be mercilessly crushed by the roller of this pseudo-culture? Imagine how useless the most energetic work on the part of the individual teacher must be, who would fain lead a pupil back into the distant and evasive Hellenic world and to the real home of culture, when in less than an hour, that same pupil will have recourse to a newspaper, the latest novel, or one of those learned books, the very style of which already bears the revolting impress of modern barbaric culture—"

"Now, silence a minute!" interjected the philosopher in a strong and sympathetic voice. "I understand you now, and ought never to have spoken so crossly to you. You are altogether right, save in your despair. I shall now proceed to say a few words of consolation."

CHAPTER SIX

Research, Education and Instruction

From *The Idea of the University* (1923/1960)

KARL JASPERS

Translated, H. A. T. Reiche and H. F. Vanderschmidt, this selection is taken from *The Idea of the University*, 1960, Edited by Karl Deutsch, With Preface by O. L. Zangwill, Published by Peter Owen, London, United Kingdom.

Editors' Note

Karl Jaspers was an existential philosopher though of an unusual kind. For him, philosophy had legitimate interests both in knowledge and in 'existenz'. In particular, Jaspers had a sympathy for the kind of philosophy that sought to underwrite science but was concerned that it was liable to over-reach itself. Neither science nor such a philosophy could in themselves supply meaning. Ultimately, 'everything essentially real is for me only by virtue of the fact that I am I myself' (Jaspers, 1971).

Against such a background, it was inevitable that, in his thinking about the university, Jaspers should adopt an inclusive outlook; but there was more to it than that. Jaspers taught philosophy at the University of Heidelberg from 1921 until being suspended by the Nazis in 1937, Jaspers standing by his refusal to support the Nazi regime throughout World War II. *The Idea of the University* was written at the end of the war, and we can glimpse in it Jaspers' sense of interconnectivity and the potential of the university to aid both personal development and societal development.

The extract here, 'Research, Education and Instruction' constitutes chapter four of *The Idea of the University*. The chapter title alone indicates Jaspers' sense of there being interconnections between the responsibilities that befall the University, in bringing together a concern for spirit, human existence and reason. This is not just a matter of joining the functions of the university, bringing teaching and research close together, but is also a matter of the spirit of the university itself. 'An infinite cosmic order', 'care', 'intellectual conscience', 'civilization', 'indivisible whole', 'unity', 'philosophical point of view', awakening, 'freedom', 'self-sacrificing' and personal 'responsibility': terms such as these (all in the chapter reproduced here) are indicative not only of Jaspers' sense of wholeness but of the university as a space of untrammelled enquiry and as a 'spirit of adventure'.

RB

Recommended Reading

Jaspers, K. (1971). *Philosophy of Existence.* Philadelphia, PA: University of Pennsylvania.

* * * * *

The student comes to the university in order to study the arts and sciences and to prepare himself for a profession. Despite the apparent clarity of his task and situation the student is frequently perplexed. Overwhelmed by the sheer mass of what can be learned he wants to know what is of chief importance. Orientation lectures, practice sessions, and syllabi only partially help to overcome his difficulties. In the last analysis he must find his own way in the world of lectures, laboratories and seminars.

But the student expects even more from the university. To be sure, he studies a special field and has in mind a definite profession. Still, the university with its aura of tradition represents to him the unity of all branches of learning. He respects this unity and expects to experience it, and through it to arrive at a well-founded *Weltanschauung*. He wants to arrive at truth, wants to gain a clear view of the world and of people. He wants to encounter wholeness, an infinite cosmic order. Science and learning are essentially of the spirit: they seek relations to the totality of all there is to be known.

Yet even with all this, youth is not satisfied. The young person has a heightened sense of the seriousness of life since he is aware of the weighty decisions still ahead. He feels plastic, full of possibilities. He is aware that what will become of him largely depends upon himself. He feels that his daily life is what counts, every hour, every living impulse. The young person wants to learn either by apprenticing himself to a master, through self-discipline, or through frank discussion among friends similarly motivated.

One's expectations arc only seldom fulfilled at a university. The first rush of enthusiasm does not last. Perhaps the student never had been quite clear about what he wanted, what he was doing. At any rate, he becomes disillusioned, confused. He ceases striving and loses himself in blind alleys. He studies for examinations only and judges everything according to what ·use it will have for examinations. He considers his period of study as a painful transitional period before his professional life can begin. The latter now holds the promise of salvation. He says that he is probably too stupid to grasp the essentials, resigns himself to practicing his specialty. On the other hand, his originally creative enthusiasms may lose their vitality and become a matter of lip service. He becomes lazy in his work, wants to grasp the idea, unity, profundity directly without any disagreeable effort which to his way of thinking grasps only trivia. He thinks that by reading a few good books he is doing scholarly work. He finally perverts true effort to the point where he seeks an edifying frame of mind, rather than scholarship, and mistakes the classroom for the pulpit.

If he is lucky, the individual student makes his own way, a way that leads to development and purpose, guided only by his personal intuition. Ultimately, he who does not know where he is going goes the farthest. Reflection on the overall implications of his proposed work will not directly help any man to get his bearings. But it will help him indirectly by making him aware of possibilities and limitations and thus prevent confusion. The aspiring scholar will reflect on the broader questions of direction, order and aims of his work. For the will to know implies the will to understand clearly what one is doing. Our discussion here aims to assist this quest for intellectual clarity as a way of life, a form of human existence.

Three things are required at a university: professional training, education of the whole man, research. For the university is simultaneously a professional school, a cultural centre and a research institute. People have tried to force the university to choose between these three possibilities. They have asked what it is that we really expect the university to do. Since, so they say, it cannot do everything it ought to decide upon one of these three alternatives. It was even suggested that the university as such be dissolved, to be replaced by three special types of school: institutes for professional training, institutes for general education possibly involving a special staff, and research institutes. In the idea of the university, however, these three are indissolubly united. One cannot be cut off from the others without destroying the intellectual substance of the university, and without at the same time crippling itself. All three are factors of a living whole. By isolating them, the spirit of the university perishes.

Research

Within the life of the university teachers and students are driven by a single motive, man's basic quest for knowledge. For every advance in knowledge, however, stubborn, indefatigable work is necessary. This work involves three factors:

1) Work in its narrower sense consists of learning and practicing, widening one's realm of knowledge and mastering methods. Work is the basis of everything else. Work more than anything stands in need of discipline and order. It is most time-consuming and can be initiated at any time. Only hard work can lay the indispensable foundations, can fashion our tools, and can supply the necessary method through which to express and check any new discovery, as well as the actual verification of what would remain mere conjecture. No one can fail to respect the sheer discipline and endurance of persistent effort. The student should start in on this work immediately as he has learned it in school. "The sooner we realize," says Goethe, "that there is a systematic way, call it craft or call it art, of augmenting our natural endowments, the happier we are." But whoever boasts about his craftsman like competence and thinks that it suffices to make his contribution valuable is lost in a morass of materials and technique. Sheer industry is not above resenting enviously and ignobly any genuine intellectual competence with its far broader scope.
2) If work is not to be just endless drudgery, if there is to be meaning in it, it needs something which cannot be attained through good will alone. Ideas which are not rational but truly intuitive first give impetus to the scientist, invest his discoveries with importance. Ideas grow and move. They cannot be compelled by will alone. They grow, however, only for those people who are steadily at work. "Conjectures" are unpredictable and incalculable. That which alone causes learning to thrive-something unclear, opaque to reason and impossible to manufacture just this demands devoted care. The man who does intellectual research belongs to that group of men who must "forever think about their subject," who are thoroughly permeated by their work. His is not the compartmentalization of life into work and amusement. One's way of life is a requisite condition for ideas, especially if these are to be taken seriously. Many a man has had a good idea but uncaring has soon forgotten it.
3) Above and beyond mere industry the scholar and scientist has an intellectual conscience. While he realizes that everywhere he must trust to luck and right instinct, he strives at the same time for conscious and honest control

> over his creative impulses. Unthinking industry without aims, mere feeling and belief, mere consent and edification which do not in turn impel him to a creativity of his own run equally counter to his conscience. The scholar tries to relate chance and isolated occurrences to a whole. He strives for continuity, resists arbitrary interruption of a line of thought. But he does interrupt it when his conscience compels him to follow up some idea which might lead him further. He then turns to pursue this intensively. He is as distrustful of frequent reorientations as he is of absolute continuity along a single line of thought. Because he strives for the ultimate implications of his ideas and wishes to bring these out in his work, he is little concerned with what is merely fashionable or current. But he is concerned with the present, with the present moment as the incarnation of eternity. He is able to seclude himself. He knows that no one on the outside can judge whether or not he is proceeding correctly. His intellectual conscience decides for him. No outside advice can lighten the burden of his responsibility.

It is the responsibility of the university to promote intellectual work based on these three elements.

The process of learning deals with definite subject matter. Nothing is exempt from this radical quest for knowledge. Whatever exists in the world should be brought into the scope of the university so as to become object for study. Knowledge cannot be created exclusively by the mind. Only the mathematician and the logician are self-contained in this sense and need not go beyond everyday experience. The student at all times requires material for empirical observation. Because the university realizes this, it furnishes him with additional aids, such as collections, libraries and clinics. Materials for study and research or pictures of them, apparatus and experimental equipment are also made available.

Yet inanimate objects alone do not make up all that there is to be known. Mind is intrinsically alive. A given historical period and civilization can achieve genuine self-awareness. It does so when its thinking members stand in a relationship of "give and take" with their own time, when they associate with intellectually productive people. The university exists against the undefinable background of an intellectual atmosphere, a human "give and take" that cannot be induced by an act of will or organization, but either is or is not there. Groups and personal relationships of an incalculable sort are formed. The university is impoverished if this human-intellectual lifeblood ceases to pulse through its veins, or if only pedants and philistines continue to concern themselves with living material alien to them as human beings. It is impoverished if there is only philology, no philosophy, only technology, but no theory, endless facts but no ideas.

The always limited world of the university is broadened by travel, by admitting visiting scholars, by broad and personally deep relationships, by foreign connections, or if the university contributes its personnel to some practical tasks which others like doctors serve on a permanent basis. All such practical activity may strengthen the idea of the university, provided it can be shared, turned into ideas, and evoke a response in the community of scholars.

If research is to be the task of the university then this task is realizable at the university only in the face of many conflicting obligations. Some have therefore concluded that it would be better to have institutes for pure research alone, unburdened by any other duties. Such research institutes have in fact been organized and turned out good work. Yet fundamentally they remain offshoots of the university. In the long run they will flourish only in association with the university. They are dependent on the university for their supply of new talent. Moreover, research in itself depends on access to the whole of knowledge, and the opportunity of exchange with all sorts of specialists. Where research institutes are not tied to special places by the nature of their research, they do well to locate in university towns. For a certain time a specialized project can have astounding success, especially in the natural sciences. But the meaning and creative perpetuation of research can only be preserved if it maintains a lively exchange with the whole of knowledge. The individual scientist or scholar may profit from spending a certain length of time, or even the remainder of his life, at a research institute, relieved from the other duties of a university. Yet .what he has achieved was accomplished .in living exchange with the scholarly community to which he might some day return. Moreover; teaching itself is often—even most of the time—stimulating to research.

Above all, teaching vitally needs the substance which only research can give it. Hence the combination of research and teaching is the lofty and inalienable basic principle of the university. This combination is sound not because it is an economy measure, nor because this combination alone financially enables the scientist or scholar to do his research, but because ideally the best research worker is also the best and only teacher. The research worker may be pedagogically inept, that is, he may be inept in transmitting bare facts. Yet he alone can bring the student into contact with the real process of discovery, hence with the spirit of science rather than with dead results which can be committed to memory. He is the spirit of scientific inquiry come to life; in communication with him one can sec knowledge as it genuinely exists. He awakens similar impulses in his students. He directs his students to the source of knowledge. Only he who himself does research can really teach. Others only pass on a set of pedagogically arranged facts. The university is not a high school but a higher institution of learning.

The university has professional schools preparing its graduates for jobs that can only be filled by people with basically scientific outlook. This requires a familiarity with research and method, as distinct from specialized training in the narrower sense. The best preparation for these special professions is not memorization of a closed body of knowledge but training and development of the faculties for scholarly and scientific thinking. This alone can lay the foundation for further intellectual and scientific training throughout life. The university can only lay the basis for professional training; practice alone brings mastery. The university should provide the best possible conditions for this eventual growth through practice.

The young person must learn how to ask questions. He must study something systematically, get to the bottom of it. He need not, however, carry the sum total of factual knowledge about in his head. Wherever this is the case, it is of no lasting value. After examinations, one quickly forgets. The decisive factor after this is not the body of fact learned, but one's judgment. What matters then is not factual knowledge by itself but the ability and initiative to go out and get the facts on one's own, to think about them effectively, to know what questions to ask. Not memorizing facts but contact with living research imparts this ability. Technical detail, outlines and the like are not excluded but are simply left to textbook study. A bare fifty years ago people used to say that "an institution of higher learning is not a high school." It is certainly a good idea to cover in one's theoretical study as many of the practically useful materials as is possible. But the most important factors even so remain: an active intellect, the ability to grasp problems and to pose questions, the mastery of method.

By its very name the university is a "universe."[1] Discovery and research constitute an indivisible whole-departmentalization notwithstanding. The university deteriorates if it becomes an aggregate of specialized schools alongside of which it tolerates the· so-called "general education" as mere window dressing and vague talk in generalities. Scholarship depends on a relation to the whole. Individual disciplines are meaningless apart from their relation to the whole of knowledge. Therefore it is the intention of the university to impart to its students a sense of the unity both of his own particular field of study and of all knowledge. The whole business of schooling, the mastery of routine and of a body of facts, becomes harmful if it loses this sense of relatedness to the ideal of learning or actually prevents the student from living up to this ideal.

The university, then, must provide the professions with a twofold foundation. It must instil a growing lifelong commitment to the scientific outlook as well as to

---

1 In origin this meant a "universe" of teacher and student, but it has long since shifted its meaning to the one indicated above.

the search for the unity of knowledge. These two are requisite for all intellectual professions, which are the professions involving more' than the routine practice of specialized technique. The doctor, the teacher, the administrator, the judge, the clergyman, the architect, are each in his own way professionally concerned with man as a whole, and the conditions of human life as a whole. Preparation for these professions is unthinking and inhuman if it fails to relate us to the whole and to develop our perceptiveness, to show the wide scope of knowledge or to make us think philosophically. Deficiencies in professional routine which are bound to exist at the time when the degree is conferred can be eliminated with practice. Basic deficiencies in scholarly and scientific training are irremediable.

Everyone engaged in an intellectual profession is bound to think in scholarly terms. The true scholar or scientist, however, is he who can persist in the effort of protracted thinking without losing sight of the whole. Hence the best way of imparting practical scientific training is to encourage the habit of research.

To address oneself to the whole is what is called the "philosophical" point of view. All science is "philosophical" in this sense, so long as it does not neglect the end for the means, and so lose itself and its ideal in a concern for cataloguing words and facts, for apparatus, collections, techniques, or isolated phenomena. According to Kant it is the dignity, the absolute value of philosophy which lends value to all other branches of knowledge. This does not mean that everyone should study philosophy. Many a man has evinced his philosophical impulse not only in his novel way of posing questions but in his very attacks upon "philosophy in general." Yet the philosophy that matters is the one at work within science and human life itself, as against the mere vocabulary and jargon of philosophy, which is usually what the detractors of philosophy mean to attack. What matters is the philosophical impulse from which research proceeds, the idea which gives research direction, and the meaning which gives it value and ends of its own. That type of philosophical thought has value which can shape and motivate the scientist and scholar, that philosophy, in short, which permeates the whole of the university. The existence of special chairs for philosophy and of a special department for philosophy, where philosophy can flourish without apparent contact with the whole, is justifiable only on purely administrative and pedagogical grounds.

Education as Formation of the Mind

Formal education, like tradition, generally tends to be dependent upon particular forms of social organization. The changes in educational outlook parallel the changes which a nation undergoes in the course of its history. The unifying factor in education reflects the dominance in each case of a given social body, e.g., church, class, nation. Education could be described as the manner by which these social bodies perpetuate themselves from generation to generation. Hence education becomes transformed when there are social revolutions. Moreover, attempts at social innovations turn to pedagogical questions first. Because of this, considerations of the significance and methods of education inevitably include the larger question of state and society. Blueprints for the good society such as Plato's *Republic* treat political and educational organization as co-extensive. Education prepares each individual to be a member of society and, conversely, society is the means of the individual's education.

Let us consider some aspects of education from the point of view of the historical changes to which they have been subject. The social need of the times determines what will be included in the curriculum. Theological knowledge is required in preparation for the ministry; training in the skills of using language, for a humanistic education. For the education of the Greek gentleman a knowledge of myth and legend is required. Today, the importance of sociology, economics, technology, natural science and geography is stressed. Education changes with cultural ideals. The way schools are organized mirrors the social structure. In the past diverse types of educational systems have been attempted such as schools for the several estates, academies for the nobility and private instruction for aristocrats and patricians. All democracies demand common public education because nothing makes people so much alike as the same education.

Apart from sociological and historical considerations, we can distinguish three basic forms of education:

1) Scholastic instruction. This type of education is limited to the mere "transmission" of the tradition. The teacher only reproduces, he is not himself active in original research. All knowledge has been systematized. Certain authors and books are considered authoritative. The role of the teacher is an impersonal one; he is a representative who may be replaced by anyone else who is qualified. All material is reduced to formulae. The medieval teacher dictated a text to his students and commented upon it. The availability of textbooks has made dictating superfluous. But the underlying idea of medieval education is by no means dead today. The student subordinates himself to some system of thought which shelters him yet without thereby subordinating him to any one personality. Knowledge is frozen for all time into an orderly world picture. Here the student is interested only in what is fixed and permanent, wants to assimilate results, and like the pupil in Goethe's Faust wants to take home results in "black and white." The scholastic approach continues to be indispensable to Western rationalism.

2) Apprenticeship. Of chief importance here is not an impersonal tradition, but a personality felt to be unique. The reverence and love rendered to the master's person have something of worship in them. The distance between master and pupil derives not merely from a quantitative difference (of two generations), but in addition, from an inherent qualitative one. The person of the master exerts an authority with a marvellous power. A wide variety of motives comes into play here. There is the need to subordinate oneself, the desire to avoid responsibility, the relief experienced through association with greatness, coupled with the enhancement of one's sense of self-importance and the need for a discipline sterner than any we can impose on ourselves.
3) In Socratic education, the teacher and his student ought to stand on the same level. Both are meant to be free. No hard and fast educational system exists here, rather endless questioning and ultimate ignorance in the face of the absolute. Personal responsibility is carried to its utmost and is nowhere alleviated. Education is a "midwifery," in which the student is helped to give birth to his abilities and powers. He is awakened to an awareness of his own capacities, he is not compelled from without. What counts is not the accident of empirical individuality but our true self which emerges in the process of self-realization. The Socratic teacher resists his students' urge to make him their authority and master. Herein lies the greatest temptation for students. He turns them away from himself and back onto themselves; he hides in paradoxes, makes himself inaccessible. The intimate relationship between student and teacher here is not one of submission, but of a contest for truth. The teacher knows that he is only human, demands that his students differentiate between human and divine.

In all three types of education respect is a dominant factor. In scholastic education respect focuses on a tradition visible in the very hierarchy of social structure. In apprenticeship-training respect focuses on the personality of the master; in Socratic education, on the transcendent status of mind which imposes on human life the burden of straddling two worlds.

Respect is indispensable to education. Without it, industriousness at best remains. Respect is the very substance of all education. Man's humanity requires his realization of the absolute. Without it all would be meaningless.

Within the world this absolute can be reflected on three levels: on the corporate level, such as the social group for which one is being prepared, the state, or an institutionalized form or religion; on an individual level; or on both levels simultaneously.

To the extent that its substance becomes problematic, education becomes rigid. Respect is artificially maintained through deliberate secrecy exercised by those in authority. It is maintained also by the demand of blind obedience to a personal authority, and by awakening map's desire for submission. Mere "fulfilment of duty" becomes a substitute for work in behalf of what is essential in education. Instead of striving for one's best achievement, people will seek to gratify their ambitious vanity for recognition and status. The memorization of supposedly useful data replaces the transformation of the entire man by his education. Instead of affirming a given educational ideal with their whole persons such people are only interested in acquiring quickly-to-be-forgotten facts for an examination which supposedly stamps them as educated.

All formal education is free to choose one of these three methods of education above discussed. But it presupposes the value of the educational substance communicated. Without faith in this value no real education can exist, only pedagogical technique.

Once the substance of education has become problematic, the faith in it wavering, the question as to what are the aims of education poses itself. It is a hopeless undertaking, however, to seek such ideals in a manner that ignores the actual historical situation and our own real aims, if, in short, one seeks these ideals in isolation from our own lives. This is the reason why educational slogans such as the following don't amount to much: development of special aptitudes, moral improvement, broadening one's frame of reference, character building, national pride, strength and independence, ability to express oneself, development of the personality, creation of a unifying sense of common cultural tradition, etc.

Education at a university is Socratic by its very nature. It is not the whole of one's education, nor is it like the instruction one receives in high school. University students are adults, not children. They are mature, have full responsibility for themselves. Professors do not give them assignments or personal guidance. Freedom, the all-important factor, is irreconcilable with even so impressive a training as that which has been traditionally identified with the monastic orders and military academies. This type of submission to rigid training and leadership keeps the individual from experiencing a genuine will to know. It blocks the development of human independence that admits no other source or tie than God Himself.

University education is a formative; process aiming at meaningful freedom. It takes place through participation in the university's intellectual life.

Education is not a task to be pursued in isolation. This is why, next to the principle that research and teaching are indivisible, we have a second principle which states that research and teaching are in fact inseparable from the educational process as a whole. Research and professional schooling have an educative effect precisely because they do not just transmit facts and knowledge, but awaken ideas of unity and develop a scientific attitude. To be sure, this development of active intelligence is still less than the training of the whole man. That training involves more. Nevertheless, university education is an integral component of it.

A university so conceived educates in a way which is neither indefinable nor yet definitive. It educates by involving the rational and philosophic impulse, so decisive for the whole man, in its unbounded commitment to the spirit of inquiry and clarification. To the extent that it succeeds in involving the whole man, it enhances his proper humanity, what the Romans termed man's *Humanitas*: the listening to arguments, understanding, the ability to think along with the viewpoints of others, honesty, discipline and consistency. But this type of personality is a spontaneous by-product, not a conscious goal. If education is set up toward this end in isolation from scholarship, what is lost is precisely the intellectual development aimed for. Do we want a thin "humanistic" education which instead of philological, methodical schooling teaches results, offers beautiful objects to be observed, enjoyed and talked about? Do we desire an educational process which reaches deeply into the soul, which directs itself toward religious needs? The university is not a church, no religious order, no mystery, nor is it a place for prophets and apostles. Its principle is to furnish all tools and offer all possibilities in the province of the intellect, to direct the individual to the frontiers, to refer the learner back to himself for all his decisions, to his own sense of responsibility. This sense of responsibility has become awakened through his learning and is brought through it to the highest possible level and the clearest awareness. The university demands a ruthless will to know. Since learning and personal initiative go hand in hand; the university aims for the broadest possible development of independence and personal responsibility. Within its sphere, it respects no authority other than truth in its infinite variety, the truth which all are seeking and yet no one can claim to possess in final and complete form.

The idea of the university derives its educational force from the primary human will to know. It gives the educated man both sureness of purpose and at the same time great humility. Insight alone cannot decide the purpose or ultimate goal of existence. One clear and ultimate purpose is this at any rate: the world wants to be understood. Research belongs to the university not only because it is the basis of training for the professions, but because the university itself exists for research, fulfils its meaning through research. The student is the scholar and scientist-to-be. He will remain philosophically and intellectually oriented for the duration of his life, if he allows himself to grow along with his thinking, even where his way of shaping reality is practical rather than theoretical, a way no less productive than scientific and scholarly achievement measured in terms of published output.

To live freely in the world of ideas is on first inspection fraught with danger for the student. He is thrown back upon his own resources since such a mode of life, thrives only on one's own responsibility. From the freedom of teaching springs the freedom of learning. No authority, no rules and regulations, no supervision of studies such as are found in high schools must be allowed to hamper the university student. He is free to "go to the dogs." It has often been said that you have to risk your young men if you want to get a generation of men. There is a place certainly for scholastic Instruction, for learning in its narrower sense, and for practice in methods. But the student is free to choose how extensively he wants to participate in this instruction, and when he can get on with books alone, without benefit of teachers.

Ideally the relation between professor and student involves a Socratic equality of status with a mutual stress on standard not on authority. Intellectual excellence, not mediocrity, sets the tone. We live and work together under the common obligation of calling one another to the highest of standards in thought and performance. Our enemies are smug self-satisfaction and a Philistine attitude. We have a basic desire to be near those whom we admire. Love for the great man, whose very existence makes the greatest demands on us, lends us wings. Still the relation remains Socratic. Nobody becomes authority. The grain of sand remains free and independent next to the cliff. For even the grain of sand IS substance. The recognition of an intellectual aristocracy implies making demands upon oneself only, never entitles one to feel superior or make demands upon others. Two things fundamentally unite all members of the university, whether teachers or students; a common calling to exert themselves as if for the very highest attainment, and at the same time, the constant pressure to live up to that calling and prove themselves. It is best in this connection not to indulge in extensive self-analysis, yet on the other hand not to demand outside recognition.

It has been said that students should become leaders of their people. Some have even conceived the strange notion of a school for future leaders. Such notions violate the idea of the university. Leaders come from all classes and occupations. Expert knowledge is attainable not only at a university. Academic training has no monopoly on expert knowledge. It is all well and good to demand "intellectuality" of a leader. In reality, however, leaders are often made of very different stuff. The world is no Platonic Republic, ruled by philosophers. Will to power, resoluteness, deliberation, an eye for the realities of the moment, practical experience and success, as well as special traits of character, are the important qualities. Leaders may well come from academic circles. But generally the type of person found in academic professions is not a leader type. The clergyman, the doctor, the teacher, is certainly a "leader" in a limited sense, either because of his formal authority (which has nothing to do with the idea of the university), as long as this is recognized in the society in which he lives; or he may be a "leader" by virtue of his humanity and spirituality, which manifest themselves in his individual personality. These are again and again put to question, and are never a matter of personal claim. Or he may be a leader because of his expert knowledge, which proves itself useful in his specialty.

Instruction

The mechanics of instruction involve lectures, seminars and laboratories in small private groups, and discussions between two people.

Lectures have held pre-eminence in teaching for ages. They present the materials to be learned in such a way that the listener can visualize how and for what reasons they were collected. Bare facts can be gathered from books. In lectures the listener takes notes and is compelled to think "bout the lecture. He prepares himself for lectures by doing experiments, studying books, and extending his knowledge.

One cannot establish a standard for good lectures. If they are good they have a special quality which cannot be imitated. Their intended meaning differing widely with the personality of the lecturer, is valuable in each case. There are lectures which aim to instruct and personally involve the listener, which seek to hold him intellectually; and there are lectures where the speaker, totally oblivious to his audience, engages in a monologue about research in progress, yet even so manages to impart a sense of genuine participation in genuine research. Lectures which aim to sum up an entire subject are in a class by themselves. They are indispensable, for they awaken the impulse to envisage the whole, provided thorough work on the details is being pushed at the same time. Such lectures should be given only by the most mature professors drawing upon the sum total of their life's work. There should therefore be general lectures by the most outstanding professors ·on each of the basic subjects treated as wholes.

Fundamental disciplines are those whose specific content has universal significance. As against auxiliary subjects and special techniques, their every detail is not an end in itself, but symbolizes the entire cognitive process. Disciplines whose specialized details succeed in mirroring the whole are by that token universal in character. There are textbooks which manage to convey the universality implicit in such disciplines. The manner in which a given discipline investigates its materials reveals the extent to which it is a fundamental discipline.

In the past decades lectures have been subject to much criticism. They are said to be a one-sided affair which encourages a passive attitude on the part of the listener, that any sign as to whether the listener has understood and assimilated the lecture is lacking, that the subject of the lecture is usually better stated in books and can be learned more quickly from these. These objections apply to poor lectures which repeat a dead body of knowledge identically from year to year, or to lectures which are little more than an easy informal flow of talk. Lectures are of value when they become a genuine part of a professor's life work, when they are prepared with care and at the same time inimitably reflect contemporary intellectual life.

Such lectures belong to what is irreplaceable in tradition. The memory of outstanding scholars lecturing accompanies one throughout life. The printed lecture, perhaps even taken down word for word is only a pale residue. True, what is of value in the lecture, its content, still communicates in printed form. But the lecturer himself presents this content in such a way as to suggest the total context which motivates his scholarship. Through his tone, his gestures, the real presence of his thinking the lecturer can unconsciously convey the "feel" of the subject. No doubt this can only be conveyed by the spoken word and only in a lecture-not in conversation or discussion. The lecture situation evokes something from the teacher which would remain hidden without it. There is nothing artificial about his thinking, his seriousness, his questioning, his perplexity. He allows us to take part in his innermost intellectual being. This great value is lost the moment it becomes contrived. Right away the result is affectation, rhetoric, pathos, artificial formulas, effects, demagoguery, shamelessness. Hence there are no rules for the preparation of a good lecture. One needs to do no more than to take the matter seriously: to consider the lecture a high point in one's professional responsibility and achievement, finally to renounce all artificiality. In the century and a half of important lectures from Kant to Max Weber it has become evident that even if the speaker falters and makes mistakes in his speech, if his sentences are grammatically incomplete or wrong, if his voice is not effective-none of these things is able to destroy the profound effect of the lecture if its intellectual substance is communicated. Lecture notes convey no more than a weak reflection of actual lectures. Yet even in the absence of personal recollection our imagining what they must have been like can be a challenge to us.

In seminars and laboratory work methods are mastered through practical contact with materials, apparatus and concepts which are studied by concrete example. By his own initiative the student may extend his understanding of these matters. Mastery of techniques occupies the greater amount of effort. We shall not take up the methods of teaching appropriate to different fields and their different technical facilities. Many fields have at their disposal a firm pedagogical tradition to serve as skeleton, not as substitute for instruction.

These seminars and laboratories are designed to acquaint us directly with the subject matter and the elements of learning. They differ basically from courses which merely transmit information, courses which make up for the lack of intellectual initiative on the part of students unable to do better and more rapid work on their own. For in every detail the whole is always implicitly and indirectly present. Textbook knowledge is only incidentally referred to and briefly reviewed in class so as to make the student aware where he has to fill in gaps on his own. The essential factor is to train one's perceptions through personal collaboration on the frontiers of knowledge. The kind of work which best motivates independent study is that which, presupposing general textbook knowledge, deals with a particular problem and goes straight to the heart of the matter. Textbooks by themselves are tiresome. Conversely, to chain oneself to a single object makes one narrow. Each gives life to the other.

Finally, education may take the form of discussion. Questions of basic importance are brought up in small groups, all members of which participate actively. This, in turn, will induce some of the participants to conclude the discussion alone with the teacher in a serious and lively give and take. Here student and teacher meet one another on the same level, as is the ideal. Together they will strive to formulate the problem with such clarity and precision as will awaken impulses in each by himself to make solid, personal contributions later on.

Teaching at the university must not be allowed to "get into a rut." Wherever teaching is intellectually alive it cannot help taking personal form: paradoxically only when the professor has a truly objective approach to ideas does his teaching have genuine individuality. Digressions which are simultaneously objective and personal combine with the special needs of the moment to keep teaching fresh and lively.

Teaching is one thing when it addresses itself to the average student, quite another when it addresses itself to a gifted few. The basic difference between school and university is that in schools the teacher must teach all the students entrusted to him. In the university, however, he has no such obligation. University education is meant for a number of selected people who are filled with a very special intellectual zeal and have sufficient mental equipment to do the work. In effect, the people who attend the university are an average group of people who have been able to acquire the necessary preparation. The weeding-out process is therefore up to the university.

The prospective student should have the following qualities: a desire for objectivity and an irrepressible self-sacrificing drive to intellectual attainment. These qualities cannot be objectively detected ahead of time. Only a minority of people possess these qualities, which in addition, are distributed in a wholly unpredictable way. They can be cultivated and made effective only indirectly. Yet it is to this minority that the university must direct itself if it is to live up to its own ideal standards. The true student can be relied on to make his way amid the difficulties and mistakes inevitable and necessary for intellectual growth, unperplexed by the mass of courses offered. Selectivity and discipline guide his studies. We must be prepared to accept, perhaps even welcome, the fact that the rest, at a loss for guidance, will learn next to nothing. Artificial guides such as the syllabi, curricular and other technical devices which convert the university into a school, are in conflict with the ideal of the university. They have resulted from adapting the university to the needs of the average student, on the grounds that the great mass of students should be made to learn enough at least to pass the examinations. This line of reasoning, appropriate enough to the school, is detrimental to the university, where the students are adults, even considering no more than their ages.

Nonetheless, university instruction cannot centre around the handful of superlative students. Rohde, the historian of Greek/religion, thought that out of one hundred students ninety-nine do I not understand the teacher and the one hundredth does not need him. If true, that would be disheartening. University education addresses itself not to the few geniuses or to the mediocre average, J but to that minority who while capable of growth and of initiative, nevertheless stand in need of instruction.

Some instruction geared to the abilities of the less gifted and lazy students who are the average is probably indispensable. By and large, however, university education is different. Lectures and seminars which are slightly over the student's head and so spur him on to increased effort are better than full comprehension purchased at the price of over-simplification. Independent reading and study in laboratories, collections and travelling must complement formal classroom work from the very start. Where instruction is geared to the pace of the brightest among the promising minority already mentioned the mediocre majority of students will have to exert themselves. All are working under a standard which no one entirely satisfies. Respect for the intellectually first-rate must provide all with an incentive to exert themselves to the utmost of their abilities.

Lectures follow one another according to some general order and plan. The sequence in which the beginner hears them is not unimportant. Hence compulsory study plans have come into being. In this way, however, university study ends up being strait-jacketed. The university is turned into a school in order to achieve a satisfactory average with statistical certainty. This leads to the destruction of the university. As you stifle the student's freedom to learn as he sees fit you stifle the life of the mind. The life of the mind is never more than a chance achievement amid a sea of failure and frustration. It is always something over and above average performance. Both student and teacher are unhappy when chained to curricula and syllabi, to tests and mediocre standards. An atmosphere of uninspired and uninspiring common sense may well produce satisfactory mastery of technical "know how" and testable factual information. Such an atmosphere, however, stifles genuine understanding and the spirit of adventure in research.

CHAPTER SEVEN

The Self-Assertion of the German University

Address Delivered on the Solemn Assumption of the Rectorate of the University Freiburg 1933/34: Facts and Thoughts (1933/1985)

MARTIN HEIDEGGER

From Gunther Neske & Emil Kettering (Eds.), *Martin Heidegger and National Socialism*, New York: Paragon House, 1990, pp. 5–13.

Editors' Note

'The Self-Assertion of the German University' a speech Heidegger delivered on 27 May 1933 after his election as head of Freiburg University is seen as his most infamous political text and a sign of his compromise with the principles of National Socialism. What has been called 'The Heidegger Controversy' erupted with the publication of Victor Farias' (1989) *Heidegger and Nazism* that called into question Heidegger's political beliefs and the extent of his engagement with Nazism. The Rectoral Address utilises the basic concepts of Greek philosophy—*poièsis* enlightened by *technè* (or production, putting into a work the truth disclosed by a knowhow), praxis (or action) and *theoria* (or contemplation)—and registers the strong influence of Plato's politics. It focuses on the philosophical reappropriation of original Greek ontology in relation to the factical life of the human Dasein, and its enlarged project beyond an individual Dasein to the Dasein of the German people as a whole. The 'Controversy' has been one of the longest running disputes in philosophy and the humanities and generated a great deal of commentary now further heightened after the publication of the 'Black Notebooks.' *Schwarze Hefte* 2014–2015, volumes 94–96 of Heidegger's *Collected Works* (*Gesamtausgabe*) demonstrate Heidegger's anti-Semitism and highlight his claim that Jews had become one of the central figures of the modern rootless and man-centred 'machination' (*Machenschaft*) and were collectively responsible for their own industrial genocide. Heidegger had defended himself a number of time claiming that he was an apolitical thinker until his assumption of the rectorate accepting the post and party membership reluctantly as a means to protect the university from political interference. One of the central difficulties that this text poses is a paradox presented to us by one of the West's greatest philosophers who despite his protestations to the contrary remained convinced that Nazism with its obsession about 'World Jewry' and its unbridled racism could ever represent a solution to modernity and the 'decline of the West'.

MP

Recommended Reading

Farias, Victor (1989). *Heidegger and Nazism*. Philadelphia, Temple University Press.

Heidegger, Martin (2014). *Überlegungen XII–XV* (*Schwarze Hefte* 1939/41), *Gesamtausgabe* 96, Frankfurt, Klostermann.

Heidegger, Martin (2015). *Anmerkungen I–V*, *Gesamtausgabe* 97, Frankfurt, Klostermann.

* * * * *

The assumption of the rectorate is the commitment to the *spiritual* leadership of this institution of higher learning.[1] The following of teachers and students only awakens and strengthens through a true and common rootedness in the essence of the German university. This essence, however, only gains clarity, rank, and power if the leaders, first and foremost and at any time, are themselves led—led by the relentlessness of that spiritual mission that forces the destiny of the German people into the shape of its history.

Do we know about this spiritual mission? Whether we do or not, the question must inevitably be faced: *are* we, teachers and students of this "high" school, truly and commonly rooted in the essence of the German university? Does this essence

1 Translator's note. Here Heidegger uses *hohe Schule*. Like the more common word *Hochschule, hohe Schule* means "institution of higher education." However, the word has a special aura, especially in the way Heidegger uses it. I have thus chosen to translate it later in the text as "'high' school."

have genuine strength to shape our existence [*Dasein*]?[2] Only if we fundamentally *will* this essence. But who would want to doubt this? The dominant characteristic of the university's essence is generally thought to be its "self-administration"; it is to be preserved. However—have we really fully considered what this claim to self-administration demands of us?

Self-administration means that we set ourselves our own task and determine the way and manner of its realization ourselves, so that in doing so we ourselves will be what we ought to be. But do we know *who we ourselves* are, this body of teachers and students of the highest school of the German people? Can we know this at all without the most constant and unsparing *self examination*?

Neither awareness of the present state of the university nor acquaintance with its previous history are enough to guarantee sufficient knowledge of its essence—unless we first, with clarity and severity, delimit this essence for the future, and in such self-limitation, *will* it, and in such willing, *assert* ourselves.

Self-administration can only exist when it is grounded in self-examination. Self-examination, however, can only take place in the strength of the German university's *self-assertion*. Will we carry it out? And how?

The self-assertion of the German university is the primordial, common will to its essence. We regard the German university as the "high" school that, grounded in science and by means of science, educates and disciplines the leaders and guardians of the destiny of the German people. The will to the essence of the German university is the will to science as will to the historical spiritual mission of the German people as a people that knows itself in its state [Staat]. *Together*, science and German destiny must come to power in the will to essence. And they will do so and *only* will do so, if we—teachers and students—on *the one hand*, expose science to its innermost necessity and, *on the other hand*, are able to stand our ground while German destiny is in its most extreme distress.

However, we will not experience the essence of science in its innermost necessity as long as we—when speaking of the "new concept of science"—only contest the self-sufficiency and lack of presuppositions of an all-too-contemporary science. Such action is merely negative. Hardly looking back beyond the past decades, it becomes a mere semblance of a true struggle for the essence of science.

If we want to grasp the essence of science, we must first face the decisive question: Should there still *be* science for us in the future, or should we let it drift toward a rapid end? It is never unconditionally necessary that science should be

2 Translator's note. Throughout Heidegger's rectorial address, I have translated *Dasein* as "existence." I have interpreted Heidegger's use of *Dasein* here to mean just that and have decided not to use the untranslatable technical term *Dasein*.

at all. But if there should be science and if it should be *for us* and *through us*, then under what condition can it truly exist?

Only if we again place ourselves under the power of the *beginning* of our spiritual-historical existence. This beginning is the departure, the setting out, of Greek philosophy. Here, for the first time, Western man rises up, from a base in a popular culture [*Volkstum*] and by means of his language, against the *totality of what is* and questions and comprehends it as the being that it is. All science is philosophy, whether it knows and wills it—or not. All science remains bound to that beginning of philosophy. From it science draws the strength of its essence, assuming that it still remains at all equal to this beginning.

Here we want to regain two distinguishing properties of the original Greek essence of science for *our* existence.

An old story was told among the Greeks that Prometheus had been the first philosopher. Aeschylus has this Prometheus utter a saying that expresses the essence of knowing:

> τέχυη δάυάγκης ἀσθευεστέρα μακρῷ
> (Prom. 514, ed. Wil).

"Knowing, however, is far weaker than necessity." That means that all knowing about things has always already been surrendered to the predominance of destiny and fails before it.

Precisely because of this, knowing must unfold its highest defiance. Only then will the entire power of the concealedness [*Verborgenheit*] of what is rise up and knowing will really fail. In this way, what is opens itself in its unfathomable inalterability and lends knowing its truth. In this Greek saying on the creative impotence of knowledge, one all too readily hopes to find a prototype for a knowing that is based purely on itself, when actually such knowing has forgotten its own essence. This knowing is interpreted for us as the "theoretical" attitude. But what does θεωρία mean to the Greeks? It is said: pure contemplation, which only remains bound to the matter in question and all that it is and demands. This contemplative behavior is said, with reference to the Greeks, to be pursued for its own sake. But this reference is mistaken. For on the one hand, "theory" is not pursued for its own sake, but only in the passion to remain close to and under the pressure of what is. On the other, the Greeks fought precisely to comprehend and carry out this contemplative questioning as one, indeed as *the* highest, mode of human ἐνέργεια, of human "being-at-work." They were not concerned with aligning practice with theory. Rather, the reverse was true: theory was to be understood as the highest realization of genuine practice. For the Greeks, science is not a "cultural asset" but the innermost determining center of all of popular [*volklich*] and national [*stoat/Wit*] existence. The Greeks thought science not merely a means of bringing the unconscious to consciousness, but the power that hones and encompasses all of existence.

Science is the questioning standing of one's ground in the midst of the constantly self-concealing totality of what is. This active perseverance knows about its impotence in the face of destiny.

This is the initial essence of science. But does this beginning not already lie two and half millennia behind us? Has not the progress of human actions changed science as well? Certainly! The Christian-theological interpretation of the world that followed and the later mathematical-technological thinking of the modern age have distanced science, both in time and in its concerns, from its beginning. But this does not mean that the beginning has been overcome, let alone that it has been negated. Assuming that the primordial Greek science is indeed something great, then the be-ginning of this greatness remains what is greatest. The essence of science could not even be emptied out or used up, as is happening today despite all the results and "international organizations," if the greatness of the beginning did not still endure. The beginning still is. It does not lie behind us, as something that was long ago, but stands before us. As what is greatest, the beginning has passed in advance over all that is to come and thus already over us as well. The beginning has invaded our future. There it stands as the distant command to us to catch up with its greatness.

Only if we resolutely submit to this distant command to regain the greatness of this beginning, only then will science become the innermost necessity of our existence. Otherwise it will remain an accident into which we fall or the dispassionate contentment of a safe occupation, serving to further a mere progress of information.

But if we submit to the distant command of the beginning, science must become the fundamental happening of our spiritual and popular [volklich] existence.

And if our most authentic existence itself stands before a great transformation, and if it is true what that passionate seeker of God and last German philosopher, Friedrich Nietzsche, said: "God is dead"—and if we must be serious about this forsakenness of modern human beings in the midst of what is, then what is the situation of science?

Then, the initial, awed perseverance of the Greeks in the face of what is transforms itself into a completely uncovered exposure to the hidden and uncertain; that is, the questionable. Questioning is then no longer merely a preliminary step that is surmounted on the way to the answer and thus to knowing; rather, questioning itself becomes the highest form of knowing. Questioning then unfolds its most authentic strength to unlock the essential in all things. Questioning then forces our vision to focus, with the utmost simplicity, on the inevitable.

Such questioning shatters the encapsulation of the sciences in separate specialities, brings them back from their boundless and aimless dispersal in individual fields and corners, and directly exposes science once again to the productivity and blessing of all world-shaping powers of human-historical existence, such as nature, history, language; people, custom, state; poetry, thought, faith; disease, madness, death; law, economy, technology.

If we will the essence of science understood as the questioning, uncovered standing one's ground in the midst of the uncertainty of the totality of what is, then this will to essence will create for our people its world of innermost and most extreme danger, i.e. its truly spiritual world. For "spirit" is not empty cleverness, nor the noncommittal play of wit, nor the boundless drift of rational dissection, let alone world reason; spirit is the primordially attuned, knowing resoluteness toward the essence of Being. And the spiritual world of a people is not the superstructure of a culture any more than it is an armoury filled with useful information and values; it is the power that most deeply preserves the people's earth- and blood-bound strengths as the power that most deeply arouses and most profoundly shakes the people's existence. Only a spiritual world guarantees the people greatness. For it forces the constant decision between the will to greatness and the acceptance of decline to become the law for each step of the march that our people has begun into its future history.

If we will this essence *of* science, then the teachers of this university must really advance to the outermost post, endangered by constant uncertainty about the world. If they stand their ground there; that is to say, if a common questioning and a communally tuned saying arises from there—in essential nearness to the pressing insistence of all things—then they will gain the strength for leadership. For what is decisive in leading is not just walking ahead of others but the strength to be able to walk alone, not from obstinacy or a craving for power, but empowered by the deepest purpose and the broadest obligation. Such strength binds to what is essential, selects the best, and awakens the genuine following of those who have new courage. But we do not need to first awaken this following. German students are on the march. And *whom* they are seeking are those leaders through whom they want to elevate their own purpose so that it becomes a grounded, knowing truth, and to place it into the clarity of interpretive and effective word and work.

Out of the resoluteness of the German students to stand their ground while German destiny is in its most extreme distress comes a will to the essence of the university. This will is a true will, provided that German students, through the new Student Law,[3] place themselves under the law of their essence and thereby first define this essence. To give oneself the law is the highest freedom. The much-lauded "academic freedom" will be expelled from the German university; for this freedom was not genuine because it was only negative. It primarily meant lack of

3 Translator's note. Proclaimed on 1 May 1933, the *neue Studentenrecht* sought to organize students according to the *Führerprinzip* in an effort to integrate the universities into the National Socialist state.

concern, arbitrariness of intentions and inclinations, lack of restraint in what was done and left undone. The concept of the freedom of the German student is now brought back to its truth. In future, the bond and service of German students will unfold from this truth.

The *first* bond binds to the national community [*Volksgemeinschaft*]. It obligates to help carry the burden of and to participate actively in the struggles, strivings, and skills of all the estates and members of the people. From now on, this bond will be fixed and rooted in the existence of the student by means of *Labor Service* [*Arbeitsdienst*].

The *second* bond binds to the honor and the destiny of the nation in the midst of all the other peoples. It demands the readiness, secured by knowledge and skill and tightened by discipline, to give the utmost in action. In future, this bond will encompass and penetrate the entire existence of the student as *Military Service* [*Wehrdienst*].

The *third* bond of the students binds them to the spiritual mission of the German people. This people works at its fate by opening its history to all the overwhelming world-shaping powers of human existence and by continually fighting for its spiritual world anew. Thus exposed to the most extreme questionableness of its own existence, this people wills to be a spiritual people. It demands of itself and for itself that its leaders and guardians possess the strictest clarity of the highest, broadest, and richest knowledge. Young students, who at an early age have dared to act as men and have extended their willing to the future destiny of the nation, force themselves, from the very ground of their being, to serve this knowledge. These students will no longer permit *Knowledge Service* [*Wissensdienst*] to be a dull and rushed training for a "distinguished" profession. Because the statesman and the teacher, the doctor and the judge, the minister and the architect lead the existence of people and state, because they guard and hone it in its fundamental relations to the world-shaping powers of human being, these professions and the education for them are entrusted to Knowledge Service. Knowledge does not serve the professions but the reverse: the professions effect and administer that highest and essential knowledge of the people concerning its entire existence. But for us this knowledge is not the dispassionate taking note of essences and values as such, but the most severe endangerment of existence in the midst of the overwhelming power of what is. The very questionableness of Being forces the people to work and fight and forces it into its state [*Staat*], to which the professions belong.

The three bonds—by the people, to the destiny of the state, in spiritual mission—are *equally primordial* to the German essence. The three services that arise from it—Labor Service, Military Service, and Knowledge Service—are equally necessary and of equal rank.

The primordial and full essence of science, whose realization is our task, provided we submit to the distant command of the beginning of our spiritual-historical existence, is only created by knowledge about the people that actively participates and by knowledge about the state's destiny that always keeps itself prepared, both at one with knowledge about the spiritual mission.

It is *this* science that is meant when the essence of the German university is delimited as the "high" school that, grounded in science and through science, educates and disciplines the leaders and guardians of the German people.

This primordial concept of science obligates us not only to "objectivity," but, above all, to make our questioning in the midst of the historical-spiritual world of the people essential and simple. Indeed, it is only then that objectivity can truly ground itself—i.e., discover its nature and its limit.

Science, in this sense, must become the power that shapes the body of the German university. This contains a twofold task: Teachers and students, each in their own way, must become *seized* and *remain* seized by the concept of science. At the same time, however, this concept of science must intervene in and rearrange the basic forms in which the teachers and students each act in a scientific community: in the *faculties* and as *student bodies of specific departments* [*Fachschaften*].

The faculty is a faculty only if it becomes capable of spiritual legislation, and, rooted in the essence of its science, able to shape the powers of existence that pressure *it* into the *one* spiritual world of the people.

The student body of a certain department is a student body only if it places itself in the realm of this spiritual legislation from the start and thus tears down departmental barriers and overcomes the staleness and falseness of superficial professional training.

At the moment when faculties and departmental student bodies set the essential and simple questions of their science into motion, teachers and students are already encompassed by the *same* final necessities and pressing concerns of the existence of people and state.

The unfolding of the primordial essence of science, however, demands such a degree of rigor, responsibility, and superior patience that, in comparison, the conscientious adherence to or the eager alteration of established procedures hardly matter.

But if the Greeks needed three centuries just to put the *question* of what knowledge is onto the right ground and on a secure track, *we* have no right to assume that the elucidation and unfolding of the essence of the German university will occur in the current or coming semester.

But there is *one* thing we do know from the indicated essence of science: The German university will only gain shape and power if the three services primordially coalesce to become *one* formative force. That is to say:

The teachers' will to essence must awaken to the simplicity and breadth of knowledge about the essence of science and thus grow strong. The students' will to essence must force itself to rise to the highest clarity and discipline of knowing and integrate, demanding and determining, engaged knowledge [*Mitwissenschaft*] about the people and its state into the essence of science. The two wills must confront one another, ready for *battle*. All abilities of will and thought, all strengths of the heart, and all capabilities of the body must be unfolded *through* battle, heightened *in* battle, and pre-served *as* battle.

We choose the knowing battle of those who question, and we profess with *Carl von Clausewitz*:[4] "I renounce the frivolous hope of salvation by the hand of accident."

This battle community of teachers and students, however, will only recreate the German university into a place of spiritual legislation and establish in it the center of the most disciplined preparation for the highest service to the people in its state if teachers and students arrange their existence more simply, more unsparingly, and more frugally than all the other members of their people [*Volksgenossen*]. All leading must concede its following its own strength. All following, however, bears resistance in itself. This essential opposition of leading and following must not be blurred let alone eliminated.

Battle alone keeps this opposition open and implants in the entire body of teachers and students that basic attitude that allows self-limiting self-assertion empower resolute self-examination to come to genuine self-administration.

Do we, or do we not, will the essence of the German university? It is up to us whether, and to what extent, we concern ourselves with self-examination and self-assertion, not just in passing, but starting from its foundations, or whether we—with the best of intentions—merely change old institutions and add new ones. No one will keep us from doing this.

But no one will even ask us whether we do or do not will, when the spiritual strength of the West fails and its joints crack, when this moribund semblance of a culture caves in and drags all forces into confusion and lets them suffocate in madness.

Whether this will or will not happen depends solely on whether we, as a historical-spiritual people, still and once again will ourselves—or whether we no longer will ourselves. Each individual *participates* in this decision even when, and especially when, he evades it.

But we do will that our people fulfil its historical mission.

We do will ourselves. For the young and the youngest strength of the people, which is already reaching beyond us, *has* already *decided* the matter.

---

4 Translator's note. Carl von Clausewitz (1780–1831), for many years head of the Prussian War College, was the author of the influential *Vom Krieg* (On War).

But we will only fully understand the magnificence and greatness of this new departure when we carry within us that profound and far-reaching thoughtfulness that gave ancient Greek wisdom the saying:

τά … μεγλα πάυτα ἐπιφαλη …
[All that is great stands in the storm …]
(Plato, Republic, 497 d. 9).

CHAPTER EIGHT

The Idea of the University

Learning Processes (1987)

JÜRGEN HABERMAS

Translated by John R. Blazek, this selection by Jürgen Habermas is taken from Volume 41 of *New German Critique* (Spring–Summer, 1987), pp. 3–22. This Special Issue on the Critiques of the Enlightenment, published by New German Critique and Duke University Press, retrieved from http://www.jstor.org/stable/488273

Editors' Note

For half a century, through his philosophical and theoretical writings, Jürgen Habermas has been attempting to advance the basis for a more rational society and indeed world order. Since the Enlightenment, reason has been deployed to provide a legitimation of 'modern' society but Habermas has contended that the kind of reason that has taken hold is an unduly limited form of reason, being instrumental and technical and so neglecting human communication and the 'life-world'.

The university is not immune from these processes of advancing rationality, as we see in the extract here. Ever since its foundations, but particularly in its early nineteenth Germanic elaborations, the forms of reason sustained by the university were held to have edifying potentials, both at the personal and at the societal levels. The idea of the university, accordingly, was a significant idea, embracing the university both as a knowledge-based institution and as a resource for aiding the formation and development of the social and personal realms. However, with the advance both of mass higher education and the incorporation of the university into knowledge production systems, it is no longer clear that such a narrative any more holds water. Now, the university has been differentiated into so many sub-systems. In the process, the various kinds of unifying features characteristic of the past university—unifying different kinds of knowledge, unifying research and teaching, unifying forms of reason, unifying inquiry with the life-world, unifying universality with particularities—are all in jeopardy, if they are not lost forever.

Habermas' response to this situation is optimistic. A 'normative ideal' of the university may be found still in the argumentation that attaches to formal inquiry. These are not simply the efforts of lone individuals but are collaborative 'learning processes'. To speak of collaboration does not as such imply consensus. To the contrary, 'discursive disputes … carry the promissory note of generating surprising arguments'. Certainly, there is no straightforward carry-over into the life-world, either at personal or social levels but there is an embodying here of a 'communicative rationality, the forms of which modern societies must employ to understand themselves'.

RB

Recommended Reading

Habermas, J. (1971). *Towards a Rational Society*. London: Heinemann. (Especially chapters 1, 2 and 3).

* * * * *

In the inaugural issue of *Die Wandlung* [The Transformation], a journal founded shortly after the war by Karl Jaspers, Alfred Weber, Dolf Sternberger and Alexander Mitscherlich, there appeared the text of a lecture by Jaspers entitled "The Renewal of the University." It had been held in 1945 to mark the reopening of the University of Heidelberg upon the philosopher's return from inner immigration to reassume his Chair in Philosophy. Emphasizing the opportunity for a new beginning, Jaspers took up the central theme of his 1923 book "The Idea of the University," which was republished in 1946. Fifteen years later, in 1961, the book appeared in a revised edition.[1] In the intervening period, Jaspers saw his hopes disappointed. Yet here Jaspers still proceeds from the premises of that sociology which had been implicit to German Idealism: An institution remains functional only so long as it vitally embodies its inherent idea. Should its spirit evaporate, an

1 K. Jaspers and K. Rossmann, *Die Idee der Universitdt* (Heidelberg, 1961).

institution will petrify into something merely mechanical, like a soulless organism reduced to dead matter.

Not even the university can continue to form a whole once the unifying bond of its corporative consciousness dissolves. The functions the university fulfils for society must preserve an inner connection with the goals, motives and actions of its members. In this sense the university should institutionally embody, and at the same time motivationally anchor, a life form which is intersubjectively shared by its members, and which even bears an exemplary character. What since Humboldt has been called "the idea of the university" is the project of embodying an ideal life form. Moreover, this idea does not limit itself to one of the many particularized life forms of early bourgeois society, but—thanks to its intimate connection with science and truth—to something universal, something prior to the pluralism of social life forms. The idea of the university points to principles of formation according to which *all* forms of objective spirit are structured.

Even disregarding this extravagant claim to exemplary status, isn't the very premise that a vast and extraordinarily complex structure such as the modern university system be permeated and sustained by a mode of thought shared by all its members, unrealistic in the extreme? Couldn't Jaspers have learned years earlier from Max Weber that the organizational reality into which the functionally specified subsystems of a highly differentiated society imbed themselves rests on wholly different premises? The functional capability of such institutions depends precisely on a *detachment* of their members' motivations from the goals and functions of the organization. Organizations no longer embody ideas. Those who would bind organizations to ideas must restrict their operative range to the comparatively narrow horizon of the life world intersubjectivity shared by their members. Thus, one of the many reverential articles with which the *Frankfurter Allgemeine* overindulged the University of Heidelberg on its 600th anniversary came to the sobering conclusion: "The assertion of unbroken faithfulness to Humboldt is the life-lie of our universities. They no longer have a formative idea."[2] From this standpoint, all those reformers who, like Jaspers, have appealed (and with ever weaker voices still appeal) to the *idea* of the university, belong to those purely defensive minds whose cultural criticism is rooted in a hostility to all forms of modernization.

It is undeniable that Jaspers shared that bourgeois cultural pessimism which formed the background ideology of the German Mandarins. But he was not the *only* one who, during the arguments of the 1960s for a long-overdue reform of the universities, reached back to ideas of the 19th century Prussian university reformers. In 1963, two years after the new edition of Jaspers' book, Helmut Schelsky entered

2 K. Reumann, "Verdunkelte Wahrheit," *Frankfurter Allgemeine Zeitung* 24 March 1986.

the discussion with a piece bearing the title "Solitude and Freedom." And two years after this, the final draft of a long-debated SDS position paper appeared with the title "The University in a Democracy."[3] Three documents of reform, from three generations, each offering a different perspective. Each marks a steadily increasing distance from Humboldt—and a growing sobriety concerning the idea of the university. Yet despite generational differences (and an evident intellectual reorientation since the end of the war), none of the three parties is able fully to abandon the notion that the central issue remained the critical renewal of this very idea.

Twenty years and a half-heartedly executed, in part already retracted organizational reform of the universities separate us today from those attempts to give the university a new character in light of its renewed idea. What can we learn from the past two decades? Must the university, on its way towards functional specialization within an ever more swiftly differentiating system of knowledges, discard like an empty shell what once had been called its "idea?" Or does the frame which universities provide for scientific learning processes still account for a bundle of integrated functions which, while perhaps not in need of a normative self-image, nevertheless requires a somehow shared self-understanding of the university's members—traces of a corporative consciousness?

II

Perhaps a look at the external development of the universities will suffice to answer these questions. The expansion in education after World War II was a worldwide phenomenon which led Talcott Parsons to speak of an "educational revolution." In the German Reich between 1933 and 1939, the number of students had been cut in half, dropping from 121,000 to 56,000. In 1945, in the area later to become the Federal Republic, only 15 universities were left in existence. Already by the mid-1950s, 50 universities could again accommodate about 150,000 students. In the early 1960s, the course was set for a deliberate expansion of the post-secondary educational sector, and since that time the number of students has quadrupled. Today over a million students receive education at 94 universities.[4] Of course, such absolute figures only reveal their true significance when compared with international trends.

---

3 W. Nitsch, U. Gerhardt and C. Offe, *Hochschule in der Demokratie* (Neuwied, 1965).

4 Not considered are 94 additional Trade Universities and Art Academies. See H. Kohler and J. Naumann, Trends der Hochschulentwicklung, *Recht der Jugend und des Bildungswesens* 6:32 (1984): 419 ff. An overview can be found in *Max Planck Institut für Bildungsforschung: Das Bildungswesen in der Bundesrepublik* (Hamburg, 1984) 228 ff.

In almost all Western industrial societies, the trend towards extending formal education began after World War II and continued until the end of the 1970s; in the developed socialist nations, the same expansion phase was concentrated in the 1950s. UNESCO figures show that, in the period between 1950 and 1980, secondary school attendance rates went from 30 to 80 percent; the corresponding university rates jumped from barely 4 percent to 30 percent. The parallels in the educational expansion of the various industrial societies become even clearer if we compare the selectivity of the educational system in the Federal Republic with that of the US, Great Britain, France and East Germany (as is done in the forthcoming Second Educational Report of the MPI for Educational Research). Although the national education systems have completely different structures, and despite the differences in their political and economic systems, the same orders of magnitude are reported for the highest qualification levels. If one defines the educational elite by higher academic achievements (usually by completion of a dissertation [*Promotion*]), it comprises between 1.5 percent and 2.6 percent of those born in a given year; if one defines it by completion of the most important forms of academic study (B.A., Master's, or State Examinations), the share lies between 8 percent and 10 percent. The authors of the Second Educational Report pursued their international comparisons into areas of qualitative specialization and found, for example, that publication rates and other external indicators of scholarly productivity in particular fields approximated one another to a surprisingly high degree—completely independent of whether the national university systems were more openly structured, or more sharply oriented towards selectivity and the formation of elites.

Furthermore, despite their stubborn resistance to government-mandated reforms, German universities have changed in more than just their quantitative dimensions. The most salient characteristics of a specifically German heritage have been smoothed away. Antiquated hierarchies were dismantled along with the *Ordinarien*-university; and with a certain leveling of status, the Mandarin ideology, too, lost its basis. External and internal differentiations have allowed teaching and research to become more specialized. In sum, even in their internal structures, West Germany's mass universities have come to resemble those of other industrial nations.

A more distanced perspective derived from international comparisons thus yields a picture which practically compels one to adopt a functionalist interpretation. According to this view, the general patterns of social modernization have also determined university developments (ones which began in West Germany a decade later than they did in East Germany or the other Western countries). During the period of greatest acceleration, educational expansion generated ideologies in step with this. It appears that the dispute between reformers and defenders of the status quo was conducted by both sides under the false premise that the issue was whether to renew or retain the idea of the university. Within this ideological framework, a process took place which neither of the parties had desired—something the rebelling students fought against as "technocratic university reform." Although labelled reform, it appeared that in fact only a new cycle had been initiated in the differentiation process of the scientific system—one which had become functionally autonomous here as it had everywhere else. From this perspective, universities present themselves as part of a system requiring less and less normative integration in the heads of professors and students the more it becomes self-regulating via systemic mechanisms and the more it orients itself to the environments of the economy and the planning administration. The pragmatic recommendations of the National Science Advisory Council, which demanded a shift of emphasis in favor of disciplinary autonomy and a differentiation of research and theory, fit all too well into this picture.[5]

Of course, the intellectual and political reserve of the Advisory Council leaves room for further interpretations. The cautious recommendations don't necessarily imply the kind of functionalist reading which seems to converge with the currently popular neoconservative models of interpretation. On the one hand, many favor a functionally differentiated scientific system, one for which the normatively integrating power of an intellectual center anchored in corporative self-understanding would only be a hindrance. Yet, on the other hand, anniversaries always provide convenient occasions to cloak the university's systemic autonomy by rhetorically affirming an earlier tradition of a wholly different, *normatively* intended autonomy. Thus veiled, the flows of information between the now functionally autonomous subsystems (for example, between the universities and the economic-military-administrative complex), can be all the more discreetly coordinated. In this view, a sense of tradition retains only compensatory value; an awareness of tradition counts as much as the size of the gaps that it is called upon to fill in a university robbed of its formative idea. Of course, sociologically considered, this neoconservative interpretation could again be merely the reflection of a business cycle that moves independently of the themes and theories to which it gave rise.

The activist educational policy initiated in West Germany during the overdue modernization push at the beginning of the 1960s was sustained until the end of the Great Coalition by a substantial consensus of all parties; during Brandt's government, the Federal Republic experienced an upswing in the educational policy sector—and the start of a polarization between the political parties on these issues. In 1974, the downswing finally began. Educational policy was hit from both sides by the onsetting economic crisis: university graduates faced worsened labor market

5 See *Wissenschaftsrat: Empfehlungen und Stellungnahmen* (1984); *Wissenschaftsrat: Empfehlungen zum Wettbewerb im deutschen Hochschulsystem* (1985).

conditions, while on the cost and financing side, the universities suffered from the government's fiscal crisis.[6] Thus what the neoconservatives today view as a "realistic reorientation" of educational policy can also be seen as a recession phenomenon in the realm of educational planning, largely explainable in purely economic and political terms.[7] However, even if the educational up- and down-swings cut through all themes and theories, the functionalist interpretation which dominates today is still not simply to be accepted at face value. Processes of differentiation which have accelerated over the last two decades need not be brought under a single systems theoretical description leading to the conclusion that the universities have now completely outgrown the horizon of the life world.

Empirically, it appears to be an open question whether the stimuli behind the growth of knowledge wouldn't finally become paralyzed were they to specialize exclusively on the function of research. Scientific productivity might well depend upon the university's form, in particular upon that interplay of research with the training of future students, the preparation for academic careers, the participation in general education, cultural self-understanding and public opinion formation.

The universities are still rooted in the life world through this interpenetration of functions. So long as this connection is not completely torn asunder, the idea of the university is still not wholly dead. But the complexity and internal differentiation of this connection shouldn't be underestimated. When the classical German university was born, the Prussian reformers projected an image of it which suggested an oversimplified connection between scientific learning processes and the life forms of modern societies.

In what follows, I wish to recall the classical idea as held by Schelling, Humboldt and Schleiermacher, and then examine the three variants of its renewal offered by Jaspers, Schelsky and the SDS reformers.

III

Humboldt and Schleiermacher associate two notions with the idea of the university. First, they are concerned with the problem of how modern science, freed

6 K. Hiifner, J. Naumann, H. Köhler and G. Pfeffer, *Hochkonjunktur und Flaute: Bildungspolitik in der BRD* (Stuttgart, 1986).

7 An indication of this are the uneven developments in educational reform proposals from one country to the next. For example, last year 50 professors at the Collège de France presented to the President recommendations for educational reform which in their goals and tenor were very reminiscent of the reform climate in the Federal Republic during the 1960s. Recommendations inspired by Pierre Bourdieu appeared in *Neue Sammlung* 3:25 (1985).

from the supervision of religion and the church, can be institutionalized without endangering its autonomy—whether through the authority of the government which secures the external existence of science, or through pressures from the side of the occupational and economic system, with its interest in the useful applications of scientific work. Humboldt and Schleiermacher see the solution to the problem in a governmentally organized autonomy of science which would protect the university from both political interventions and economic imperatives. At the same time—and this is the second notion—Humboldt and Schleiermacher want to explain why it is in the interest of the state itself to guarantee to the university the external organizational form of an internally unlimited freedom. Both thinkers were convinced that, if only scientific work were turned over to the dynamics of research processes, the universities would serve as focal points for moral culture, and indeed for the spiritual life of the nation generally.[8]

These two notions combine to form the idea of the university, and to explain several of the more striking characteristics of the German university tradition. They make comprehensible 1) the affirmative attitude of an apolitical science toward state authorities, 2) the defensive attitude of the university *vis-à-vis* professional training, and 3) the key position of the philosophical faculty within the university as well as the emphatic significance attributed to science for culture and society as a whole. Thus, the idea of the university produces, on the one hand, a promising emphasis on scientific autonomy which points to the functional independence of the scientific system. Of course, this scientific autonomy is supposed to be perceived only in "solitude and freedom," at a clear distance from bourgeois society and the political public sphere. And on the other hand, the idea of the university produces the general, culture-shaping power of a science in which the totality of the life world should reflexively concentrate itself.

The reformers of that age could envision the scientific process as a narcissistically self-enclosed process of research and teaching, since the *unity of teaching and research* was an integral demand of German Idealism. Whereas today discussions at the cutting edge of research and the presentation of this state of knowledge for purposes of instruction are two quite different things, Schelling (in his "Lectures on the Methodology of Academic Study") still could maintain that the

8 "At the very least there is as little decent and noble life for the state as there is for the individual as long as one fails to attach a general meaning to the always narrowed competence in the area of official science. For the acquisition of all this knowledge the state as well as the individual makes as a natural and necessary pre-requisite that it be grounded in science and that it be reproduced and completed through science." (F. Schleiermacher, "Gelegentliche Gedanken über Universitäten im deutschen Sinn (1808)," *Die Idee der deutschen Universität*, ed. E. Anrich [Darmstadt, 1959] 226).

construction of philosophic thought itself gave rise to the form of its pedagogical presentation.[9]

In the same manner, the university was to owe its inner connection to the life world to the totalizing power of idealism. The reformers attributed to philosophy a unifying power with respect to (as we would say today) cultural tradition, to socialization and to social integration. Idealist Philosophy was first of all encyclopedically structured and would thus assure both unity amidst the multiplicity of scientific disciplines and the unity of science with art and morality. Philosophy commended itself as a form which reflected the whole of culture. Secondly, its Platonistic character was expected to assure the unity of training and general education. More specifically: as ideas are comprehended they simultaneously enter into the knower's moral character, thus freeing it from all one-sidedness. This elevation to the Absolute opens the way for the all-around development of the individual person. Finally, the self-reflexive basis of idealistic philosophy promised the unity of science and enlightenment. While today philosophy has become a subject that draws the esoteric interest of specialists, a notion of philosophy which proceeds from the self-reference of the knowing subject and develops all substantive knowledge along the path of a reflexive movement of thought could simultaneously satisfy both the specialist's esoteric interest in science and the layman's exoteric interest in self-understanding and enlightenment.[10] Since philosophy, as Hegel would put it, expresses its age in thought, it should replace the socially integrative power of religion with the reconciliatory power of reason. Fichte could therefore envision that a university which institutionalized such a science would become the birthplace of a future, emancipated society, the very focus of national cultivation.[11]

The risky and improbable aspect of this university idea (as encountered in the famous founding documents) first becomes clear when one realizes just what conditions would have had to be fulfilled for the successful *institutionalization* of such a philosophical science—a science which, solely through its inner structure, was intended to simultaneously make possible and guarantee (1) the unity of research and teaching, (2) the unity of the sciences, (3) the unity of science and general education, and (4) the unity of science and enlightenment.

Strictly understood, the unity of research and teaching meant that teaching and learning would only be conducted in a manner necessary for the innovative

---

9 F. W. J. Schelling, "Vorlesungen uiber die Methode des akademischen Studiums (1802)," *Die Idee der deutschen Universitäit* 20.

10 E. Martens and H. Schnidelbach, *Philosophie-Grundkurs* (Hamburg, 1985) 22 ff.

11 J. G. Fichte, "Deduzierter Plan einer in Berlin zu errichtenden höheren Lehranstalt," *Die Idee der deutschen Universität* 217.

process of scientific progress. Science should be able to reproduce itself in the sense that the professors would train their own successors. The future researcher is the sole goal for which the university of researching scholars assumes the task of training. This view retained a certain plausibility for the philosophy faculty at least, so long as university professors replenished their ranks from the circle of *Gymnasium* teachers previously trained by them.

The idea of the unity of the sciences could only continue to gain force if philosophy in fact advanced to become the fundamental science [*Grund-wissenschaft*] of the unified natural sciences and humanities. That is the significance of the polemic against "bread-and-butter" sciences, against the dispersion into specialized schools, against the derivative quality of those faculties which find "their unity not in knowledge directly, but rather in some external occupation."

In institutional terms, the unity of science and general education presupposed the unity of teachers and students.[12] This cooperatively structured, fundamentally egalitarian and complementary relationship was to be realized in the discursive forms of the seminar. But this soon became irreconcilable with the more formal organization which quickly developed in the hierarchically designed research institutes of the natural sciences.

A final extravagance was the idea of the unity of science and enlightenment, inasmuch as it burdened the autonomy of the sciences with the expectation that, within its walls, the university could anticipate in microcosm a society of free and equal citizens. However, from the start it was unclear how this enlightening and emancipatory assignment could go hand in hand with the apolitical reserve the university was expected to maintain as the price for the political supervision of its freedom.

These institutional preconditions for an implementation of the fundamental idea of the German university were either non-existent from the start, or they became ever less capable of fulfilment during the course of the 19th century. First, a differentiated occupational system required academic preparation for more and more professional careers. In the long run, the advanced schools for engineering, commerce, pedagogy and art couldn't remain outside the universities. Secondly, the empirical sciences, which had emerged from the womb of the philosophical faculty, followed an ideal of procedural rationality which condemned to failure all attempts at encyclopedically embedding their substantive contents within an

---

12 W. Humboldt, "Über die innere und aussere Organisation der hoheren wissenschaftlichen Anstalten (1810)," *Ibid.* 217.

all-encompassing philosophical interpretation.[13] This emancipation of the empirical sciences sealed the destruction of all metaphysical world views. In the midst of a pluralism of privatized religious beliefs [*Glaubensmaechten*], philosophy also lost its monopoly on interpreting culture as a whole.

Thirdly, science advanced to become an important productive force in industrial society. For example, pointing to Liebig's Institute in Giessen, the state government in Baden emphasized as early as 1850 the "extraordinary importance of chemistry for agriculture."[14] The natural sciences forfeited their role of providing a world view in favor of producing technically useful knowledge. Thus, working conditions for research were tailored less to the functions of general education than to the functional imperatives of the economy and administration. Finally, academic education in Germany served to define a special class of academics, a social class of *Bildungsbürger* following the model of the upper-level civil servant.[15] However, the establishment of a clear professional differentiation between popular and academic education confirmed class structures which negated both the universalist intent of the university idea and the promise it had held for an emancipation of society as a whole.[16]

To the extent that there was a growing awareness of these tendencies, the idea of the university had to be mobilized all the more vigorously against the "facts"—until it degenerated to the ideology of a professional class with high social prestige. For the humanities and social sciences, Fritz K. Ringer identifies the period of decline of the German Mandarins as the years between 1890 and 1933.[17] In the sheltered inwardness enjoyed by these Mandarins, the neo-humanist educational ideal was deformed into the intellectually elitist, apolitical, conformist self-conception of an internally autonomous institution that remained far removed from practice while intensively conducting research.[18]

Of course, one must also see the positive side. In both forms—as idea as well as ideology—the idea of the university contributed to the brilliance and the internationally incomparable success of German university science throughout the 19th century, and even up to the 1930s of our own century. In particular, the state-organized scientific autonomy had consigned differentiation of scientific disciplines to the internal dynamic of the research processes themselves. Under the protection of an only

13 See my review of Ringer's book: "Die deutschen Mandarine," *Philosophische-Politische Profde* (Frankfurt a.M., 1981) 485 ff.

14 J. Klüwer, *Universität und Wissenschaftssystem* (Frankfurt a.M., 1983) 1.

15 L. von Friedeburg, "Elite-elitAr?," *Ordnung und Unordnung*, ed. G. Becker (Weinheim, 1986) 23 f.

16 T. Ellwein, *Die deutsche Universität* (Kinigstein, 1985) 124 ff.

17 F. K. Ringer, *The Decline of the German Mandarins* (Cambridge, Mass., 1969).

18 See for this thesis J. Klüwer.

superficially adopted educational humanism, the natural sciences had quickly won their autonomy and, for all their positivism, became a fruitful model even for the humanities and social sciences.[19] At the same time, the ideology of the German Mandarins lent the universities a strong corporative self-consciousness, winning them support from the *Kulturstaat*, and recognition throughout society. And last but not least, the utopian surplus inherent to the university idea also preserved a critical potential which from time to time could be revived for a renewal of the institutions.

IV

That, at any rate, was the belief of reformers in the early 1960s. The first impulses toward renewal after 1945 had been insufficient. Apart from material shortages, there prevailed a deep exhaustion of the corporative self-consciousness. The idea of the university, in the traditional form of the Mandarin consciousness, had still survived the Nazis; but given its demonstrated impotence against (or even complicity with) the Nazi regime, it stood convicted of lacking any substance. And yet, even on the defensive after 1945, traditionalists of the Humboldtian idea were strong enough to stave off well-meant attempts at reform, and to strike a deal with the pragmatically-minded colleagues on the Science Advisory Council [*Wissenschaftsrat*], set up in the late 1950s. Thus, the unavoidable quantitative growth of the universities took place as an expansion within otherwise unaltered structures.[20]

In this situation, Jaspers again returned to Humboldt; Schelsky and the SDS students attempted a critical appropriation of this heritage—while maintaining a certain social-scientific distance by prefacing their reform proposals with a sober diagnosis of those structural transformations the universities had undergone in the meantime. In the background, one already finds international comparisons of educational sociologists, demand analyses from educational economists and civil rights postulates of educational politicians. Schelsky summarizes all this with the term "self-propelling dynamics" [*Sachgesetzlichkeiten*], for these processes have a systemic

---

19 "The danger that humans only expend themselves in outer, environment modifying actions and then bind everything, other people and themselves, to this object level of action. This new form of human self-alienation, which can rob oneself and the other of inner identity, this new metaphysical temptation of humankind contains the danger that the creator loses himself in his work, the builder in his constructions. People are horrified at the thought of transferring themselves into self-produced objectivity, into a constructed being, and yet they work unceasingly on furthering this very process of scientific-technical self-objectification." (H. Schelsky, *Einsamkeit und Freiheit* [Hamburg, 1963] 299).

20 See T. Ellwein 238.

character and produce structures which detach themselves from the life world. They undermine the corporative consciousness of the university, exploding those fictions of unity which Humboldt, Schleiermacher, Fichte and Schelling once hoped to establish through the totalizing power of philosophic reflection. Interestingly enough, though, Schelsky no more favored a simple compliance of the universities with these systemic imperatives than did the leftist reformers. He did not opt for the sort of permanent technocratic reform which has meanwhile become established practice. This is surprising: The theory of technocracy Schelsky developed around the same time would have led one to expect this. Instead, he dipped into the fund of Humboldtian ideas in order to stress the need to "shape" the "self-propelling dynamics":

> The decisive point now is that these "objective tendencies" are one-sided ..., that countervailing forces must come into play, ones which will not arise automatically but can only be generated by creative efforts.[21]

The ever-differentiating system of sciences should not simply coalesce with the economy, technology and administration, but rather should remain rooted in the life world via the complex bundle of its classic functions. And again, this interplay of functions should be explained by the structure of science itself.

Thus, the theoretically ambitious reform initiatives of the early 1960s again recommenced from the concept of a science which was still credited with a (somehow) unifying power; again the university was conceived as only the institutional embodiment of this idealist power. Naturally, the position of philosophy *vis-à-vis* the sciences had meanwhile changed to such a degree that philosophy itself no longer formed the heart of the differentiating scientific fields. But what should assume the vacant position? Was it really necessary to retain the idea of a unity of the sciences? The totalizing power of the scientific process could certainly no longer be thought of as a synthesis and secured by a metaphysical connection to the world as a whole. Totalizing theories of that sort were no longer available.

Jaspers offers a comparatively conventional answer. He admits that the rationality of the open-ended, purely methodically determined sciences is wholly procedural and can no longer provide a substantive unity amidst the unpredictably splintering canon of disciplines. Yet Jaspers still wants to reserve a special role for philosophy *vis-à-vis* the now emancipated disciplines, even though philosophy had been forced to the margins and reduced to the tasks of illuminating *Existenz* and of analyzing *das Umgreifende*. The sciences are said to *require* the leadership of philosophy, because only philosophy can secure the motivation for an unconditional desire for knowledge and the attitude of scientific thinking. Thus, philosophy at

---

21 H. Schelsky 275.

least retains the role of a guardian of the idea of the university—and thus avocation as the pacemaker of reforms.

Schelsky's reflections are less idealistic. He replaces philosophy with a theory of science, dividing the specialized fields into three formal categories: the natural sciences, the social sciences and the humanities. Individual fields develop autonomously, but the three categories with their specific forms of knowledge are each in their own way functionally intermeshed with modern society. They can no longer be collectively encompassed by philosophical reflection. Rather, a philosophical type of thinking now emerges from inside the sciences and settles within each discipline as its corresponding form of self-reflection. Thus, an equivalent emerges for the now fictive unities of the Humboldtian university:

> Inasmuch as philosophy arises from the specialized sciences and, in making these its object, critically transcends them, it indirectly regains as its object the whole of scientific civilization. Inasmuch as it explores the limits and conditions of the particular sciences, it holds them open ... against blinding social constraints.[22]

During this same period, I myself became an advocate of a type of critique of science intended to explain the interrelations among methodologies, global background assumptions and functional contexts of application and developed in my book *Knowledge and Human Interests*.[23] I held the same hopes as Schelsky: That in this dimension of critical self- reflection, the relations of research processes to the life world could be rendered transparent; not just the relations to the applications and implementations of scientific knowledge, but above all the relations to culture as a whole, to socialization processes, to the continuation of tradition and to general issues in the public sphere.

A second element of the Humboldtian heritage was also revived with these reform initiatives. I am referring to the exemplary significance given to scientific autonomy, beyond the constitutional guarantee of freedom of teaching and research. Jaspers understood by scientific autonomy the realization of an international communication net which would protect the free state from the total state.[24] Schelsky gave to this view a personalistic, existentialist note: scientific autonomy meant a distancing from, and a moral sovereignty over pressures arising from the "self-propelling dynamics," the system's imperatives of state and economy.

---

22 *Ibid.* 290.

23 J. Habermas, "Universität in der Demokratie—Demokratisierung der Universität," *Kleine politische Schrifen* I–IV [Frankfurt a.M., 1981] 110 ff. and 134 ff.

24 K. Jaspers and K. Rossmann 33 f.

And both the authors of the SDS position paper and leftist reformers joined in the defence of what was then called the democratization of the university, with the expectation of stimulating practices of participatory self-administration.

Here is not the place to offer an evaluation of the organizational reforms which were then actually carried out; rather, I must content myself with the general observation that those goals indebted to a critical appropriation of the university idea have not been realized. In a postscript added in 1970 to a new edition of his book, Schelsky explained the failure of the reforms by the fact that the science system, under the pressure of a sharp rise in complexity, had undergone a high degree of differentiation and thus "could no longer be held together in its various functions by a shared self-image."[25] I think that the term "self-image" [*Leitbild*] betrays a reliance upon premises which were in fact too naive to keep pace with the dynamics of differentiation in the various fields of research. Take first the idea of a unifying self-reflection of the disciplines. The assumption that a form of reflection not springing from the logic of research itself could be grafted onto it was obviously unrealistic. The history of the modern sciences (Kuhn, etc.) teaches us that "normal science" is characterized by routines and by an objectivism which protects everyday research from unnecessary problematizations. Advances in self-reflection are triggered by crises, but even then the replacement of degenerating paradigms by new ones proceeds more like a natural process (Toulmin). Where, by contrast, reflection on fundamental questions and critique of science are continually conducted, they establish themselves—like philosophy itself—as just one more specialty among many others. Equally unrealistic was the expectation that participation of all involved groups would alone be enough to fill the self-administration of the universities with political vitality—especially when the government had to force reforms through against the will of the professors. But if the inner integrity of the university cannot be saved even under these revised premises, mustn't we admit that this institution can get along perfectly well without that fond notion it once had of itself? Does anything remain upon which an integrating self-understanding of universities could be founded?

V

The view suggested by systems theory is equally unrealistic. Luhmann assumes that all spheres of social action are held together beneath the level of normative orientations by value-neutral steering mechanisms such as money or administrative power. For systems theory, the integrating force of ideas and institutions belongs *a priori* to

25 H. Schelsky 243.

the superstructure above a substratum of flows of communication, which are systemically linked without requiring any further norms. Systems theory doesn't even ask whether this *can* be valid for all spheres of action, e.g., for cultural action systems like the science system. Until now, the heart of the science system has been located in a *function-concentrating* institution—in the universities, which by no means have outgrown the horizon of the life world in the style of, for example, capitalist corporations or international agencies. There is one experience which speaks against such system-theoretical overgeneralization, which Schelsky formulated this way:

> The unique aspect in the institutional development of the modern university resides in the fact that, in its case, functional differentiation occurred within the same institution, one which thus experienced scarcely any loss of function through transferral of tasks to other agencies. On the contrary, one could even speak of an enrichment of functions, at least of an increase in significance and of a broadening of the university's functional areas over the last hundred years of its development.[26]

Thus Talcott Parsons, in his book on the American university, proceeds from the assumption that the university system simultaneously fulfils four functions: the central function of (1) research and the reproduction of the academic personnel coincides with (2) professional training (and the production of new information and technologies) on the one hand, and (3) general education and (4) contributions to cultural self-understanding and intellectual enlightenment, on the other. Parsons offers as his example the American university system, with its clear institutional differentiation, and assigns the first three of those functions mentioned to different institutions—the graduate schools, the professional schools and the colleges. But each of these institutions is again so differentiated internally that each (with varying emphasis) branches out again towards all the other functional areas. Only the fourth function does not have a carrier institution of its own. This is filled by the intellectual role of the professors. If one considers that Parsons locates in this fourth function not only outwardly directed efforts of enlightenment addressed to the public, but also reflection upon the role of the sciences themselves and upon the relationship existing between the spheres of cultural value (science, morality, and art), one realizes that this catalogue of functions reproduces in a slightly different guise exactly what the Prussian reformers once had described as the "unities": the unity of research and teaching, the unity of science and general education, the unity of science and enlightenment and the unity of the sciences.

Of course, the significance of this last idea has changed substantially, for the openly differentiated multiplicity of scientific disciplines no longer represents per

---

26 *Ibid.* 267.

se the medium which can tie all these functions together. Yet today, as earlier, the university learning processes do not simply stand in an inner connection to the reproductive functions of the life world. Going beyond mere academic career preparation, they contribute to general socialization processes by introducing students to the mode of scientific thinking, i.e., to the adoption of a hypothetical attitude *vis-à-vis* facts and norms. Going beyond the acquisition of expert knowledge, they contribute to intellectual enlightenment by offering informed interpretations and diagnoses of contemporary events, and by taking concrete political stands. Going beyond mere reflection on methodology and basic theory, they contribute to the self-understanding of the sciences within the whole of culture by supplying theories of science, morality, art and literature. It is rather the very form of organizing scientific learning processes in the medium of academic discourse which still roots the highly differentiated and specialized disciplines in the life world via the simultaneous fulfilment of those various functions.

Of course, the differentiation of specific fields demands a correspondingly sharp differentiation within the university. Here, from different institutional vantage points, different groups perceive the various functions as bearing varying weights. The corporative consciousness has consequently boiled down to an intersubjectively shared awareness that, while it is true others may be "doing science" in differing ways, taken altogether they fulfil not only a single, but rather an entire complex of functions. The fact that the functions remain tied together, however, can hardly still be attributed, as Schelsky thought, to the binding power of the normative self-image of the German university. And one might ask: would that even be desirable?

The corporative self-understanding of the university would be in even deeper trouble if it were anchored in something like a normative ideal, for ideas come and go. The essence of the old university idea was that it was supposed to have been grounded in something more stable than just the content of particular ideas—it was to be anchored, procedurally anchored, in the scientific process itself. But if science or the scientific method is no longer suitable as such an anchor, since the multiplicity of disciplines no longer leaves room for the totalizing power of either an all-encompassing philosophy or even for the mere self-reflection of science arising from the individual disciplines themselves, what could then possibly serve to ground an integrated self-understanding of the corporative body?

The answer is already to be found in Schleiermacher:

> The first law of all efforts aimed at knowledge (is): communication. Nature herself has clearly enunciated this law in the impossibility of producing something, even if only for oneself, without language. Thus, purely from the drive for knowledge itself ... one can derive all the associations necessary for its satisfaction, all the various types of communication and community necessary for enhancing knowledge.

I borrow here one of Schleiermacher's "Occasional Thoughts on the German Conception of the University"[27] without sentimentality, because I seriously believe that it is the communicative or discursive forms of scientific argumentation which in the final analysis hold the learning processes together in their various functions. Schleiermacher viewed the notion that "a scientific person could live shut off by himself in solitary labors and undertakings" as a "sheer delusion." However much he appears to work alone in the library, at his writing desk, or in the laboratory, his learning processes are inextricably interwoven with a public "community of investigators" (Peirce). The various disciplines have constituted themselves within specialized internal public spheres, and they can retain their vitality only within these structures—associations, annual conferences, journals, etc. The specialized internal public spheres coalesce and branch apart again in the university's programs. What Humboldt said of the communicative association of professors and their students is true not only for the ideal form of the seminar, but also for the normal form of scientific work:

> If they (students and younger colleagues) were not to gather voluntarily around the teacher, then he should seek them out in order to get closer to his goal by combining his more experienced powers (which for that very reason, however, tend also to be more easily one-sided and less vital) with their weaker power, which is still impartially and courageously striving in all directions.[28]

I can assure you that this sentence no less faithfully describes the working presuppositions of the more solidly organized operation of a Max-Planck Institute than it does that of a philosophy seminar. Even outside the university, scientific learning processes still retain certain features of their roots in the universities. They all live from the stimulating and productive power of discursive disputes that carry the promissory note of generating surprising arguments. The doors stand open, and at any moment a new face can suddenly appear, a new idea can unexpectedly arrive.

I would like to avoid repeating the mistake of stylizing the "community of investigators" as something exemplary. The egalitarian and universalistic content of their forms of argumentation expresses only the norms of scientific discourse, not those of society as a whole. But they share in a pronounced way that communicative rationality, the forms of which modern societies (which are decidedly not a *Leitbild* from the past) must employ to understand themselves.

---

27 *Die Idee der deutschen Universität* 224.
28 *Ibid.* 378.

CHAPTER NINE

The Idea of the University, Yesterday, Today, Tomorrow

From *Hans-Georg Gadamer on Education, Poetry, and History Applied Hermeneutics* (1992)

HANS-GEORG GADAMER

Translated by Lawrence Schmidt and Monica Reuss, this selection by *Hans-Georg Gadamer* is taken from *Hans-Georg Gadamer on Education, Poetry, and History: Applied Hermeneutics* (1992), Edited by Dieter Misgeld and Graeme Nicholson, Published by the State University of New York Press, Albany, New York.

Editors' Note

Hans-Georg Gadamer, a student of Martin Heidegger, was a German philosopher of hermeneutics well known for his highly influential *Truth and Method* (1960). From the Platonic-Aristotelian perspective Gadamer developed a dialogical philosophy that embodied Heidegger thinking and avoids both subjectivism and relativism. His project of philosophical hermeneutics looked to reveal the nature of human understanding as the basic ontological process of humankind. Famously Gadamer argued against the Enlightenment's 'prejudice against prejudice' (considered as prejudgement or preunderstanding). In interpretation both the text and the interpreter stand in a particular historical tradition that is based on a linguisticality that enable the interpretation of a text as a fusion of horizons that enables understanding. Understanding takes place as an event in the linguistically mediated happening of tradition. Dialogue or 'conversation' becomes the model for the interpretation of a text: interpretation is a result of the historical and linguistic situatedness of human knowing where being underlies and makes language possible. *Hans-Georg Gadamer on Education, Poetry, and History* consists of three parts: The Philosopher in the University; Hermeneutics, Poetry, and Modern Culture, and; Europe and the Humanities. Gadamer in the chapter in question writes of the shift from *doctrina* to *research* to investigate the Idea of the University in its connection with science and participation in research.

MP

Recommended Reading

Gadamer, Hans-Georg (1960, 1989). *Truth and Method* 1989b, *Truth and Method*, 2nd rev. ed. (1st English edn, 1975), trans. by J. Weinsheimer and D. G. Marshall, New York: Crossroad.

* * * * *

The theme which was proposed to me for today was specifically introduced to this university by the model and precedent of my predecessor, Karl Jaspers. So I will follow the suggestion to reflect upon how we today evaluate the university in terms of its idea and reality. In discussing this subject matter I would claim a double justification. One is the detachment of age which allows me to view the university of today from a distance of almost two decades during which I have not been an active member of this university. The other is that the universal concern of the philosopher is to seek distance, to preserve this as a basic value and, yes, even to recognize this as a fundamental human responsibility.

I wish to present my reflections as a free sequence of remarks and not as a commemorative speaker. I wish rather to express what affects me. When I chose the title, "The Idea of the University—Yesterday, Today, Tomorrow," I did not intend to undertake a historical review or a prophetic prognosis. Rather I will try to order my thoughts from the perspective of today which always stands between yesterday and tomorrow. Although I repeat the title of Jaspers' three public statements concerning the idea of the university from the years 1923, 1945, and 1961, that also does not mean that I will follow this sequence nor hold the same position. Everyone must come to terms with reality in their own way and I believe that whoever wants to come to terms with reality has to recognize that ideas and reality always belong together and are always apart.

I would like to briefly remind you that the specific structure of the university which developed in our German culture has, in the meantime, become a model for universities in many countries around the world. Humboldt's founding of the University of Berlin expressed a Prussian-Protestant critique of the more or less orthodox style of teaching and learning during the Enlightenment. We are conscious of this model as embodying this critique. That however implies that we are conscious of the critical situation in which this idea began to seek its reality. Knowing this, we may be convinced that it is not something completely new and perhaps also not something completely bad when a nation—or even humanity—knows itself to be in a critical situation. At any rate it was truly a critical situation when, at the time of the most pitiful and darkest degradation of the Prussian nation, Humboldt's reform of the university undertook the political and cultural renewal of the university and provided for academic freedom. It became the model for the nineteenth and twentieth centuries. Certainly there were and are ideologically influenced universities, for example in the Catholic tradition and in places of state-funded atheism. But that does not at all change the fact that everywhere the idea of the university, as it has developed in the last two centuries, concerns the transition from *doctrina* to *research*. Or as Wilhelm yon Humboldt defined it: the transition to "science, which has not yet been completely discovered." We call it research and find the idea of the university to be closely connected to participation in research. Taking part in scientific research is not however a preparation for a profession in which science is to be applied, but rather means "education" [*Bildung*]. This word is, of course, not a very popular word any more, and it has forfeited its true meaning when it began to mark the class difference between the educated class and the uneducated.

Humboldt himself was not so much concerned with the teaching achievements of the professors or with the output of scientific research when he founded the university on the idea of education. What he wished to denote with this word was not opposition to the uneducated, but is explicable as being against developing the university into a professional school. It meant, therefore, opposition to the expert [*Facbmann*]. The word, education, signified a distancing from everything profitable and useful. In its elevated sense, the "science, which has not yet been completely discovered," means "living with ideas." This should unify the youth at the university and is intended to disclose through knowledge the horizon for all of reality and thereby also to open the possibility of surpassing this reality. Two things are required for this, solitude and freedom. Humboldt, one of the most introverted great intellectuals, understood solitude particularly well. And freedom, the struggle for which has constituted the world-historical fate of humanity, was supposed to especially become possible by this "living with ideas" at the university. The freedom to structure one's studies and the solitude of research were the important founding values of this idea of the university. That one is always also concerned to make these values productive in preparation for the professions of political life was self-evident for Humboldt. Lawyers and doctors were clearly the ones in whose professional preparation at the university the humanistic idea of renewing classical education was first formulated in our history. This occurred in order to enable them to work together with the clergy and teachers on the new task. To transmit to them the idea of education was exactly the point of Humboldt's new action. That this could occur through participating in research was certainly an ideal which could be accomplished by a greater number of students in the earlier stages of Humboldt's reform than is possible today. And nevertheless today it is still the goal of our actual efforts.

We have thereby reached our own problem. We must become aware of the critical situation in which the university finds itself today. We live in the time of industrial society. The time, which I would like to review with you in order to understand our situation, is the time when industrial society formed and when the task of the university found itself placed in an unusual and new relationship of tension with practical living. Today research is not conducted exclusively at the university. It has even become difficult to conduct research at a university in such a manner that the student can at all participate in the formative ideas. We will need to discuss the reasons for this critical situation and we will only be able to look to ourselves for help. We must recognize that industrial society through its structuring of the whole way of life indirectly affects the university. This is particularly due to the enormous explosion of the costs which are required for research today. And because of this, industry has made funds available to the universities for some time. In order to justify universities and research institutes, and what they can and should be, besides responding to the dominant interest in the economy, one has used, for decades, a differentiation which does not exist. I mean the difference between applied research and basic research. In truth there can be no other research except basic research. That means there is no other type of research except research which in its own activity is not concerned about the practical and pragmatic purposes which may be related to it. The freedom of the will to know consists exactly in pursuing to the end all possible doubts and one's own possible self-critique. So it is already indicated that the situation of the university in modem society is necessarily a critical one. It must seek to discover a balance between the duty to prepare students for a profession and the duty to educate which lies in the essence and activity of research. Not without reason has the characteristic word for industrial work, namely the word "industry" [*Betrieb*], been extended into the research sector. We speak unreservedly of the research industry and regard our place of work as an industrial institution. In fact, all the professions we know are dependent upon the research industry and teaching industry—the doctor, the lawyer, the economist, the minister, and not to forget all the teachers who through their profession indirectly have the broadest area of influence in the modern state. We need to think through the continual opposition between the educational task of the university and the practical utility which society and the state expect from it.

Yesterday and today. Let us look at yesterday from today. I do not mean to refer to the long history of the university but to the particular development of the university in the industrial epoch and that means at the same time the epoch of the alienation of education [*Bildung*]. Naturally this does not concern just a particular German phenomenon. The question is posed within a world process. However, we must examine and explicate this general problem from the particular conditions of our own history, our own academic institutions and our way of life. This is the central question of the industrial epoch of the nineteenth and the slowly ending twentieth century. So for a long time the continued effect of Humboldt's university reform was directed toward a university for the bourgeois elite. We should recognize that for such an elite this institution was excellent, recognized throughout the world and often used as an exemplar. But we should also recognize the developmental law of our civilization: increasing scientific specialization has to be paid for with a decline of education [*Bildung*]. Finally, we must recognize that the place of the "academic world" within the whole society has become doubtful.

Recalling my own university days, I began during the First World War while Wilhelm the Second still ruled and then continued my studies in the difficult first years after the war. We all know how difficult the living conditions had become then in Germany. With honorable exertion the Republic attempted to make available to all parts of the German populace the old and traditional form of elite education, which had been supported by the bourgeoisie and in part by the nobility. The academic profession became the legitimate goal of all those who felt their intellectual capabilities and talents would enable them to study, at least in principle. That was the end of the old traditional form, which a social class had established for itself. When I became a student, student life still occurred in traditional fraternities with all their old customs which had survived from one generation to the next in the fraternities' associations and their ideals. But fundamentally it was not the fraternity student but the free student who sought his form of life and his friendships at the university. Along with this, we should remember that the emancipation from the parents' home, which had always been associated with the initiation of one's studies, had also delegated a certain educational role to the landlady of the student, which earlier had been accomplished in the corporate forms of military service and the fraternities. Since this education no longer exists, it appears to me that we have lost something today. The youth today are presented with a new task of self-education which is not supported by any institutions. At this point I must relate my experience in other countries, for example, how impressed I am with the level of self-education in American students. It is astounding how these rowdies, whose parents may not even completely trust them, become in a few years polite, disciplined, and very reasonable young people. Never during a visit has an American student not asked me after ten minutes if he would be permitted to have just a moment longer of my time. American students have always done this—a German student does not in general say this. Certainly it pleases me when one wishes to speak with me longer. But I also admire the degree of reciprocal education which has been accomplished there, where every visitor has learned to show consideration for other possible visitors and for the time taken from the professor.

Clearly, at that earlier time, one studied under different conditions. I remember that when I was a student at Marburg the 3,000th student received a gold watch from the city, because one was so pleased over this increase. Today we are rather in the opposite situation. Today we would be willing to present much more than a golden watch to that student who would symbolize a decrease in the number of students from 30,000 to 3,000. We would reward in him the return to a sensible relationship between teachers and students, and therefore, the return to an actual chance for education which would be truly compatible with our teaching and research duties.

It is not my intention to romantically portray my own academic youth. The difficulties which the young Weimar Republic had to overcome are well known also in the sphere of the university. Especially at the university one could clearly observe how little German society was prepared for its task of parliamentary democracy and how a system for selection was missing which was truly supported by all classes. Not a very encouraging aspect of life at the university then. On the other hand, as a student in the university, one could have experienced, perhaps better than at any other time, how the unmastered weight of tradition encumbered the German university, which before had formed an elite society. Nevertheless, one can say that in the Weimar Republic a living tension existed between the ideological preconditioning through the earlier German tradition and the searching and creating of new ideals. This created a genuine freedom which found expression in the free choice of interests for the teachers as well as for the learners. The false nationalistic and reactionary ideology, which was already developing at the universities during the Weimar era and which then led to Nazi control, is known. What one does not know so well, either abroad or in the younger generation which surrounds us today, is how this fascist ideologizing at the universities, which came to dominate with Hitler's seizure of power, was defeated after a few years by the students themselves. This led to the use of terror by the party and secret police. Due to the insanity of the war and its criminal continuation, this terrorizing became ever worse, especially for the academic youth. On the whole one should not be misled: only in extreme cases was there an ideologizing of science and academic teaching, about which one now would prefer not to be reminded. But these cases were avoided by the reasonable student who sought education and knowledge.

Now we have reached the present and its most recent history, i.e., the epoch which began with the reconstruction of a free university and society. Clearly at that time the problems of today's university had already emerged. At first a kind of restoration madness dominated, namely, the idea that in modern industrial society there could be something like a "pouvoir neutre," a neutral position, for the academic institution of the university within the state. The major point of my presentation will be to demonstrate that that is not the case. Freedom will not be guaranteed us, if we do not know how to use the small space of freedom which has been left us. So the reconstruction of Heidelberg University began with the incentive not to again be dependent upon a tradition which no longer sustains and is dead. On the other side, the incentive was to transpose what was alive and valuable in this tradition into new forms. Therefore, we in Heidelberg have attempted—I have also participated in this since 1949—to give a new structure to student life, the living together of the student body, and thereby to create a new tradition. This failed due to the students themselves—for very sincere reasons. The gap between those who had returned from the war and the inexperienced young people who came to the university as greenhorns at the end of the 1940s, did not permit a unification, from which a tradition could have developed within student life. Thus the leadership was missing which could have created a common life for the students according to their own desires. Finally, the real problem of our academic existence erupted with the enrolment explosion. No one in the whole world was really prepared for this. This as well was a worldwide event. In our German tradition we were especially poorly prepared. Because we were still guided by the idea that academic education meant to direct one toward research and at least to participate in research. This was an ideal that had been preserved within the bourgeois culture of schooling and education in the nineteenth century, although by the beginning of the twentieth century it had already degenerated into a mere system of certification. With the change to a mass university, structural problems had to occur for which, in the sheer quantitative expansion of the universities, we have not found the institutional forms.

The result is a threefold alienation which has afflicted the community of teachers and learners and their position in society. First is the obvious relationship between the academic teacher and his students which characterized the previous

Universitas Scholarum. The address "fellow-student" [*Kommilitone*] is derived from the existence and functioning of this community, because we all understood ourselves to be in the same "militia," whether professors or students. This has clearly become a problem which can in principle no longer be solved. Fortunately, surrounding each professor who has something to say, there are those who gather around him not just for the purpose of achieving a grade and completing a good examination but who also come into personal contact with him. The circle which forms around each academic teacher in the natural sciences and medicine is prescribed to some degree by other regularities. Here the place in the laboratory or in the internship allows a direct relationship among the researchers, teachers, and students. However, even in this case, the availability of research directors will be lessened by the administrative bureaucratization to which one must devote too much of one's time. But wherever such restrictions, caused by the means and modes of work, prevent direct contact between the teacher and student, it has become an unsolvable problem to handle the unlimited number of students. Statistically it is almost impossible to express how poor the relationship between the number of teachers and students is in Germany and in a few other similarly under-developed European countries. I do not exactly know the situation in the East. In any case, the adherence to forms of academic teaching, which we still defend for carefully considered reasons, confronts the teaching professor of today with overwhelming problems—and naturally the student has to pay for this, for he is not able to find the proper access to his teacher. Therefore, the student encounters the truly didactic, namely the role model, almost exclusively as standing behind a rostrum. In most academic disciplines, the augmentation of teachers by using assistants cannot be considered a solution to this shortage.

The second alienation, which affects professors just as much as students, is the alienation of the sciences from one another. Where is the *Universitas Literature* considering the fragmentation and departmentalization which has become unavoidable due to the large size of institutions? Obviously this fragmentation leads to the disintegration of the university into professional schools, which are more or less tightly sealed from each other. One tried everything possible so that the organization of the newly formed departments would not become too meaningless and the organic relationships would not be too greatly sundered. But a disruption of the intellectual communication which belongs to a university unavoidably occurred. In the daily routine of teaching, the sciences know all too little about each other; in the area research it may be better. Again the students have to foot the bill.

The third is perhaps the most serious problem. I remind you that Humboldt viewed the actual purpose of studying at a university not to be attending lectures or completing good essays on small research assignments for a seminar or something similar, but "living with ideas." This has become enormously difficult for today's student. The alienation occurs especially between student and student and between oneself and the society in which the students live. It is almost as if a new profession has been created for being a student. There are economic and social reasons for this. But anyone who takes his studies seriously certainly knows that his position as a student is only the preparation for a real place in society, and that means for a profession. In our German society, because of its structure and history, this is also a unique problem which grew from the peculiar merits of our scientific culture.

Let us now attempt to look from today toward tomorrow. Not as a seer does, although the Homeric seer, the Greek seer, was one characterized by not being able to know the future without knowing the past and present. Here we are concerned with a fundamental problem: I mean the independence [*Abseits*] of the academic world. What happens to the idea of the university in a society which induces in those who are growing up an ever increasing distrust in its way of life, so that every appeal is only heard with mistrust? How should the idea of education through participation in research, which may still be the actual attraction to academic studies, be made possible in reality?

Where else can the idea be if not in reality? There is a thought in Plato which we need to consider in this case. It states: one cannot even imagine a city where the idea of a city is completely lost and no longer recognizable at all. That is surely also our task, not to imagine an idea as a distant guiding image but to learn to recognize it in concrete reality. That includes in our case the task of recognizing and justifying the independence of the academic world. It would be an illusion, to which the German academic has all too long succumbed, to still dream of a *res publica literaria*, a republic of intellectuals, which would be an autonomous world based on old privileges from the Middle Ages or established with the formation of nations in modern times, and so embodying and guaranteeing the idea of academic freedom. Our task is rather to give a new definition to academic freedom. We live in a modern industrial world, in a modern bureaucratic state, in a thoroughly organized system of social life, upon which we all depend, and in this system we have been allotted a modest space of freedom. Within it occurs our effectivity as inquiring teachers and inquiring learners, and it is truly a privilege to be exempted in various important matters from the tight net of modern professional life and from political calculations. Here romantic ideas of guarantees for academic freedom are out of place. We will need other justifications for our activity, and we must develop them.

There is still another independence which is no less vital and unavoidable, even if it may appear to be precarious in the social reality of our time. I mean the distance from practical activity, which is implanted in the essence of this large institution of research and teaching. One understands the transition from this world of research and teaching to the practical activity of a profession and the unique relearning that must then occur. It is therefore common to accuse the university of being divorced from real life, and one contemplates improvements. However, I do not believe that this independence of the academic world is something which we could or should alter through reforms and modifications in the institutional arrangement of the whole or through an opening of it to so-called real life. We are concerned here with a much deeper problem. It is not limited to teaching and learning nor to knowledge and ability at the university alone. I am here approaching a subject matter which I may partially claim as my own. This does not mean that I will now conduct a technical philosophical lecture. I will also not lose sight of the fact that we are concerned with a special case of learning and teaching when we consider the uniqueness which characterizes human social life. This no longer concerns just the situation of German education and the idea of the German university, but concerns a basic anthropological problem which exists in all schools and educational institutions in all cultures. It concerns the position of humans in nature. The central point is that humans, as opposed to animals, are in a special manner social beings which have moved beyond the impulses, instincts, and hierarchies which otherwise determine life in nature. Nevertheless human beings and their life processes are also undeniably part of nature.

Aristotle attempted in his politics to point out the constants of our human nature which constitute the foundations for the political task of ordering and directing human life. He declared it to be a decisive step in nature when it granted humans language, a system of communication which surpasses those used by animals of so many species. And with language we received distance and thereby pretence, lies, self-deception, in short all the great ambiguities of our human existence. Evidently they are connected with the distinctive characteristic of human beings: to find means and ways for distant goals, to sacrifice for distant goals, and in general, to be able to subordinate instinctual impulse, fear, or desire. To use our own concepts: to accept the whole asceticism connected with work. We may actually perceive work as something specifically human because it is achieved by a continual denial of impulses. It appears to me that all this is implied by the unique human possession of language. We live this dangerous distance to ourselves, which possesses an eery presence in the impulses of the human soul as, for example, the phenomenon of suicide shows, or is seen in the terrible legacy of war against one's own kind not known elsewhere in nature. If one recognizes this, then one understands that the exceptionally dangerous characteristic of humans—to achieve distancing and the bridging of distance—has the effect of blocking natural impulses and instinctual urges. But it also demands we construct the possibility of living together and the structures for living together. All this is demanded of us. The Greeks had a word for this, which Aristotle used in such a context; it is *syntheke*, the common establishment of common values. The whole legal system with all its limitations, the whole of our institutions and morals, the whole of what modern psychology calls "socialization," all this grows from this difficult distinctive characteristic of humans. A never-ending process of learning occurs which does not end in knowledge. To remain incomplete is the fate of our desire to learn and know. Religions have known to seek and find their emotionally powerful answer. In the history of the Western world an answer has developed, the Greek answer, which is continually being revived by us. It is the answer connected with the concept of *theoria*, theoretical knowledge. This ideal of *theoria* presents itself to the Greeks through the model of the divine, a spirit which perceives and finalizes itself and everything else. However, the Greeks never forgot that this ideal of theory—of living in pure observation or thinking which sees the things as they are—is not a straightforward human inheritance but, in the best case, a possible accomplishment which always remains restricted and bounded. Given their constricted practical and political life, there was no need to tell the Greeks how limited the free space of theory was. It is the same for us. Society offers and grants us a free space of a limited type. The free space of theory is not offered as a privilege to a particular class but as a human possibility, which is never totally unrealized in any person and which we have been given to develop to a higher degree for everyone.

It is not a new problem that persons having received a theoretical training are often disappointed when they have to face practical life. This transition always entails a new learning and often a renunciation of the abstract, exotic, and unpragmatic knowledge which one had absorbed. This problem appears to me to be necessarily connected to the fundamental problem of desiring to know and needing to know, which is the very essence of human nature, and implies a dislodging from the path of natural life. In a famous allegory Plato presented the whole problem to us in an unforgettable manner. It is the story of the cave where humans are chained. They may only look at the wall where shadows are passing. Through careful observation they learn the series of ever repeating forms, which are depicted there. Experience means for them that one begins to know and to say what comes next—until one who is so chained is set free, turned around and led out of the cave—to the sun and bright day of the true world. But, if one is then finally forced to return to the cave from the bright day, then he will be ridiculed by those who have remained chained because of his dazed and blind state which prohibits him from finding his way about due to the sudden darkness. The story which I tell has its point for our circumstance. It portrays the insurmountable tension between true knowledge, which is knowledge in the bright light of the universal and binding, and pragmatic correctness, adroitness and prudence, which we practice in specific situations. In both cases insurmountable prejudices threaten. From the side of those who always followed only pragmatic adroitness, that they will perceive the newly arrived from outside as completely blind. The others, who may believe that they have understood the truth, may be tempted to scorn the thankless enterprise of attempting to discover order within the darkness of this cave existence. In this story it is already understood with total clarity: a free thinking, which is bound by no political, economic, psychological, or emotional restrictions, cannot even exist. Life must always enter into new restrictions. Within the restrictions of our social life, in the fateful framework into which each one has been placed by birth and experience, it is important to preserve the free space which one has been allotted. I believe we can draw conclusions from this story for our own thought and perhaps also find an answer to the questions which afflict our youth: how can the free space be found where they can realize their own possibilities?

The modern mass university imposes three forms of alienation upon us all, teachers and learners. I wish to discern the positive possibilities which still remain for us. The first thing that we must learn is that the freedom which permits us a theoretical orientation in our life must be seen by us as a task and not just as a bestowed present. This task is enormously difficult. For we live in a society which, in order to preserve its own order, teaches and rewards adopting to and fitting into its institutionalized structures of being. Society trains us in all that—to use the image—like shadowy forms pass on the cave wall and where discovering order is the pragmatic wisdom of all. What can the university be in this situation? Considering the large number of students today, I do not overestimate the extent to which participation in research is an actual possibility. But even a faint awareness that there are people here who as participants in research speak to them and take a position in questions which concern everyone, is already something. The alienation between teachers and learners may become a little less when we understand what it means to nevertheless see in existence a kind of *universitas scholarum* as opposed to the molding of social consciousness by the powers of the present, accomplished as it is through the struggle of ideologies and interests, the struggle of competitive life in a modern society. That is, when we encounter the existence of the *universitas scholarum*, still free in its seclusion. Here one can still participate in research out of theoretical interest and without asking *cui bono* (whom does it please?). Thus one is free from censorship and reprimand, be it by a government which already knows the truth or be it by the economic system for whose flourishing and functioning everything else is concerned. This participation in research does not so much mean, as the novice may perhaps think, that one is actually able to make one's own contributions to research. The most noble mediation between us few teachers and the great mass of students consists of all those who at least attempt an authentic accomplishment of their own in research. Success is perhaps not granted to all, but a professor without students who attempt to enter science would be robbed of his best interpreters, best mediators.

What I mean by this is especially that inquiry and research produce poor television viewers and newspaper readers. We always ask: What is the motivation? What interests are being expressed? Why are we being informed about this? Is the aim to keep us within the limits of an administered social order? The interaction with research, even in the limited forms which are today still possible for everyone, assures that one can again risk one's own judgment and need not simply agree to opinions. I see this as the most noble task presented the student of today. And yet this is exactly what one criticizes in us and in him—that we give no ideological direction, not even instructions concerning how to act in the future concrete situations of professional life. Of course, we already know and think it appropriate that the educated student will be exposed to a new shock when, after his studies, he has to enter into professional life and come to terms with pressures to conform. Fellow students, every student who has taken his studies seriously, should be aware that he has received something: to risk his own judgments and not simply to allow himself to be manipulated.

The second alienation which I discussed concerned the specialization of the sciences and the separation of the whole field of knowledge from skill, even in the field of the "Litterae." The contemporary university is disintegrating into many specialties. Here as well I have no illusions. The researcher himself is influenced by the pressure to specialize. He is thereby enclosed within the boundaries of his own knowledge. And teaching is even more deeply affected. Becoming older one especially experiences this. One may still take note of the development of new tendencies in the research of one's own discipline, which one may still observe with the open-minded attitude of a genuine spirit of research. But one is nevertheless excluded. Already it is not easy for the researcher and the one who lives with science to keep up with his own discipline. Nevertheless, it remains true that only those teachers who can freely question their own prejudgments, and who have the capacity to imagine the possible, can help students develop the ability to judge and the confidence to think for themselves. That we criticize ourselves and that others criticize us is the authentic breath of life for every true academic and researcher. This is not always comfortable. I do not propose that to be criticized is comfortable. Every person is then a little distressed and doubts himself still more than he usually does. This is true for teachers as well as for learners—and to have chosen this is our lot.

Now for the third question. What I find to be most dangerous in our situation is that it has become so unbelievably difficult just to discover an existing authentic solidarity. I believe it is important to keep one's eyes open in order to discover where it exists. To a limited extent and for a time in the family; nobody who has been embraced by a family for an extended time should discount that he has once known solidarity. Also the emancipation from the family usually, if not always, means entering into a new solidarity by making friends, becoming acquainted with the working milieu, or whatever else it may be. In short, the free community of those who come together in solidarity has not ceased to accept us, even if we, as citizens in our state, have this general position of independence, which is not always appreciated and does not qualify us as good democrats.

Let me conclude. We should have no illusions. Bureaucratized teaching and learning systems dominate the scene, but nevertheless it is everyone's task to find his free space. The task of our human life in general is to find free spaces and learn to move therein. In research this means finding the question, the genuine question. You all know that as a beginner one comes to find everything questionable, for that is the privilege of youth to seek everywhere the novel and new possibilities. One then learns slowly how a large amount must be excluded in order to finally arrive at the point where one finds the truly open questions and therefore the possibilities that exist. Perhaps the most noble side of the enduring independent position of the university—in political and social life—is that we with the youth and they with us learn to discover the possibilities and thereby possible ways of shaping our own lives. There is this chain of generations which pass through an institution, like the university, in which teachers and students meet and lose one another. Students become teachers and from the activity of the teachers grows a new teaching, a living universe, which is certainly more than something known, more than something learnable, but a place where something happens to us. I think this small academic universe still remains one of the few precursors of the grand universe of humanity, of all human beings, who must learn to create with one another new solidarities.

PART TWO

The English and Scottish (Liberal) Tradition

CHAPTER TEN

A Discourse on the Studies of the University. A Discourse (1833), Psalm CXVI. 17, 18, 19

From *A Discourse on the Studies of the University* (1833)

ADAM SEDGWICK

This excerpt is taken from *A Discourse on the Studies of the University*, by Adam Sedgwick, 1969, with Introduction Eric Ashby and Mary Anderson. Published by Leicester University Press, Leicester, United Kingdom. Originally published in 1833.

Editors' Note

Adam Sedgwick a professor of geology at Cambridge University was one of the founders of modern geology proposing various geological scales and the Cambrian period mainly based on the investigation of rock strata. In 1819 Sedgwick helped to found the Cambridge Philosophical Society at a time when 'philosophy' still based on its medieval use signified any research outside medicine and theology. The Society was established with the aim 'of promoting scientific inquiry, and of facilitating the communication of facts connected with the advancement of Philosophy and Natural History'. This was an age when geology as a part of natural history was one of the leading sciences used to establish evolution with strong implications for theology and philosophy. Indeed, Sedgwick comments on the use of the word in relation to 'the exact sciences' and indicates that his aim is to trace the connection between the physical sciences and natural theology with the idea of establishing a moral system based on the supremacy of conscience yet subservient to 'Christian truth.' Sedgwick welcomed Lyell's theories on uniformitarian geology and trained Darwin as a field geologist even although he later rejected Darwin's evolutionary theory by means of natural selection, preferring to hold an organic conception of the world in the eyes of God. *Discourse on the Studies of the University* (1833) emphasised the place of geology within the tradition of natural theology and strongly criticised utilitarian moral philosophy. As Sedgwick remarks in the Preface the 'discourse' was delivered at the Chapel at Trinity College on 'the classical, metaphysical and moral studies of the University.'

MP

Recommended Reading

Background Note on Adam Sedgwick, Adam Sedgwick Collection, American Philosophical Society. Retrieved from http://www.amphilsoc.org/collections/view?docId=ead/Mss.B.Se25L-ead.xml;query=;brand=default

* * * * *

I will offer to thee the sacrifice of thanksgiving, and will call upon the name of the Lord. I will pay my vows unto the Lord now in the presence of all his people. In the courts of the Lord's house, in the midst of thee, O Jerusalem. Praise ye the Lord.

How beautiful and how varied are the forms of praise and thanksgiving in the book of Psalms! They appear as the outpourings of a grateful heart before God for the glories of his creation—for succour in the hour of danger—for deliverance from affliction—for national privileges—and for anticipated salvation. There is an earnestness in many of them that lays hold upon our strongest sympathies: for (without speaking of their inspired and prophetic character) they may be truly said to spring from feelings which are natural to every man who is not utterly debased, and in the exercise of which generous tempers ever take delight. The words I have chosen are the conclusion of a Psalm composed by one who had been raised up from some great affliction—*his soul had been delivered from death, his eyes from tears, and his feet from falling*. I quote them however with no reference to the purpose for which they were first uttered, but because they are well fitted for the occasion that brings us together—to *offer in the courts of the Lord's house the sacrifice of thanksgiving, and to call upon the name of the Lord.*

A well disciplined mind may perhaps learn to see everything with an eye of faith, so as to find, in all the dispensations of Providence, a motive for the exercise of holiness. But many of us are, I fear, too little endowed with a spirit leading to a contemplation of God in the common bounties of his creation: our spiritual sluggishness requires something' more exciting than sensations arising from large and general views of God's providence—something which comes immediately to our own hearts and bosoms, and seems to bear upon our personal happiness. When the body is weighed down by sickness, or the spirits sunk by present affliction, the glories of this world fade away before us; and we seek, or at least as Christian men we ought to seek, our proper consolation in looking to that heavenly kingdom which suffers no change, and into which sorrow finds no entrance: and after the clouds lately gathered round us are passed away and we are conscious of a great deliverance, the feelings of our hearts (unless quite dead to religious sense) will burst forth in the language of praise and thanksgiving. In like manner, though perhaps in less degree, on the national anniversary, the religious festival, or the solemn commemoration, thoughts seemingly extinct within us will start into new life, and trains of association will arise, lifting our thoughts above the selfishness and sensuality of the world, and fixing them on our noblest destinies.

And let me here observe, that the fact of our receiving impressions like these (however interrupted, and by whatever means excited), is an evidence that the spirit of religion is not dead within us. By the blessing of God, the spark now burning but dimly may be excited to a flame, which shall refine the corruptions of our hearts, and become the animating principle of our lives. On this account, every visitation tending to alienate our affections from the world ought to be considered as the warning voice of God addressed to ourselves, and not to be despised; and every solemnity of religion (whether public or private), having the power of touching the heart and acting on our better feelings, is to be regarded as a merciful invitation of God, and never to be rejected.

Sentiments such as these are surely fitted for the occasion on which we meet; to return thanks to God for the mercies he has vouchsafed to us—to recount the names of those pious benefactors to whom we owe the peaceful abode of learning and science wherein we dwell—to place before the mind's eye those illustrious men who have inhabited this our Zion, and obtained for themselves a name imperishable as the records of our race. These men are to us in the place of a glorious ancestry, urging us by their example to an emulation of their deeds; and we are unworthy sons if we turn a deaf ear to that voice by which they still seem to speak to us.

Among them were found many to join the foremost rank of those who in ancient times emancipated this country from spiritual bondage; to partake in the great work of translating the records of our faith into our native tongue, and to put forth their whole intellectual strength in diffusing the light of Christian truth among the people.

In their lists we read the name of Bacon, who, gifted almost with prophetic spirit, was enabled to climb the Pisgah of science, and point out the land of promise to those who were to follow him—of Newton, who after having achieved, by his single arm, the conquest of the natural world, was not puffed up, but gave God the glory; combining, with powers which never fell to the share of any other man, the simplicity of a child, and the humility of a Christian—of Ray, who saw the finger of God in the whole frame-work of animated nature, and within these very walls taught the listeners to comprehend the meaning of those characters he himself had first interpreted—of Barrow, the learned and the wise, the inventive philosopher, the manly reasoner, the eloquent and single minded christian moralist—and of many other illustrious men, whose very names time would fail me to tell, who having had their minds braced by the studies of this place, and their hearts sanctified by the wisdom from above, devoted themselves to the high and sacred office of extending the empire of truth.

And surely the happiness we enjoy and the names we this day commemorate, require something more from us than the gratitude of the lips—something more than a formal and heartless ceremonial. We are here met at our annual celebration where these, mighty men have met before; we are worshipping at the altar where they worshipped, we are treading on their ashes, and looking on their tombs, and every thing around us is sanctified by their genius.

Circumstances like these have ever exerted a powerful influence on generous natures. If heathen men have felt them, and made them the topics of exhortation and the mainsprings of national honour, how much more ought they to affect us who are assembled as a Christian brotherhood. We believe that the glorious names we commemorate are not those of men who have perished without hope; but that having fought the good fight in this life, they have received a crown of glory in that which is to come. They seem to speak to us from their tombs, but with no earthly voice, encouraging us by their example, and telling us to be firm and of good cheer in this our pilgrimage—that beyond the dark portal to which we all are hurrying there is a land of promise—and that treading in the steps where they have trodden, and guided by the heavenly hand which guided them, we ourselves may reach that land and dwell with them in everlasting glory.

The influence of domestic example is I think to be recognized in the institutions of every nation. In all of them, under some form or other, we find the traces of hereditary rank and of transmitted authority: and in infant societies, those institutions did not, I believe, commence in assumed physical superiority, but rather in the experience of moral fitness.

It is not wise for us' too nicely to canvass the decrees of Omnipotence: some of them we can partially comprehend—some of them must ever remain hidden from our sight. We are however justified in saying that in the moral as in the physical world, God seems to govern by general laws: and when he declares to us, that he will visit the sins of the fathers on their children; and that he will have mercy on thousands in them that love him and obey him; we hear not a new and despotic annunciation contrary to the ordinary operations of his moral government; but rather we hear a formal promulgation and a higher sanction of them. It is true as a matter of fact, that some races and kindreds are favoured above the rest of men—that God shows mercy to them in thousands, spreading among them the light of truth, and exalting them above the other nations of the earth. But these temporal blessings, I repeat, are not violations, but examples of the moral government of God; for in the nature of things they only co-exist with the exercise of those moral and intellectual qualities which bind men and families together, and form the very sinews of national strength. When the lessons and the examples of virtue fail, the nation's strength fails with them; the voice of eloquence, and the maxims of wisdom are no longer heard within its walls, and its proudest monuments soon moulder into the dust; or if they remain at all, are visited in after times as mighty ruins, serving only to contrast its former glory with its present desolation.

It is then our bounden duty to reflect, that our sentiments and our conduct do not terminate with ourselves. Every man however humble his station and feeble his powers, exercises some influence on those who are about him for good or for evil: and these influences emanating again as from a fresh center, are propagated onwards—and though diluted by new motives, and modified by new circumstances at each transmission, so as in common cases to be lost to the eye of man, they may still go on producing a silent effect to the remotest generations; and thus become, under Providence, a part of the appointed means by which a nation's glory is continued, and its strength upheld.

What I have said of nations, is true also of families or households like our own. If we have received a goodly inheritance we ought to transmit it unimpaired to our children. It matters not to us that the light of truth has been shed abroad by those who have gone before us, if we be living in intellectual darkness. It is not our honour, but our shame, that the wise and good have d welt within these walls, if they have now no living representatives. Self-examination is therefore among the most important duties of this solemnity; nor is it to be a mere idle and inoperative retrospect, but must be followed by prayer against intellectual pride and presumptuous sins.—prayer for support in those resolves of which our consciences approve—prayer above all for that spirit which will lift us above the temptations of the world. If we be endowed with this temper, we bring a hallowed offering to the altar, and cannot doubt that the incense of our praise will mount up to the throne of grace, and bring down a blessing on our household.

By the arrangements of Providence, things which to us seem good and evil are so blended in this life, that in the annual celebration of societies like our own, we are seldom permitted to meet with feelings of unmixed joy. In thinking of the past glories of our body and of the mighty minds by which its animation has been continued, it is impossible for anyone who has dwelt within its walls but a few short years, not to be struck with the changes in its moral aspect—not to be reminded of early prospects blighted, of the links of friendship severed—not to have impressed upon his memory, that hearts but as yesterday warm with kindness, and tongues glowing with the accents of genius, are now cold and inanimate. The song of praise and the voice of thanksgiving ought therefore to be heard as notes of preparation; telling us that this is not our abiding city—that with all the good things it contains, and the goodly recollections belonging to it, it is but a halting place in the great pilgrimage of life—and that before another returning festival the names of some of us may be also written on the long scroll of those who are departed.

These, my brethren, seem to be sentiments not merely fitted for the occasion on which we meet, but such as must force themselves on every serious and reflecting mind. I must however content myself with this short allusion to them, as the time does not allow me to dwell on them any farther.

Leaving then these general topics, I proceed to speak of this as a place of sound learning and christian education, and to inquire what ought to be the conduct of the understanding during the course of our academic studies before we enter on the great theatre of life. What I am now saying, though I hope not altogether unfitting to other ears, is chiefly addressed to the younger members of our household.

In the first place, let me put before you a law and condition of your being, of great influence in the formation of your characters. Impressions independent of the will, whether produced directly through the senses, or by trains of association within the mind, gradually lose their power by repetition: but habits, whether of mind or body depending on a previous determination of the will, gain strength by their very exercise, so as at length to become a part of ourselves and an element of our happiness. It is to the operation of this law that we must refer some of the strangest contradictions in human nature. What a melancholy contrast we too often find between the generous temper of youth, and the cold calculating spirit of a later period! between the actions of a man at one time of his life and those of another! I believe there is not one whom I am now addressing, who, if he reflect at all, will not acknowledge how much the cold hand of time has already chilled some of his better feelings. Now it is absolutely certain, that sensuality and other sins to which by nature man is prone, will do their work in marring the image of God, and (unless opposed by some countervailing principle) will end in habits making a wreck both of soul and body. In such a state of things a man becomes utterly spell-bound—*he is in the gall of bitterness and the bonds of iniquity*, and has no power to help himself; and the hand of God alone can help him.

I am not now contending for the doctrine of moral necessity; but I do affirm that the moral government of God is by general laws; and that it is our bounden duty to study those laws, and as far as we can to turn them to our account. As far, at least, as this world is concerned, the feelings on which we act in early life may and do diminish in their intensity, and yet we may go on in a course, honourable to ourselves and useful to our country, mainly by what is called the force of habit. Of what vast importance it is then, to those I am now addressing, many of whom have barely reached the dawn of manhood, to lay a good foundation against the coming time, by fostering habits of practical kindness, and self control—by mental discipline and study—by cultivating all those qualities which give elevation to the moral and intellectual character—in one word, by not wavering between right and wrong, but by learning the great lesson of acting strenuously and unhesitatingly on the light of conscience.

The studies of this place, as far as they relate to mere human learning, divide themselves into three branches.

First. The study of the laws of nature, comprehending all parts of inductive philosophy.

Secondly. The study of ancient literature—or in other words, of those authentic records which convey to us an account of the feelings, the sentiments, and the actions, of men prominent in the history of the most famous empires of the ancient world. In these works we seek for examples and maxims of prudence and models of taste.

Thirdly. The study of ourselves, considered as individuals and as social beings. Under this head are included ethics, and metaphysics, moral and political philosophy, and some other kindred subjects of great complexity, hardly touched on in our academic system, and to be followed out in the more mature labours of after-life. Our duty here is to secure a good foundation on which to build; and to this end we must inquire what ought to be the conduct of the mind in entering on any of these great provinces of human learning.

I

A study of the laws of nature for many years has been, and I hope ever will be, held up to honour in this venerable seat of the discoveries of Newton. But in this, as in every other field of labour, no man can put aside the curse pronounced on him—that by the sweat of his brow he shall reap his harvest. Before he can reach that elevation from whence he may look down upon and comprehend the mysteries of the natural world, his way is steep and toilsome, and he must read the records of creation in a strange, and to many minds, a repulsive language, which rejecting both the senses and the imagination, speaks only to the understanding. But when this language is once learnt, it becomes a mighty instrument of thought, teaching us to link together the phenomena of past and future times; and gives the mind a domination over many parts of the material world, by teaching it to comprehend the laws by which the actions of material things are governed. To follow in this track, first trodden by the immortal Newton—to study this language of pure unmixed truth, is to be regarded not only as your duty, but your high privilege. It is no servile task, no ungenerous labour. The laws by which God has thought good to govern the universe are surely subjects of lofty contemplation; and the study of that symbolical language by which alone these laws can be fully deciphered, is well deserving of your noblest efforts. Studies of this kind not merely contain their own intellectual reward, but give the mind a habit of abstraction, most difficult to acquire by ordinary means, and a power of concentration of inestimable value in the business of life. Were there any doubt of this, I would appeal to modern examples, and point out a long list of illustrious men, who after being strengthened by our severe studies and trained in our discipline have borne off the prize in the intellectual conflicts of their country. But I need not attempt to prove what no one is prepared to deny.

Are there, however, no other consequences of these studies beyond those I have pointed to? The moral capacities of man must not be left out of account in any part of intellectual discipline. Now these severe studies are on the whole favourable to self-control; for, without fastening on the mind through the passions and the senses, they give it not merely a power of concentration, but save it from the languor and misery arising from vacuity of thought—the origin of perhaps half the vices of our nature.

Again, the study of the higher sciences is well suited to keep down a spirit of arrogance and intellectual pride: for, in disentangling the phenomena of the material world, we encounter things which hourly tell us of the feebleness of our powers, and material combinations so infinitely beyond the reach of any intellectua1 analysis as to convince us at once of' the narrow limitation of our faculties. In the power of grasping abstract truth, and in the power of linking together remote truths by chains of abstract reasoning, we *may* be distinguished from the lower orders of the beings placed around us; but, in the exercise of these powers, we bear perhaps no resemblance whatsoever to the supreme intellect. Applied to an Almighty Being with the attribute of ubiquity, in whose mind all things past and to come co-exist in eternal presence, time and space have no meaning, at least in that sense in which they are conditions of our own thoughts and actions. To him all truth is as by intuition; by us truth is only apprehended through the slow and toilsome process of comparison. So that the powers and capacities, forming the very implements of our strength, are also the indications of our weakness. In some of our capacities, we may perhaps exhibit a faint shadow of a portion of our Maker's image; but in the reasoning power, of which we sometimes vainly boast, we bear to him, I believe, no resemblance whatsoever.

Simplicity of character, humility, and love of truth, ought therefore to be (and I believe generally have been) among the attributes of minds well trained in Philosophy. After all that has been done since the thoughts of man were first turned to the phenomena of the material world—after all the boasted discoveries of science, from the first records of civilization, down to our own days—those glorious passages of the Old Testament, contrasting the power and wisdom of God in the wonders of his creation, with man's impotence and ignorance, have still, and ever will continue to have, not merely a figurative or poetical, but a literal application. *Gird up now thy loins like a man; for I will demand of thee, and answer thou me.*[1] *Where wast thou when I laid the foundations of the earth? declare, if thou hast understanding.... Whereupon are the foundations thereof fastened? or who laid the corner-stone thereof; when the morning-stars sang together, and all the sons of God shouted for joy? Or who shut up the sea with doors, when it brake forth, as if it had issued out of the womb? When I made the cloud the garment thereof, and thick darkness a swaddling band for it. ... and said, Hitherto shalt thou come, but no further: and here shall thy proud waves be stayed? ... Where is the way where light dwelleth? and as for darkness, where is the place thereof. ... Knowest thou it, because thou wast then born? or because the number of thy days is great?*

Before such an interrogator, we can only bow in humble adoration. The study of the laws of nature may strengthen and exalt the intellectual powers: but strange must be our condition of self-government and tortuous our habits of thought, if such studies be allowed to co-exist with self-love and arrogance and intellectual pride.

A study of the Newtonian philosophy, as affecting our moral powers and capacities (the subject I am now pressing on your thoughts), does not terminate in mere negations. It teaches us to see the finger of God in all things animate and inanimate, and gives us an exalted conception of his attributes, placing before us the clearest proof of their reality; and so prepares, or ought to prepare, the mind for the reception of that higher illumination, which brings the rebellious faculties into obedience to the divine will.

---

1 Job, chap. xxxviii.

We learn, by experiment, the different actions and relations of the material things around us, and we find them bound together by a law of mutual attraction. Following our master of philosophy in the loftiest generalization recorded in the history of mankind, we attribute this property, found in the matter on the surface of our planet, to every other mass of matter within the limits of the visible universe. We bring our generalization to the test of observations of a new and certain kind, and we find that it is true. We find that no parts of the visible universe are insulated from the rest; but that all are knit together by the operation of a common law. We follow this law into its remotest consequences, and we find it terminating in beauty, and harmony, and order.[2]

---

2 The paragraph here referred to requires no explanation to anyone instructed in the first principles of physical astronomy. The following note is addressed exclusively to those who are unacquainted with the severe parts of inductive philosophy.

In order to understand the nature and importance of Newton's discoveries, we must remember that, in the preceding century, the Copernican system had been promulgated; and that Kepler, after incredible labour, had established the following general propositions on the evidence of direct observations.

1. That if each planetary orbit be considered as a space traced out by a line drawn from the sun to the revolving body; this line traces out equal successive areas in equal successive times.
2. That the planets move in elliptical orbits, having the sun in a common focus.
3. That the squares of the times of revolution of the several planets and the cubes of their distances from the sun, are in a fixed proportion to each other.

It must also be admitted that, before the discoveries of Newton, there was current in the philosophic world, a vague and general notion of some material action of the planets on each other. No one, for example, doubted that the tides were some how or other influenced by the moon: and, perhaps no one who had adopted the Copernican system, and speculated on the nature of mechanical motion, could doubt that the planets were affected by some action or p power emanating from the sun. Before the time of Newton, no one had, however, ventured to promulgate any definite or numerical law of gravitation; still less had anyone, on the assumption of a definite law, demonstrated a single fundamental proposition in astronomy. What had been done by preceding philosophers, takes no more from the glory of Newton than the predictions of Seneca take away from the honor of Columbus.

If anyone anticipated Newton, in the application of the law of gravitation to the system of the Universe, it was Kepler, and not Hook, as has been sometimes erroneously asserted. Hook did not demonstrate a single fundamental proposition in astronomy; and Newton, I believe, preceded him in the very speculations on which his claims have been sometimes set up. For we must remember that Newton, when a very young man, had just notions of the nature of a central force; and that he endeavoured to prove, by calculation, that the moon was held in its orbit by the sole force of the earth's attraction; and failed, only because the distance of the moon had been falsely estimated by practical astronomers. Leaving,

Again, if we commence our examination of the natural world with the small portions of matter which surround us, and following our induction in a new

---

however, mere historical discussion, let us consider one or two of the early steps of his philosophic progress.

He first appeared as the improver of Ule elements of mechanical philosophy, giving the laws of motion a generality they had not before, and extending their application to the investigation of motions arising from the combined action of many forces. Starting, then, with the laws of motion (which, in the first instance, may be regarded as an enunciation of material phenomena ascertained by direct experiment) his next grand generalization led him to extend these laws to all the bodies of the solar system; and, combining this assumption with the first proposition of Kepler (above quoted), he at once demonstrated that, the planetary bodies are retained in their orbits by a force tending to the center of the sun. Combining this demonstrated truth with the second proposition of Kepler (above quoted), he then went on to prove, by a new and most refined geometry, that the force, emanating from the sun, must vary inversely as the square of the distance from its center; or, in other words, must diminish in the exact proportion in which the square of the distance increases. Having once established this great truth, he then proved that the third proposition of Kepler was a necessary consequence of the demonstrated law of central force. Nothing can be conceived more perfect than this induction; which, starting with laws ascertained by observation, ascended by successive demonstrations, and proved that the most striking phenomena of the solar system were necessary truths involved in the operation of one single mechanical law.

By a similar train of demonstrative reasoning, Newton proved that the planets act on the several satellites revolving round them according to the same law by which the sun acts on them; and that the moon is retained in her orbit by the same power which on the earth's surface, brings a heavy body to the ground. Generalizing the truths at which he had so far arrived by demonstrative reasoning, and asserting of gravitation only what was known of its nature by direct experiment at the earth's surface, he proved that the center of each planet may be considered as a distinct center of a force, not primarily impressed upon the center; but derived as a secondary phenomenon from the combined action of every particle composing the planetary mass; and he also demonstrated (with a skill almost supernatural, considering the feeble instruments at that time placed within his hands), that the irregularities of the moon's motions are necessary consequences of the universal law of material action.

Again, knowing as a matter of fact that the planets are not perfect spheres, he proved that their forms are necessary effects of his own theory: and combining these conclusions with the law of universal gravitation, he proved, by most subtile calculations, that certain irregularities in the annual motion of the earth (producing the phenomena of equinoctial precession) are the necessary consequences of the sun's action on the mass of a spheroidal body.

In tracing out the consequences of the law of gravitation, and explaining the minute secular inequalities of the heavenly bodies, much, no doubt, was left by him unfinished. But he had lighted the way for those who were to follow, had given them the key whereby the mysteries direction, resolve them into their elements, and unravel the laws of their combination; we see at every step new cause for wonder, new objects for admiration.

---

of the kingdoms of nature were to be unlocked and had laid foundations of every part of that superstructure which has been since reared only by the united labours of the philosophic world. The refined geometry of Newton, however beautiful as a mode of exhibiting known truths, is thrown aside as an implement of discovery. "It was like the bow of Ulysses, which none but its master could bend;" and the difficult questions of physics are now assailed by weapons of greater power.* We must not however forget, that he was a great inventor in pure mathematics: and though he had not made a single optical experiment, nor taken a step in expounding the laws of the material world, he would still have had an exalted place in the philosophic history of man.

* *Discourse on the Study of Natural Philosophy*, by Sir John Herschel, p. 273.

Of the theory of universal gravitation, in the form it has at length assumed, it is not too much to say, that it can be changed by no hand but that which first impressed on matter the laws whereby it continues to be governed. Should man be ever permitted to ascend to some higher universal law, binding together the phenomena of light, heat, magnetism, and all the other subtile agents of our system, still no part of the foundations of physical astronomy would be shaken, and the utmost change to be introduced into It would be a trifling modification of the mere language of some of its propositions.

In the following words (taken from the preface of the first edition of the *Principia*) Newton has recorded with great simplicity, his own method of arriving at philosophic truth. *Omnis philosophiæ difficultas in eo versari videtur, ut a phænomenis moiuum investigemus vires naturæ, deinde ab his viribus demonstremus phænomena reliqua. Ex phænomenis igitur cælestibus, per propositiones mathematice demonstratas, derivantur vires Gravitatis, quibus corpora ad solem et planetas singulos tendunt: deinde, ex his viribus, per propositiones etiam mathermaticas, deducuntur motus planetarum, cometarum, lunæ, et maris.*

Near the end of his book of Optics, he writes in the same philosophic spirit—"As in mathematics, so in natural philosophy, the investigation of difficult things by the method of analysis ought ever to precede the method of composition. This analysis consists in making experiments and observations, and in drawing general conclusions from them by induction, and admitting of no objections against the conclusions, but such as are taken from experiments, or other certain truths. For hypotheses are not to be regarded in experimental philosophy. And although the arguing from experiments and observations by induction be no demonstration of general conclusions, yet it is the best way of arguing which the nature of things admits of, and may be looked upon as so much the stronger, by how much the induction is more general. And if no exception occur from phenomena, the conclusion may be pronounced generally. But if at any time afterwards any exception shall occur from experiments, it may then begin to be pronounced with such exceptions as occur. By this way of analysis we may proceed from compounds to ingredients, and from motions to the forces producing them; and in general, from effects to their causes, and from particular causes to more general ones, till the argument end in the most general. This is the method of *analysis*.

Every portion of the matter we tread beneath our feet (however insignificant as an object of sense) propagates its influence through all space, and is felt in the

---

And the *synthesis* consists in assuming the causes discovered, and established as principles, and by them explaining the phenomena proceeding from them and proving the explanations."

The former of these methods when applied to the investigation of physical phenomena, has long been known by the term *induction*: the latter, in one of the writings of Sir John Herschel, is called the method of *deduction*. This word had nearly been forgotten, but was wanted, and is again becoming current in the language of philosophy.

In the method of analysis and induction Newton stands without a rival in the history of man; whether we regard the boldness and certainty of his generalizations or the inventive skill by which he linked together truths before his time sterile and unconnected. In the power of deductive reasoning, he may perhaps have had some equals; but it must ever be difficult to form any just comparison of the intellectual powers of men labouring during distinct periods in the advance of science.

Deductive reasoning is the consummation of exact science, and its importance is shewn in two ways—First, in deducing from first principles, physical truths already known by observation; in which view, it not only offers the highest possible confirmation of the principle from which we start, but it assists and perfects the results of observation. Secondly, ill deducing consequences hitherto concealed in the unexplored regions of nature. Such were some of the great secular inequalities, and astronomical periods discovered by Laplace—and such (to quote more recent instances) was the conical refraction brought to light by Professor Hamilton, and the modifications of Newton's coloured rings predicted by Professor Airy before they had ever been exhibited by any experimental test.*

* On the effects of inductive and deductive habits of thought on the mind of man, see two very original and beautiful chapters in the latter part of a work published during the past year by the Rev, W. Whelwell. *Astronomy and General Physics considered with reference to Natural Theology*.

It must however be obvious, that deductive reasoning can never have any value, except when we have to do with the laws of fixed and unchangeable elements: without this condition it leads only to the extension and complication of error. In moral and psychological questions (for example) where all the elements are ill defined, the analytic is the only method of approaching truth. Logic may teach us to disentangle sophistry, to marshal our ideas, and to limit our conclusions: but it cannot, without a miracle, draw fixed consequences from unfixed elements. Those who, on psychological questions, have dealt in the forms of deductive proof, have perhaps done the least harm when they have allowed the imagination entirely to usurp the seat of reason. Their works may then amuse and instruct mankind, though not perhaps in the way the authors first intended. But the affectation of the language of synthetic demonstration on moral questions, has, almost without exception, been followed by practical evils; giving rise to a train of shallow reasoners, venders of trifling propositions, or propagators of antisocial paradoxes.

remotest regions of the universe. However small the particle of dust we trample on, it may present traces of a mechanism subservient to the complicated functions of a living being; or it may be a compound inorganic body, possessing properties of indefinite complexity: and though it be what we call a simple substance, still it is held together by its own laws of cohesion; it is composed of elements not brought together fortuitously, but in obedience to a fixed law, by which they are congregated in definite proportions, and grouped in symmetry and order. Not only is every portion of matter governed by its own laws, but its powers of action on other material things are governed also by laws subordinate to those by which its parts are held together. So that in the countless changes of material things and their countless actions on each other, we find no effect which jars with the mechanism of nature; but all are the harmonious results of dominant laws.

Again, if we pass from the consideration of things visible and tangible to the subtle and imponderable agents of the material world, we not only witness the manifestation of their powers in every physical change and every combination, but we know that some of them, and we may perhaps suppose that all of them, are diffused uninterruptedly through every portion of the universe. We are certain that the material of light is at least as far extended as the force of gravitation. It places us at once in physical contact with the remotest bodies of our created system, and by its vibrations they become manifest to us through our visual sense. There is, therefore, no portion of space, however small or however distant, which is not filled at all times with subtle matter—which does not every moment transmit material influences, in number complexity and rapidity beyond the grasp of thought, yet never anomalous or fortuitous but governed by fixed laws, and subservient to ends most important in the economy of nature, and essential to the very existence of sentient beings.

In speaking of the laws of nature and of the harmonious changes resulting from their action, in spite of ourselves we fall into language in which we describe the operations of intelligence: and language, let me observe, was never formed by a convention of learned men, or constructed on the scheme of an hypothesis. It is the true offspring of our intellectual nature and bears the image of such ideas as rise up of necessity in the mind, from our relation to the things around us. If we forget him in our thoughts, with our lips at least we must do homage to the God of nature. What are the laws of nature but the manifestations of his wisdom? What are material actions hut manifestations of his power? Indications of his wisdom and his power co-exist with every portion of the universe. They are seen in the great luminaries of heaven—they are seen in the dead matter whereon we trample—they are found in all parts of space, remote as well as near, which we in our ignorance sometimes regard as mere vacuities—they are unceasing—they are unchangeable.[3]

---

3 When the great bodies of our system are described as revolving *in vacuo* about the sun, we merely understand by such words, that they revolve in a space offering no sensible resistance to their motions; and even this assumption must now be modified, for the most attenuated of these bodies (the comets) probably meet with a resistance sensibly changing the periods of their return. That Newton did not suppose the existence of an extensive vacuum within the limits of our system, is evident from his speculations respecting the nature of light and the cause of gravitation; and in the tenth proposition in the third book of the Principia, he gives the following reason for supposing, that the motions of the planets may be continued for an indefinite period of time; *si ascendatur in cœlos ubi pondus medii, in quo planetæ moventur, diminuitur in immensum, resistentia prope cessabit.**

* See also the concluding parts of Newton's Optics especially Queries 18, 19, 20, and 28.

We may perhaps make the words this note refers to, somewhat better understood by taking an imaginary case. Let us suppose a sentient being sustained in any part of our system, which is not occupied by the grosser matter of the planetary bodies, and endowed with a power of sight as great as in our own when assisted by the best telescope yet invented. To such a being, all the bodies of our system would at once become visible, and the firmament around would be seen by him, glittering with the light of many million stars. But we must remember that each of these shining points is seen only through the intervention of a beam of light sent down by it directly to the eye. There is, therefore, not a single point in the empty spaces of our system, through which millions of beams of light do not pass unceasingly, yet with a material action so subtile that one beam interferes not with another, but each passes onward, as if moving by itself—the sole messenger from the centre of light to the sentient beings of the universe.

In general considerations like these the mind seems to lose its power, and becomes almost bewildered; and if we call in the aid of calculation, though we build on demonstration and clothe our results in numbers, our conclusions seem, perhaps more than ever, removed from the grasp of sense. If we accept the theory (considered. by some of those who have most deeply studied it, as well established as the theory of gravitation) which derives the sensation of sight from vibrations propagated through an elastic ether, by the visible object to the eye; then is each beam of light but a part of a distinct system of vibrations, every wave of which diverges through space with a sustained velocity sufficient to carry it eight times round the earth in a single second, and each wave is followed by another at so short an interval, that 100,000 of them are packed within the space of every inch. Millions of such sys· terns of vibrations pass, then, unceasingly through every point of visible space, yet without disorder and confusion: so that each system of waves goes on unobstructed by the others, preserving the individual powers impressed upon it, and through them ministering to the wants of millions of sentient beings.

Our knowledge of the complicated fabric of the material universe (even in those parts we sometimes describe as mere vacuities) does not end here. There is not a point in any

Contemplations such as these lift the soul to a perception of some of the attributes of God; imperfect it may be, but still suited to the condition of our being. But are thoughts like these to pass through the mind and produce only a cold acquiescence? Are we to dwell in the perpetual presence of God and yet dishonour him by the worship of ourselves, and refuse to him the homage of our humble praise? Such were not the feelings of the holy Psalmist, when, contrasting his own feebleness with the all-pervading wisdom and power of God, he was kindled as by fire from heaven, and burst out into rapturous expressions of adoration. *Whither shall I go from thy spirit? or whither shall I flee from thy presence? If I ascend up into heaven, thou art there: if I make my bed in hell, behold, thou art there. If I take the wings of the morning, and dwell in the uttermost parts of the sea; Even there shall thy hand lead me, and thy right hand shall hold me. If I say, Surely the darkness shall cover me; even the night shall be light about me. Yea, the darkness hideth*

---

portion of our system through which millions of material influences (implied indeed in the law of universal gravitation) are not constantly transmitted. That they differ from the subtile material action last considered is certain; yet no one will deny that they belong to some mode of material action, though he knows nothing of the mechanism whereby they are propagated and maintained.

Had there been any extended vacuities in the universe, it might, perhaps, have been said that such portions of space were without any manifestation of the Godhead. But what has been stated is enough to shew that there are no such places within the ken of our senses or the reach of our thoughts. That God is every where is the language of revealed religion; that God manifests his power every where is, in like manner, the voice of natural religion spoken through the universal domination of material laws.

Considerations like these fill the mind with feelings of the vastness of the power and skill employed in the mechanism of the world; yet, of the great Architect himself and of the materials employed by him, they give no adequate notion whatsoever. Still we are (in part at least) permitted to ascend up to the laws impressed on matter, and to see how they have been adapted to each other, so as to work together for a common end, and to minister to the wants of man and his fellow beings; and this is enough for the argument built upon such knowledge.

Truth depends not on authority: but it may be well to fortify this conclusion by two quotations from the latter part of Newton's Optics. "Though every true step made in this philosophy brings us not immediately to the knowledge of the first Cause, yet it brings us nearer to it, and on that account is to be highly valued." Again, he writes "If natural philosophy in all its parts, by pursuing this method (of analysis and induction), shall at length be perfected, the bounds of moral philosophy will be also enlarged. For, so far as we can know by natural philosophy what is the first Cause, what power he has over us, and what benefits we receive from him; so far our duty towards him, as well as towards one another, will appear to us by the light of nature."

not from thee: but the night shineth as the day: the darkness and the light are both alike to thee.[4]

How any believer can deny the reality of a natural religion when he reads those passages in the Bible where its power is so emphatically acknowledged, is more than I can understand. We are told by St. Paul, that even the Gentiles are without excuse, *for the invisible things of God from the creation of the world are clearly seen, being understood by the things which are made, even his eternal power and Godhead.*[5] Yet I have myself heard it asserted within these very walls, that there is no religion of nature, and that we have no know ledge of the attributes of God or even of his existence, independently of revelation. The assertion is, I think, mischievous, because I believe it untrue: and by truth only can a God of truth be honoured, and the cause of true religion be served.

But there is another class of objectors, who not only adopt this cold and unnatural conclusion, but rejecting revelation along with it, banish utterly all thought of God from the world. It is indeed true, as these objectors state, that all material changes are governed by fixed laws, and that the present condition of all material things is but a natural consequence of these laws operating on that condition of matter which preceded the phenomena we contemplate. They rest their strength, as far as I understand their meaning, in this immutability of the laws of nature: and having, with much labour, deciphered a portion of these laws, and having traced the ordained movements of the material world without ever thinking of the Being by whom these movements were directed, they come at length to deify the elements themselves, and to thrust the God of nature from his throne. But where is the reasonableness of this conclusion? The unchangeableness of the laws of nature is not only essential to the well being, but to the very existence of creatures like ourselves. The works of our hands are liable to perpetual change, from caprice, from violence, or from natural decay: but in the material laws ordained by God, there are no such indications, because they partake of the perfections of his attributes, and are therefore unchangeable.

The single-minded writers of the New Testament, having their souls filled with other truths, thought little of the laws of nature: but they tell us of the immutable perfections of our heavenly Father, and describe him as a being in *whom is no variableness or shadow of turning*. The religion of nature and the religion of the Bible are therefore in beautiful accordance; and the indications of the Godhead, offered by the one, are well fitted to give us a livelier belief in the promises of the other. So far from offering any foundation for an atheistical argument, the constancy of

4 Psalm cxxxix, 7–12.
5 Rom, i. 23.

the laws of nature, might, I think, have been almost anticipated by a well ordered mind, though unacquainted with the great discoveries of physics: and should the framer of the universe have other changes in reserve for the material world beyond those that follow the laws by which he has already in part revealed himself to us, we have no right to suppose that such changes can be known or understood by beings like ourselves—so feeble in capacity—so limited in time—and confined to such a speck of the universe.

But after all, we do contemplate something more than a mere succession of material changes. We find that these changes are limited by an adjusting power, and tend to a condition of equilibrium, and that the ultimate results of the laws of nature are harmony and order. We find them operating in different portions of space with endless complexity, and yet producing effects perfectly adapted to each other. We see innumerable portions of matter not only obeying laws common to all matter, but acted on by new laws subservient to vital powers; and by these laws gradually moulded into a beautiful form and mechanism—suite at once to all the complicated functions of a sentient being, and to all the material elements which surround it. Are we to believe that there can be such beautiful and harmonious movements in the vast mechanism of nature, and yet think that the spirit of God hath not brooded over term, and that his hand hath not guided them? Can we see in every portion of the visible world the impress of wisdom and power, and yet believe that these things were not foreseen in the Divine Mind, and these ends not contemplated before he called the universe into being?

The external world proves to us the being of a God in two ways, by addressing the imagination, and by informing the reason. It speaks to our imaginative and poetic feelings, and they are as much a part of ourselves as our limbs and our organs of sense. Music has not charms for the deaf, nor has painting for the blind; and all the touching sentiments and splendid imagery borrowed by the poet from the world without, would lose their magic power, and might as well be presented to a cold statue as to man were the no preordained harmony between his mind and the material things around him. It is certain that the glories of the external world are so fitted to our imaginative powers as to give them a perception of the Godhead, and a glimpse of his attributes; and this adaptation is a proof of the existence of God, of the same kind (but of a greater or less power according to the constitution of our individual minds) with that we derive from the adaptation our senses to the constitution of the material world.

The heavens declare the glory of' God and the firmament sheweth his handy work.[6] Here is a direct assertion—an appeal to the heart and not to the understanding;

---

6 Psalm xix, 1.

and every unsophisticated heart will be in unison with it. *The fool hath said in his heart there is no God: corrupt are they and have done abominable iniquity.*[7] In this passage the denial of God is coupled in the mind of the sacred poet with foul and sensual sin. And is not such a union justified by experience? A soul corroded by sensual sin can ill reflect the pure image of God—can ill discern the indications of his will in the glories of his creation.

Leaving, however the proofs of an intelligent cause from connexion between the external world and our imaginative powers, let us once more glance our eye over the proofs which appeal to the reasoning faculties. The mind becomes bewildered among the countless movements continually going on, and the perpetual changes produced by material actions, of which we see neither the beginning nor the end: but we find repose in the study of animated nature.

Every being possessing life may first be considered apart from the rest of nature. Its bodily organs are produced by powers of vast complexity and understood only in their effects—confined in their operation to the individual being, and entirely separate from the ordinary modes of atomic action. Yet these organs thus elaborated, exhibit throughout a perfect mechanism, in all its parts (as far as we can comprehend them) exactly fitted to the vital functions of the being. Contrivance proves design: in every organic being we survey (and how countless are the forms and functions of such beings!) we see a new instance of contrivance and a new manifestation of an intelligent superintending power.

This proof is so strong that it never has been and never can be gainsaid. It is in vain that we attempt to shut out the belief in an intelligent Creator by referring all phenomena to a connected succession of material causes, not one of which is fully comprehended. This thought should indeed fill us with deep humility, but takes not from us the fair inductions of our reason. We do not understand that complicated material action by which the God of nature builds up the organic structure of a sentient being: but we do, in part at least, comprehend the adaptation of its mechanism to various ends, and we see those ends accomplished: and this is enough to warrant our conclusion.

An uninstructed man sees a piece of mechanism, and from the form and the acting of its external parts (though he comprehend neither its whole structure not its objects) is certain that it is the work of a skilful hand. Another man understands all its complicated movements, but knows not the nature of the moving power in which they originate. A third can explain the alternate expansions and condensations of an elastic vapour and point out this action as the origin and support of the whole propelling force. At length we find one, who will not only explain the whole

7 Psalm liii, 1.

mechanism from first to last; but tell us of the nature of its materials, of the places whence they were derived, of the modes of their fabrication, of the manner in which they were put together, and of all the effects of their combined action. But it is not necessary to know all this to be certain of an intelligent contriver. The first observer drew this conclusion rightly from what he saw, though he comprehended little of these complicated movements. And after all, what relation does the most skilful mechanist bear to is workmanship? He does not create one particle of matter—he does not supersede one law of nature: but using the matter created to his hands, and forming and combining it in subordination to the laws impressed on it, and obtains a series of results—foreseen in his own mind and determined in his will before he commenced the building of his fabric.

Something like this we can trace in the development of organic beings. They are formed of matter, which was created, and governed by its own laws, anterior to their existence: they are matured by a regulated succession of material actions: when perfected, they exhibit an exquisite combination of mechanical contrivances, and organs fitted to carry them into effect. To such a structure are superadded vital functions and appetencies, which (like the moving force of a complicated engine) put all its parts into motion, and compel them to obey the laws of their destination. The external forms of organic bodies we can study, their functions we can observe, their internal mechanism we can partly trace: but when we consider the vital powers connected with their origin and development, we find ourselves among phenomena out of the ken of our senses, and removed beyond our intellectual grasp; and are compelled to acknowledge our utter ignorance. But, on this account to exclude an intelligent contriver, would not be more wise, that for a man to assert the fortuitous concourse of the wheels of a machine, because he knew not the power by which is was set in motion.

It is in vain that we attempt to banish an intelligent Creator, by referring all changes organic and in organic, to a succession of constant material actions, continued during an eternity of past time. Were this true, it would not touch our argument: and every clear instance of organic contrivance or material adaptation, would be a phenomenon unexplained, except on the supposition of a contriver. It would only prove that, in a certain portion of space, God had thought fit to give a constant manifestation of his wisdom and power through an indefinite period of duration, The eternity of material forms is, however, but a dream of vain philosophy, unfounded in reason or analogy; and, as far at least as organic nature is concerned, contradicted by the plainest physical records of the past world.

Assuming, then, that the structure of every being, endowed with life, demonstrates the existence of an intelligent overruling power, to what more does the conclusion lead us?—To the inevitable belief that all inanimate nature is also the production of the same overruling intelligence. As all parts of matter are bound together by fixed and immutable laws; so all parts of organic nature are bound to the rest of the universe, by the relations of their organs to the world without them, If the beautiful structure of organic bodies prove design, still more impressive is the proof, when we mark the adaptation of their organs to the condition of the material world, By this adaptation, we link together all nature, animate and inanimate, and prove it to be one harmonious whole, produced by one dominant intelligence.

The organs of sense and the materials around them are related to each other in the way of adaptation, but not in the way of cause and effect. The eye is not formed by the vibrations of light, nor the ear by the pulsations of the air. Had this been the case, such beings as the blind and the deaf would never have been heard of; for no being can be removed from the influence of those elements, The eye and the ear are formed in the womb by the mysterious operations of organic secretion and assimilation, before the pulsations of the air have ever reached the ear, or the vibrations of light have ever acted on the visual sense. They are examples of beautiful mechanism demonstrating design; but they are adapted only to a future condition of the being; and so also demonstrate a provident intelligence. Should anyone deny conclusions such as these, I can only reply that his mind is differently constituted from my own, and that we have no common ground on which to build a reasonable argument.

By the discoveries of a new science (the very name of which has been but a few years engrafted on our language), we learn that the manifestations of God's power on the earth have not been limited to the few thousand years of man's existence. The Geologist tells us, by the clearest interpretation of the phenomena which his labours have brought to light, that our globe has been subject to vast physical revolutions. He counts his time not by celestial cycles, but by an index he has found in the solid framework of the globe itself. He sees a long succession of monuments each of which may have required a thousand ages for its elaboration. He arranges them in chronological order; observes on them the marks of skill and wisdom, and finds within them the tombs of the ancient inhabitants of the earth. He finds strange and unlooked-for changes in the forms and fashions of organic life during each of the long periods he thus contemplates. He traces these changes backwards through each successive era, till he reaches a time when the monuments lose all symmetry, and the types of organic life are no longer seen. He has then entered on the dark age of nature's history; and he closes the old chapter of her records.—This account has so much of what is exactly true, that it hardly deserves the name of figurative description.

Geology, like every other science when well interpreted, lends its aid to natural religion. It tells us, out of its own records, that man has been but a few years a dweller on the earth; for the traces of himself and of his 'works are confined to the last monuments of its history. Independently of every written testimony, we therefore believe that man, with all his powers and appetencies, his marvellous structure and his fitness for the world around him, was called into being within a few thousand years of the days in which we live—not by a transmutation of species, (a theory no better than a phrensied dream), but by a provident contriving power. And thus we at once remove a stumbling block, thrown in our way by those who would rid themselves of a prescient first cause, by trying to resolve all phenomena into a succession of material actions, ascending into an eternity of past time.

But this is not the only way in which Geology gives its aid to natural religion. It proves that a pervading intelligent principle has manifested its power during times long anterior to the records of our existence. It adds to the great cumulative argument derived from the forms of animated nature, by shewing us new and unlooked-for instances of organic structure adjusted to an end, and that end accomplished. It tells us that God has not created the world and left it to itself, remaining ever after a quiescent spectator of his own work: for it puts before our eyes the certain proofs, that during successive periods there have been, not only great changes In the external conditions of the earth, but corresponding changes in organic life; and that in every such instance of change, the new organs, as far as we can comprehend their use, were exactly suited to the functions of the beings they were given to. It shews intelligent power not only contriving means adapted to an end: but at many successive times contriving a change of mechanism adapted to a change of external conditions; and thus affords a proof, peculiarly its own, that the great first cause continues a provident and active intelligence.

I forhear to dwell on other questions deeply connected with this science—proofs of a higher temperature, as shewn by the organic forms of the old world—indications of the same thing, in the crystalline structure of the lower strata, and the masses on which they rest—and further proofs derived from the figure of the earth itself. The spheroidal form of the earth seems to have preceded all geological phenomena, and makes probable the condition of primeval fusion: and, following in the same train of thought, we have only to imagine another accession of heat, and the whole earth must have been dissipated through planetary space, and have appeared (were there then an eye like our own to behold it) as a mere expanded nebulosity.

Speculations like these, starting at least from actual phenomena, are not without their use. For, without lowering one jot the proof of a preordaining intelligence, they point, through a long succession of material changes, towards a beginning of things, when there was not one material quality fitted to act on senses like our own; and thus they take from nature that aspect of unchangeableness and stern necessity which has driven some men to downright atheism, and others to reject all natural religion.

If, then, our planetary system was gradually evolved from a primeval condition of matter, we may well believe, that every material change within it, from first to last, has been but a manifestation of the Godhead, and an emanation from his immediate will—or we may suppose, that new powers have, by an act of creative interference, been impressed on it at successive epochs of its changes; and that these new powers, working together with the old, may have brought about the next system of material conditions[8]—or, if it be thought more conformity with what we see of the modes of material action, to suppose that the primeval system contained within itself the elements of every subsequent change, then is the primeval matter to the matured system of the world, as the seed to the plant, or the egg to the living creature. Following for a moment the last of these hypotheses—shall this embryo of the material world contain within itself the germ of all the beauty and harmony, the stupendous movements and exquisite adaptations of our system—the entanglement of phenomena, held together by complicated laws, but mutually adjusted so as to work together to a common end—and the relation of all these things to the functions of beings possessing countless superadded powers, bound up with life and volition? And shall we then satisfy ourselves, by telling of laws of atomic action, of mechanical movements, and chemical combinations; and dare to think1 that in so doing, we have made one step towards an explanation of the workmanship of the God of nature? So far from ridding ourselves, by our hypothesis, of the necessity of an intelligent first cause, we give that necessity a new concentration, by making every material power, manifested since the creation of matter, to have emanated from God's bosom by a single act of omnipotent prescience.

Leaving, however, these subjects of lofty speculation, and retracing our steps from the first condition of created matter towards the order of things now going on before us, we see from the form and structure of the solid masses on the surface of the earth, that many parts of it have been elaborated during successive periods of time; and if we cannot point out the first traces of organic life, we can find, at least, an indication of its beginning. During the evolution of countless succeeding ages, mechanical and chemical laws seem to have undergone no change; but tribes of sentient beings were created, and lived their time upon the earth. At succeeding epochs, new tribes of beings were called into existence, not merely as the progeny of those that had appeared before them, but as new and living proofs of creative

8 This second hypothesis (though perhaps less philosophical than either of the other two) is suggested by the analogy of the repeated changes of organic species alluded to above, each of which can be regarded only as a positive creative interference.

interference: and though formed on the same plan, ann. bearing the same marks of wise contrivance, oftentimes as unlike those creatures which preceded them, as if they had been matured in a different portion of the universe and cast upon the earth by the collision of another planet. At length, within a few thousand years of the days in which we live (a period short indeed if measured by the physical monuments of time past), man and his fellow beings are placed upon the earth. Of the whole creation, he alone has an appetence for abstract truth—he alone sees material powers, and by the capacity of his mind, grasps at them not as accidents, but phenomena under some ruling law—and, in describing them, he uses language (and what is language but the connected natural signs of internal thoughts I) in which, in spite of himself, he describes the operations of intelligence and power. He turns these laws to his own account; by his own volition works upon them, and produces consequences important to himself and foreseen in his own mind: and thus he learns, from what he has done himself, and from the constitution of his intellectual nature, to see in all things around him contrivance and causation. All nature is but the manifestation of a supreme intelligence, and to no being but him, to whom is given the faculty of reason, can this truth be known. By this faculty he becomes the lord of created beings, and finds all matter, organic and inorganic, subservient to his happiness, and working together for his good. A part of what is past he can comprehend; something even of the future he can anticipate; and on whatever side he looks, he sees proofs, not of wisdom and power only, but of goodness.

But these abstract powers form not the whole immaterial part of man. He has moral powers and capacities unsatisfied with what he sees around him. He longs for a higher and more enduring intellectual fruition—a nearer approach to the God of nature: and seeing that every material organ, as well as every vital function and capacity in things around him is created for an end, he cannot believe that a God of power and goodness will deceive him; and on these attributes he builds his hopes of continued being, and future glory.

This is the true end to which the religion of nature points. Her light may be but dim, and beyond the point to which she leads us there may *be a way which the vulture's eye hath not seen, the lion's whelp hath not trodden, nor the fierce lion passed*—a cold and dismal region, where our eyes behold none but the appalling forms of nature's dissolution: but here our heavenly Father deserts us not; he lights a new lamp for our feet, and places a staff in our hands, on which we may lean securely *through the valley of the shadow of death*, and reach and dwell in a land where death and darkness have heard the doom of everlasting banishment.

In ending this portion of my discourse, let me exhort you not only to mingle thoughts like these with your abstract studies, but to give them an habitual personal application—to seek above all things a spirit of single-mindedness and humility—to believe yourselves in the perpetual presence of God—to adore him in the glories of his creation—to see his power and wisdom in the harmony of the world-his goodness and his providence in the wonderful structure of living beings—not merely to admit these things as general truths, but to make yourselves familiar with them by frequent trains of reasoning founded on such examples as are continually before you.[9]

---

9 It has been sometimes objected to natural religion that it misleads men by a dim and deceitful light, on matters clearly put before them in the word of God. The objection is sound, so far as it applies to those who set up natural, in the place of revealed truth: but it is invalid in any other sense, as it strikes at the root of all knowledge that is not religious. If the conclusions of natural religion be true, then must they well deserve our study; and they are of no small moral worth, provided they be kept in their proper place, and in subordination to truths of a higher kind. Were all men honest believers in the word of God, then could the inductions of natural religion add nothing to the strength of their convictions of his being and providence. But to doubting minds, entangled in the mazes of a false philosophy, or lost perhaps in sense, and unused to any severe exercise of thought, the ready inductions of natural religion may bring convictions of the greatest moral worth—at moments too, when proofs of a different kind would be denied all access to the understanding. Moreover, the habit of contemplating God through the wonders of the created world and its adaptation to the wants of man, is not only compatible with firm religious belief, but with the highest devotional feeling; as is proved by passages, almost without number, in the sacred poetry of the Bible.

The chief ground, however, for urging the habitual study of natural religion upon those to whom the preceding discourse is addressed, is the belief that it is a wholesome exercise for the understanding. In rising, step by step, to an apprehension of the great laws of the material world, it is surely well for us to have ever present to our thoughts the conviction that these laws are but a manifestation of the will of a preordaining mind; and in noting the countless relations of material things around us, and their fitness for each other, we surely ought not to shut our eyes to the ever living proofs of wisdom and creative power. The study of the kingdoms of nature, conducted in such a spirit, not only strengthens and elevates the natural powers of man, but tends, I believe, to produce a cheerful sobriety of thought most favourable to the reception of sound religious impressions. Such appears to have been the temper of Paley, especially during the latter years of his life: and in mentioning his name, I cannot but urge on all those who are commencing their academic course, the habitual study of his delightful work on Natural Theology. It is hardly possible to read this book without catching some part of the Author's spirit; and if this spirit be gained, we shall then find the material world with a new life breathed into it, and speaking a language which, to those uninstructed in its meaning, may fall upon the ear without suggesting a single appropriate train of thought.

Since the preceding discourse was delivered, some very important and elaborate treatises have appeared (and others are in progress), enforcing different parts of the great argument to be drawn from final causes. It is, I think, impossible that any one of them, or all of them

To deny all natural religion is not more strange than to commence a system of moral philosophy by denying the existence of moral feelings. It is, I think, to deny

---

together, should supersede the work of Paley. They may expand and enforce his argument by new and pregnant illustrations; and they may supply some deficiencies in his work, especially in the part that treats of the adaptation of the mechanical laws of the universe to each other, and to the wants of man. With one part of the mechanical argument he has indeed attempted to grapple; but not, I think, with the same power he has put forth in the other portions of this volume.

To comment on the treatises just alluded to would be quite out of place in a note like this: but I may be allowed to rejoice, in common with many other Members of the University, at the appearance of a work (referred to in a former note, p. 85) which, combining a philosophic view of the highest generalizations of exact science with an original and well-sustained argument drawn from the universal proofs of wisdom and design, falls in admirably with the course of reading of our best class of students. It is assuredly not too much to say, that this author has well earned the honor of tilling up a chasm in the moral literature of his country.

Paley has stated with his usual clearness and skill the importance of comparative anatomy to the doctrine of final causes.* The philosophic anatomist tells us that the organs at each animal may be described as parts of a machine well fitted together, and exactly suited to the functions they have to perform. He reasons from the function to the organ, or from the organ to the function, with perfect confidence; and in cases too where the living type has been never seen. This adaptation may now be called a law of organic structure; and it has been proved only by patient observation, like every other inductive physical truth. When once established it becomes the animating principle of every department of natural history: both helping us in the arrangement of known object, and in the interpretation of new phenomena. To form an adequate notion of the importance of this law, we have only to bear in mind how it enabled Cuvier to reassemble the scattered organs of many beings of a former world—to determine their place in the scale of animated nature—and to reason on their functions with as much clearness as if they were themselves still living before him.

* Natural Theology, Chap. XII.

In passing from one order of beings to another as they stand arranged in a museum of comparative anatomy, we see a continued repetition of the same organs, yet in each successive instance we find them changed in a greater or less degree in their proportions and manner of adjustment. This most striking fact bears directly on the argument for design. "Whenever we find a general plan pursued, yet with such variations in it as are, in each case, required by the particular exigency of the subject to what it is applied, we possess, in such plan and such adaptation, the strongest evidence that can be afforded of intelligence and design; an evidence which the most completely excludes every other hypothesis." This view of the argument admits of endless illustrations. To each man those instances are the best that spontaneously offer themselves to his mind. The real difficulty is to teach men first to enter on such trains of thought, and to shake off that torpor in which their senses seem often to be steeped.

that very constitution of our minds on which the fabric of our religious character must be built. How such a character is matured and upheld I do not now inquire:

Paley's instances are well put, and full of meaning: I will endeavour to add one or two familiar examples to them, though at the risk of extending this note to an unreasonable length.

Of all the solid parts of the animal frame, the most obviously mechanical are the jaws and teeth; we know, in each instance, the office they have to perform, and we know that they perform it well. Let us then examine, in a museum of anatomy, the jaws of some one order of animals—for example, the carnivorous. In each instance we find cutting teeth in front, sharp fangs on the sides, and molar teeth in the back part of the jaws. The molar teeth rise into sharp lance-shaped points of hard enamel, and overlap each other in the upper and lower jaw, like the edges of a pair of shears. We see at once an apparatus well fitted for tearing and for clipping flesh, and, in some cases, fitted also for cracking bones; but not at all suited for grinding the seeds or stalks of vegetables. Let us then observe the manner in which the jaws are fitted to one another. At each end of the lower jaw rises a well defined transverse process, working in a corresponding depression of the skull; in short the jaws work together by a firm hinge, allowing them to open and shut like a pair of shears, but admitting of no grinding motion. That such an articulation is important for the carnivorous animal no one can doubt, who has observed how ill a pair of scissors perform their office with a loose hinge. Thus we see, from one end to the other, an implement well suited for its work, and all its parts in good adjustment. But all these nice adjustments would be lost, were there not levers attached to the jaw, and muscles to work the levers—were not each part of the animal frame adapted to all the other parts—and were not the instincts; and appetites of the animal such as are fitted to give to this frame-work its appropriate movement.

Let us then turn to another order of animals of strongly contrasted habits—for example, the ruminating. We find the lower jaw armed with incisor teeth, working against a hard callous pad, placed upon the upper. This prevents the animal from inflicting a severe bite, but enables it readily to crop grass and to tear off the stalks of vegetables. The sharp fangs are wanting; but, were this the place for the observation, we might shew how it is protected from the fiercer beasts by the instinct of fear combined with aC1He senses and great fleetness—by gregarious habits—and by formidable weapons of defence placed on its brow, and given, be it observed, to none of the carnivorous tribes. Its flat topped molar teeth are not formed for cutting, but for grinding; and its jaws are loosely fitted together, so as to allow of a grinding movement. With a change of form ill one part, is a change of adjustment in another, and the parts continue to work well together. Had the articulation of the carnivorous jaw remained unchanged, the herbivorous tooth could not have performed its office. But we have not yet done with the adjustments. In the ruminating animal, the enamel is not all placed on the top of the tooth, as in the carnivorous; but is arranged in deep vertical layers, alternating with bony matter; and this arrangement, in all states of the tooth, secure!' a rough grinding surface. These layers are arranged in irregular curves running lengthwise in the jaw, and their convex and concave portions are so delicately opposed in the upper and lower jaw, as to produce, during a lateral movement (like that of a cow chewing the cud), but among persons of intellectual habits, it depends for its commencement, mainly on the conduct of the mind in early life: and during the changes of advancing years cannot perhaps be so well upheld by any ordinary means as by a steady habit of

---

the greatest possible quantity of friction. Again, we might go on and shew the adaptation of the muscles of the head to the apparatus here described; and, beginning with the jaw, we might go through the whole animal frame and prove that all the parts were skilfully contrived and fitted together so as to minister to the wants of the beings they belong to.

Let us next see what is the structure of the jaw in animals, of some different and intermediate order. Perhaps the best for our selection, are the *rodentia*, or gnawers. Like the ruminating animals, they are without fangs; but they have long sharp cutting teeth, meeting together like a pair of pinchers. That these implements are useful to the creatures possessing them, no one can doubt. It is by their help that the beaver saws down a tree for his water-dam, that the rat gnaws his way through a board, and that the squirrel drills a hole through the shell of a nut, and extracts the kernel. Most of the animals of this order are herbivorous, and therefore ground their food with flat-topped molar teeth. But how is this duty to be performed, as the front teeth lock together in such a way as to make a transverse grinding movement almost impossible? It is provided for by a new adjustment. A process of the lower jaw works in a depression of the skull, as in the carnivorous order.

The articulation admits however of more play, and its direction instead of being transverse, is length-wise, and thus allows the lower jaw to rub, like a carpenter's plane, backwards and forwards upon the upper. Everyone must have been struck with this movement who has seen a rabbit eating the leaf of a cabbage. The work of nature would still be left incomplete, were there not also a corresponding adjustment in the enamel of each tooth. We find then, on inspection, that the enamel of the molar teeth is arranged in vertical layers (as in the *ruminantia*) and that they form a good grinding surface; but the direction of the layers is now transverse to the jaw. This is what it ought to be, in order that the teeth may work to the best advantage. The layers of enamel are transverse to the teeth, for the same reason that the iron of a carpenter's plane is transverse to the direction in which the workman uses it. But this is not the only new adjustment in the teeth of those animals. The incisors being implements of perpetual use, are renewed by perpetual growth; there is a special provision for their support in a bent socket, and being enamelled only in front they are always kept sharp. By the very act of gnawing, the hinder part of the incisor wears away quicker than the fore part, and in that way always preserves a sharp inclined edge like that of an adze or chisel—the very form that is wanted by the animal. It is not enough to say that all these adjustments are complete; what would be their value, were not the muscular frame also fitted to them, and the animal powers such as to call them into action?

These instances are among the most obvious and well-known, in comparative anatomy, and have been quoted on that very account. The same kind of reasoning might be applied to the organs of all animated beings; and there is literally no end to the examples of mechanical adjustment. Considered in this way, they put the proofs of contrivance and design in the clearest point of view, and give the argument a unity and connexion it cannot have by the mere consideration of detached instances.

seeing, and adoring with thankfulness of heart, the wisdom and goodness of God in the wonders and bounties of his creation. The materials for thoughts like these are placed abundantly around us.

To many minds, the forms of natural knowledge presented in the abstractions of severe science, are cold and uninviting: but if we follow them with the light of other kindred studies, such as those I have endeavoured faintly to shadow out, we bring down the fire from heaven which at once gives them movement and animation.

Once for all, and by way of recapitulation, we see the proofs of wisdom and design in the structure of every being endowed with life. The argument is cumulative; each instance being perfect in its kind. We see the proofs of wisdom still more clearly when we review the classes and orders of animated nature; for we find the God of nature working upon a plan, and adapting the same organs to different ends, by a series of' delicate mechanical adjustments. Our argument gains strength as we ascend to a consideration of the mechanical laws impressed on matter: for law implies a lawgiver, and without that notion the word law is without meaning. Still more strengthened is our argument as we learn to comprehend the exquisite adaptation of these laws to the organs and functions of all living beings. We see, then, through all nature, animate and inanimate, but one unbroken impress of wisdom and power: and the conclusion at which man thus arrives, elevates his intellectual condition, and falls in with the appetencies of his moral nature. Surely then we may conclude with Paley, that the world around us proceeds from design and intelligence—"intelligence properly and strictly so called, including under that name foresight, consideration, and reference to utility. … 'After all the schemes of a reluctant philosophy, the necessary resort is to a Deity. The marks of *design* are too strong to be gotten over—design must have a designer—that designer must have been a person—that person is God'."*

* Paley's Nat. Theol. End of Chap. Xxiii.

CHAPTER ELEVEN

Preparatory Remarks and of the Subjects of University Teaching

From *On the Principles of English University Education* (1837)

WILLIAM WHEWELL

These excerpts are taken from *On the Principles of English University Education*, The Rev. W. Whewell, 1837. Published by John W. Parker, London, United Kingdom.

Editors' Note

William Whewell was a genuine polymath in an era before the industrial separation of the disciplines. He published work in the sciences (geology, physics, astronomy, mechanics, economics) as well as philosophy, theology and poetry, translating the works of Goethe. He won a scholarship to Trinity College, Cambridge later becoming a Master, Fellow, tutor and finally professor of philosophy devoted to 'moral theology.' He was responsible for mapping the history of inductive reasoning in science, publishing two major works attempting to systemise the sciences—*History of the Inductive Sciences* (1837) and *The Philosophy of the Inductive Sciences* (1840). As an opponent of British empiricism and in particular John Stuart Mill he asserted with Kant the *a priori* nature of necessary truth. His *Principles* is divided into three chapters devoted in turn to the subjects of university teaching, direct and indirect teaching, and discipline with an Appendix on 'Thoughts on the Study of Mathematics as a part of a Liberal Education.' In his Prefatory Remarks he writes: 'The considerations which I here offer to the public on the subject of Education, have been suggested by a long and somewhat laborious course of researches on the principles and history of science, and by many years' experience as a tutor in a principal College of the University of Cambridge.' In this work he argues for the extension of university teaching to science suggesting that while science subjects 'do not constitute the *culture*, they *belong* to the information of a well-educated man' (p. 42).

MP

* * * * *

Prefatory Remarks

The considerations which I here offer to the public on the subject of Education, have been suggested by a long and somewhat laborious course of researches on the principles and history of science, and by many years' experience as a tutor in a principal College of the University of Cambridge. I trust, therefore, that I shall stand absolved from all suspicion of approaching so important a subject without due thought and preparation. I have for some time intended, on the first occasion of comparative leisure, to state my views on the points here treated of; and I should have done so, in the same manner, and probably nearly at the same time as I have done, whether or not other pamphlets on questions connected with the English Universities had appeared. I request the reader, therefore, not to mix me up in his thoughts with any controversies which may happen to be going on at this time. I mean not to express any disrespect to persons engaged in such controversies; but I must take the liberty of saying, that I have neither sought nor shunned the discussion of any questions on which they may happen to have touched.

There is another controversy, to which some part of the following pages may appear to have reference; the question of the comparative value of *Mathematics*, and of certain other studies which have been termed *Philosophy*, as instruments of Education. An Edinburgh reviewer, in a criticism upon a former publication of mine, maintained that the study of mathematics is, for such a purpose, useless or prejudicial; and recommended the cultivation of "philosophy" in its place. In a letter to the Editor of the Review, (which I published,) I expressed my willingness to discuss the subject at a future time; and, referring to the mathematical course of this University, as my example of mathematical education, I requested to be informed, by description, or by reference to books, what that "philosophy" was, which the reviewer was prepared to contend for, as a better kind of education.

I considered this as a proceeding, in the courtesy of literary combat, equivalent to sending my opponent the measure of my weapon, and begging to be furnished with the dimensions of his. When, therefore, the reviewer, in reply, flatly refused[1] "to perplex the question by a compliance with Mr. Whewell's misplaced request," I certainly considered myself as freed from any call to continue the controversy. No adherent of the reviewer could expect me to refute a proposition which the author himself did not venture to enunciate in an intelligible form. And, therefore, in the present book, I do not at all profess to discuss the question of the value of mathematics, and other kinds of philosophy, with reference to the reviewer's assertions, but simply so far as it is brought before me by the general course of my reflections.

I must also observe, that my remarks, at present, will be bounded within the limits of my title. I do not undertake to examine the subject of education in general, but the *Education of Universities*; nor again, of Universities in general, but of *English* Universities. Moreover, I am far from intending or hoping to treat the subject, even thus limited, fully and completely; my purpose is merely to offer certain Considerations, having reference to the general *Principles* on which the work of English Universities is and must be conducted, rather than to their actual condition and their proceedings in detail. I trust, however, that the Principles which I shall endeavour to establish, are so far substantial and practical, that their application to the real business of Universities will be obvious and immediate.

A formal division of my subject might appear as if I intended to exhaust it, and might mislead the reader, since, as I have said, such is not my purpose. But it will, I think, add to the clearness of what I have to say, to divide my Considerations into three chapters; of which, the *first* will refer to the *matter* taught, and mainly to the question of what may be termed Practical and Speculative Teaching—the *second* chapter will have reference to the *manner* of teaching, and to the relative value of the Direct and Indirect Methods of instruction—the *third* chapter will treat of that superintendence and control, besides the mere teaching of the understanding, which, under the name of *Discipline*, has hitherto been considered a part of the office of English Universities. On all these subjects I trust I shall be able to point out certain large and weighty alternatives of principle, between which, in all our Universities, old or new, we must necessarily choose; and I hope I shall be abl. to give satisfactory reasons in favour of that choice which I venture to recommend. I now proceed to my task.

---

1 Edin. Rev. No. VXXVII.

Of the subjects of University teaching

Section 1: Of the distinction of practical and speculative teaching

There are two modes of teaching, which, in a general view, may be broadly distinguished from each other. In the one mode the lecturer expounds to his audience the doctrines or results of some branch of knowledge, the speculations of antecedent philosophers, or his own, while the office of the audience is only to attend to him, to listen, to receive, think on, and treasure up what the speaker delivers, without being called upon themselves to take any active Fart; without being required to produce, to test, or to apply the knowledge thus acquired. In another mode of teaching, the learner has not merely to listen, but to do something himself; not merely to receive, but to produce his knowledge: as when the mathematical student proves the proposition which is enunciated by his teacher, or solves a problem proposed to him; or when the classical scholar renders Horace or Thucydides into English. The former I call *speculative*, the latter, *practical* teaching. And I must beg the reader to recollect the manner in which I use these terms; namely, with reference to the *mode* of teaching, not the possible application of the *subject* taught. It is because geometry is taught thus *practically*, and not because it is what is commonly called "practical knowledge," that I designate the cultivation of geometry, in the manner which prevails in English Universities, as Practical Teaching. In their marked forms, these two kinds of teaching are very clearly distinguished. Lectures uncombined with any questions or practical demands on the learner, are familiar to us in our own Universities, in those of foreign lands, in the metropolis, and in the provinces; as modes of treating of physics and metaphysics, geology and political economy, taste and politics. All such lectures I speak of as speculative teaching, since they are employed in delivering to the hearer the doctrine adopted by the teacher, in a speculative form. Practical teaching, where the scholar, with voice, pen, or pencil, follows the track pointed out to him, and is constantly brought back into it when he deviates, are still more familiar; for by this method we learn everything that, in the most peculiar sense, we learn at all. It is by such a process that we become able to read, to write, to cast accounts, to translate Latin and Greek, to speak French and German, to solve equations, to obtain our own results in the highest branches of mathematics. The teaching of mothers and fathers, of schools, and a great part of the teaching of our English Universities, has hitherto been of this practical kind.

Now we may observe, that when we come to such branches of literature and science as are likely to be selected for the matter of University teaching, some of these branches naturally and almost inevitably require to be taught practically, while others as clearly are more fitted for the speculative mode of teaching. Languages and mathematics are of the former kind; but many of the sciences, and those especially which are wide and varied in their topics, which involve doubtful or newly-established principles, of which the foundations are constantly undergoing changes, can hardly be taught otherwise than speculatively. Such subjects are, for example, geology, political economy, and, as appears to me, metaphysics. In such subjects as these, the student may listen, and may acquire such knowledge as the teacher possesses; but he is not, and cannot be called upon, as a part of the teaching, to do something which depends on the knowledge thus acquired, He may follow with the clearest apprehension, and it may be, with full and well-founded conviction, the views which are presented to him by the teacher; but still he is passive only; he is a spectator, not an actor, in the intellectual scene. He does not interpret and employ a peculiar acquired language, as he does in his classical reading, or his algebraical calculations.

What I have called practical teaching prevails in the Colleges of our English Universities. A large portion of the teaching, in those institutions, has always consisted, as it still does, of exercises, in which the pupil translates his Greek or Latin author, proves his proposition, or solves his equation, in the hearing or under the eye of his tutor; or answers interrogatories, in which he has to produce the knowledge which he has acquired. I believe this to have been the mode of teaching employed among us from the earliest times. In that College, at least, of which I know most, such a method is enjoined in the statutes. Disputations are to be constantly held in the chapel; verses written and affixed in the hall; and the lecturers are to employ half an hour in expounding their author, but a whole hour in examining their class.[2] But besides these practical lectures, we have always had lectures of the speculative kind, delivered by the University professors. Such lectures on history, morals, political economy, law, medicine, anatomy, geology, botany, mineralogy, chemistry, the mechanical sciences, and other subjects, have constantly been going on in our Universities; and have, especially of late years, often excited very great attention. We may, therefore, distinguish our practical and speculative teaching, as *college lectures* and *professorial lectures*—and such a distinction corresponds to the phraseology commonly in use among us.

It may be said, that with professorial lectures examinations may be combined, and that such lectures may thus be converted into practical teaching. Nor do I

2 Lectorum singuli horam in dies singulos quibus legere tenentur in classe suâ examinandâ consumant; dimidiatam vero in authore interpretando. *Stat. Trin. Coll. Cant. cap. 9mo, De Lectorum Officio.*

intend to deny that, under certain conditions, which I shall afterwards endeavour to determine, this effect may be produced. But without now entering into this subject, I trust that the main features of the distinction, which I am trying to point out, of the two kinds of teaching, are already sufficiently clear.

Now it must be observed that, though all branches of science and speculation, old and new, fixed and moveable, may be made the subjects of exposition in lectures, practical teaching is applicable only to a limited range of subjects—those, namely, in which principles having clear evidence and stable certainty, form the basis of our knowledge; and in which, consequently, a distinct possession of the fundamental ideas enables a student to proceed to their applications, and to acquire the habit of applying them in every case with ease and rapidity. The idea of space, of number, of the general relations of grammar and the force of language, are necessary and immutable parts of the furniture of the human mind. And mathematics and languages, which are the development and working of these ideas, can be practically taught, for we can appeal to these ideas, and familiarize the mind with a series of vast and varied, yet certain consequences, to which they lead. But when we come to the wider physical sciences, we can only present the facts as a matter of observation, and the speculation as dependent on the facts. Here there is no room for acquiring habits of interpretation which can be tested by the teacher. And in sciences which are not physical, as morals or metaphysics, the philosophy of history, or of taste, the instruction is still more inevitably of the speculative kind. The teacher must be content to tell, and the learner to receive, what has been thought, or ought to be thought, on these subjects. He does not, by learning them, acquire a new faculty, which he must practically exercise. Such subjects as I have just described, may, perhaps, without impropriety, be distinguished by the collective title of "philosophy;" and if this be allowed, it will, I think, appear, that *philosophy* is only fitted for speculative, as *mathematical and classical* studies are for practical, teaching. In saying this, I do not at all profess to know, whether I am employing the term "philosophy," in the sense attached to it by other persons, who may have written on the subject; but it may, I think, designate appropriately a large class of studies, all of which admit of the same mode of communication to the student.

In such studies, moreover, even if examinations be added to lectures, they can hardly constitute a practical teaching; for in such instances, the knowledge which lectures convey, is either merely retained in the memory, or is employed as material for further speculation by the student, and is not assimilated and convened into a practical habit of intellectual action. Examinations, therefore, in these cases, may test the goodness of the memory, and the clearness of the apprehension or general faculties; and we may also conceive examinations of a higher kind, that call out the powers of original thought, and detect the activity of talent and genius. But the trial of mere memory and clear headedness is not practical teaching, in the same sense as the acquisition of a power of interpretation or calculation; and the higher kind of examination which we have mentioned, presupposes that practical teaching of which we here speak, and is not to be confounded with it. And thus, even with the addition of examinations on subjects of general philosophy, there will still remain, between those studies and the mathematical and classical pursuits of the English Universities, that difference which I describe by calling the former speculative teaching.

Thus the distinction of speculative and practical instruction, which at first sight appears to be a difference of the manner of teaching, is found, on examination, to imply a difference of the subjects taught. When we have determined that we will teach practically, we have decided that we must lecture, not on philosophy, not on metaphysics or speculative morals, or political economy, but on subjects of a different kind—on the works of Greek and Latin authors; the properties of space and number—the laws of motion and force.

Of course, I mean only, that *so far* as we teach practically, we must select such subjects. Nothing prevents us, and as I have said, we have not been prevented, from giving, in addition to our college courses, professorial lectures on all the other subjects which I have mentioned. But it is not on that account the less important to my purpose, to keep the consideration of the two kinds of study distinct. It is obvious also, that, in many cases, the same subject admits of being dealt with in both ways. We may not only ascertain that our pupils can translate Sophocles, but we may present to them the widest speculative views at which critics have arrived, respecting the history and structure of the Greek language, or the Greek drama. We may enter into discussions respecting the metaphysical grounds of the axioms of geometry, the 'processes of algebra, the laws of motion. Such speculations and discussions are of the highest interest and value; but it is easy to see that they are something in addition to the teaching of Greek and mathematics. They add immensely to the value of the practical acquisition of language and mathematical habits, but they presuppose the acquisition; and when these philosophical views are substituted for the practical instruction, they are altogether empty and valueless as means of education.

But I do not here insist upon this point. In the present section, my object was to distinguish the two systems, before I compared them. Trusting that the distinction is now sufficiently clear, I proceed to the comparison. And this I shall consider with reference to such points as these: the effect on the intellectual and on the moral character of those who are educated, and on the general progress of national culture and civilisation.

Section 2: Of the effect of practical teaching on the intellectual habits

The advantages which belong to the study of mathematics, as an intellectual discipline, have been often stated by various persons. I may repeat language which I have already used—"In mathematics, the student is rendered familiar with the most perfect examples of strict inference; compelled habitually to fix his attention on those conditions on which the cogency of the demonstration depends; and, in the mistaken or imperfect attempts at demonstration made by himself or others, he is presented with examples of the most natural fallacies, which he sees exposed and corrected." My Edinburgh reviewer[3] expressed a wish, that these latter "novel assertions had been explained and exemplified;" and obviously, was really at a loss to understand them, although they refer to the daily occurrences of the lecture-room. This is a curious proof how entirely practical teaching is lost sight of, amid the speculations of his school. I may observe, too, as I have done elsewhere,[4] that reasoning, as a practical habit, is taught with peculiar advantage by mathematics, because we are, in that study, concerned with long chains of reasoning, in which each link hangs from all the preceding. "The language contains a constant succession of short and rapid references to what has been proved already; and it is justly assumed, that each of these brief movements helps the reasoner forwards in a course of infallible certainty and security. Each of these hasty glances must possess the clearness of intuitive evidence, and the certainty of mature reflection: and yet must leave the reasoner's mind entirely free to turn instantly to the next point of his progress. The faculty of performing they are learnt, among professional men and practical applications. If they are wished for as information, they stand on the same ground as the higher physical sciences, of which we have spoken above, so far as the arguments there employed are applicable to them. But this "practical knowledge" can never stand in the place of a really liberal education, nor in the smallest degree supersede the necessity of the studies we have pointed out, if such an education be our object.

* * *

Section 7: On the moral effect of practical and speculative teaching

Besides the communication to the student of the matter taught, there are certain collateral effects of the two kinds of' teaching, which are well worthy of notice. I will speak briefly of a few of these.

---

3 Review of Thoughts on the Study of Mathematics, p. 127.

4 Mechanical Euclid, with Remarks on Mathematical Reasoning, p. 14.4.

Mathematical doctrines are fixed and permanent; no new system of geometry can supersede the old. The old truths will always be true, and always essential. Not only so, but even the old books remain in use. Euclid has never been superseded, and never will be so without great detriment to education. And if Archimedes had written a treatise on Mechanics, in extent and form similar to that of Euclid on Geometry, such a work would probably have been one of our best instruments of education at the present day.

In *philosophical* doctrines, on the contrary, a constant change is going on. The commentator supersedes the original author, or at least becomes equally important: the systematiser is preferred to him who first threw out the same thoughts in a less regular form. Or else a revolution takes place; the old system is refuted; a new one is erected, to last its little hour, and wait its certain doom, like its predecessor. There is nothing old, nothing stable, nothing certain, in this kind of study. Change is constantly taking place; change is constantly looked for. Novelty is essential, in order to command attention or approbation. The car rolls on; old objects glide back; the point of view changes. The student knows, or at least cannot but suspect, that his teacher and his teacher's creed are but for a day; and that what is demonstrated to be true, will be found hereafter to be a truth so imperfect, that it is best put out of sight.

Now I conceive it cannot be doubted that the mind of a young man employed mainly in attending to teachers of this latter kind, must fail to acquire any steady and unhesitating conviction of the immutable, and fixed nature of truth, such as the study of mathematics gives. This constant change in the system of received doctrines must unsettle and enfeeble his apprehension of all truths. He has no time, he has no encouragement, to take up the doctrines that are placed before him, and to study them till he is firmly possessed of them, secure that their certainty and value can never alter. He lives among chances and has not the heart to labour patiently for treasures that may be ravished from him by the next revolution. The state of Germany, for instance, has of late years been as unfavourable to the intellectual welfare of its students, as the condition of the most unstable government of the East is, to the material prosperity of its subjects. A great philosophical conquest is made by Kant, and a universal empire is supposed to be on the point of being established. But Fichte, who began with being a follower of Kant, ends by deposing him. Schelling carries away the allegiance of Germany from Fichte; and then Hegel becomes more powerful than any of his predecessors; and a younger Fichte raises the standard against all these rulers. And thus, with dire shedding of ink, revolution after revolution succeeds.

Now amid all this change and fear of change, how can any man eat tranquilly of the fruit of his own field, under his own vine and fig-tree? How can he cultivate his own thoughts, and possess in a tranquil and even spirit the knowledge and the habits of mind which he has acquired! He cannot feel or relish old and familiar truths, such as mathematical sciences deal with. He cannot be content with such conclusions as can be obtained by the way of demonstration. He becomes almost inevitably himself a wide and restless speculator; criticising what has already been done in philosophy; attempting to guess what will be the next step; and destitute, not only of those clear ideas, and those habits of exact thought, through which alone any real advances in knowledge can be appropriated by the student, but devoid also of that steady belief in the permanent nature and value of speculative truth, which is an essential virtue of the understanding.

Again; another mode in which this speculative teaching operates unfavourably, as I conceive, upon students, is this—it places them in the position of critics instead of pupils. In mathematical and other practical teaching, the teacher is usually, and almost necessarily, much the superior of his scholar in the knowledge which they cultivate together; and the scholar cannot but feel this, and must consequently be led to entertain a docile and confiding disposition towards his instructor. On the other hand, when a system is proposed which offers its claims to him it claims to him, and asks his assent, which he may give or refuse, he feels himself placed in the situation of an equal and a judge, with respect to his professor. And if, as is very likely to be the case with active-minded young speculators, he goes through several phases of philosophical opinion, and gives his allegiance to a succession of teachers, he can hardly fall to look upon them with a self-complacent levity, which involves little of respect. He will probably think of his masters much as the poet speaks of the objects of his transient admiration whom he chronicles.

The gentle Henrietta then,
And a third Mary next did reign,
And Joan, and Jane, and Andria;
And then a pretty Thomasine,
And then another Katharine,
And then a long *et cetera*.

Now this want of docility, confidence, and respect, when it prevails in the student towards his teacher, cannot, I think, be looked upon otherwise than as a highly prejudicial feeling, and one which must destroy much of the value and usefulness of the education thus communicated.

The difference of the subjects which are recommended by different persons as suitable for University teaching, does in fact depend upon an entire difference in the views and temper of the authors of the recommendations. In the teaching of Universities, a *spirit* of respect, or a spirit of *criticism*, may be appealed to.

According to the first system, we must select subjects which consist of undoubted truths, and works of unquestioned excellence, and must require the student to familiarise himself with these. Such subjects are mathematical studies, and the best classical authors. According to the other system, we take subjects in which we endeavour to .draw the student's attention by our mode of treating them, and to carry his conviction with us by our arguments. In this system, we invite him to inquire for himself; to accept or reject according to his best judgment; to examine all doctrines boldly and thoroughly. This *critical* system it is which rejoices to have *philosophy* for its subject, and has shown alike its vigour and its tendency by the rapid succession of prevalent systems.

I do not at all hesitate to say, that the *respectful* system appears to me the proper line of education. I conceive that the student ought to have, placed before him, something which is of a stable and permanent kind; in which it is a good mental exercise to struggle with the apparent objections, because it is certain that by effort and practice they may be overcome:—and in which it has been ascertained that admiration is not the result of novelty, or of some transient bearing upon the feelings of the age. The *critical* system seems to me to be properly addressed, not to students who are undergoing education, but to philosophers who have already been completely educated. Nor can I believe, that to put young men in such a position, at a period of their lives when they ought to be quietly forming their minds for future action, can have any other result than to fill them with a shallow conceit of their own importance; to accustom them to deliver superficial and hasty judgments; and to lead them to take up new systems, with no due appreciation of the knowledge, thought, and gravity of mind, which are requisite for such a purpose. If this course educates a man for anything, it educates him to be a judge of philosophical systems—an office which few Englishmen will ever have to fill.

I believe that this opinion of the effect of the two, modes of university education has been confirmed by the actual result. The practical education of the English universities has produced men fitted for practical life. I need not dwell upon this. I have already noticed how well the training of the college appears to prepare men to become good lawyers. I will add, that I conceive our physicians to be the first in the world, and that I ascribe their excellence mainly to the practical course of general culture which they receive in the Universities; which does what no merely professional education can do; and of which the effects are seen, when the professional employments bring into play the intellectual habits. Our clergy derive inestimable advantages from the cast of their university education; and if clerical education among us be capable of improvement, this certainly will not be brought about by the substitution of the philosophy of Schelling and Hegel for the mathematics of Euclid and Newton. That our Universities educate men to be legislators, statesmen, and magistrates of some practical power and skill, no one can doubt, except he who thinks that this little island has, for the last three hundred years, run an unprosperous course, and held an undistinguished place in Europe. For-the fortunes of nations are determined, under Providence, by their practical leaders, and men are formed by their education.

In Germany and France, we are told that there prevails among the young men of the Universities a vehement and general hostility to the existing institutions of their country. I know not how truly this is said; but I conceive that such a consequence may, naturally flow from an education which invokes the critical spirit, and invites it to employ itself on the comparison between the realities of society and the dreams of system-makers.

I shall not here prosecute this subject further, since my object is to hasten onto some principles which apply more intimately to that process of instruction which has hitherto existed in the English Universities. But I hope I have made it appear that, distinguishing the two systems of education as I have done, we may, with nearly equal propriety, treat of them as *practical* and *speculative* teaching; or on the one hand *mathematics* combined with *classics*, and on the other *philosophy*; or *college* lectures, and *professorial* lectures—and may look upon them as exemplifying a *respectful* and a *critical* spirit. And I hope I have satisfied the reader that (allowing fully the value and use of philosophy and of professorial lectures in their due place, of which I may afterwards speak) we could not abandon the practical teaching, the mathematical and classical studies, and the College lectures of our Universities, without great loss to the intellectual training of our youth, without destroying highly beneficial feelings which exist between them and their teachers, and without putting in serious and extensive jeopardy the interests of the civilisation of England and of the world.

CHAPTER TWELVE

Knowledge Its Own End

From *The Idea of the University* (1852)

JOHN HENRY NEWMAN

This selection is taken from Part 1: University Teaching: Discourses, 2nd Edition of *The Idea of a University*, by John Henry Newman, 2009. This is The Integral Unabridged text, published for UCD International Centre for Newman Studies, by Ashfield Press, Dublin, Republic of Ireland. Text set in Plantin by Ashfield Press, as a simile of Longman's ninth edition of 1889.

Editors' Note

Arguably, *The Idea of a University* by J. H. Newman is the most famous book on the topic ever written. While, in the twenty-first century, homage is often paid in equal parts to both Newman and to W von Humboldt, it is Newman's book that inspires in the modern age, a phenomenon that owes much to the lucidity and humanity of its prose.

John Henry Newman was both a theologian and an educationalist. His stature in the first guise ultimately led to his becoming a Cardinal—having converted to Rome from the Anglican tradition—and, following his death, to sainthood. And yet, on account especially of *The Idea of a University*, it is probably for his educational ideas and, thereby, as an educationalist, that he is most remembered. *The Idea of a University* is not, in fact, a unitary book but a collection of 'discourses', lectures and essays, that Newman worked up mainly in 1852 primarily on the occasion of his being appointed Rector of a new Catholic University in Dublin, Ireland. Together, they provide what has often been described as the foremost account of the liberal idea of the university.

'Liberal' was a term that runs through the discourses and was, therefore, a term that Newman used unashamedly. It is important, though, that it be understood that, by the term 'liberal', Newman had in mind not the humanities or the 'liberal arts' or, indeed, any content or subject matter as such. What Newman had in mind was an educational orientation, an educational spirit, indeed. It was an orientation marked out by other favoured terms and ideas such that, in his conception of the university, knowledge 'was its own end', that it should lead to a 'philosophical outlook', that it should be open to all forms of knowledge (which, after all, 'forms one whole' and so constitutes 'universal knowledge') and that it should aid an 'ascent' of the mind. Newman was not against work or instrumental activities but they should not provide the raison d'être of a university education. Far from such an enlargement of mind not being useful, it was a 'good' that was 'always useful'. One may be forgiven for wondering whether these ideas—of an enlarging of the mind, of a sense of the unity of knowledge, of knowledge as a good in itself—do not have some merit, *suitably reinterpreted*, in the twenty-first century.

RB

*****

A university may be considered with reference either to its Students or to its Studies; and the principle, that all Knowledge is a whole and the separate Sciences parts of one, which I have hitherto been using in behalf of its studies, is equally important when we direct our attention to its students. Now then I turn to the students, and shall consider the education which, by virtue of this principle, a University will give them; and thus I shall be introduced, Gentlemen, to the second question, which I proposed to discuss, viz, whether and in what sense its teaching, viewed relatively to the taught, carries the attribute of Utility along with it.

1

I have said that all branches of knowledge are connected together, because the subject-matter of knowledge is intimately united in itself, as being the acts and the work of the Creator. Hence it is that the Sciences, into which our knowledge may be said to be cast, have multiplied bearings one on another, and an internal sympathy, and admit, or rather demand, comparison and adjustment. They complete, correct, balance each other. This consideration, if well-founded, must be taken into account, not only as regards the attainment of truth, which is their common end, but as regards the influence which they exercise upon those whose education consists in the study of them. I have said already, that to give undue prominence to one is to be unjust to another; to neglect or supersede these is to divert those from their proper object. It is to unsettle the boundary lines between science and science, to disturb their action to destroy the harmony which binds them together. Such a proceeding will have a corresponding effect when introduced into a place of education. There is no science but tells a different tale, when viewed as a portion of a whole, from what it is likely to suggest when taken by itself, without the safeguard, as I may call it, of others.

Let me make use of an illustration. In the combination of colours, very different effects are produced by a difference in their selection and juxtaposition; red, green, and white, change their shades, according to the contrast to which they are submitted. And, in like manner, the drift and meaning of a branch of knowledge varies with the company in which it is introduced to the student. If his reading is confined simply to one subject, however such division of labour may favour the advancement of a particular pursuit, a point into which I do not here enter, certainly it has a tendency to contract his mind. If it is incorporated with others, it depends on those others as to the kind of Influence which it exerts upon him. Thus the Classics, which in England are the means of refining the taste, have in France subserved the spread of revolutionary and deistical doctrines. In Metaphysics, again, Butler's Analogy of Religion, which has had so much to do with the conversion to the Catholic faith of members of the University of Oxford, appeared to Pitt and others who had received a different training, to operate only in the direction of infidelity. And so again, Watson, Bishop of Llandaff, as I think he tells us in the narrative of his life, felt the science of Mathematics to indispose the mind to religious belief, while others see in its investigations the best parallel, and thereby defence, of the Christian Mysteries. In like manner, I suppose, Arcesilas would not have handled logic as Aristotle, nor Aristotle have criticized poets as Plato; yet reasoning and poetry are subject to scientific rules.

It is a great point then to enlarge the range of studies which a University professes, even for the sake of the students; and, though they cannot pursue every subject which is open to them, they will be the gainers by living among those and under those who represent the whole circle. This I conceive to be the advantage of a seat of universal learning, considered as a place of education. An assemblage of learned men, zealous for their own sciences, and rivals of each other, are brought, by familiar intercourse and for the sake of intellectual peace, to adjust together the claims and relations of their respective subjects of investigation. They learn to respect, to consult, to aid each other. Thus is created a pure and clear atmosphere of thought, which the student also breathes, though in his own case he only pursues a few sciences out of the multitude. He profits by an intellectual tradition, which is independent of particular teachers, which guides him in his choice of subjects, and duly interprets for him those which he chooses. He apprehends the great outlines of knowledge, the principles on which it rests, the scale of its parts, its lights and its shades, its great points and its little, as he otherwise cannot apprehend them. Hence it is that his education is called "Liberal." A habit of mind is formed which lasts through life, of which the attributes are, freedom, equitableness, calmness, moderation, and wisdom; or what in a former Discourse I have ventured to call a philosophical habit. This then I would assign as the special fruit of the education furnished at a University, as contrasted with other places of teaching or modes of teaching. This is the main purpose of a University in its treatment of its students.

And now the question is asked me, What is the *use* of it? and my answer will constitute the main subject of the Discourses which are to follow.

2

Cautious and practical thinkers, I say, will ask of me, what, after all, is the gain of this Philosophy, of which I make such account, and from which I promise so much. Even supposing it to enable us to exercise the degree of trust exactly due to every science respectively, and to estimate precisely the value of every truth which is anywhere to be found, how are we better for this master view of things, which I have been extolling? Does it not reverse the principle of the division of labour? will practical objects be obtained better or worse by its cultivation? to what then does it lead? where does it end? what does it do? how does it profit? what does it promise? Particular sciences are respectively the basis of definite arts, which carryon to results tangible and beneficial the truths which are the subjects of the knowledge attained; what is the Art of this science of sciences? what is the fruit of such a Philosophy? what are we proposing to effect, what inducements do we hold out to the Catholic community, when we set about the enterprise of founding a University?

I am asked what is the end of University Education, and of the Liberal or Philosophical Knowledge which I conceive it to impart: I answer, that what I have already said has been sufficient to show that it has a very tangible real and sufficient end, though the end cannot be divided from that knowledge itself. Knowledge is capable of being its own end. Such is the constitution of the human mind that any kind of knowledge, if it be really such, is its own reward. And if this is true of all knowledge, it is true also of that special Philosophy, which I have made to consist in a comprehensive view of truth in all its branches, of the relations of science to science, of their mutual bearings, and their respective values. What the worth of such an acquirement is, compared with other objects which we seek,—wealth or power or honour or the conveniences and comforts of life, I do not profess here to discuss; but I would maintain, and mean to show, that it is an object, in its own nature so really and undeniably good, as to be the compensation of a great deal of thought in the compassing, and a great deal of trouble in the attaining.

Now, when I say that Knowledge is, not merely a means to something beyond it, or the preliminary of certain arts into which it naturally resolves, but an end sufficient to rest in and to pursue for its own sake, surely I am uttering no paradox, for I am stating what is both intelligible in itself, and has ever been the common judgment of philosophers and the ordinary feeling of mankind. I am saying what at least the public opinion of this day ought to be slow to deny, considering how much we have heard of late years, in opposition to Religion, of entertaining, curious, and various knowledge. I am but saying what whole volumes have been written to illustrate, viz., by a "selection from the records of Philosophy, Literature, and Art, in all ages and countries, of a body of examples, to show how the most unpropitious circumstances have been unable to conquer an ardent desire for the acquisition of knowledge."[1] That further advantages accrue to us and redound to others by its possession, over and above what it is in itself, I am very far indeed from denying; but, independent of these, we are satisfying a direct need of our nature in its very acquisition; and, whereas our nature, unlike that of the inferior creation, does not at once reach its perfection but depends, in order to it, on a number of external aids and appliances, Knowledge, as one of the principal of these, is valuable for what its very presence in us does for us after the manner of a habit, even though it be turned to no further account, nor sub serve any direct end.

3

Hence it is that Cicero, in enumerating the various heads of mental excellence, lays down the pursuit of Knowledge for its own sake, as the first of them. "This pertains most of all to human nature," he says, "for we are all of us drawn to the pursuit of Knowledge; in which to excel we consider excellent, here as to mistake, to err, to be ignorant, to be deceived, is both an evil and a disgrace."[2] And

---

1 Pursuit of Knowledge under Difficulties. Introd.

2 Cicero Offic. init.

he considers Knowledge the very first object to which we are attracted, after the supply of our physical wants. After the calls and duties of our animal existence, as they may be termed, as regards ourselves, our family, and our neighbours, follows, he tells us, "the search after truth. Accordingly, as soon as we escape from the pressure of necessary cares, forthwith we desire to see, to hear, and to learn; and consider the knowledge of what is hidden or is wonderful a condition of our happiness."

This passage, though it is but one of many similar passages in a multitude of authors, I take for the very reason that it is so familiarly known to us; and I wish to observe, Gentlemen, how distinctly it separates the pursuit of Knowledge from those ulterior objects to which certainly it can be made to conduce, and which I suppose solely contemplated by the persons who would ask of me the use of a University or Liberal Education. So far from dreaming of the cultivation of Knowledge directly and mainly in order to our physical comfort and enjoyment, for the sake of life and person, of health, of the conjugal and family union, of the social tie and civil security, the great Orator implies, that it is only after our physical and political needs are supplied and when we are "free from necessary duties and cares," that we are in a condition for "desiring to see, to hear, and to learn." Nor does he contemplate in the least degree the reflex or subsequent action of Knowledge, when acquired, upon those material goods which we set out by securing before we seek it; on the contrary, he expressly denies its bearing upon social life altogether, strange as such a procedure is to those who live alter the rise of the Baconian philosophy, and he cautions us against such a cultivation of it as will interfere with our duties to our fellow-creatures. "All these methods," he says, "are engaged in the investigation of truth, by the pursuit of which to be carried off from public occupations is a transgression of duty. For the praise of virtue lies altogether in action; yet intermissions often occur, and then we recur to such pursuits; not to say that the incessant activity of the mind is vigorous enough to carry us on in the pursuit of knowledge, even without any exertion of our own." The idea of benefiting society by means of "the pursuit of science and knowledge" did not enter at all into the motives which h would assign for their cultivation.

This was the ground of the opposition which the elder Cato made to the introduction of Greek Philosophy among his countrymen, when Carneades and his companions, on occasion of their embassy, were charming the Roman youth with their eloquent expositions of it. The fit representative of a practical people, Cato estimated everything by what it produced; whereas the Pursuit of Knowledge promised nothing beyond Knowledge: itself. He despised that refinement or enlargement of mind of which he had no experience.

4

Things, which can bear to be cut off from everything else and yet persist in living must have life in themselves; pursuits, which issue in nothing, and still maintain their ground for ages, which are regarded as admirable, though they have not as yet proved themselves to be useful must have their sufficient end in themselves, whatever it turns out to be. And we are brought to the same conclusion by considering the force of the epithet, by which the knowledge under consideration is popularly designated. It is common to speak of "*liberal* knowledge," of the "*liberal* arts and studies," and of a "*liberal* education," as the especial characteristic or property of a University and of a gentleman; what is really meant by the word? Now, first, in its grammatical sense it is opposed to *servile*; and by "servile work" is understood as our catechisms inform us, bodily labour, mechanical employment, and the like, in which the mind has little or no part. Parallel to such servile works are those arts, if they deserve the name, of which the poet speaks,[3] which owe their origin and their method to hazard, not to skill; as, for instance, the practice and operations of an empiric. As far as this contrast may be considered as a guide into the meaning of the word, liberal education and liberal pursuits are exercises of mind, of reason, of reflection.

But we want something more for its explanation, for there are bodily exercises which are liberal, and mental exercises which are not so. For instance, in ancient times the practitioners in medicine were commonly slaves; yet it was an art as intellectual in its nature, in spite of the pretence, fraud, and quackery with which it might then, as now, be debased, as it was heavenly in its aim. And so in like manner, we contrast a liberal education with a commercial education or a professional; yet no one can deny that commerce and the professions afford scope for the highest and most diversified powers of mind. There is then a great variety of intellectual exercises, which are not technically called "liberal;" on the other hand, I say, there are exercises of the body which do receive that appellation. Such, for instance, was the palæstra, in ancient times; such the Olympic games, in which strength and dexterity of body as well as of mind gained the prize. In Xenophon we read of the young Persian nobility being taught to ride on horseback and to speak the truth; both being among the accomplishments of a gentleman. War, too, however rough a profession, has ever been accounted liberal, unless in cases when it becomes heroic, which would introduce us to another subject.

Now comparing these instances together, we shall have no difficulty in determining the principle of this apparent variation in the application of the term which I am examining. Manly games, or games of skill, or military prowess,

---

3 Τέχνη τύχην εστερξε και τύχη τέχνην. *Vid.* Arist. Nic. Ethic. vi.

though bodily, are, it seems, accounted liberal; on the other hand, what is merely professional, though highly intellectual, nay, though liberal in comparison of trade and manual labour, is not simply called liberal, and mercantile occupations are not liberal at all. Why this distinction? because that alone is liberal knowledge, which stands on its own pretensions, which is independent of sequel, expects no complement, refuses to be *informed* (as it is called) by any end, or absorbed into any art, in order duly to present itself to our contemplation. The most ordinary pursuits have this specific character, if they are self-sufficient and complete; the highest lose it, when they minister to something beyond them. It is absurd to balance, in point of worth and importance, a treatise on reducing fractures with a game of cricket or a fox-chase; yet of the two the bodily exercise has that quality which we call "liberal," and the intellectual has it not. And so of the learned professions altogether, considered merely ~s professions; although one of them be the most popularly beneficial, and another the most politically important, and the third the most intimately divine of all human pursuits, yet he very greatness of their end, the health of the body, or of the commonwealth, or of the soul, diminishes, not increases, their claim to the appellation "liberal," and that still more, if they are cut down to the strict exigencies of that end. If, for instance, Theology, instead of being cultivated as a contemplation, be limited to the purposes of the pulpit or be represented by the catechism, it loses,—not its usefulness, not its divine character, not its meritoriousness (rather it gains a claim upon these tides by such charitable condescension),—but it does lose the particular attribute which I am illustrating; just as a face worn by tears and fasting loses its beauty, or labourer's hand loses its delicateness;—for Theology exercised is not simple knowledge, but rather is art or a business making use of Theology. And thus it appears that even what is supernatural need not be liberal, nor need a hero be a gentleman, for the plain reason that one idea is not another idea. And in like manner the Baconian Philosophy, by using its physical sciences in the service of man, does thereby transfer them from the order of Liberal Pursuits to, I do not say the inferior but the distinct class of the Useful. And, to take a different instance, hence again, as is evident, whenever personal gain is the motive, still more a distinctive effect has it upon the character of a given pursuit; thus racing, which was a liberal exercise in Greece, forfeits its rank in times like these, so far as it is made the occasion of gambling.

All that I have been now saying is summed up in a few characteristic words of the great Philosopher. "Of possessions," he says "those rather are useful, which bear fruit; those *liberal, which tend to enjoyment*. By fruitful, I mean, which yield revenue; by enjoyment, where *nothing accrues of consequence beyond the using*."[4]

---

4 Aristot. Rhet. i. S.

5

Do not suppose, that in thus appealing to the ancients, I am throwing back the world two thousand years, and fettering Philosophy with the reasonings of paganism. While the world lasts, will Aristotle's doctrine on these matters last, for he is the oracle of nature and of truth. While we are men, we cannot help, to a great extent, being Aristotelians, for the great Master does but analyze the thoughts, feelings, views, and opinions of humankind. He has told us the meaning of our own words and Ideas, before we were born. In many subject-matters, to think correctly, is to think like Aristotle; and we are his disciples whether we will or no, though we may not know it. Now, as to the particular instance before us, the word "liberal" as applied to Knowledge and Education, expresses a specific idea, which ever has been, and ever will be, while the nature of man is the same, just as the idea of the Beautiful is specific, or of the Sublime, or of the Ridiculous, or of the Sordid. It is in the world now, it was in the world then; and, as in the case of the dogmas of faith, it is illustrated by a continuous historical tradition, and never was out of the world, from the time it came into it. There have indeed been differences of opinion from time to time, as to what pursuits and what arts came under that idea, but such differences are but an additional evidence of its reality. That idea must have a substance in it, which has maintained its ground amid these conflicts and changes, which has ever served as a standard to measure things withal, which has passed from mind to mind unchanged, when there was so much to colour, so much to influence any notion or thought whatever, which was not founded in our very nature. Were it a mere generalization, it would have varied with the subjects from which it was generalized; but though its subjects vary with the age, it varies not itself. The palæstra may seem a liberal exercise to Lycurgus, and illiberal to Seneca; coach driving and prize-fighting may be recognized in Elis, and be condemned in England; music may be despicable in the eyes of certain moderns, and be in the highest place with Aristotle and Plato,—(and the case is the same in the particular application of the idea of Beauty, or of Goodness, or of Moral Virtue, there is a difference of tastes, a difference of judgments)—still these variations imply, instead of discrediting, the archetypal idea, which is but a previous hypothesis or condition, by means of which issue is joined between contending opinions, and without which there would be nothing to dispute about.

I consider, then, that I am chargeable with no paradox, when I speak of a Knowledge which is its own end, when I call it liberal knowledge, or a gentleman's knowledge, when I educate for it, and make it the scope of a University. And still less am I incurring such a charge, when I make this acquisition consist, not in Knowledge in a vague and ordinary sense, but in that Knowledge which I have especially called Philosophy or, in an extended sense of the word, Science; for whatever claims Knowledge has to be considered as a good, these it has in a higher degree when it is viewed not vaguely, not popularly, but precisely and transcendently as Philosophy. Knowledge, I say, is then especially liberal, or sufficient for itself, apart from every external and ulterior object, when and so far as it is philosophical, and this I proceed to show.

6

Now bear with me, Gentlemen, if what I am about to say, has at first sight a fanciful appearance. Philosophy, then, or Science, is related to Knowledge in this way:—knowledge is called by the name of Science or Philosophy, when it is acted upon, informed, or if I may use a strong, figure, impregnated by Reason. Reason is the principle of that intrinsic fecundity of Knowledge, which to those who possess it, is its especial value, and which dispenses with the necessity of their looking abroad for any end to rest upon external to itself. Knowledge, indeed, when thus exalted into a scientific form, is also power; not only is it excellent in itself, but whatever such excellence may be, it is something more, it has a result beyond itself. Doubtless; but that is a further consideration, with which I am not concerned. I only say that, prior to its being a power, it is a good; that it is, not only an instrument, but an end. I know well it may resolve itself into an art, and terminate in a mechanical process, and in tangible fruit; but it also may fall back upon that Reason which informs it, and resolve itself into Philosophy. In one case it is called Useful Knowledge, in the other Liberal. The same person may cultivate it in both ways at once; but this again is a matter foreign to my subject; here I do but say that there are two ways of using Knowledge, and in matter of fact those who use it in one way are not likely to use it in the other, or at least in a very limited measure. You see, then, here are two methods of Education; the end of the one is to be philosophical, of the other to be mechanical; the one rises towards general ideas, the other is exhausted upon what is particular and external. Let me not be thought to deny the necessity, or to decry the benefit, of such attention to what is particular and practical, as belongs to the useful or mechanical arts; life could not go on without them; we owe our daily welfare to them; their exercise is the duty of the many, and we owe to the many a debt of gratitude for fulfilling that duty. I only say that Knowledge, in proportion as it tends more and more to be particular, ceases to be knowledge. It is a question whether Knowledge can in any proper sense be predicated of the brute creation; without pretending to metaphysical exactness of phraseology, which would be unsuitable to an occasion like this I say, it seems to me improper to call that passive sensation, or perception of things, which brutes seem to possess by the name of Knowledge. When I speak of Knowledge, I mean something intellectual, something which grasps what it perceives through the senses; something which takes a view of things; which sees more than the senses convey; which reasons upon what it sees and while it sees; which invests it with an Idea. It expresses itself, not in a mere enunciation, but by an enthymeme: it is of the nature of science from the first, and in this consists its dignity. The principle of real dignity in Knowledge, its worth, its desirableness, considered irrespectively of its results, is this gem within it of a scientific or a philosophical process. This is how it comes to be an end in itself; this is why it admits of being called Liberal. Not to know the relative disposition of things is the state of slaves or children; to have mapped out the Universe is the boast, or at least the ambition, of Philosophy.

Moreover, such knowledge is not a mere extrinsic or accidental advantage, which is ours today and another's tomorrow, which may be got up from a book, and easily forgotten again, which we can command or communicate at our pleasure, which we can borrow for the occasion, carry about in our hand, and take into the market; it is an acquired illumination, it is a habit, a personal possession, and an inward endowment. And this is the reason, why it is more correct, as well as more usual, to speak of a University as a place of education, than of instruction, though, when knowledge is concerned, instruction would at first sight have seemed the more appropriate word. We are instructed, for instance, in manual exercises, in the fine and useful arts, in trades, and in ways of business; for these are methods, which have little or no effect upon the mind itself, are contained in rules committed to memory, to tradition, or to use, and bear upon an end external to themselves. But education is a higher word; it implies an action upon our mental nature, and the formation of a character; it is something individual and permanent, and is common spoken of in connexion with religion and virtue. When, then, we speak of the communication of Knowledge as being Education, we thereby really imply that the Knowledge is a state or condition of mind; and since cultivation of the mind is surely worth seeking for its own sake, we are thus brought once more to the conclusion, which the word "Liberal" and the word "Philosophy" have already suggested, that there is a Knowledge which is desirable, though nothing come of it, as being of itself a treasure, and a sufficient remuneration of years of labour.

7

This, then, is the answer which I am prepared to give to the question with which I opened this Discourse. Before going on to speak of the object of the Church in taking up Philosophy, and the uses to which she puts it, I am prepared to maintain that Philosophy is its own end, and, as I conceive, I have now begun the proof of it. I am prepared to maintain that there is a knowledge worth possessing for what it is, and not merely for what it does; and what minutes remain to me today I shall devote to the removal of some portion of the indistinctness and confusion with which the subject may in some minds be surrounded.

It may be objected then, that, when we profess to seek Knowledge for some end or other beyond itself whatever It be, we speak intelligibly; but that, whatever men may have said, however obstinately the idea may have kept its ground from age to age, still it is simply unmeaning to say that we seek Knowledge for its own sake, and for nothing else; for that it ever leads to something beyond itself, which therefore is its end, and the cause why it is desirable;—moreover, that this end is twofold, either of this world or of the next; that all knowledge is cultivated either for secular objects or for eternal; that if it is directed to secular objects, it is called Useful Knowledge, if to eternal, Religious or Christian Knowledge;—in consequence, that if, as I have allowed, this Liberal Knowledge does not benefit the body or estate, it ought to benefit the soul; but if the fact be really so, that it is neither a physical or a secular good on the one hand, nor a moral good on the other, it cannot be a good at all, and is not worth the trouble which is necessary for its acquisition.

And then I may be reminded that the professors of this Liberal or Philosophical Knowledge have themselves, in every age, recognized this exposition of the matter, and have submitted to the issue in which it terminates; for they have ever been attempting to make men virtuous; or, if not, at least have assumed that refinement of mind was virtue, and that they themselves were the virtuous, portion of mankind. This they have professed on the one hand; and on the other, they have utterly failed in their professions, so as ever to make themselves a proverb among men, and a laughing-stock both to the grave and the dissipated portion of mankind, in consequence of them. Thus they have furnished against themselves both the ground and the means of their own exposure, without any trouble at all to anyone else. In a word, from the time that Athens was the University of the world, what has Philosophy taught men, but to promise without practising, and to aspire without attaining? What has the deep and lofty thought of its disciples ended in but eloquent words? Nay, what has its teaching ever meditated, when it was boldest in its remedies for human ill, beyond charming us to sleep by its lessons, that we might feel nothing at all? like some melodious air, or rather like those strong and transporting perfumes, which at first spread their sweetness over everything they touch, but in a little while do but offend in proportion as they once pleased us. Did Philosophy support Cicero under the disfavour of the fickle populace, or nerve Seneca to oppose an imperial tyrant? It abandoned Brutus, as he sorrowfully confessed, in his greatest need, and it forced Cato, as his panegyrist strangely boasts, into the false position of defying heaven. How few can be counted among its professors, who, like Polemo, were thereby converted from a profligate course, or like Anaxagoras, thought the world well lost in exchange for its possession? The philosopher in Rasselas taught a superhuman doctrine, and then succumbed without an effort to a trial of human affection.

"He discoursed," we are told, "with great energy on the government of the passions. His look was venerable, his action graceful, his pronunciation clear, and his diction elegant. He showed, with great strength of sentiment and variety of illustration, that human nature is degraded and debased, when the lower faculties predominate over the higher. He communicated the various precepts given, from time to time, for the conquest of passion, and displayed the happiness of those who had obtained the important victory, after which man is no longer the slave of fear, nor the fool of hope … He enumerated many examples of heroes immoveable by pain or pleasure, who looked with indifference on those modes or accidents to which the vulgar give the names of good and evil."

Rasselas in a few days found the philosopher in a room half darkened, with his eyes misty, and his face pale. "Sir," said he, "you have come at a time when all human friendship is useless; what I suffer cannot be remedied, what I have lost cannot be supplied. My daughter, my only daughter, from whose tenderness I expected all the comforts of my age, died last night of a fever." "Sir," said the prince, mortality is an event by which a wise man can never be surprised; we know that death is always near, and it should therefore always be expected." "Young man," answered the philosopher, "you speak like one who has never felt the pangs of separation." "Have you then forgot the precept," said Rasselas, "which you so powerfully enforced? … consider that external things are naturally variable, but truth and reason are always the same." "What comfort," said the mourner, "can truth and reason afford me? Of what effect are they now, but to tell me that my daughter will not be restored?"

8

Better, far better, to make no professions, you will say, than to cheat others with what we are not, and to scandalize them with what we are. The sensualist, or the man of the world, at any rate is not the victim of fine words, but pursues a reality and gains it. The Philosophy of Utility, you will say, Gentlemen, has at least done its work; and I grant it,—it aimed low, but it has fulfilled its aim. If that man of great intellect who has been its Prophet in the conduct of life played. false to his own professions, he was not bound by his philosophy to be true to his friend or faithful in his trust: Moral virtue was not the line in which he undertook to instruct men; and though, as the poet calls him, he were the "meanest" of mankind, he was so in what may be called his private capacity and without any prejudice to the theory of induction. He had a right to be so, if he chose for anything that the Idols of the den or the theatre had to say to the contrary. His mission was the increase of physical enjoyment and social comforts;[5] and most wonderfully, most awfully has he fulfilled his conception and his design. Almost day by day have we fresh and fresh shoots, and buds, and blossoms, which are to ripen into fruit, on that magical tree of Knowledge which he planted, and to which none of us perhaps, except the very poor, but owes, if not his present life, at least his daily food, his health, and general well-being. He was the divinely provided minister of temporal benefits to all of us so great, that, whatever I am forced to think of him as a man, I have not the heart, from mere gratitude, to speak of him severely. And, in spite of the tendencies of his philosophy, which are, as we see at this day, to depreciate, or to trample on Theology, he has himself, in his writings, gone out of his way, as if with a prophetic misgiving of those tendencies, to insist on it as the instrument of that beneficent Father,[6] who, when He came on earth in visible form, took on Him first and most prominently the office of assuaging the bodily wounds of human nature. And truly, like old mediciner in the tale, "he say diligently at his work, and hummed, with cheerful countenance, a pious song;" and then in turn "went out singing into the meadows so gaily, that those who had seen him from afar might well have thought it was a youth gathering flowers for his beloved, instead of an old physician gathering healing herbs in the morning dew."[7]

Alas, that men, in the action of life or in their heart of hearts, are not what they seem to be in their moments of excitement, or in their trances or intoxications of genius,—so good, so noble, so serene! Alas, that Bacon too in his own

5 It will be seen that on the whole I agree with Lord Macaulay in his Essay on Bacon's Philosophy. I do not know whether he would agree with me.

6 De Augment. iv. 2, *Vid.* Macaulay's Essay; *Vid.* also "In principia operis ad Deum Patrem, Deum Verbum, Deum Spiritum, preces fundimus humillimas et ardentissimas, ut hurnani generis ærurnnarum memores, et peregrinationis istius vitæ, in quâ dies paucos et malos terimus, *novis suis eleemosynis, per manus nostras*, familiam humanam dotare dignentur. Atque illud insuper supplices rogamus, ne *humana divinis officiant*; neve *ex reseratione viarum sensûs*, et accensione majore luminis naturalis, *aliquid incredulitatis* et noctis, animis nostris erga divina mysteria oboriatur," etc. *Præf.* Instaur. Magn.

7 Fouque's *Unknown Patient.*

way should after all be but the fellow of those heathen philosophers who in their disadvantages had some excuse for their inconsistency, and who surprise us rather in what they did say that in what they did not do! Alas, that he too, like Socrates or Seneca, must be stripped of his holy-day coat, which looks so fair, and should be but a mockery amid his most majestic gravity of phrase; and, for all his vast abilities, should, in the littleness of his own moral being, but typify the intellectual narrowness of his school! However, granting all this, heroism after all was not his philosophy:—I cannot deny he has abundantly achieved what he proposed. His is simply a Method whereby bodily discomforts and temporal wants are to be most effectually removed from the greatest number; and already, before it has shown any signs of exhaustion, the gifts of nature, in their most artificial shapes and luxurious profusion and diversity, from all quarters of the earth, are, it is undeniable, by its means brought even to our doors, and we rejoice in them.

9

Useful Knowledge then, I grant, has done its work; and Liberal Knowledge as certainly has not done its work,—that is, supposing, as the objectors assume, its direct end, like Religious Knowledge, is to make man better; but this I will not for an instant allow, and, unless I allow it, those objectors have said nothing to the purpose. I admit, rather I maintain, what they have been urging, for I consider Knowledge to have its end in itself. For all its friends, or its enemies, may say, I insist upon it, that it is as real a mistake to burden it with virtue or religion as with the mechanical arts. Its direct business is not to steal the soul against temptation or to console it in affliction, any more than to set the loom in motion, or to direct the steam carriage; be it ever so much the means or the condition of both material and moral advancement, still, taken by and in itself, it as little mends our hearts as it improves our temporal circumstances. And if its eulogists claim for it such a power, they commit the very same kind of encroachment on a province not their own as the political economist who should maintain that his science educated him for casuistry or diplomacy. Knowledge is one thing, virtue is another; good sense is not conscience, refinement is not humility, nor is largeness and justness of view faith. Philosophy, however enlightened, however profound, gives no command over the passions, no influential motives, no vivifying principles. Liberal Education makes not the Christian, not the Catholic, but the gentleman. It is well to be a gentlemen, it is well to have a cultivated intellect, a delicate taste, a candid, equitable, dispassionate mind, a noble and courteous bearing in the conduct of life;—these are the connatural qualities of a large knowledge; they are the objects of a University; I am advocating, I shall illustrate and insist upon them; but still, I repeat, they are no guarantee for sanctity or even for conscientiousness, they may attach to the man of the world, to the profligate, to the heartless,—pleasant, alas, and attractive as he shows when decked out in them. Taken by themselves, they do but seem to be what they are not; they look like virtue at a distance, but they are detected by close observers, and on the long run; and hence it is that they are popularly accused of pretence and hypocrisy, not, I repeat, from their own fault, but because their professors and their admirers persist in taking them for what they are not, and are officious in arrogating for them a praise to which they have no claim. Quarry the granite rock with razors, or moor the vessel with a thread of silk; then may you hope with such keen and delicate instruments as human knowledge and human reason to contend against those giants, the passion and the pride of man.

Surely we are not driven to theories of this kind, in order to vindicate the value and dignity of Liberal Knowledge. Surely the real grounds on which its pretensions rest are not so very subtle or abstruse, so very strange or improbable. Surely it is very intelligible to say, and that is what I say here, that Liberal Education, viewed in itself, is simply the cultivation of the intellect, as such, and its object is nothing more or less than intellectual excellence. Everything has its own perfection, be it higher or lower in the scale of things; and the perfection of one is not the perfection of another. Things animate, inanimate, visible, invisible, all are good in their kind, and have a *best* of themselves, which is an object of pursuit. Why do you take such pains with your garden or your park? You see to your walks and turf and shrubberies; to your trees and drives; not as if you meant to make an orchard of the one, or corn or pasture land of the other, but because there is a special beauty in all that is goodly in wood, water, plain, and slope, brought all together by art into one shape, and grouped into one whole, Your cities are beautiful, Your palaces, your public buildings, your territorial mansions, your churches; and their beauty leads to nothing beyond itself, There is a physical beauty and a moral: there is a beauty of person, there is a beauty of our moral being, which is natural virtue; and in like manner there is a beauty, there is a perfection, of the intellect, There is an ideal perfection in these various subject-matters, towards which individual instances are seen to rise, and which are the standards for all instances whatever, The Greek divinities and demigods, as the statuary has moulded them, with their symmetry of figure, and their high forehead and their regular features, are the perfection of physical beauty, The Heroes, of whom history tells, Alexander, or Cæsar, or Scipio, or Saladin, are the representatives of that magnanimity or self-mastery which is the greatness of human nature, Christianity too has its heroes, and in the supernatural order, and we call them Saints, The artist puts before him beauty of feature and form; the poet, beauty of mind; the preacher, the beauty of grace: then intellect too, I repeat, has its beauty, and it has those who aim at it, To open the mind, to correct it, to refine it, to enable it to know, and to digest, master, rule, and use its knowledge, to give it power over its own faculties, application, flexibility, method, critical exactness, sagacity, resource, address, eloquent expression, is an object as intelligible (for here we are inquiring, not what the object of a Liberal Education is worth, nor what use the Church make of it, but what it is in itself), I say, as object as intelligible as the cultivation of virtue, while, at the same time, it is absolutely distinct from it.

10

This indeed is but a temporal object, and a transitory possession; but so are other things in themselves which we make much more of and pursue. The moralist will tell us that man, in all his functions, is but a flower which blossoms and fades, except so far as a higher principle breathes upon him, and makes him and what he is immortal. Body and mind are carried on into an eternal state of being by the gifts of Divine Munificence; but at first they do but fail in a failing world; and if the powers of intellect decay, the powers of the body have decayed before them, and, as an Hospital or an Alms-house, though its end be ephemeral, may be sanctified in the service of religion, so surely may a University, were it nothing more than I have as yet described it. We attain to heaven by using this world well, though it is to pass away; we perfect our nature, not by undoing it, but by adding to it what is more than nature, and directing it towards aims higher than its own.

CHAPTER THIRTEEN

Inaugural Address at the University of St. Andrews, February 1st, 1867 (1867)

JOHN STUART MILL

Inaugural Address at St. Andrews, Given February 1st, 1867, By John Stuart Mill. Published by Longmans, Green, Reader, and Dyer, London, United Kingdom. Published by The Library of Victoria University, Toronto, Retrieved from http://oll.libertyfund.org/titles/255

Editors' Note

Much has been written about the John Stuart Mill as one of the most influential thinkers of the nineteenth century whose theories and works shaped the modern liberal tradition and its institutions including the freedom of the individual against the state. The Inaugural Address was delivered by Mill on being installed as Rector of the University in 1867. His own education at which he excelled learning Greek and Latin at an early age and works in chemistry and experimental physics focused on objective and disinterested analysis which he in part blamed for his crisis and depression beginning in 1826 from which he emerged through the cultivation of the sentiments. As he puts it in his Autobiography: 'I, for the first time, gave its proper place, among the prime necessities of human well-being, to the internal culture of the individual. I ceased to attach almost exclusive importance to the ordering of outward circumstances, and the training of the human being for speculation and for action. I had now learnt by experience that the passive susceptibilities needed to be cultivated as well as the active capacities, and required to be nourished and enriched as well as guided. … The cultivation of the feelings became one of the cardinal points in my ethical and philosophical creed' (p. 147). He agrees with Newman that universities should discharge the function of advanced schools and that assumed opposition between literature and science is absurd but holds that it is beyond the power of the university to educate morally or religiously.

MP

* * * * *

In complying with the custom which prescribes that the person whom you have called by your suffrages to the honorary presidency of your University should embody in an Address a few thoughts on the subjects which most nearly concern a seat of liberal education; let me begin by saying, that this usage appears to me highly commendable. Education, in its larger sense, is one of the most inexhaustible of all topics. Though there is hardly any subject on which so much has been written, by so many of the wisest men, it is as fresh to those who come to it with a fresh mind, a mind not hopelessly filled full with other people's conclusions, as it was to the first explorers of it: and notwithstanding the great mass of excellent things which have been said respecting it, no thoughtful person finds any lack of things both great and small still waiting to be said, or waiting to be developed and followed out to their consequences. Education, moreover, is one of the subjects which most essentially require to be considered by various minds, and from a variety of points of view. For, of all many-sided subjects, it is the one which has the greatest number of sides. Not only does it include whatever we do for ourselves, and whatever is done for us by others, for the express purpose of bringing us somewhat nearer to the perfection of our nature; it does more: in its largest acceptation, it comprehends even the indirect effects produced on character and on the human faculties, by things of which the direct purposes are quite different; by laws, by forms of government, by the industrial arts, by modes of social life; nay even by physical facts not dependent on human will; by climate, soil, and local position. Whatever helps to shape the human being; to make the individual what he is, or hinder him from being what he is not—is part of his education. And a very bad education it often is; requiring all that can be done by cultivated intelligence and will, to counteract its tendencies. To take an obvious instance; the niggardliness of Nature in some places, by engrossing the whole energies of the human being in the mere preservation of life, and her over-bounty in others, affording a sort of brutish subsistence on too easy terms, with hardly any exertion of the human faculties, are both hostile to the spontaneous growth and development of the mind; and it is at those two extremes of the scale that we find human societies in the state of most unmitigated savagery. I shall confine myself, however, to education in the narrower sense; the culture which each generation purposely gives to those who are to be its successors, in order to qualify them for at least keeping up, and if possible for raising, the level of improvement which has been attained. Nearly all here present are daily occupied either in receiving or in giving this sort of education: and the part of it which most concerns you at present is that in which you are yourselves engaged—the stage of education which is the appointed business of a national University.

The proper function of a University in national education is tolerably well understood. At least there is a tolerably general agreement about what a University is not. It is not a place of professional education. Universities are not intended to teach the knowledge required to fit men for some special mode of gaining their livelihood. Their object is not to make skilful lawyers, or physicians, or engineers, but capable and cultivated human beings. It is very right that there should be public facilities for the study of professions. It is well that there should be Schools of Law, and of Medicine, and it would be well if there were schools of engineering, and the industrial arts. The countries which have such institutions are greatly the better for them; and there is something to be said for having them in the same localities, and under the same general superintendence, as the establishments devoted to education properly so called. But these things are no part of what every generation owes to the next, as that on which its civilization and worth will principally depend. They are needed only by a comparatively few, who are under the strongest private inducements to acquire them by their own efforts; and even those few do not require them until after their education, in the ordinary sense, has been completed. Whether those whose specialty they are, will learn them as a branch of intelligence or as a mere trade, and whether, having learnt them, they will make a wise and conscientious use of them or the reverse, depends less on the manner in which they are taught their profession, than upon what sort of minds they bring to it—what kind of intelligence, and of conscience, the general system of education has developed in them. Men are men before they are lawyers, or physicians, or merchants, or manufacturers; and if you make them capable and sensible men, they will make themselves capable and sensible lawyers or physicians. What professional men should carry away with them from a University, is not professional knowledge, but that which should direct the use of their professional knowledge, and bring the light of general culture to illuminate the technicalities of a special pursuit. Men may be competent lawyers without general education, but it depends on general education to make them philosophic lawyers—who demand, and are capable of apprehending, principles, instead of merely cramming their memory with details. And so of all other useful pursuits, mechanical included. Education makes a man a more intelligent shoemaker, if that be his occupation, but not by teaching him how to make shoes; it does so by the mental exercise it gives, and the habits it impresses.

This, then, is what a mathematician would call the higher limit of University education: its province ends where education, ceasing to be general, branches off into departments adapted to the individual's destination in life. The lower limit is more difficult to define. A University is not concerned with elementary instruction: the pupil is supposed to have acquired that before coming here. But where does elementary instruction end, and the higher studies begin? Some have given a very wide extension to the idea of elementary instruction. According to them, it is not the office of a University to give instruction in single branches of knowledge from the commencement. What the pupil should be taught here (they think), is to methodize his knowledge: to look at every separate part of it in its relation to the other parts, and to the whole; combining the partial glimpses which he has obtained of the field of human knowledge at different points, into a general map, if I may so speak, of the entire region; observing how all knowledge is connected, how we ascend to one branch by means of another, how the higher modifies the lower, and the lower helps us to understand the higher; how every existing reality is a compound of many properties, of which each science or distinct mode of study reveals but a small part, but the whole of which must be included to enable us to know it truly as a fact in Nature, and not as a mere abstraction.

This last stage of general education destined to give the pupil a comprehensive and connected view of the things which he has already learnt separately, includes a philosophic study of the Methods of the sciences; the modes in which the human intellect proceeds from the known to the unknown. We must be taught to generalize our conception of the resources which the human mind possesses for the exploration of nature; to understand how man discovers the real facts of the world, and by what tests he can judge whether he has really found them. And doubtless this is the crown and consummation of a liberal education: but before we restrict a University to this highest department of instruction—before we confine it to teaching, not knowledge, but the philosophy of knowledge—we must be assured that the knowledge itself has been acquired elsewhere. Those who take this view of the function of a University are not wrong in thinking that the schools, as distinguished from the universities, ought to be adequate to teaching every branch of general instruction required by youth, so far as it can be studied apart from the rest. But where are such schools to be found? Since science assumed its modern character, nowhere: and in these islands less even than elsewhere. This ancient kingdom, thanks to its great religious reformers, had the inestimable advantage, denied to its southern sister, of excellent parish schools, which gave, really and not in pretence, a considerable amount of valuable literary instruction to the bulk of the population, two centuries earlier than in any other country. But schools of a still higher description have been, even in Scotland, so few and inadequate, that the Universities have had to perform largely the functions which ought to be performed by schools; receiving students at an early age, and undertaking not only the work for which the schools should have prepared them, but much of the preparation itself. Every Scottish University is not a University only, but a High School, to supply the deficiency of other schools. And if the English Universities do not do the same, it is not because the same need does not exist, but because it is disregarded. Youths come to the Scottish Universities ignorant, and are there taught. The majority of those who come to the English Universities come still more ignorant, and ignorant they go away.

In point of fact, therefore, the office of a Scottish University comprises the whole of a liberal education, from the foundations upwards. And the scheme of your Universities has, almost from the beginning, really aimed at including the whole, both in depth and in breadth. You have not, as the English Universities so long did, confined all the stress of your teaching, all your real effort to teach, within the limits of two subjects, the classical languages and mathematics. You did not wait till the last few years to establish a Natural Science and a Moral Science Tripos. Instruction in both those departments was organized long ago: and your teachers of those subjects have not been nominal professors, who did not lecture: some of the greatest names in physical and in moral science have taught in your Universities, and by their teaching contributed to form some of the most distinguished intellects of the last and present centuries. To comment upon the course of education at the Scottish Universities is to pass in review every essential department of general culture. The best use, then, which I am able to make of the present occasion, is to offer a few remarks on each of those departments, considered in its relation to human cultivation at large: adverting to the nature of the claims which each has to a place in liberal education; in what special manner they each conduce to the improvement of the individual mind and the benefit of the race; and how they all conspire to the common end, the strengthening, exalting, purifying, and beautifying of our common nature, and the fitting out of mankind with the necessary mental implements for the work they have to perform through life.

Let me first say a few words on the great controversy of the present day with regard to the higher education, the difference which most broadly divides educational reformers and conservatives; the vexed question between the ancient languages and the modem sciences and arts; whether general education should be classical—let me use a wider expression, and say literary—or scientific. A dispute as endlessly, and often as fruitlessly agitated as that old controversy which it resembles, made memorable by the names of Swift and Sir William Temple in England and Fontenelle in France—the contest for superiority between the ancients and the moderns. This question, whether we should be taught the classics or the sciences, seems to me, I confess, very like a dispute whether painters should cultivate drawing or colouring, or, to use a more homely illustration, whether a tailor should make coats or trousers. I can only reply by the question, why not both? Can anything deserve the name of a good education which does not include literature and science too? If there were no more to be said than that scientific education teaches us to think, and literary education to express our thoughts, do we not require both? And is not any one a poor, maimed, lopsided fragment of humanity who is deficient in either? We are not obliged to ask ourselves whether it is more important to know the languages or the sciences. Short as life is. and shorter still as we make it by the time we waste on things which are neither business, nor meditation, nor pleasure, we are not so badly off that our scholars need be ignorant of the laws and properties of the world they live in, or our scientific men destitute of poetic feeling and artistic cultivation. I am amazed at the limited conception which many educational reformers have formed to themselves of a human being's power of acquisition. The study of science, they truly say, is indispensable: our present education neglects it: there is truth in this too, though it is not all truth: and they think it impossible to find room for the studies which they desire to encourage, but by turning out, at least from general education, those which are now chiefly cultivated. How absurd, they say, that the whole of boyhood should be taken up in acquiring an imperfect know—ledge of two dead languages. Absurd indeed: but is the human mind's capacity to learn, measured by that of Eton and Westminster to teach? I should prefer to see these reformers pointing their attacks against the shameful inefficiency of the schools, public and private, which pretend to teach these two languages and do not. I should like to hear them denounce the wretched methods of teaching, and the criminal idleness and supineness, which waste the entire boyhood of the pupils without really giving to most of them more than a smattering, if even that, of the only kind of knowledge which is even pretended to be cared for. Let us try what conscientious and intelligent teaching can do, before we presume to decide what cannot be done.

Scotland has on the whole, in this respect, been considerably more fortunate than England. Scotch youths have never found it impossible to leave school or the university having learnt somewhat of other things besides Greek and Latin; and why? Because Greek and Latin have been better taught. A beginning of classical instruction has all along been made in the common schools: and the common schools of Scotland, like her Universities, have never been the mere shams that the English Universities were during the last century, and the greater part of the English classical schools still are. The only tolerable Latin grammars for school purposes that I know of, which had been produced in these islands until very lately, were written by Scotchmen. Reason, indeed, is beginning to find its way by gradual infiltration even into English schools, and to maintain a contest, though as yet a very unequal one, against routine. A few practical reformers of school tuition, of whom Arnold was the most eminent, have made a beginning of amendment in many things: but reforms, worthy of the name, are always slow, and reform even of governments and churches is not so slow as that of schools, for there is the great preliminary difficulty of fashioning the instruments: of teaching the teachers. If all the improvements in the mode of teaching languages which are already sanctioned by experience, were adopted into our classical schools, we should soon cease to hear of Latin and Greek as studies which must engross the school years, and render impossible any other acquirements. If a boy learnt Greek and Latin on the same principle on which a mere child learns with such ease and rapidity any modem language, namely, by acquiring some familiarity with the vocabulary by practice and repetition, before being troubled with grammatical rules—those rules being acquired with tenfold greater facility when the cases to which they apply are already familiar to the mind; an average schoolboy, long before the age at which schooling terminates, would be able to read fluently and with intelligent interest any ordinary Latin or Greek author in prose or verse, would have a competent knowledge of the grammatical structure of both languages, and have had time besides for an ample amount of scientific instruction. I might go much further; but I am as unwilling to speak out all that I think practicable in this matter, as George Stephenson was about railways, when he calculated the average speed of a train at ten miles an hour, because if he had estimated it higher, the practical men would have turned a deaf ear to him, as that most unsafe character in their estimation, an enthusiast and a visionary. The results have shewn, in that case, who was the real practical man. What the results would shew in the other case, I will not attempt to anticipate. But I will say confidently, that if the two classical languages were properly taught, there would be no need whatever for ejecting them from the school course, in order to have sufficient time for everything else that need be included therein.

Let me say a few words more on this strangely limited estimate of what it is possible for human beings to learn, resting on a tacit assumption that they are already as efficiently taught as they ever can be. So narrow a conception not only vitiates our idea of education, but actually, if we receive it, darkens our anticipations as to the future progress of mankind. For if the inexorable conditions of human life make it useless for one man to attempt to know more than one thing, what is to become of the human intellect as facts accumulate? In every generation, and now more rapidly than ever, the things which it is necessary that somebody should know are more and more multiplied. Every department of knowledge becomes so loaded with details, that one who endeavours to know it with minute accuracy, must confine himself to a smaller and smaller portion of the whole extent: every science and art must be cut up into subdivisions, until each man's portion, the district which he thoroughly knows, bears about the same ratio to the whole range of useful knowledge that the art of putting on a pin's head does to the field of human industry. Now, if in order to know that little completely, it is necessary to remain wholly ignorant of all the rest, what will soon be the worth of a man, for any human purpose except his own infinitesimal fraction of human wants and requirements? His state will be even worse than that of simple ignorance. Experience proves that there is no one study or pursuit, which, practiced to the exclusion of all others, does not narrow and pervert the mind; breeding in it a class of prejudices special to that pursuit, besides a general prejudice, common to all narrow specialties, against large views, from an incapacity to take in and appreciate the grounds of them. We should have to expect that human nature would be more and more dwarfed, and unfitted for great things, by its very proficiency in small ones. But matters are not so bad with us: there is no ground for so dreary an anticipation. It is not the utmost limit of human acquirement to know only one thing, but to combine a minute knowledge of one or a few things with a general knowledge of many things. By a general knowledge I do not mean a few vague impressions. An eminent man, one of whose writings is part of the course of this University, Archbishop Whately, has well discriminated between a general knowledge and a superficial knowledge. To have a general knowledge of a subject is to know only its leading truths, but to know these not superficially but thoroughly, so as to have a true conception of the subject in its great features; leaving the minor details to those who require them for the purposes of their special pursuit. There is no incompatibility between knowing a wide range of subjects up to this point, and some one subject with the completeness required by those who make it their principal occupation. It is this combination which gives an enlightened public: a body of cultivated intellects, each taught by its attainments in its own province what real knowledge is, and knowing enough of other subjects to be able to discern who are those that know them better. The amount of knowledge is not to be lightly estimated, which qualifies us for judging to whom we may have recourse for more. The elements of the more important studies being widely diffused, those who have reached the higher summits find a public capable of appreciating their superiority, and prepared to follow their lead. It is thus too that minds are formed capable of guiding and improving public opinion on the greater concerns of practical life. Government and civil society are the most complicated of all subjects accessible to the human mind: and he who would deal competently with them as a thinker, and not as a blind follower of a party, requires not only a general knowledge of the leading facts of life, both moral and material, but an understanding exercised and disciplined in the principles and rules of sound thinking, up to a point which neither the experience of life, nor any one science or branch of knowledge, affords. Let us understand, then, that it should be our aim in learning, not merely to know the one thing which is to be our principal occupation, as well as it can be known, but to do this and also to know something of all the great subjects of human interest: taking care to know that something accurately; marking well the dividing line between what we know accurately and what we do not: and remembering that our object should be to obtain a true view of nature and life in their broad outline, and that it is idle to throw away time upon the details of anything which is to form no part of the occupation of our practical energies.

It by no means follows, however, that every useful branch of general, as distinct from professional knowledge, should be included in the curriculum of school or university studies. There are things which are better learnt out of school, or when the school years, and even those usually passed in a Scottish university, are over. I do not agree with those reformers who would give a regular and prominent place in the school or university course to modem languages. This is not because I attach small importance to the knowledge of them. No one can in our age be esteemed a well-instructed person who is not familiar with at least the French language, so as to read French books with ease; and there is great use in cultivating a familiarity with German. But living languages are so much more easily acquired by intercourse with those who use them in daily life; a few months in the country itself, if properly employed, go so much farther than as many years of school lessons; that it is really waste of time for those to whom that easier mode is attainable, to labour at them with no help but that of books and masters: and it will in time be made attainable, through international schools and colleges, to many more than at present. Universities do enough to facilitate the study of modem languages, if they give a mastery over that ancient language which is the foundation of most of them and the possession of which makes it easier to learn four or five of the continental languages than it is to learn one of them without it. Again, it has always seemed to me a great absurdity that history and geography should be taught in schools; except in elementary schools for the children of the labouring classes, whose subsequent access to books is limited. Who ever really learnt history and geography except by private reading? and what an utter failure a system of education must be, if it has not given the pupil a sufficient taste for reading to seek for himself those most attractive and easily intelligible of all kinds of knowledge? Besides, such history and geography as can be taught in schools exercise none of the faculties of the intelligence except the memory. A University is indeed the place where the student should be introduced to the Philosophy of History; where Professors who not merely know the facts but have exercised their minds on them, should initiate him into the causes and explanation, so far as within our reach, of the past life of mankind in its principal features. Historical criticism also—the tests of historical truth—are a subject to which his attention may well be drawn in this stage of his education. But of the mere facts of history, as commonly accepted, what educated youth of any mental activity does not learn as much as is necessary, if he is simply turned loose into an historical library? What he needs on this, and on most other matters of common information, is not that he should be taught it in boyhood, but that abundance of books should be accessible to him.

The only languages, then, and the only literature, to which I would allow a place in the ordinary curriculum, are those of the Greeks and Romans; and to these I would preserve the position in it which they at present occupy. That position is justified, by the great value, in education, of knowing well some other cultivated language and' literature than one's own, and by the peculiar value of those particular languages and literatures.

There is one purely intellectual benefit from a knowledge of languages, which I am specially desirous to dwell on. Those who have seriously reflected on the causes of human error, have been deeply impressed with the tendency of mankind to mistake words for things. Without entering into the metaphysics of the subject, we know how common it is to use words glibly and with apparent propriety, and to accept them confidently when used by others, without ever having had any distinct conception of the things denoted by them. To quote again from Archbishop Whately, it is the habit of mankind to mistake familiarity for accurate knowledge. As we seldom think of asking the meaning of what we see every day, so when our ears are used to the sound of a word or a phrase, we do not suspect that it conveys no clear idea to our minds, and that we should have the utmost difficulty in defining it, or expressing, in any other words, what we think we understand by it. Now it is obvious in what manner this bad habit tends to be corrected by the practice of translating with accuracy from one language to another, and hunting out the meanings expressed in a vocabulary with which we have not grown familiar by early and constant use. I hardly know any greater proof of the extraordinary genius of the Greeks, than that they were able to make such brilliant achievements in abstract thought, knowing, as they generally did, no language but their own. But the Greeks did not escape the effects of this deficiency. Their greatest intellects, those who laid the foundation of philosophy and of all our intellectual culture,

Plato and Aristotle, are continually led away by words; mistaking the accidents of language for real relations in nature, and supposing that things which have the same name in the Greek tongue must be the same in their own essence. There is a well-known saying of Hobbes, the far-reaching significance of which you will more and more appreciate in proportion to the growth of your own intellect: "Words are the counters of wise men, but the money of fools." With the wise man a word stands for the fact which it represents; to the fool it is itself the fact. To carry on Hobbes' metaphor, the counter is far more likely to be taken for merely what it is, by those who are in the habit of using many different kinds of counters. But besides the advantage of possessing another cultivated language, there is a further consideration equally important. Without knowing the language of a people, we never really know their thoughts, their feelings, and their type of character; and unless we do possess this knowledge, of some other people than ourselves, we remain, to the hour of our death, with our intellects only half expanded. Look at a youth who has never been out of his family circle: he never dreams of any other opinions or ways of thinking than those he has been bred up in; or, if he has heard of any such, attributes them to 'some moral defect, or inferiority of nature or education. If his family are Tory, he cannot conceive the possibility of being a Liberal; if Liberal, of being a Tory. What the notions and habits of a single family are to a boy who has had no intercourse beyond it, the notions and habits of his own country are to him who is ignorant of every other. Those notions and habits are to him human nature itself; whatever varies from them is an unaccountable aberration which he cannot mentally realize: the idea that any other ways can be right, or as near an approach to right as some of his own, is inconceivable to him. This does not merely close his eyes to the many things which every country still has to learn from others: it hinders every country from reaching the improvement which it could otherwise attain by itself. We are not likely to correct any of our opinions or mend any of our ways, unless we begin by conceiving that they are capable of amendment: but merely to know that foreigners think differently from ourselves, without understanding why they do so, or what they really do think, does but confirm us in our self-conceit, and connect our national vanity with the preservation of our own peculiarities. Improvement consists in bringing our opinions into nearer agreement with facts; and we shall not be likely to do this while we look at facts only through glasses coloured by those very opinions. But since we cannot divest ourselves of preconceived notions, there is no known means of eliminating their influence but by frequently using the differently coloured glasses of other people: and those of other nations, as the most different, are the best.

But if it is so useful, on this account, to know the language and literature of any other cultivated and civilized people, the most valuable of all to us in this respect are the languages and literature of the ancients. No nations of modem and civilized Europe are so unlike one another, as the Greeks and Romans are unlike all of us; yet without being, as some remote Orientals are, so totally dissimilar, that the labour of a life is required to enable us to understand them. Were this the only gain to be derived from a knowledge of the ancients, it would already place the study of them in a high rank among enlightening and liberalizing pursuits. It is of no use saying that we may know them through modem writings. We may know something of them in that way; which is much, better than knowing nothing. But modem books do not teach us ancient thought; they teach us some modem writer's notion of ancient thought. Modem books do not shew us the Greeks and Romans; they tell us some modem writer's opinions about the Greeks and Romans. Translations are scarcely better. When we want really to know what a person thinks or says, we seek it at first hand from himself. We do not trust to another person's impression of his meaning, given in another person's words; we refer to his own. Much more is it necessary to do so when his words are in one language, and those of his reporter in another. Modem phraseology never conveys the exact meaning of a Greek writer; it cannot do so, except by a diffuse explanatory circumlocution which no translator dares use. We must be able, in a certain degree, to think in Greek, if we would represent to ourselves how a Greek thought: and this not only in the abstruse region of metaphysics, but about the political, religious, and even domestic concerns of life. I will mention a further aspect of this question, which, though I have not the merit of originating it, I do not remember to have seen noticed in any book. There is no part of our knowledge which it is more useful to obtain at first hand—to go to the fountain head for—than our knowledge of history. Yet this, in most cases, we hardly ever do. Our conception of the past is not drawn from its own records, but from books written about it, containing not the facts, but a view of the facts which has shaped itself in the mind of somebody of our own or a very recent time. Such books are very instructive and valuable; they help us to understand history, to interpret history, to draw just conclusions from it; at the worst, they set us the example of trying to do all this; but they are not themselves history. The knowledge they give is upon trust; and even when they have done their best, it is not only incomplete but partial, because confined to what a few modem writers have seen in the materials, and have thought worth picking out from among them. How little we learn of our own ancestors from Hume, or Hallam, or Macaulay, compared with what we know if we add to what these tell us, even a little reading of contemporary authors and documents! The most recent historians are so well aware of this, that they fill their pages with extracts from the original materials, feeling that these extracts are the real history, and their comments and thread of narrative are only helps towards understanding it. Now it is part of the great worth to us of our Greek and Latin studies, that in them we do read history in the original sources. We are in actual contact with cotemporary minds; we are not dependent on hearsay; we have something by which we can test and check the representations and theories of modem historians. It may be asked, why then not study the original materials of modem history? I answer, it is highly desirable to do so; and let me remark by the way, that even this requires a dead language; nearly all the documents prior to the Reformation, and many subsequent to it, being written in Latin. But the exploration of these documents, though a most useful pursuit, cannot be a branch of education. Not to speak of their vast extent, and the fragmentary nature of each, the strongest reason is, that in learning the spirit of our own past ages, until a comparatively recent period, from contemporary writers, we learn hardly anything else. Those authors, with a few exceptions, are little worth reading on their own account. While, in studying the great writers of antiquity, we are not only learning to understand the ancient mind, but laying in a stock of wise thought and observation, still valuable to ourselves; and at the same time making ourselves familiar with a number of the most perfect and finished literary compositions which the human mind has produced—compositions which, from the altered conditions of human life, are likely to be seldom paralleled, in their sustained excellence, by the times to come.

Even as mere languages, no modem European language is so valuable a discipline to the intellect as those of Greece and Rome, on account of their regular and complicated structure. Consider for a moment what grammar is. It is the most elementary part of logic. It is the beginning of the analysis of the thinking process. The principles and rules of grammar are the means by which the forms of language are made to correspond with the universal forms of thought. The distinc tions between the various parts of speech, between the cases of nouns, the moods and tenses of verbs, the functions of particles, are distinctions in thought, not merely in words. Single nouns and verbs express objects and events. many of which can he cognized by the senses: but the modes of putting nouns and verbs together, express the relations of objects and events, which can be cognized only by the intellect; and each different mode corresponds to a different relation. The structure of every sentence is a lesson in logic. The various rules of syntax oblige us to distinguish between the subject and predicate of a proposition, between the agent, the action, and the thing acted upon; to mark when an idea is intended to modify or qualify, or merely to unite with, some other idea; what assertions are categorical, what only conditional; whether the intention is to express similarity or contrast, to make a plurality of assertions conjunctively or disjunctively; what portions of a sentence, though grammatically complete within themselves, are mere members or subordinate parts of the assertion made by the entire sentence. Such things form the subject-matter of universal grammar; and the languages which teach it best are those which have the most definite rules, and which provide distinct forms for the greatest number of distinctions in thought, so that if we fail to attend precisely and accurately to any of these, we cannot avoid committing a solecism in language. In these qualities the classical languages have an incomparable superiority over every modern language, and over all languages, dead or living, which have a literature worth being generally studied.

But the superiority of the literature itself, for purposes of education, is still more marked and decisive. Even in the substantial value of the matter of which it is the vehicle, it is very far from having been superseded. The discoveries of the ancients in science have been greatly surpassed, and as much of them as is still valuable loses nothing by being incorporated in modem treatises: but what does not so well admit of being transferred bodily, and has been very imperfectly carried off even piecemeal, is the treasure which they accumulated of what may be called the wisdom of life: the rich store of experience of human nature and conduct, which the acute and observing minds of those ages, aided in their observations by the greater simplicity of manners and life, consigned to their writings, and most of which retains all its value. The speeches in Thucydides; the Rhetoric, Ethics, and Politics of Aristotle; the Dialogues of Plato; the Orations of Demosthenes; the Satires, and especially the Epistles of Horace; all the writings of Tacitus; the great work of Quintilian, a repertory of the best thoughts of the ancient world on all subjects connected with education; and, in a less formal manner, all that is left to us of the ancient historians, orators, philosophers, and even dramatists, are replete with remarks and maxims of singular good sense and penetration, applicable both to political and to private life: and the actual truths we find in them are even surpassed in value by the encouragement and help they give us in the pursuit of truth. Human invention has never produced anything so valuable, in the way both of stimulation and of discipline to the inquiring intellect, as the dialectics of the ancients, of which many of the works of Aristotle illustrate the theory, and those of Plato exhibit the practice. No modern writings come near to these, in teaching, both by precept and example, the way to investigate truth, on those subjects, so vastly important to us, which remain matters of controversy, from the difficulty or impossibility of bringing them to a directly experimental test. To question all things; never to turn away from any difficulty; to accept no doctrine either from ourselves or from other people without a rigid scrutiny by negative criticism, letting no fallacy, or incoherence, or confusion of thought, slip by unperceived; above all, to insist upon having the meaning of a word clearly understood before using it, and the meaning of a proposition before assenting to it; these are the lessons we learn from the ancient dialecticians. With all this vigorous management of the negative element, they inspire no scepticism about the reality of truth, or indifference to its pursuit. The noblest enthusiasm, both for the search after truth and for applying it to its highest uses, pervades these writers, Aristotle no less than Plato, though Plato has incomparably the greater power of imparting those feelings to others. In cultivating, therefore, the ancient languages as our best literary education, we are all the while laying an admirable foundation for ethical and philosophical culture. In purely literary excellence—in perfection of form—the pre-eminence of the ancients is not disputed. In every department which they attempted, and they attempted almost all, their composition, like their sculpture, has been to the greatest modem artists an example, to be looked up to with hopeless admiration, but of inappreciable value as a light on high, guiding their own endeavours. In prose and in poetry, in epic, lyric, or dramatic, as in historical, philosophical, and oratorical art, the pinnacle on which they stand is equally eminent. I am now speaking of the form, the artistic perfection of treatment: for, as regards substance, I consider modem poetry to be superior to ancient, in the same manner, though in a less degree, as modem science: it enters deeper into nature. The feelings of the modem mind are more various, more complex and manifold, than those of the ancients ever were. The modem mind is, what the ancient mind was not, brooding and self-conscious; and its meditative self-consciousness has discovered depths in the human soul which the Greeks and Romans did not dream of, and would not have understood. But what they had got to express, they expressed in a manner which few even of the greatest modems have seriously attempted to rival. It must be remembered that they had more time, and that they wrote chiefly for a select class, possessed of leisure. To us who write in a hurry for people who read in a hurry, the attempt to give an equal degree of finish would be loss of time. But to be familiar with perfect models is not the less important to us because the element in which we work precludes even the effort to equal them. They shew us at least what excellence is, and make us desire it, and strive to get as near to it as is within our reach. And this is the value to us of the ancient writers, all the more emphatically, because their excellence does not admit of being copied, or directly imitated. It does not consist in a trick which can be learnt, but in the perfect adaptation of means to ends. The secret of the style of the great Greek and Roman authors, is that it is the perfection of good sense. In the first place, they never use a word without a meaning, or a word which adds nothing to the meaning. They always (to begin with) had a meaning; they knew what they wanted to say; and their whole purpose was to say it with the highest degree of exactness and completeness, and bring it home to the mind with the greatest possible clearness and vividness. It never entered into their thoughts to conceive of a piece of writing as beautiful in itself, abstractedly from what it had to express: its beauty must all be subservient to the most perfect expression of the sense. The *curiosa felicitas* which their critics ascribed in a pre-eminent degree to Horace, expresses the standard at which they all aimed. Their style is exactly described by Swift's definition, "the right words in the right places." Look at an oration of Demosthenes; there is nothing in it which calls attention to itself as style at all: it is only after a close examination we perceive that every word is what it should be, and where it should be, to lead the hearer, smoothly and imperceptibly into the state of mind which the orator wishes to produce. The perfection of the workmanship is only visible in the total absence of any blemish or fault, and of anything which checks the flow of thought and feeling, anything which even momentarily distracts the mind from the main purpose. But then (as has been well said) it was not the object of Demosthenes to make the Athenians cry out "What a splendid speaker!" but to make them say "Let us march against Philip!" It was only in the decline of ancient literature that ornament began to be cultivated merely as ornament. In the time of its maturity not the merest epithet was put in because it was thought beautiful in itself; nor even for a merely descriptive purpose, for epithets purely descriptive were one of the corruptions of style which abound in Lucan, for example: the word had no business there unless it brought out some feature which was wanted, and helped to place the object in the light which the purpose of the composition required. These conditions being complied with, then indeed the intrinsic beauty of the means used was a source of additional effect, of which it behoved them to avail themselves, like rhythm and melody of versification. But these great writers knew that ornament for the sake of ornament, ornament which attracts attention to itself, and shines by its own beauties, only does so by calling off the mind from the main object, and thus not only interferes with the higher purpose of human discourse, which ought, and generally professes, to have some matter to communicate, apart from the mere excitement of the moment, but also spoils the perfection of the composition as a piece of fine art, by destroying the unity of effect. This, then, is the first great lesson in composition to be learnt from the classical authors. The second is, not to be prolix. In a single paragraph, Thucydides can give a clear and vivid representation of a battle, such as a reader who has once taken it into his mind can seldom forget. The most powerful and affecting piece of narrative perhaps in all historical literature, is the account of the Sicilian catastrophe in his seventh book, yet how few pages does it fill! The ancients were concise, because of the extreme pains they took with their compositions; almost all moderns are prolix, because they do not. The great ancients could express a thought so perfectly in a few words or sentences, that they did not need to add any more: the modems, because they cannot bring it out clearly and completely at once, return again and again, heaping sentence upon sentence, each adding a little more elucidation, in hopes that though no single sentence expresses the full meaning, the whole together may give a sufficient notion of it. In this respect I am afraid we are growing worse instead of better, for want of time and patience, and from the necessity we are in of addressing almost all writings to a busy and imperfectly prepared public. The demands of modem life are such—the work to be done, the mass to be worked upon, are so vast, that those who have anything particular to say—who have, as the phrase goes, any message to deliver—cannot afford to devote their time to the production of masterpieces. But they would do far worse than they do, if there had never been masterpieces, or if they had never known them. Early familiarity with the perfect, makes our most imperfect production far less bad than it otherwise would be. To have a high standard of excellence often makes the whole difference of rendering our work good when it would otherwise be mediocre.

For all these reasons I think it important to retain these two languages and literatures in the place they occupy, as a part of liberal education, that is, of the education of all who are not obliged by their circumstances to discontinue their scholastic studies at a very early age. But the same reasons which vindicate the place of classical studies in general education, shew also the proper limitation of them. They should be carried as far as is sufficient to enable the pupil, in after life, to read the great works of ancient literature with ease. Those who have leisure and inclination to make scholarship, or ancient history, or general philology, their pursuit, of course require much more, but there is no room for more in general education. The laborious idleness in which the school-time is wasted away in the English classical schools deserves the severest reprehension. To what purpose should the most precious years of early life be irreparably squandered in learning to write bad Latin and Greek verses? I do not see that we are much the better even for those who end by writing good ones. I am often tempted to ask the favourites of nature and fortune, whether all the serious and important work of the world is done, that their time and energy can be spared for these *nugæ difficiles*? I am not blind to the utility of composing in a language, as a means of learning it accurately. I hardly know any other means equally effectual. But why should not prose composition suffice? What need is there of original composition at all? if that can be called original which unfortunate schoolboys, without any thoughts to express, hammer out on compulsion from mere memory, acquiring the pernicious habit which a teacher should consider it one of his first duties to repress, that of merely stringing together borrowed phrases? The exercise in composition, most suitable to the requirements of learners, is that most valuable one, of retranslating from translated passages of a good author: and to this might be added, what still exists in many Continental places of education, occasional practice in talking Latin. There would be something to be said for the time spent in the manufacture of verses, if such practice were necessary for the enjoyment of ancient poetry; though it would be better to lose that enjoyment than to purchase it at so extravagant a price. But the beauties of a great poet would be a far poorer thing than they are, if they only impressed us through a knowledge of the technicalities of his art. The poet needed those technicalities: they are not necessary to us. They are essential for criticizing a poem, but not for enjoying it. All that is wanted is sufficient familiarity with the language, for its meaning to reach us without any sense of effort, and clothed with the associations on which the poet counted for producing his effect. Whoever has this familiarity, and a practiced ear, can have as keen a relish of the music of Virgil and Horace, as of Gray, or Bums, or Shelley, though he know not the metrical rules of a common Sapphic or Alcaic. I do not say that these rules ought not to be taught, but I would have a class apart for them, and would make the appropriate exercises an optional, not a compulsory part of the school teaching.

Much more might be said respecting classical instruction, and literary cultivation in general, as a part of liberal education. But it is time to speak of the uses of scientific instruction: or rather its indispensable necessity for it is recommended by every consideration which pleads for any high order of intellectual education at all.

The most obvious part of the value of scientific instruction, the mere information that it gives, speaks for itself. We are born into a world which we have not made; a world whose phenomena take place according to fixed laws, of which we do not bring any knowledge into the world with us. In such a world we are appointed to live, and in it all our work is to be done. Our whole working power depends on knowing the laws of the world—in other words, the properties of the things which we have to work with, and to work among, and to work upon. We may and do rely, for the greater part of this knowledge, on the few who in each department make its acquisition their main business in life. But unless an elementary knowledge of scientific truths is diffused among the public, they never know what is certain and what is not, or who are entitled to speak with authority and who are not: and they either have no faith at all in the testimony of science or are the ready dupes of charlatans and impostors. They alternate between ignorant distrust, and blind, often misplaced, confidence. Besides, who is there who would not wish to understand the meaning of the common physical facts that take place under his eye? Who would not wish to know why a pump raises water, why a lever moves heavy weights, why it is hot at the tropics and cold at the poles, why the moon is sometimes dark and sometimes bright, what is the cause of the tides? Do we not feel that he who is totally ignorant of these things, let him be ever so skilled in a special profession, is not an educated man but an ignoramus? It is surely no small part of education to put us in intelligent possession of the most important and most universally interesting facts of the universe, so that the world which surrounds us may not be a sealed book to us, uninteresting because unintelligible. This, however, is but the simplest and most obvious part of the utility of science, and the part which, if neglected in youth, may be the most easily made up for afterwards. It is more important to understand the value of scientific instruction as a training and disciplining process, to fit the intellect for the proper work of a human being. Facts are the materials of our knowledge, but the mind itself is the instrument: and it is easier to acquire facts, than to judge what they prove, and how, through the facts which we know, to get to those which we want to know.

The most incessant occupation of the human intellect throughout life is the ascertainment of truth. We are always needing to know what is actually true about something or other. It is not given to us all to discover great general truths that are a light to all men and to future generations; though with a better general education the number of those who could do so would be far greater than it is. But we all require the ability to judge between the conflicting opinions which are offered to us as vital truths; to choose what doctrines we will receive in the matter of religion, for example; to judge whether we ought to be Tories, Whigs, or Radicals, or to what length it is our duty to go with each; to form a rational conviction on great questions of legislation and internal policy, and on the manner in which our country should behave to dependencies and to foreign nations. And the need we have of knowing how to discriminate truth, is not confined to the larger truths. All through life it is our most pressing interest to find out the truth about all the matters we are concerned with. If we are farmers, we want to find what will truly improve our soil; if merchants, what will truly influence the markets of our commodities; if judges, or jurymen, or advocates, who it was that truly did an unlawful act, or to whom a disputed right truly belongs. Everytime we have to make a new resolution or alter an old one, in any situation in life, we shall go wrong unless we know the truth about the facts on which our resolution depends. Now, however different these searches for truth may look, and however unlike they really are in their subject-matter, the methods of getting at truth, and the tests of truth, are in all cases much the same. There are but two roads by which truth can be discovered; observation, and reasoning: observation, of course, including experiment. We all observe, and we all reason, and therefore, more or less successfully, we all ascertain truths: but most of us do it very ill, and could not get on at all were we not able to fall back on others who do it better. If we could not do it in any degree, we should be mere instruments in the hands of those who could: they would be able to reduce us to slavery. Then how shall we best learn to do this? By being shewn the way in which it has already been successfully done. The processes by which truth is attained, reasoning and observation, have been carried to their greatest known perfection in the physical sciences. As classical literature furnishes the most perfect types of the art of expression, so do the physical sciences those of the art of thinking. Mathematics, and its application to astronomy and natural philosophy, are the most complete example of the discovery of truths by reasoning; experimental science, of their discovery by direct observation. In all these cases we know that we can trust the operation, because the conclusions to which it has led have been found true by subsequent trial. It is by the study of these, then, that we may hope to qualify ourselves for distinguishing truth, in cases where there do not exist the same ready means of verification.

In what consists the principal and most characteristic difference between one human intellect and another? In their ability to judge correctly of evidence. Our direct perceptions of truth are so limited; we know so few things by immediate intuition, or, as it used to be called, by simple apprehension that we depend for almost all our valuable knowledge, on evidence external to itself; and most of us are very unsafe hands at estimating evidence, where an appeal cannot be made to actual eyesight. The intellectual part of our education has nothing more important to do, than to correct or mitigate this almost universal infirmity—this summary and substance of nearly all purely intellectual weakness. To do this with effect needs all the resources which the most perfect system of intellectual training can command. Those resources, as every teacher knows, are but of three kinds: first, models, secondly rules, thirdly, appropriate practice. The models of the art of estimating evidence are furnished by science; the rules are suggested by science; and the study of science is the most fundamental portion of the practice.

Take in the first instance mathematics. It is chiefly from mathematics we realize the fact that there actually is a road to truth by means of reasoning; that anything real, and which will be found true when tried, can be arrived at by a mere operation of the mind. The flagrant abuse of mere reasoning in the days of the schoolmen, when men argued confidently to supposed facts of outward nature without properly establishing their premises, or checking the conclusions by observation, created a prejudice in the modern, and especially in the English mind, against deductive reasoning altogether, as a mode of investigation. The prejudice lasted long, and was upheld by the misunderstood authority of Lord Bacon; until the prodigious applications of mathematics to physical science—to the discovery of the laws of external nature—slowly and tardily restored the reasoning process to the place which belongs to it as a source of real knowledge. Mathematics, pure and applied, are still the great conclusive example of what can be done by reasoning. Mathematics also habituates us to several of the principal precautions for the safety of the process. Our first studies in geometry teach us two invaluable lessons. One is, to lay down at the beginning, in express and clear terms, all the premises from which we intend to reason. The other is, to keep every step in the reasoning distinct and separate from all the other steps, and to make each step safe before proceeding to another; expressly stating to ourselves, at every joint in the reasoning, what new premise we there introduce. It is not necessary that we should do this at all times, in all our reasonings. But we must be always able and ready to do it. If the validity of our argument is denied, or if we doubt it ourselves, that is the way to check it. In this way we are often enabled to detect at once the exact place where paralogism or confusion get in: and after sufficient practice we may be able to keep them out from the beginning. It is to mathematics, again, that we owe our first notion of a connected body of truth; truths which grow out of one another, and hang together so that each implies all the rest; that no one of them can be questioned without contradicting another or others, until in the end it appears that no part of the system can be false unless the whole is so. Pure mathematics first gave us this conception; applied mathematics extends it to the realm of physical nature. Applied mathematics shews us that not only the truths of abstract number and extension, but the external facts of the universe, which we apprehend by our senses, form, at least in a large part of all nature, a web similarly held together. We are able, by reasoning from a few fundamental truths, to explain and predict the phenomena of material objects: and what is still more remarkable, the fundamental truths were themselves found out by reasoning; for they are not such as are obvious to the senses, but had to be inferred by a mathematical process from a mass of minute details, which alone came within the direct reach of human observation. When Newton, in this manner, discovered the laws of the solar system, he created, for all posterity, the true idea of science. He gave the most perfect example we are ever likely to have, of that union of reasoning and observation, which by means of facts that can be directly observed, ascends to laws which govern multitudes of other facts—laws which not only explain and account for what we see, but give us assurance beforehand of much that we do not see, much that we never could have found out by observation, though, having been found out, it is always verified by the result.

While mathematics, and the mathematical sciences, supply us with a typical example of the ascertainment of truth by reasoning; those physical sciences which are not mathematical, such as chemistry, and purely experimental physics, shew us in equal perfection the other mode of arriving at certain truth, by observation, in its most accurate form, that of experiment. The value of mathematics in a logical point of view is an old topic with mathematicians, and has even been insisted on so exclusively as to provoke a counter-exaggeration, of which a well-known essay by Sir William Hamilton is an example: but the logical value of experimental science is comparatively a new subject, yet there is no intellectual discipline more important than that which the experimental sciences afford. Their whole occupation consists in doing well, what all of us, during the whole of life, are engaged in doing, for the most part badly. All men do not affect to be reasoners, but all profess, and really attempt, to draw inferences from experience: yet hardly anyone, who has not been a student of the physical sciences, sets out with any just idea of what the process of interpreting experience really is. If a fact has occurred once or oftener, and another fact has followed it, people think they have got an experiment, and are well on the road towards shewing that the one fact is the cause of the other. If they did but know the immense amount of precaution necessary to a scientific experiment; with what sedulous care the accompanying circumstances are contrived and varied, so as to exclude every agency but that which is the subject of the experiment—or, when disturbing agencies cannot be excluded, the minute accuracy with which their influence is calculated and allowed for, in order that the residue may contain nothing but what is due to the one agency under examination; if these things were attended to, people would be much less easily satisfied that their opinions have the evidence of experience; many popular notions and generalizations which are in all mouths, would be thought a great deal less certain than they are supposed to be; but we should begin to lay the foundation of really experimental knowledge, on things which are now the subjects of mere vague discussion, where one side finds as much to say and says it as confidently as another, and each person's opinion is less determined by evidence than by his accidental interest or prepossession. In politics, for instance, it is evident to whoever comes to the study from that of the experimental sciences that no political conclusions of any value for practice can be arrived at by direct experience. Such specific experience as we can have, serves only to verify, and even that insufficiently, the conclusions of reasoning. Take any active force you please in politics, take the liberties of England, or free trade: how should we know that either of these things conduced to prosperity, if we could discern no tendency in the things themselves to produce it? If we had only the evidence of what is called our experience, such prosperity as we enjoy might be owing to a hundred other causes, and might have been obstructed, not promoted, by these. All true political science is, in one sense of the phrase, *a priori*, being deduced from the tendencies of things, tendencies known either through our general experience of human nature, or as the result of an analysis of the course of history, considered as a progressive evolution. It requires, therefore, the union of induction and deduction, and the mind that is equal to it must have been well disciplined in both. But familiarity with scientific experiment at least does the useful service of inspiring a wholesome scepticism about the conclusions which the mere surface of experience suggests.

The study, on the one hand, of mathematics and its applications, on the other, of experimental science, prepares us for the principal business of the intellect, by the practice of it in the most characteristic cases, and by familiarity with the most perfect and successful models of it. But in great things as in small, examples and models are not sufficient: we want rules as well. Familiarity with the correct use of a language in conversation and writing does not make rules of grammar unnecessary; nor does the amplest knowledge of sciences of reasoning and experiment dispense with rules of logic. We may have heard correct reasonings and seen skilful experiments all our lives—we shall not learn by mere imitation to do the like, unless we pay careful attention to how it is done. It is much easier in these abstract matters, than in purely mechanical ones, to mistake bad work for good. To mark out the difference between them is the province of logic. Logic lays down the general principles and laws of the search after truth; the conditions which, whether recognised or not, must actually have been observed if the mind has done its work rightly. Logic is the intellectual complement of mathematics and physics. Those sciences give the practice, of which Logic is the theory. It declares the principles, rules, and precepts, of which they exemplify the observance.

The science of Logic has two parts; ratiocinative and inductive logic. The one helps to keep us right in reasoning from premises, the other in concluding from observation. Ratiocinative logic is much older than inductive, because reasoning in the narrower sense of the word is an easier process than induction, and the science which works by mere reasoning, pure mathematics, had been carried to a considerable height while the sciences of observation were still in the purely empirical period. The principles of ratiocination, therefore, were the earliest understood and systematized, and the logic of ratiocination is even now suitable to an earlier stage in education than that of induction. The principles of induction cannot be properly understood without some previous study of the inductive sciences: but the logic of reasoning, which was already carried to a high degree of perfection by Aristotle, does not absolutely require even a knowledge of mathematics, but can be sufficiently exemplified and illustrated from the practice of daily life.

Of Logic I venture to say, even if limited to that of mere ratiocination, the theory of names, propositions, and the syllogism, that there is no part of intellectual education which is of greater value, or whose place can so ill be supplied by anything else. Its uses, it is true, are chiefly negative; its function is, not so much to teach us to go right, as to keep us from going wrong. But in the operations of the intellect it is so much easier to go wrong than right; it is so utterly impossible for even the most vigorous mind to keep itself in the path but by maintaining a vigilant watch against all deviations, and noting all the byways by which it is possible to go astray—that the chief difference between one reasoner and another consists in their less or greater liability to be misled. Logic points out all the possible ways in which, starting from true premises, we may draw false conclusions.

By its analysis of the reasoning process, and the forms it supplies for stating and setting forth our reasonings, it enables us to guard the points at which a fallacy is in danger of slipping in, or to lay our fingers upon the place where it has slipped in. When I consider how very simple the theory of reasoning is, and how short a time is sufficient for acquiring a thorough knowledge of its principles and rules, and even considerable expertness in applying them, I can find no excuse for omission to study it on the part of any one who aspires to succeed in any intellectual pursuit. Logic is the great disperser of hazy and confused thinking: it clears up the fogs which hide from us our own ignorance, and make us believe that we understand a subject when we do not. We must not be led away by talk about inarticulate giants who do great deeds without knowing how, and see into the most recondite truths without any of the ordinary helps, and without being able to explain to other people how they reach their conclusions, nor consequently to convince any other people of the truth of them. There may be such men, as there are deaf and dumb persons who do clever things, but for all that, speech and hearing are faculties by no means to be dispensed with. If you want to know whether you are thinking rightly, put your thoughts into words. In the very attempt to do this you will find yourselves, consciously or unconsciously, using logical forms. Logic compels us to throw our meaning into distinct propositions, and our reasonings into distinct steps. It makes us conscious of all the implied assumptions on which we are proceeding, and which, if not true, vitiate the entire process. It makes us aware what extent of doctrine we commit ourselves to by any course of reasoning, and obliges us to look the implied premises in the face, and make up our minds whether we can stand to them. It makes our opinions consistent with themselves and with one another, and forces us to think clearly, even when it cannot make us think correctly. It is true that error may be consistent and systematic as well as truth; but this is not the common case. It is no small advantage to see clearly the principles and consequences involved in our opinions, and which we must either accept, or else abandon those opinions. We are much nearer to finding truth when we search for it in broad daylight. Error, pursued rigorously to all that is implied in it, seldom fails to get detected by coming into collision with some known and admitted fact.

You will find abundance of people to tell you that logic is no help to thought, and that people cannot be taught to think by rules. Undoubtedly rules by themselves, without practice, go but a little way in teaching anything. But if the practice of thinking is not improved by rules, I venture to say it is the only difficult thing done by human beings that is not so. A man learns to saw wood principally by practice, but there are rules for doing it, grounded on the nature of the operation, and if he is not taught the rules, he will not saw well until he has discovered them for himself. Wherever there is a right way and a wrong, there must be a difference between them, and it must be possible to find out what the difference is; and when found out and expressed in words, it is a rule for the operation. If anyone is inclined to disparage rules, I say to him, try to learn anything which there are rules for, without knowing the rules, and see how you succeed. To those who think lightly of the school logic, I say, take the trouble to learn it. You will easily do so in a few weeks, and you will see whether it is of no use to you in making your mind clear, and keeping you from stumbling in the dark over the most outrageous fallacies. Nobody, I believe, who has really learnt it, and who goes on using his mind, is insensible to its benefits, unless he started with a prejudice, or, like some eminent English and Scottish thinkers of the past century, is under the influence of a reaction against the exaggerated pretensions made by the schoolmen, not so much in behalf of logic as of the reasoning process itself. Still more highly must the use of logic be estimated, if we include in it, as we ought to do, the principles and rules of Induction as well as of Ratiocination. As the one logic guards us against bad deduction, so does the other against bad generalization, which is a still more universal error. If men easily err in arguing from one general proposition to another, still more easily do they go wrong in interpreting the observations made by themselves and others. There is nothing in which an untrained mind shows itself more hopelessly incapable, than in drawing the proper general conclusions from its own experience. And even trained minds, when all their training is on a special subject, and does not extend to the general principles of induction, are only kept right when there are ready opportunities of verifying their inferences by facts. Able scientific men, when they venture upon subjects in which they have no facts to check them, are often found drawing conclusions or making generalizations from their experimental knowledge, such as any sound theory of induction would shew to be utterly unwarranted. So true is it that practice alone, even of a good kind, is not sufficient without principles and rules. Lord Bacon had the great merit of seeing that rules were necessary, and conceiving, to a very considerable extent, their true character. The defects of his conception were such as were inevitable while the inductive sciences were only in the earliest stage of their progress, and the highest efforts of the human mind in that direction had not yet been made. Inadequate as the Baconian view of induction was, and rapidly as the practice outgrew it, it is only within a generation or two that any considerable improvement has been made in the theory; very much through the impulse given by two of the many distinguished men who have adorned the Scottish universities, Dugald Stewart and Brown.

I have given a very incomplete and summary view of the educational benefits derived from instruction in the more perfect sciences, and in the rules for the proper use of the intellectual faculties which the practice of those sciences has suggested. There are other sciences, which are in a more backward state, and tax the whole, powers of the mind in its mature years, yet a beginning of which may be beneficially made in university studies, while a tincture of them is valuable even to those who are never likely to proceed further. The first is physiology; the science of the laws of organic and animal life, and especially of the structure and functions of the human body. It would be absurd to pretend that a profound knowledge of this difficult subject can be acquired in youth, or as a part of general education. Yet an acquaintance with its leading truths is one of those acquirements which ought not to be the exclusive property of a particular profession. The value of such knowledge for daily uses has been made familiar to us all by the sanitary discussions of late years. There is hardly one among us who may not, in some position of authority, be required to form an opinion and take part in public action on sanitary subjects. And the importance of understanding the true conditions of health and disease—of knowing how to acquire and preserve that healthy habit of body which the most tedious and costly medical treatment so often fails to restore when once lost, should secure a place in general education for the principal maxims of hygiene, and some of those even of practical medicine. For those who aim at high intellectual cultivation, the study of physiology has still greater recommendations, and is, in the present state of advancement of the higher studies, a real necessity. The practice which it gives in the study of nature is such as no other physical science affords in the same kind, and is the best introduction to the difficult questions of politics and social life. Scientific education, apart from professional objects, is but a preparation for judging rightly of Man, and of his requirements and interests. But to this final pursuit, which has been called *par excellence* the proper study of mankind, physiology is the most serviceable of the sciences, because it is the nearest. Its subject is already Man: the same complex and manifold being, whose properties are not independent of circumstance, and immovable from age to age, like those of the ellipse and hyperbola, or of sulphur and phosphorus, but are infinitely various, indefinitely modifiable by art or accident, graduating by the nicest shades into one another, and reacting upon one another in a thousand ways, so that they are seldom capable of being isolated and observed separately. With the difficulties of the study of a being so constituted, the physiologist, and he alone among scientific enquirers, is already familiar. Take what view we will of man as a spiritual being, one part of his nature is far more like another than either of them is like anything else. In the organic world we study nature under disadvantages very similar to those which affect the study of moral and political phenomena: our means of making experiments are almost as limited, while the extreme complexity of the facts makes the conclusions of general reasoning unusually precarious, on account of the vast number of circumstances that conspire to determine every result. Yet in spite of these obstacles, it is found possible in physiology to arrive at a considerable number of well-ascertained and important truths. This therefore is an excellent school in which to study the means of overcoming similar difficulties elsewhere. It is in physiology too that we are first introduced to some of the conceptions which play the greatest part in the moral and social sciences, but which do not occur at all in those of inorganic nature. As, for instance, the idea of predisposition, and of predisposing causes, as distinguished from exciting causes. The operation of all moral forces is immensely influenced by predisposition: without that element, it is impossible to explain the commonest facts of history and social life. Physiology is also the first science in which we recognize the influence of habit—the tendency of something to happen again merely because it has happened before. From physiology, too, we get our clearest notion of what is meant by development or evolution. The growth of a plant or animal from the first germ is the typical specimen of a phenomenon which rules through the whole course of the history of man and society—increase of function, through expansion and differentiation of structure by internal forces. I cannot enter into the subject at greater length; it is enough if I throw out hints which may be germs of further thought in yourselves. Those who aim at high intellectual achievements may be assured that no part of their time will be less wasted, than that which they employ in becoming familiar with the methods and with the main conceptions of the science of organization and life.

Physiology, at its upper extremity, touches on Psychology, or the Philosophy of Mind: and without raising any disputed questions about the limits between Matter and Spirit, the nerves and brain are admitted to have so intimate a connection with the mental operations, that the student of the last cannot dispense with a considerable knowledge of the first. The value of psychology itself need hardly be expatiated upon in a Scottish university; for it has always been there studied with brilliant success. Almost everything which has been contributed from these islands towards its advancement since Locke and Berkeley, has until very lately, and much of it even in the present generation, proceeded from Scottish authors and Scottish professors. Psychology, in truth, is simply the knowledge of the laws of human nature. If there is anything that deserves to be studied by man, it is his own nature and that of his fellow-men: and if it is worth studying at all, it is worth studying scientifically, so as to reach the fundamental laws which underlie and govern all the rest. With regard to the suitableness of this subject for general education, a distinction must be made. There are certain observed laws of our thoughts and of our feelings which rest upon experimental evidence, and, once seized, are a clue to the interpretation of much that we are conscious of in ourselves, and observe in one another. Such, for example, are the laws of association. Psychology, so far as it consists of such laws—I speak of the laws themselves, not of their disputed applications—is as positive and certain a science as chemistry, and fit to be taught as such. When, however, we pass beyond the bounds of these admitted truths, to questions which are still in controversy among the different philosophical schools—how far the higher operations of the mind can be explained by association, how far we must admit other primary principles—what faculties of the mind are simple, what complex, and what is the composition of the latter—above all, when we embark upon the sea of metaphysics properly so called, and enquire, for instance, whether time and space are real existences, as is our spontaneous impression, or forms of our sensitive faculty, as is maintained by Kant, or complex ideas generated by association; whether matter and spirit are conceptions merely relative to our faculties, or facts existing *per se* and in the latter case, what is the nature and limit of our knowledge of them; whether the will of man is free or determined by causes, and what is the real difference between the two doctrines; matters on which the most thinking men, and those who have given most study to the subjects, are still divided; it is neither to be expected nor desired that those who do not specially devote themselves to the higher departments of speculation should employ much of their time in attempting to get to the bottom of these questions. But it is a part of liberal education to know that such controversies exist, and, in a general way, what has been said on both sides of them. It is instructive to know the failures of the human intellect as well as its successes, its imperfect as well as its perfect attainments; to be aware of the open questions, as well as of those which have been definitively resolved. A very summary view of these disputed matters may suffice for the many; but a system of education is not intended solely for the many: it has to kindle the aspirations and aid the efforts of those who are destined to stand forth as thinkers above the multitude: and for these there is hardly to be found any discipline comparable to that which these metaphysical controversies afford. For they are essentially questions about the estimation of evidence; about the ultimate grounds of belief; the conditions required to justify our most familiar and intimate convictions; and the real meaning and import of words and phrases which we have used from infancy as if we understood all about them, which are even at the foundation of human language, yet of which no one except a metaphysician has rendered to himself a complete account. Whatever philosophical opinions the study of these questions may lead us to adopt, no one ever came out of the discussion of them without increased vigour of understanding, an increased demand for precision of thought and language, and a more careful and exact appreciation of the nature of proof. There never was any sharpener of the intellectual faculties superior to the Berkeleian controversy. There is even now no reading more profitable to students—confining myself to writers in our own language, and notwithstanding that so many of their speculations are already obsolete—than Hobbes and Locke, Reid and Stewart, Hume, Hartley, and Brown: on condition that these great thinkers are not read passively, as masters to be followed, but actively, as supplying materials and incentives to thought. To come to our own cotemporaries, he who has mastered Sir William Hamilton and your own lamented Ferrier as distinguished representatives of one of the two great schools of philosophy, and an eminent Professor in a neighbouring University, Professor Bain, probably the greatest living authority in the other, has gained a practice in the most searching methods of philosophic investigation applied to the most arduous subjects, which is no inadequate preparation for any intellectual difficulties that he is ever likely to be called on to resolve.

In this brief outline of a complete scientific education, I have said nothing about direct instruction in that which it is the chief of all the ends of intellectual education to qualify us for—the exercise of thought on the great interests of mankind as moral and social beings—ethics and politics, in the largest sense. These things are not, in the existing state of human knowledge, the subject of a science, generally admitted and accepted. Politics cannot be learnt once for all, from a text-book, or the instructions of a master. What we require to be taught on that subject, is to be our own teachers. It is a subject on which we have no masters to follow; each must explore for himself, and exercise an independent judgment. Scientific politics do not consist in having a set of conclusions readymade, to be applied everywhere indiscriminately, but in setting the mind to work in a scientific spirit to discover in each instance the truths applicable to the given case. And this, at present, scarcely any two persons do in the same way. Education is not entitled, on this subject, to recommend any set of opinions as resting on the authority of established science. But it can supply the student with materials for his own mind, and helps to use them. It can make him acquainted with the best speculations on the subject, taken from different points of view: none of which will be found complete, while each embodies some considerations really relevant, really requiring to be taken into the account. Education may also introduce us to the principal facts which have a direct bearing on the subject, namely the different modes or stages of civilization that have been found among mankind, and the characteristic properties of each. This is the true purpose of historical studies, as prosecuted in an University. The leading facts of ancient and modern history should be known by the student from his private reading: if that knowledge be wanting, it cannot possibly be supplied here. What a Professor of History has to teach, is the meaning of those facts. His office is to help the student in collecting from history what are the main differences between human beings, and between the institutions of society, at one time or place and at another: in picturing to himself human life and the human conception of life, as they were at the different stages of human development: in distinguishing between what is the same in all ages and what is progressive, and forming some incipient conception of the causes and laws of progress. All these things are as yet very imperfectly understood even by the most philosophic enquirers, and are quite unfit to be taught dogmatically. The object is to lead the student to attend to them; to make him take interest in history not as a mere narrative, but as a chain of causes and effects still unwinding itself before his eyes, and full of momentous consequences to himself and his descendants: the unfolding of a great epic or dramatic action, to terminate in the happiness or misery, the elevation or degradation, of the human race; an unremitting conflict between good and evil powers, of which every act done by any of us, insignificant as we are, forms one of the incidents; a conflict in which even the smallest of us cannot escape from taking part, in which whoever does not help the right side is helping the wrong, and for our share in which, whether it be greater or smaller, and let its actual consequences be visible or in the main invisible, no one of us can escape the responsibility. Though education cannot arm and equip its pupils for this fight with any complete philosophy either of politics or of history, there is much positive instruction that it can give them, having a direct bearing on the duties of citizenship. They should be taught the outlines of the civil and political institutions of their own country, and in a more general way, of the more advanced of the other civilized nations. Those branches of politics, or of the laws of social life, in which there exists a collection of facts or thoughts sufficiently sifted and methodized to form the beginning of a science, should be taught *ex professo*. Among the chief of these is Political Economy; the sources and conditions of wealth and material prosperity for aggregate bodies of human beings. This study approaches nearer to the rank of a science in the sense in which we apply that name to the physical sciences, than anything else connected with politics yet does. I need not enlarge on the important lessons which it affords for the guidance of life, and for the estimation of laws and institutions, or on the necessity of knowing all that it can teach in order to have true views of the course of human affairs, or form plans for their improvement which will stand actual trial. The same persons who cry down Logic will generally warn you against Political Economy. It is unfeeling, they will tell you. It recognizes unpleasant facts. For my part, the most unfeeling thing I know of is the law of gravitation: it breaks the neck of the best and most amiable person without scruple, if he forgets for a single moment to give heed to it. The winds and waves too are Very unfeeling. Would you advise those who go to sea to deny the winds and waves—or to make use of them, and find the means of guarding against their dangers? My advice to you is to study the great writers on Political Economy, and hold firmly by whatever in them you find true; and depend upon it that if you are not selfish or hard-hearted already. Political Economy will not make you so. Of no less importance than Political Economy is the study of what is called Jurisprudence; the general principles of law; the social necessities which laws are required to meet; the features common to all systems of law, and the differences between them; the requisites of good legislation, the proper mode of constructing a legal system, and the best constitution of courts of justice and modes of legal procedure. These things are not only the chief part of the business of government, but the vital concern of every citizen; and their improvement affords a wide scope for the energies of any duly prepared mind, ambitious of contributing towards the better condition of the human race. For this, too, admirable helps have been provided by writers of our own or of a very recent time. At the head of them stands Bentham; undoubtedly the greatest master who ever devoted the labour of a life to let in light on the subject of law; and who is the more intelligible to non-professional persons, because, as his way is, he builds up the subject from its foundation in the facts of human life, and shows by careful consideration of ends and means, what law might and ought to be, in deplorable contrast with what it is. Other enlightened jurists have followed with contributions of two kinds, as the type of which I may take two works, equally admirable in their respective times. Mr. Austin, in his Lectures on Jurisprudence, takes for his basis the Roman law, the most elaborately consistent legal system which history has shewn us in actual operation, and that which the greatest number of accomplished minds have employed themselves in harmonizing. From this he singles out the principles and distinctions which are of general applicability, and employs the powers and resources of a most precise and analytic mind to give to those principles and distinctions a philosophic basis, grounded in the universal reason of mankind, and not in mere technical convenience. Mr. Maine, in his treatise on Ancient Law in its relations to Modem Thought, shews from the history of law, and from what is known of the primitive institutions of mankind, the origin of much that has lasted till now, and has a firm footing both in the laws and in the ideas of modem times; shewing that many of these things never originated in reason, but are relics of the institutions of barbarous society, modified more or less by civilization, but kept standing by the persistency of ideas which were the offspring of those barbarous institutions, and have survived their parent. The path opened by Mr. Maine has been followed up by others, with additional illustrations of the influence of obsolete ideas on modem institutions, and of obsolete institutions on modern ideas; an action and reaction which perpetuate, in many of the greatest concerns, a mitigated barbarism: things being continually accepted as dictates of nature and necessities of life, which, if we knew all, we should see to have originated in artificial arrangements of society, long since abandoned and condemned.

To these studies I would add International Law; which I decidedly think should be taught in all universities, and should form part of all liberal education. The need of it is far from being limited to diplomatists and lawyers; it extends to every citizen. What is called the Law of Nations is not properly law, but a part of ethics: a set of moral rules, accepted as authoritative by civilized states. It is true that these rules neither are nor ought to be of eternal obligation, but do and must vary more or less from age to age, as the consciences of nations become more enlightened and the exigencies of political society undergo change. But the rules mostly were at their origin, and still are, an application of the maxims of honesty and humanity to the intercourse of states. They were introduced by the moral sentiments of mankind, or by their sense of the general interest, to mitigate the crimes and sufferings of a state of war, and to restrain governments and nations from unjust or dishonest conduct towards one another in time of peace. Since every country stands in numerous and various relations with the other countries of the world, and many, our own among the number, exercise actual authority over some of these, a knowledge of the established rules of international morality is essential to the duty of every nation, and therefore of every person in it who helps to make up the nation, and whose voice and feeling form a part of what is called public opinion. Let not any one pacify his conscience by the delusion that he can do no harm if he takes no part, and forms no opinion. Bad men need nothing more to compass their ends, than that good men should look on and do nothing. He is not a good man who, without a protest, allows wrong to be committed in his name, and with the means which he helps to supply, because he will not trouble himself to use his mind on the subject. It depends on the habit of attending to and looking into public transactions, and on the degree of information and solid judgment respecting them that exists in the community, whether the conduct of the nation as a nation, both within itself and towards others, shall be selfish, corrupt, and tyrannical, or rational and enlightened, just and noble.

Of these more advanced studies, only a small commencement can be made at schools and universities; but even this is of the highest value, by awakening an interest in the subjects, by conquering the first difficulties, and inuring the mind to the kind of exertion which the studies require, by implanting a desire to make further progress, and directing the student to the best tracks and the best helps. So far as these branches of knowledge have been acquired, we have learnt, or been put into the way of learning, our duty, and our work in life. Knowing it, however, is but half the work of education; it still remains, that what we know, we shall be willing and determined to put in practice. Nevertheless, to know the truth is already a great way towards disposing us to act upon it. What we see clearly and apprehend keenly, we have a natural desire to act out. "To see the best, and yet the worst pursue," is a possible but not a common state of mind; those who follow the wrong have generally first taken care to be voluntarily ignorant of the right. They have silenced their conscience, but they are not knowingly disobeying it. If you take an average human mind while still young, before the objects it has chosen in life have given it a turn in any bad direction, you will generally find it desiring what is good, right, and for the benefit of all; and if that season is properly used to implant the knowledge and give the training which shall render rectitude of judgment more habitual than sophistry, a serious barrier will have been erected against the inroads of selfishness and falsehood. Still, it is a very imperfect education which trains the intelligence only, but not the will. No one can dispense with an education directed expressly to the moral as well as the intellectual part of his being. Such education, so far as it is direct, is either moral or religious; and these may either be treated as distinct, or as different aspects of the same thing. The subject we are now considering is not education as a whole, but scholastic education, and we must keep in view the inevitable limitations of what schools and universities can do. It is beyond their power to educate morally or religiously. Moral and religious education consist in training the feelings and the daily habits; and these are, in the main, beyond the sphere and inaccessible to the control of public education. It is the home, the family, which gives us the moral or religious education we really receive: and this is completed, and modified, sometimes for the better, often for the worse, by society, and the opinions and feelings with which we are there surrounded. The moral or religious influence which a University can exercise, consists less in any express teaching, than in the pervading tone of the place. Whatever it teaches, it should teach as penetrated by a sense of duty; it should present all knowledge as chiefly a means to worthiness of life, given for the double purpose of making each of us practically useful to his fellow-creatures, and of elevating the character of the species itself; exalting and dignifying our nature. There is nothing which spreads more contagiously from teacher to pupil than elevation of sentiment: often and often have students caught from the living influence of a professor, a contempt for mean and selfish objects, and a noble ambition to leave the world better than they found it, which they have carried with them throughout life. In these respects, teachers of every kind have natural and peculiar means of doing with effect, what everyone who mixes with his fellow-beings, or addresses himself to them in any character, should feel bound to do to the extent of his capacity and opportunities. What is special to a University on these subjects belongs chiefly, like the rest of its work, to the intellectual department. A University exists for the purpose of laying open to each succeeding generation, as far as the conditions of the case admit, the accumulated treasure of the thoughts of mankind. As an indispensable part of this, it has to make known to them what mankind at large, their own country, and the best and wisest individual men, have thought on the great subjects of morals and religion. There should be, and there is in most universities, professorial instruction in moral philosophy; but I could wish that this instruction were of a somewhat different type from what is ordinarily met with. I could wish that it were more expository, less polemical and above all less dogmatic. The learner should be made acquainted with the principal systems of moral philosophy which have existed and been practically operative among mankind, and should hear what there is to be said for each: the Aristotelian, the Epicurean, the Stoic, the Judaic, the Christian in the various modes of its interpretation, which differ almost as much from one another as the teachings of those earlier schools. He should be made familiar with the different standards of right and wrong which have been taken as the basis of ethics: general utility, natural justice, natural rights, a moral sense, principles of practical reason, and the rest. Among all these, it is not so much the teacher's business to take a side, and fight stoutly for someone against the rest, as it is to direct them all towards the establishment and preservation of the rules of conduct most advantageous to mankind. There is not one of these systems which has not its good side; not one from which there is not something to be learnt by the votaries of the others; not one which is not suggested by a keen, though it may not always be a clear, perception of some important truths, which are the prop of the system, and the neglect or undervaluing of which in other systems is their characteristic infirmity. A system which may be a whole erroneous, is still valuable, until it has forced upon mankind a sufficient attention to the portion of truth which suggested it. The ethical teacher does his part best, when he points out how each system may be strengthened even on its own basis, by taking into more complete account the truths which other systems have realized more fully and made more prominent. I do not mean that he should encourage an essentially sceptical eclecticism. While placing every system in the best aspect it admits of, and endeavouring to draw from all of them the most salutary consequences compatible with their nature, I would by no means debar him from enforcing by his best arguments his own preference for some one of the number. They cannot be all true; though those which are false as theories may contain particular truths, indispensable to the completeness of the true theory. But on this subject, even more than on any of those I have previously mentioned, it is not the teacher's business to impose his own judgment, but to inform and discipline that of his pupil.

And this same clue, if we keep hold of it, will guide ns through the labyrinth of conflicting thought into which we enter when we touch the great question of the relation of education to religion. As I have already said, the only really effective religious education is the parental—that of home and childhood. All that social and public education has in its power to do, further than by a general pervading tone of reverence and duty, amounts to little more than the information which it can give; but this is extremely valuable. I shall not enter into the question which has been debated with so much vehemence in the last and present generation, whether religion ought to be taught at all in universities and public schools, seeing that religion is the subject of all others on which men's opinions are most widely at variance. On neither side of this controversy do the disputants seem to me to have sufficiently freed their minds from the old notion of education, that it consists in the dogmatic inculcation from authority, of what the teacher deems true. Why should it be impossible, that information of the greatest value, on subjects connected with religion, should be brought before the student's mind; that he should be made acquainted with so important a part of the national thought, and of the intellectual labours of past generations, as those relating to religion, without being taught dogmatically the doctrines of any church or sect? Christianity being a historical religion, the sort of religious instruction which seems to me most appropriate to a University is the study of ecclesiastical history. If teaching, even on matters of scientific certainty, should aim quite as much at showing how the results are arrived at, as at teaching the results themselves, far more, then, should this be the case on subjects where there is the widest diversity of opinion among men of equal ability, and who have taken equal pains to arrive at the truth. This diversity should of itself be a warning to a conscientious teacher that he has no right to impose his opinion authoritatively upon a youthful mind. His teaching should not be in the spirit of dogmatism, but in that of enquiry. The pupil should not be addressed as if his religion had been chosen for him, but as one who will have to choose it for himself. The various Churches, established and unestablished, are quite competent to the task which is peculiarly theirs, that of teaching each its own doctrines, as far as necessary, to its own rising generation. The proper business of a University is different: not to tell us from authority what we ought to believe, and make us accept the belief as a duty, but to give us information and training, and help us to form our own belief in a manner worthy of intelligent beings, who seek for truth at all hazards, and demand to know all the difficulties, in order that they may be better qualified to find, or recognize, the most satisfactory mode of resolving them. The vast importance of these questions—the great results as regards the conduct of our lives, which depend upon our choosing one belief or another—are the strongest reasons why we should not trust our judgment when it has been formed in ignorance of the evidence, and why we should not consent to be restricted to a one-sided teaching, which informs us of what a particular teacher or association of teachers receive as true doctrine and sound argument, but of nothing more.

I do not affirm that an University, if it represses free thought and enquiry, must be altogether a failure, for the freest thinkers have often been trained in the most slavish seminaries of learning. The great Christian reformers were taught in Roman Catholic Universities; the sceptical philosophers of Prance were mostly educated by the Jesuits. The human mind is sometimes impelled all the more violently in one direction, by an over-zealous and demonstrative attempt to drag it in the opposite. But this is not what Universities are appointed for—to drive men from them, even into good, by excess of evil. a University ought to be a place of free speculation. The more diligently it does its duty in all other respects, the more certain it is to be that. The old English Universities, in the present generation, are doing better work than they have done within human memory in teaching the ordinary studies of their curriculum; and one of the consequences has been, that whereas they formerly seemed to exist mainly for the repression of independent thought, and the chaining up of the individual intellect and conscience, they are now the great foci of free and manly enquiry, to the higher and professional classes, south of the Tweed. The ruling minds of those ancient seminaries have at last remembered that to place themselves in hostility to the free use of the understanding, is to abdicate their own best privilege, that of guiding it. A modest deference, at least provisional, to the united authority of the specially instructed, is becoming in a youthful and imperfectly formed mind; but when there is no united authority—when the specially instructed are so divided and scattered that almost any opinion can boast of some high authority, and no opinion whatever can claim all; when, therefore, it can never be deemed extremely improbable that one who uses his mind freely may see reason to change his first opinion; then, whatever you do, keep, at all risks, your minds open: do not barter away your freedom of thought. Those of you who are destined for the clerical profession are, no doubt, so far held to a certain number of doctrines, that if they ceased to believe them they would not be justified in remaining in a position in which they would be required to teach insincerely. But use your influence to make those doctrines as few as possible. It is not right that men should be bribed to hold out against conviction—to shut their ears against objections, or, if the objections penetrate, to continue professing full and unfaltering belief when their confidence is already shaken. Neither is it right that if men honestly profess to have changed some of their religious opinions, their honesty should as a matter of course exclude them from taking a part for which they may be admirably qualified, in the spiritual instruction of the nation. The tendency of the age, on both sides of the ancient Border, is towards the relaxation of formularies, and a less rigid construction of articles. This very circumstance, by making the limits of orthodoxy less definite, and obliging everyone to draw the line for himself, is an embarrassment to consciences. But I hold entirely with those clergymen who elect to remain in the national church, so long as they are able to accept its articles and confessions in any sense or with any interpretation consistent with common honesty, whether it be the generally received interpretation or not. If all were to desert the church who put a large and liberal construction on its terms of communion, or who would wish to see those terms widened, the national provision for religious teaching and worship would be left utterly to those who take the narrowest, the most literal, and purely textual view of the formularies; who, though by no means necessarily bigots, are under the great disadvantage of having the bigots for their allies, and who, however great their merits may be, and they are often very great, yet if the church is improvable, are not the most likely persons to improve it. Therefore, if it were not an impertinence in me to tender advice in such a matter, I should say, let all who conscientiously can, remain in the church. A church is far more easily improved from within than from without. Almost all the illustrious reformers of religion began by being clergymen: but they did not think that their profession as clergymen was inconsistent with being reformers. They mostly indeed ended their days outside the churches in which they were born; but it was because the churches, in an evil hour for themselves, cast them out. They did not think it any business of theirs to withdraw. They thought they had a better right to remain in the fold, than those had who expelled them.

I have now said what I had to say on the two kinds of education which the system of schools and universities is intended to promote—intellectual education, and moral education: knowledge and the training of the knowing faculty, conscience and that of the moral faculty. These are the two main ingredients of human culture; but they do not exhaust the whole of it. There is a third division, which, if subordinate, and owing allegiance to the two others, is barely inferior to them, and not less needful to the completeness of the human being; I mean the aesthetic branch; the culture which comes through poetry and art, and may be described as the education of the feelings, and the cultivation of the beautiful. This department of things deserves to be regarded in a far more serious light than is the custom of these countries. It is only of late, and chiefly by a superficial imitation of foreigners, that we have begun to use the word Art by itself, and to speak of Art as we speak of Science, or Government, or Religion: we used to talk of the Arts, and more specifically of the Fine Arts: and even by them were vulgarly meant only two forms of art. Painting and Sculpture, the two which as a people we cared least about—which were regarded even by the more cultivated among us as little more than branches of domestic ornamentation, a kind of elegant upholstery. The very words "Fine Arts" called up a notion of frivolity, of great pains expended on a rather trifling object—on something which differed from the cheaper and commoner arts of producing pretty things, mainly by being more difficult, and by giving fops an opportunity of pluming themselves on caring for it and on being able to talk about it. This estimate extended in no small degree, though not altogether, even to poetry; the queen of arts, but, in Great Britain, hardly included under the name. It cannot exactly be said that poetry was little thought of; we were proud of our Shakespeare and Milton, and in one period at least of our history, that of Queen Anne, it was a high literary distinction to be a poet; but poetry was hardly looked upon in any serious light, or as having much value except as an amusement or excitement, the superiority of which over others principally consisted in being that of a more refined order of minds. Yet the celebrated saying of Fletcher of Saltoun, "Let who will make the laws of a people if I write their songs" might have taught us how great an instrument for acting on the human mind we were undervaluing. It would be difficult for anybody to imagine that "Rule Britannia" for example, or "Scots wha hae," had no permanent influence on the higher region of human character; some of Moore's songs have done more for Ireland than all Grattan's speeches: and songs are far from being the highest or most impressive form of poetry. On these subjects, the mode of thinking and feeling of other countries was not only not intelligible, but not credible, to an average Englishman. To find Art ranking on a complete equality, in theory at least, with Philosophy, Learning, and Science—as holding an equally important place among the agents of civilization and among the elements of the worth of humanity; to find even painting and sculpture treated as great social powers, and the art of a country as a feature in its character and condition, little inferior in importance to either its religion or its government; all this only did not amaze and puzzle Englishmen, because it was too strange for them to be able to realize it, or, in truth, to believe it possible: and the radical difference of feeling on this matter between the British people and those of France, Germany, and the Continent generally, is one among the causes of that extraordinary inability to understand one another, which exists between England and the rest of Europe, while it does not exist to anything like the same degree between one nation of Continental Europe and another. It may be traced to the two influences which have chiefly shaped the British character since the days of the Stuarts: commercial money-getting business, and religious Puritanism. Business, demanding the whole of the faculties, and whether pursued from duty or the love of gain, regarding as a loss of time whatever does hot conduce directly to the end; Puritanism, which looking upon every feeling of human nature, except fear and reverence for God, as a snare, if not as partaking of sin, looked coldly, if not disapprovingly, on the cultivation of the sentiments. Different causes have produced different effects in the Continental nations; among whom it is even now observable that virtue and goodness are generally for the most, part an affair of the sentiments, while with us they are almost exclusively an affair of duty. Accordingly, the kind of advantage which we have had over many other countries in point of morals—I am not sure that we are not losing it—has consisted in greater tenderness of conscience. In this we have had on the whole a real superiority, though one principally negative; for conscience is with most men a power chiefly in the way of restraint—a power which acts rather in staying our hands from any great wickedness, than by the direction it gives to the general course of our desires and sentiments. One of the commonest types of character among us is that of a man all whose ambition is self-regarding; who has no higher purpose in life than to enrich or raise in the world himself and his family; who never dreams of making the good of his fellow-creatures or of his country an habitual object, further than giving away, annually or from time to time, certain sums in charity; but who has a conscience sincerely alive to whatever is generally considered wrong, and would scruple to use any very illegitimate means for attaining his self-interested objects. While it will often happen in other countries that men whose feelings and whose active energies point strongly in an unselfish direction, who have the love of their country, of human improvement, of human freedom, even of virtue, in great strength, and of whose thoughts and activity a large share is devoted to disinterested objects, will yet, in the pursuit of these or of any other objects that they strongly desire, permit themselves to do wrong things which the other man, though intrinsically, and taking the whole of his character, farther removed from what a human being ought to be, could not bring himself to commit. It is of no use to debate which of these two states of mind is the best, or rather the least bad. It is quite possible to cultivate the conscience and the sentiments too. Nothing hinders us from so training a man that he will not, even for a disinterested purpose, violate the moral law, and also feeding and encouraging those high feelings, on which we mainly rely for lifting men above low and sordid objects, and giving them a higher conception of what constitutes success in life. If we wish men to practice virtue, it is worth while trying to make them love virtue, and feel it an object in itself, and not a tax paid for leave to pursue other objects. It is worth training them to feel, not only actual wrong or actual meanness, but the absence of noble aims and endeavours, as not merely blamable but also degrading: to have a feeling of the miserable smallness of mere self in the face of this great universe, of the collective mass of our fellow creatures, in the face of past history and of the indefinite future—the poorness and insignificance of human life if it is to be all spent in making things comfortable for ourselves and our kin, and raising ourselves and them a step or two on the social ladder. Thus feeling, we learn to respect ourselves only so far as we feel capable of nobler objects: and if unfortunately those by whom we are surrounded do not share our aspirations, perhaps disapprove the conduct to which we are prompted by them—to sustain ourselves by the ideal sympathy of the great characters in history, or even in fiction, and by the contemplation of an idealized posterity: shall I add, of ideal perfection embodied in a Divine Being?

Now, of this elevated tone of mind the great source of inspiration is poetry, and all literature so far as it is poetical and artistic. We may imbibe exalted feelings from Plato, or Demosthenes, or Tacitus, but it is in so far as those great men are not solely philosophers or orators or historians, but poets and artists. Nor is it only loftiness, only the heroic feelings, that are bred by poetic cultivation. Its power is as great in calming the soul as in elevating it—in fostering the milder emotions, as the more exalted. It brings home to us all those aspects of life which take hold of our nature on its unselfish side, and lead us to identify our joy and grief with the good or ill of the system of which we form a part; and all those solemn or pensive feelings, which, without having any direct application to conduct, incline us to take life seriously, and predispose us to the reception of anything which comes before us in the shape of duty. Who does not feel a better man after a course of Dante, or of Wordsworth, or, I will add, of Lucretius or the Georgics, or after brooding over Gray's Elegy, or Shelley's Hymn to Intellectual Beauty? I have spoken of poetry, but all the other modes of art produce similar effects in their degree. The races and nations whose senses are naturally finer and their sensuous perceptions more exercised than ours receive the same kind of impressions from painting and sculpture: and many of the more delicately organized among ourselves do the same. All the arts of expression tend to keep alive and in activity the feelings they express. Do you think that the great Italian painters would have filled the place they did in the European mind, would have been universally ranked among the greatest men of their time, if their productions had done nothing for it but to serve as the decoration of a public hall or a private *salon*? Their Nativities and Crucifixions, their glorious Madonnas and Saints, were to their susceptible Southern country-men the great school not only of devotional, but of all the elevated and all the imaginative feelings. We colder Northerns may approach to a conception of this function of art when we listen to an oratorio of Handel, or give ourselves up to the emotions excited by a Gothic cathedral. Even apart from any specific emotional expression, the mere contemplation of beauty of a high order produces in no small degree this elevating effect on the character. The power of natural scenery addresses itself to the same region of human nature which corresponds to Art. There are few capable of feeling the sublimer order of natural beauty, such as your own Highlands and other mountain regions afford, who are not, it least temporarily, raised by it above the littlenesses of humanity, and made to feel the puerility of the petty objects which set men's interests at variance, contrasted with the nobler pleasures which all might share. To whatever avocations we may be called in life, let us never quash these susceptibilities within us, but carefully seek the opportunities of maintaining them in exercise. The more prosaic our ordinary duties, the more necessary it is to keep up the tone of our minds by frequent visits to that higher region of thought and feeling, in which every work seems dignified in proportion to the ends for which, and the spirit in which, it is done; where we learn, while eagerly seizing every opportunity of exercising higher faculties and performing higher duties, to regard all useful and honest work as a public function, which may be ennobled by the mode of performing it—which has not properly any other nobility than what that gives—and which, if ever so humble, is never mean but when it is meanly done, and when the motives from which it is done are mean motives. There is, besides, a natural affinity between goodness and the cultivation of the Beautiful, when it is real cultivation, and not a mere unguided instinct. He who has learnt what beauty is, if he be of a virtuous character, will desire to realize it in his own life— will keep before himself a type of perfect beauty in human character, to light his attempts at self- culture. There is a true meaning in the saying of Goethe, though liable to be misunderstood and perverted, that the Beautiful is greater than the Good; for it includes the Good, and adds something to it: it is the Good made perfect, and fitted with all the collateral perfections which make it a finished and completed thing. Now, this sense of perfection, which would make us demand from every creation of man the very utmost that it ought to give, and render us intolerant of the smallest fault in ourselves or in anything we do, is one of the results of Art cultivation. No other human productions come so near to perfection as works of pure Art. In all other things, we are, and may reasonably be, satisfied if the degree of excellence is as great as the object immediately in view seems to us to be worth: but in Art, the perfection is itself the object. If I were to define Art, I should be inclined to call it, the endeavour after perfection in execution. If, we meet with even a piece of mechanical work which bears the marks of being done in this spirit—which is done as if the workman loved it, and tried to make it as good as possible, though something less good would have answered the purpose for which it was ostensibly made—we say that he has worked like an artist. Art, when really cultivated, and not merely practiced empirically, maintains, what it first gave the conception of, an ideal Beauty, to be eternally aimed at, though surpassing what can be actually attained; and by this idea it trains us never to be completely satisfied with imperfection in what we ourselves do and are: to idealize, as much as possible, every work we do, and most of all, our own characters and lives.

And now, having travelled with you over the whole range of the materials and training which a University supplies as a preparation for the higher uses of life, it is almost needless to add any exhortation to you to profit by the gift. Now is your opportunity for gaining a degree of insight into subjects larger and far more ennobling than the minutiae of a business or a profession, and for acquiring a facility of using your minds on all that concerns the higher interests of man, which you will carry with you into the occupations of active life, and which will prevent even the short intervals of time which that may leave you, from being altogether lost for noble purposes. Having once conquered the first difficulties, the only ones of which the irksomeness surpasses the interest; having turned the point beyond which what was once a task becomes a pleasure; in even the busiest after-life, the higher powers of your mind will make progress imperceptibly, by the spontaneous exercise of your thoughts, and by the lessons you will know how to learn from daily experience. So, at least, it will be if in your early studies you have fixed your eyes upon the ultimate end from which those studies take their chief value—that of making you more effective combatants in the great fight which never ceases to rage between Good and Evil, and more equal to coping with the ever new problems which the changing course of human nature and human society present to be resolved. Aims like these commonly retain the footing which they have once established in the mind; and their presence in our thoughts keeps our higher faculties in exercise, and makes us consider the acquirements and powers which we store up at any time of our lives, as a mental capital to be freely expended in helping forward any mode which presents itself of making mankind in any respect wiser or better, or placing any portion of human affairs on a more sensible and rational footing than its existing one. There is not one of us who may not qualify himself so to improve the average amount of opportunities, as to leave his fellow creatures some little the better for the use he has known how to make of his intellect. To make this little greater, let us strive to keep ourselves acquainted with the best thoughts that are brought forth by the original minds of the age; that we may know what movements stand most in need of our aid, and that, as far as depends on us, the good seed may not fall on a rock, and perish without reaching the soil in which it might have germinated and flourished. You are to be a part of the public who are to welcome, encourage, and help forward the future intellectual benefactors of humanity; and you are, if possible, to furnish your contingent to the number of those benefactors. Nor let anyone be discouraged by what may seem, in moments of despondency, the lack of time and of opportunity. Those who know how to employ opportunities will often find that they can create them: and what we achieve depends less on the amount of time we possess, than on the use we make of our time. Ton and your like are the hope and resource of your country in the coming generation. All great things which that generation is destined to do, have to be done by some like you; several will assuredly be done by persons for whom society has done much less, to whom it has given far less preparation, than those whom I am now addressing. I do not attempt to instigate you by the prospect of direct rewards, either earthly or heavenly; the less we think about being rewarded in either way, the better for ns. But there is one reward which will not fail you, and which may be called disinterested, because it is not a consequence, but is inherent in the very fact of deserving it; the deeper and more varied interest you will feel in life: which will give it tenfold its value, and a value which will last to the end. All merely personal objects grow less valuable as we advance in life: this not only endures but increases.

The End

CHAPTER FOURTEEN

Sweetness and Light

From *Culture and Anarchy* (1869)

MATTHEW ARNOLD

This selection is taken from *Culture and Anarchy*, by Matthew Arnold, 1960, Edited with Introduction by J. Dover Wilson. Published by The University Press, Cambridge, United Kingdom, Originally published in 1932, Reprinted (with corrections) 1935.

Editors' Note

Matthew Arnold, son of Thomas Arnold headmaster of Rugby School, was a major Victorian poet with Tennyson and Browning, and literary and cultural critic who worked as an inspector of schools. He wrote *Culture and Anarchy* his central work between 1867 and 1869 as a series of periodical essays. As an expansion of his earlier attacks in 'The Function of Criticism' Arnold attacks the philistinism of Victorian England: culture as 'the study of perfection,' is opposed to the prevalent 'anarchy' of a new democracy without standards and without a sense of direction. Arnold classifies English society into Barbarians, Philistines and Populace. The Philistines in his mind were the most influential for their strength and energy and the mission was to both educate and humanize them. He was greatly concerned at the passage of the Reform Act of 1867 that enfranchised part of the urban male working class for the first time and sought to find a means that could cope with its effects. As a self-proclaimed Christian humanist Arnold argued against both Bentham and Mill the followers of utilitarianism on the one hand, and the defenders of the liberal reform, on the other. Arnold appealed to the authority of 'culture' as the means by which the social and political confusion of the times could be overcome. As he writes in the Preface, added in 1975: 'The whole scope of the essay is to recommend culture as the great help out of our present difficulties; culture being a pursuit of our total perfection by means of getting to know, on all the matters which most concern us, the best which has been thought and said in the world, and, through this knowledge, turning a stream of fresh and free thought upon our stock notions and habits, which we now follow staunchly but mechanically, vainly imagining that there is a virtue in following them staunchly which makes up for the mischief of following them mechanically.'

MP

*****

The disparagers of culture make its motive curiosity; sometimes, indeed they make its motive mere exclusiveness and vanity. The culture which is supposed to plume itself on a smattering of Greek and Latin is a culture which is begotten by nothing so intellectual as curiosity; it is valued either out of sheer vanity and ignorance, or else as an engine of social and class distinction, separating its holder like a badge or title, from other people who have not got it. No serious man would call this *culture*, or attach any value to it, as culture, at all. To find the real ground for the very differing estimate which serious people will set upon culture, we must find some motive for culture in the terms of which may lie a real ambiguity; and such a motive the word *curiosity* gives us.

I have before now pointed out that we English do not, like the foreigners, use this word in a good sense as well as in a bad sense.[1] With us the word is always used in a somewhat disapproving sense. A liberal and intelligent eagerness about the things of the mind may be meant by a foreigner when he speaks of curiosity, but with us the word always conveys a certain notion of frivolous and unedifying activity. In the *Quarterly Review*, some little time ago, was an estimate of the celebrated, French critic, M. Sainte-Beuve, and a very inadequate estimate it in my judgment was. And its inadequacy consisted chiefly in this: that in our English way it left out of sight the double sense really involved in the word *curiosity*, thinking enough was said to stamp M. Sainte-Beuve with blame if it was said that he was

1 "I have before now pointed out," etc.: v. *Ess.* Crit. l, p. 16. In the *Quarterly Review* some time ago: i.e. Jan. 1866. M. Sainte-Beuve (1804–69): v. Editor's Introduction, p. xix.

impelled in his operations as a critic by curiosity, and omitting either to perceive that M. Sainte-Beuve himself, and many other people with him, would consider that this was praise worthy and not blameworthy, or to point out why it ought really to be accounted worthy of blame and not of praise. For as there is a curiosity about intellectual matters which is futile, and merely a disease, so there is certainly a curiosity,—a desire after the things of the mind simply for their own sakes and for the pleasure of seeing them as they are,—which is, in an intelligent being, natural and laudable. Nay, and the very desire to see things as they arc, implies a balance and regulation of mind which is not often attained without fruitful effort, and which is the very opposite of the blind, and diseased impulse of mind which is what we mean to blame when we blame curiosity. Montesquieu says:—"The first motive which ought to impel us to study is the desire to augment the excellence of our nature, and to render an intelligent being yet more intelligent."[2] This is the true ground to assign for the genuine scientific passion, however manifested, and for culture, viewed simply as a fruit of this passion; and it is a worthy ground, even though we let the term *curiosity* stand to describe it.

But there is of culture another view, in which not solely the scientific passion, the sheer desire to see things as they are, natural and proper in an intelligent being, appears as the ground of it. There is a view in which all the love of our neighbour, the impulses towards action, help, and beneficence, the desire for removing human error, clearing human confusion, and diminishing human misery, the noble aspiration to leave the world better and happier than we found it,—motives eminently such as are called social,—come in as pan of the rounds of culture, and the main and pre-eminent pan. Culture is then properly described not as having its origin in curiosity, but as having its origin in the love of perfection; it is *a study of perfection*. It moves by the force, not merely or primarily of the scientific passion for pure knowledge, but also of the moral and social passion for doing good. As, in the first view of it, we took for its worthy motto Montesquieu's words: "To render an intelligent being yet more intelligent!" so, in the second view of it, there is no better motto which it can have than these words of Bishop Wilson: "To make reason and the will of God prevail!"

Only, whereas the passion for doing good is apt to be overhasty in determining what reason and the will of God say, because its turn is for acting rather than thinking, and it wants to be beginning to act; and whereas it is apt to take its own conceptions, which proceed from its own state of development and share in all the imperfections and immaturities of this, for a basis of action; what distinguishes

---

2 Montesquièu (1689–1755): the French political philosopher, author of *De L'Esprit des Lois*.

culture is, that it is possessed by the scientific passion as well as by the passion of doing good; that it demands worthy notions of reason and the will of God, and does not readily suffer its own crude conceptions to substitute themselves for them. And knowing that no action or institution can be salutary and stable which is not based on reason and the will of God, it is not so bent on acting and instituting, even with the great aim of diminishing human error and misery ever before its thoughts, but that it can remember chat acting and instituting are of little use, unless we know how and what we ought to act and to institute.

This culture is more interesting and more far-reaching than that other, which is founded solely on the scientific passion for knowing, But it needs times of faith and ardour, times when the intellectual horizon is opening and widening all round us, to flourish in. And is not the close and bounded intellectual horizon within which we have long lived and moved now lifting up, and are not new lights finding free passage to shine in upon us? For a long time there was no passage for them to make their way in upon us, and then it was of no use to think of adapting the world's action to them. Where was the hope of making reason and the will of God prevail among people who had a routine which they had christened reason and the will of God, in which they were inextricably bound, and beyond which they had no power of looking? But now the iron force of adhesion to the old routine,–social, political, religious,—has wonderfully yielded; the iron force of exclusion of all which is new has wonderfully yielded. The danger now is, not that people should obstinately refuse to allow anything but their old routine to pass for reason and the will of God, but either that they should allow some novelty or other to pass for these too easily, or else that they should underrate the importance of them altogether, and think it enough to follow action for its own sake, without troubling themselves to make reason and the will of God prevail therein. Now, then, is the moment for culture to be of service, culture which believes in making reason and the will of Cod prevail, believes in perfection, is the study and pursuit of perfection, and is no longer debarred, by a rigid invincible exclusion of whatever is new, from getting acceptance for its ideas, simply because they are new.

The moment this view of culture is seized, the moment it is regarded not solely as the endeavour to see things as they are, to draw towards a knowledge of the universal order which seems to be intended and aimed at in the world, and which it is a man's happiness to go along with or his misery to go counter to,—to learn, in short, the will of God,—the moment. I say, culture is considered not merely as the endeavour to *see* and *learn* this, but as the endeavour, also, to make it *prevail*, the moral, social and beneficent character of culture becomes manifest. The mere endeavour to see and learn the truth for our own personal satisfaction is indeed a commencement for making it prevail, a preparing the way for this, which always serves this, and is wrongly, therefore, stamped with blame absolutely in itself and not only in its caricature and degeneration. But perhaps it has got stamped with blame, and disparaged with the dubious title of curiosity, because in comparison with this wider endeavour of such great and plain utility it looks selfish, petty, and unprofitable.

And religion, the greatest and most important of the efforts by which the human race has manifested its impulse to perfect itself,—religion, that voice of the deepest human experience,—does not only enjoin and sanction the aim which is the great aim of culture, the aim of setting ourselves to ascertain what perfection is and to make it prevail; but also, in determining generally in what human perfection consists, religion comes to a conclusion identical with that which culture,—culture seeking the determination of this question through *all* the voices of human experience which have been heard upon it, of art, science, poetry, philosophy, history, as well as of religion, in order to give a greater fulness and certainty to its solution,—likewise reaches. Religion says: *The kingdom of God is within you*; and culture, in like manner, places human perfection in an *internal* condition, in the growth and predominance of our humanity proper, as distinguished from our animality: It places it in the ever-increasing efficacy and in the general harmonious expansion of those gifts of thought and feeling which make the peculiar dignity, wealth, and happiness of human nature. As I have said on a former occasion: "It is in making endless additions to itself,' in the endless expansion of its powers, in endless growth in wisdom and beauty, that the spirit of the human race finds its ideal. To reach this ideal, culture is an indispensable aid, and that is the true value of culture."[3] Not a having and a resting, but a growing and a becoming, is the character of perfection as culture conceives it; and here, too, it coincides with religion.

And because men are all members of one great whole, and the sympathy which is in human nature will not allow one member to be indifferent to the rest or to have a perfect welfare independent of the rest, the expansion of our humanity, to suit the idea of perfection which culture forms, must be a *general* expansion. Perfection, as culture conceives it, is not possible while the individual remains isolated. The individual is required, under pain of being stunted and enfeebled in his own development if he disobeys, to carry others along with him in his march towards perfection, to be continually doing all he can to enlarge and increase the volume of the human stream sweeping thitherward. And here, once more, culture lays on us the same obligation as religion, which says, as Bishop Wilson has admirably put it, that "to promote the kingdom of God is to increase and hasten one's own happiness."

---

3 "As I have said on a former occasion": v. *A French Eton* (ed. 1892), pp. 116–17.

But, finally, perfection,—as culture, from a thorough disinterested study of human nature and human experience learns to conceive it,—is a harmonious expansion of *all* the powers which make the beauty and worth of human nature, and is not consistent with the over-development of anyone power at the expense of the rest. Here culture goes beyond religion, as religion is generally conceived by us.

If culture, then, is a study of perfection, and of harmonious perfection, general perfection, and perfection which consists in becoming something rather than in having something, in an inward condition of the mind and spirit, not in an outward set of circumstances,—it is clear that culture, instead of being the frivolous and useless thing which Mr. Bright, and Mr. Frederic Harrison, and many other Liberals are apt to call it, has a very important function to fulfil for mankind. And this function is particularly important in our modern world, of which the whole civilisation is, to a much greater degree than the civilisation of Greece and Rome, mechanical and external, and tends constantly to become more so. But above all in our own country has culture a weighty part to perform, because here that mechanical character, which civilisation tends to take everywhere, is shown in the most eminent degree. Indeed nearly all the characters of perfection, as culture teaches us to fix them, meet in this country with some powerful tendency which thwarts them and sets them at defiance. The idea of perfection as an *inward* condition of the mind and spirit is at variance with the mechanical and material civilisation in esteem with us, and nowhere, as I have said, so much in esteem as with us. The idea of perfection as a *general* expansion of the human family is at variance with our strong individualism, our hatred of all limits to the unrestrained swing of the individual's personality, our maxim of "every man for himself." Above all the idea of perfection as a *harmonious* expansion of human nature is at variance with our want of flexibility, with our inaptitude for seeing more than one side of a thing, with our .intense energetic absorption in the particular pursuit we happen to be following. So culture has a rough task to achieve in this country. Its preachers have, and are likely long to have, a hard time of it, and they will much oftener be regarded, for a great while to come, as elegant or spurious Jeremiahs, than as friends and benefactors. That, however, will not prevent their doing in the end good service if they persevere. And meanwhile, the mode of action they have to pursue, and the sort of habits they must fight against, ought to be made quite clear for everyone to see who may be willing to look at the matter attentively and dispassionately.

Faith in machinery is, I said, our besetting danger; often in machinery most absurdly disproportioned to the end which this machinery, if it is to do any good at all, is to serve; but always in machinery, as if it had a value in and for itself. What is freedom but machinery? what is population but machinery? what is coal but machinery? what are railroads but machinery? what is wealth but machinery?

what are even, religious organisations but machinery? Now almost every voice in England is accustomed to speak of these things as if they were precious ends in themselves, and therefore had some of the characters of perfection indisputably joined to them. I have before now noticed Mr. Roebuck's stock argument for proving the greatness and happiness of England as she is, and for quite stopping the mouths of all gainsayers.[4] Mr. Roebuck is never weary of reiterating this argument of his, so I do not know why I should be weary of noticing it. May not every man in England say what he likes?"—Mr. Roebuck perpetually asks; and that, he thinks, is quite sufficient, and when every man may say what he likes, our aspirations ought to be satisfied. But the aspirations of culture, which is the study of perfection, are not satisfied, unless what men say, when they may say what they like, is worth saying,—has good in it, and more good than bad. In the same way the *Times*, replying to some foreign strictures on the dress, looks, and behaviour of the English abroad, urges that the English ideal is that everyone should be free to do and to look just as he likes. But culture indefatigably tries, not to make what each raw person may like, the rule by which he fashions himself; but to draw ever nearer to a sense of what is indeed beautiful, graceful, and becoming, and to get the raw person to like that.

And in the same way with respect to railroads and coal. Everyone must have observed the strange language current during the late discussions as to the possible failure of our supplies of coal. Our coal, thousands of people were saying, is the real basis of our national greatness; if our coal runs short, there is an end of the greatness of England. But what *is* greatness?—culture makes us ask. Greatness is a spiritual condition worthy to excite love, interest, and admiration; and the outward proof of possessing greatness is that we excite love, interest, and admiration. If England were swallowed up by the sea tomorrow, which of the two, a hundred years hence, would most excite the love, interest, and admiration of mankind,—would most, therefore, show the evidences of having possessed greatness,—the England of the last twenty years, or the England of Elizabeth, of a time of splendid spiritual effort, but when our coal, and our industrial operations depending on coal, were very little developed? Well, then, what an unsound habit of mind it must be which makes us talk of things like coal or iron as constituting the greatness of England, and how salutary a friend is culture, bent on seeing things as they are, and thus dissipating delusions of this kind and fixing standards of perfection that are real!

---

4 Mr. Roebuck's stock argument: J. A. Roebuck (1801–79), a prominent radical politician of the Benthamite school. Arnold often refers to him, since his utterances provided useful examples of Benthamite extravagance. Cf. *Ess. Crit.* 1, p. 21 and *A French Eton* (ed. 1895), p. 102. The quotation comes from a speech made at Sheffield. Cf. p. 121.

Wealth, again, that end to which our prodigious works for material advantage are directed,—the commonest of commonplaces tells us how men are always apt to regard wealth as a precious end in itself; and certainly they have never been so apt thus to regard it as they are in England at the present time. Never did people believe anything more firmly, than nine Englishmen out often at the present day believe that our greatness and welfare Ire proved by our being so very rich. Now, the use of culture is that it helps us, by means of its spiritual standard of perfection, to regard wealth as but machinery, and not only to say as a matter of words that we regard wealth as but machinery, but really to perceive and feel that it is so. If it were not for this purging effect wrought upon our minds by culture, the whole world, the future as well as the present, would inevitably belong to the Philistines.[5] The people who believe most that our greatness and welfare are proved by our being very rich, and who most give their lives and thoughts to becoming rich, are just the very people whom we call Philistines. Culture says: "Consider these people, then, their way of life, their habits, their manners, the very tones of their voice; look at them attentively; observe the literature they read, the things which give them pleasure, the words which come forth out of their mouths, the thoughts which make the furniture of their minds; would any amount of wealth be worth having with the condition that one was to become just like, these people by having it?" And thus culture begets a dissatisfaction which is of the highest possible value in stemming the common tide of men's thoughts in a wealthy and industrial community, and which saves the future, as one may hope, from being vulgarised, even if it cannot save the present.

Population, again, and bodily health and vigour, are things which are nowhere treated in such an unintelligent, misleading, exaggerated way as in England. Both are really machinery; yet how many people all around us do we see rest in them and rail to look beyond them! Why, one has heard people, fresh from reading certain articles of the *Times* on the Registrar-General's returns of marriages and births in this country, who would talk of our large English families in quite a solemn strain, as if they had something in itself beautiful, elevating, and meritorious in them; as if the British Philistine would have only to present himself before the Great Judge with his twelve children, in order, to be received among the sheep as a matter of right!

But bodily health and vigour, it may be said, are not to be classed with wealth and population as mere machinery; they have a more real and essential value. True; but only as they are more intimately connected with a perfect spiritual condition than wealth or population are. The moment we disjoin them from the idea of a

5 The Philistines: v. note, p. 100.

perfect spiritual condition, and pursue them, as we do pursue them, for their own sake and as ends in themselves, our worship of them becomes as mere worship of machinery, as our worship of wealth or population, and as unintelligent and vulgarising a worship as that is. Everyone with anything like an adequate idea of human perfection has distinctly marked this subordination to higher and spiritual ends of the cultivation of bodily vigour and activity. "Bodily exercise profiteth little; but godliness is profitable unto all things," says the author of the Epistle to Timothy. And the utilitarian Franklin says just as explicitly:—"Eat and drink such an exact quantity as suits the constitution of thy body, *in reference to the services of the mind.*"[6] But the point of view of culture, keeping the mark of human perfection simply and broadly in view, and not assigning to this perfection, as religion or utilitarianism assign to it, a special and limited character,—this point of view, I say, of culture is best given by these words of Epictetus: "—It is a sign ἀφυία," says he,—that is, of a nature not finely tempered,—"to give yourselves up to things which relate to the body; to make, for instance, a great fuss about exercise, a great fuss about eating, a great fuss about drinking, a great fuss about walking, a great fuss about riding.[7] All these things ought to be done merely by the way: the formation of the spirit and character must be our real concern." This is admirable; and, indeed, the Greek word εὐφυία, a finely tempered nature, gives exactly the notion of perfection as culture brings us to conceive it: a harmonious perfection, a perfection in which the characters of beauty and intelligence are both present, which unites "the two noblest of things," —as Swift, who of one of the two, at any rate, had himself all too little, most happily calls them in his *Battle of the Books*, "—the two noblest of things, *sweetness and light.*"[8] The εὐφνής is the man who tends towards sweetness

---

6 The utilitarian Franklin: Benjamin Franklin (1706–90), the American politician, scientist and philosophical writer. Arnold is quoting from the Autobiography (1817), his best known work.

7 Epictetus: Stoic philosopher, born c. A.D. 60, v. essay on Marcus Aurelius in *Ess. Crit.* 1.

8 "*Battle of the Books . . . sweetness and light*": Arnold borrows more than the phrase "sweetness and light" from Swift. In the story Swift tells of the Bee and the Spider may be found the origin of Arnold's distinction between the man of culture and the Philistine. The spider boasts of his web, for all the world like Bright boasting of the industrial prowess of England, "I am a domestic animal, furnished with a native stock within myself. This large castle (to show my improvements in the mathematics) is all built with my own hands, and the materials extracted altogether out of my own person." Whereupon the Bee asks "Whether is the nobler of the two, that which by a lazy contemplation of four inches round, by an overweening pride, feeding and engendering on itself, turns all into excrement and venom, producing nothing at all but flybane and cobweb; or that which by a universal range, with long search, much study, true judgment and distinction of things, brings home honey and wax." The Spider, as Aesop then points out, is the type of the moderns, the Bee

and light; the ἀφνής, on the other hand, is our Philistine. The immense spiritual significance of the Greeks is due to their having been inspired with this central and happy idea of the essential character of human perfection; and Mr. Bright's misconception of culture, as a smattering of Greek and Latin, comes itself, after all, from this wonderful significance of the Greeks having affected the very machinery of our education, and is in itself a kind of homage to it.

In thus making Sweetness and light to be characters of perfection, culture is of like spirit with poetry, follows one law with poetry. Far more than on our freedom, our population, and our industrialism, many amongst us rely upon our religious organisations to save us.[9] I have called religion a yet more important manifestation of human nature than poetry, because it has worked on a broader scale for perfection, and with greater masses of men. But the idea of beauty and of a human nature perfect on all its sides, which is the dominant idea of poetry, is a true and invaluable idea, though it has not yet had the success that the idea of conquering the obvious faults of our animality, and of a human nature perfect on the moral side,—which is the dominant idea of religion,—has been enabled to have; and it is destined, adding to itself the religious idea of a devout energy, to transform and govern the other.

The best art and poetry of the Greeks, in which religion and poetry are one, in which the idea of beauty and of a human nature perfect on all sides adds to itself a religious and devout energy, and works in the strength of that, is on this account of such surpassing interest and instructiveness for us, though it was,—as, having regard to the human race in general, and, indeed, having regard to the Greeks themselves, we must own,—a premature attempt, an attempt which for success needed the moral and religious fibre in humanity to be more braced and developed than it had yet been. But Greece did not err in having the idea of beauty, harmony, and complete human perfection, so present and paramount. It is impossible to have this idea too present and paramount; only, the moral fibre must be braced too. And we, because we have braced the moral fibre, are not on that account in the right way, if at the same time the idea of beauty, harmony, and complete human perfection, is wanting or misapprehended amongst us; and evidently it is wanting or misapprehended at present. And when we rely as we do on our religious organisations, which in themselves do not and cannot give us this idea, and think we have done enough if we make them spread and prevail, then, I say, we fall into our common fault of over-valuing machinery.

---

of the ancients who have "by infinite labour and search, and ranging through every corner of nature" filled their "hives with honey and wax, thus furnishing mankind with the two noblest of things, which are sweetness and light."

9 "Far more … to save us": omitted in ed. I.

Nothing is more common than for people to confound the inward peace and satisfaction which follows the subduing of the obvious faults of our animality with what I may call absolute inward peace and satisfaction,—the peace and satisfaction which are reached as we draw near to complete spiritual perfection, and not merely to moral perfection, or rather to relative moral perfection. No people in the world have done more and struggled more to attain this relative moral perfection than our English race has. For no people in the world has the command to *resist the devil*, to *overcome the wicked one*, in the nearest and most obvious sense of those words, had such a pressing force and reality. And we have had our reward, not only in the great worldly prosperity which our obedience to this command has brought us, but also, and far more, in great inward peace and satisfaction. But to me few things are more pathetic than to see people, on the strength of the inward peace and satisfaction which their rudimentary efforts towards perfection have brought them, employ, concerning their incomplete perfection and the religious organisations within which they have found it, language which properly applies only to complete perfection, and is a far-off echo of the human soul's prophecy of it. Religion itself, I need hardly say, supplies them in abundance with this grand language. And. very freely do they use it; yet it is really the severest criticism of such an incomplete perfection as alone we have yet reached through our religious organisations.[10]

The impulse of the English race towards moral development and self-conquest has nowhere so powerfully manifested itself as in Puritanism. Nowhere has Puritanism found so adequate an expression as in the religious organisation of the Independents. The modern Independents have a newspaper, the *Nonconformist*, written with great sincerity and ability. The motto, the standard, the profession of faith which this organ of theirs carries aloft, is: "The Dissidence of Dissent and the Protestantism of the Protestant religion." There is sweetness and light, and an ideal of complete harmonious human perfection! One need not go to culture and poetry to find language to judge it. Religion, with its instinct for perfection, supplies language to judge it, language too which is in our mouths every day.[11] "Finally, be of one mind, united in feeling," says St. Peter. There is an ideal which judges the Puritan ideal: "The Dissidence of Dissent and the Protestantism of the Protestant religion!" And religious organisations like this are what people believe in, rest in, would give their lives for! Such, I say, is the wonderful virtue of even the beginnings of perfection, of having conquered even the plain faults of our animality that the religious organisation which has helped us to do it can seem to us something precious, salutary, and to be propagated, even when it wears such a brand of imperfection on its forehead

---

10 "And very freely … yet it": omitted in ed. I, which reads "which" instead.

11 "… language too … every day": omitted in ed. I. Independents: i.e. Congregationalists.

as this. And men have got such a habit of giving to the language of religion a special application, of making it a mere jargon, that for the condemnation which religion itself passes on the shortcomings of their religious organisations they have no ear; they are sure to cheat themselves and to explain this condemnation away. They can only be reached by the criticism which culture, like poetry, speaking a language not to be sophisticated, and resolutely testing these organisations by the ideal of a human perfection complete on all sides, applies to them.

But men of culture and poetry, it will be said, are again and again failing, and failing conspicuously, in the necessary first stage to a harmonious perfection, in the subduing of the great obvious faults of our animality, which it is the glory of these religious organisations to have helped us to subdue. True, they do often so fail. They have often been without the virtues as well as the faults of the Puritan; it has been one of their dangers that they so felt the Puritan's faults that they too much neglected the practice of his virtues. I will not, however, exculpate them at the Puritan's expense. They have often failed in morality, and morality is indispensable And they have been punished for their failure, as the Puritan has been rewarded for his performance. They have been punished wherein they erred; but their ideal of beauty, of sweetness and light, and a human nature complete on all its sides, remains the true ideal of perfection still; just as the Puritan's ideal of perfection remains narrow and inadequate, although for what he did well he has been richly rewarded. Notwithstanding the mighty results of the Pilgrim Fathers' voyage, they and their standard of perfection are rightly judged when we figure to ourselves Shakespeare or Virgil,—souls in whom sweetness and light, and all that in human nature is most humane, were eminent,—accompanying them on their voyage, and think what intolerable company Shakespeare and Virgil would have found them! In the .same way let us judge the religious organisations which we see all around us. Do not let us deny the good and the happiness which they have accomplished; but do not let us fail to see clearly that their idea of human perfection is narrow and inadequate, and that the Dissidence of Dissent and the Protestantism of the Protestant religion will never bring humanity to its true goal. As I said with regard to wealth: Let us look at the life of those who live in and for it,—so I say with regard to the religious organisations. Look at the life imaged in such a newspaper as the *Nonconformist*,—a life of jealousy of the Establishment, disputes, tea-meetings, openings of chapels, sermons; and then think of it as an ideal of a human life completing itself on all sides, and aspiring with all its organs after sweetness, light, and perfection![12]

---

12 "… the *Nonconformist*": a weekly Congregational paper founded in 1841 and edited by Edward Miall, v. note, p. 87.

Another newspaper, representing, like the Nonconformist, one of the religious organisations of this country, was a short time ago giving an account of the crowd at Epsom on the Derby day, and of all the vice and hideousness which was to be seen in that crowd; and then the writer turned suddenly round upon Professor Huxley, and asked him how he proposed to cure all this vice and hideousness without religion.[13] I confess I felt disposed to ask the asker this question: and how do you propose to cure it with such a religion as yours? How is the ideal of a life so unlovely, so unattractive, so incomplete, so narrow, so far removed from a true and satisfying ideal of human perfection, as is the life of your religious organisation as you yourself reflect it, to conquer and transform all this vice and hideousness?[14] Indeed, the strongest plea for the study of perfection as pursued by culture, the clearest proof of the actual inadequacy of the idea of perfection held by the religious organisation,—expressing, as I have said, the most wide-spread effort which the human race has yet made after perfection,—is to be found in the state of our life and society with these in possession of it, and having been in possession of it I know not how many hundred years. We are all of us included in some religious organisation or other; we all call ourselves, in the sublime and aspiring language of religion which I have before noticed, *children of God*. Children of God;—it is an immense pretension I—and how are we to justify it? By the works which we do, and the words which we speak. And the work which we collective children of God do, our grand centre of life, our city which we have builded for us to dwell in, is London! London, with its unutterable external hideousness, and with its internal canker of *publicè egestas, privatim opulentia*,—to use the words which Sallust puts into Cato's mouth about Rome,—unequalled in the world![15] The word, again, which we children of God speak, the voice which most hits our collective

---

13 Prof. Huxley: T. H. Hurley (1825–95), scientist and agnostic. A friend of Arnold, though they differed on many points. He criticized Arnold in an address on "Science and Culture" (1880) delivered at Birmingham (v. *Science and Education*, no. vi) and Arnold replied in "Literature and Science" printed in *Nineteenth Century*, April, 1884 (v. *Discourses in America*, no. ii). The personal relations between the two men are well illustrated by the following letter from Huxley, dated July 8, 1869:

> My dear Arnold—Look at Bishop Wilson on the sin of covetousness and then inspect your umbrella stand. You will there see a beautiful brown smooth-handled umbrella which is not your property. Think of what the excellent prelate would have advised and bring it with you next time you come to the Club. The porter will take care of it for me.—Ever yours faithfully, T. H. Huxley.

14 "… so incomplete": ed. I omits this.

15 "… *publicè egestas, privatim opulentia*": cf. *A French Eton* (p. 20), "With us' it is always the individual that is filled, and the public that is sent empty away."

thought, the newspaper with the largest circulation in England, nay, with the largest circulation in the whole world, is the *Daily Telegraph*![16] I say that when our religious organisations,—which I admit to express the most considerable effort after perfection that our race has yet made,—land us in no better result than this, it is high time to examine carefully their idea of perfection, to see whether it does not leave out of account sides and forces of human nature which we might turn to great use; whether it would not be more operative if it were more complete. And I say that the English reliance on our religious organisations and on their ideas of human perfection just as they stand, is like our reliance on freedom, on muscular Christianity,[17] on population, on coal, on wealth,—mere belief in machinery, and unfruitful; and that it is wholesomely counteracted by culture, bent on seeing things as they are, and on drawing the human race onwards to a more complete, a harmonious perfection.[18]

Culture, however, shows its single-minded love of perfection, its desire simply to make reason and the will of God prevail, its freedom from fanaticism, by its attitude towards all this machinery, even while it insists that it is machinery. Fanatics, seeing the mischief men do themselves by their blind belief in some machinery or other,—whether it is wealth and industrialism, or whether it is the cultivation of bodily strength and activity, or whether it is a political organisation,—or whether it is a religious organisation,—oppose with might and main the tendency to this or that political and religious organisation, or to games and athletic exercises, or to wealth and industrialism, and try violently to stop it. But the flexibility which sweetness and light give, and which is one of the rewards of culture pursued in good faith, enables a man to see that a tendency may be necessary, and even, as a preparation for something in the future, salutary, and yet that the generations or individuals who obey this tendency are sacrificed to it, that they fall short of the hope of perfection by following it; and that its mischiefs are to be criticised, lest it should take too firm a hold and last after it has served its purpose.

Mr. Gladstone well pointed out, in a speech at Paris, and others have pointed out the same thing,—how necessary is the present great movement towards wealth and industrialism, in order to lay broad foundations of material well-being for the society of the future.[19] The worst of these justifications is, that they are generally addressed to the very people engaged, body and soul, in the movement in question;

16 "... the largest circulation in the whole world": v. note, p. 8 "Mr. G. A. Sala."
17 "... muscular Christianity: a reference to Charles Kingsley who was said to preach this type of religion.
18 "... complete, a harmonious perfection": ed. I reads "complete perfection."
19 "Mr. Gladstone ... at Paris": probably in connexion with the great Industrial Exhibition of 1867.

at all events, that they are always seized with the greatest avidity by these people, and taken by them as quite justifying their life; and that thus they tend to harden them in their sins. Now, culture admits the necessity of the movement towards fortune-making and exaggerated industrialism, readily allows that the future may derive benefit from it; but insists, at the same time, that the passing generations of industrialists,—forming, for the most part, the stout main body of Philistinism,—are sacrificed to it. In the same way, the result of all the games and sports which occupy the passing generation of boys and young men may be the establishment of a better and sounder physical type for the future to work with. Culture does not set itself against the games and sports; it congratulates the future, and hopes it will make a good use of its improved physical basis; but it points out that our passing generation of boys and young men is, meantime, sacrificed. Puritanism was perhaps necessary to develop the moral fibre of the English race, Nonconformity to break the yoke of ecclesiastical domination over men's minds and to prepare the way for freedom of thought in the distant future; still, culture points out that the harmonious perfection of generations of Puritans and Nonconformists has been, in consequence, sacrificed, Freedom of speech may be necessary for the society of the future, but the young lions of the *Daily Telegraph* in the meanwhile are sacrificed.[20] A voice for every man in his country's government may be necessary for the society of the future, but meanwhile Mr. Beales and Mr. Bradlaugh are sacrificed.[21]

Oxford, the Oxford of the past, has many faults; and "she has heavily paid for them in defeat, in isolation, in want of hold upon the modern world. Yet we in Oxford, brought up amidst the beauty and sweetness of that beautiful place, have not failed to seize one truth:—the truth that beauty and sweetness are essential characters of a complete" human perfection. When I insist on this, I am all in the faith and tradition of Oxford. I say boldly that this our sentiment for beauty and sweetness, our sentiment against hideousness and rawness, has been at the bottom of our attachment to so many beaten causes, of our opposition to so many triumphant movements. And the sentiment is true, and has never been wholly defeated, and has shown its power even in its defeat. We have not won our political battles, we have not carried our main points, we have not stopped our adversaries' advance, we have not marched victoriously with the modern world; but we have told silently upon the mind of the country, we have prepared currents of feeling which sap our adversaries' position when it seems gained, we have kept up our own communications with the future. Look at the Course of the great movement which shook Oxford to its centre some thirty years ago! It was directed, as anyone who reads

20 "Puritanism was perhaps necessary": ed. I reads "Puritanism was necessary."

21 Mr. Beales and Mr. Bradlaugh: v. Editor's Introduction, pp. xxv–xxvi.

Dr. Newman's *Apology* may see, against "what in one word may be called 'Liberalism.' Liberalism prevailed; it was the appointed force to do the work of the hour; it was necessary, it was inevitable that it should prevail. The Oxford movement war broken, it failed;[22] our wrecks are scattered on every shore:"–

> Quæ regio in terris nostri non plena laboris?[23]

But what was it, this Liberalism, as Dr. Newman saw it, and as it really broke the Oxford movement? It was the great "middle-class Liberalism, which had for the cardinal points of its belief the Reform Bill of 1832, and local self-government, in politics; in the social sphere, free-trade, unrestricted competition, and the making of large industrial fortunes; in the religious sphere, the Dissidence of Dissent and the Protestantism of the Protestant religion. I do not say that other and more intelligent forces than this were not opposed to the Oxford movement: but this was the force which really heat it; this was the force which Dr. Newman felt himself fighting with; this was the force which till only the other day seemed to be the paramount force in this country, and to be in possession of the future; this was the force whose achievements fill Mr. Lowe with such inexpressible admiration, and whose rule he was so horror struck to see threatened.[24] And where is this great force of Philistinism now? It is thrust into the second rank, it is become a power, of yesterday, it has lost the future.[25] A new power has suddenly appeared, a power which it is impossible yet to judge fully, but which is certainly a wholly different force from middle-class Liberalism; different in its cardinal points of belief, different in its tendencies in every, sphere. It loves and admires neither the legislation of middle-class Parliaments, nor the local self-government of middle-class vestries, nor the unrestricted competition of middle-class industrialists, nor the dissidence of middle-class Dissent and the Protestantism of middle-class Protestant religion.

---

22 The Oxford movement was broken, it failed: v. Editor's Introduction, p. xiii. In 1869 Liberal Churchmanship seemed everywhere triumphant. Essays and Reviews had appeared in 1860 and its authors escaped official condemnation as heretics; Bishop Colenso (v. note, p. 181) published a still more startling book in 1862 and likewise survived. Meanwhile Wilberforce, the leader of the High Church party, was twice disappointed of a hoped for succession to the archiepiscopal throne and in 1863 the latitudinarian Stanley was appointed Dean of Westminster (v. note, p. 8).

23 "Quæ regio in terris nostri non plena laboris?" What part of the world is not full of our calamities? Aeneid, 1, 460.

24 "Mr. Lowe": Robert Lowe (1811–92), Viscount Sherbrooke. v. Editor's Introduction; pp. xiv, xxiii.

25 "It is thrust into the second rank ... the future": referring to the Reform Act of 1867 which first gave the vote to the working classes, v. Editor's Introduction, pp. xxiii–xxviii.

I am not now praising this new force, or saying that its own ideals are better; all I say is, that they are wholly different. And who will estimate how much the currents of feeling created by Dr. Newman's movement, the keen desire for beauty and sweetness which it nourished, the deep aversion it manifested to the hardness and vulgarity of middle-class Liberalism, the strong light it turned on the hideous and grotesque illusions of middle-class Protestantism,—who will estimate how much all these contributed to swell the tide of secret dissatisfaction which has mined the ground under the self-confident Liberalism of the last thirty years, and has prepared the way for its sudden collapse and supersession? It is in this manner that the sentiment of Oxford for beauty and sweetness conquers, and in this manner long may it continue to conquer!

In this manner it works to the same end as culture, and there is plenty of work for it yet to do. I have said that the new and more democratic force which is now superseding our old middle-class Liberalism cannot yet be rightly judged. It has its main tendencies still to form. We hear promises of its giving us administrative reform, law reform, reform of education, and 1 know not what; but those promises come rather from its advocates, wishing to make a good plea for it and to justify it for superseding middle class Liberalism, than from clear tendencies which it has itself yet developed. But meanwhile it has plenty of well-intentioned friends against whom culture may with advantage continue to uphold steadily its ideal of human perfection; that this is *an inward spiritual activity, having for its characters increased sweetness, increased light, increased life, increased sympathy*. Mr. Bright, who has a foot in both worlds. the world of middle-class Liberalism and the world of democracy, but who brings most of his ideas from the world of middle-class Liberalism in which he was bred, always inclines to inculcate that faith in machinery to which, as we have seen, Englishmen are so prone, and which has been the bane of middle-class Liberalism. He complains with a sorrowful indignation of people who "appear to have no proper estimate of the value of the franchise;" he leads his disciples to believe,—what the Englishman is always too ready to believe,—that the having a vote, like the having a large family, or a large business, or large muscles, has in itself some edifying and perfecting effect upon human nature. Or else he cries out to the democracy,—"the men," as he calls them, "upon whose shoulders the greatness of England rests,"—he cries out to them: "See what you have done![26] I look over this country and see the cities you have built, the railroads you, have made, the manufactures you have produced, the cargoes which freight the ships of the greatest mercantile navy the world has ever seen! I see that you

26 "See what you have done", etc. From a speech of Dec. 4, 1866, v. Public Addresses, ed. T. Rogers. p. 373.

have converted by your labours what was once a wilderness—these islands, into a fruitful garden; I know that you have created this wealth, and are a nation whose name is a word of power throughout all the world." Why, this is just the very style of laudation with which Mr. Roebuck or Mr. Lowe debauch the minds of the middle classes, and make such Philistines of them. It is the same fashion of teaching a man to value himself not on what he *is*, not on his progress in sweetness and light, but on the number of the railroads he has constructed; or the bigness of the tabernacle he has built.[27] Only the middle classes are told they have done it all with their energy, self-reliance, and capital, and the democracy are told they have done it all with their hands and sinews. But teaching the democracy to put its trust in achievements of this kind is merely training them to be Philistines to take the place of the Philistines whom they are superseding; and they too like the middle class will be encouraged to sit down at the banquet of the future without having on a wedding garment, and nothing excellent can then come from them. Those who know their besetting faults, those who have watched them and listened to them, or those who will read the instructive account recently given of them by one of themselves, the *Journeyman Engineer*,[28] will agree that the idea which culture sets before us of perfection,—an increased spiritual activity, having for its characters increased sweetness, increased light, increased life, increased sympathy,—is an idea which the new democracy needs far more than the idea of the blessedness of the franchise, or the wonderfulness of its own industrial performances.

Other well-meaning friends of this new power are for leading it, not in the old ruts of middle-class Philistinism, but in ways which are naturally alluring to the feet of democracy, though in this country they are novel and untried ways. I may call them the ways of Jacobinism.[29] Violent indignation with the past, abstract systems of renovation applied wholesale, a new doctrine drawn up in black and white for elaborating down to the very smallest details a rational society for the future,—these are the ways of Jacobinism. Mr. Frederic Harrison and other disciples of Comte,[30]—one of them, Mr. Congreve,[31] is an old friend of mine, and I am glad to have an opportunity of publicly expressing my respect for his talents and character,—are among the friends of democracy who are for leading it in paths of this

27 "... the bigness of the tabernacle": a reference to Spurgeon, v. note, p. 20.

28 "... the *Journeyman Engineer*": v. p. 238.

29 "Jacobinism": i.e. revolutionary principles.

30 Comte, Auguste (1789–1857), founder of Positivism, at once a philosophy aiming at a unification of all knowledge and a religion based upon the worship of Humanity.

31 Mr. Congreve: Richard Congreve (1818–99), founder of the Positivist community in London; educated at Rugby with Arnold, who calls him "acquaintance" in ed. I and ed. 2, but alters it to "friend" in ed. 3.

kind. Mr. Frederic Harrison is very hostile to culture, and from a natural enough motive; for culture is the eternal opponent of the two things which are the signal marks of Jacobinism,—its fierceness, and its addiction to an abstract system.[32] Culture is always assigning to system-makers and systems a smaller share in the bent of human destiny than their friends like. A Current in people's minds sets towards new ideas; people are dissatisfied with their old narrow stock of Philistine ideas, Anglo-Saxon ideas, or any other; and Some man, some Bentham[33] or Comte, who has the real merit of having early and strongly felt and helped the new current but who brings plenty of narrowness and mistakes of his own into his feeling and help of it, is credited with being the author of the whole current, the fit person to be entrusted with its regulation and to guide the human race.

The excellent German historian of the mythology of Rome, Preller, relating the introduction at Rome under the Tarquins of the worship of Apollo, the god of light, healing, and reconciliation, will have us observe that it was not so much the Tarquins who brought to Rome the new worship of Apollo, as a current in the mind of the Roman people which set powerfully at that time towards a new worship of this kind, and away from the old run of Latin and Sabine religious ideas. In a similar way, culture directs our attention to the natural Current there is in human affairs and to its continual working, and will not let us rivet our faith upon anyone man and his doings. It makes us see, not only his good side, but also how much in him was of necessity limited and transient; nay, it even feels a pleasure, a sense of an increased freedom and of an ampler future, in so doing.

I remember, when I was under the influence of a mind to which I feel the greatest obligations, the mind of a man who was the very incarnation of sanity and clear sense, a man the most considerable, it seems to me, whom America has yet produced,—Benjamin Franklin,[34]—I remember the relief with which, after long feeling the sway of Franklin's imperturbable common-sense, I came upon a project of his for a new version of the Book of Job, to replace the old version, the style of which, says Franklin, has become obsolete, and thence less agreeable. "I give," he continues, "a few verses, which may serve as a sample of the kind of version I would

---

32 "... abstract system": Arnold is here drawing freely upon Burke's *Reflections on the Revolution*.

33 Bentham: Jeremy Bentham (1748–1832), the founder of Utilitarianism, the reformer of the criminal code, the leader of philosophic radicalism which inspired the Liberalism of the age. Cf. p. 67 and the preface to *Ess. Crit.* 1. It is easy to make fun of Bentham's notions about Plato, of his style, and of his crotchets, but no other single man has exercised a more profound influence upon modern England (v. Dicey, *Law and Opinion in England*). The worse, Arnold would reply, for England! For to him Benthamism was the philosophic expression of the Englishman's "worship of machinery."

34 Benjamin Franklin: v. note, p. 53.

recommend." We all recollect the famous verse in our translation: "Then Satan answered the Lord and said: 'Doth Job fear God for nought?'" Franklin makes this: "Does Your Majesty imagine that Job's good conduct is the effect of mere personal attachment and affection?" I well remember how when first I read that, I drew a deep breath of relief, and said to myself: "After all, there is a stretch of humanity beyond Franklin's victorious good sense!" So, after hearing Bentham cried loudly up as the renovator of modern society, and Bentham's mind and ideas proposed as the rulers of our future, I open the *Deontology*.[35] There I read: "While Xenophon was writing his history and Euclid teaching geometry, Socrates and Plato were talking nonsense under pretence of talking wisdom and morality. This morality of theirs consisted in words; this wisdom of theirs was the denial of the matters known to every man's experience." From moment of reading that, I am delivered from the bondage of Bentham! the fanaticism of his adherents can touch me no longer; I feel the inadequacy of his mind and ideas for supplying the rule of human society, for perfection.

Culture tends always thus to deal with the men of a system, of disciples, of a school; with men like Comte or, the late Mr. Buckle,[36] or Mr. Mill.[37] However much it may find to admire in these personages, or in some of them, it nevertheless remembers the text: "Be not ye called Rabbi I" and it soon passes on from any Rabbi.[38] But Jacobinism loves a Rabbi; it does not want to pass on from its Rabbi in pursuit of a future and still unreached perfection; it wants its Rabbi and his ideas to stand for perfection, that they may with the more authority recast the world; and for Jacobinism, therefore, culture,—eternally passing onwards and seeking,—is an impertinence and an offence. But culture, just because it resists this tendency of Jacobinism to impose on us a man with limitations and errors of his own along with the true ideas of which he is the organ, really does the world and Jacobinism itself a service.

35 *Deontology or Science of Morality*: published after Bentham's death in 1834 in 2 vols.

36 Mr. Buckle: Henry Thomas Buckle (1821–62). author of *A History of Civilisation in England* (1857–6 I), which had an immense and world-wide circulation, and was an attempt to trace historic factors to geographical causes.

37 Mr. Mill: John Stuart Mill (1806–73), economist, philosopher, radical, a disciple of Bentham (v. above), whose Utilitarianism he softened and humanised. Cf. *James and John Stuart Mill on Education*, another volume in the present series. Arnold describes him in *A French Eton* (p. 156) as "not perhaps the great spirit that some of his admirers suppose, but ... a singularly acute, ardent, and interesting man ... capable of following lights that led him away from the regular doctrine of philosophical radicalism." Cf. *Ess. Crit.* 1, 348.

38 "Be not ye called Rabbi!" Matth. xxii. 8.

So, too, Jacobinism, in its fierce Hatred of the past and of those whom it makes liable for the sins of the past, cannot away with the inexhaustible indulgence proper to culture, the consideration of circumstances, the severe judgment of actions joined to the merciful judgment of persons. "The man of culture is in politics," cries Mr. Frederic Harrison, Hone of the poorest mortals alive! "Mr. Frederic Harrison wants to be doing business, and he complains that the man of culture stops him with a "turn for small fault-finding, love of selfish ease, and indecision in action." Of what use is culture, he asks, except for "a critic of new books or a professor of *belles lettres*?" Why, it is of use because, in presence of the fierce exasperation which breathes, or rather, I may say, hisses, through the whole production in which Mr. Frederic Harrison asks that question, it reminds us that the perfection of human nature is sweetness and light. It is of use because, like religion,—that other effort after perfection,—it testifies that, where bitter envying and strife are, there is confusion and every evil work.

The pursuit of perfection, then, is the pursuit of sweetness and light. He who works for sweetness works in the end for light also; he who works for light works in the end for sweetness also. But he who works for sweetness and light united,[39] works to make reason and the will of God prevail. He who works for machinery, he who works for hatred, works only for confusion. Culture looks beyond machinery, culture hates hatred; culture has one great r passion, the passion for sweetness and light. It has one even yet greater!—the passion for making them *prevail*. It is not satisfied till we *all* come to a perfect man; it knows that the sweetness and light of the few must be imperfect until the raw and unkindled masses of humanity are touched with sweetness and light. If I have not shrunk from saying that we must work for sweetness and light, so neither have I shrunk from saying that we must have a broad basis, must have sweetness and light for as many as possible. Again and again I have insisted how those are the happy moments of humanity, how those are the marking epochs of a people's life, how those are the flowering times for literature and art and all the creative power of genius, when there is a *national* glow of life and thought, when the whole of society is in the fullest measure permeated by thought, sensible to beauty, intelligent and alive. Only it must be *real* thought and *real* beauty; *real* sweetness and *real* light. Plenty of people will try to give the masses, as they call them, an intellectual food prepared and adapted in the way they think proper for the actual condition of the masses. The ordinary popular literature is an example of this way of working on the masses. Plenty of people will try to indoctrinate the masses with the set of ideas and judgments constituting the

---

39 "He who works for sweetness ... sweetness and light united": ed. 2 substitutes the single "He who works for sweetness and light."

creed of their own profession or party. Our religious and political organisations give an example of this way of working on the masses. I condemn neither way; but culture works differently. It does not try to teach down to the level of inferior classes; it does not try to win them for this or that sect of its own, with ready-made judgments and watchwords. It seeks to do away with classes; to make the best that has been thought and known in the world current everywhere; to make all men live in an atmosphere of sweetness and light, where they may use ideas, as it uses them itself, freely,—nourished and not bound by them.[40]

This is the *social idea*; and the men of culture are the true apostles of equality. The great men of culture are those who have had a passion for diffusing, for making prevail, for carrying from one end of society to the other, the best knowledge, the best ideas of their time; who have laboured to divest knowledge of all that was harsh, uncouth, difficult, abstract, professional, exclusive; to humanise it, to make it efficient outside the clique of the cultivated and learned, yet still remaining the *best* knowledge and thought of the time, and a true source, therefore, of sweetness and light. Such a man was Abelard in the Middle Ages,[41] in spite of all his imperfections; and thence the boundless emotion and enthusiasm which Abelard excited. Such were Lessing[42] and Herder[43] in Germany, at the end of the last century; and their services to Germany were in this way inestimably precious. Generations will pass, and literary monuments will accumulate, and works far more perfect than the works of Lessing and Herder will be produced in Germany; and yet the names of these two men will Jill a German with a reverence and enthusiasm such as the names of the most gifted masters will hardly awaken. And why?[44] Because they *humanised* knowledge; because they broadened the basis of life and intelligence; because they worked powerfully to diffuse sweetness and light, to make reason and the will of God prevail. With Saint Augustine they said: "Let us not leave Thee alone to make in the secret of thy knowledge, as thou didst before the creation of the firmament, the division of light from darkness; let the children of thy spirit, placed in their firmament, make their light shine upon the earth, mark the division

---

40 "It seeks to do away with classes ... bound by them": I follow the ed. 2 text here, Arnold in 1869 omitting the words "to make the best ... current everywhere" and reading "where they use" for "and use."

41 Abelard (1079–1142): the great scholastic philosopher, who was for a time the centre of extraordinary intellectual ferment at the University of Paris.

42 Lessing (1729–81): the great German critic.

43 Herder (1744–1803): a writer of inferior merit to Lessing, but with considerable reputation in his own and Arnold's time. His ideas were of a sort to interest Arnold, and were no unlike those which form the staple of *Culture and Anarchy*.

44 "And why?" Omitted in ed. I.

of night and day, and announce the revolution of the times; for the old order is passed, and the new arises; the night is spent, the day is come forth; and thou shalt crown the year with thy blessing, when thou shalt send forth labourers into thy harvest sown by other hands than theirs; when thou shalt send forth new labourers to new seed-times, whereof the harvest shall be not yet."

CHAPTER FIFTEEN

Aim and Basis

From *The Crisis in the University* (1949)

SIR WALTER MOBERLY

This selection is taken from *The Crisis in the University*, by Sir Walter Moberly, 1949. Published for the Christian Frontier Council, By SCM Press Ltd, London, United Kingdom.[1]

Editors' Note

Walter Hamilton Moberly (1881–1974) was a professor of philosophy who served as Vice-Chancellor of the University of Manchester and chairman of the UK's University Grants Committee (1935–1949). A committed Christian, his book 'The Crisis in the University' offered a way of reconstructing universities in the aftermath of World War II in a way that paid attention to Christianity but not unduly so. Although he was a graduate of Oxford, both his career—in the University of Birmingham and University College Exeter—and his position on the University Grants Committee doubtless helped to forge in him a concern for all the universities in the UK. Indeed, 'The Crisis in the University' was remarkable

1 SCM Press Ltd, London, the original publisher of this selection, has confirmed that they no longer have any record of who maintains the copyright for this text. The author is deceased. The Volume Editors did their best to find the copyright holder of this chapter.

in attempting to provide an overarching philosophy for the university system as a whole.

The crisis to which Moberly sought to draw attention was not an economic crisis (although in the immediate aftermath of World War II the UK universities were in a difficult situation) but was at once moral, cultural and educational in character. Just what was the place and role of the university to be in a world that appeared to be fragmenting and without clear purpose or even values? No less than carving out a sense of the university as providing some of the resources for societal reconstruction lay at the heart of Moberly's book. But, in turn, grave problems arose, for universities, in Moberly's view, had failed to live up to their potential.

All too often, universities have been content—he argued—to rest on unexamined presuppositions; for instance, of a ready-to-hand neutrality rather than a self-conscious commitment. And they had failed to constitute themselves as centres of vigorous cross-disciplinary and critical inquiry, living out fully their intellectual freedom. As a result, fundamental questions had been ducked: how shall a person live? What principles might serve the world? Students had too often been allowed to complete their studies without facing up to such matters. Consequently, 'the cultural failure of the universities is seen in the students. In recent years large numbers of these have been apathetic and have had neither wide interests nor compelling convictions'. 'The Crisis in the University' does nothing less that lay out principles to combat this grave situation and may well, therefore, speak to later generations.

RB

* * * * *

We come now to the most crucial; and the hardest part of our task. At this time of crisis, in the middle of the twentieth century and after two world-wars, what positive convictions, if any, should the British universities embody? In our earlier chapters we have painted a picture of disintegration, and we have disallowed various attempts at re-integration. What then is our own alternative? To what extent should a university concern itself with philosophies of life, and should it stand positively for any particular philosophy of life? If so, what should that be; and in what way should it be exemplified (e.g. by inculcation to students, tests for teachers etc.)? What responsibility has a university for the philosophies of life of its members? We ourselves are writing as Christian believers, desiring to bring Christian insight to the problem, 'How can the university be the university?' but we have already ruled out the view that definite Christian conviction can, now or in any near future, be the basis of integration. At what then can we legitimately aim, and what can we reasonably ask others to concede? These are the most fundamental questions that can possibly be asked about universities;' and yet it is just on these issues that, both within and outside the universities, there is most obviously confusion or disharmony.

We confess frankly that in answering these questions we can only make a small beginning. At best what we have to offer is an interim report. As we see it, neither the general intellectual situation nor the mind of the general body of Christians in the university world, admits at present of anything more. Much further thinking and experimenting needs to be done, and the most we can hope is to contribute some stimulus towards it. But to shirk this central question altogether would make nugatory everything else we have to say. However crude or superficial our treatment, all that we have said so far leads up to it and all that is to follow springs from it.

1 The Open Forum

As a minimum, even if the university is officially neutral on ultimate issues, its neutrality should be 'positive' and not 'negative.' That is it should not exclude or discourage discussion of these, frequently burning, questions but should actively promote and stimulate it. We borrow the term 'positive neutrality' from International Student Service, whose experience in this respect is highly relevant. In addition to its relief work, I.S.S. has for many years brought together in conference groups of students and staff, for frank discussion of the most controversial and explosive questions. In this way it has successfully brought together such apparently unmixable groups as Jews and Arabs, Orangemen and Sinn Feiners, Dutch and Indonesians, etc., to discuss the very questions which divide and inflame them. The basis of unity which makes possible the plainest of speaking without rupture is, first, solidarity as university men and women, and, secondly, personal fellowship engendered in living together throughout the conference. Such conferences are, in a high degree, educational to all who take part ill them. There you meet face to face those who hold opinions and sentiments antagonistic to your own. You become aware of such views not only at long range, as something misguided and perverse to be refuted, but as the sincere convictions of men with whom you are ill immediate personal fellowship. They come alive to you and the members of each group take a notable step towards imaginative understanding of just those factors which they have been most liable to overlook. Disagreement may still be deep, but much misunderstanding will have been removed; and when, in later life, some of these students hold key positions, their decisions are likely to be more intelligent and responsible than they would otherwise have been. But, in order to perform this function, it is necessary that I.S.S., as an organization, should be uncommitted to any side in regard to the vexed questions debated at its conferences. Otherwise it would be unable to assemble the parties.

This analogy may be applied to the university. The university 'must be a community within which the chief contemporary intellectual positions ... may enter into a living encounter with one another.' At the very least, fundamental questions must not be ignored but must be asked and examined radically. How shall a man live? What are the things which really matter and what is their relative importance? To what sort of world have we to adjust ourselves? 'Here arises the responsibility of the universities. They are inheritors of the Greek tradition of candid and intrepid thinking about the fundamental issues involved in the life of the individual and of the community and of the Greek principle that' the unexamined life is no life for man '... Certainly it is no part of the duty of a university to inculcate any particular philosophy of life. But it is its duty to assist its students to form their own philosophies of life, so that they may not go out into the world maimed and useless. It should stimulate and train them, not of course necessarily to think alike, but at least to think, and to think strenuously about the great issues of right and wrong, of liberty and government, on which both for the individual and for the community, a balanced judgment is essential to a rational life.'[2] The vital principle of democracy is that differences are hammered out in discussion. But the discussion which goes on in a university may be defective, either because it omits the really vital issues or because it treats them only at a superficial level. The radical discussion that is required is difficult and daunting, because it may not leave oneself unchanged. Yet of course to say this is easier than to mean it; and, to mean it in occasional 'hours of insight,' is easier than to do so steadily and effectively through 'days of gloom.'

How does one live? Every sane and civilized man must perforce have some rudimentary working philosophy of life, however unconscious or uncritical. From hour to hour he must make decisions and do what seems best to him. Not to take such choices seriously and simply to drift is infra-human; and it is unworthy of a university man or woman not to relate them to the live issues of the time or, in so doing, to be duller or more purblind than he can help. It ought to be impossible, though it is actually common, to go through a university without ever feeling this challenge at the deep level where real decisions are made. 'Upon leaving the university the foundations for an intelligent personal theory of the world and of life should have been laid.'[3] Here a university, however neutral officially, has a heavy responsibility. Somehow it should impress on its students the urgency of deliberation and decision. It may be unable to offer them an agreed *Weltanschauung*. But if

---

2 U.G.C. Report, p. 32.

3 Paulsen, *The German Universities*, E. T., p. 308.

it cannot speak with one voice, let it speak through its teachers with several voices. The one thing unforgivable is to be silent.

If this is our policy, we must recognize that it involves the frank abandonment of the old effort to protect the student from influences that are dangerous and unsettling. In the latter part of the nineteenth century Christian parents shuddered at the exposure of their sons in the universities to infidelity and lamented the disappearance of 'security from proselytism and infectious scornfulness';[4] and the Christian leaders fought long and strenuously against the admission of teachers without guarantee of Christian belief. Their attitude is stated clearly by Liddon in a letter to William Bright written in 1868. 'Speaking absolutely, we know that religious truth can take care of itself ... But in the concrete and particular case of young men living together, tempted to every sort of moral mischief, and eager to get rid in their worst moments of the sanctions and control of religion; it is no disparagement to religious truth to say that it does need protection ... To treat Oxford undergraduates as in all respects men, appears to me the greatest possible mistake ... The question is ... whether the sons of Christian parents are for all time to come to be made over to infidel teachers of history and philosophy, with an undisputed right to teach them infidelity.'[5] Similarly, in Charlotte Yonge's novel, *The Daisy Chain*, when Norman May while at Oxford reads some German criticism and speculation by which his faith is temporarily shaken, his father blames his rash folly; to meddle with the accursed books was to run into temptation and to taste poison. Such an attitude is understandable, but it is misguided; and it is far less plausible now than it was in Liddon's day. The dangers are incidental to growing up, and the student is to be treated as an adult. Christian training at the university level ought to include being confronted by, and not being safeguarded from, other ways of thinking. This is a tension which is inseparable from being an educated adult in a world so deeply divided as is ours. No doubt it may be urged that such a tension is all very well for the abler student, but that, to bear it, is beyond the capacity of the weaker brother. But the answer must be that such a 'weaker brother' is probably out of place in a university, and certainly his needs cannot be allowed to determine university procedure. Faith, no more than virtue, should be 'fugitive and cloistered.' Such a faith must be insecure for it is one to which the holder has no real right. It is indeed Newman who, wiser than his allies, denies that the best way of learning to swim in troubled waters is never to have gone into them. In his famous tribute to the Oxford of eighty years ago, Matthew Arnold enumerates among her charms that she was 'so unravaged by the fierce

4 Keble's words quoted in *Life of Pusey*, III, p. 400.

5 *Life*, pp. 132, 133.

intellectual life of our century.' But that is a thing which no university has any business to be; for the university, intellectual innocence is not a virtue but a vice.

On the same fundamental educational principle-that the student is to be regarded as an adult-the tradition that the teacher should abstain from participation in radical discussion of ultimate questions, and should be reticent about his own views, must be rejected as a false idol equally with the tradition of protecting the student. The teacher of children may reasonably scruple to express to them opinions conflicting with the beliefs of their parents or the general sense of the community. But that is because children have not yet come to years of discretion and are not yet capable of weighing and judging for themselves. At the university stage there is no excuse for depriving students of the means and responsibility of judgment or of sheltering them from its difficulties. It is a boon to students to know 'what are the personal convictions of a sincere and serious man with respect to the great problems of life and the world to which such a man has devoted deep and serious thought.'[6] To communicate these frankly must not be regarded as a breach of professional etiquette, while to have none to communicate is a mark of professional incapacity. Thus, as Christian teachers ourselves, we claim freedom to express with a clear conscience our Christian convictions and our grounds for them. But we recognize that the same freedom must be conceded to those who differ from us. It is, for example, the right of Professor J. B. S. Haldane as of Mr. C. S. Lewis. This applies not only to 'out of school' activities, to the evening meeting of the Conservative or the Labour Club, the Student Christian Movement or the Rationalist Society, but also to the lecture room.

It is true that there remains an essential distinction between university teaching and propaganda, a distinction which both Fascists and Communists have tended to obliterate. The teacher should not suppress his convictions for fear of being accused of proselytism; yet it is not his primary concern to make proselytes. His immediate task is to aid understanding rather than to impel his pupils towards, or away from, any prescribed type of action, to supply them with data for forming intelligent judgments of their own rather than to enlist them as disciples. But among those data should be his own conclusions and the reasons which have led him to them.

2 The Reopening of Communications

To be such a forum as we have described is a minimum requirement, but is it enough? Can a university rightly leave commitment to its individual members

6 Paulsen, *op. cit.*, p. 241.

and confine itself corporately to holding the ring? This attitude has recently been sharply challenged by Mr. Arnold Nash writing from a Christian standpoint. 'The liberal democratic university' he says 'by rejecting any real attempt to discern and then to teach a unified conception of life, refuses to be a university.'[7] Does not a university stultify itself if there is no coherent scheme of life for which it stands, no coherent picture of the universe which it presents? Is not that intellectual anarchy? It does not behave so spinelessly in regard to the special sciences. When it is a question of the master-science to which all these are subordinate, is the university in effect to sit back and say, 'God bless you my boys, go to it'? On that showing it is all-important for the individual student or teacher to choose a way of life and, when so doing, to have heard the best that can be said for all sides' but, for the university officially, they are all on a level, whether fascist, communist, liberal-humanitarian or Christian. Students would then be like a jury which hears the witnesses and the speeches of the advocates but is without the help of any judicial summing up. But can anyone honestly believe this who to-day is a consenting party to the denazification of the German universities?

In the special sciences no one advocates so complete an embargo on corporate commitment. 'The accepted technique of teaching chemistry does not Imply that the Phlogiston theory has as much to be said for it as the Atomic theory.'[8] Alchemy, Astrology and Phrenology are not given equal hospitality with the recognized sciences. Nor is it so in the homes and schools from which students come. Any philosophy of life may there be inculcated only half-heartedly and ineffectively, it may be implicit rather than explicit; but It can hardly be absent entirely. Are we then at the university stage of education tacitly to confess the insincerity of the earlier stages by our inability corporately to adhere to any consistent *Weltanschauung*? Would not such an inhibition be irresponsible and almost pathological? That is certainly the view of the 'scientific humanists.' The universities, says Brian Simon in the last words of *A Student's View of the Universities*[9] should 'ally themselves with the forces of progress all over the world to overthrow the enemies of culture and science.' This is also the clear implication of Professors Bernal and Hogben. The question here is not one of the use of tests or of proscription, that shall be considered later.'[10] It is not whether the heretic shall be tolerated, or even in some sense welcomed, in the university. It is whether all distinction between orthodoxy and heresy shall, in principle, be annihilated.

---

7 *The University and the Modern World*, p. 35.
8 Hogben, *op. cit.*, p. 143.
9 p. 142.
10 See below, pp. 156ff.

In any case is not the supposed corporate neutrality quite unreal and impracticable? A university may indeed be neutral in theory. It may abstain from identifying itself publicly with any particular philosophy of life. But in practice it is impossible to plan its studies or its corporate life except by reference to some standard of values, implied if not expressed. It is impossible to have a rational standard of values in the absence of any clear Image of the ends of human existence and that entails some conception of the nature of man and of the world. Without that, either the university will be merely chaotic—a conclusion in which no one can acquiesce—or its working philosophy will be surreptitious, unthought out and uncriticized. Such a university will be wanting in intellectual honesty; it will be too timid to make clear even to itself the body of convictions by which it is really animated. Now, in some forms of community, dominance by such a hotch-potch of sentiments, habits and archetypal ideas may pass muster. Thus Burke asserts the superior value of communal prejudices in comparison with reasoning; the presumption being that, through the operation of 'the survival of the fittest,' the prevailing prejudices are those which the course of ages has shown to be salutary. It is often maintained that the British temperament is such that our conclusions are more likely to be sound than our reasoning to be valid, and that it is therefore a mistake for us to try to rationalize too much. But can a university possibly be satisfied to base its attitude in regard to the deepest matters on sloppy thinking and conventional prejudice and to substitute 'One does feel' for 'I believe'? In adopting a *Weltanschauung* and commending a way of life, must not its thought be as thorough, intrepid and relentless as it is in the special sciences? If anything in this region is to be handed on to students, must it not be a coherent and articulate philosophy? Otherwise the university is involved in the absurdity which F. H. Bradley long ago pointed out, that it is permitted to think only so long as it does not think strictly.

* * *

Vital as is the need for a common and coherent philosophy of life there is a prior and more modest but still more urgent task. Professor Emmet most pertinently continues—'We no longer live in a common civilization which speaks a common intellectual language. Hence we are beset by the problem of communication.'[11] There can only be a genuine integration where minds are really in touch with, and really meet, one another; and this is just what is not happening at present. The university, like the contemporary intellectual scene generally, is a Babel. There is/

---

11 *Op. cit.*, p. 221.

no common means of intercourse because the different sections dwell in different intellectual worlds. The first need is to restore communication.

The situation is like that which at present exists between the Great Powers. They have no common philosophy and no hope of arriving at one in any near future. They must somehow work together; and yet it is all but impossible to do so when their objectives and presuppositions are diverse. Any agreements they make are in the highest degree precarious, since they are prompted by different motives and are differently interpreted; and, in case of divergences there are no common standards to which appeal can be made. In these circumstances the immediate object of statesmen from month to month must be to reach some *modus vivendi*, however temporary and unsatisfactory, so as to gain time in which some more thorough job may be attempted. And if all full and frank communication is prevented by the existence of an 'iron curtain,' that must be removed before there can be any real progress towards understanding. Similarly, in the university world, the equivalent of an iron curtain shuts off different groups from all but superficial mental contact with one another. They inhabit different imaginative worlds and have different sets of instinctive convictions.[12] Behind the differences in their conscious opinions lie those deeper differences in the habitual, and no longer noticed, mental categories ill terms of which they think and the unconscious assumptions and basic acceptances which largely determine their respective altitudes. In the ordinary way such differences are never resolved. Thus a Christian theologian or philosopher may enter into public controversy with a scientist of Marxist outlook, and each may in some degree impress other people. But hardly ever does either make the least impression on the either. This is not because they are impervious to reason, but because their minds never really meet. The 'man convinced against his will' who refuses to change his mind need not be simply pig-headed or perverse. The reasons for his belief which he has been able to adduce may have been roughly handled; but he feels obscurely that his real reasons are multifarious and elusive and that they have not been touched. It is what is at the back, rather than at the front, of the mind that is decisive, and this is rarely brought into the picture.

Here the question is no longer of teachers talking freely to students but of their talking freely to one another. One day at an educational conference a hard-bitten pagan administrator heard a divine speak in the traditional language of Christian devotion and was so bored and alienated that he barely restrained himself from walking out. But then there followed another representative of the Churches who spoke in the language of the plain man. The administrator listened with keen interest. At the end he whispered to his neighbour, 'You know, *I could*

12 *cf.* Whitehead, *Science and the Modern World*, p. 5.

talk to that man. We might not agree, but I could talk to him.' A real contact had been established where before there was none. That is what needs doing at a thousand points throughout the universities. The theologian and the engineer, the doctor, the chemist and the lawyer, Sir Richard Livingstone and Professor Bernal, Mr. C. S. Lewis and Professor J. B. S. Haldane, the Provost of King's and Professor Hogben, must learn how to talk to one another on the radical level at which their 'instinctive convictions' are brought into the open and their minds really make contact. When they do, things will really begin to happen: Till they do, no talk of an integrated philosophy of life for the university will be more than talk. A deeper critical awareness of our own 'instinctive convictions' and of those of our own group may be the first requisite for understanding those of others. It is a two-way traffic that is required. 'Real life is meeting,' and the university needs much more of it. It is the penetrative imagination which can go behind what another man says to his real mind that we most need to cultivate, and our chief object in so doing must be, not to refute him, but to understand him and to learn from him. The deep reverence for personality which is inherent in Christianity makes this specially incumbent on Christians. This will involve two things. The first is a deeper and more resolute self-analysis than most of us have hitherto attempted or are likely to find at all palatable; so that we may become aware of the real grounds of our thinking and feeling and behaving as we normally do. The second is a patient and sustained effort to enter into the minds of colleagues whose interests or philosophies of-life are remote from our own, in order to understand and appreciate, not only what they believe, but why they believe it. Neither of these tasks can be accomplished quickly or easily. Merely to find a psychological formula by which to interpret our own or other people's minds is not to perform but to evade them.

3 Special Academic Postulates

Though the intellectual situation does not yet admit of any agreed systematic philosophy, certain basic values, elementary and elemental are already implied in our common living and action. If it were no; so there would be no real bond between us. However highly we rate the importance of freedom of thought, we must rest it on some basis of conviction. The university is engaged in a co-operative quest for truth. But such a quest itself presupposes agreement in some underlying value-judgment, held, not as a tentative hypothesis, but with absolute assurance. We cannot without absurdity have an open mind about the value of having an open mind.

At ordinary times such basic principles may well be below the threshold of consciousness. Habit and custom may supply enough of a common pattern for practical purposes. Indeed it is arguable that institution such as the British Empire gets on better because we do not try to work out its principles too precisely. But when basic values are threatened, as they have been in the last ten years, it becomes necessary to defend them, and to defend them we must know clearly what we have to defend. It is necessary to disentangle the essential values on which no compromise is possible from fortuitous and possibly undesirable accretions which may well be dispensed with. As Karl Mannheim puts it, 'Our democracy has got to become militant if it is to survive … The new militant democracy will develop a new attitude to values … It will have the courage to agree on some basic values, which are acceptable to everybody who shares the traditions of Western civilization.' And he enumerates 'those basic virtues and values—such as brotherly love, mutual help, decency, social justice, freedom, respect for the person, etc.—which are the basis of the peaceful functioning of a social order.'[13]

What then are 'the basic values and virtues' which our universities to-day should commend, for which they should stand and on which they should endeavour to build their corporate' life? What are the credentials by which they are to be recognized? They have two sources. First, there are certain specific assumptions and convictions without which the work of the university cannot go on. They are inherent in the job; but they may be imperilled either from within by some 'treason of the intellectuals,' or from without by political dictation as they obviously were in Hitlerite Germany. It is only those with personal experience of the working of a university from within who can determine what these are. In this respect there falls on them a special duty of vigilance; and here they have to lead, and not merely to follow public opinion. Secondly, there are other basic values, more general in character, which the universities share with the whole community. It is true that the British universities, though not State universities, are in effect communal institutions, inasmuch as they represent the whole community rather than any particular section. Hence, in general, the basic values they presuppose can only be those acknowledged by the community in which they are set. For such a university to assume any special colour, whether Christian, Communist, or Bourgeois Individualist, which is not that of the nation as a whole would be illegitimate. But Mannheim's contention still remains;—are there not some fundamental values, recognized and respected to-day by the British people? If so, should they not be acknowledged and exemplified by the British universities? In this Section we shall be concerned with the former set of assumptions; the latter will be discussed in the following Section.

---

13 Diagnosis of Our Time, p. 7.

Here we are concerned with assumptions on which, as academic people engaged in doing our job, we cannot be neutral, since that would be to saw off the branch on which we are sitting. The university is a Guild; it is perhaps the greatest of the Guilds which have come down to us from the Middle Ages. But every Guild evolves its own professional standards and principles of craftsmanship and its own professional ethic; e.g., the Goldsmiths, the Merchant Taylors, the Royal Colleges of Medicine and Surgery, the Inns of Court, etc. Of all such codes there are three characteristics to be noted. First, it is the members of the Guild rather than the public who are competent to be their judge and to decide what their code should be and what is, or is not, an offence against it. *Cuique in sua arte credendum.* The innovator has to make good his case before a body of educated opinion, a jury of his peers. It is true that professional opinion tends to be unduly conservative. But reforms, and even revolutions, can only come from within. If the practice of surgery is revolutionized, it is by no quack with his panacea, but by a Lister who has himself been subjected to the fundamental disciplines. Secondly, the Guild-members are not merely the judges, but the rightful guardians of their professional principles. Against the client who wants his lawyer or doctor to do something unprofessional, sometimes against popular clamour or governmental pressure, the Guild-members have a moral responsibility for maintaining their standards. For instance—to confine ourselves to illustrations which have ceased to be controversial—it is now clear that both Fascists in Italy and Nazis in Germany imposed on their universities procedures which were not only morally wrong but professionally disastrous. Thirdly, a Guild normally accepts responsibility for the professional training of its members. It initiates novices into the theory as well as the practice of the craft; and it teaches these with authority as a set, not only of tentative hypotheses, but of articles of faith.

The special quality of such presuppositions is that they are inherent and not extrinsic. With others we may be suspicious that some sectional or outside interest is trying to capture and exploit the university, to make it an instrument for the service of some purpose other than its own, to superimpose on it some particular pattern, political, religious, social, or even aesthetic, to force it into some framework which does not properly belong to it. But such natural resentment and resistance should not blind us to the fact that there are some presuppositions inherent in the undoubted task of the university, some postulates without which it cannot proceed. Some such postulates indeed each Faculty has peculiar to itself; related, that is, to its special field and method of study. But, over and above these, there are some which are common to the university as a whole. For instance, the engineer and the theologian may be largely ignorant, uninterested and even unsympathetic concerning each other's work. But they recognize each other as genuinely engaged in the pursuit of discovery and learning and as paying allegiance to some common intellectual standards; and, on that ground, they recognize each other as colleagues. If it were not so, they would have no business to be in the same university, and each must be striving to oust the other.

Apart from discussing *what* these presuppositions are, it is important to recognize *that* they are and that they may need to be defended. But if we are to defend them, we must seek to analyse them and to distinguish the authentic from the spurious. In what then do they consist? Much further thought needs to be given to this question. What follows is a tentative attempt to discern and describe some of them. But it is only a beginning; it is offered as the launching rather than the conclusion of a discussion.

First there is the conviction that the things of the mind are worth pursuing, developed to an intensity at which it becomes an intellectual passion. Without this intellectual passion the members of a university staff become only a kind of academic civil service, doing a routine job with reasonable efficiency, but uninspired and uninspiring. They communicate no glow because they feel none. Everyone who is acquainted with universities from the inside knows that here is the difference between mechanism and life. Of course this is a platitude, but it needs insisting on; for, in some ways, the utilitarianism fashionable to-day is against its recognition. In this matter we need to preserve a delicate balance. Only yesterday it was important to repudiate academic isolationism-the precious intellectual dwelling complacently in his ivory tower, content to keep himself unspotted from the world. To-day it is equally important to repudiate the thoroughgoing utilitarian, who assigns to the pursuit of truth a function merely ancillary to the attainment of comfort or power by the community. An institution whose interest in truth was confined to the knowledge how to do or to make or to mend things would not be a university.

As Christians we are especially concerned to maintain this balance. On the one hand we welcome an insistence that thinking should be responsible and should lead to action and engage the whole man rather than reflect a detached and merely speculative curiosity. On the other hand, the supreme Christian experience is not in action but in worship (which includes contemplation, and even, in a sense, enjoyment, as well as action). For the Christian, truth is one aspect of the being of God, and to treat with contumely the cult of truth for its own sake comes near to repudiating the cult of God for his own sake. This has been put very clearly by the philosopher, F. H. Bradley, in a famous passage, 'Some in one way and some in others, we seem to touch and have communion with what is beyond the visible world. In various manners we find something higher, which both supports and humbles, both chastens and transports us. And with certain persons the intellectual effort to understand the universe is a principal way of thus experiencing the Deity. No one probably who has not felt this, however differently he might express it, has ever cared much for metaphysics. And wherever it has been felt strongly, it has been its own justification.'[14] Bradley is speaking primarily of philosophy. But what he says, holds good of 'the intellectual effort to understand the universe' in detail as well as in the gross. That is, it applies to academic study as a whole.

A second postulate is the duty of intellectual thoroughness. In the university, arguments must be followed wherever they lead, however unexpected, and they must be followed through relentlessly to the end, however unwelcome. In the conventional detective story, the great detective, called in by friends of the suspected man to refute the police theory, warns them that, once engaged, he will regard it as his duty to discover and to reveal the whole truth whether that is favourable to his client or not; the university acknowledges the same obligation. In other departments of life there is room for conventions into whose objective basis no exact scrutiny is made, in which indeed there is often an undefined, but tacitly agreed, element of 'Let's pretend.' Examples are the rites of Freemasons and other Friendly Societies, the institution of Christmas as it exists for that large majority of our people who have no firm religious conviction, or the rights and powers of the Crown. For practical purposes it is needless, and sometimes undesirable, to probe or analyse these too precisely. Such a twilight between belief and disbelief has its legitimate place in some spheres of life, but it has no legitimate place in a university. For the university it is a canon that thinking must be of the utmost strictness that the subject matter permits and slovenly thinking is taboo. Nor can there be any forbidden territory. Loyalty to this obligation is one aspect of intellectual integrity, as are the two or three which follow.

The next postulate, closely related, is the obligation to be meticulously accurate in dealing with empirical evidence. It is true that we have already disclaimed the simple-minded view that truth is attainable by nothing but faithful reception and reporting of empirical data, and we have laid stress on the vital part played by schemes of interpretation. But the empirical data are also vital, and even those whose schemes of interpretation differ widely may be held together by a common intellectual conscience in the observation, recording and taking account of such data. The classical scholar must reject the most ingenious or seductive emendation

---

14 Bradley is careful to preserve balance. For he continues on the next page, 'There is no calling or pursuit which is a private road to the Deity. And assuredly the way through speculation on ultimate truth, though distinct and legitimate, is not superior to others. There is no sin, however prone to it the philosopher may be, which philosophy can justify so little as spiritual pride.'

as soon as the manuscript evidence contradicts it. The historian must note and report evidence that seems to contradict the interpretation to which he has previously committed himself equally with evidence that confirms it. As to the scientist, Darwin's declaration is classical, 'I have endeavoured to keep my mind free so as to give up any hypothesis however much beloved ... as soon as facts are shown to be opposed to it.'[15] Apart from such a conscience there could be no common ground, or even room for argument, between different schools of thought. As it has been put, 'there is a kind of inner demon which says' Come off it, 'when we are indulging in ingenious feats of explaining things away in the interests of our own point of view, political, religious or philosophical.' The evil consequences of the lack of such a conscience were seen in an extreme form in Nazi Germany. According to Dr. Jaspers the Nazi biological theories were due to 'a closed mind, which translated all reasons to the contrary into confirmations.'[16]

Fourthly, there is the obligation to approach controversial questions with the temper of the judge rather than of the advocate or the notorious 'expert witness.' This is totally distinct from tepidity or from a disposition to compromise. It is the fruit of a passion for the whole truth as against half-truths, for proportion as against one-sidedness. It springs from a high sense of intellectual responsibility, whose possessor is on his guard against adopting an opinion more easily because, for instance, it pleases or shocks, amuses or impresses, and is doubly watchful and critical of the unconscious operation on his mind of his own pet prejudices and sympathies. This is an obligation more easily acknowledged than observed, for the influence of non-rational and mainly unconscious motives, even on minds of very fine intellectual quality, is much more pervasive than has been realized till lately. A rare example of self-knowledge and self-mastery is shown, again, by Darwin. In his autobiographical fragment he speaks of his 'golden rule that whenever a published fact, a new observation or thought came across me which was opposed to my general results, to make a memorandum of it without failing at once; for I had found by experience that such facts and thoughts were far more apt to escape from the memory than favourable ones.'[17]

An aspect of this judicial temper is fair-mindedness in dealing with the opinions of others, particularly those which are uncongenial and opposed to one's own. This is .required: not only or mainly for the sake of courtesy and good feeling, but in the interest of truth. In controversial questions, all opinions held at all widely among persons technically qualified to form an opinion at all are part of the data

15 *Life*, I, p. 105.
16 See his inaugural address at the re-opening of Heidelberg University, October, 1945.
17 *Op. cit.* I, p. 87.

for judgment. There is a prima facie presumption, not of course that each of these is free from error or amounts even to a half-truth, but that it is not mere nonsense, that there is at least 'something in it.' So long as views which we reject seem to us nothing but 'fool opinions,' we ought to feel uncomfortable and insecure; for the probability is that we have failed to understand them or to take account of the grounds on which they are held. We are only fully entitled to reject them finally when we have first understood why they seem plausible to those who hold them and then have seen further. A merely combative attitude is untrue to the university spirit. That spirit is expressed by Henry Sidgwick when, writing amusedly in his diary of a visit to Keble College and of his friendship with the Anglo-Catholic, Edward Talbot, he says, 'We agree in two characteristics which are quite independent of formal creeds—a belief that we *can* learn, and a determination that we *will* learn, from people of the most opposite opinions.'[18]

The fifth postulate insists on freedom of thought and publication. It is closely linked with the sense of responsibility on which we have just insisted; for responsible thinking must be allowed to find its own way, even at the risk of error, and be met by open argument. In Dr. Jaspers' words, the university 'claims freedom of teaching and learning as the condition of the responsible independence of professors and students.' If the intellectual conscience is to operate, it must not be constricted and hampered by extraneous interference. As the scholar or scientist will resist internal motives other than the pursuit of truth, so he will resist external pressure which must deflect it. This does not imply a reversion to the 'Liberal' conception of the university in its old form, for the university need not be neutral or indifferent or take Gallio for its model. But it springs from a conviction that expulsion or silencing of heretics involves a worse evil than any which it can avert. The university is no place for the mass-production or mass-repression of opinion. The methods of the Commissar and the drill-sergeant are wholly out of place. The attempt to find a short cut involves a short-circuit.

This needs emphasis because it may be endangered. The besetting sin of academic liberalism, it is now widely recognized, was to shirk practical decisions because of the difficulty of reaching theoretical certainty; though in fact people are constantly called on to take such decisions on. a basis of probability only. But that is not sufficient ground for pretending that greater theoretical certainty has been attained than the evidence warrants, for trying to manufacture it by non-rational means or for closuring the theoretical debate in the academic arena.

The university, as a community in pursuit of truth, needs the potential contributions of all its members who are capable of original thought. To rule out in

18 *Memoir*, p. 403.

advance those who quit certain prescribed lines, contradicts its central purpose. The Miltonic argument is still valid. 'They are the troublers and dividers of unity who neglect and permit not others to unite with those dissevered pieces which are yet wanting to the body of Truth. To be still searching what we know not, by what we know, still closing tip truth to truth as we find it (for all her body is homogeneal and proportional), this is the golden rule in theology as well as in arithmetic and makes up the best harmony in a Church; not the forced and outward union of cold and neutral, and inwardly divided minds.' For *Church* read *University*, and this passage retains all its force. Any 'forced and outward union' does not assist, but inhibits, the genuine union of tested conviction.

* * *

Our last postulate is the conviction that the university has indeed a social responsibility, but that this is first and foremost a responsibility for focussing the community's intellectual conscience. No doubt it has also some measure of responsibility for the community's moral conscience. An eminent German scientist is quoted by Professor Bernal as saying, 'I do not know anything about politics and I do not want to know anything about politics, because if I keep out of it I do not see how they can do anything to me';[19] and while such irresponsibility may be extenuated by the peculiar strain, most of us would agree that it cannot be justified. But that sort of responsibility falls on the individual teacher rather than on the university corporately, it falls on him as citizen rather than 'as professor, and it is one which he shares with multitudes of his fellow-citizens. But the university's distinctive responsibility—the task which no one else can perform—is to be the university; that is, to be a place where the criticism and evaluation of ideas is continually being carried forward, where nonsense can be exposed for what it is, and where the intellectual virtues rooted in sincerity of mind are being fostered and transmitted. Of course this intellectual conscience is not a monopoly of the university, but no other institution has an equal opportunity of engendering and of nourishing it. There are many other services which the university can render to the community,'[20] but they will be 'Greek gifts' if they are given at the expense of this quintessential service. The university will betray the community, as well as lose its own soul, if it allows itself to be so anxious and troubled about many things as to miss the one thing needful.

On these academic postulates there are two general comments to be made. First, of course it is not suggested that universities are places where these convictions are

19 *Op. cit.*, p. 395.
20 See Chapter IX below.

regularly lived up to and the appropriate virtues practised. On the contrary, if we say that, in these respects, we are blameless, we deceive ourselves; the evil that we would not, we constantly do. But they are the standards which, by common consent, we acknowledge and hold in honour, and to which we appeal in judging our own and our colleagues' performance. Insofar as we have offended against them, we repudiate and condemn our own action. Secondly, they are put forward as 'rules of the guild,' tacitly agreed working assumptions, found to be necessary to good workmanship in our craft. Probably most university teachers, at least in Great Britain, would assent to them. If they are criticized, it is more likely to be as platitudes than as paradoxes. But some, if not all, of them have far-reaching implications in the sphere of ethics, of anthropology and even of ontology. If their acknowledgment does not absolutely necessitate a particular philosophy of life, it is at least true that to some philosophies of life they are thoroughly congenial and to others highly antipathetic.

4 Basic communal values

Those basic assumptions which the British universities share with the nation may themselves be subdivided.

a. Universal

Some are common to all universities anywhere, to El Azhar, Peiping and Calcutta equally with Oxford, Paris or Harvard. The convulsions of the last fifteen years have made clear that there are some values or principles which are indispensable to civilized existence. This was typified at an annual conference of International Student Service shortly before the War. The German representatives were troubled by the relief work done in Great Britain and other countries, which at that time was mostly for refugees from Nazi persecution; but they were ready to be pacified by an assurance that the basis of this work was purely humanitarian and in no way 'ideological.' But at the critical moment the British relief secretary jumped up and, speaking with much feeling, said, 'Of course, I.S.S. is neutral, on ordinary political questions. But there are *certain elementary conditions of civilization* for which we do stand.' In the words of Dr. Kotschnig, the war was widely felt to be not only a conflict between different political and economic systems, but a 'clash of mutually exclusive worlds of thought and aspiration.'[21] It was a war not between one civi-

---

21 *Slaves Need No Leaders*, p. 11.

lized Power and another, but between civilization and barbarism; and in such a war the real mind of all civilized persons and learned bodies, whether expressed or not, must perforce be on one side.

Deeper than all differences of moral judgment is the difference between those who make moral judgments at all and those who do not. It is the old issue between Socrates and Thrasymachus; and it is the issue on which, humanly speaking, the fate of the world in the next few years seems to hang. What is in question is, whether those who hold power will recognize any moral standards as objective and binding on them, and as having a *de jure* authority superior to their own inclinations or interests. The problem of power is the problem of our age. But all civilization has depended on the recognition of some restraint to naked power. The universality of the recognition of the 'Tao,' that is of the existence of 'moral law' having authority, has already been pointed out in Chapter IV above. This recognition is part of the common cultural heritage of civilization. Here then is something for which the universities of the world must stand. For our own universities, this principle was applied eighty years ago by the chief philosopher of Liberalism. In his Rectorial Address to the St. Andrew's students, J. S. Mill laid down that the proper end of their studies was that they should become 'more effective fighters in the battle between good and evil,' and that universities should have a pervading tone of reverence and duty. In this he was at one with Carlyle, Shaftesbury and Pusey, and indeed with Confucius, Marcus Aurelius and Kabir.

Mr. Lewis's examples go to show that the traditional wisdom of different civilizations includes, not only a recognition of Duty as something peremptory and absolute, but a good deal of agreement about the kinds of conduct which Duty enjoins. Here only one or two examples can be given. One is the duty of reasonableness. When Hitler first came into power, a distinguished German who was then in this country remarked that this event was the triumph of irrationalism and betokened an uprush of forces from the psychic underworld. That is something towards which universities cannot be neutral, for it is a condition of civilization that the beast in man should be subjected to the man in man. Another duty is good faith. 'Keeping of faith,' says Locke, 'belongs to man as man and not as a member of society.' No reasons of State or business excuse a breach of covenant; without mutual trust, social intercourse becomes impossible. Another duty, important though hard to define, is that of a good will of man towards man, a certain freemasonry between fellow-members of the species which is the exact opposite of the natural enmity affirmed by Hobbes, a disposition to treat others as friends so long as they do not show themselves to be enemies.

On this basis the peoples of all civilized communities can meet. Here the universities of the world cannot be neutral, since civilization cannot be neutral. If any student or teacher advocates irrationalism or Machiavellianism or inhumanity, he may indeed be tolerated for reasons we have already given; but he is definitely a 'dissenter' and unrepresentative, for in this respect his mind IS in contradiction with the mind of any university.

b. Western

Secondly, there are some further principles which are common to the contemporary civilization of the West. Europe and America have a common cultural heritage, derived mainly from Greece, Rome and Palestine. There are some truths concerning the good life and the conditions of attaining it on which these are agreed, and one function of Western education will be to pass them on. 'Our society, like any society, rests on common beliefs and a major task of education is to perpetuate them.' This is the contention of the Harvard Report, *General Education in a Free Society*. The writers are clear that an educational system must have some common purpose which holds it together; that, in the United States, this purpose once was to make Christians citizens, that in existing conditions it can be so no longer, and that some alternative must be found on which the Christian and Humanist, Professor Niebuhr and Mr. Lippmann, can unite and that the source of such an alternative is to be found in 'the intellectual forces which have shaped the Western mind.'[22] Of these forces Christianity is one, but it is one among others.

The Nazis proclaimed a 'war against the West.' In so doing they recognized, though by repulsion, that there was a moral tradition, common, e.g., to the Latin and to the Anglo-Saxon peoples, which constituted a standing obstacle and rebuke to their aims and methods. This again is more easily perceived than analysed. But it is not hard to identify some judgments characteristic of the Western mind. First there is a certain activism, a sense that it is normally right to be up and busy. An obstacle is something to be removed; an evil is something to be redressed. Fatalism is not a Western creed, and it is no accident that Applied Science is a Western product. Secondly, from Greece has come the conception of the good life as embodying the cardinal virtues of wisdom, temperance, courage and justice; and from Rome an ingrained respect for law and order. Fatalistic and irresponsible inertia, unbridled indulgence of appetite or self-will, cowardice in all its forms, in justice and anarchy, are decisively condemned by our Western tradition. Thirdly, there is a Palestinian element in our Western heritage. Though the extent of its survival to-day is disputed its place in the historic tradition is not. 'The Christian

22 *Op. cit.*, p. 44.

virus or elixir is in our Western blood.'[23] This deepens the Roman demand for even-handed justice by adding a respect for the individual as possessing rights and responsibilities. The Harvard writers define their moral basis as being the dignity of man and his duty toward his fellow-men. But, however defined, its practical importance lies in what it excludes. Men are never to be treated simply as slaves or cannon-fodder, as beasts of burden or as material for scientific experiment. Whoever holds otherwise is a heretic. On such issues Western civilization has not an open mind but a firm conviction. It is against this moral heritage that so much that has happened in Europe in the last fifteen years is a gross offence.

c. British

Thirdly, over and above those principles which they share with the universities of other countries, there are certain basic values for which the British universities may legitimately stand, since they are inherent in the British way of life. They are a part of the heritage which, in 1940, our people rallied to defend. Our political history notoriously suggests that there is some such common, national, basis of belief. Our party-differences have not been carried to an extreme. After a General Election, the party newly returned to power does not undo the bulk of the work of its predecessors. The outlook which Mr. Churchill and Mr. Attlee have in common is more important than the things in which they differ. The national unity in time of war only expresses and reveals an underlying unity of standard and of purpose which is there all the time.

From this unity there arises directly the first of these basic values. That is tolerance, or, as it has been recently described, 'our habit of 'not killing one another.' The parties to our contentions are not implacable. The sombre drama of Thucydides, Book III, has not been enacted 'in England's green and pleasant land.' Class-war has not hitherto disrupted our society as it has disrupted others. No doubt this trait has its reverse side, a lack of intellectual thoroughness and moral intensity. But, primarily, it is based on tacit recognition of a fellowship more fundamental than all the Isms that divide us. 'Fraternity' is that one of the revolutionary triad which we rate most highly.

A second of our national basic values is illustrated by the paradox that this country is the home both of the 'Rule of Law' and of the 'Sovereignty of Parliament.' We can dispense with legal checks on the sovereign body because, in practice, the moral authority of tradition and the informal pressure of public opinion give sufficient security that it will not abuse its powers. Similarly, we can dispense

23 Toynbee, *op. cit.*, V. p. 190.

with the police-state, because we can rely on a 'general habit of spontaneous cohesion and conformity; people take their places in the queue without being hectored by someone in uniform. Irrespective of party, we believe in ordered liberty and in self-discipline. With this goes an ingrained belief that a balance between continuity and change is both needful and possible. In making alterations the style of the building should be preserved; but' 'a state without the means of some change is without the means of its conservation.' So we cherish the *critic* on the hearth, and 'His Majesty's Opposition' is one of our most characteristic institutions.

A third of our basic values is represented by the conviction that, Democracy is meaningful and right.'[24] Of course 'democracy' is a highly ambiguous term. But, in this context, it clearly does not imply any particular political arrangement; it signifies a broad ethical test by which political arrangements are to be judged. As such a test, it seems to be twofold. On the one hand, it emphasizes the claim of every man to consideration. Government should be, for the people.' 'The poorest he that is in England hath a life to live as the richest he.' That strikes a chord to which something deep in our nature responds. On the other hand, it expresses the community's need of the active co-operation of all its members in ordering the common life; and, seen from the opposite angle, this is the right—and obligation—of every man to a share in responsibility. In some real sense government must be by the people.

All this is fairly obvious. These are values which few persons of influence in our universities would question. Humanists, whether theocentric or anthropocentric, can easily agree upon them. But, so far, they are vague and superficial. In quiet times they may supply a common ground on which we can get along without digging deeper. But are they deeply rooted enough to enable us to stand against the impassioned communist or fascist at a time when events are forcing on us, in the most practical and insistent form, the question: Do we really believe what we have supposed ourselves to believe, and, if so, with what depth of conviction do we believe it? At this level a further question is unavoidable. In the body of common conviction, unformulated but actually operative, which the British universities share with the British people, how far, and in what sense, is there a definitely Christian ingredient? There is no suggestion here of reviving the idea of a 'Christian university' which we have definitely rejected in the previous Chapter. But, if there is any significant sense in which it was 'Christian civilization' that the nation defended in 1940' it may follow that the culture which British universities diffuse should in some degree be a Christian culture.

---

24 We take this phrase from the Harvard Report, where it is used to express the basic presupposition of American Universities.

5 Do these values include a Christian ingredient?

Among the British universities to-day, broadly speaking, the ancient do, and the modern do not, make formal acknowledgment of a Christian basis. Which are right, and with which is the future? Is the Christian profession of Oxford, Cambridge and the Scottish universities only a historical survival, having no longer real point or meaning, a venerable facade behind which there is only emptiness? Ought Cambridge, equally with Chicago or even with Calcutta, to preserve an official neutrality between Christianity and other religions or between religion and rationalism? Or is the absence of Christian orientation and Christian profession in 'Redbrick' an unnecessary and crippling impoverishment? Behind this lies the question: In what sense, if in any, is the British people still a Christian people? On this the only comment which can be made with confidence is, that the answer is not simple or easy, and anyone who thinks it is rules himself out of court. In the nature of the case, any answer must be impressionistic and cannot admit of demonstration, and, in attempting an answer, academic people speak with no special authority; yet, in practice, some answer must be presupposed.

* * *

c. An Alternative Diagnosis

Our present communal condition of mind is not simple but extremely complex. To depict it accurately and in due proportion is hard. It would certainly be false to represent the mind of the nation as still predominantly Christian, but neither is it clearly pagan or completely secularized. A penetrating diagnosis is contained in Mr. T. S. Eliot's *The Idea of a Christian Society*.[25] He starts with two propositions which are common ground to writers of different schools. On the one hand, much of our heritage is Christian. Our forefathers had a Christian map of the world. That is their mental world-picture, or the frame-work within and with reference to which they saw particular events, was Christian. Their 'culture,' in Ortega's sense of the word; the body of convictions, conscious or unconscious, which under ay their moral judgments and by which they purported to direct their lives, was largely derived from the Bible. On the other hand the British nation is vastly less Christian than it used to be. It has undergone a drastic, and ever accelerating, process of secularizing. The traditional order of life as it existed for instance for the villagers of Gray's *Elegy* and for countless earlier and several later generations,

25 See also Professor John Baillie's Riddell Lectures—*What is Christian Civilization*?

has been disrupted. Church and churchyard have lost their pivotal position. 'The bosom of his Father and his God' is no longer a simple and natural climax for the poet. For the common mind indeed 'Nature' has silently displaced God as the ultimate basis to which all other things are referred.

But Mr. Eliot adds three further propositions which, if accepted, must radically modify the reasonable aim of the body of Christians, both in the nation and in the university. First, though the destructive process has already gone far and may go further, it is still incomplete. Our present state is transitional and not pagan or wholly secular; it differs widely from that prevailing in India or China or again in the Soviet Union. It is true that it cannot be long maintained; either the secularization will be completed or there will be a revivification of Christianity. But the issue is still open.

Secondly, 'we have to-day a culture which is mainly negative, but which, so far as it is positive, is still Christian.'[26] So far as there is a national conscience, it is still mainly Christian in colouring. With the majority of people for whom the Christian picture has faded out, no alternative body of convictions, serving as an effective guide to existence, has yet taken its place. There is only a vacuum; in practice they belong nowhere and give no whole-hearted allegiance to anything. 'The religion of the Englishman,' that is, the cause or causes for which, when roused, he is impelled to sacrifice everything, and even life itself if need be, is Christian in origin. In wartime it was often remarked that we were much surer of what we were fighting *against* than of what we were fighting *for*. But, when analysed, those values which we felt in our bones to be menaced by Hitler, and which Churchill incited us to defend, are what our nation first received as Christian values. It acquired them, not as self-subsistent truths but, as the consequence of certain beliefs about the nature of man and of the universe. The large number of our countrymen who sprang to their defence, but who have, individually, abandoned Christian worship and Christian belief, are putting their trust in a plant which has been severed from its roots, or as has often been said, they are having on their capital.

Thirdly, the issue cannot long remain open. Some of the factors producing the present precarious equilibrium are evanescent. The present residual Christianity will die out, so far as the public scene is concerned, unless it undergoes a revivification. 'The choice before us is between the formation of a new Christian culture and the acceptance of a pagan one. Both involve radical changes.'

Mr. Eliot's book was published in 1939, and, since then, events have moved swiftly towards a climax. In Europe, the war with its attendant atrocities, the overrunning of so many countries by the Nazi régime, and the resistance movements

---

26 *Op. cit.*, p. 13.

with their heroic and anarchic features, have combined to disturb rudely thick layers of convention and comfort which ordinarily conceal from men the reality of themselves and of the world. In this country we have experienced the imminent menace of annihilation, the awakening of 1940 bringing a renewed sense of mission, wide recognition abroad and a call to moral leadership, and the partial but still retrievable lapse since the end of hostilities. In the next twenty or thirty years, the future of the world may depend, and the future of the British Commonwealth almost certainly does depend, on whether we are able to stand for a way of life, as coherent and as whole-heartedly embraced as any other, but saner and more convincing. That remains to be seen. Our own belief is that it will depend on a recovery of our Christian heritage and its bold readaptation to contemporary facts. The burden of proof seems to rest on those who think it can be done otherwise.

What is the upshot? The British people to-day is not 'Christian,' except in a debased sense of the word which is therefore better avoided. But its imagination, its ethos and its sentiment are, to a very substantial extent, *Christianized*. This is also true of the universities. The full Christian faith cannot now, or in any near future, be the working basis of the British universities any more than of the nation. But it is not impossible or necessarily illegitimate, that the pattern of their organization and studies, and the character of their corporate life, should be given deliberately a certain degree of consciously Christian orientation. It is not for the university, in its official capacity, to attempt the work of evangelization. The university cannot itself be the sower of the seed, though it can give him his opportunity. But it can, and should provide a soil which will he favourable to growth and not so and that the seed withers nor so full of thorns that It IS choked.

But what i9 thc moral? If the situation is as open as we have described it have universities within the nation or Christians within the university nothing to do but to wait and see which way things will go? Are the determining factors wholly outside their control. Or is there any initiative which they can nightly and effectively take?

* * *

7 Conclusion

If our universities are to rise to the height of the times, the first, and quite inescapable, requirement is that they shall concentrate far more attention on the deep and difficult issues of the day. There must be no more tacit conspiracy of silence. Convictions must be explored and tested to their roots. Next, communications must be re-opened. Contact must be made and the issue must be joined, not at the ordinary level of debate, but at the level at which convictions are really formed. If, at this level, agreement on a basic philosophy of life were possible, that would invigorate the whole work of the universities and their contribution to the world; but nothing like a modern 'Summa' is conceivable for a long time to come. Yet, though unformulated and unsystematic, the acceptance of some basic values is implied in the normal attitudes of British university teachers and students as of the British people generally, and there are others more special to the university; and for practical purposes these can be regarded as axiomatic.

So much very many critics would be willing to concede. 'But,' they will ask, 'why cannot you stop at that?' We agree in commending certain virtues and in condemning certain vices; and, on that basis, we can work in harmony on practical Issues which come up for decision in Faculty, Senate or Council. We do not agree, and are not likely to agree, on ultimate questions. Why then force to the front questions which must divide us? This is a time of transition. The ground is still heaving, the day for permanent building is not yet. In intellectual, as in physical, construction we must still 'make do' with temporary expedients.

Such an attitude might be reasonable in less desperate times. But 'safety first,' to let well alone, *quieta non movere*, to wait for the secular movement of thought to come to a natural climax, is no missionary policy for Great Britain in the world to-day, .or for the universities in Great Britain. It may sound plausible in our own pleasant, and seldom war-scarred, Common Rooms; it would be much less so in the universities of Central Europe. If we are to 'withstand in the evil day, and, having done all, to stand,' there must be no gaps and no weakness in our armour: The 'truth' with which we 'gird our loins' must be comprehensive and thoroughly grounded. Otherwise we shall succumb to strange gospels which are more coherent, and more firmly held than our own. Whatever our basic values are, national and academic, we need to make them much clearer and to develop and deepen them, if we are to play the rôle in the world, to which we were called in 1940, and to which leaders as far apart as Winston Churchill and Sir Stafford Cripps would agree that we are called to-day.

In these basic values there is certainly a Christian ingredient. No doubt it is extremely hard to estimate its present extent and significance. Equally honest observers may well differ widely in their estimates; and, even among our own group there is at least some nuance of difference. Christian teachers should not ask their colleagues to accept in advance any wider commitment of the university to a Christianized orientation than those colleagues are disposed to concede. But they should claim elbow-room to show themselves a 'creative minority,' if they can. All will then depend on whether they have enough spiritual energy and political wisdom to demonstrate to others that a growing Christianization of 'the impersonal configuration of our common life' is what sound reason and the common good require.[27] Yet in their own minds, they will be well aware that they can only hope to have such energy and wisdom, if they open themselves in extraordinary measure to be vehicles of the grace of God.

Some of the lines on which such a policy may be worked out in practice will be considered in the later chapters. What is possible and legitimate varies from university to university. But for Christian teachers and students everywhere, if we have ears to hear, there is sounding, through the course of events, a trumpet-call for action. Almost audibly, the voice of the Lord is heard, saying, 'Whom shall I send and who will go for us?'

27 ct. Maritain, *op. cit.*, 'J p. 168.

CHAPTER SIXTEEN

The Idea of the University

From *Education and the University A Sketch for an 'English School'; English Literature in Our Time and the University* (1967)

F. R. I. LEAVIS

This selection is taken from the 2nd Edition of *Education & the University: A Sketch for an 'English School'*, 1979, by, F. R. Leavis. Published by Cambridge University Press, Melbourne, Australia.

Editors' Note

F. R. Leavis taught English, primarily at the University of Cambridge, England, and had an abiding interest in the idea of the University. Accurate as it may be, this statement seriously underplays Leavis' stature and position at each point. For Leavis himself, at any rate, he lived and even *was* both English and Cambridge; and his commitments to English literature and Cambridge and his concern for universities were intimately interwoven. English literature was integral, as he saw it, not just to Cambridge but for any proper realisation of the university in the modern era. What was in question, ultimately, was no less than culture and civilisation in—as a he saw it—a threatening age. 'Intelligence', 'life', 'vitality', 'human', 'collaboration' and 'creativity' were just a few of his favoured terms and related concerns. And all of these concerns were pursued with a passion that took no prisoners. Even his appearance, with a plain white open-necked shirt and modest dress, spoke of a spartenness and an integrity of will.

In his language—in his assault on a 'Technologic-Benthamite civilisation'—and in his vigour in taking on those who would not sympathise with his outlook, Leavis formed a determined adversary. Famously, he took on C. P. Snow in 'the two cultures' debate in England in the 1960s. C. P. Snow was a scientist who also wrote novels and argued that no-one could be thought as cultured unless they had some understanding of the basic concepts and theories of science (he pointed to the significance of the second law of thermodynamics). Leavis attacked this position, in effect claiming that Snow failed to understand the idea of culture.

Leavis revolutionised English literature as a university subject at Cambridge and that influence spread outwards across universities and into the teaching of English in schools. He insisted on close attention to texts in a dialogical pedagogy: 'this is so, isn't it?' was his approach, looking to the formation of a third world of interactive engagement, beyond the worlds of the text as an object and the individual's private and possibly prejudiced response. He founded the journal Scrutiny, to develop a larger debate in the construction of an interdisciplinary inquiry. Partly through his iconoclasm and partly through his unforgiving style, he was unable to gain the recognition his efforts over decades deserved (Cambridge never accorded him the title of 'professor') and he lived out the last years of his academic life in the (English) University of York.

RB

Recommended Reading

Cranfield, S. (2016). *F. R. Leavis: The Creative University.* Dordrecht: Springer.

MacKillop, I. and Storer, R. (eds) (1995). *F. R. Leavis: Essays and Documents.* Sheffield: Sheffield Academic Press.

Snow, C. P. (1978). *The Two Cultures and A Second Look.* Cambridge: Cambridge University Press.

Storer, R. (2009). *F. R. Leavis.* Routledge: London.

* * * * *

This closeness of connection between the character of a society and the character of its education cannot be too strongly stressed. Schools and colleges are not something apart from the social order to which they belong. They are that order trying to prepare its youth for participation in its own activities. And a society can only teach the hopes, the knowledge, the values, the beliefs which it has.

Alexander Meiklejohn, *The Experimental College.*

Using the same epigraph on another occasion the present writer opened with this commentary:

> If these depressing considerations leave some of us (in. eluding Dr. Meiklejohn) still arduously interested in education, it must be because it is still possible to believe that the obvious drift—or drive—of civilization doesn't exhaustively represent 'the hopes, the knowledge, the values, the beliefs' of the society to which we belong. And it is in fact in that society conventionally assumed that education should be in some ways concerned with countering certain characteristic tendencies of civilization. Those of us who are not completely pessimistic are committed to believing that this assumption is in some measure justified by a correspondent reality, one which we ought to do our utmost to make more effective.
>
> In bold moments a complementary proposition to Dr. Meiklejohn's may perhaps be thrown out: namely, that schools and colleges are, or should be, society trying to preserve and develop a continuity of consciousness and a mature directing sense of value—a sense of value informed by a traditional wisdom. Any serious notion of education would seem to invoke both propositions. Their reconciliation in practice, things being as they are to-day, cannot be provided for by any simple formula. A complete and happy reconciliation would clearly involve more than educational reform.

I indicate here the nature both of the problem that must be faced by anyone to-day who proposes to take education seriously, and of the faith in which he must face it. He will inevitably find himself thinking of the problem as one of resisting the bent of civilization in our time—of trying to move against the stream. But if resistance and countermovement were all there were to it, the effort would not be worth making. Those who find it worth making must feel it to be the insistence of essential human needs; needs manifested in a certain force of tradition that they, in promoting the effort, represent and are endeavouring, by bringing it to greater consciousness of ends and means and urgencies, to strengthen and direct. In despondent moments they may feel that urgency manifests itself today in something like a completeness of unconsciousness, and that it is misleading to speak of any relevant tradition as having force. Nevertheless they have to recognize that, actually, cultural tradition relevant to their aims is active and potent in many ways in the life of the community, and notably in education.

I am concerned in these pages with liberal education at the university level (if something effective cannot be done at that level, it would seem vain to hope much of efforts in education at other levels). The universities are recognized symbols of cultural tradition—of cultural tradition still conceived as a directing force, representing a wisdom older than modern civilization and having an authority that should check and control the blind drive onward of material and mechanical development, with its human consequences. The ancient universities are more than symbols; they, at any rate, may fairly be called foci of such a force, capable, by reason of their prestige and their part in the life of the country, of exercising an enormous influence. Much has been compromised there; there, too, unconsciousness gains—it both spreads and deepens; but they are still in more than form representatives of humane tradition.

'Humane tradition' may seem a vague concept. I don't think that an attempt to define it by an enumeration of its contents would help. It seems to me better to point to English literature, which is unquestionably and producibly 'there,' and to suggest that the 'literary tradition' that this unquestionable existence justifies us in speaking of might also be called a vague concept. And the relation of 'literary tradition' to 'humane tradition' is plainly not the mere external one of a parallel. Here, it may be said in passing, we have a reason for making a scheme of liberal education centre in the study of English literature. But this is a head to be returned to later. The business at the moment is to suggest in what way a serious effort in education must be conceived as the effort of a cultural tradition at maintaining continuity—or in what way such an effort is conceived to be so in these pages.

For I think it worth insisting on the difference, as I see it, between the present approach and the Humanism of Irving Babbitt. It occurred to me to make the dissociation because Mr. T. S. Eliot, referring at the Malvern Conference (in a complimentary way) to an essay of mine the substance of which is included in this book, used the word 'humanist' in commenting on the approach.[1] The accompanying mention of Irving Babbitt made the bracketing force of the word plain. The difference, I might start by saying, is that, whereas Humanism is a doctrine and Irving Babbitt's aim is to state and establish it in general theoretical terms, my own aim is to deal in doctrine, theory and general terms as little as possible. The main concern of these pages is with methods and tactics; these are what, keeping as close as possible to the practical, they offer. Of course, certain assumptions are implied; these are what I am stating now.

I assume that the attempt to establish a real liberal education in this country-to restore in relation to the modern world the idea of liberal education-is worth making because, in spite of all our talk about disintegration and decay, and in spite of what we feel with so much excuse in our many despondent moments, we still have a positive cultural tradition. Its persistence is such that we can, in attempting at an ancient university an experiment in liberal education, count on a sufficient measure of agreement, overt and implicit, about essential values to make it unnecessary

1 *Malvern, 1941. Being the Proceedings of the Archbishop of York's Conference.* See Mr. Eliot's address, and, in particular, pages 205 and 208.

to discuss ultimate sanctions, or provide a philosophy, before starting to work. This I assume; and I believe further that what is unnecessary is best avoided. That is, the kind of effort I have in mind would be the effort of an actual living tradition to bring itself to a focus, and would see itself—or feel itself-in terms of the carrying-on of a going concern. It may be said that here I am offering theory and doctrine; their drift, then, is that we should deal as much as possible in the concrete, the actual and the particular, and not expend ourselves overmuch on the definition or exploration of values and sanctions in the abstract.

Criticizing Babbitt's Humanism Mr. Eliot says:

> It is not at all that Mr. Babbitt has misunderstood any of these persons, or that he is not fully acquainted with the civilization out of which they sprang. On the contrary, he knows all about them. It is rather, I think, that in his interest in the messages of individuals—messages conveyed in books—he has tended merely to neglect the conditions. The great men whom he holds up for our admiration and example are torn from their contexts of race, place and time. And in consequence, Mr. Babbitt seems to me to tear himself from his own context.

Here the difference between Humanism and the approach in question in these pages comes out plainly enough. It is a central aim of Babbitt's Humanism that invites this criticism; the aim of arriving with the aid of (among others) Confucius, Buddha, Socrates and Erasmus at definitions of an ideal Humanism or Humanist. But the business of working out in practice at an ancient English university the means of rehabilitating the function of the 'humanities' involves, as I see it, no such undertaking. It is advisedly that I particularize' ancient English university': the preoccupation is not with the generalities of philosophical and moral theory and doctrine, but with picking up a continuity; carrying on and fostering the essential life of a time-honoured and powerful institution, in this concrete historical England. And the preoccupation of the students in the contemplated school would not be with this and the other selected exemplar-man or book, 'torn from their context of race, place and time.' At the centre of the work, in a way and under conditions to be discussed, would be a study of the literature of their own language and country—the most intimate kind of study, that is, of a concrete tradition. And a study of tradition in literature involves a great deal more than the literary.

Of course, it is the preoccupation with cultural values as human and separable from any particular religious frame or basis, the offer at a cultural regeneration that is not to proceed by way of a religious revival, that prompts the description 'humanist.' Literary criticism must, in this sense, always be humanist; whatever it may end in, it must be humanist in approach, in so far as it is literary criticism and not something else. It seems to me obvious that the approach needed in education must be in the same way humanist. The study of English literature, and not the less so for being controlled by a strict critical discipline, necessarily leads the student, by a variety of approaches, to consider the relation of humane culture to religion, and the place of religion in civilization. The conclusions drawn from such a study may often concur with those expressed by Mr. Eliot in his essay on *The Humanism of Irving Babbitt.* Whether or not this is likely to be so for students who haven't started as adherents of a religious creed there is no immediate need to discuss. The point is that, whatever else may be necessary, there must in any case be, to meet the present crisis of civilization, a liberal education that doesn't start with a doctrinal frame, and is not directed at inculcating one. The Christian comments that the culture represented by such an education is incomplete, and for him, perhaps, the frame will always be there. And when he says that the cultural tradition we belong to and must aim to preserve is in very important senses Christian he commands assent. But this is the age, not of Dante or of Herbert, but of T. S. Eliot; and Eliot's genius, which is of the kind that makes a poet profoundly representative, runs to that marvellous creative originality in the use of language because he cannot, for the ordering of his experience in poetry of directly religious preoccupation, make anything like that direct use of a received doctrinal frame or conceptual apparatus which for Dante or Herbert was natural or inevitable—though the aspiration of Eliot's poetry is given in the declared Anglo-Catholicism and classicism of s prose.

In such an age the business of quickening and concentrating into strong conscious life the cultural sensibility in which tradition has its effective continuance (for the nature of the problem answers to this kind of account) will not be forwarded by any proposal that implies conditions at all analogous to those of the age of Dante. The education that will forward the attainment of a real order cannot offer a comprehensive order either as a scheme mapping out and articulating the fields of study in their inevitable relation to a centre of significance, or as a rewarding realization that is to be the goal. The prevailing spirit must be tentative, and if we are to find an analogy with which to suggest the nature of the key discipline we must go to *Burnt Norton*, *Coriolan*, and the other poems of that group rather than to the *Divina Commedia*.[2] Principles, of course, are implied in the measure of tacit agreement—the 'sensibility'—that makes the kind of effort possible, and the discipline would certainly involve exploring them; but to make it a matter of trying

---

2 See Appendix I, below. The point is of such radical importance, and the analogy has so close a bearing on the present argument, that I print here my immediately relevant discussion of T. S. Eliot's later poetry—a discussion that appeared as a review when *The Dry Salvages* was published.

to impose in advance the order that can only be expected to emerge in course of time, if things go well with civilization, would be vain.

This, then, is by way of explaining in what sense the present approach is 'humanist,' and of suggesting that, if the kind of education proposed may perhaps be judged 'liberal' in more than one sense of the adjective, nevertheless not all of those who insist on the necessity of a religious approach will feel themselves bound to judge that the endeavour after that kind of educational improvement is no matter for active countenance and co-operation.

The aim is to keep as close as possible to the concrete, and to deal with general considerations-in-terms related as immediately as possible to practice—or to particular proposals conceived as practical. Prevailing practice and prevailing conditions being what they are, what suggestions—given the measure of actual and tacit agreement about ends that can be counted on for working purposes might reasonably be made for initiating, at an ancient university, a serious attempt to work out an answer to the educational problem? Any proposals worth advancing at all would involve changes drastic enough to give the advocacy something of a quixotic look to those who know the academic world, but the intention is the reverse of Utopian. So much is it the reverse that the charges of presumption and impertinence will hardly in any case be avoided; but I am convinced that a profitable approach must be by way of practical suggestions directed at particular actual conditions.

Some preliminary canvassing of general considerations is, of course, indispensable. A good tactical opportunity for it was provided, when a start was made some ten years ago in *Scrutiny* towards working out the present approach, by the timely appearance of two American texts: a book, *The Experimental College*, by Alexander Meiklejohn, and an essay, *Thoughts after Flexner*, by Brooks Otis. The book reported an actual experiment in liberal education made at the University of Wisconsin; the essay appeared in a short-lived periodical, *The New Frontier*, run by young graduates of well-known eastern universities.

The setting contemplated by the two authors in their approaches to the common problem is fairly suggested by this, from Dr. Meiklejohn's book:

> Our first aim is not to get liberal thinking done excellently, but to get it done at all. In a word, we must recognize that the drift of American life is against those forms of liberal thinking which seem most essential to its welfare (p: 138).

—a passage that relates interestingly to that quoted as epigraph to this chapter. For 'drift of American life,' of course, we can read' drift of modern life'; American conditions are the conditions of modern civilization, even if the 'drift' has gone further on the other side of the Atlantic than on this. On the one hand there is the enormous technical complexity of civilization, a complexity that could be dealt with only by an answering efficiency of co-ordination—a co-operative concentration of knowledge, understanding and will (and 'understanding' means not merely a grasp of intricacies, but a perceptive wisdom about ends). On the other hand, the social and cultural disintegration that has accompanied the development of the inhumanly complex machinery is destroying what should have controlled the working. It is as if society, in so complicating and extending the machinery of organization, had incurred a progressive debility of consciousness and of the powers of co-ordination and control—had lost intelligence, memory and moral purpose. (Of course—but I had better be explicit—no metaphysic of the collective is implied here; the figurative expressions translate into such terms as my tradition, intellectual moral and humane and Mr. Brooks Otis s 'capable and influential group of human beings.'[3]) The inadequacy to their function of statesmen and labour-leaders is notorious, depressing and inevitable, and in our time only the very naive have been able to be exhilarated by the hopes of revolutionaries. The complexities being what they are, the general drift has been technocratic, and the effective conception of the human ends to be served that accompanies a preoccupation with the smooth running of the machinery tends to be a drastically simplified one. The war, by providing imperious immediate ends and immediately all-sufficient motives, has produced a simplification that enables the machinery, now more tyrannically complex than ever before, to run with marvellous efficiency. The greater is the need for insisting on the nature of the problem that the simplification doesn't solve, and on the dangers that, when the war is over, will be left more menacing than before, though not necessarily more attended to.

It was a romantic and irresponsible vision that in the Marxising days, acclaimed a human triumph that was to emerge out of catastrophe, and it is a philistine obtuseness that (whatever it may call itself) sees a human triumph in any Utopian consummation of the process of the capitalist era. The problem is to avoid both a breakdown of the machinery and its triumph—a final surrender to it of the human spirit. 'The great social problem of today,' says Mr. Otis, 'has thus become entirely a matter of controlling the machine (the machine on which the 'machinery of civilization depends). There can be no control without (to revert to the metaphors of 'organism' and 'mind') a higher co-ordination. An urgently necessary work, consequently, is to explore the means of bringing the various essential kinds of specialist knowledge and training into effective

3 All such "schemes" [of social re-organization] indeed become Utopian and futile in exact proportion to their lack of support by a sufficiently capable and influential group of living human beings. …'

relation with informed general intelligence, humane culture, social conscience and political will. Here, in this work, we have the function that is pre-eminently the university's; if the work is not done there it will not be done anywhere.

The general problem as Mr. Otis states it is to restore 'The unity of the Educated Class, and the unity of the Educated Mind in terms of the ideas of its own age.' Of the intellectuals of the past he says admirably:

> The important point is that they represented the centre of the civilization of their age—not particular and isolated aspects of it, but the whole of it. They had, of course, their varying occupations, their special ignorances—but they were in general aware of their own world at all points. With their common *lingua franca*, their common stock of knowledge, and their common social status they gradually developed an idea of what the truly' educated' man should be like, what his role in society should be, and in particular what responsibility he had for himself and his world. *This class—in short—may be said to have definitely represented and been responsible for civilization in their time.*

Any such 'centre'—centre of co-ordination and of consciousness, one may say, pressing Mr. Otis into the context of those metaphors already used—has been virtually lost in the process of disintegration; the process to be discussed in terms of rapid change, mass-production, levelling-down, and, Mr. Otis emphasizes, specialization. Specialization represents the problem in the form in which it confronts one when one is asked how, in practice, the function ascribed to the university is, or can be, performed. It is Mr. Otis's charge that, in American universities, hardly any serious show is made of performing it. 'The task is … to devise an education whose method and content will supply to its recipients sufficient common premises and ideas to give them an effective unity and a consequent effective influence on the problems of their own time—to give, in other words, meaning and a common function to the "educated" man … *par excellence* the man who is responsible for civilization.' But the academic world is part of the contemporary world, and the university itself has been disabled for the task by the process that makes the task so urgent: the idea of liberal culture has been defeated and dissipated by advancing specialization; and the production of specialists (Mr. Otis can cite so distinguished a reformer as Dr. Flexner) tends to be regarded as the supreme end of the university, its *raison d'être*.

Specialization, of course, is inevitable (though some kinds are not so obviously necessary as others); the problem is to bring the special sciences and studies into significant relation—to discover how to train a kind of central intelligence by or through which they can, somehow, be brought into relation. About the kind of relation into which they can be brought it is not easy to say anything brief and convincing. We cannot lay our plans in the expectation of producing even one modern Leonardo da Vinci, and, on the other hand, a smattering, or even a good deal more, of half a dozen specialisms doesn't make an educated mind. As Mr. Otis says: 'Our great present educational problem is to devise a method of "cultural" instruction which will—in the modern world—take the place of the old "liberal arts."' What he goes on to say enforces the difficulty of the problem:

> This implies—as is indeed self-evident—an enormous effort of synthesis. It is more—infinitely more—than any mere rearrangement of curriculum, which will 'require' so many' courses' (survey, orientation or what not) illustrating so many facets of the universe, from the standpoint of eminent Specialists in these facets. An education which aims to present the *basic* ideas that express the civilization of our time, must be the result of a genuine philosophical and historical unification, which will exhibit the actual interplay of ideas, influences, and forces, and which will chart in some way their direction and give some glimmer of their meaning. It might not be too much to say that we need for our own age what the *Summa* of Thomas Aquinas was for his.

So stated, the difficulty might well seem paralysing. Our age will, before it can stand in hope of its *Summa*, have been turned into something very different from what it is now. But education cannot wait upon the synthesis, and the 'enormous effort' that makes the synthesis possible will not be merely philosophical; it will be the effort that creates an age, and the educational effort will be an essential part of it. In fact, if we are to restore our chilled courage after Mr. Otis's admirable theoretical statement of the problem we must turn to Dr. Meiklejohn's account of the practical experiment. Where the preoccupation is with immediate practice we find, for 'synthesis,' this:

> The principle here involved is that the greatest need of education just now is coherence, unity of interest and intention. On the one hand, it is imperative that in any group which plans for liberal teaching the different fields of knowledge shall be represented. The diverse elements in the human, the intellectual situation, must all be present. But, on the other hand, the essential task is that of bringing these elements into order, into meaning. And for the accomplishing of that purpose the Advisers are persuaded that the smallness of the planning group is a prime requisite. It must be possible, it must be arranged, that all members of the teaching force shall have genuine and intimate intellectual acquaintance with one another. This is another way of saying that the teachers, as they attempt to educate their pupils, must themselves be gaining education from one another, and from their common enterprise. They must be trying to create the wisdom which they wish to impart.

This passage (it is representative of Dr. Meiklejohn's book) brings home how little the problem can be properly envisaged with an eye fixed narrowly upon the desired student-product of an educational regime—envisaged, that is, in terms merely of a standard 'educated man' to be produced. And the 'common enterprise' described by Dr. Meiklejohn had, we remind ourselves, a university as a background—a background that, ideally, would have been very much more than merely that, for a university should be an inclusive and more complex 'common enterprise.'

In fact, at this point a fresh approach seems indicated. No English reader of Dr. Meiklejohn and Mr. Otis can fail to perceive that the practical problem in this country will be appreciably different from theirs, the 'background' here being so different from that exhibited or implied in their references. It is time to consider what there is to start from here. Perhaps, where the older English universities are concerned, there is something to be set against the general American advantage of greater plasticity. Those who are close to a strong conservative tradition are apt to be more aware of its disadvantages, yet It must be confessed that even Harvard, in the glimpses afforded by Mr. Otis, appears to have suffered a great deal more from the last half-century of civilization than Oxford and Cambridge have done. At any rate, let us take stock of what we are given, to start from, here.

It has, then, to be recognized that a not altogether inconsiderable, if very small, minority do contrive to get something of an education (in the relevant sense of the word) at Oxford and Cambridge, as things are. If the process of their production is considered, it is clearly not to be accounted for in terms of curricula, formal studies and official instruction. Curricula, at the best, give opportunities, and if these are profited by it is mainly owing to the stimulus derived from the general ambience, to the education got in that school of unspecialized intelligence which is created in informal intercourse—intercourse that brings together intellectual appetites from specialisms of all kinds, and from various academic levels. It is, it might be said, because they are so much more than educational institutions that the older universities have this measure of educational virtue.

The effect of these considerations is to suggest a restatement of the problem. We have not to debate whether it is to produce specialists or the 'educated man' that the university should exist. Its essential function involves the production of both—though to say 'the educated man' is perhaps misleading. The problem is to produce specialists who are in touch with a humane centre, and to produce a centre for them to be in touch with; but this centre is not best conceived as a standard' educated man.' There will be 'educated men' with various stresses, various tendencies towards specialization. There will be—as there happily are-specialists who will be classifiable equally as 'educated men.' Ortega y Gasset, as quoted by Mr. Otis, speaks of the 'peculiar brutality and aggressive stupidity with which a man comports himself when he knows a great deal about one thing and is totally ignorant of the rest.' Even a specialist who merely knows that there is a centre will be better than that. And even the mere specialist to whom this degree of education cannot be ascribed will, in his complacent barbarism, be less completely cut off from the centre if he is in touch with fellow specialists who are themselves, in some measure, not uneducated.

Seen in this light, the problem of maintaining a 'centre'—a centre that shall favour the utmost possible of communication and co-ordination—does not take on any less importance. And though the functioning of a university, actually and ideally, is so far from being merely a matter of formal provision and official machinery, these can obviously further as well as frustrate: the practical problem is to make such provision a. shall innervate the actual functioning, the essential process associated above with informal intercourse. This end would be most effectively sought, it is clear, by experiment in the spirit and manner of the Experimental College. And at this point it is relevant to remind the reader of the education gained by the teachers at Madison from their 'common enterprise,' and to suggest once more that the 'common enterprise,' ideally, would involve a wider active co-operation, and so a larger profit, than it was Dr. Meiklejohn's business to take note of.

In fact, what we find ourselves contemplating is the problem of contriving, in an actual university, to come substantially nearer to realizing the 'Idea of a University.' How to produce the 'educated man'-the man of humane culture who is equipped to be intelligent and responsible about the problems of contemporary civilization—this is a truly urgent study, but a study that apart from an adequate preoccupation with the Idea of a University is likely to end in despair. If the universities make it possible to hope something of education, that is because their function, fully performed, comprises so much more than any talk of education—or of research and scholarship—can suggest. The full performance of their inclusive function involves the performance of many functions. By way of indicating the general nature of the inclusive function as it is conceived here I perhaps may quote—there is, I think, some point in the quoting-what I have written elsewhere:

> A university of its very nature (or 'idea'), if it is one at all, asserts a contrary view of cultural tradition to the Marxian: a view of cultural tradition as representing the active function of human intelligence, choice and will; that is, as a spiritual force that can direct and determine. The promoters of *Scrutiny* didn't say that they were bent, in their zeal on behalf of I the function of criticism,' on vindicating at the same time 'the Idea of a University': they may well have felt that to put it in those terms would have been presumptuous and impolitic (they were none of them of any academic importance). But in planning to do in their own way what clearly couldn't be done in the old, they were consciously appealing to the idea that it was more than ever the *raison d'être* of a university to be) amid the material pressures and dehumanizing complications of the modern world, a focus of humane consciousness, a centre where, faced with the specializations and distractions in which human ends lose themselves,

> intelligence, bringing to bear a mature sense of values, should apply itself to the problems of civilization.

Contemplation of the Idea doesn't conduce to satisfaction with the actual. A relating of specialisms in a nonspecialist centre of consciousness—this is not a process that, from within an ancient university, one is apt to be very much aware of. A distinguished war-time migrant remarked to me recently that he found Cambridge, with all its advantages, surprisingly content to be an agglomeration of departments and special studies. In spite of the unsurpassed opportunities for intercourse across the departmental and specialist frontiers, and in spite of its being so much urged in favour of the college system that it favours such intercourse, he found little evidence that the use made of these opportunities amounted to much. It was to this lack of communication, this failure in general intellectual life, that he attributed the neglect in Cambridge of his own field of work, the Social Sciences; and he added that they involved so much bringing together of different special studies that the institution of a school of the Social Sciences would tend very strongly to promote the kind of intercourse the failure of which we were deploring. And it is certainly true that, where the disease and the debility have gone so far, there seems little hope of improvement unless in some kind of formal academic provision designed to bring specialisms into communication. My own postulate, of course, is that, while more than one such move is to be desired, one is pre-eminently necessary—one that should aim at creating a real centre in a school of the humanities: without such a centre, a university, whatever essential functions it performs and whatever improvements are attempted, will remain calamitously remote from the Idea.

The effort, then, to work out the means of educating liberally at the university level must be seen as at the same time an effort to create such a centre or focus within the university. To put it in these terms may seem portentous in the light of the particular proposals that follow. But even the most modest achievement of the kind would be gain, and what seemed insignificant in relation to the complex magnitude of the university might have, directly and indirectly, wide consequences-would have, if the achievement were, on however modest a scale, a real one.

What, then, might be done towards making a School of English a real humane focus in a university, pre-eminently representative of the Idea, and capable of discharging the function of the university in the matter of liberal education?—For seeing the problem in this way, and holding this approach to be the most promising, I have already thrown out some hints of reason, and these, I hope, will have been adequately reinforced by the time the lines of the kind of experiment I should like to see undertaken have been sketched.

Literature and the University

The Wrong Question.* From *English Literature in our Time & the University* (1969)

This selection is taken from *English Literature in our Time & the University*, F. R. Leavis, 1969, From the Clark Lectures 1967. Published by Chatto & Windus, London, United Kingdom.

* * * * *

English literature in our time—I am concerned in these lectures with that. If I had said 'in *my* time' it would have tended to have a different effect. For there have been great and rapid changes in the last forty years. This fact is an essential consideration for my particular theme, though not, perhaps, in the way I may be immediately taken to intimate: what would ordinarily be suggested by 'literary history' is not my proposed business.

Change is insisted on in this passage from the front page of the *Times Literary Supplement* for May 19, 1966—a passage that is a pregnant text for me, inviting me to define positively the nature of my preoccupation:

> 'It seems inconceivable that higher education could be both a large system and a comprehensive one, and yet universities remain essentially the same as they have been;

---

* Excerpt (Chapter 1, pp. 37–60) from: Leavis, F. R. (1969). *English Literature in our times & the university. The Clark Lecturers, 1967*. London, United Kingdom: Chatto & Windus.

> indeed there is a lack of historical perspective about Lord Robbins's comments that implies an idea of an eternal university, that belies the evidence of rapid social change in their students—and their teachers. As for their other function, have universities always been the source of the best ideas in our civilization? Name a great novelist who was a don; apart from Housman, most poets, I think, have been outside the university net?'

The article is a review of the report of the Franks Commission and of Lord Robbins's *The University and the Modern World*, a collection of his addresses. I don't want to defend Lord Robbins, and I should have liked to be able to say that my sympathies were with the reviewer, who is critical of Lord Robbins's assumptions and mode of thought. But I can't. The whole article is depressingly documentary—words the force of which (I mean the last two) will have come out, I hope, before long. It confirms my sense of the great need there is to get attention for the considerations I want to put forward—and it makes me feel (as I have felt from time to time during the last forty years) that I would rather discuss the function of the university with a mathematician or a physicist than with an academic humanist, which is what I take the reviewer to be.

The aspect of change represented by the passage I have quoted that I want to emphasize regards the latter part of it, and it is one of which the author is unconscious:

> Have universities always been the source of the best ideas in our civilization? Name a great novelist who was a don; apart from Housman, most poets, thinkers and creators have been outside the university net.

It is no new thing for an academic humanist to be blind and blank and urbanely unconcerned in that way. What I have to dwell on is the frightening truth that the blindness and blankness and unconcern are today general. You don't, of course, settle the question, how important or unimportant have Oxford and Cambridge been to English literature in the past, by asking how many dons were great novelists or great poets and offering us Housman. You say nothing to the point. You merely show your lack of interest in the nature of a civilization, and in the conditions out of which a great literature grows and by which it is kept alive.

A literature grows out of a culture. A great poet, though he may have a profound influence on his native language by his supremely creative use of it (it developed and is kept living in creative use), didn't create it. Shakespeare had an immeasurably great influence upon English, but couldn't have done so had he not inherited in it a rich, supple and exquisitely vital language. The indebtedness of Shakespearian English to the universities (though Shakespeare was notoriously *not* a classical or an English don) was immense—a subject on which a first year man reading 'English' could write at least a page or two, and which a maturer student of distinguished mind, choosing it for a piece of original work, could make very much more of than a language specialist—or a linguistician—is likely (I believe) to have provided for in his implicit canons of relevance, or to be predisposed to applaud, or to see the point of.

I will say no more on this head—and I have said nothing about the University Wits. I will only add that, not merely to Shakespeare, but to the subsequent creators of modern English literature it has mattered in most vital ways (and not merely materially) that England contained an educated class and an educated public. No one will contend that the universities 'had nothing to do with *their* existence.

The points I have made are obvious. I don't for a moment suggest that the writer in the *Times Literary Supplement* is inclined to question them, or to question that Oxford and Cambridge have had the greatest importance in English life and civilization. What I am calling attention to is the portentous significance of his being, when taking part in the debate, which isn't merely theoretical, about the urgent need to expand, multiply and modernize the universities, able to dismiss with such unconscious irresponsibility all suggestion that the universities have had a vital function in relation to English literature. In doing that—this is the truth for which I aim at getting a full and real recognition—he is lightly dismissing the function that, in our world (which becomes every year more completely what it is), only the university can perform. 'Lightly' is the word: his article is an unconscious tribute to the potency of the technologico-Benthamite climate in which we live. The function of the university towards the sciences will in any case be performed—provision for *them* is in no danger of being neglected: the humane function, that which gives the sciences their human meaning and their *raison d'être*, can be left to—what? The Sunday papers? If the idea of the university is not understood in the university itself, and is not fought for, with fierce, informed and resolute conviction there, where in our world will it be, and by whom?

I have perhaps made it plain by now that my associated insistences—on the university and on English literature—are two emphases in the expression of the same basic concern. It is the concern that it was Arnold's distinction to have given expression to and that makes the conception of the function of criticism he stands for—*he* made It part of the English-speaking cultural heritage—a significant development. Contemplating, in an earlier phase of it than ours, the advance of industrial civilization, he saw that something new was happening to humanity, and that England and America in especial were exposed to a new kind of menace. It is that which he has in mind when he expresses his fear that England will become a 'greater Holland'. This is obviously a recoil from triumphant materialism, affluent and unleavened. Whether or not the way of expressing it is fair to Holland, there can be no doubt about the essential nature of the fear; the Arnoldian context—the immediate one and the general context of essays and pamphlets—makes it perfectly plain. It is that the massive and rapid growth of material civilization, the changes in human habit and the human condition brought about by technological advance, will entail a lapse of that creatively human response to economic fact, to the inescapable exigencies of life and material circumstance, which a cultural tradition *is*—is, while it remains a living power in the present.

Arnold saw, and said, that to preserve continuity—continuity of cultural consciousness—a more conscious and deliberate use of intelligence was needed than in the past. This is the meaning of the stress he laid upon poetic tradition (literature for him *was* poetry), and of his preoccupation with 'centrality', with defining the idea of 'authority' in matters of taste and judgment, and with standards. If we are inclined to comment that his prescription, for all his command of urbane irony, looks pathetically unrealistic in relation to the menace it has in view, we should remind ourselves of a difference between his time and ours that we tend to forget: in the England he was addressing there was a large and immensely influential educated class. He himself comments on this fact explicitly, as well as implying everywhere his awareness of it, and his reliance on it. But, as his work in the field of education and such essays as that on 'Equality' testify, he was far from resting in a complacent ease of mind about the cultural advantage England enjoyed in the existence of this social class which shared (he accepted for his purpose that description) the education and manners of the governing class, and—or, if you like, and yet—supported the Victorian intellectual reviews. He was too generous and fastidious humanly to be satisfied, and, moreover, with his eye on the inevitable coming economic, social and political transformations, he saw the dangers inherent in that ambiguity, the 'educated class'—or 'educated classes'.

It was the main concern of his life to promote in this country the steps and the process that should create (this being their ideal aim) a class of the educated—a class that could be definable and thought of as essentially and unequivocally that, in dissociation from the idea of social privilege, or social privilege as ordinarily cried out against, detested and prized (even by Lord Snow). Or perhaps it would be better to say, not thought of as class at all—though it is well to insist that there must be a community of the 'educated' that can never be a majority. No one minds-even in America—there being an *élite* of athletes. To be both brief and unambiguous in this matter is difficult, and perhaps I had better add to what I have said that Arnold had no designs *against* the actual 'educated class' that had produced him and his ideals, and that mattered so much to him and made it possible for him to energize with hope. It mattered so much because it represented the possibility of an effective appeal to standards. And what I mean by this has so essential an importance for my theme that I must now, even at the cost of some insistence on what ought to be truism—and at the cost of saying what some here will have heard me say before, try to make it plain, if I can, beyond any misunderstanding. In that attempt I have a more difficult task than Arnold had—or, perhaps I had better say, was conscious of having.

The word 'standards' is not the less necessary because, like so many of the most important words in our field of discourse, its use can't be justified by the kind of definition the prompt logic of the enemy demands. One can't long discuss the study of literature and the unavoidableness of critical judgments *without* using it. And when I try to explain what 'standards' are, what is their nature and authority as we, students of literature and (therefore) critics, are concerned with them, my underlying and essential preoccupation is not merely or mainly theoretical, but brings together very intimately my disquiet at the actual state of criticism in the English speaking world, my conception of what literary studies should be at the university, and my sense of the idea of a university as it needs to be fostered—and realized—in the technological age.

How, then, when the question of 'standards'—the challenge to explain what they are, or the problem of exorcizing misconceptions—comes up in the way in which it does come up for the literary critic, how as a literary critic does he deal with it? How, as a literary critic, should he deal with it?

In this insistence on 'literary critic' I have a reason: I wish to intimate that I am not proposing to attempt a philosophical discussion. I'm not much interested in establishing in any thorough-going theoretical way that the phrase 'the standards of literary criticism', means something; that their basis must be this, and their nature that. On the other hand, I *am* very much preoccupied with vindicating literary criticism as a specific discipline—a discipline of intelligence, with its own field, and its own approaches within that field. And in particular I am preoccupied with insisting that there is an approach to the problem of 'standards' that is proper to the field of literary criticism and to the literary critic as such—that you don't need to be a philosopher to make it.

Let me add at once that with this preoccupation goes—as, when it is seriously entertained, there must, I think, go—a concern for the critical function in contemporary actuality; for the function of criticism as, in sum, it is performed or not performed, and as it ought to be performed, here in our day in England. I indicate here one aspect of the difficulty of dealing with the problem of standards: you can neither separate it off, nor deal with it in the abstract. You can't profitably discuss the standards of criticism apart from the purposes and the methods, or apart from the actual functioning of criticism in the contemporary world. And apart from the ability to arrive at intelligent and sensitive judgments in the concrete—except, that is, as informed by critical experience—understanding of the nature of critical judgment in the abstract can amount to little. To consider the nature of 'standards' involves considering the function of criticism in the full sense of that phrase, and apart from intelligence about the actual functioning in the world as we know it (where, that is, we have the closest access to the concrete), that consideration will hardly achieve a living strength, the strength of real understanding. Real understanding in fact, can't be a mere theoretical matter; it will entail real critical engagement in relation to the contemporary scene.

I am emboldened to say elementary things when I remember—and I remember because the pronouncement was directed against me and an endeavour, in which I was involved, to ensure that there should be a play of serious criticism upon the contemporary scene, that not so very long ago an Editor of the *Times Literary Supplement* pronounced, in a British Council publication: 'There is ... no desirable life of the mind of which literary reviews are an essential component, and in which fixed standards of criticism gain a kind of legal backing.' To emphasize the force of 'fixed standards' he spoke also of 'imposing accepted values'-and spoke as if that were something I myself notoriously advocated. No one, then, who knows what 'standards' are and what is the nature of critical authority *could* talk of 'fixed standards' or of 'providing them with a legal backing', and no one who understands the nature of a judgment could talk of 'imposing accepted values'. Essentially, as I've said before (I suppose) in a good many places-but the point has to be made and much hangs on it, a critical judgment has the form, 'This is so, isn't it?'. And the concurrence appealed for must be real, or it serves no critical purpose, and, if he suspects insincerity or mere politeness, can bring no satisfaction to the critic—to the critic *as* critic.

What, of its very nature, the critical activity aims at, in fact, is an exchange, a collaborative exchange, a corrective and creative interplay of judgments. For though my judgment asks to be confirmed and appeals for agreement that the thing is *so*; the response I expect at best will be of the form, 'Yes, but', the 'but' standing for qualifications, corrections, shifts of emphasis, additions, refinements. The process of personal judgment from its very outset, of course, is in subtle ways essentially collaborative, as my thinking is—as any use of the language in which one thinks and expresses one's thoughts *must* be. But the functioning of criticism demands a fully overt kind of collaboration. Without a many-sided real exchange—the implicitly and essentially collaborative interplay by which the object, the poem (for example) in which the individual minds meet, and, at the same time, the judgments concerning it, are established, the object, which we think of as 'there' in a public world for common contemplation, isn't really 'there'.

What, under the head of Practical Criticism, we call analysis is a creative, or re-creative, process. It's a more deliberate following-through of that process of creation in response to the poet's words (a poem being in question) than any serious reading is. It is a re-creation in which, by a considering attentiveness, we ensure a more than ordinary faithfulness and fullness. And actually when one is engaged in analysis one is engaged in discussion, even if only implicitly. That is a point I made in saying that a judgment has the form, 'This is so, isn't it?' One is engaged in discussion of ...?—the poem, which is there *for* discussion only in so far as those discussing have each recreated it.

The discussion is an effort to establish the poem as something standing in a common world between those discussing, and thus to justify our habitual assumption that it does so stand. It's 'there' only when it's realized in separate minds, and yet it's not merely private. It's something in which minds can meet, and our business is to establish the poem and meet in it. Merely private, on the one hand, and, on the other, public in the sense that it can be produced in a laboratory, or tripped over—the poem is neither: the alternatives are not exhaustive. There is a third realm, and the poem belongs to that. I take courage for this reminder, for this repetition, for this insistence on the elementary, because, as I hope to bring out with the appropriate cogency—it's at any rate the purpose of these lectures, a great deal more than literary criticism is involved, just as the *rationale* of literary criticism involves a great deal more than this term itself, with its limiting adjective, might seem to imply.

Also, I wanted to say: this is as far as the literary critic *qua* literary critic need go epistemologically or metaphysically. It's all very familiar-with the familiarity of things that are so fundamental, so necessarily taken for granted, that we don't ordinarily bother to recognize them. If difficulty should seem to be caused by the demand for full conscious recognition (which is necessary when it's a question of justifying the pretensions of criticism, and the implicit pretensions of literature and art in general, and all mature interest in literature and art) the critic can say: 'But consider language.' A language—apart from the conventional signs and symbols for it—is really *there*, it really exists in full actuality, only in individual users; it is *there* only as its idioms, phrases, words and so on, with the meaning, intention, force in which their life resides, are uttered and meant by me (for example) and taken by you. Do they then belong to the public world (you can't point to them), or are they merely personal and private? We know that the brisk 'either-or' doesn't meet the case.

And language, in the full sense, in the full concrete reality that eludes the cognizance of any form of linguistic science, does more than provide an analogue for a 'culture' in that full sense which very much concerns us, but eludes the immense body of important people who share Lord Robbins's outlook; it is very largely the essential life of a culture. And literature, of course, is a mode or manifestation of language.

What in all this I have been trying to bring into clear and full recognition is the collaborative-creative nature of criticism; and I have my eye now particularly on the word 'standards'. Criticism is concerned with establishing the poem—or the novel—as an object of common access in what is in some sense a public world so that when we differ about it we are differing about what is sufficiently the same thing to make differing profitable. But the establishing of the poem (or the novel) is the establishing of a value. Any reading of it that takes it *as* a work of art involves an element of implicit valuation. The process, the kind of activity of inner response and discipline, by which we take possession of the created work is essentially the kind of activity that completes itself in a value judgment.

Of course, here again the enemy has his opportunity. Valuation isn't a simple idea, and the process of 'valuing' isn't in simple analogy with putting a price on. 'Value', in fact, is another of those essential words which, as needed for our purposes, don't lend themselves to the kind of definition necessary for effective defence against the indifference that, in a Benthamite and egalitarian world, so rapidly becomes overt hostility. I'm avowing that when I say that 'value' is inextricably bound up with 'significance'. And so far from valuing being a matter of bringing up a scale, a set of measures, or an array of fixed and definite criteria to the given work, every work that makes itself felt as a challenge evokes, or generates, in the critic a fresh realization of the grounds and nature of judgment. A truly great work is realized to *be* that because it so decidedly modifies—alters—the sense of value and significance that judges. That is what is testified to in the commonplace that a great artist creates the taste by which he is appreciated.

'Creates' is the right word: in the effect on the public's power to respond and realize, the effect on taste-to accept that word for the moment (though it carries a most inadequate suggestion), creative genius achieves the completion of its distinctive work. D. H. Lawrence makes that point in the answer he gave to a question put to him, very near the end of his life, about the nature of the artist's impulsion-his drive: 'One writes out of one's moral sense; for the race, as it were'. On 'moral'—and that it should carry, even for the use in which the critic finds it necessary, the odour of an unpleasant or bad word is a symptom of our time-the immediately relevant commentary again comes from Lawrence.

> The true artist doesn't substitute immorality for morality. On the contrary, he always substitutes a finer morality for a grosser. As soon as you see a finer morality, the grosser becomes relatively immoral.

It is when we feel that the radical criteria are notably challenged that the word 'moral' comes up; it comes up *because* they are challenged, and is our response to the realization. About Lawrence one might say that his moral perception is a manifestation of his genius, being the fineness of his sense of life—his sense of the difference between what makes *for* life and what makes against it. But to say that is to invite the comment that it is a large proposition, and 'life' is a large word. What is life? The advantage the critic enjoys when justifying such uses as he has to make of the word, and of his other indispensable terms, is that he has the work of a creative writer in front of him; he is preoccupied with referring as sensitively, faithfully and closely to that as he is able. The terms are prompted by the created thing, and he in turn gives them, for the reader, their charge of special meaning, their due specific force, by means, essentially, of a tact of particular reference to the given work as present that is the aim-in the evoked experience of it, the evoked recall (a critical process that is, in its wholly subservient and instrumental way, itself creative).

From time to time, as I was preparing these lectures, I felt that I had overworked that last adjective and must both become more sparing of it and do some revisionary elimination. But prescription, I found, was one thing, and performance another; and, further, I found myself reflecting that my theme of its very nature entailed so much the kind of insistence directed by Blake against the cultural tyranny he associated with the names of Newton and Locke that to avoid a frequent use of the word was impossible. Blake was the human protest on behalf of life against the repression of creativity represented by the prevailing ethos of the 18th century—life, he insisted, was essentially creative in a way denied not only by the prepotence of Newton and Locke in the dominant spirit of 'civilized' and final commonsense, but by the very language—the modes and conventions of utterance—established firmly as belonging to the basic nature of things and the spirit of civilization, and accepted as natural. The emphasis Blake lays on art and the artist is one with his insistence on the creativeness of perception.

The civilization we live in presents a more formidable menace to life, and, in saying that, I see the justification of my reference to Blake in the force, peculiarly appropriate to my purpose, that the word 'life' now has, thus associated with Blake's kind of insistence on an essential creativeness—'creativeness' itself being given the right charge of meaning. The generality of my proposition has, then (I hope), for those I am addressing, the directed point and the edge it has in my own mind. The menace, the sense of its lethal insidiousness, was (as so often) borne in on me with disturbing vividness quite recently, when I listened to a paper on Newman's *Idea of a University*. The paper was distinguished, informed by wide experience, and provocative of question and comment; but, as I knew, effective discussion of fundamentals is improbable, indeed almost impossible, in a large assembly. Nevertheless, since no one, when the time for discussion came, seemed anxious to speak first, I opened by saying briefly what I most wanted to say. It was roughly this:

> 'I didn't, Sir, like your dividing the business of the university under two heads: one, handing things on (the word "tradition" came in here), and the other, creating new knowledge. It prejudices the upshot at the very beginning—unless challenged. What I am most concerned for that comes under your "handing things on" is rather to be called "maintaining a continuity", and perhaps I can make clear the difference I have in mind by adding immediately that for "continuity" you can substitute "a life"—"maintaining a life". Consider the life of a language: a language is maintained in *use*—use by a community in response to changing conditions and a changing civilization, and the use that maintains it is creative.'

The reader of the paper saw my point, but as I expected, it wasn't taken up in discussion. But towards the close a speaker who had shown himself notably articulate remarked, glancing back over what had been said, that I, he gathered, was a vitalist. I could only reply that I didn't see how that word helped. I felt, in fact, nonplussed; very few, it was plain, had taken my meaning, and I recognized that an attempt to convey it on that kind of occasion was an enterprise absurdly out of the question. No thought of any philosophy or intellectual system, of course, had been in my mind; I merely meant to evoke in my hearers a strong present sense of what they of course knew, and to insist on its crucial relevance.

But did they know it? Do people know it? They do and they don't. The problem of getting them to recognize it is very like the problem of getting people to recognize what they take for granted, what they implicitly assume, when they formulate and advance a critical judgment and engage in the critical discussion to which it leads.

The 'handing-on', then, for which it is recognized (in a kind of way) that provision has to be made in the conception of a new university isn't a mere matter of handing on—handing over—tools, data, inert equipment, externalities to be taken possession of as such, conquered provinces, technical know-hows. In its vital nerve (and if it hasn't one, it's nothing), and most essentially, it's a matter of carrying on a vital continuity in which the promoters and executants are already involved in such a way that, but for their being so involved, there would have been no conception, no planning, and no point in founding a university. They have, that is, a common culture in which (say), for all their differences, agnostics, Catholics and diverse kinds of Protestant can work together for common human ends. Such a cultural tradition, like the language that is at the heart of it, has been formed and kept living—that is, changing in response to changing conditions (material, economic and so on)—by continuous collaborative renewal. The participants tend to be hardly conscious of the basic values and assumptions they share, but it is the sense of something basic shared that makes possible the assumption (for instance) that there is point in founding new universities.

The state, however, of being hardly conscious, or mainly unconscious, illustrated by the episode I have just related, won't do in the civilization that sweeps us on. Without a human effort of a kind the need for which Lord Robbins and his associates have given no sign of being aware of, an effort directed and sustained by intelligent purpose, the new universities—the universities in sum—will merely be a part of the process by which, whatever provision is made for philosophy, psychology and the social sciences, the world comes to assume invincibly, to the immense impoverishment of life, that a rising 'standard of living' is a sufficient account of human ends. That is the significance of the uninhibited frankness with which Lord Robbins avows his solidarity with Lord Snow.

What, of course, I have virtually been saying is that the unprecedented civilization to which we are committed demands a new, or a more strongly positive, conception of the university and its function. The great and most menacing change brought about by the technological revolution is that it has almost destroyed the creative cultural process, of which the finer operation in that continuous renewal which maintained the human world of values and significances and spiritual graces is on the point of death; it has turned the business of human adjustment to changing material conditions into a reductive process, largely determined by business profit. The worker earns the wherewithal and the leisure to enjoy a higher standard of living by work that has little interest for him and little human meaning; it is something to be got behind him so that he can get away to live—before the telly, over the pools form, in the bingo hall, in the car. Technology, and the financial appetites, mechanisms and potencies produced by it, have determined his culture for him and saved him the trouble.

It wasn't my purpose to develop this particular branch of the theme; but I wanted to remind you that the facts it points to concern vitally, not merely the industrial workers directly affected, but all of us, including those of us whose business is with English literature-which achieved its greatness in another kind of human world. And I will now revert to that matter of 'standards', which I left hanging in the air—a matter on which, as everyone knows, the technological revolution has a bearing. The term 'standards' presents itself when there is question of getting recognition for the justice—or the absurdity—of judgments affirming (explicitly or implicitly) relative value and importance. It's a representative use, for instance, when I say that the general acceptance, in England, of Hemingway as a great writer, or the spectacle of an academic critic going out of his way to pronounce a Kingsley Amis novel a 'serious study in amorality', would have been possible only in a period marked by a collapse of standards. We talk about 'standards', in fact, at times when it is peculiarly hard to invoke standards with effect. And they can be 'there' to be invoked with effect by the critic only in the existence of an educated public capable of responding intelligently, and influential enough to make its response felt. I need say no more by way of defining standards. They depend on, they are a manifestation of, that collaborative interplay in which the poem is established as something in which minds can meet, which maintains the life of a language, which creates the essential values and significances of the human world, which creates a culture.

When one speaks of the lapse of standards what one is pointing to is the fact that it is hard for the critic to believe in any decisive influence represented by any public his work can be supposed to imply. It isn't that there aren't many intelligent and cultivated persons about, enough to be a potential influence of great value, whose 'yes, but-', or whose 'no', is of the kind the critic needs, but they don't form an effective public; they don't really form a public at all.

To bring out the force of that truth one can adduce the fact—it is at least very suggestive—that the whole of the English-speaking world can't, or won't, maintain, on ordinary business lines, a single serious critical journal. The related fact is that such performance of the current function of criticism as can be alleged is what we see in the review pages of the weeklies and the Sunday papers, and it certainly doesn't imply the existence of a public that entertains and exacts a serious conception of the critical function.

The theme is one I needn't enlarge upon. The relevance of the present alarm about the difficulty of keeping a newspaper going on a circulation of a mere million or two is plain. If the advance of technology and the conditions of a technological civilization mean that a 'quality' newspaper must have an immense advertising revenue, then the editorial policy must be one that ensures an immense circulation, and the review-columns that make the formal salute to literary culture will, judged as an offer to perform the function of criticism, be contemptible. And the reviewing in the 'intellectual' weeklies will be indistinguishable in general quality from that in the Sunday papers. The same kinds of writer, very largely the same writers, write in both and are most of them in other ways actively engaged in the culture of the technological age; and as for the cultural standards of their smaller and superior public, the Sunday papers (like the review columns of the *Guardian*) in any case give us them.

Now there is no question of trying to reverse, or halt, the advance of technology. There can be no restoring the wheelwright's shop or the conditions of production that integrated work organically with a living culture and associated it in a major way with the creative human response. But that doesn't mean that we must, or should, leave the human heritage, the cultural continuity, to lapse and let technology henceforward dictate, unchecked by any human wisdom or human sense more mature than Lord Robbins's. There is a dreadful blank unconsciousness to be faced, as Lord Robbins unconsciously testifies; but there is also in humanity an instinct of self-preservation to appeal to—a sense of vital needs thwarted and starved by technologico-Benthamite civilization.

The university, in so far as it is more than a centre and nursery of the sciences, a technological institute, or a collocation of specialist departments, is the representative of that instinct, and the organ through which society has to make the sustained effort (one directed by collaborative intelligence and a full human responsibility) to keep those needs recognized and provide our civilization with memory and mature purpose. Although, as I pointed out in commenting on that odd and significant dismissive attitude of the writer in the *Times Literary Supplement,* the university has always had a major importance in relation to the country's cultural life—an importance (the immediate emphasis) for creative literature, its function was never so vital as it is now: living continuity used to be maintained in many ways in the functioning of the general life of society—in the life of the home, for instance, and of the local milieu, and there was not that destructive action on the creative heritage and the human positive response which characterizes the mechanisms of civilization in our time—characterizes them to such a tune that, in the resulting amnesia and passivity, the destructiveness isn't recognized as such. As things are now, if provision is not made for the focused and fostered insight, purpose and effort of continuity, the heritage is lost, abandoned to oblivion, and mankind faces a fate more certain than the feared nuclear cataclysm. I recall Mr Owen Barfield's recent comment-a retort to naive neo-Wellsian euphoria—on that transatlantic world which confronts us with our own imminent future.

> I had not thought death had undone so many

—a sentence that, with its dual context, you know. The only possible provision, the only possible organ, is the university-to recognize which fact is to recognize the context of organic life the university must have in the country at large, will draw its strength from, and will foster.

When I say that the university as a centre of consciousness for the community must have its centre in an English school, I don't mean anything of the kind that was meant when we were told, at Cambridge, forty years ago: 'Poetry will save us'. Nor do I mean that in some hierarchy of esteem English comes first. But the need is for a focal centre; and a focus of cultural continuity can only be in English. English literature, magnificent and matchless in diversity and range, and so full and profound in its registration of changing life, gives us a continuity that is not yet dead. There is no other; no other access to anything approaching full continuity of mind, spirit and sensibility—which is what we desperately need.

CHAPTER SEVENTEEN

The Idea of the University,* 1950

From *The Voice of Liberal Learning: Michael Oakeshott on Education* (1989)

MICHAEL OAKESHOTT

This selection is taken *The Voice of Liberal Learning: Michael Oakeshott on Education*, Michael J. Oakeshott, 1989, Edited with Introduction by Timothy Fuller. Published by Yale University Press, New Haven, CT.

Editors' Note

Michael Oakeshott was primarily a political philosopher. However, during the course of his intellectual life, he wrote essays on the nature of education, particularly university education, and six of these were collected together (by Timothy Fuller) to form the volume entitled *The Voice of Liberal Learning*.

By the term 'liberal' here, Oakeshott had in mind that universities should offer a space free from the exigencies and press of the world, from 'the here and now'. A liberal education 'is liberated from the distracting business of satisfying human wants'. However, 'becoming educated is itself an emancipation' not merely *from*

* *Editorial note:* This piece, first published in *The Listener*, is in part a distillation of 'The Universities' (pp. 127–8). However, it contains some new material and provides a succinct introduction to Oakeshott's thought on the subject, and is therefore reproduced here in its entirety.

the world but is a positive space in which one's humanity might be developed. The university was to offer, thereby, a special kind of space, for reflection, thought, study and engagement with the different modes of experience that had evolved over centuries and which had come to constitute civilisation itself. Universities, accordingly, should offer the 'gift of an interval', in which this kind of disinterested study could take place. A university education, so conceived, was both a conversation in itself and an entry into and an engagement with the conversations of humanity.

This liberal learning was not for practice in any straightforward sense even if it might inform practice. Nor was it 'socialization' and nor mere 'collective understanding'. Rather, it was a matter of the development of mind. 'Mind ... is the intelligent activity in which man [sic] may understand and explain processes which cannot understand and explain themselves.' This is a self-avowedly 'conservative' philosophy of the university and learning and it is explicitly at odds, for example, with Oakeshott's contemporary, Walter Moberly, who saw in the universities a potential to assist the social and moral development of the world and who sought to overcome a paradox of the university being at once 'autonomous' and as 'useful to the community'. For Oakeshott, this is tantamount to having 'the best of both worlds' and is shot through with 'incoherence'. There *is* a 'genuine crisis in the universities', that of 'how to avoid destruction at the hands of men [sic] who have no use for their characteristic virtues, men who are convinced only that "knowledge is power".'

RB

Recommended Reading

O'Sullivan, N. (2011). The place of enlightenment in Michael Oakeshott's conception of liberal education. *Politeja 3*(17), 5–16. Retrieved from http://www.michael-oakeshott-association.com/files/NOS11.pdf

* * * * *

It is a favourite theory of mine that what people call ideals' are 'purposes' are never themselves the source of human activity; they are shorthand expressions for the real spring of conduct, which is a disposition to do certain things and a knowledge of how to do them. Human beings do not start from rest and spring into activity only when attracted by a purpose to be achieved. To be alive is to be perpetually active. The purposes we attribute to particular kinds of activity are only abridgements of our knowledge of how to engage in this or that activity.

This, for example, is obviously so in the activity we call 'science'. Scientific activity is not the pursuit of a premeditated end; nobody knows or can imagine where it will reach. There is no perfection, prefigured in our minds, which we can set up as a standard by which to judge current achievements. What holds science together and gives it its impetus and direction is not a known purpose to be achieved, but the knowledge scientists have of how to conduct a scientific investigation. Their particular pursuits and purposes are not superimposed upon that knowledge, but emerge within it. Or again, a cook is not a man who first has a vision of a pie and then tries to make it; he is man skilled in cookery, and both his projects and his achievements spring from his skill. Or, to take a third example, a man may think he has a 'mission' in life, and he may think that his activity is governed by this 'mission'. But, in fact, it is the other way about; his missionary activity consists n knowing how to behave in a certain way and in trying to behave in that way; and what he calls his 'mission' is only a shorthand expression of this knowledge and endeavour.

For this reason, the current talk about the 'mission' and the 'function' of a university goes rather over my head; I think I can understand what is intended, but it seems to me an unfortunate way of talking. It assumes that there is something called 'a university', a contrivance of some sort, something you could make another of tomorrow if you had enough money, of which it is sensible to ask, What is it 'for'? And one of the criticisms of contemporary universities is that they are not as clear as they ought to be about their 'function'. I am not at all surprised. There is plenty that might properly be criticized in our universities, but to quarrel with them because they are not clear about their 'function' is to make a mistake about their character. A university is not a machine for achieving a particular purpose or producing a particular result; it is a manner of human activity. And it would be necessary for a university to advertise itself as pursuing a particular purpose only if it were talking to people so ignorant that they had to be spoken to in baby-language, or if it were so little confident of its power to embrace those who came to it that it had to call attention to its incidental charms. My impression, however, is that our universities have not yet sunk so low as to make this necessary. They may not know what they are 'for', they may be very hazy about their 'function', but I think they do know something that is much more important—namely, how to go about the business of being a university. This knowledge is not a gift of nature; it is a knowledge of a tradition, it has to be acquired, it is always mixed up with error and ignorance, and it may even be lost. But, it is only by exploring this sort of knowledge (which I believe not to have been lost) that we can hope to discover what may be called the 'idea' of a university.

A university is a number of people engaged in a certain sort of activity: the Middle Ages called it *Studium*; we may call it 'the pursuit of learning'. This activity is one of the properties, indeed one of the virtues, of a civilized way of living; the scholar has his place beside the poet, the priest, the soldier, the politician and the man of business in any civilized society. The universities do not, however, have a monopoly of this activity. The hermit scholar in his study, an academy famous for a particular branch of learning, a school for young children, are each participants in this activity and each of them is admirable, but they are not universities. What distinguishes a university is a special manner of engaging in the pursuit of learning. It is a corporate body of scholars, each devoted to a particular branch of learning: what is characteristic is the pursuit of learning as a co-operative enterprise. The members of this corporation are not spread about the world, meeting occasionally or not at all; they live in permanent proximity to one another. And consequently we should neglect part of the character of a university if we omitted to think of it as a place. A university, moreover, is a home of learning, a place where a tradition of learning is preserved and extended, and where the necessary apparatus for the pursuit of learning has been gathered together.

Of the scholars who compose a university, some may be expected to devote an unbroken leisure to learning, their fellows having the advantage of their knowledge from their conversation and the world benefiting, perhaps, from their writings. A place of learning without this kind of scholar could scarcely be called a university. Others, however, will engage themselves to teach as well as to learn. But here again, it is the special manner of the pedagogic enterprise which distinguishes a university. Those who come to be taught at a university have to provide evidence that they are not merely beginners; and not only do they have displayed before them the learning of their teachers, but they are offered a curriculum of study, to be followed by a test and the award of a degree. Three classes of person, then, go to compose a university as we know it—the scholar, the scholar who is also a teacher, and those who come to be taught, the undergraduates. And the presence of these three classes, and the relations that prevail between them, determine the distinctive place of a university in the wider enterprise we call the pursuit of learning.

Let us consider the activity of these three classes. Everyone who knows anything about it, knows that there is a difference between the pursuit of learning and the acquisition of information. It is a subtle difference, for an ill-informed man can scarcely be called a learned man. But a scholar is something more than a picker-up of unconsidered trifles: he knows something about what he is looking for, and he can distinguish between what he knows and what he does not know. The world's contempt for the 'poor pedant' is often mistaken; it judges the scholar's activity by its use, and finds it pedantic when it appears useless. But this is a false standard; what is reprehensible is not the pursuit of knowledge which has no immediate use, nor that attention to detail which is unavoidable in scholarship, but that blind groping about among fragments of learning which are known only as fragments into which scholarship sometimes degenerates. This does not happen as often as the world thinks; and perhaps it is less liable to happen in a university than elsewhere.

There is, indeed, no simple way of determining what composes the world of learning; no clear reason—such as usefulness—can be found to justify its parts. They do not represent a premeditated purpose, but a slowly changing tradition. As the years pass, new studies rise above the horizon and old studies are rejuvenated by coming in contact with the new. Unavoidably, each scholar is something of a specialist who cultivates a chosen field. But it rarely happens that this is a very narrow field, and a scholar may often be found turning from one study to another or poking his nose into something which is not his chief business. Nevertheless, the pursuit of learning may have the appearance of a fragmentary enterprise; and even if we suspect that this is what it looks like when seen only from the outside, it will not seem far-fetched to enquire whether some superior integrating force is not wanted to give coherence and proportion to the whole pursuit. Do we not need a map, it may plausibly be asked, a map on which the relations between the parts of the world of learning are clearly displayed? Would not the whole thing be better for a little glue to hold it together? And some who feel most strongly about this are to be found filling in the interstices between the sciences with a sticky mess called 'culture', in the belief that they are supplying a desperate need. But both the diagnosis and the remedy spring from a sad misconception.

The world of learning needs no extraneous cement to hold it together; its parts move in a single magnetic field, and the need for go-betweens arises only when the current is gratuitously cut off. The pursuit of learning is not a race in which the competitors jockey for the best place, it is not even an argument or a symposium; it is a conversation. And the peculiar virtue of a university (as a place of many studies) is to exhibit it in this character, each study appearing as a voice whose tone is neither tyrannous nor plangent, but humble and conversable. A conversation does not need a chairman, it has no predetermined course, we do not ask what it is 'for', and we do not judge its excellence by its conclusion; it has no conclusion, but is always put by for another day. Its integration is not superimposed but springs from the quality of the voices which speak, and its value lies in the relics it leaves behind in the minds of those who participate.

The scholar, then, is one who knows how to engage in the activity of learning; his natural voice is not that of the preacher or of the instructor. Yet it is not surprising that among scholars should be found teachers, and that university should be a place where one might go with the expectation of learning something. Not every scholar will have the sympathy that makes a great teacher, but every genuine scholar unavoidably imparts to those capable of recognizing it something of his knowledge on how to pursue learning. His power to teach springs from the force and inspiration of his knowledge, from his immersion in the pursuit of learning, which may be felt even by those little touched with the ambitions of a scholar. And even those whose learning and sympathy are ready, those who are pre-eminently capable of imparting what they know, must be expected to be something different from assiduous instructors. They may be trusted to know the rules, but they will not be much concerned to teach conclusions. One may go to some sorts of art schools and be taught ten ways of drawing a cat of a dozen tricks to remember in painting an eye, but the scholar as teacher will teach, not how to draw or to paint, but how to see. He may be easily articulate, or he may find it difficult to throw off his own doubts and hesitancies, but, since he is a scholar, it does not belong to his character to speak with no voice in particular, and he will have nothing to do with vulgarization of learning which regards it merely as a means to passing an examination or winning a certificate.

But a university may be credited with a power to teach which goes beyond that of its individual scholars. It is not an academy drawing its inspiration from a single pre-eminent man; it is a body of scholars who supply one another's imperfections, both personal and scholastic. It accommodates many different sorts of teacher, and each sort draws its power from its intercourse with other sorts. When we commend the easily articulate don who has a ready answer for all our questions, we should remember that he is not simply a superlatively lively mind but is often the spokesman for the less articulate and perhaps more profound and original minds with which he is in daily communication: without them he would hardly exist. A university, then, is an institution peculiarly well adapted to the weakness and ignorance of mankind because its excellence does not depend upon the appearance of a universal genius, though it knows how to make room for one, should one emerge. Moreover, like the House of Commons or an old established business, it imparts something without having expressly to teach it; and what it imparts in this way is at least the manners of the conversation.

The scholar, the teacher, and lastly those who come to be taught, the undergraduate: he, or she, also has a distinctive character. First, he is not a child, not a beginner. He has already had his schooling elsewhere, and has learned enough, morally and intellectually, to take a chance with himself upon the open sea. He is neither a child nor an adult, but stands in a strange middle moment of life when he knows only enough of himself and of the world which passes before him to wish to know more. He has not yet found what he loves, but neither is he jealous of time, of accidents, or of rivals. Perhaps the phrase from the fairy tale suits him best he has come to seek his intellectual fortune. But, further, he is not the first who has passed from school to university, he is not like a stranger who knows nothing of what to expect, so that everything has to be explained to him on his arrival in words of one syllable. And if the tradition to which he belongs has already taught him anything, it will have taught him that he will not find his intellectual fortune, once and for all, in three years at a university. He is, therefore, we may suppose, in tune with what he is to find and is prepared to make use of it.

And what does he find? If he is not unlucky, he finds a strongly flowing current of activity, men and women engaged in the pursuit of learning, and an invitation to participate in some manner in this activity. This invitation is extended alike to those already touched by an ambition for a life of learning and to those who have no such ambition. A university is not a contrivance for making scholars; its ideal is not a world populated solely by scholars. For about 400 years in England the education of the would-be scholar and of the man of the world has been the same, and this tradition belongs to our idea of a university.

Beyond this, a university would be found to offer the undergraduate a limited variety of studies from which to make his choice; for, of course, it is discriminating about what it teaches, and not everything that engages the attentions of its scholars is thought suitable for undergraduate study. Where this particular selection of subjects came from, it would be hard to say. Some are old, others new; some—like medicine and law—have a semi-professional appearance, others have little direct connection with the world outside. Certainly none of these studies owes its place in a university curriculum to any reason so simple as its professional usefulness or because the knowledge concerned is easy to teach or easy to test. Indeed, the only characteristic common to them all is that of being a recognized branch of scholarship; in each the pursuit of learning is reflected and consequently each has within itself—when we drink deeply of it—a power to educate. Together they represent, at least in outline, the conversation which is being carried on in the university; and the undergraduate would never be tempted to mistake his university for an institute in which only one voice was heard, or for a polytechnic in which only the mannerisms of the voices were taught.

This, then, to the undergraduate, is the distinctive mark of a university; it is a place where he has the opportunity of education in conversation with his teachers, his fellows and himself, and where he is not encouraged to confuse education with training for a profession, with learning the tricks of a trade, with preparation for future particular service in society or with the acquisition of a kind of moral and intellectual outfit to see him through life. Whenever an ulterior purpose of this sort makes its appearance, education (which is concerned with persons, not functions) steals out of the back door with noiseless steps. The pursuit of learning for the power it may bring has its roots in a covetous egoism which is not less egoistic or less covetous when it appears as a so-called 'social purpose', and with this a university has nothing to do. The form of its curriculum has no such design; and the manner of its teaching teachers interested in the pupil himself, in what he is thinking, in the quality of his mind, in his immortal soul, and not in what sort of a schoolmaster or administrator he can be made into—the manner of this teaching has no such intention.

But further, a university has something else to offer the undergraduate, and I take this to be its most characteristic gift because it is exclusive to a university and is rooted in the character of university education as neither a beginning nor an end, but a middle. A man may at any time in his life begin to explore a new branch of learning or engage in fresh activity, but only at a university may he do this without a rearrangement of his scarce resources of time and energy; in later life he is committed to so much that he cannot easily throw off. The characteristic gift of a university is the gift of an interval. Here is an opportunity to put aside the hot allegiances of youth without the necessity of at once acquiring new loyalties to take their place. Here is a break in the tyrannical course of irreparable events; a period in which to look round upon the world and upon oneself without the sense of an enemy at one's back or the insistent pressure to make up one's mind; a moment in which to taste the mystery without the necessity of at once seeking a solution. And all this, not in an intellectual vacuum, but surrounded by all the inherited learning and literature and experience of our civilization; not alone, but in the company of kindred spirits; not as a sole occupation, but combined with the discipline of studying a recognized branch of learning; and neither as a first step in education (for those wholly ignorant of how to behave or think) nor as a final education to fit a man for the day of judgement, but as a middle. This interval is nothing so commonplace as a pause to get one's breath; no young man or woman, I take it, would say 'Thank you' for an opportunity of that sort; it is not the cessation of activity, but the occasion of a unique kind of activity.

It would be difficult to determine the generation of this remarkable opportunity. Perhaps it sprang (as Lucretius imagines human limbs to have sprung) from there being people who, in varying degrees, could make use of it. At all events, I think it is the one thing that every university in Europe, in some measure, provides for its undergraduates. The enjoyment of it depends upon some previous preparation (no man ignorant of what he should have learned in the nursery could expect to make use of it), but it does not depend on any definable pre-existing privilege or upon the absence of the necessity of earning one's living in the end—it is itself the privilege of being a 'student', the enjoyment of *schole*—leisure. One might, hazarding a misunderstanding, reduce this to a doctrine about the character of a university; one might call it the doctrine of the interim. But the doctrine would be no more than a brief expression of what it felt like to be an undergraduate on that first October morning. Almost overnight, a world of ungracious fact had melted into infinite possibility; we who belonged to no 'leisured class' had been freed for a moment from the curse of Adam, the burdensome distinction between work and play. What opened before us was not a road but a boundless sea; it was enough to stretch one's sails to the wind. The distracting urgency of an immediate destination was absent, duty no longer oppressed, boredom and disappointment were words without meaning; death was unthinkable. But it belongs to the character of an interim to come to an end; there is a time for everything and nothing should be prolonged beyond its time. The eternal undergraduate is a lost soul.

And what of the harvest? Nobody could go down from such a university unmarked. Intellectually, he may be supposed to have acquired some knowledge, and, more important, a certain discipline of mind, a grasp of consequences, a greater command over his own powers. He will know, perhaps, that it is not good enough to have a 'point of view', that what we need is *thoughts*. He will not go down in possession of an armoury of arguments to prove the truth of what he believes; but he will have acquired something that puts him beyond the reach of the intellectual hooligan, and whatever has been the subject of his study he may be expected to be able to look for some meaning in the things that have greatly moved mankind. Perhaps he may even have found a centre for his intellectual affections. In short, this period at a university may not have equipped him very effectively to earn a living, but he will have learned something to help him lead a more significant life. And morally—he will not have acquired an outfit of moral ideas, a new reach-me-down suit of moral clothing, but he will have had an opportunity to extend the range of his moral sensibility, and he will have had the leisure to replace the clamorous and conflicting absolutes of adolescence with something less corruptible.

The pursuit of learning, like every other great activity, is unavoidably conservative. A university is not like a dinghy which can be jiggled about to catch every transient breath of wind. The critics it should listen to are those who are interested in the pursuit of learning, not those who find a university imperfect because it is not something other than it is. But somehow or other the idea of a university in recent years has got mixed up with notions such as 'higher education', 'advanced training', refresher courses for adults' -things admirable in themselves, but really very little to do with a university. And it is time something was done to unravel the confusion. For these ideas belong to a world of power and utility, of exploitation, of social and individual egoism, and of activity, whose meaning lies outside itself in some trivial result or achievement and this is not the world to which a university belongs; it is not the world to which education in the true sense belongs. It is a very powerful world; it is wealthy, interfering and well-meaning. But it is not remarkably self-critical; it is apt to mistake itself for the whole world, and with amiable carelessness it assumes that whatever does not contribute to its own purposes is somehow errant. A university needs to beware of the patronage of this world, or it will find that it has sold its birthright for a mess of pottage; it will find that instead of studying and teaching the languages and literatures of the world it has become a school for training interpreters, that instead of pursuing science it is engaged in training electrical engineers or industrial chemists, that instead of studying history it is studying and teaching history for some ulterior purpose, that instead of educating men and women it is training them exactly to fill some niche in society.

A university, like everything else, has a place in the society to which it belongs, but that place is not the function of contributing to some other kind of activity in the society but of being itself and not another thing. Its first business is with the pursuit of learning there is no substitute which, in a university, will make up for the absence of this—and, secondly, its concern is with the sort of education that has been found to spring up in the course of this activity. A university will have ceased to exist when its learning has degenerated into what is now called research, when its teaching has become mere instruction and occupies the whole of an undergraduate's time, and when those who came to be taught come, not in search of their intellectual fortune but with a vitality so unroused or so exhausted that they wish only to be provided with a serviceable moral and intellectual outfit; when they come with no understanding of the manners of conversation but desire only a qualification for earning a living or a certificate to let them in on the exploitation of the world.

The Definition of a University, 1967*

From *The Journal of Educational Thought* (1967)

This selection by Michael J. Oakeshott is taken from *The Journal of Educational Thought*, 1967—December, Volume 2, Number 3. Published by The University of Calgary, Alberta, Canada.

* * * * *

The world is unusually full of doubts and confusion, and among them is a very considerable confusion about the nature of a university and the character of a university education. Perhaps this confusion is greatest in those parts of the world where, because universities are an old-established feature of the landscape, they have, until recently, been accepted without very much reflection. Moreover, universities have always been manifold and somewhat ambiguous institutions which naturally resist attempts to define their character. But the creation of many new universities, the appearance of students in large numbers who come with mixed and uncertain expectations, as well as other changes, have shaken us out of the mood of acceptance into a mood of reflection. All over the world universities have now got used to hearing themselves talked about in general terms.

---

* Following is the text of a lecture presented at The University of Calgary on April 4, 1967.

I do not think this is a supremely desirable situation to be in. I would, myself, much prefer to be a member of a confident going concern, not eaten up with doubts about what it is doing or with guilt for not having done it better in the past, and thus able to bend myself to a task which has not degenerated into being itself problematic. But one must take one's time as one finds it, and do one's best to participate in its own peculiar urgencies.

Nevertheless, I feel I ought to ask your forgiveness for reverting to a now rather hackneyed theme. I do so, however, not to sow further doubts, but to try to resolve some which already assail us. In short, I speak as a believer, not (in this matter) as a critical sceptic.

I will make my beginning with a university as a place of learning and teaching.

Learning is the comprehensive activity in which we come to know ourselves and the world around us. It is a paradoxical activity: it is doing and submitting at the same time. And its achievements range from merely being aware to what may be called understanding and being able to explain.

In each of us it begins at birth; and it takes place, not in some ideal abstract world, but in the local world we inhabit. For the individual it terminates only in death; for a civilization it can end only with the collapse of a characteristic manner of life which may deprive us, for the time being, of anything very much to be learned. Sometimes the process of learning is suspended while we use or enjoy what we have learned. But the suspension is, perhaps, never either decisive or complete: there is probably a component of 'learning,' and not merely having learned,' in every notable performance.

By learning I mean an activity possible only to an intelligent capable of choice and self-direction in relation to its own impulses and to the world around it. These, of course, are pre-eminently human characteristics; and, as I understand it, only human beings are capable of learning.

A learner is not the passive recipient of impressions, or one whose accomplishments spring from mere reactions to circumstances; nor is he one who attempts nothing he does not know how to achieve. He is a creature of wants rather than needs, of recollection as well as memory; and he wants to know what to think and what to believe as well as what to do. Learning is conduct not behaviour. In short, these analogies of clay and wax, of receptacles to be filled and empty rooms to be furnished have nothing to do with learners and learning. And the only way to decisively to abolish man is to understand him to be capable of learning by understanding him as a creature capable only of conditionable reflexes for whose behaviour the now modish word 'syndrome' is appropriate.

What distinguishes human beings is not their unusual long period of helplessness and dependence, nor is it (as Aristotle thought) their ability to speak to one another are to engage in rational discourse: these are merely symptoms of man human character. What distinguishes them is that each is born an heir to an inheritance to which he can succeed only in a process of learning.

If this inheritance were a landed estate, the heir would expect to succeed automatically on the death of his father or on coming of age. It would be conveyed to him by lawyers, and the most that would be expected of him would be legal acknowledgement.

But the inheritance I speak of is not like this. What every man is born an heir to his inheritance of human achievements; an inheritance of feelings, emotions, images, visions, thoughts, beliefs, ideas, understandings, intellectual and practical enterprises, languages, relationships, organizations, religions, canons and maxims of conduct, procedures, rituals, skills, works of art, books, musical compositions, tools, artifacts and utensils.

The components of this inheritance are beliefs, not physical objects; facts not 'things'; 'expressions' which have means or uses which require to be understood because they are the 'expressions' of human minds. The starry heavens above and the moral law within, no less than Dante's *Divina Commedia* and the city of London, are human achievements.

Now, this world of human achievement can be entered, possessed and enjoyed only in a process of learning. A 'picture' may be purchased, but one cannot merely purchase an understanding of it. And I have called this world 'our common human inheritance' because to enter it is the only way of becoming a human being, and to inhabit it is to be a human being. It is into this world that the child, even in its earliest adventures in awareness, initiates itself. Not only may it be entered only by learning, but there is, in fact, nothing else to learn. If, from one point of view, the analogies of wax and clay are inappropriate to learning, from another point of view the analogies of sagacious apes and accomplished horses are no more appropriate. These admirable creatures have no such inheritance; they may only be trained to react to a stimulus and to perform tricks.

But this inheritance is an historic achievement; it is 'positive' and not 'necessary'; it is contingent upon circumstances, it is miscellaneous and incoherent; it is what human beings have achieved, not by the impulsion of a final cause, but by exploiting the opportunities of fortune and by means of their own efforts. It comprises the standards of conduct to which from time to time they have given their preferences, the pro-and con-feelings to which they have given their approval or disapproval, the intellectual enterprises they have happened upon and pursued, the duties they have imposed upon themselves, the activities they have delighted in, the hopes they have entertained and the disappointments they have suffered. The notions of 'finished' and 'unfinished' are equally inapplicable to it. It does not deliver to us a clear and unambiguous message; it offers advice and suggestion, recommendations, aids to reflection, rather than directives. It has been put together, not by designers, but by men who knew only dimly what they did. It is not like a packet of seeds which, implanted in the mind of a learner, must blossom well or ill according to their own inevitable character; it is a packet of thoughts, without any fixed potentiality, ready to become whatever the learner can make of them.

And this, perhaps, points the way out of what has become the most famous dilemma of all who think about learning and education. Is learning to be understood as acquiring knowledge, or is it to be regarded as a process in which the learner makes the most of himself?

Learning to the student of to-day, highly conscious that he is something on his own account and not particularly humble in his attachment to 'self-expression,' seems often a kind of imprisonment; what he seeks is emancipation from what he thinks of as the dead hand of the past.

But, in fact, this discrepancy between entering into and possessing a human inheritance and making the most of himself is an illusion. 'Self-realization' for human beings is not, of course, the realization of an exactly predetermined end which requires only favourable circumstances in order that it shall be achieved. But neither is this self an infinite, unknown potentiality which an inheritance of human achievement is as likely to thwart as to promote. Selves are not rational abstractions, they are historic, circumstantial personalities; indeed, they are themselves among the components of this world of human achievements. And there is no other way for a human being to make the most of himself than by learning to recognize himself in the mirror of this inheritance of human achievement.

To learn is not to be put in touch with what is dead, nor is it to be obliged to rehearse the social history of mankind. Death is a feature of the natural, not the human world; and it is only in nature that generation involves a boring process of recapitulating all the earlier stages of life. To inherit this world of human achievement is often to possess oneself of what does not lie on the surface of the present world, of much that has come to be neglected, and of something, even, that for the time being is forgotten. And to know only what is in current use is to become acquainted with only an attenuated version of this inheritance. To see oneself reflected in the mirror of the current modish world is to see a sadly distorted image of a human being; for there is nothing to encourage us to believe that what has captured current fancy is the most valuable part of our inheritance, or that what is better survives more readily than what is worse. And nothing of this human inheritance survives which is not cared for by human beings.

This, then, is learning and the general character of what' there is to be learned. I will come back to it later to consider what part a university has to play in it.

Meanwhile, let us for a moment consider the activity of teaching, for that too is something that belongs to a university.

Teaching is a practical activity in which a person already learned imparts his learning to his pupils. No doubt one may properly be said to learn from books, from gazing at the sky or listening to the waves (so long as one's disposition is that mixture of activity and submission we call curiosity), but to say that the book, the sky or the sea has 'taught' us anything, or that we have taught ourselves, is to speak the language of unfortunate metaphor. The counterpart of the teacher is not the learner in general, but the pupil. This does not mean that I subscribe to the prejudice which attributes all learning to teaching—especially in a university, where to be a pupil and to be taught is not at all the only path to learning. It means only that the office of teacher is one that bears consideration on its own account.

The activity of a teacher is, then, specified in the first place by the character of his partner. The ruler is partnered by the citizen, the physician by his patient, the master by his servant, the commander by his subordinates, the lawyer by his client, the prophet by his disciple, the clown by his audience, the hypnotist by his subject, and both the trainer and the tamer by creatures whose aptitudes are for being trained and tamed. Each of these is engaged in practical activity, but it is not teaching; each has a partner, but it is not a pupil. Like the ruler, or the hypnotist, the teacher communicates something to his partner; his peculiarity is that what he communicates is appropriate to a partner who is a pupil—it is something that can be received only by learning.

It is difficult to think of any circumstances where learning may be said to be impossible. Of course, in some conditions it will take place more rapidly and more successfully than in others; but in principle, it does not depend upon any specifiable degree of attention, and it is not uncommon to find oneself to have learned without knowing how or when it happened. Thus, the random utterances of anyone, however foolish or ignorant, may serve to enlighten a learner, who receives from them as much or as little as he happens to be ready to receive, and receives often what the speaker himself did not know or did not know he was conveying.

But such casual utterances are not teaching; and he who scatters them is not, properly speaking, a teacher. Teaching is the deliberate and intentional initiation of a pupil into the world of human achievement, or into some part of it. The teacher is one whose utterances (or silences) are designed to promote this initiation in respect of a pupil—that is, in respect of a learner whom he recognizes to be ready to receive what he has resolved in communicate. In short, a pupil is a learner known to a teacher, a learner for whom he has taken specific responsibility; and teaching, properly speaking, is impossible in his absence.

The part of the teacher, then, is to hold up the mirror of human achievement before a pupil; and to hold it in such a manner that it reflects not merely what has caught the fancy of a current generation, but so that it reflects something which approximates more closely to the whole of that inheritance. His business (indeed, this may be said to be his peculiar quality as an agent of civilization) is to release his pupils from servitude to the current dominant feelings, emotions, images, ideas, beliefs and even skills, and to bring to their notice what the current world may have neglected or forgotten.

Nevertheless, engaged in initiating his pupils into so contingent an inheritance, the teacher may be excused for thinking that he needs some assurance of its worth. For, like others, he may have a superstitious prejudice against the human race and be satisfied only when he can feel himself anchored to something for which fallible human beings are not responsible. But he must be urged to have the courage of his human circumstances. This man-made inheritance, of which he is the living custodian, contains everything to which value is attributable; it is the ground and context of every judgment of better or worse. If there were a mirror of perfection which he could hold up to his pupils, he might be expected to prefer it to this home-made article. But there is no such mirror. He may be excused if he finds the present dominant image of civilized life too disagreeable to impart with any enthusiasm to his pupils. But if he has no confidence in any of the standards of worth written into this inheritance of human achievement, he had better not be a teacher. His hold upon the mirror would be too unsteady; he would have nothing to teach.

There is an ancient oriental image which recognizes this account of our circumstances and this relation between learner and teacher. In it the child is understood to owe its physical life to its father, a debt to be acknowledged with appropriate respect. But initiation into this world of human achievements is owed to the Sage, the teacher; and this debt is to be acknowledged with profound reverence—for to whom can a man be more deeply indebted than to those to whom he owes, not his mere existence, but his participation in a genuinely human life?

This then is the world into which we are born—a world made by human beings: the object of all learning and the subject of all teaching. What place does a university occupy within it?

Clearly, a university, as a place where learning goes on (a place, indeed, devoted to learning), may be specified by the sort of people who enter its doors—their age, their earlier attainments in learning and the sort of learning they are now in search of.

For nobody, is a university the first attempt he has made to possess himself of his human inheritance, nor will it be his last. The conventional age at which a boy or a girl enters a university differs in different parts of the world, but everywhere it is preceded by,' school days.' Thus, a university may be recognized as a place in which our human inheritance is laid out in a manner appropriate to learners who are not beginners.

This tells us something, but not very much. And it does not suggest a distinction which I think it is important to observe. A university as a place where a number of young people are gathered together for a few of the most impressionable years of their career on earth will inevitably be the place where many will find themselves acquiring interests which will be with them for life: making decisions which, for themselves, may be momentous; entering into relationships which may be the most durable they will ever enjoy—all of which may be thought of as 'learning.' There is, then, on the one hand what may happen to a student in these years and in these circumstances, and what he happens upon. And, from this point of view, all that need be said is that those who make and manage universities should recognize that this is what a university will unavoidably be for its students. One of the advantages of being at a university should be that these things, which happen to all human beings at about that time of life, shall happen in more rather than less favourable circumstances. On the other hand, a university is not merely a scene of happenings; it is an institution designed to give something specific to those who have come to it. And in discussing the nature of a university what I want to consider is the gifts it intentionally offers, and not the chance opportunities it affords. A railway station affords shelter from the rain, a place of *rendezvous*, and has a hundred other potential uses; but what it specifically offers is a train service. What is a university in terms of its intentional design?

Those who have got beyond the view that a university is a place of 'after school' or of 'higher' learning often recommend us to think of it as a place where a particular part, by no means the whole, of our human inheritance is displayed for the learner; namely, that part which may be called specifically *intellectual*: here are to be found the fruits of human reflective intelligence gathered together and cared for. One can, perhaps, see what is meant by this; but it leaves me in doubt about what exactly it is intended to exclude, and the suspicion that it will exclude some things which I would not want to exclude. Perhaps, it is intended to set on one side all that part of our human inheritance which is composed of emotional attitudes, pro-and con-feelings, visions, longings, aspirations and the moral adventures of mankind. But I do not myself see this as more than a rather arbitrary distinction; and as I have interpreted it, the whole of this human inheritance is to be regarded as the work of the human mind, the product of human intelligence. Moreover, this picture makes a university look too much like a warehouse for my liking. This being so, I prefer to go on another tack in trying to distinguish what learning and teaching in a university is specifically concerned with.

This inheritance of human accomplishments—which we may call a civilization—may, from one point of view, be seen as a collection of skills which together define and make possible a current manner of living. Acquiring one of these skills—that of a lawyer, a doctor, an accountant, a farmer or a commercial traveller—is taking possession of a part of this inheritance of human achievement in a process of learning.

Each of these skills has an intellectual component. In some it is greater than others; and a rough measure of this intellectual component is to be found in the length of time it takes to acquire the skill concerned. Thus, in this view of it, a civilization has the naive appearance of things known and skills practised which are entailed in a current manner of living. This manner of living is never completely coherent; there are new skills on their way in, and old skills on their way out. And every skill in use is, we may suppose, being improved.

Now, what is learned in this respect has three important characteristics. First, for most people, what is learned is a single skill. No doubt, there are jacks-of-all-trades; but, in respect of skills, our inheritance of human achievement has become so complicated that our current way of living depends very much on people who have so high a degree of proficiency that no man is likely to be master of more than one skill. Learning, here, is a highly specialized activity. Secondly, learning one of these skills which keep a current society going is acquiring a specific body of information, and being able to use it with ease and assurance. This body of information is strictly limited (though it may in some cases be large), and it does not significantly look outside itself. It is naturally concerned with the latest achievements of human thought in relation to a particular skill. And thirdly, learning one of these skills is learning *how* to do something which is needed to keep a current society going: the achievements of this learning are all exhibited in the practice of this skill.

Thus, when a civilization is recognized as a collection of skills, each representing a human achievement, which make possible and sustain a current manner of living, learning may be recognized as a man fitting himself to fill a specific place in his society and to satisfy a current demand. Nobody learns skills which are never practised.

Now, to regard our inheritance of human achievements as a collection of skills to be learned, and of inventions, devices and enterprises in which we have learned to impress ourselves upon the world, exploit its natural resources, and to make it the sort of place we want to live in, is one way of looking at it; but it is not the only way. Those who hand on these skills from generation to generation, each adding its own improvements, are certainly agents of civilization; but this is not all there is to be handed on. And, in my view, a university, and learning in a university, represents a different and complementary way of regarding this inheritance. For this inheritance of human achievement, which we can succeed to only in a process of learning, and in relation to which we become and are human beings, contains something else; namely, the various enterprises of understanding and explaining ourselves and the world we find ourselves in. And these are what I think a university is concerned with.

This, you may think, is a distinction without a difference. "Surely," you may say, "these practical skills entail an understanding both of ourselves and the components of the world we live in. And surely there is a lot which goes on in universities, and has always gone on in universities, which is indistinguishable from teaching and learning the skills which sustain a manner of living. Perhaps universities have been more concerned with those skills which have a large intellectual component; nevertheless, these are among the most important of the practical skills which we use in impressing ourselves on the world." Yes. There is truth in both these observations, but they lie to one side of what I am suggesting.

Learning a practical skill is acquiring appropriate information and knowing how to use it to achieve desired results. What is to be learned appears as reliable conclusions reached, facts established and useable. No doubt much of this information is to be recognized as the product of enterprises designed to enlarge our understanding of ourselves and the world. But, properly speaking, it is a by-product. For there is an important difference between learning which is concerned with the degree of understanding necessary to practise a skill and learning which is expressly focussed upon an enterprise of understanding and explaining. In the one case, what is to be learned appears as a result detached from the process in which it was acquired; but in the other case, what is to be learned is how to participate in an enterprise of understanding which may or may not yield detachable results.

A 'science,' for example, for the learner of a practical skill, is a collection of information capable of being used; but a 'science' in a university is an intellectual pursuit, an explanatory manner of thinking and speaking, being explored. From time to time, no doubt, it may throw off these useable pieces of information; but to do so is not its business. Doctrines, ideas, facts and theories which are invested elsewhere to yield practical profits (like the Mendelian theory of biological inheritance or the molecular structure of matter), in a university are recognized as temporary achievements, valued solely for their explanatory value, in an enterprise of understanding which is, in principle, both endless and autonomous. A 'science' in a university does not have even the appearance of being a warehouse in which items of information are stored, ready for use.

Thus, when a student, entering a university, chooses for himself a field of study—chemistry, biology, economics, sociology—which in some cases may look all too like the opportunity of acquiring the knowledge necessary to practise a skill, what he is really doing is choosing to be initiated into one of the great explanatory enterprises which belong to his human inheritance.

Moreover, there are many enterprises of understanding pursued in universities, like history or philosophy, which cannot be expected to throw off any such by-products of readily useable conclusions and which, consequently, may scarcely be mistaken for anything but autonomous enterprises of understanding.

In short, our inheritance of human achievements includes, not only the skills we need for transforming the world, but also (and independently) these great, autonomous, enterprises of understanding ourselves and the world. And, whatever the adventitious appearances to the contrary, it is with these that learning at a university is concerned. It is participation in this which is the common character of all the faculties of a university; it is this common character which makes nonsense of the modish notion of 'two cultures'; and it is this common engagement in understanding which gives to the activity of teaching in a university its distinctive character. For teaching, here, is not imparting information; it is holding up the mirror of a civilization in such a manner that what is to be seen in it is men thinking, men engaged in the supremely intellectual activity of understanding the world.

Moreover, it is the manner in which teaching is carried on in a university which stands in the way of our mistaking these enterprises of understanding merely for other skills, perhaps less immediately useful than the practical skills, but nevertheless sharing the common characteristics of all skills.

In a university, a 'science' is taught by one who is actually engaged in exploring it, history is taught by historians, philosophy by philosophers. But students who come to study a 'science' or history or philosophy are not regarded as apprentices to a particular explanatory skill. It is possible that some of them will become 'scientists,' or historians, but the vast majority will not. And what a teacher in a university is doing, is not educating successors to himself (though some of his pupils may turn out to be this); it is imparting to his pupils some familiarity with one of these enterprises of understanding as autonomous intellectual pursuits. What he is doing is showing them what it is like to think as a 'scientist' or as an historian.

And, here, perhaps, there is a certain oddity in the situation. For long enough it has been believed that, even for people who are to spend the rest of their lives in practical occupations of one sort or another, it is a good thing for them to spend three or four years, at this time in their lives, not in learning a professional skill, but in becoming acquainted with some of the great enterprises of human understanding and explanation—becoming acquainted, that is, with what may be recognized as the 'academic' attitude towards the world. It has been believed that one who is not himself going to be a 'scientist,' or an historian, or a philosopher is not wasting his time acquiring, not some information (which might always come in useful), but some insight into what it is to be a 'scientist' or an historian. This is the belief' which, in a certain sense, constitutes a university as a place of education. And, although I cannot say where it sprang from, I do not think it is either an eccentric belief, or one incapable of being defended.

No literature can consist entirely of masterpieces. The circumstantial context of masterpieces is a vast body of writings of less than this quality, and a public educated by them to recognize and appreciate the masterpiece. And, in somewhat the same manner, the great enterprises of understanding pursued by human beings depend upon the appreciation of men who can recognize them, and even be excited by them, but who do not and cannot actually participate in them. Thus, the university student of 'science,' though he may never himself become a scientist in the strict sense, plays a not unimportant part in making possible the explanatory enterprise we call a 'science.' Indeed, I believe he plays a more important and less equivocal part in this than the man who merely uses, in a practical enterprise of exploitation, the information and ideas which are the usable by-products of scientific thinking.

Moreover, the most important gift of a university to the society in which it has place is not the provision of the useful by-products thrown off by some enterprises of understanding, but the opportunity it offers, to many or few, of not going through life without having had a glimpse, though perhaps no more than a glimpse, of that part of their human inheritance to which these enterprises belong: the opportunity to possess more completely than falls to the lot of everybody the whole of this inheritance of human endeavour and achievement.

A society aware of its human inheritance, brought up to value it and take pride in it, and recognizing that none of it can be possessed except in a process of learning and that some of it is not to be judged by its immediate usefulness—such a society will be disposed to afford as much as it reasonably can from its resources for its university, and for the sort of education that goes on in universities. Clearly, this will not be the first charge on a pioneer society: the homestead, the schoolhouse, the church and the market-place may be expected to come before the university; and the farmer, the soldier, the man of business, the lawyer, the politician, even the poet and the players of musical instruments, will come before the scholar. But, in our notion of a civilized society, something will be lacking until the university makes its appearance. And when it appears it will be recognized to be an association of persons engaged in caring for and attending to this inheritance of enterprises of understanding. It will be concerned, not merely to keep this intellectual inheritance intact, but to be continuously recovering what has been lost, restoring what has been neglected, collecting together what has been dissipated, repairing what has been corrupted, reconsidering, reshaping and reorganizing these advantages of human understanding.

Its scholars will live at what is called "the frontiers of knowledge"; and they will recognize themselves as engaged in intellectual pursuits rather than as gatherers or custodians of a store of information. And their pupils will be spectators at performances, and will carry away with them (when the time comes to go out into the world) whatever glimpses, impressions or insights they may have acquired of such men at work.

For there is something properly and unavoidably 'cloistered' about a university. Its pursuits have only an oblique relationship to the world in which immediate usefulness is the criterion of importance. It is a luxury—not in the sense that what it supplies is superfluous to all but the very sophisticated, but in the sense that this belongs to the world of human wants rather than to the world of human needs.

Not being comparable to a light-industry (having no product, in the strict sense), nor to a store (having no sales-list of items for disposal), a university is apt to confound the accountants. Profit and loss, cost and return on capital are not easily calculable; indeed, there is something inappropriate in making the calculations. It illustrates the truth that there is nothing great in the world that does not involve waste, and that the human propensity to avoid waste (which has itself been erected into a science) is, perhaps, one of our greatest intellectual vanities. But to me, at least, the tendency of modern universities to become immensely costly affairs, both relatively and absolutely, is regrettable. If they were poorer they might be better—so long as their poverty was recognized as an opportunity to go more warily in setting up new (and often not very well-considered) faculties, or for the exclusion of distracting frills.

But universities or proto-universities having appeared—that is, associations of scholars engaged in exploring the great human enterprises of intellectual understanding—their recognition as valuable educational institutions opens up some difficult questions. Who are to enjoy the benefits of an education of this kind?

Clearly, there will be some who, by native ability and by their willingness to submit to the discipline of academic study and by their willingness to endure the detachments and privations it entails, single themselves out as appropriate. These, let me say again, are not confined to those who have discovered in themselves a vocation for scholarship; they will include also others who, though they will never be scholars, are reluctant to pass through life without having become acquainted with some of the great intellectual pursuits of mankind. And, although there may be ways of discovering who these are, and the relation between their abilities and their ambitions, these devices will not be infallible, even if the criterion itself remains uncorrupted.

But, as generation succeeds to generation, and the life of the student—largely on account, not of the academic opportunities a university expressly offers, but because of what it affords as a scene of happenings—begins to acquire an irresistible allure, the claim not to be excluded from it begins to appear as the claim not to be excluded from one of the major pleasures of civilized life.

And when, added to this, having enjoyed the life of a student, and having, perhaps, acquired a university degree, is recognized as conferring a desirable social status and perhaps opening the door, not merely to the 'learned professions,' but to the wonderland of personal fortune, wealth and prosperity, then we have before us a situation recognizably our own.

Let me say something about each of these components of this situation. *What* I recall as the experience of going to a university is the sense of entering upon a life from which, so far as may be, the sordid ambitions and the collective inanities of the world had been magically excluded; the feeling of being emancipated from the pressures of immediate achievement; the offer of an opportunity to look around, without enemies at one's back, and without having to come to immediate decisions; the release from old commitments entered into in the semi-conscious years of childhood, and the absence of haste to contract new ones; the leisure, the sense of adventure and the companionship of others of the same kind; the opportunity to make mistakes without having to pay heavily for them: and all this, not in a vacuum or in a museum but surrounded by the inherited learning, literature and experience of our civilization and by men engaged in exploring this inheritance and adding to it; and not as a sole occupation, but combined with the discipline of study. And *when* I recall it, it seems to me so valuable an experience that I would not know how to deny it to anybody. Yet, it was what it was, in virtue of the fact that it corresponded to the wants and expectations of the great majority of my companions; and if we had imposed upon it different wants and different expectations, it would have dissolved, leaving behind only the little which was able to withstand the invasion.

I could not have written off as merely illegitimate the wants and expectations of such invaders. I could not do this even if they were the desire for well-digested useful information to be handed to them on a plate; the desire for the opportunity, not to learn to think, but to shout mindless and barbaric slogans to one another; the desire to win the easy victories which fall to a feeble *libido dominandi* exercised over the diffidence of half-formed and uncertain personalities; or even merely the desire to live at ease and postpone the time when the simple but inexorable demands of adult life have to be responded to. But I cannot avoid the conclusion that a university handed over to the satisfaction of these wants and expectations, or their like, has ceased to be a university; and that this is the main consideration to be taken into the account when we consider the place of university education in a society.

In respect of the other component of our situation—our recognition of a university career as the passport to social prestige, to power and to emolument—there is this to be said. I think we have gone too far in this direction. In exaggerating the esteem which attaches to this qualification we have depressed the esteem which has hitherto attached to many others, and we are prejudicing the appearance of new ways of acquiring esteem. Those who have been to a university have had the opportunity of acquiring some admirable qualities, and many of them have actually acquired them; but we are wrong to confine our admiration to these. There are many others, for which a university is not the natural seed-bed, and these should not be excluded from our esteem. Moreover, if we accord this exclusive esteem to a university education, we shall end by imposing upon universities a distracting and corrupting engagement—that of providing for the education of everybody who, for whatever reason, we are to admit to our esteem. And that way lies ruin.

Those who have passed their lives in universities are not so vain as to have chosen this engagement for themselves; it is something which, in present circumstances, they are liable to have imposed upon them, not merely by designing governments, but also, and more powerfully, by the less detectable pressures of our single-minded modern societies. In a civilization which has sold itself to the plausible ethics of productivity and in doing so has given itself a narrow path upon which to tread, and in societies which have begun to think of themselves, more and more, in the exclusive terms of 'an economy,' it is only to be expected that universities should be pressed into the common pattern, and be made servants of the social purpose. But in these circumstances, they become institutions in need of care and protection; not because what they have to offer is something to be ashamed of, but because it seems to grow daily less relevant to those current wants which have won our exclusive attention. This single-minded endeavour to provide for the needs of a technological society has been seen by some as an opportunity for university education to win the applause of those who have hitherto been doubtful or indifferent. But this is not so; what such an endeavour seeks is only the adventitious by-products of the great enterprises of human understanding and explanation. And universities, the custodians of these enterprises, are, at best, offered a package-deal with regard to the students they take and what they are to be taught, which entails partial surrenders; and, at worst, they find themselves wholly suborned.

'Academic freedom' has become a cant phrase in the mouths of well-meaning but muddled advocates. But, in fact, it can sustain only one meaning: the freedom to be academic, the freedom of a university to pursue its explorations of the enterprises of human understanding and to initiate successive generations of students into this intellectual inheritance. It is false friends, rather than open enemies, we should beware of; those whose friendly gestures and offers of help are all too often incitements to desert. The time may come when, in the face of the vulgarity of a single-minded devotion to the exploitation of the world and of the barbarism of instant affluence, learning will have to hide its head, and universities will survive only by the exercise of the courage of their calling and by becoming retreats devoted to keeping alive, in hostile circumstances, the great disinterested enquiries of mankind. But that time is not yet. Universities still have some genuine and discerning friends, many of whom have themselves never enjoyed the opportunities they offer; and there are students, alive to the enchantment of the pursuit of understanding, and for whom a university education, uncorrupted, and with all its ardours and severities, is an answer to their hopes, desires and expectations. And to these friends, all who love learning and who do not believe that learning is the only thing in life, are humbly grateful.

CHAPTER EIGHTEEN

The Central Problem

From *Universities between Two Worlds* (1974)

WILLIAM ROY NIBLETT

This selection is taken from *Universities between Two Worlds*, by W. Roy Niblett, 1974. Published by University of London Press Ltd., London, United Kingdom.*

Editors' Note

Roy Niblett had a life-long fascination about and passion for education. 'Life-long' here takes on a particular meaning. Niblett died (in 2005) just short of his ninety-ninth birthday and he was active almost until his last day.

After teaching in a school, Niblett became successively a lecturer and then (in 1945) a professor of education. As a professor education, Niblett had what was for him the enjoyable task of supporting the work of local colleges of education in their preparation of school teachers.

Subsequently (in 1959), Niblett moved from the north of England to London, to be both (the first) Professor of Higher Education and Dean of the Institute of Education. Although he formally retired in 1968, Niblett continued to be very

* Disclaimer: Although the editors and publisher made every effort to locate the copyright holders of W. Roy Niblett's *Universities between Two Worlds* (1974), no copyright holder was found, in which case this text has been treated as if it were in the public domain.

active, not only writing but continuing to be part of discussion groups and forums, many of which he himself established over decades. Through his career, Niblett was also much in demand to serve on national committees concerned with the development of higher education. He was a member of the University Grants Committee for many years and chaired its sub-committee on halls of residence (the matter of students living well together being a matter dear to his heart).

As well as being vitally interested in higher education, Niblett was also a practising Christian and while the latter rarely intruded into his scholarship, it surely supplied a concern with the individual. For Niblett, students were never a mass but were individuals, with their own possibilities and potential. Accordingly, in much of his writing—as in the extracts here from his book '*Universities between Two Worlds*'—Niblett developed a critique of the emerging dominant view of higher education. As he saw it, higher education was becoming overly focused on the acquisition of technical knowledge. In the process, a sense of the student as a person, with personal values and feelings, was being neglected. This concern had, as its context, a wider concern that the world itself—especially through the power of science and technology—was becoming preoccupied with 'control over nature' and that 'human nature' was itself becoming instrumentalised (not Niblett's word!) as a result.

We see these concerns vividly in the extracts here. Niblett brings up 'the question of what human life is for' and observes that 'more mastery of a technical sort will not in itself solve [such a question]'. Niblett warns of 'an impoverishment of the authority of reason itself' and to address that matter calls for nothing less than 'turning a corner in our whole concept of higher education'. Niblett presses the case, therefore, for 'learning of a more directly "felt" experiential kind', and gives examples from across many disciplines as to what this could look like in teaching approaches.

A 'detachment from any personal involvement in life' was anathema to Niblett, for whom 'an (interior) understanding of feeling [and] valuing' could count as knowledge every bit as 'external' facts and measurement. 'Something [was] wrong with our theory of knowledge if we divorce knowing from being in such a way.' Indeed, 'the job of civilising and sensitising … students both morally and aesthetically [was becoming] the more imperative in a world [of consumption and gratification]' Universities, accordingly, need 'to link the affective with the cognitive', and so be both 'places of knowledge and places with spirit'.

RB

* * * * *

The problems facing higher education at the start of the 1970s are obviously very great and very many. But essentially they stern from the difficulty of educating young people brought up in a society so uncertain and confused as ours about its own objectives, at a time when an enormous increase in our technical accomplishment and control over nature and human nature has occurred. Any solution demands a moral insight and moral choices that are products of a profoundly humane temper, one very different from that likely to be produced by an education directed to the production of technical skills, however complex and demanding of intelligence.

For example, with the perfecting or near perfecting of contraceptive devices for men and women—and the availability of abortion in case of 'mistakes'—a different situation presents itself from the one which has hitherto obtained. One can react by playing down the importance or significance of sexual experience, marriage and the family. But that involves risks of enfeebling sources of value and of principle which are parts of the heritage of western civilisation. Maybe we can dry up such sources and do without them. But we have few substitutes for them likely to be as good or ones that enable us to face as many of the facts about human love, responsibility and mortality. There is a certain lack of depth and imagination in some of the advocates of every kind of sexual freedom which makes one wonder if they are not already influenced by a technological manipulative frame of mind, far more escapist than they are aware of.

Another example comes from the power which technological knowledge seems to be about to put into men's hands of breeding future human beings with close control over their inherent capacities, intelligence, even temperament. Cloning—that is the breeding of a whole sequence of absolutely identical beings—has already proved possible in the case of frogs. It may or may not ever be possible in the case of men, but whatever the degree of exactitude with which we can choose the sort of people we want to have peopling the earth a nearer approach to it is fearsomely likely. This leaves us with some extremely difllicultchoices to make: What kinds of human beings are most human? How important do we really think a cold analytical intelligence to be relative to kindness, understanding and capacity for affection? The more fundamental the choices which technology puts it within our power to make, the more important imaginative insight and foresight become, and the more important is moral judgement. But such qualities and capacities are not of a technical kind; they are themselves the attributes of human beings, not of automata. They may perhaps be developed by education, including tertiary education, though primary and secondary education may well be more important. What is certain is that they cannot simply be created without a perception—not itself technological in nature—that they are desirable and humane.

Again, there is the application of technological knowledge to control the size of the world's population or of the population of any part of the world. It is agreed already on all hands that we cannot go on indefinitely, or indeed for much longer, allowing the peoples of the earth to grow in number at anything like their present rate. But on what principles should we limit the proportions of black, brown, white and yellow? Should we seek to stabilise world population at its present size? the number alive fifty years ago? or the probable numbers fifty years hence? The kind of judgement called for is not one to be made simply according to food supply, the number it is possible at maximum to support with the amount of nourishment attainable or theoretically obtainable. Questions of standards of living are involved, and not material standards only. The question of what human life is *for* is not far off. That is not a technological question but one with philosophical, moral and religious elements in it.

Clearly, a type of higher education which concentrates on the production of technological men is not in itself sufficient; it grows less and less so the more advanced our technological knowledge becomes. It is not contended that we can, or could possibly, educate a generation of people who will know definitively or in detail the answers to these particular problems or to the many others facing us. What is contended is that any adequate form of tertiary education should awaken minds to a realisation that more mastery of a technical sort will not in itself solve them for us. It is not enough even to equip men and women to be well informed in general, experts in one or more special fields, tolerant, lucid in argument and able to apply their knowledge. What of capacity for personal experience? for personal recognition of moral authority? for facing the fact of human finiteness? If we simply say that it is not the business of the college or the university to be concerned with such things we are trading out of the real situation; as we are if we maintain that the only source of authority is logical deduction from observed facts. This is to perpetuate if not enhance the impoverishment of the authority of reason itself, only one of whose main criteria, as we saw in Chapter I, is of this type. An understanding of the kind of authority which has personal roots as well as that which is more impersonal is emphatically something which a higher education should be concerned to produce. That, however, means turning a corner in our whole concept of higher education. It may be that higher, as distinct from further, education cannot long survive unless we do turn this corner—and face the practical consequences involved.

The fact is that higher education has to become a lot more responsible than it has been, both socially and personally. We have not, I think, by any means as yet realised the extent of the revolution required in the next fifty years to make it so: the changes of assumption that are called for, the changes of orientation, the changes of content.

The basis on which so much of the content of higher education has so far rested is that personal experiences and social values are not as real or in the last resort as important as physical entities, hard facts and verifiable laws—the facts of history and of petrology; of physiology and of linguistics; the laws of mathematical reasoning and of climatology. A strict detachment and neutrality, we have argued, and argued logically, are indispensable if we are to understand the world and eventually perhaps the universe itself, with personal hopes and desires discounted—at times, it may be, heroically. The search therefore has been for an empirical method free as far as may be possible from feelings, biases, presuppositions. If the whole truth can never be discovered, at least this is the way patiently and gradually to find out more and more of it: it would be stupid and self-deceptive to imagine that there are other reliable routes.

I do not for a moment doubt that approaches to knowledge through experiment, theorem and deduction must be continued—and continued with energy and resolution. But by themselves they are not enough. If we lose the capacity for learning of a more directly 'felt' experiential kind we shall sacrifice more than we can possibly afford. We shall deplete our humanity. In such circumstances, higher education can and will betray us.

What must be emphasised is that the approach to knowledge through experiment and deduction itself involves a number of assumptions—for instance that it is possible to be detached without having made presuppositions; that 'facts' can be isolated from experiences. But we depend in all our perception or testing of fact—both mathematical and scientific fact-upon the ways in which we apprehend time, space and sequence. There is an element of interpretation in our observation of every phenomenon. Even in our ways of isolating phenomena from one another we depend upon common human traditions in feeling, sensing and interpreting. We separate out the act of observing and examining an entity from the act of imagining what it might be like to be that entity—dividing the physical from the animal, and the animal from the human, worlds. But we do this at least in part for convenience, not because the nature of things causes us to do so. In deducing and creating a theory about the laws of the physical world a scientist looks at his electrons from an external viewpoint. He assumes that, at any rate for his purposes, they are all identical and from his detached examination they may be as nearly as can matter. But so, of course, may the individuals in a crowd of human creatures seem, especially if they are of a different colour and belong to a different race from ourselves. What is more significant, however, is that in the case of human beings we do not confuse them clinically, as physiological or even psychoanalytic specimens, with knowing them as friends, knowing what it feels like to be them, realising something of their uniqueness as individuals, different from ourselves but in a measure understandable because we know something of what it is like to be us. The assumption that every sheep or every cell or every electron is 'the same' as every other may be totally justifiable for certain purposes; but nonetheless it remains an assumption.

An historian much more obviously relies both upon self-understanding and upon traditions in interpreting what happened in past situations. In imagining what took place in a particular case he makes use of his estimate of what is possible and probable in the natural order and in human nature. The view of the world which he has will in part determine what events in the past he notices at all, or takes to be significant. Victory, material prosperity, success, for example, he will normally estimate as more important and desirable than defeat and failure. Those who are daily engaged in the use of methods of history and science can be fully occupied without devoting a great deal of attention to the presuppositions they are using.

Sociologists and psychologists habitually rely upon a good deal of understanding of themselves and their own way of reacting, or nearly reacting, to the world to secure data for their subject. It would be impossible to know anything about instincts, or repressions, or compensation, or social pressure, if no one knew from personal experience what these things meant or could mean. A text-book knowledge of such entities is only likely to be useful occasionally-for examination purposes, if those. To *understand* them we are dependent upon ability to understand ourselves and to go on thence to identify ourselves with other humans by a leap of sympathy. There are many assumptions concealed within such a process for all of us—for example that our own personalities are continuing realities; that the personalities of other people are in major ways like our own; that identity is a viable concept; and that people can be socialised and individualised in differing degrees. 'We have', says Professor George Woods (1965), 'no satisfactory images or concepts of the identity or continuity of the life of a personal being. But we have no persisting doubt of our own existence and we are not wholly without some notion of what it means to be, and to be an active personal being' (p. 8). It is this kind of fact with which most teachers in higher education have had few dealings, at any rate as teachers, and of which they have taken too little account.

It is because the world in which we live as persons is one in which we share common experiences that we can understand one another at all. We can observe and study our experiences; we can detach ourselves from them for particular purposes. But we are dependent upon them as men for interest, feeling, perception, individuality. It is impossible to live a life from the outside; to sense, to love, to value, to understand, depend upon capacity at least sometimes to be inside. To ensure on the one hand a strong awareness of the objectively measurable and its importance in our civilisation and to encourage on the other an awareness of one's own sensings, impulses, affections, insights, must be among the objects of a general education. 'A culture survives principally', as Philip Rieff (1966) has said, 'by the power of its institutions to bind and loose men in the conduct of their affairs with reasons which sink so deeply into the self that they become commonly and implicitly understood-with that understanding of which explicit belief and precise knowledge of externals would show outwardly like the tip of an iceberg.' It is easy to 'fail to take into account the degree of intimacy with which this comprehensive interior understanding ... binds even the ignorants of a culture to a great chain of meaning' (pp. 2–3).

The theory of knowledge which has been dominant in our time tends, as I have suggested, to take man's own capacity for experiencing, his feelings of his own significance, even his own sense of responsibility, too little into account. A psychology which speaks entirely in terms of 'behaviour', apart from its danger of treating human reactions only by reference to animal ones, can deprive us of even the possibility of actions that are moral. It counts them as irrelevant. A sociology which sees all social movements as outcomes of material or economic causes does not allow for our hopes of freedom, our workings of conscience, our feelings of responsibility. 'A human being, making a responsible decision and dedicating himself to action', says Michael Polanyi in *Education and the Nature of Man* (1967), 'can be understood only by responding to his situation as if it were one's own.' Systems of explanation which would avoid such involvement are defective. 'There is', he goes on, 'a hierarchy of levels in the universe ... each higher level demanding a deeper participation for understanding it' and this offers hopes of a 'perspective in which we can once more place first things first: the living above the inanimate, man above the animal and the duties of man above man' (p. 15). Yet many teachers of the subjects in the higher education spectrum apparently seek a complete detachment from any personal involvement in life or situations. Nor do their systems of explanation necessitate such an involvement at any point.

How at this rate are we ever to come to a view which takes all the factors into account, including those insights, that love, that personal responsibility, which we sometimes undeniably feel? There is undoubtedly a disinclination in many academic circles to reckon with such feelings. Let us, it is said, stick to our lasts and talk of what we can observe and/or prove with some certainty. But if it is not the business of the thinkers and teachers in universities to attend to such matters, whose business is it? Moral judgements are implicit in many of the procedures and most of the policies we follow or agree to in the world outside. Such judgements need to be brought up into consciousness as far as may be. Does not an agricultural scientist who advocates the development of bigger and more economically run broiler houses base his advocacy upon a series of value judgements? The advocate of broiler houses can no doubt claim that by this means good cheap food can be provided, at a reasonable profit to the producer, for large numbers of people in our overpopulated world. But the feeding of multitudes at such a cost to the rights even of animals may well add to human moral insensitivity. To promote broiler houses because they produce more much-needed food does not end the responsibility of the agricultural scientist. He has solved, in part, one problem: that of feeding people. His method has created another: cruelty to chickens. He recognises this, probably, but condones the cruelty on grounds of the greater importance of people. He has not recognised the next resulting problem: the extra degree of de-humanisation and of desensitisation which will certainly result for some from habitual indulgence in a condoned cruelty. He must now face this next responsibility, which is to devise a non-cruel method of producing cheap chickens—one which does not deny the animals their rights. Instead of broiler birds we may almost unnoticingly go on to produce broiler men: indeed we may already be on the way to doing that. The general moral temperature may be lowered.

The experimental neurologist at work on his monkeys may cause them extreme suffering and degradation, but may be able to justify his usage of them by the hope that eventually human lives may be extended or relieved from almost unendurable pain. He will have to decide himself the way out of his moral dilemma. The very job of carrying out his experiments with monkeys day by day may tend to blunt his moral sense. Unless he is careful, human beings too may be used experimentally in a way which comes to seem to him as defensible as using monkeys. The distinguished American neurosurgeon, Irving S. Cooper (1969), writes: 'A few years ago during an international meeting of neurologists and neurosurgeons, an eminent professor, one of the most brilliant innovators in modern neurosurgery, in describing an operation which carried considerable risk and was extremely difficult for the patient to endure, said, "We do not advocate nor are we embarking on any therapeutic regime. It is an experiment". He then outlined the technical difficulties and dangers inherent in the procedure, concluding, "all of this cannot be thought of in any way as a therapeutic procedure". No one rose to argue that this type of procedure, performed on a human being by a surgeon who states that it is not a therapeutic procedure, is absurd' (p. 109).

The responsibilities of surgeons are not limited to performing their operations with as much compassion for the patient as possible nor to restoring him to health or sanity. In future more often than now surgeons and medical scientists will have to decide whether and when to transplant organs from one human being to another in order to improve his capacities or functioning. What 'improvement' can be effected in a man or woman without making them different in their identity from what they were before? What changes of personality may legitimately be brought about? And what are the limits of justification in such a matter? The more man gets control over his environment and takes charge of his own development the more his decisions must incorporate a moral element and the more important will be his concept of what attributes are most desirable in human beings. We may defend the growing of two blades of grass where one grew before, or the fattening up of pigs, or the addition of chemical preservatives to breakfast cereals, on the grounds of the increase to human prosperity and health that these policies may bring. But what is an 'improvement' in human evolution? Planners need to be more than manipulators: they need an understanding of what it really means to be man and to have values in control of the manipulation. Such values are not simply proclamations of goals or of ends but affect at every stage the choice of what means shall be used to attain them.

The educator may sometimes have to choose whether it is more important for students at a given time to add to their knowledge and technical skills or to their experiences-and what levels or quality of experience they may be most in need of. When we are told that research has shown that watching T.V. not merely adds greatly to knowledge but imparts a wider vocabulary and enables children to be more vicariously experienced, what are the criteria for determining whether the experiences are important or desirable? We are assured by Professor Hilde Himmelweit (1958) of the London School of Economics that 'children who watch T.V. develop a more objective response to many situations'. But is this a substitute for feeling themselves into a range of situations which it would be good for them to understand or chiefly an inoculation against manifestations of life which they would find insupportable if involved in them themselves? Research workers in education and psychology are themselves sometimes deficient and unpractised in these very sorts of insight and 'experiencing power'.

A distinction is to be drawn between knowledge which includes an understanding of feeling, loving, acts of valuing, and knowledge which is external, concerned with facts, measurement, the 'behaviour' of things. Both kinds are indispensable to a properly human and a properly humane life. The kind of personal and moral commitment which is the mark of the civilised man is not an irrationality. A sense of purpose that is intelligent includes an analytic and deductive exercise of mind but does not stop there.

By and large, universities today are much better at imparting knowledge and techniques that are what I have called 'external' than at fostering either aesthetic or moral awareness. They are more interested in training experts than experiencers. The university graduate rarely lacks a good deal of knowledge; he is more likely to lack an ability to find much meaning in life, to keep in touch with himself, or a sense that the past-even his own past-in any real sense belongs to him.

Most of the vast numbers of students entering higher education in Britain, the United States and many other countries, in the next quarter of a century will be looking to their period in a college or university or polytechnic to fit them for a profession or to give them expertise to equip them to survive in the technological world they will live in. Because money is limited, it is likely that more will be studying part-time. Staffing ratios will be lower, though more and cleverer devices to help their instruction will be available, so more of their education will be self-directed. In Britain, as we have seen, a large percentage of the extra students will go to polytechnics rather than to universities; more will be living at home rather than in colleges or halls or lodgings or flats. But in universities far too many of the courses we give are conventionally academic and unconsciously designed to transform the brighter by gradual stages into professors. And we have hoped that somehow this recipe will work for the rest as well. Such a programme is obviously inappropriate now and will become even more so as greater numbers of students crowd into higher education.

Yet the job of civilising and sensitising these students both morally and aesthetically will be the more imperative in a world becoming more adept year by year at making men into performers, consumers made contented only by more consumption, people able to gratify the maximum number of desires in a given period of time, but finally left at the mercy of their merciless instincts—like smaller modern Faustuses or Don Juans. And all in the name of progress.

What is the answer? Ought higher education to be ill the least concerned with the challenge? One can of course declare that this is not an educational problem at all; or if an educational problem, one for churches, governments or political parties-anything rather than colleges and universities, whose task is to pursue knowledge through rational inquiry and to discipline reason in a narrower sense.

I do not believe that that is a realistic position in the period ahead. Something is wrong with our theory of knowledge if we divorce knowing from being in such a way. Detachment is for the sake of living-not an end in itself. And life in a barrel, even a well-padded one, on its way over Niagara has all too short a date. Higher education must not merely broaden a student's sense of social responsibility, arousing in the potential expert an interest in the social consequences of practising his expertise. We must meet the more far-reaching and far more difficult challenge of sending him back to first principles and getting him to consider what is worthwhile in life.

There is no one recipe that will be successful in more than a fraction of the cases. But the direction of effort must be to broaden that sense of social responsibility once it has been aroused. The chemist who becomes concerned with the problem of effluents, the farmer who becomes alarmed at the side effects of spraying crops, the builder made aware of the social consequence of high-rise blocks-these are still a long way from necessarily being interested in the good life in general, or the links between social and personal. But they are at least a bit closer to considering the key question: how do we know that something, that anything, is worthwhile? As soon as that point is reached, hope glimmers, though the glimmer can easily fade if there is nobody to fan it to flame. And so often the teacher of agriculture, or chemistry, or surgery, or business administration or building is not good at such fanning.

How do we know something is worthwhile? The answer always involves an act of experiencing and an act of recognising the significance of the experience. First, we have personal feelings; second, we become aware of the feelings; third, we judge their importance.

For many people, music, literature, a film, a personal betrayal, a sudden bereavement, the breakup of a love affair, may bring experience, but they do not link these things with anything they regard as education. They believe that education is learning things for use. The problem of how to connect using with experiencing at a deep enough level is the primary educational problem. It is this problem that causes Ivan Illich to advocate deschooling; that we should abandon our schools and colleges altogether because they cheat us of life.

That may be a counsel of despair. But the alternative is almost as drastic. How do we get our students to recognise any authority other than finite knowledge: knowledge won as a result of carrying on a kind of offensive against an implacable world, knowledge retained with difficulty at least till the examination is over or the essay has been written? I do not want to underestimate the value of this kind of knowledge. One of the enormous benefits which technology brings is that though the world may be implacable, if you can get the mastery over just one small bit of it you can become implacable too. You can do something in a world where most people feel impotent. This important kind of knowledge is finite and demonstrable. Evidence exists for it, and it takes logic, determination and strenuousness to achieve and prove it. But, as I have argued, there is also the knowledge yielded by evaluating our personal experiences. Unless we can judge these experiences, we have no way of learning to value anything else.

Western civilisation is full of people like Martha in the gospel story, busily attending to what they think are their proper jobs, and it is supremely difficult to get our students of technology or management or even philosophy itself to stop attending to those jobs for a moment and listen (so that they discover what they already know). Yet such listening is one way to find meaning in things and therefore to be able to judge their worth. Most conventional kinds of study, whether of the sciences or the humanities, are associated with effort. They discount the relaxation indispensable to experiencing. Much that is essential in education, I would maintain, is not research-minded; it is concerned with the parts of life that technical study neatly avoids; personal suffering, personal happiness, good and evil, commitment, the mysterious, the inextricable mixture of human motives. *Hamlet, The Marriage of Figaro,* Willa Cather's *Death Comes for the Archbishop*, Greek myth, the powerful sculpture of the Mayas-all are dense with meaning that awaits our understanding. How are we to become quite enough, individual enough, to realise their meaning or our own need? I have no easy answer. But I believe, all the same, that the ultimate alternative may be the destruction or rebuilding of the college, the graduate school, higher education itself, as we know them. For to educate people to be experts in a world that no longer has any meaning is a kind of madness and may come to be recognised as the madness it is.

> 'We know the answers, all the answers.
> It is the questions that we do not know.[1]

And without putting the questions searchingly to ourselves, the answers will be illusory.

What is a consumer society for? What is progress in aid of? I suspect that it is these questions that we should, with a desperate urgency, be asking; and that unless we can ask them at a level of understanding that it takes imagination and humanity to reach, we cannot really answer them at all. We need both intellect and lively affection, both capacity to analyse and capacity to feel, if we are to find any answers that have lasting meaning.

---

1 Louis Macneice.

Universities between Two Worlds

From *Universities between Two Worlds* (1974)

This selection is taken from *Universities between Two Worlds*, by W. Roy Niblett, 1974. Published by University of London Press Ltd., London, United Kingdom.

* * * * *

We have been suggesting that today universities are between two worlds both chronologically and ideologically. It remains to sum up and to deduce the consequences of the position taken.

The period 1950–70 saw a rapid enlargement of the world's population, with great strides taken in many countries in the development of society. People's expectations grew fast of what life had to offer them in opportunity and affluence. The period 1970–2000 is likely to see even more rapid changes. The population of the world still increases alarmingly and there is greater need than ever before for planning and the application of rigorous scientific thought. That combination is likely to yield far more leisure—or unemployment—for the majority of people, but it may well call for a smaller, not a larger, *proportion* of sheer experts highly trained in the universities of Europe and the United States. This for two reasons. First, with many more countries developing systems of higher education of their own, the extent of their dependence upon the products of the universities of other countries will be lessened, though it will still remain appreciable. Secondly, while the increased centralisation, mechanisation and sophistication of life may well stimulate the demand for limited numbers of inventors and administrators of high quality, who will compete for the jobs available, the demand for graduates with a rather lesser expertise, though a first class intelligence, may be reduced, if not in their absolute numbers at least in the percentage of the population involved. In other words the market for 'top' experts may be strong even in comparison with the present day; but we may find that the densely populated world is producing a superfluity of experts at other levels, even if each only works a fifteen- or twenty-hour week. In this situation should not many universities and polytechnics and other institutions of higher education contract in size or close down altogether?

By no means. But what will become more and more clear is that their main job is no longer that of producing technological experts. The period of their history in which that was taken for granted will be seen as transitional. The world into which mankind will be moving will be one needing more, not less, education, but an education which tries to cater for human development more directly. Of course universities must still train people who will be able to tackle the technical problems—for example the problem of feeding the vast extra number of mouths; of travelling faster and more often; of an urban world. If they trade out from doing this, they will not belong to the modem world anymore and will certainly be replaced by institutions which are more useful.

But if universities drift into becoming places of multitudinous utility—without, it may be, altogether realising the fact—it will be only a matter of time before it becomes clear that this is reductionism and that their quality cannot be measured in terms of productivity alone. The personal and social progress which matters even more is in mental span, moral development, range of imaginative apprehension. People will need to be helped to develop further and more sensitively their powers of enjoyment, their sense of purpose, their capacity for empathy and moral action. And they will need to do this as individuals, not merely as imitators of others.

It used to be common for the elite members of a society to act as the transmitters of the moral code and upholders, at any rate publicly, of the view of the world or the religious faith which all the other members would be expected to adopt which they would indeed find it natural to adopt. Kings and leaders told their people what they should believe. 'Then King Darius wrote unto all people, nations and languages that dwell in all the earth: "Peace be multiplied unto you. I make a decree, that in every dominion of my kingdom men tremble and fear before the God of Daniel", (Daniel VI, vv, 25–6). For most of the world's history so far, people could be experts technically—they could be carpenters, farmers, merchants, soldiers, scribes—and function efficiently and happily without any high degree of individualisation. One hardly needed to arrive at convictions that were individual on any deep matter: one simply and naturally adopted those of one's society. In clothes, manners, nationalism and patriotism, one followed the fashions of one's class or one's occupation. There might be different elites to respect for different sectors of one's life—princes who formed an elite, bishops and priests who formed an elite, doctors, lawyers, grandparents. The sources of most of the authority even over the mature man or woman were almost always outside him. He might be a master of his craft but morally he was an obedient servant. He was obedient to the rules given him from without, not dependent upon his own insights save in small degrees.

The general direction of the evolution of our society now, especially for its more intelligent members, is and must continue to be towards greater and greater individual awareness and self-dependence. The words elite and elitist have in our time acquired a sinister sound. One of the animating impulses for men in many countries is towards more equality. Nor will they be content for long if for prince and bishop are substituted big-businessman or clever scientist. These may well be respected as experts within their range of competence, as financial manipulators, ingenious inventors or whatever. But that is very different from their being regarded as authorities or guides on how life should be lived. It is no far step from this position to one in which universities and other places of higher education could come to be accepted within their range of competence as useful, even indispensable, service stations for the modern world—but as little or nothing more. We may ask their professors to see round more of the corners ahead than we can ourselves; we may ask universities to solve more complicated problems than we are capable of doing; and to be great reservoirs of knowledge and skill. But we hesitate to ask them to be places of reflection or thought except for specific and directed technological, scholarly or research enterprises.

The fact is, however, that maintenance of the trust of a people in those who have been highly educated, its powerful civil servants and its scientists for example, is dependent upon their having not only knowledge but vision too. The universities from which they come are expected to play their part in securing both. Society in spite of its hesitancies finds that it does need people—many of them in universities-to feed it with imaginative ideas, some of fundamental import. Through the years its own direction of development has been altered, by men whose ideas, whether or not they were themselves at a university, have been given effective currency by the missionary work of such places. In the past two hundred years these have included Kant, Goethe, Coleridge, Darwin, Marx, Kierkegaard, Nietzsche, Durkheim, Freud.

Any system of higher education is going in future to be more and more dependent both for its financing and for the degree of freedom given to it or to any of its parts upon the public's faith in it. This in some part certainly depends on the recognition by people of its usefulness, but it depends too on their recognition, whether overt or covert, that it stands for values less immediate and definable than use. Even public readiness to respect research has within it an ingredient or two other than an anticipation of larger crops, more effective drugs, more ingenious weapons, better transport, however surely these are expected dividends. There is also a suspicion, however faint sometimes, that to know the truth is important, whether it be in our favour or not; that insight matters, as do knowledge, logic, justice and sense of purpose. Any institution which shows that it values these will, in a free country, be given a certain respect.

This is the basic justification for according a higher measure of academic freedom to institutions of higher education. Unless, however, they continue to deserve it and are widely felt to deserve it, they are always, and will always be, in danger of losing it.

An enlightened state, an enlightened local education authority, an enlightened religious denomination, may give an institution of higher education almost, if not quite, all the freedom it can use. But each may be tempted on occasion to say: 'It is imperative now for us to have people who will make themselves efficient instruments for national or industrial or denominational purposes: soldiers, machine minders, staunch defenders of given doctrines, who will obey the rational only as we see it'. In these circumstances it may be part of the mission of the university, and of other places of higher education also, to put such—it may be quite necessary—obedience into its temporary place while standing for, and proclaiming, the importance of both a wider imagination and a wider reason. For most purposes and for much of the time institutions of higher education may not need any more autonomy than they are allowed by those who sponsor them. But on occasion they may need, and should be able to come under, an umbrella which is the joint and conscious property of all those institutions. Because of the need in a community for thought, foresight and understanding, and the dangers that civilisation will be engulfed, a university cannot without betraying itself opt out of the situation.

A university, however, may not be willing to accept other institutions of higher education as companions under an umbrella, for another reason than a temptation to sit pretty to its social responsibilities. It may, as we have seen, have too limited a concept of the nature of rationality and of ways of attaining it and regard quite a number of subjects of study which are pursued in other institutions of higher education as too unintellectual for recognition. The adjective 'rigorous' an excellent word in its place—can be used unreasonably to confine the territory of reason itself. How far should a university ever have to hear about, let alone seriously consider as studies, such subjects as drama, creative music, social work, sculpture, housecraft, physiotherapy? It should, even if it is at the apex of the hierarchy, certainly care about them. It is bad in almost every way for universities to be ivory towers with impermeable walls. Such subjects need not be abhorrent if they too are studied in an environment where intelligence is respected and the dominant values are both evaluative and distinctively humane. The making of the syllabuses for such subjects and the teaching of courses in them should of course 'be in the hands of the relevant experts. As it is, applied subjects with a not necessarily much larger theoretical basis abound in both universities and polytechnics—from dairy farming to estate management, from concrete engineering to dentistry, from transportation studies to marketing.

A time of financial stringency such as the one we have now entered challenges our priorities robustly. The state may decide that higher education is both too important and too expensive to be left to the academics and it will interfere directly and vigorously. But systems planning and cost benefit analysis by themselves solve no moral question. A calculating rationalism is not capacious enough in its presuppositions about human nature. Nor is it any answer to what Alvin Toffler has recently called 'the quiescent but still simmering disaffection of youth'.

Most departments in institutions of higher education of all types want to modify presuppositions—though not always enough—as well as to impart facts and skills. Their teachers want students to acquire knowledge and to develop a capacity to examine evidence with detachment, but also to develop fairmindedness, tolerance, convictions and confidence in facing the world. Few teachers in polytechnics, or universities, at bottom want their students to be careerists in their orientation and nothing more.

In both kinds of institution they fail to make this sufficiently clear. If higher education-whether pursued in universities or polytechnics-is going to be able to help as it should to counter the drift and the tendency to dissolution of our time, its teachers need to be more in touch with themselves and with each other, and to face more unitedly the underlying task they have in common.

In the thinking about the content of higher education too small a part is being played by those who think from first principles, too large a part by the activists and planners. But what the former have to say, if it could be made forcefully articulate, could do much to compel us to go back to principles at a time when to do that is vital. Men—including the economists and planners—know at heart so much more than they say or even reckon with. And it is knowledge at this level that we need to draw upon.

To cater for national and personal needs adequately is, then, a job common to universities and polytechnics. Their students are equally human beings; and many in future will be having part of their higher education in one type of institution and part in another. If Britain has been rather disenchanted with its universities in the last half-dozen years, it could easily become just as disappointed with its polytechnics, towards the end of another half-dozen—especially if they produce only functionaries, however efficient, and not educated men and women.

No doubt polytechnics hope increasingly not to lay themselves open to this charge. University teachers and polytechnic teachers have a large measure of freedom to teach in the way they want, and, in considerable degree, what they want. The wanting, however, often lacks sufficient range and depth. Universities and polytechnics are not adequately mission-oriented, in social or in human terms. No one wants the polytechnics to imitate the universities. But that they will more and more be complementary parts of one higher education system needs emphasising. Underneath the necessary and desirable differences, they have civilising and moral objectives in common. Methods of attaining these call for much continuing joint discussion and a deeper understanding of what is involved.

Governments, as we said earlier, tend to pay institutions of higher education to produce experts of the sorts they judge they most need, experts who as technology advances tend to acquire more and more power to affect the daily lives of millions. It is particularly for the institutions who educate to degree level to produce graduates who have a necessary fear of the consequences of the exercise of their own power; and foresight enough to control those consequences, as far as may be, on behalf of us all. In the long run no doubt it is this achievement that governments will be willing to pay most for—in respect and even in hard cash; but if it is too long a run men may have lost much of their humanity *en route*, with few noticing that it has happened. The higher education system of any advanced country is certainly going to continue to comprise a diversity of institutions with overlapping functions. It is important that differences in immediate objective and of administrative control should not obscure their underlying community of purpose.

Throughout this book it is the importance of the personal education of the student that has been stressed: in reaching down to the sources of authority there is no possible substitute for insights that come individually if they are to come at all. Some of them will be insights into the absoluteness of the objectivity of fact, of 'the armies of unalterable law' which govern the behaviour of the universe as it is encountered or seen. Some will be insights less magisterial but more intimate.

Ben Jonson's *Timber* quotes a passage from the *Famosa Apologia* of the physician Mayerne—a passage from which incidentally the motto of the University of Lancaster is taken. '*Patet omnibus veritas,*' it begins—'Truth lies open to all, it is not yet anyone's possession. Much of it is left even for those to come. Nothing is more hostile to truth than to take away freedom to speculate.' Yes, indeed, but only some *kinds* of truth will be yielded by an attitude of speculation, even in higher education. The direction in which men look will affect and limit what they are able to see. Truth may lie open to all, but only to the extent and from the directions that they lie open to receive it. Men are so often 'distraught by expectancy', to use Rilke's phrase, that it is only with difficulty that they will notice what they are not expecting, or almost expecting, to see. It follows, as I have implied in earlier chapters, that the education of the inward glance is of fundamental importance: it is this which affects the evidence we shall be able to recognise as authoritative or even be able to recognise as evidence at all.

Places of higher education need to widen the area of their search for truth. Unless they do they will lack the communication with some of the sources of authority essential to the giving of the leadership, and producing the kind of men, needed if the world is not to relapse into a new barbarism. Our reliance on technology cannot but increase; yet we are at the stage of having lost the faith that science in itself is good or its ethical neutrality really trustworthy. New contacts with the sources of illumination, and therefore of authority, are imperative.

In his *Mission of the University*, Ortega y Gasset (1946) declares in his typically emphatic way that the culture of the Middle Ages was a way of looking at things. It involved the system of ideas concerning the world and humanity which the man of that time possessed; it was a repertory of convictions which became the effective guide of his existence. 'Life is a chaos, a tangled and confused jungle in which man is lost. But his mind reacts against the sensation of bewilderment: he labours to find "roads", "ways" through the woods in the form of clear, firm ideas concerning the universe, positive convictions about the nature of things. The ensemble, or system, of these ideas, is culture in the true sense of the term; it is precisely the opposite of external ornament. Culture is what saves human life from being a mere disaster; it is what enables man to live a life which is something above meaningless tragedy or inward disgrace' (pp. 43–4).

Higher education, I believe, needs to develop new orientations. The answer on the part of the universities cannot be in their concentrating upon being multiversities alone; nor upon their withdrawing into a concentration on pure scholarship and research. They must remain places of personal and civilising education for an actual and living society. They need in other words to link the world of scholarship and research with that of action, to link the affective with the cognitive. They need to be both places of knowledge and places with spirit; in touch both with the objective and with the subjective. In such a linkage there is bound to be conflict. 'Is it the task of the university to be a clerisy, self-consciously guarding the past and seeking assertively to challenge the new? Or is it just a bazaar, offering Coleridge and Blake, Burckhardt and Nietzsche, Weber and Marx as antiphonal prophets, each with his own call? No consensual answer is possible, perhaps because the university is no longer the citadel of the traditional mode—only the simple-minded can believe it is—but an arena in which the critics once outside the Academy have, like the tiger (or Tyger) once outside the gates of society, found a place—deservedly—within. And the tension between past and future, mind and sensibility, tradition and experience, for all its strains and discomfitures, is the only source for maintaining the independence of inquiry itself' (Bell, 1966, p. 149).

At anyone moment of time if the university is alive such tension, vitally held, may be perceived as present as strenuously as it is in one of the world's great bridges-the Maracaibo Lake Bridge in Venezuela, the Verrazano Suspension Bridge at the entrance to New York harbour, the Severn Bridge at the Beachley-Aust crossing; as it is in the pity and terror brought together in a great Greek or Elizabethan play; or in the straining sexual opposites united and evolvingly fulfilled in a great Mozartian duet like 'Là ci darem la mano' in *Don Giovanni*. The kind of knowledge the university has to convey is knowledge that is still alive, still leaving experiences behind it. It is in the experiencing afresh again and again that the educative power of knowledge rests. That word 'rests' is full of a calm activity.

To say that a place of higher education should produce an elite is to say among other things that it should produce more people who have access to their own experiences and can evaluate them. It is through such people that a direction of looking is mediated. We catch presuppositions and assumptions from people who hold them. But what is the range and scope of the personal involvement brought into the reckoning? Is the content of higher education to be limited to those kinds of knowledge and skill which will be contributed only by an observer who has learned to be detached and unmoved? Is 100,000,000 always to be 10^4 x 10^4 or sometimes to be ten thousand times ten thousand? Unless places of higher education in future serve mankind in more than clever but utilitarian ways they will deservedly if slowly come to forfeit confidence. For in spite of all our planning they will fail of real purpose, fail to bridge the gap between the world of the past and that of the future, between the world outside man and the world within him.

CHAPTER NINETEEN

The Vernacular Basis of Scottish Humanism

From *The Democratic Intellect: Scotland and Her Universities in the Nineteenth Century* (1961)

GEORGE ELDER DAVIE

This selection is taken from *The Democratic Intellect: Scotland and Her Universities in the Nineteenth Century*, by George Elder Davie, 1981, published by Edinburgh University Press, Edinburgh, Scotland. Originally published in 1961.

Editors' Note

It is not often recognized that whereas England had two universities for over six hundred years until the 1830s, Scotland had four universities from the late mediaeval period (Aberdeen, St Andrews, Glasgow and Edinburgh). Other major differences that have characterised the Scottish situation are those of a broad four-year undergraduate curriculum and a higher participation rate than that evident in the English higher education system. These matters are relevant in understanding Davie and his book on *The Democratic Intellect.*

Davie was a Scot and was a lecturer in philosophy, first at Edinburgh, then at Queen's University, Belfast and then again at Edinburgh. In much of his work, Davie was at pains to bring out Scottish distinctiveness in its academic culture, which had long taken its bearings from the breadth and philosophical leanings of continental

Europe compared with the more specialist and more immediately utilitarian character of the English academic culture. A yet further difference lay in the close connection of the English universities with the (Anglican) church whereas the Scottish universities possessed a strong 'intellectual-secular element' (as Davie himself put it in his Introductory essay, p. xii), closely bound in with 'Metaphysical Scotland' (p. xii).

The sub-title of *The Democratic Intellect* is 'Scotland and Her Universities in the Nineteenth Century'. In other words, universities, on Davie's view, had to be understood against the background of a wider cultural and social background. Indeed, in nineteenth century Scotland, it was hoped that 'the universities would assume responsibility for the nation's spiritual leadership' (p. xvi) and 'to neutralise the inequalities of scholastic and family backgrounds' (p. xvii). Accordingly, 'general studies of a non-utilitarian kind were given pride of place in the curriculum and, as in France, the path … lay through compulsory philosophy' (p. xvii). Here, in 'ideals so un-English as these' (p. xvii) lay the value of the national ideal of 'the democratic intellect' (p. xix). The intellect was crucial in reflecting, sustaining and developing a Scottish identity, but it needed to be at once independent of church, broad, philosophical and democratic.

RB

* * * * *

During the nineteenth century, according to Professor Saunders, the partisans of classicism constituted a powerful pressure-group of questionable tendency, well-meaning but narrow-minded.

> The Commissioners proposed to make the classics the basis of advanced literary, philosophical and scientific study. … They were intimately persuaded that no other studies were better fitted either to inform the taste, or exercise the faculties of youth, or to create a love of freedom, and a spirit of generous and manly independence. The example of English education was familiar and increasingly potent. It was also the age of Greek independence, and classical humanism. The Hellenic tradition was to be introduced to a people whose 'civility' was inspired by the Reformation and the Enlightenment, whose educational tradition emphasised equality of opportunity, whose higher education had been associated with the professions and their practice, and whose contemporary enthusiasm was for science as applied to a wide range of human affairs. These circumstances might make the new cultural element the more necessary, but it was open to argument that a liberal education and its attributes—freedom, equilibrium, calmness, moderation and wisdom—could be more directly developed out of the accepted intellectual interests of the people.[1]

1 L. Saunders, Scottish Democracy, pp. 3 j 8–9.

Saunders's account of the situation points to the possibility of a revised estimate of the place of Classical Humanism in traditional Scottish education. Granted the Scots were very backward in Greek as compared with other Western nations, especially the English and the Germans, yet their deficiency in pure classics was to a certain extent neutralised by a profound respect for the classical ideals of moderation and balance. The ideal of a tripartite course including science and philosophy as well as literature was never lost sight of in Scotland, in the way that happened in the Southern seats of learning. In particular, the educational arrangements in the North seemed designed to prevent the undue predominance of classical philology, and, apparently, even in the seventeenth century, the claim was already being made by patriots like Sir Thomas Urquhart that whereas the English Universities were interested in the knowledge of mere words, the chief concern of the Scottish Universities was with the knowledge of things.

This view of the situation would seem to be confirmed by what the Scottish classicists themselves said. Thus, Andrew Dalzel, Professor of Greek in Edinburgh in Walter Scott's time, used to complain that the low state of classical studies in Scotland was due to the Presbyterian educational settlement in the seventeenth century: 'if it had not been for the confounded Solemn League and Covenant, we would have made as good longs and shorts as they'. So too, John Burnet, Professor of Greek in St Andrews about a century later, attributed the Scottish backwardness in Greek to the victory in the seventeenth century of an educational policy which gave a priority to philosophy and science. The decisive fact about the Scottish Universities, he said, was that the mediaeval curriculum of Grammar, Logic, Ethics, Physics survived both the Revival of Learning and the Reformation. There were of course attempts to give classical philology the predominance it received elsewhere, but these were all 'defeated by our old enemies, the philosophy regents'. In consequence, the classical and literary part of the curriculum virtually remained down to the nineteenth century what it had been in the Middle Ages—Latin without Greek.[2]

The distinctive feature of classical studies in the hereditary Scottish curriculum was thus, as Burnet saw that in the seventeenth century settlement they had to accommodate themselves to the ideal of a general education which aimed at doing justice to philosophy and to science as well as to literature. The tie-up with philosophy and science prevented Scottish classicism from getting out of touch with life.

2 Burnet's essay on the classics at St Andrews in *Votiva Tabella*, the volume commemorating the quincentenary of the University In 1911.

Looked at in this light, the peculiar classical tradition encouraged by the seventeenth-century settlement might even be regarded as a very considerable educational achievement. Its great aim apparently was to perpetuate the ideals of the Renaissance in a land dominated by Presbyterian democracy, and to impress on future generations of Scots that the cultural legacy of their Protestantism included not merely the stern moralism of the Reformers but also the broad Humanism of the Scottish Latin poets. Accordingly, Scottish educational policy proceeded to treat George Buchanan as a classic; his translation of the *Psalms* became a set book side by side with Horace's odes, and held a chief place in the Scottish curriculum from the middle of the seventeenth century to the middle of the nineteenth century. At the same time, the other Scottish Latin poets were not entirely forgotten, so far at least as their works might subserve the grand policy of combining the values of Humanism with the values of Hebraicism, and hence, as Professor Clarke notes in his *History of Classical Education in Great Britain and Ireland*, the General Assembly in 1740 recommended to Scottish schools the reading of Arthur Johnston's paraphrase of the Song of Solomon.

This aim of perpetuating the cultural values of the Renaissance Humanists did not—as one might have expected—inspire a pedagogic policy of keeping alive the practice of Latin versification after the model of Johnston, Buchanan, Mark Alexander Boyd and the rest. On the contrary, as Professor Clarke points out, the Scottish educationists were opposed to the idea of including in the syllabus compulsory exercises in making Latin verses, and argued explicitly that versification in the dead languages would have cultural value only when—as in the case of Buchanan and Johnston—the prompting to write came from inspiration and natural bent. The effect of this policy of discouraging verse-making was that, by the eighteenth century, the practice had entirely died out in Scotland, whereas in England it maintained its place in the curriculum and was held in great esteem.

Under the Scottish settlement, these changes in the classical curriculum, while they involved a loss in accurate knowledge—hence Dalzel's complaint about longs and shorts—nevertheless seem to have induced a compensating gain in breadth, and, according to a fairly unanimous tradition, the classes of Humanity (as Latin was appropriately called) were notable for promoting 'a love of literature in general'. The Humanistic spirit, in fact, perpetuated itself in the Scottish classrooms in the form of a lively interest in questions of literary appreciation and aesthetic standards, and, in practice, a curriculum which put Buchanan's psalms on a level with Horace's odes seems to have provided a stimulus to a tradition of comparative criticism. Buchanan's Latin psalms were contrasted on the one hand with the poetry of Virgil and Horace, and on the other hand with the poetry of the Authorised Version, and teachers would point out to their classes both his failures and his felicities. Or again, Buchanan's polemical works in prose served as useful reminders to the young Scots that classical art need not be the prerogative of an aristocracy or a monarchy, but might equally be made a vehicle of the democratic ideal. In this way, the Scottish approach to classics, avoiding a narrow exclusiveness, was able to see beyond ancient literature to modern literature, and teachers were not afraid to illustrate the literary quality of Horace or Virgil by means of an appropriate quotation from poetry in English or even in Scots.

This Scottish practice of introducing into the Latin classroom the general questions of criticism and aesthetics was, of course, condemned by Oxonians[3] as yet one more instance of the Scottish vice of premature intellectualism, and of unseasonable addiction to metaphysics. It was a mistake to encourage young students to take general views: generalisation, if it was ever to be undertaken, was for the mature alone. Worse still, the generalities about literature were based on a scanty reading-list of a handful of poems by Buchanan, Horace, etc. No doubt these poems had been judiciously appreciated and even enthusiastically analysed, but there were not enough of them to provide a proper foundation for induction.

Whatever the truth of this, the Scottish ideal did indubitably inspire a love of literature in general and, in addition, it kept alive in Scotland the tradition of an intellectual and philosophical approach to Classical Scholarship.

The range of studies now familiarly known as 'Eng. Lit.' rose to prominence in the Scottish Universities as the result not of academic policy but of spontaneous interest on the part of the students. The beginning of the movement can perhaps be fixed in 1841 when W. E. Aytoun[4] appointed to the Edinburgh Chair of Rhetoric, introduced a shift of emphasis from the study of general principles to the historical outline of English literature, in the hope of increasing his audience.

---

3 Shairp, *The Wants of the Scottish Universities* (18) 6), p. 14.

4 See Eric Frykman's book W. E. Aytoun, Pioneer Professor of English. It has been pointed out to me that Spalding, Aytoun's predecessor in the chair, very likely had lectured on the history of literature, witness his History of English Literature which he published in 18)3, when at St Andrews. No doubt this is so, but the really significant fact is, I think, that the subject which mattered most for Spalding was Rhetoric (see the Edinburgh University Examination papers for the period of Spalding's professorship (1840–4)) and also his impressive little treatise on Rhetoric of 1839).

One can bring out more clearly still the peculiar contribution of Aytoun's tenure of the chair by noting that his successor David Masson, as usual loyal to the intellectual inheritance of Scotland, made a brave attempt to restore the credit of Rhetoric. Students' notes of his lectures, preserved in Edinburgh University, show that Masson's predominating interest was in Rhetoric rather than the history of English Literature. He gave Rhetoric flew life by treating it as 'the theory of literature', sometimes with considerable philosophical subtlety.

Apparently the response of the students was remarkable, and the numbers of the class rose in little over a decade from 30 to '30. The Royal Commission of 1818, impressed with the new development, recommended the creation of chairs in the subject in all four Universities, and at the same time enjoined the inclusion of a new compulsory paper in English literature alongside the traditional compulsions of Logic and Ethics, Latin and Greek, Mathematics and Physics.

The success of Aytoun's class was no doubt due chiefly to his conscientiousness as a teacher of English composition, but it would seem that he also met a social need by a new and popular treatment of the vexed question of the cultural symbiosis between the Scots and the English, which the rising generation—a generation containing men like Lorimer, Masson and Clerk Maxwell—apparently took very seriously. 'I have', Aytoun wrote a friend in 1853 (the year in which began Lorimer's movement preaching the cause of academical patriotism) 'a great class this winter, which adds to all my other discomforts, for the youths have caught the spirit of the time and are all Young Scotlanders, eager to write and make speeches and are frantic for reputation.'[5]

Among the topics engrossing these young patriots, one would be the treatment of the Scottish literary heritage in this new class of English Literature. The issue was more than a merely academic matter, and involved questions embarrassing to the pride of the Scots as a cultural group. The difficulty was in fact the old one ever present since the Union—that, while wholeheartedly supporting the adoption of English as the language of serious literature, they were uneasy about the implied slight to the native tongue, and to the literary record of their ancestors in it; and even the most decided opponents of Scots had their moments of divided loyalties. The normal voice of Beattie, for example, is that which says of the Gentle Shepherd that 'to a Scotchman who thoroughly understands the language and is aware of its vulgarity, it appears ludicrous from the contrasts between meanness of phrase, and dignity or seriousness of sentiment; and this gives a farcical air even to the most affecting parts of the poem, and occasions an impropriety of a peculiar kind'. But in addition to Beattie the anglicising critic, there appears at least once a Beattie who is a sturdy patriot in cultural matters.

> Our fine new fangle sparks, I grant ye,
> Gie poor auld Scotland mony a taunty;
> They're grown sae ungertfu' and vaunty,
>   And capernoited,
> They guide her like a cankered aunty,
>   That's deaf and doited.

---

5 Sir Theodore Martin, Memoir on Aytoun, p. 141.

Sae comes of ignorance, I trow,
It's this that crooks their ill-faured mou'
Wi' jokes sae course, they gar fouk spue
For downright sconner.
For Scotland wants not sons enew,
To do her honour.

I here might gie a screed of names,
Dawties of Heliconian dames!
The foremost place Gawin Douglas
That canty priest.
And wha can match the first King James
For sang and jest?

From the time of David Hume (b. 1711) to that of Aytoun (b. 1813), each new generation had to struggle with the question of what to do about the literary inheritance in Scots. A stable solution was far to seek, and men like Beattie oscillated between the insincere alternative of being more English than the English, and the impolitic alternative of a reversion to the postures of pre-Union patriotism. Finally, however, the success of Burns, of Scott and of the Ballads both north and south of the Tweed, created a new situation, and opened the way to establishing a convention, satisfactory enough to the susceptibilities of the larger nation as of the smaller, which would give Scottish literature a due place as a dependent of English literature and end the unsettled relations between the two.

The principle of the compromise was, it appears, the then fashionable distinction between art-poetry and folk-poetry. The glory of England, it was held, lay in its great tradition of art-poetry. Scotland was weak in art-poetry, and its main contributors in this field—'the Scotch Chaucerians'—were a Northern extension of the Southern tradition. As if by compensation, however, Scotland was strong in folk-poetry. In a specimen of one of his public lectures which has survived, we find Professor Aytoun applying in a forcible and intelligent way to this problem of the relation of English to Scottish poetry 'the distinction between natural poetry which is minstrelsy and artificial poetry which in default of a better name you may call aesthetical composition'. He argues that there is a connection between the Scottish tradition of poetry as natural and the democratic basis of Scottish society. The English devotion to artificial poetry is due to the stratifications and segregations of Southern society.

> There is nothing national in either Spencer or Milton or Pope, or Dryden, or Byron, or Wordsworth, or many more. They are great poets, no doubt, but the people don't sympathise with them, though portions of the intellectual and educated classes may

> do so; and taking them altogether, what kind of congruity either of sentiment or of form do you find in their work? But take Burns and Scott and Hogg, and Motherwell, and Allan Cunningham, with their predecessors David Lyndsay and Allan Ramsay and Robert Fergusson—they are adored of the people. And why? Because they are minstrels and because they embody in vivid strains the emotions, thoughts—nay, prejudices, if you will—which are most rife in the national bosom.[6]

Much of what Aytoun says here is in line with the Northern cultural tradition, but the distinctive tendency of his criticisms obscured the intricate balance of the national ideal of democracy *plus* intellectualism, by stressing the former to the exclusion of the latter. He did indeed maintain the national values up to a point, as when he insisted that 'most of the English poets want universality' in the sense of their being unable to appeal simultaneously (as the Scottish poets can) both to the unlearned many and to the learned few. But he left one with the impression that the limited appeal of the English poets was due to their employment of philosophical ideas and of elaborate diction whereas the Scottish poets reached a wider audience only by avoiding intellectuality and artistry.

Thus, in the very circles responsible for pioneering this new British subject of English Literature a convention arose of refusing the traditions of Scottish learning credit for the distinctive excellence of Scottish poetry. English poetry no doubt was seen against a background of classical scholarship, by which it had been profoundly influenced. But in the North the peculiar weakness of Scottish poets (unlike poets of other countries) was the spiritual poverty of their cultural environment.

This point of view was formulated, simultaneously, south of the border as well as north of it, and indeed it received its classic expression in Matthew Arnold's well-known passage on Burns's background.

> As we draw towards the end of the eighteenth century, we are met by the great name of Burns. We enter now on times where the personal estimate of poets begins to be rife, and where the real estimate of them is not reached without difficulty. But in spite of the disturbing pressures of personal partiality, of national partiality, let us try to reach a real estimate of the poetry of Burns.
>
> The real Burns is of course in his Scotch poems. Let us boldly say that of much of this poetry, a poetry dealing perpetually with Scotch drink, Scotch religion and Scotch manners, a Scotchman's estimate is apt to be personal. A Scotchman is used to this world of Scotch drink, Scotch religion and Scotch manners; he has a tenderness for it; he meets its poet half-way. In this tender mood he reads pieces like Holy Fair or Halloween. But this world of Scotch drink, Scotch religion, and Scotch manners is

6 Ibid., p. 233.

> against a poet, not for him, when it is not a partial countryman who reads him; for in itself, it is not a beautiful world, and no one can deny that it is of advantage to a poet to deal with a beautiful world. Burns's world of Scotch drink, Scotch religion and Scotch manners is a harsh, a sordid, a repulsive world; even the world of his Cotter's Saturday Night is not a beautiful world.

What Arnold offered us was in fact a new version of the 'ploughman poet' view of Burns. The famous Scottish educational system, he thought, in so far as it affected Burns at all, was not a help but a hindrance to him, because of its thoroughly illiberal character. Apparently Arnold in Oxonian fashion equated culture with the study of Greek, and thus for him the Scots had little culture because they had little Greek.

> The Scotch ... as the state of their universities shows, have at present little notion of *la grande culture*. Instead of guarding, like the Germans, the *wissenschaftliche Geist* of their universities, they turn them into mere school-classes; and instead of making the student, as in Germany, pass to the university through the *prima* of a high school, Scotland lets the University and the High School of Edinburgh compete for school-boys; and the University recruits its Greek classes from the 3rd or 4th forms of the High School. Accordingly, while the aristocratic class of Scotland is by its bringing up, its faults, its merits, much the same as the aristocratic class in England, the Scorch middle class is, in *la grande culture*, not ahead of the English. But so far as intellectual culture has industrial value, makes a man's business work better and helps him to get on in the world, the Scotch middle class has thoroughly appreciated it and sedulously employed it, both for itself and the class whose labour it uses; and here is their superiority to the English and the reason for the superiority of Scotch skilled labourers and Scotch men of business everywhere.[7]

---

7 Matthew Arnold, Schools and Universities of the Continent, pp. 255–6. It may be noted that in Scotland there was considerable resentment at the failure of men like Arnold to realise the predominant role of philosophy in the Scottish Universities. 'Some people both north and south of the Tweed are found in these days not infrequently to talk and write as if the Universities of Scotland were simply large Public Schools of the English type, and of a rather inferior sort. They look to the school subjects that are taught—Latin, Greek and Mathematics -and disregard, or have a very vague idea of the kind of instruction given in them. The discussion of the Scottish Universities is apt to take a one-sided course and to be restricted to questions of the degree ·of classical preparation with which the students enter, or ought to enter. All through these discussions, there is thus little perception or recognition that these Universities have been from their foundation, and throughout history, seminaries of Mental Philosophy ... In older times, as now [philosophy] is the strong and cultivated faculty [of the Scottish student].' From the opening paragraphs of John Veitch's article on 'Philosophy in Scotland' contributed to the second volume of Mind (1877), pp, 74–5.

In passages like these, Arnold lent the powerful support of his critical authority to the peculiar system of literary history in Britain which men like Aytoun were making fashionable in the new chairs of English Literature. Arnold presumably held that the English tradition constituted the cultural mainstream of literature in Britain and that the distinctively Scottish contribution to literature was significant only in virtue of being a tributary of this Southern stream. In Arnold's case, indeed, the crucial consideration had to do with critical standards and intellectual background. The essential difference for him between the Northern stream of poetry and the Southern was that the latter, for all its faults and insularity, had closer links with the European movement of ideas, culture and scholarship. In a certain sense, no doubt, Scotland inherited an ancient academic tradition of a distinctive kind, but Arnold was sure that its values had been permeated by the most benighted and illiberal spirit, and that, far from serving as an inspiration to Scottish poetry, it had stood to it in the role of a grim step-mother, of 'a cankered aunty, Deaf and doited'—to quote Beattie's ironical phrase.

It is, we believe, possible to trace the influence of this new theory of the significance of Scottish poetry, expounded by Aytoun and Arnold, in the changes which took place in the character of the textbook treatment of the subject. It has become customary in histories of literature in Britain and even in monographs on literature in the North to leave out of account the distinctive system of education and of culture which constituted the social background to Scottish poetry. A standard text-book treatment gradually developed which differed in the most extreme way from the approach found in the pioneer books on the subject—books like David Irvine's *Lives of the Scottish Poets* (1810) and Alexander Campbell's *Introduction to the History of Poetry in Scotland* (1798). What constituted the differentiating factors of books like these latter two was the 'preliminary dissertations on the literary history of Scotland', the aim of which was to make clear that over the development of Scottish poetry there presided a set of cultural values very different indeed from those obtaining in England, but not, on that account, inferior, and indeed having close and independent ties with the main European movement of culture, ideas and scholarship.

Let us begin with Irvine's discussion of the cultural background to literature in Scotland. He was sensitive (in a way that Campbell was not) to the Scottish weakness in Greek, and up to a point acknowledged the justice of English criticisms. 'The common practice of excluding the Greek tongue from the Grammar schools ought to be exploded as highly pernicious' to cultural standards. However, he would not like to see the rise among the Scots of the sort of exclusive devotion to classics found in England. The best thing for Scotland would be a due balance between classics and philosophy.

At the same time, Irvine insisted that the strength of the North in philosophy, history and philosophical criticism more than compensated for its weakness in philology, at any rate in comparison with the South.

> The philosophical and historical productions of Scottish authors who have flourished within the last fifty years are more generally diffused over the Continent than the similar compositions by their English contemporaries. In England, there is reason to believe philosophy has begun to languish, and productions which the English applaud in unqualified terms would in a Scottish University be rejected as nugatory.

The trouble with the English, he goes on, is that their devotion to philology perverts their philosophy.

> In the Southern universities, words are more carefully studied than things, and the effects of this plan may often be traced in the writings of their most distinguished members; an accurate knowledge of the niceties of ancient languages is often found accompanied by little study of enlarged investigation. The mere study of words is productive of no beneficial consequences. Writers who feel the conscious pride of philology are apt to treat of every subject in a trifling, if not a pedantic manner; the temporal rights and eternal concerns of mankind must be discussed like points of prosody or syntax.[8]

Irvine was noticeably inexplicit about his purpose in discussing at considerable length differences between the Northern and the Southern intellectual backgrounds in the preface to the lives of the Scottish poets. We may conjecture that he wished to reply to English criticisms of the intellectual poverty of Scottish poetry. If the English saw only shallow ideas in Scottish poetry, the reason probably was that they had notoriously peculiar notions, as compared with other nations, as to what constituted an idea profound and philosophical. On the other hand, Scottish philosophy had an international reputation, and the chief Scottish poets had been deeply influenced by it. Thus, in Irvine's account, it was noted that the three poets intermediate between Ramsay and Burns—Ross, Fergusson and Geddes—were all University men, and that Burns himself had read the common-sense philosophers with understanding. No doubt the standpoint of these poets was not philosophical by Southern standards, but perhaps in this department Southern standards were not worth much.

The other book, by Alexander Campbell, published in 1798, covered much the same ground from a somewhat different point of view. Here, too, the starting-point

8 David Irvine, Lives of the Scottish Poets, Vol. I, pp. 176–82.

was apparently the recognition that in Burns, two years dead, Scotland had produced a great poetic genius, and thus the aim of this book, like Irvine's, was to explain to the world the 'miracle' of Burns, by surveying the cultural heritage of his country and putting his work in relation to that of his predecessors. Campbell accordingly (like Irvine) wished to show that Scotland was not a barbarous country, but, being more of a naïve patriot, he gave a much less guarded account of what traditional artistic standards actually were like.

Not being very sophisticated, Campbell was, in particular, unashamed of IUs country's traditional devotion to Latin to the exclusion of Greek, and he gave an admiring account of the importance the memory of Scottish Humanism had as an inspiration and a model for the vernacular literature. We are left with the impression that just as Scottish literature since 1800 has been dominated by the image of Robert Burns, so between 1600 and 1800 the Scottish literary ideal was in a remarkably similar way identified with the career of George Buchanan. In the first place, we find whole-hearted enthusiasm for Buchanan's poetry.

> If the historian is accused of partiality, the poet stands confessed as the rival of Virgil himself in beauty and variety of description; his tragedies may bear comparison with those of Euripides, Aeschylus, or any of the ancients.[9]

What is more, this poet is also held up—in somewhat the same way as Burns—as the pattern of humanity for Scotsmen.

> Thus we see Buchanan, while yet in the flower of manhood, with a heart full of strong and voluptuous passions, the imagination of a poet, the mind of a philosopher, the craft and subtlety of a statesman—all, all buried in the humble station of a school-master.[10]

Campbell overdid things here, but it is true that literary Scots idolised the memory of Buchanan, and that at the mention of his name an unwonted enthusiasm found expression in the chill, restrained prose of men like Dugald Stewart and Sir James Mackintosh.

'The first name of that period', said the latter, 'who united elegant learning to original and masculine thought was Buchanan, and he too seems to have been the first scholar who caught from the ancients the noble flame of republican enthusiasm. This praise is merited by his neglected, though incomparable, tract *De Jure Regni* in which the principles of popular politics and the maxims of free

---

9 Alexander Campbell, Introduction to the History of Poetry in Scotland (Edinburgh, 1798), p. 7J.

10 Ibid., p. 73.

government are delivered with a precision and an energy which no former age has equalled and no succeeding has excelled.'[11]

There were no doubt many Scots who would not follow Stewart and Mackintosh in their admiration for Buchanan's liberalism, yet his quality of style and his poetic power formed a rallying point for national sentiment; accordingly, Campbell proceeded to suggest that Buchanan must have provided the Scots with a model for their verse compositions both in English and in the vernacular.

> The only apology for having detained the reader by the way is that the poetical works of Buchanan have, for upwards of two centuries, been read at our grammar schools and universities, and while our youth performed their academic exercises with diligence and attention, the art of poetry hath been greatly advanced, while perusing the work of this great master.[12]

According to Campbell, then, the cultural background of Scottish poetry comprised a combination of the Humanist tradition and of the philosophical tradition of the country.

> While the masterly compositions of Buchanan formed part of the classes in the humanity course at OUI Universities, a spirit of poetry, genuine and pure, infused itself in our general range of studies, which expanded the finer feelings of the soul, while the intellectual faculties deepened in tone. Thus, true philosophy moved on in majestic grandeur, while the muses strewed the path with sweetest flowers that led to the temple of fame, where now the names of Hutcheson, Smith and Reid appear engraven by the steady hand of truth, on the altar consecrated to science and virtue.[13]

One might be inclined to doubt Campbell's suggestion of a connection between the idolisation of Buchanan and the efforts to revive the tradition of poetry in Scots, but, in fact, it turns out that there is something to the story. There is a definite linkage between the Humanist legacy and the vernacular movement, in the sense that those scholars who did most to preserve the prestige of Buchanan as a classic text for Latin classes in Scotland were also the same men who did most to encourage the idea of the Scottish tongue as being as suitable a vehicle for classic poetry as any other modern language. It was in this spirit that the long-lived Ruddiman produced editions both of Gavin Douglas's Scots translation of the Aeneid, and of George Buchanan's works. Moreover, this tradition did not die with Ruddiman in 1757, but was alive almost a hundred years later in Dr Melvin,

---

11 Sir James Mackintosh, Vindiciae Gallicae. Miscellaneous Works (18p) p. 609.
12 Campbell, Introduction to the History of Poetry, p. 78.
13 Ibid., p. 211.

the celebrated Rector of Aberdeen Grammar School. Here, for example, is a reminiscence of Melvin by Sir William Geddes in which the persisting influence of Ruddiman is brought home.

'Melvin's acquaintance with Scottish learning was second only to his knowledge of the Latin classics, and the by-ways of Scottish classical learning interested him very much, such as the questions [both intimately associated with Ruddiman] as to the rival versions of the Psalms of Buchanan and Arthur Johnston or as to the Gavin Douglas version of the Aeneid of which he considered that Scotland might well feel proud. As regards later and more modern Scotch, it is not known that he had any special penchant beyond a perfect familiarity with Robert Burns',[14] but in his teaching he 'would light up the old poets [of Rome] with instances from Burns or Ramsay', often drawing attention to their weaknesses by comparison with the Latin poets.

Significantly enough, it is quite clear that this combined interest in Scots and Latin, far from being a provincial pedantry peculiar to Ruddiman and Melvin, was a genuine prolongation of the Humanist Renaissance spirit which cherished the patriotic ambition of bringing the vernacular up to the civilised level of classical Latin as a literary instrument. Melvin, it was pointed out, 'was more than a Grammarian: he had a refined literary taste manifested not only in Latin prose but in Latin verse, and not only in stately English but in pithy Scots'. We have it on good authority that his peculiarly classicist preoccupation with the excellence of Latin as a model arose chiefly because he was contrasting the ancient language not with modern English but with modern Scots, in the spirit of patriotic Humanism.

'Melvin's scholarship', said Hill Burton, 'did not arise from the peculiar call to the dry analysis of a dead language. He was a man of bright active intellect and fine taste; and that he should have come to use, as the tool of his intellectual activity, the language of Rome instead of that of his own country was probably incidental—possibly it may have been due to the shyness of competing in the language of England with Englishmen, which lingered long in Scotland, especially among those whose opportunities of mingling with the world happened to be limited.'[15]

As late as the eighteen-fifties, therefore, there could survive in Britain a few critics, of high intellectual culture, who did not feel at home with the modern English language, and who were still preoccupied with the Renaissance problem of the literary inadequacy of the native Scots—by this time much broken down—by comparison with classical Latin.

14 Masson, Melvin (189), pp. 91–2 (abbreviated).

15 Ibid., p. 8.

To bring out the depth and seriousness of this cultural tradition let us add to the accounts of Melvin by Geddes and Hill Burton that by David Masson. The last indeed is much more touched with the anglicising spirit than the two others, much more impressed with the idea that, in Melvin's time, Scots was as dead a language as Latin. His account will, therefore, be the less suspect of exaggeration. Modern readers will be more ready to accept from him, than they would from the more naive Geddes, the verdict that, from an intellectual and literary point of view, Melvin was quite able to hold his own with the nineteenth-century partisans of the so-called 'world languages', and that the weakness of his position was due chiefly to the overwhelming weight of external social pressure.

Unlike the generality of Scottish Classicists, Melvin was a stickler for accuracy in Latin at least, and his students at both University and School were unusually well drilled in longs and shorts. This almost English passion for dry detail was however counterbalanced by an un-English readiness to wax publicly enthusiastic about the literary quality of the poetry read, and to supply the class with critical analyses justifying this enthusiasm.

'Never did Melvin leave a passage of peculiar beauty of thought, expression or sound, without rousing us to a sense of its peculiarity, and impressing it upon us by reading the passage himself, eloquently and lovingly, so as to give effect to it. Over a line like Virgil's description of the Cyclopes working at the anvil "Illi inter sese magna vi bracchia tollunt", he would linger with real ecstasy, repeating it again and again with something of a tremble of excitement in his grave voice. Perhaps, however, it was in expounding his favourite Horace that he rose oftenest to what may be called the higher criticism. It was really beautiful to hear him dissect a passage in Horace, and then put it together again, thrillingly complete. Once or twice, he would delight us by the unexpected familiarity of an illustration of a passage in Horace by a parallel passage from Burns. The unexpected familiarity, I have called it; for, though his private friends knew how passionately fond he was of Bums, how he had his poems by heart and often on his lips, and was, moreover, learned in Scottish poetry and the old Scottish language generally, this was hardly known in the school and it startled us to hear our Rector suddenly quoting Scotch.'[16]

By Melvin's time the values of this humanist scholarship were becoming unfashionable among influential Scots; and, in consequence, Melvin was never elected to the Professorship which might have given him a platform adequate to the range of his intellectual interests. His death saw the end of the tradition,

16 Masson, Memories of Two Cities, pp. 234–70.

and indeed in his life his powers never had full scope. Melvin, however—Masson pointed out—accepted the situation, although not without some cost of 'self-repression'.

> The Melvin that we came afterwards to know in his own house and library had many tastes and interests of an intellectual kind that one could hardly have surmised in the Melvin of the Grammar School. I have already mentioned his fondness for old Scottish poetry; and I find that, as early as 1825, when he was still only undermaster in the school, he had assisted Jamieson in the preparation of the two-volume supplement to his *Dictionary of the Scottish language*, published in that year; and his services are specially acknowledged in the preface to that work. But as he kept to himself to the last, as one of his private recreations, this knowledge of Scottish philology, so, even of his Latin philology—it was but a sifting of the purest wheat that he gave to his pupils. Though, in teaching them, he drew Latin only from what he considered the wells of Latin undefiled, his own erudition was vast in the Latin literature of all styles and epochs. He had in his library, as I have said, an extra-ordinary collection of the Medieval Latinists. Then his excursion among the grammarians and in the history of modern Latinity were unknown to us. We had the results, but of the masses of material we heard but little. Of his admiration for Buchanan we were quite aware because Buchanan's psalms were amongst the books read; and the beauty of his Latinity became a subject of comment; but of Arthur Johnston, the Aberdonian, whom also Melvin admired we heard, but heard but incidentally. In all this, there must have been self-repression.[17]

To judge from Masson, one might gather that the tradition of Scottish Humanism, though still intellectually confident, had by Melvin's time, so to speak, gone underground, in the sense of being ashamed to appear in public. There is likely exaggeration here, and it is clear from other accounts that by no means all the young Aberdonians were as 'startled' to hear their Rector of the Grammar School quote Scotch or even speak Scotch as Masson. Even while making this qualification, however, one may concede that Masson's account is not altogether misleading, and one gets the general impression that a man like Melvin might be shy of revealing his enthusiastic adherence to the Ruddiman tradition before the more genteel of the boys.

Because Scottish Humanism was losing its influence even in Aberdeen by the beginning of Victoria's reign, one must not suppose that the authority of the Humanists had never been very firmly established. It seems clear that Ruddiman enjoyed a considerable prestige among the Scots-writing Scots as a fountain of critical principles, and that his edition of Gavin Douglas's *Aeneid* stimulated

---

17 Ibid.

poets to form projects of rendering in Scots the parts of Virgil left untranslated by Douglas, and of thus equipping the language to be a medium for poetic classics. Indeed there is some evidence that Robert Fergusson's unfulfilled plans to translate the *Georgies* and the *Eclogues* were due to the encouragement of the Ruddiman family.[18] It is also likely that this Ruddiman idea of emulating Gavin Douglas was the origin of the actual specimen-version of the first *Eclogue* made by Alexander Geddes, as well as of his attempts to devise a mode of spelling Scots which would eliminate somewhat the look of being a vulgarised version of English. Finally, it may be noted that the same influences may well have been active in Alexander Ross in the sense that he was a good Latinist, consciously aiming at a more serious sort of pastoral poetry in Scots.

The three men represented by literary historians like Campbell and Irvine as the immediate predecessors of Burns were therefore all influenced by the Humanist traditions of Scottish Latinity. What, it may be asked, had all this to do with Burns, who had not done much more than look at a Latin grammar? Burns encountered this Ruddiman tradition of Scottish Humanism at least in the person of the closest friend he made in his Edinburgh days, William Nicoll. Not merely was Nicoll, master at the Edinburgh High School, a connoisseur of elegant Latinity, remembered as much for his good taste as his rough brutality; but, it seems, the class he took between 1774 and 1795 was that in which Buchanan's psalms were read, and in which Ruddiman's refined critiques would be studied. This boon-companion of Burns was an active defender of the continuing force of the Scottish Humanist heritage in the Edinburgh High School, and when Alexander Adam, the headmaster, tried to supersede Ruddiman's text-books, Nicoll and the other three under-masters joined forces to oppose this departure from the general Scottish pedagogical practice, and after a ten years' struggle got the Town Council to forbid their head to replace the traditional book. Indeed, it would appear that the climax of this successful defence of Scottish Humanism coincided more or less with the publication of Burns's Kilmarnock edition, and with his first arrival in Edinburgh.

No doubt, this indirect link with the Latinists hardly constitutes Burns an heir of Scottish Humanism, but it may serve to bring out in a new way that quality of a trained intelligence which Edinburgh noted in him. On the intellectual side in particular, Burns, according to Irvine's account of his cultural inheritance, was no tyro, and he was apparently able to hold his own in philosophical argument with Dugald Stewart and the aesthetician Archibald Alison, to judge by Stewart's

18 See M. MacDiarmid's edition of the Poems of Robert Fergusson, Vol. I, pp. 34–7. See also A Choice Collection of Scots Poems edited by Walter Ruddiman, Edinburgh, 1766.

reference to an evening the three of them spent together. Indeed, David Masson shrewdly suggests that the universality of Burns's poetry, as compared with that of his immediate predecessors in the vernacular vein, derives largely from Burns's assimilation of the detached philosophic spirit of the Common Sense school. Hence Burns is arguably the heir of Scottish Philosophy, if not of Scottish Latinity.

Francis Jeffrey, in his critique of an 1808 edition of the poems, insists on the high intellectual level of Burns's social background, tracing it to the quickening effect of the Enlightenment, as popularly diffused by the educational system, on the pre-existing Presbyterian cast of mind. Jeffrey notes the remarkable extent to which young men, confined to a remote and agricultural province, were able to develop something of the same sort of intellectual and philosophical interests as the Edinburgh and Glasgow students did in their debating societies. Indeed, Jeffrey, in describing this side of Burns's background, speaks in much the same language as he used in describing before the Royal Commission his own student days:

> it is impossible to read the productions of Burns, along with his history, without forming a higher idea of the intelligence, tastes and accomplishments of our peasantry than most of those in higher ranks are disposed to entertain. … His epistles to his brother poets, in the ranks of small farmers and shopkeepers in the adjoining villages—the existence of a book-society and a debating-club among persons of that description, and many other incidental traits in his sketches of his youthful companions -all contribute to show that not only good sense and enlightened morality, but literature and a taste for speculation, are far more generally diffused in society than is commonly imagined, and that the delights and benefits of these generous and humanising pursuits are by no means confined to those whom leisure and affluence have courted to their enjoyment.

In Burns himself, these philosophical interests were well digested, and in poem after poem, their moderating influence may be detected. In particular, the accomplished, but unfortunately little noticed 'Epistle to James Tennant' has for its main theme the philosophy of common sense in its social tool as a check on the temptation to give way, in moods of despair, to the irrationalist extremes of revivalism. No doubt, to a Matthew Arnold these lively pages constitute nothing but one more essay on the dismal theme of 'Scotch Religion', but a different view is liable to be taken by men from backgrounds and countries where intellectual discipline and the fanaticism of principle are matters of serious moment.

Burns's Scottish background thus contains depths and dimensions unguessed at by Matthew Arnold, and there was for long no kind of absolute separation between the howff of the vernacular poet and the library of the classical scholar, or the commonsense philosopher.

'Heaven knows', says Masson in his essay on Melvin, 'how Aberdeen boys (of the Grammar School—Marischal College set) whom I have since seen reel-dancing magnificently as full-grown men in the Hanover Square Rooms came by the rudiments of that accomplishment. I believe it was done by many at dead of night, on creaking floors in out-of-the-way places in the Gallowgate, with scouts on the look-out for the clergy.'

In this way Burns's Scotland exhibited in some degree the same sort of exhilarating blend of the particular and the universal which Matthew Arnold himself had so much admired in the case of Dante's Tuscany, and thus, while Burns's verse-content is so often provincial and even parochial, he manages frequently to endow these local references with international interest by the disciplined energy of his art, and, as Dr Melvin himself was fond of pointing out, it is in Burns's talent for this sort of thing that his classicality resides; and the formula followed in *We'll gar our streams and burnies shine, Up wi' the best* recalls—so Melvin would say—the approach taken by Horace in his ode celebrating the Fons Bandusia. Burns's classicality, too, is presupposed in those interesting passages in which Francis Jeffrey, from a standpoint very close to that of the Melvins and the Ruddimans, insists that he was a conscious artist and a respecter of canons broken by the Romantics.

> These gentlemen are outrageous for simplicity, and we beg to recommend to them the simplicity of Burns. He has copied the spoken language of passion and affectation, with infinitely more fidelity than they have ever done, on all occasions which properly admitted of such adaptation; but he has not rejected the helps of elevated language and habitual associations.

What we have been trying to show by resurrecting and commenting on the books on Scottish poetry published by Campbell and Irvine about 1800 is that the cultural tradition behind the revival of Scottish poetry in the eighteenth century is by no means so poverty-stricken and illiberal as Matthew Arnold thought, and that, as a matter of historical fact, the 'Scotch drink, Scotch religion and Scotch manners' were liberalised (to use Jeffrey's expression) even in remote districts by a certain infusion of Scotch philosophy and Scotch Humanism. Nowadays, indeed, these distinctive currents of Scottish learning would seem to be generally passed over in the textbooks as if they were irrelevant to the subject of Scottish vernacular poetry; but, until the beginning of the present century, a man like Masson was able to keep alive the very different view of the Scottish cultural situation which we find in Irvine and Campbell, pointing out that Burns derived his 'intellectual emphasis' from 'his predecessors, the philosophers', and recalling too that the idea of Scots as a classic medium for literature was above all kept alive by the Scottish Latinists.

CHAPTER TWENTY

The Academic and the Practical Worlds

From *The Concept of a University* (1973)

KENNETH MINOGUE

This selection is taken from *The Concept of a University*, by Kenneth Minogue, 2005. Published by Transaction Publishers, London, United Kingdom. Originally published 1973.

Editors' Note

Kenneth Minogue was born in New Zealand and, having been educated in Australia, came to forge a career in English academia. He taught at the London School of Economics from 1959, where he became a Professor. He developed a distinctive profile as a combative liberal, inveighing with wit against ideologies and the incursions of the state. More positively, he defended civility and freedom and suggested that democracy had had the unwitting consequence of reducing the space for individuals to pursue their own happiness.

His book, *The Concept of a University* (from which our extract is taken), is characteristically trenchant and forthright. Its central argument, clearly apparent in the chapter here, is that there lies 'a difference of quality between the academic and practical worlds'. This thesis is opposed to the view that Minogue saw advancing in the wider world, that of 'monism' (as he termed it). Monism, in contrast to his 'two-world doctrine', 'is the belief that there is a single world of facts for man to use …' What is the difference of quality between these two worlds? The distinction lies in that, 'in the academic world, the only relevant criterion is that of truth or falsity; in practice, on the other hand, the criterion may be summed up … as effectiveness.' Minogue grants that 'it is certainly true that the truth of beliefs is very frequently of practical value' but it is not in that characteristic—their having potential practical worth—that their value lies so far as universities are concerned.

That there should be institutions that have at their centre a diligent inquiry into understanding the world, such that 'the result of academic inquiry into anything is to produce an entity different in kind from [practical concepts]' is a strange matter. Universities, accordingly, 'must be accounted a vast and unlikely achievement'. Among other things, the concept of a university calls for a pious attitude, which is ultimately 'blind to the practicalities of its own survival'. Indeed, 'practical men can subdue the academic world by infecting it with their own sense of urgency'. All these sentiments and judgements, we may feel, have a particular poignancy today.

RB

* * * * *

The central argument of this book may be encapsulated in a fable.

Imagine a clan of people who reclaim from the wilderness a large and rambling estate. They live off the garden, breed animals for food, and bequeath what they have achieved to the children. But, above all, they build a large and complex House in which they live and produce things. Each activity—from religion to recreation—sets up a Room of its own in which to grow. Those concerned with the activity of governing claim especially spacious quarters. And in addition to these various Rooms set aside for particular activities, families and individuals manage to build smaller rooms for themselves. Mostly the House is inhabited by vigorous, healthy people who are kept busy by looking after themselves, prosecuting feuds with each other, saving their souls, and keeping themselves distracted. But in the course of generations, a few people appear who like to spend much of their time trying to put together all the beliefs held in the House into one rational belief; or wondering what stars are made of, or what lies beyond the boundaries of the estate, or just poring over old records left by inhabitants now dead and gone.

In time, these people set up a Room of their own, and in exchange for helping to look after some of the young, they are left more or less undisturbed to pursue their concerns. They organize themselves and their conversations according to different rules from those prevalent in the rest of the House. They are great collectors. They make collections of funny-shaped stones; types of leaves; of the clouds they have seen or the styles of room built they make endless lists and classifications. They accumulate old coins which once were valuable for exchange, but have now been thrown away by all the other inhabitants as no longer of interest because no longer legal tender. Books written in earlier generations to amuse the other inhabitants of the House, but now regarded as tedious and old fashioned (because much of what they refer to has been forgotten), are industriously collected by the inhabitants of what comes to be called the Academic Room. These things are valued, almost perversely as it seems to their fellow-inhabitants, precisely because no one else takes an interest in them. The Academic Room sometimes looks like a kind of intellectual foundlings home, a refuge for orphaned ideas and facts no one else wants to know.

Still, the permission to set up the Academic Room, which looked at the time rather indulgent on the part of the governors, turns out to have been a wise decision. For the inhabitants of the House do recognize the value of writing and reading (skills which it is tedious to acquire, particularly for those who prefer an outdoor life and plenty of exercise) and they are vaguely impressed by the wisdom thought to be contained in a few books surviving from much earlier times. These books are, of course, only accessible to those who have learned the usage of the Academic Room. In time, further, the better class of people in the House got into the habit of sending their children to spend part of their early lives in the Academic Room. Partly, this was just a matter of fashion, and they must all keep up with each other; but partly it came to be recognized that such a period of detachment had some practical advantages. Access of wisdom was thought to accrue to the educated; and there were times when the detachment learned in the Academic Room brought perceptible advantages to the good governing of the House. More than that, the young often came out of the Academic Room capable of seeing things that the other inhabitants had ignored, and they could sometimes bring about startling effects which revolutionized the productive rooms of the House.

The House prospered, enclosed much more ground and built new wings and more specialized outhouses. Many rooms were turned over to educational purposes, but the Academic Room, partly for the extraneous reason that the better class of people tended to go there, never lost its pre-eminence. The result was that, when there came a shakeup in the House and the domestic staff demanded that they should live as well as the better established people, it became a matter of prestige that they too should spend some time in the Academic Room. On the other hand, having got into the Academic Room, many of them could not see much point to it. The conversation was a good deal less racy than what they had been accustomed to, the excitements of passionate commitment were missing, and those old coins and old fashioned books seemed like outmoded junk.

The newcomers, being brash and self-confident, attributed this situation not to their own temperamental incomprehension but to senile incompetence on the part of the long-established custodians of the Room. Being accustomed to transform everything into their own image, they demanded a shakeup, so that the Academic Room could take its proper place in the other activities of the House.

Some of them, indeed, went further. They disliked the whole notion of a House organized in terms of Rooms with different rules. They had become addicted to parties, and believed that Rooms merely encouraged an unhealthy furtiveness. Life was only life if everyone lived out in the courtyard in continuous human contact with everyone else.

What this fable suggests is that something valuable would be lost if these changes were to be made. The point of the argument which follows is to specify what that something is. In accordance with the fable, the usage of universities is presented as a 'Room' or 'world' of its own, logically as well as institutionally distinct from other kinds of thought. Academic inquiry is a manner of seeking to understand anything at all, a manner distinguished no doubt by its motives and preoccupations, but distinguished above all by a quite different logic from that of practice. This means that there is a consistent difference in the *kind* of meaning that is found in academic discourse, by contrast with that found in the world at large. To ignore this difference, and to treat universities simply as institutions which provide educational services for society is like treating a Ming vase as a cut glass flower bowl: plausible, but crass. There is an important and neglected sense in which the belief that universities are ivory towers—an image seldom invoked these days without sneer or repudiation—is precisely true. For the purposes of this argument, then, I am asserting a two-world doctrine, and what has to be contested is the view that all knowledge forms a single continuum in which only degrees of obscurity and confusion distinguish the academic from the man in the world. We may for convenience call this—the commonest view of the matter—monism.

A good deal of popularization has taught us to admire the extraordinary growth of knowledge from the time of the 'seventeenth-century revolution' onwards. Our astonishment at our own achievements has been fed by ingenious conjectural statistics, such as the one which claims that the quantity of our knowledge currently doubles about every fifteen years, or that ninety per cent of the scientists who have ever lived are living at this moment. (The actual figures in these claims vary somewhat, as well they might, but there is clearly a lot of popular life left in both notions.) Man is here recognized to be a curious animal who collects bits of knowledge the way the squirrel collects acorns. The moment the cave-dweller had a little leisure from the business of fending off mastodons and spearing supper, he traced out the paths of rivers and tried to make sense of the stars. An important part of this monist picture of human intellectual development is that knowledge and invention went hand in hand, lire and the wheel stimulating man's thought as much as maps and theories transformed his powers. Thousands of nameless martyrs must have died as men acquired a knowledge of what plants were edible and what were poisonous. Such merely empirical accumulations of fact, however, became vastly more powerful once the lore of the priests and (to a much greater extent) the systematization of the philosophers had begun to create an integrated body of knowledge. The growth of knowledge—often interrupted, as often resumed—is the main evidence (dyspeptics would sometimes add, the *only* evidence) for the doctrine of progress. And the doctrine of progress is relevant because it is much the commonest vehicle by which monism has in recent times been carried. For if all knowledge is practical, then it can help us bring about the effects we need. The more knowledge, the more control, until we may even achieve that elusive key to human evolution: the knowledge that will give us the power to control ourselves. One possible consequence of this view of the human situation is that universities become the spearhead of human salvation, and thus the repositories of the faith of many simpler people.

Monism is the belief that there is a single world of facts for man to use, and it may best be seen in intimate association with a set of related doctrine: the doctrine of progress, the theological doctrine that God gave the fruits of the earth to man for his comfort, and the commonsense view that the point of getting to know things is to control them. The discoveries made in universities are commonly thought to be pursued in order that we may cure diseases, improve education, maintain full employment and build better mousetraps. Still, it is clear that universities are different from marketplaces, and even though the monist discounts the difference, he must give some explanation of it. Many commonsense hints are at hand to help him do so. One of the most useful is the distinction between theory and practice. Universities may be seen as dealing with general thoughts which remain sterile until they are united with a purpose and thus give rise to a practical consequence. This movement of theory into the practical world is mediated by the central concept of monism: that of *application*.

Scientific knowledge is 'applied' to the world. The university graduate 'applies' what he has learned: that is to say, he combines it with the practical problem he faces in order to generate a solution. And although there is a great deal that goes on in universities which no one does apply and which It would seem very difficult to apply, there is no doubt that this concept does describe, within its limits, something real. A similar piece of apparatus used to distinguish the practical and the academic spheres is derived from the theory of decision-making: it is the distinction between ends and means. Universities deal primarily with pure theory, and application depends upon ends generated by human desires which it is no business of the universities to inquire into. For although moral philosophers are sometimes accorded some expert status in the matter of moral ends, an academically trained engineer is no more qualified than the ordinary man to decide which bridges should be built, and where they should be built; and when it comes to making a choice between avoiding unemployment and avoiding inflation, the economist must vacate the expert's platform and step democratically back into the ranks of the citizenry. Finally, this distinction is partnered by a further distinction which by virtue of its excessive currency amongst undergraduates (who seem to pick it up as toddlers learn to say 'mamma'), has acquired all the enfeebling tedium of something available without hesitation or thought: that between a fact and a value judgement. Science, as conceived monistically, is knowledge organized with all the economy and precision that a system of symbols can supply. All evaluations have been purged from it, for an evaluation either does not raise a question of truth or falsity, or raises it only in an oblique form. By the use of these distinctions all knowledge, from the wisdom of the peasant woman to the hypotheses of the physicist, may be presented as a single continuum which, if distilled out from vagueness, ambiguity and the imponderabilities of human desiring, may be legitimately considered as essentially true or false. And underlying this view of the matter we may always discover the assumption that the only serious reason for seeking to understand things is to control them.

Monism, like all plausible beliefs, may be found both in vulgar and in sophisticated forms, but any expositor will find himself fatally drawn to the vulgar forms because, being suitable for caricature, they create nice clear outlines. Monism expresses very clearly the naive utilitarianism so common among uneducated people—a utilitarianism which takes in not only science (which is the most obviously applicable form of knowledge) but also (for example) history, which is useful because it helps us to understand our 'heritage'. Monists regard history as information revealing who are the people of past times to whom we should be grateful for what we now enjoy. The study of languages is useful in the practical business of helping us get on with foreigners. Classical languages enhance our sense of style and are said to be good training for the mind, while the study of literature is a high-level inquiry into the practical business of cultural enjoyment. Knowledge is thought of as women used to be in times of arranged marriages: some destined to the fertile marriage of application to the world, the rest ending up in the regrettable spinsterdom of the academic journal. Here is a view by which the great achievement of what journalists have called 'the knowledge explosion' will be larger and more comprehensive encyclopedias, in which knowledge is laid out for enjoyment and use. There is a fairly evident continuity between John Stuart Mill's view of knowledge and the patter of the encyclopedia salesman. Monism has the further interest for our argument that it is implied by many socially radical attacks upon the twentieth-century university. Used by radicals, however, it has a special twist: whereas the ordinary monist regards knowledge as a single pool, applied or waiting its tum for application, the radical regards it as a defective pool, from which certain important areas of knowledge are missing because their presence would encourage important political and social changes. On the radical view, the dominant capitalist class in society controls the content of this pool of knowledge so as to ensure that it will not contain anything likely to incite the oppressed to overthrow the present state of society. Consequently the militant can believe that in attacking capitalism and seeking more power within the university he is liberating the academic world from political fetters, and allowing the pool of knowledge to grow more naturally in the future. Indeed, in the Marxist version of monism, theory must always be, in the strictest sense, a reflection of practice, and any other view is taken to be not merely false, but ideological mystification.

Monism, then, is the doctrine that knowledge consists of a vast structure of interlocking facts, varying in their degree of generality and in the extent of their precision, but all describing the same world in exactly the same way. Statements about tables and statements about moving electrons are ultimately translatable one into the other, since both are descriptions of the world in which we live, and any statement about H_20 is not fundamentally different from a statement about water. Monism is, in several versions, an aggressive doctrine, particularly where it becomes a criterion of what is to be regarded as knowledge. In the form of positivism, it asserts not merely that all knowledge is of the same fundamental character, but that that character is most purely exemplified in natural science. This has led on to the attempt to exhibit historical narrative as being fundamentally scientific in its logic. If scientific explanation be always taken as the conjunction in a deductive argument of statements about initial conditions and laws of nature, then the interest of the scientist is in the laws of nature, while that of the historian resides almost exclusively in the initial conditions. Positivism is also dominant in the social sciences where behaviourism, as a criterion of permissible and impermissible evidence, has long been a badge of purity.

Within the universities, monistic beliefs tend to impose upon academic inquiry narrower limits than a straightforward concern for objectivity would otherwise suggest. And although it has long flourished within universities, there are reasons for seeing it as an intellectual rather than an academic belief. It owes a good deal to the Baconian spirit in the seventeenth century, the *philosophes* in the eighteenth, and to radical criticisms of traditional institutions in the nineteenth century. Indeed we may add, somewhat speculatively, that there are some oddities and undercurrents in the mood with which monism has been espoused. For one thing, it often has a religious and messianic look about it, so that it becomes a stick with which to beat lingering survivals of occult thinking or theological presumption. It is almost as if it were a theological doctrine to the effect that God had put men on earth to compile an enormous memorandum of knowledge, and that all the libraries of the world consisted of drafts of this ultimate product. Art is acceptable within this doctrine only as a kind of oblique statement of truths. It has the effect of turning intellectuals into the vanguard of mankind, pressing on over 'the frontiers of knowledge' into the dark and uncharted territories of ignorance. We might even suggest that monism is but one more case of that favourite pastime of modem intellectuals: indulging in fantasies of leadership. Possibly because they had by the nineteenth century grown so numerous, intellectuals began to invent for themselves conceptual 'masses' whom they might lead. Many an intellectual has since made his living out of leading 'the nation'; while many others have led an even more shadowy mass called 'the proletariat'. Positivists cast themselves as the leaders of progressive mankind, and the scourge of superstition, mystification, obscurantism and other intellectual forms of sin. They turned monism (as any doctrine can be turned) into a kind of political melodrama in which they sought to spread knowledge to the ignorant and superstitious masses whose ignorance might be seen, according to taste, as a natural result of the human situation (for every marching army has its stragglers) or as the consequence of scheming priests, kings, aristocrats and other bad men who could more easily dupe the ignorant than the educated.

Much modem enthusiasm for education has been the result of hopeful speculation along these lines. It is clear that the world at large is full of lying, deceit, superstition and self-defeating brutality: men act blindly out of passion rather than far-sightedly out of the understanding which our knowledge can bring. In this way, education has become linked with a great number of idealistic projects. Many people believe that the teaching of science promotes an objective and rational approach to life; while the teaching of classics cannot help, in the view of some teachers of classics but to dispose a man away from despotism and in favour of liberty and democracy. In these and many other beliefs and projects we may see the mark of monism, of knowledge conceived as *essentially* a single realm.

By contrast with monism, I wish to recommend a dualistic doctrine which asserts a difference of quality between the academic and the practical worlds. The difficulty lies in finding a suitable basis for this distinction. It certainly cannot be based upon intelligence, for there is no doubt that we may find in practical matters the deployment of intelligence in a scale which very commonly dwarfs anything that goes on in universities. Nor can we find such a basis in emphasizing (by a perverse contrast with monism) the very uselessness of most academic discussion, for there would seem to be nothing discussed in universities which might not, in some imaginable circumstances, become useful in practice—if only by the minimal virtue of being a piece of esoteric and precious information likely to make an impression by its very rarity. Context will not help us. We are left facing the somewhat stark question: is the practical utilization of a piece of information merely an accident (as the monist would hold) or does it somehow affect the very meaning and significance of the information?

The first observation to be made about practical beliefs would seem to be that a great number of them are false. Sometimes this falsity is important in practice—as when I spoon into my coffee a white substance I have taken to be sugar but which is, in fact, arsenic. But a great many false beliefs are just as useful as true beliefs. I can navigate my way about the globe on the assumption that the earth is Hat. Faith healers cure many people of diseases which they certainly do not understand except in a very primitive way. And a great many cures of mental illnesses are effected by a body of psychiatrists who hold mutually contradictory doctrines of the nature of the mind and the illnesses that affect it. It is further the case that we are all, in practical life, environed by things that we would rather not know, and by beliefs which we choose for reasons quite other than a concern with truth: religious beliefs, for example, or the beliefs we hold because each of us is the centre of our own small world, and seeks to keep control of what may be admitted to this world. It is a truth now much canvassed among philosophers of science that there is no theory, no matter how dotty, which will not provide confirmations. From anti-semitism to astrology, confirming instances come cheap; all kinds of inconclusivenesses of evidence are seized upon, in the thinking of the practical world, to sustain what is in many cases nothing more substantial than the belief that we *wish* to hold.

This suggests an initial basis for our distinction: in the academic world, the only relevant criterion is that of truth or falsity; in practice, on the other hand, the criterion may be summed up in portmanteau fashion as effectiveness. Truth is very frequently a part of effectiveness, but by no means the only part (or indeed, in many cases, the main part). In practice, it is often worthwhile to judge a statement as mean or generous, consoling or hurtful, reactionary or progressive, helpful or harmful: academically speaking, such things are Irrelevant. If this is so, then there will be many circumstances in which it will be beside the point—'academic' is the word commonly used—to spend time arguing about the falsity of a belief which obviously serves us perfectly well.

Now a monist, confronted with this kind of argument, would concede the point with some impatience. There are indeed false beliefs (he might concede) which will produce a required effect, but they are always second best. There is always a true belief which would produce the same effect; and further, a false belief is likely to let people down when the circumstances change. Modem astronomy may not be much better than Ptolemaic for a limited bit of navigation in the Mediterranean, but it can produce a vastly greater number of intended effects than its more primitive competitors. And while faith healers do produce some inexplicable successes, their general rate of success is vastly less than that of modem doctors: further, their practical effectiveness is restricted precisely by the fact that they have so little understanding of the reality of what they are doing. This means that their skill is something static, and incapable of the cooperative development possible to modem scientific medicine. Truth, our monist would conclude, is always the fundamental test of belief.

A good deal of this may be admitted, for it is certainly true that the truth of beliefs is very frequently of practical value. This is a difficult question, and it is rendered all the more difficult by an attitude we all commonly adopt when considering it. For in thinking of cases such as that in which a person continues smoking by blotting out of his mind the evidence connecting lung cancer and smoking, we often feel that the more truth or reality there is in people's behaviour the better. Whole artistic genres are devoted to charting the miseries of those people who are 'living a lie' and to the exhilaration and nobility which results from the moment when the falsities of their lives collapse into a climax, after which protagonist and reality live happily ever after. Vast areas of life are obviously built upon deception: upon *suppressio veri* and *suggestio falsi*. Industries, like advertising and public relations, perhaps even politics, may be plausibly seen as resting upon deceit. In a perfect world—in heaven, or the classless society, according to choice—such things would no doubt disappear, and we might all lead lives of such transparency that even privacy, the evident medium in which falsities and furtivenesses thrive, would disappear forever. Here then is a moral doctrine, loosely linked to what we have called monism, which suggests that we would all be better off if the element of falsity in practical life disappeared altogether.

In order to deal with this, we need to show that there are some elements of falsity in practical life which are necessary and cannot conceivably be removed. And it is certainly the case that there is very frequently no *available* true belief on which to act. Politicians, spies and fugitives, for example, usually assume that no one is to be trusted, and this is usually false. But the true belief (that *some* people are not to be trusted) would be of little use. Hence there is at least one kind of systematic error in some practical activities—that which comes from erring on the safe side.

A further class of useful errors is constituted of those false beliefs without which we should not act at all. The human situation is such that a good deal of essential information is concealed from us because it has not yet happened: politics and marriage, the investment of money and the building of houses, not to mention the declaration of war, are among the things which sometimes lead people into saying: 'If only I had known what I was letting myself in for, I should never have started.' Without this human propensity to act upon inadequate or quite false information, human life would be vastly different. There are also times when the false belief is the product of the passion of the present moment: a little rational reflection would bring home to anyone that a crucial belief on which an action depends is false, but the moment for that rational reflection has not yet come. Any number of heroic acts are performed in the belief that the bullet won't hit me, or that the collective act of heroism performed by our unit, or our class, or our contemporaries, will shine imperishably in the annals of humanity. Most such beliefs are false, and posterity is too busy living its own imperishable moments to have much time for saving the moments of most of its ancestors from perishing. Human beings, as the poet said, and as we hardly need telling in this century, can bear very little reality.

These considerations suggest to us that one of the primary distinctions between the academic and the practical worlds rests upon the simplest and most luminous of facts: that in a university, no one has to come to a conclusion upon which a decision must be based. A don can afford the luxury of allowing the evidence to dictate quite precisely what conclusion he will come to, and dons do, in fact, spend a great deal of their time explaining the reasons why nothing very substantial in the way of conclusions is possible. Further, even if he does come to a conclusion, any academic will soon find that it has not been locked away in the monist's grand encyclopedia as another bit of knowledge in humanity's upward climb, but that it sits astride an unstable mass of evidence which new young dons are likely to revise. In the academic world, conclusions simmer together with the evidence, and there is no paint at which they can ever be detached from it. In the practical world, on the other hand, conclusions often long outlive the evidence for them. Decisions have to be taken and minds made up. This must generally be done on what are, in academic terms, inadequate grounds. There is about the taking of decisions in the practical world an irredeemable element of improvization which renders it necessarily, not contingently, subject to error. And it is the vast achievement of establishing universities as institutions to have created conditions of life in which this constant practical pressure towards the botched or best available conclusion has been neutralized.

We have so far developed this argument with a rather simple-minded conception of truth: we have taken it to be a matter of propositions which correspond or do not correspond to the facts. A good deal of the plausibility of arguments on all philosophical questions depends upon the examples chosen. We are led in rather different directions according as we focus our minds either on 'Napoleon died in 1821' and 'water boils at 100 degrees centigrade at sea level' on the one hand, or the Heisenberg uncertainty principle or the destructiveness of the Thirty Years War on the other. In practical life, we settle for concepts which are 'near enough' and it is pedantic to make them any more precise. Practical discourse is made up of categories like friend, 'enemy', '£10 tenant', 'communist', 'good to eat', 'ripe for revolution' and the like. These are notions riddled with imprecision and often dependent upon variations of personal taste. Practical concepts frequently combine a description with an attitude towards the thing described. Furthermore, these distinctions—the way in which the infinitely divisible fabric of reality is grasped—depend upon our interests and our passions, or, in the more pompous terminology currently fashionable, upon our social and cultural orientation. Different cultures and times, different categories; and this instability is intensified by an incessant responsiveness to changing circumstances. But clearly such semantic circumstances are not suitable to the growth of science, and the problem which immediately arises is the following: is it the case that technical terminology is to practical language what surgery is to butchery? Or is it rather that the development of understanding steadily produces more serious asymmetrics between the academic and the practical than merely degree of precision?

This is clearly one of the central questions of philosophy. It is the question answered in Platonic terms by the distinction between the unstable opinion of the practical world, *doxa*, and the reasoned and organized concepts which made up what Plato called *episteme*. The distinction between a theory and a model, and the relation of both to what they purport to explain, is a modem version of similar preoccupations. Our concern is a limited one, and the view I wish to support is that the result of academic inquiry into anything is to produce an entity different in kind from the practical concept with which the inquiry began. A historian like Professor Holt begins with one Magna Carta, the ancestor of civil rights, and ends up with a view of the complicated events of the thirteenth century so very different from the popular legend that we may legitimately regard it as a different thing altogether. A scientist, starting with the projectiles which are fired from cannons, ends up with an elaborate theory of the mathematics of curves. The literary historian who, as a child, read *Gulliver's Travels* as an adventure story, uncovers a political and allegoric content by looking more closely at it in relation to Swift's life and the history of the period in which he lived. It is a common popular belief, prevalent in the practical world, to regard as 'the same thing' whatever has the same name, and to regard all such 'names' as if they were fundamentally descriptions of the real world. This tendency gives rise to the type of popular paradox typified by such statements as that a table is 'really' just a swarm of electrons. On the argument I am presenting, the world is very much more complicated and varied than this popular view would suggest, and there are very much more complicated relations between 'theory' and 'the world' than those of description. Indeed, a great deal of what must academically be regarded as the 'nonsense of the practical world' arises from taking as straightforward description academic constructions which have a much more oblique relation to what we think we see and hear. Here, in the illusion that all theory ultimately describes, we may find the epistemology upon which the monist's key concept of application rests—whatever does not fit this theory must be relegated to an inferior realm: fantasy, nonsense, advocacy or justification. It is this inferior realm which is populated with the logical *untermenschen* known as value judgements.

Monism is wrong in suggesting that the only relations between academic theory and what may popularly be called 'the real world' are those of description and application. When practical entities are taken up by academics they evolve into quite different things: they belong now in propositions which are fundamentally hypothetical and subject to ceaseless modification; they may be challenged and changed according to rules of manipulation different from those of practice, and the result is that they no longer fit the practical world. A similar change happens with the reverse traffic of academic materials being taken over for use in the practical world. Such a transfer is always merely of fragmentary parts of the academic world. The academically hypothetical becomes the technologically assumed, and the academic giving practical advice turns into a completely different kind of figure called an 'expert'. Politicians are prone to ransack books of anthropology for statements which appear to support the political position they have already taken up on the race question. Plato's notion of the philosopher king is from its author's text untimely ripp'd to support the pretensions of some ambitious elite. But thus severed, these notions resemble the coral in tropical seas, full of colour and fascination in the water, but grey and dull out of it. These are simply two kinds of adventures that may happen to ideas—in the one case, a movement towards understanding, in the other, a use for the purpose of changing the world or, what at this level of abstraction is the same thing, the prevention of change.

It is significant to note that the uses made of academic ideas in the practical world are not academically corrigible. A politician who has just made a successful use of the legend of Magna Carta in a political speech is unlikely to be very concerned if an academic comes up to him later to explain that that famous document signified something very different from the guarantee of civil liberty which had featured in the politician's speech. What interests the politician is the fact that Magna Carta is (marginally) still extant on the statute books, and that everyone in his audience will be familiar with a melodrama in which King John features as a bad king brought to book by (more or less) liberty-loving barons. An American politician in similar circumstances may well use Patrick Henry's famous statement: 'Give me liberty or give me death!' In both cases, the practical use of these historical reminiscences takes for granted that King John, the barons, and Patrick Henry were people like us, and meant the same thing by the same words. Rap Brown, in providing a Black version of this particular bit of the American legend: 'I say to America: Fuck it. Freedom or Death!', takes the legend for granted. A historian, on the other hand, will end up by treating such legends as Hollywood History: the belief that the past consists of men like us, in fancy dress.[1] And the more the historian washes our twentieth-century preoccupations out of the legend, in order to discover in its own context what was meant (in our examples) by liberty, and what was involved in the demand for judgement by peers, the less these episodes, as historically understood, have to do with the conflicts of the present time. But it is clear that in investigating these historical events and therefore, it might seem, destroying the legend, the historian is in no way attacking liberty or civil rights. The most plausible conclusion, then, would seem to be that the Magna Carta of legend is a quite different thing from the Magna Carta of the twelfth-century historian, a difference masked, as so often, by the fact that the same name covers both. And the situation grows even more complicated if we bring in the idea of Magna Carta as it affected English political ideas in the seventeenth century—an idea different from both those we have considered. In the case of a name like 'the Battle of the Boyne' we find a variety of both practical and historical events. Now it is perfectly possible to insist, with brutalist common sense, that these are simply different versions or interpretations of 'the same things'; but when it is impossible to give any account of that 'same thing' which is not also an interpretation; and when the logic of the concept as it appears in practical and in academic contexts is quite different, then it is difficult to see what is gained by this insistence on the misleadingly obvious. What is achieved is to make us the dupes of the unreflective monism embedded in some of our linguistic practices.

Our intellectual situation would appear to be such, then, that we are faced with a dilemma. For in the case of Magna Carta we find that the politician cannot use the concept unless it is anachronistic, while the historian cannot use it if it is. More generally, we have the alternative of being academic and ineffective (or irrelevant, as the term goes today) or, alternatively, practical and if not false at least

1 Intellectual historians, following Professor Butterfield, commonly refer to such legends as 'Whig History'.

unacademic. Here is a fork which, while commonly recognized in all the pejorative uses of the word 'academic', is nevertheless concealed from us by the fact that language contains vastly fewer names than concepts. Further, it would simply be a misunderstanding on his part if our monist were to counter this argument by asserting that the more truth there is in the teaching of history the better, since history has often been used in the past to reinforce unpleasantly nationalist or racialist emotions. For it is clear that what the monist seeks in this respect is not 'real history' (which teaches nothing practical to anyone) but a history seeming to encourage different moral opinions: less of 'Death to the French!' and more of 'Kameradschaft. This may well be desirable, but it is certainly not the replacement of 'false' history by true.

The cognitive dilemma, by which we are faced with a choice between being academic and ineffective, or practical and effective, makes it clear that universities must be accounted a vast and unlikely achievement. For the constant pressure of practice is such that only a set of most unusual contingencies occurring together could possibly have permitted such an institution to come into existence and to entrench itself in such organizational ways as to survive for centuries. And the paradoxical result has been, of course, an enormous boost in practical power; for the world happens to be the sort of place in which the free movement of disinterested inquiry allows the mind to arrive at places which suggest practical expedients which could not be directly approached. It required monastic attitudes, a tradition of corporate association deriving from the politics of Europe an enthusiasm for a past culture, not to mention the resourcefulness of concrete individuals, to bring universities into existence. And as one of the remoter consequences of their durability we may cite the infinite patience and skill with which archaeologists dig to recapture not treasure but the lost pas: of mankind—one of the many ways in which the academic tradition has given to Western civilization a unique place in the achievements of mankind.

It might seem that, in using historical examples I have been choosing particularly favourable ground for the argument I wish to present. It will be argued that in technology we do find a precise example of academic propositions being applied. But this would not be true. Science consists of a vast structure of hypotheses, with a good deal of interlocking, which scientists both develop by logic and imagination and test by experiment. It is an ever-changing world in which those theories which are currently accepted must be assumed liable to revision in the light of future work. Although we do, of course, recognize that 'in practice' many things have been 'Scientifically proven', this is in strict terms a vulgar expression, since proof is only properly applicable to logic and mathematics (and in a different sense, law) while scientific hypotheses may have strong Support but can never be regarded as necessary truths. No part of science can safely be regarded as beyond revision, if for no other reason than that each part IS affected by the changing context in which it must always be construed. And while scientists do often make confident judgements about what they is indubitable, they are also prone in their general behaviour to recognize just this kind of tentativeness. But this view of science is not, of course, the view taken in unsophisticated writing. The vulgar opinion is that science is a glare of findings surrounded by a penumbra of doubtful hypotheses, and scientists, like men clearing a field, steadily produce greater numbers of increasingly reliable propositions. Now if we inquire how it is that so erroneous a view of science has become so current, the answer in our terms is perfectly clear: the general public have mistaken for science a set of propositions which (though often identical in notation) are essentially practical. As with Magna Carta, two things have been taken to be one. In the case of science, tentative propositions logically and experimentally linked to other assertions similarly tentative, have been confused with the assertions—isolated from a context of inquiry and regarded as certain—which serve as the basis for action. The Western World has seen a succession of cosmologies in which the system of Ptolemy was superseded by that of Newton, and that of Newton by Einstein. But popular opinion has taken each in turn as the final pronouncement of science, popularizers have developed 'philosophies' on the same assumption, and practical men have produced effects, often very complex and successful effects, by taking for granted this or that fragment of a complex scientific system. In other words, an apparently scientific proposition when used in technology must be construed differently: it is taken as certain (which it cannot be in science) and it is sundered from a much more complex system in association with which it is scientifically to be understood.

The situation is the same, let it be added, in philosophy, which provides a special kind of rational explanation of the world we live in, but does not, and cannot, legislate about our practical concerns. If it appears to do so, then we may be certain that the legislation is not philosophy, even though it may superficially resemble it in verbal construction. Aristotle, for example, argued in the *Politics* that some men are by nature slaves, and this scandalous opinion has provoked a good deal of unease among his liberal commentators. It has vulgarly been taken as Aristotle's 'justification' of the Athenian practice. But Aristotle is simply saying that the common practice of slavery is not rationally inexplicable, and that some people are more suited to obedience than others. But what he does not say, and could not philosophically say, is that in any particular society men ought to institute slavery legally. There is no logical contradiction in accepting Aristotle's argument on slavery and supporting political democracy -indeed there are respects in which Aristotle did this himself.

The distinction between the practical and the academic worlds is exemplified in the difference between a phrase book and a grammar book. Phrase books are quick and effective, and they are based upon what experience shows to be the most commonly used words and idioms. To master a phrase book is to learn a language after the manner in which a child learns it. And as this example shows, it is by no means the case that someone who has mastered a phrase book is limited to the mechanical repetition of phrases about the pen of my aunt and the demeanour of the coachman. A little ingenuity will generate an infinite number of further possible sentences out of the phrase book, according to the skill of the user. A grammar book, on the other hand, is an analysis of the language, and the fact that grammar is not central to speaking is shown by the fact that it is taught to children who already have a fluent mastery of their language. Thereby they learn not to do the right thing, but to know why it is the right thing. A grammar book begins, of course, as a description and analysis of an actually spoken language, but in time it comes to act as a criterion of how that language ought to be spoken. It is often the case that to learn grammar is the soundest and most reliable way of learning a language; but there are other ways of doing so, and it is not uncommon to find someone who has an excellent mastery of the grammar but has difficulty in making himself understood. Further, an understanding of grammar, though it is slow and indirect eventually supplies a mastery of the language, along with its past and its possibilities, which cannot be found in the phrase book. Phrase books depend upon current practice, and therefore go out of date very quickly. Each has its advantages, each its limitations. But the grammar book, in being the paradigm of a form of learning which has its own inherent order and rationality independent of relevance and usage, exemplifies the education of the schools, while the phrase book which is responsive to what pupils wish to learn and to what is currently going on in society, is equally the paradigm of that useful learning to which we must all devote so much of our time.

There is obviously a good deal of traffic between the academic and the practical worlds: they are, after all, merely abstractions, and any academic will imaginatively participate in both. But as a proposition moves from the one world to the other, it will suffer certain significant changes. An academic theory will lose its hypothetical character and tum into a practical assumption: something taken for granted. A philosophical argument (which is a form of explanation) will turn into a justification (whose business is to defend, not to explain). Practical concepts are vague, fluid and at the mercy of their connotation; but they appear in propositions generally much more dogmatically asserted than in the academic world. Academic discourse, by contrast, tends to dissolve concepts into simpler and harder entities which may be more playfully entertained. To wonder about a concept, which is a form of playing with it, is one of the commonest gates from the one world into the other. Most beliefs are, as it were, locked firmly into place and pinned down by the practical purposes they serve. And what is irrelevant to these purposes is, by practical men, correctly dismissed as 'academic'. Everything academic began its life in the practical world, however remotely; and from the academic world, by a process of simplification, comes a stream of suggestions, assumptions, ideas to be used and abused, manners of viewing problems, and a host of other things which are indeed useful, but not in the direct form of 'application' imagined by the monist. Understanding and control must be recognized as different kinds of human activity. An interest in control focuses our mind upon what is relevant to the purpose we have in hand, while he who understands is able to follow the contours of the world as it is with a freedom unknown to the man who seeks control. We have already seen that the academic world grew out of religion, and religion very commonly adopts an attitude of piety towards at least some parts of the world. To try to control or manipulate (certain aspects of) God's handiwork is an impiety. The academic world would seem to have inherited this kind of piety with regard to everything that exists. It renounces passionate involvement, as did its monkish ancestors, and gets in return a freedom to roam wherever its inclination leads.

It should be clear from this argument that any distinction between the academic and the practical world in terms of fact and value is blind to certain crucial features of our knowledge. It is certainly true that evaluation is a practical business; but the practical world includes also the vast descriptive apparatus by which we make our way in the world. The moment a practical purpose lights up the world, what is illuminated has a different character from what the academic studies: we are back in Plato's cave. The most easily accessible logic of practice is that which has been studied since the time of the Sophists as rhetoric, for in the behaviour of speakers before courts and political assemblies we may observe a logical design which is too conspicuously directed towards the end of persuasion to be mistaken for scientific inquiry. But to concentrate our attention upon rhetoric is to notice only a small part of practice. A very large number of the beliefs we espouse are designed not to contribute to discovery, but to identify ourselves (both to ourselves and others) as members of some admirable moral class. The membership of such moral classes is not at all a hypothesis which we seriously are prepared to discuss in terms of the evidence available. We commonly formulate the moral class in such a way as to protect ourselves from evidence that might refute, and we are constantly aware of confirming, instances. Furthermore, should anyone choose to deny the moral identification we have made, it is very seldom the result of a disinterested passion, but commonly in response to some practical impulse of his own. Practical discourse is full of vagueness, vacuity, 'metaphysical' elevation, dogmatism (the logical form of shouting) and equivocation: and it is difficult to see how else people could carry on—even though precisely these devices may also be recognized as leading people into unhappiness. Philosophers of science these days commonly distinguish scientific theories from other kinds of intellectual production in terms of refutability. This is a logical criterion: but it may also plausibly be seen as a moral one. For it demands that the framer of scientific (and indeed any kind of academic) hypotheses is under an obligation to take the risk of being refuted by the evidence. He must not take refuge in the 'monster-barring' and 'concept-stretching' stratagems by which we all defend ourselves in practical life.[2] This has tempted some expositors of the academic world into the belief that it is *morally* distinct from—indeed, superior to—the practical: that in the practical world, men seek the security of moral commitment and entrench themselves behind absolutes, while the academic adventures freely wherever the evidence may take him. What academic could fail to be tempted by such an opinion? He is so often presented as belonging to a class of sedentary and prudent men that the opportunity to appear as a hero is not to be lightly brushed aside. Nevertheless, it should be remembered that the advancing of theories has its practical side, and that an academic who has advanced a hypothesis has sunk a certain amount of his identity into it. In such situations, every academic becomes familiar with the stratagems of moral trench-warfare.

For so long as we fail to recognize the duality of the academic and the practical worlds, we shall connive at a situation in which each bullies the other. The practical man has his own criteria of what is worth doing, and seeks from academics whatever may help him in his designs; monism is current in part because it is necessary to facilitate this kind of bullying. On the other hand, academics—or rather those familiar with the academic world who are in love with reason and are therefore often called rationalists—tend to believe that any human activity which is not the outcome of an explicit theory must be the result of blind impulse, and can only be improved if it is superseded by a 'theory' of its own. Graduates often come down from universities filled with a missionary zeal to see the standards of objectivity and impartiality they have learned at the university transform the world.

Still, there is no doubt that it is practicability which seeks to subdue the academic world, while any appearance to the contrary must be seen as a form of practicality using the occasionally influential garb of learning. Since it is a characteristic of the academic world to be blind to the practicalities of its own survival-indeed, to any practicalities at all-practical men can subdue the academic world by infecting

2 Stratagems described by Professor Imre Lakatos, *Criticism and the Growth of Knowledge*, London 1970.

it with their own sense of urgency! For urgency is the demand that a conclusion must be arrived at within a limited time, and is an infallible indicator of practical concerns. Urgency has often influenced academic preoccupations by means of a confusion between two kinds of 'problem', one practical, and the other academic.

Everyone is familiar with a collection of 'World Problems' or 'Great Issues of Our Time' which circulate like punchdrunk boxers through the magazine sections of the quality press; world population increase, the effect of chemicals upon the balance of nature, world government, pollution, the two cultures and the affluence gap are current examples. All of these, being practical problems, are of no academic interest whatsoever. The reason why world population is going up very fast is no mystery at all; nor is there any mystery about some of the conditions which would slow it down. The only difficulty is the entirely practical matter of how to bring some sufficient set of these conditions about, and it is only a problem for people who are interested in trying to do so. If there are interesting academic problems, they will be about genetics, or human behaviour, and thus only tangentially related to such a world problem as the 'population explosion'.

This particular implication of the distinction I am recommending will seem paradoxical to some readers and outrageous to others. For, it will be said, any of these problems might in time lead to the disappearance of human life from the earth; at the very least to its violent impoverishment. What will then become of universities? The answer is, no doubt, that if these predictions are correct then universities will disappear along with everything else human. The point, however, is that the survival of universities is not an academic concern of universities. It is, of course, an important practical concern, and it deserves attention in practical terms. But such practical responsibility does not exist in the academic world. That is indeed precisely one of its greatest attractions.

The fact that a problem is urgent, then, will be the clearest sign we can have that it is a practical problem; and as a practical problem it will be quite distinct from an academic one. Medically, the problem of cancer is two problems: a practical problem because we all want to cure the thousands who die of the disease, and a medical problem—or, rather, cluster of problems—about the behaviour of cells. It happens in this case that a solution to the academic problem may be a precondition of a solution to the practical problem: at least, this is a plausible way of looking at it. It might happen, of course, that someone might stumble across a cure for cancer, highly effective but quite mysterious. Or research might discover an explanation that did not help in curing. In the case of a cure without understanding, the practical problem would virtually have ceased, except perhaps for a certain amount of residual anxiety that the cures might merely be flukes, and that until the academic problem had been solved—i.e., until doctors worked out some idea of *why* the cure was a cure—then there would be a considerable possibility of relapse. It seems very commonly to happen in our civilization that practical problems and academic problems are to be found in clusters, and that academics may legitimately employ huge research facilities in groping with academic problems on which hinge practical matters of great weight. This has often been a fortunate circumstance for academics, as It means that social and financial support is available for what otherwise would have had to be left to one side. But it is an unfortunate circumstance in that it often leads academics to become merely research agents of practical concerns like the government, with the consequence that the coherence of academic work is impaired by the intrusion of practical concerns.

The remoteness of academic from practical concerns must be regarded not as a surviving tradition from less enlightened days, but an essential condition of the maintenance of the academic world. The practical world is one we cannot help living in, but the academic world requires special cultivation, and did not come into existence in any significant form until quite recent times. And the condition of its survival is that it should be isolated from the essentially practical task of taking decisions. In the world of practical responsibilities decisions must be taken; and if there isn't enough Information for a sound decision then a decision is risked and the fingers are crossed. But the essential concern of the academic world is with the cogency of evidence: what the evidence will suggest and what the evidence will support. Academics are, as a matter of fact, frequently turning away from the substantial issue of their discussion to consider just how far they are entitled by what they know to arrive at a conclusion. This habit of mind is peculiarly irritating if urgent questions are at stake.

It might seem that the argument that I am presenting is simply the recommendation of a remote ideal having connection either with what happens or with what is possible. There is certainly plenty of discussion suggesting that universities must modernize themselves and play their 'proper' part in society. Such discussion might persuade some readers that my description of the academic world is, if possibly desirable in some vague way, nonetheless entirely out of touch with modem realities. All that needs to be said here is that I am describing the character of a good deal of the work which is actually carried on in universities today. Much else, of course, happens in universities, much of it practical. It is exactly this 'much else' which is threatening to transform the academic world. Universities find themselves subject to government pressures and to demands that their research facilities be used in cooperation with industry. Student militants exert another kind of practical pressure. Each of these unacademic groups wants to change the universities, and each of them presents what it wants as if it were reform. Meanwhile, dons themselves are weakened by the lure of money, fame and power: all practical objectives and mightily desirable.

Some element of compromise on these matters seems eminently possible. The people who live in the academic world are, in addition to being dons, also citizens, fathers, mortgagees: they play most of the parts of modem men. It has recently been much less the case that universities are places of refuge for suitable men of a wayward, eccentric and wondering disposition. Further, it is perfectly possible for some academics to live happily in both worlds—capable of bringing their intellectual skills to bear on practical tasks without allowing this to begin colouring their vision of their academic work. But it takes a clear head, not to mention talents not universal regarded as the apex of advanced education. Consequently everyone wants to share in a university education, and many are commonly disappointed with what they find. It cannot be too highly emphasized that the distinction between the academic and the practical worlds is not a matter of status. It would be absurd to say that either was superior to the other. The only person who would try and say so would be someone who imagined that the academic world was fine and spiritual, while the practical world was vulgar and materialistic. Such a view would be a total misunderstanding of the distinction I am advancing. The practical world as I have presented it is not simply a place for supplying the material necessities of civilization; it includes, as well, man's preoccupation with the salvation of his soul, and the survival of humanity as well as the values of love and friendship.

Here then is a restatement of a common distinction between the academic and the practical worlds, a distinction which is embodied in the popular attitudes that recognize that academics are very commonly inferior practitioners, and that young men straight down from the universities, with theory pouring out of their ears, have a great deal of unlearning to do before they can become effective doctors, engineers or businessmen. It is a distinction which has to be made, now, in elaborate terms. For on my reading of the situation, the Academic Room in the House has become crowded with a new collection of people who do not quite understand what the point of the Room is. They are half impressed by what they have found, but a little baffled also. It is as if they had taken diamonds of thought for bits of shiny glass, and classical texts for yesterday's weekend reviews. They believe that the Room is out of date and in need of a shakeup. If they get their way, they will have made the Academic Room indistinguishable from the rest of the House.

PART THREE

The American (Pragmatist) Tradition

CHAPTER TWENTY-ONE

The Place of the University in Modern Life

From *The Higher Learning in America: A Memorandum on the Conduct of Universities by Business Men* (1918)

THORSTEIN VEBLEN

This is an abridged version of Chapter 1 (incorporating the first three sections of six) that serves as the Introduction to *The Higher Learning in America: A Memorandum on the Conduct of Universities by Business Men*. Published in 1918, by B. W. Huebsch, New York, NY.

Editors' Note

Thorstein Veblen was an economist and one of the leaders of the 'institutional economics' within the history of economic thought, a movement that believe in the role of institutions in shaping economic behavior in including the role of law. (New institutional economics is a recent variant). Veblen was strongly influenced by Darwin's theory of evolution, by Marx, the German historical school that rejected the individual as a unit of analysis, and pragmatism (especially Peirce). Veblen is famous for his book, *The Theory of the Leisure Class* (1899) that coins the tern 'conspicuous consumption' defined in terms of spending more money on goods than they are worth. Veblen's key insight and analysis of American universities is that they have overrun by business values that have corrupted underlying spiritual and intellectual values. He considers business values and 'accountability' are inimical to academic values. 'Disciplining' the university by market principles is seen to be antithetical to the central values of the university. Veblen offered an insightful cultural-institutional critique and line of criticism of universities almost one hundred years that has been the basis of a deafening chorus from critics across the political spectrum ever since.

MP

*****

I

In any known civilization there will be found something in the way of esoteric knowledge. This body of knowledge will vary characteristically from one culture to another, differing both in content and in respect of the canons of truth and reality relied on by its adepts. But there is this common trait running through all civilizations, as touches this range of esoteric knowledge, that it is in all cases held, more or less closely, in the keeping of a select body of adepts or specialists—scientists, scholars, savants, clerks, priests, shamans, medicinemen—whatever designation may best fit the given case.

In the apprehension of the given society within which any such body of knowledge is found it will also be found that the knowledge in question is rated as an article of great intrinsic value, in some way a matter of more substantial consequence than any or all of the material achievements or possessions of the community. It may take shape as a system of magic or of religious beliefs, of mythology, theology, philosophy or science. But whatever shape it falls into in the given case, it makes up the substantial core of the civilization in which it is found, and it is felt to give character and distinction to that civilization.

In the apprehension of the group in whose life and esteem it lives and takes effect, this esoteric knowledge is taken to embody a systematization of fundamental and eternal truth; although it is evident to any outsider that it will take its character and its scope and method from the habits of life of the group, from the institutions with which it is bound in a web of give and take. Such is manifestly the case in all the historic phases of civilization, as well as in all those contemporary cultures that are sufficiently remote from our everyday interests to admit of their being seen in adequate perspective. A passably dispassionate inquiry into the place which modern learning holds in modern civilization will show that such is also the case of this latest, and in the mind of its keepers the most mature, system of knowledge. It should by no means be an insuperably difficult matter to show that this "higher learning" of the modern world, the current body of science and scholarship, also holds its place on such a tenure of use and wont, that it has grown and shifted in point of content, aims and methods in response to the changes in habits of life that have passed over the Western peoples during the period of its growth and ascendancy. Nor should it be embarrassingly difficult to reach the persuasion that this process of change and supersession in the scope and method of knowledge is still effectually at work, in a like response to institutional changes that still are incontinently going forward.[1]

To the adepts who are occupied with this esoteric knowledge, the scientists and scholars on whom its keeping devolves, the matter will of course not appear in just that light; more particularly so far as regards that special segment of the field of knowledge with the keeping and cultivation of which they may, each and several, be occupied. They are, each and several, engaged on the perfecting and conservation of a special line of inquiry, the objective end of which, in the view of its adepts, will necessarily be the final and irreducible truth as touches matters within its scope. But, seen in perspective, these adepts are themselves to be taken as creatures of habit, creatures of that particular manner of group life out of which their preconceptions in matters of knowledge, and the manner of their interest in the run of inquiry, have sprung. So that the terms of finality that will satisfy the adepts are also a consequence of habituation, and they are to be taken as conclusive only because and in so far as they are consonant with the discipline of habituation enforced by that manner of group life that has induced in these adepts their particular frame of mind.

Perhaps at a farther remove than many other current phenomena, but none the less effectually for that, the higher learning takes its character from the manner of life enforced on the group by the circumstances in which it is placed. These constraining circumstances that so condition the scope and method of learning are primarily, and perhaps most cogently, the conditions imposed by the state of the industrial arts, the technological situation; but in the second place, and scarcely less exacting in detail, the received scheme of use and wont in its other bearings has its effect in shaping the scheme of knowledge, both as to its content and as touches the norms and methods of its organization. Distinctive and dominant among the constituent factors of this current scheme of use and wont is the pursuit of business, with the outlook and predilections which that pursuit implies. Therefore any inquiry into the effect which recent institutional changes may have upon the pursuit of the higher learning will necessarily be taken up in a peculiar degree

1 An inquiry of this kind has been attempted elsewhere: Cf. *The Instinct of Workmanship*, chapter vii, pp. 321–340; "The Place of Science in Modern Civilization", *American Journal of Sociology*. Vol. XI (March, 1906), pp. 585–609; "The Evolution of the Scientific Point of View," University of California Chronicle (1908), Vol. X, No. 4, pp. 395–416.

with the consequences which an habitual pursuit of business in modern times has had for the ideals, aims and methods of the scholars and schools devoted to the higher learning.

The Higher Learning as currently cultivated by the scholars and scientists of the Western civilization differs not generically from the esoteric knowledge purveyed by specialists in other civilizations, elsewhere and in other times. It engages the same general range of aptitudes and capacities, meets the same range of human wants, and grows out of the same impulsive propensities of human nature. Its scope and method are different from what has seemed good in other cultural situations, and its tenets and canons are so far peculiar as to give it a specific character different from these others; but in the main this specific character is due to a different distribution of emphasis among the same general range of native gifts that have always driven men to the pursuit of knowledge. The stress falls in a somewhat obviously different way among the canons of reality by recourse to which men systematize and verify the knowledge gained; which is in its turn due to the different habituation to which civilized men are subjected, as contrasted with the discipline exercised by other and earlier cultures.

In point of its genesis and growth any system of knowledge may confidently be run back, in the main, to the initiative and bias afforded by two certain impulsive traits of human nature: an Idle Curiosity, and the Instinct of Workmanship.[2]

In this generic trait the modern learning does not depart from the rule that holds for the common run. Men instinctively seek knowledge, and value it. The fact of this proclivity is well summed up in saying that men are by native gift actuated with an idle curiosity,—"idle" in the sense that a knowledge of things is sought, apart from any ulterior use of the knowledge so gained.[3] This, of course, does not imply that the knowledge so gained will not be turned to practical account. In point of fact, although the fact is not greatly relevant to the inquiry here in hand, the native proclivity here spoken of as the instinct of workmanship will unavoidably incline men to turn to account, in a system of ways and means, whatever knowledge so becomes available. But the instinct of workmanship has also another and more pertinent bearing in these premises, in that it affords the norms, or the scheme of criteria and canons of verity, according to which the ascertained facts will be construed and connected up in a body of systematic knowledge. Yet the

---

2 Cf. The Instinct of Workmanship and the State of the Industrial Arts, ch.i and pp. 30–45, 52–62, 84–89.

3 In the crude surmises of the pioneers in pragmatism this proposition was implicitly denied; in their later and more advisedly formulated positions the expositors of pragmatism have made peace with it.

sense of workmanship takes effect by recourse to divers expedients and reaches its ends by recourse to varying principles, according as the habituation of workday life has enforced one or another scheme of interpretation for the facts with which it has to deal.

The habits of thought induced by workday life impose themselves as ruling principles that govern the quest of knowledge; it will therefore be the habits of thought enforced by the current technological scheme that will have most (or most immediately) to say in the current systematization of facts. The working logic of the current state of the industrial arts will necessarily insinuate itself as the logical scheme which must, of course, effectually govern the interpretation and generalizations of fact in all their commonplace relations. But the current state of the industrial arts is not all that conditions workmanship. Under any given institutional situation,—and the modern scheme of use and wont, law and order, is no exception, workmanship is held to a more or less exacting conformity to several tests and standards that are not intrinsic to the state of the industrial arts, even if they are not alien to it; such as the requirements imposed by the current system of ownership and pecuniary values.

These pecuniary conditions that impose themselves on the processes of industry and on the conduct of life, together with the pecuniary accountancy that goes with them—the price system have much to say in the guidance and limitations of workmanship. And when and in so far as the habituation so enforced in the traffic of workday life goes into effect as a scheme of logic governing the quest of knowledge, such principles as have by habit found acceptance as being conventionally salutary and conclusive in the pecuniary conduct of affairs will necessarily leave their mark on the ideals, aims, methods and standards of science and those principles and scholarship. More particularly, standards of organization, control and achievement, that have been accepted as an habitual matter of course in the conduct of business will, by force of habit, in good part reassert themselves as indispensable and conclusive in the conduct of the affairs of learning. While it remains true that the bias of workmanship continues to guide the quest of knowledge, under the conditions imposed by modern institutions it will not be the naive conceptions of primitive workmanship that will shape the framework of the modern system of learning; but rather the preconceptions of that disciplined workmanship that has been instructed in the logic of the modern technology and sophisticated with much experience in a civilization in whose scheme of life pecuniary canons are definitive.

The modern technology is of an impersonal, matter-of-fact character in an unexampled degree, and the accountancy of modern business management is also of an extremely dispassionate and impartially exacting nature. It results that the modern learning is of a similarly matter-of-fact, mechanistic complexion, and that it similarly leans on statistically dispassionate tests and formulations. Whereas it may fairly be said that the personal equation once—in the days of scholastic learning—was the central and decisive factor in the systematization of knowledge, it is equally fair to say that in later time no effort is spared to eliminate all bias of personality from the technique or the results of science or scholarship. It is the "dry light of science" that is always in request, and great pains is taken to exclude all color of sentimentality.

Yet this highly sterilized, germ-proof system of knowledge, kept in a cool, dry place, commands the affection of modern civilized mankind no less unconditionally, with no more afterthought of an extraneous sanction, than once did the highly personalized mythological and philosophical constructions and interpretations that had the vogue in the days of the schoolmen.

Through all the mutations that have passed over this quest of knowledge, from its beginnings in puerile myth and magic to its (provisional) consummation in the "exact" sciences of the current fashion, any attentive scrutiny will find that the driving force has consistently been of the same kind, traceable to the same proclivity of human nature. In so far as it may fairly be accounted esoteric knowledge, or a "higher learning," all this enterprise is actuated by an idle curiosity, a disinterested proclivity to gain a knowledge of things and to reduce this knowledge to a comprehensible system. The objective end is a theoretical organization. a logical articulation of things known, the lines of which must not be deflected by any consideration of expediency or convenience, but must run true to the canons of reality accepted at the time. These canons of reality, or of verity, have varied from time to time, have in fact varied incontinently with the passage of time and the mutations of experience. As the fashions of modern time have come on, particularly the later phases of modern life, the experience that so has shaped and reshaped the canons of verity for the use of inquiring minds has fallen more and more into the lines of mechanical articulation and has expressed itself ever more unreservedly in terms of mechanical stress. Concomitantly the canons of reality have taken on a mechanistic complexion, to the neglect and progressive disuse of all tests and standards of a more genial sort; until in the off-hand apprehension of modern men, "reality" comes near being identified with mechanical fact, and "verification" is taken to mean a formulation in mechanical terms. But the final test of this reality about which the inquiries of modern men so turn is not the test of mechanical serviceability for human use, but only of mechanistically effectual matter-of-fact.

So it has come about that modern civilization is in a very special degree a culture of the intellectual powers, in the narrower sense of the term, as contrasted with the emotional traits of human nature. Its achievements and chief merits are found in this field of learning, and its chief defects elsewhere. And it is on its achievements in this domain of detached and dispassionate knowledge that modern civilized mankind most ingenuously plumes itself and confidently rests its hopes. The more emotional and spiritual virtues that once held the first place have been overshadowed by the increasing consideration given to proficiency in matter-of-fact knowledge. As prime movers in the tide of civilized life, these sentimental movements of the human spirit belong in the past,—at least such is the self-complacent avowal of the modern spokesmen of culture. The modern technology, and the mechanistic conception of things that goes with that technology, are alien to the spirit of the "Old Order." The Church, the court, the camp, the drawing-room, where these elder and perhaps nobler virtues had their laboratory and playground, have grown weedy and gone to seed. Much of the apparatus of the old order, with the good old way, still stands over in a state of decent repair, and the sentimentally reminiscent endeavors of certain spiritual "hold-overs" still lend this apparatus of archaism something of a galvanic life. But that power of aspiration that once surged full and hot in the cults of faith, fashion, sentiment, exploit, and honor, now at its best comes to such a head as it may in the concerted adulation of matter-of-fact.

This esoteric knowledge of matter-of-fact has come to be accepted as something worthwhile in its own right, a self-legitimating end of endeavor in itself, apart from any bearing it may have on the glory of God or the good of man. Men have, no doubt, always been possessed of a more or less urgent propensity to inquire into the nature of things, beyond the serviceability of any knowledge so gained, and have always been given to seeking curious explanations of things at large. The idle curiosity is a native trait of the race. But in past times such a disinterested pursuit of unprofitable knowledge has, by and large, not been freely avowed as a legitimate end of endeavour; or such has at any rate been the state of the case through that later segment of history which students commonly take account of. A quest of knowledge has overtly been rated as meritorious, or even blameless, only in so far as it has appeared to serve the ends of one or another of the practical interests that have from time to time occupied men's attention.

But latterly, during the past few generations, this learning has so far become an avowed "end in itself" that "the increase and diffusion of knowledge among men" is now freely rated as the most humane and meritorious work to be taken care of by any enlightened community or any public-spirited friend of civilization.

The expediency of such "increase and diffusion" is no longer held in doubt, because it has ceased to be a question of expediency among the enlightened nations, being itself the consummation upon which, in the apprehension of civilized men, the advance of culture must converge. Such has come to be the long-term common sense judgment of enlightened public opinion. A settled presumption to some such effect has found lodgment as a commonplace conviction in the popular mind, in much the same measure and in much the same period of time as the current body of systematic knowledge has taken on the character of matter of fact. For good or ill, civilized men have come to hold that this matter-of-fact knowledge of things is the only end in life that indubitably justifies itself. So that nothing more irretrievably shameful could overtake modern civilization than the miscarriage of this modern learning, which is the most valued spiritual asset of civilized mankind.

The truth of this view is borne out by the professions even of those lieutenants of the powers of darkness who are straining to lay waste and debauch the peoples of Christendom. In high-pitched concert they all swear by the name of a "culture" whose sole inalienable asset is this same intellectual mastery of matters of fact. At the same time it is only by drawing on the resources of this matter-of-fact knowledge that the protagonists of reaction are able to carry on their campaign of debauchery and desolation.

Other interests that have once been held in higher esteem appear by comparison to have fallen into abeyance,—religious devotion, political prestige, fighting capacity, gentility, pecuniary distinction, profuse consumption of goods. But it is only by comparison with the higher value given to this enterprise of the intellect that such other interests appear to have lost ground. These and the like have fallen into relative disesteem, as being sordid and insubstantial by comparison. Not that these "lower" human interests, answering to the "lower" ranges of human intellect, have fallen into neglect; it is only that they have come to be accounted "lower," as contrasted with the quest of knowledge; and it is only on sober second thought, and perhaps only for the ephemeral present, that they are so accounted by the common run of civilized mankind. Men still are in sufficiently hot pursuit of all these time-worn amenities, and each for himself is, in point of fact, more than likely to make the pursuit of such self-seeking ends the burden of his life; but on a dispassionate rating, and under the corrective of deliberate avowal, it will appear that none of these commend themselves as intrinsically worthwhile at large. At the best they are rated as expedient concessions to human infirmity or as measures of defense against human perversity and the outrages of fortune. The last resort of the apologists for these more sordid endeavours is the plea that only by this means can the ulterior ends of a civilization of intelligence be served. The argument may fairly be paraphrased to the effect that in order to serve God in the end, we must all be ready to serve the Devil in the meantime.

It is always possible, of course, that this pre-eminence of intellectual enterprise in the civilization of the Western peoples is a transient episode; that it may eventually—perhaps even precipitately, with the next impending turn in the fortunes of this civilization—again be relegated to a secondary place in the scheme of things and become only an instrumentality in the service of some dominant aim or impulse, such as a vainglorious patriotism, or dynastic politics, or the breeding of a commercial aristocracy. More than one of the nations of Europe have moved so far in this matter already as to place the primacy of science and scholarship in doubt as against warlike ambitions; and the aspirations of the American community appear to be divided—between patriotism in the service of the captains of war, and commerce in the service of the captains of finance. But hitherto the spokesmen of any such cultural reversion are careful to declare a perfunctory faith in that civilization of disinterested intellectual achievement which they are endeavouring to suborn to their several ends. That such pro forma declarations are found necessary argues that the faith in a civilization of intelligence is still so far intact as to require all reactionaries to make their peace with it.

Meantime the easy matter-of-course presumption that such a civilization of intelligence justifies itself goes to argue that the current bias which so comes to expression will be the outcome of a secure and protracted experience. What underlies and has brought on this bent in the temper of the civilized peoples is a somewhat intricate question of institutional growth, and can not be gone into here; but the gradual shifting of this matter-of-fact outlook into the primacy among the ideals of modern. Christendom is sufficiently evident in point of fact, to any attentive student of modern times. Conceivably, there may come an abrupt term to its paramount vogue, through some precipitate sweep of circumstances; but it did not come in by anything like the sudden intrusion of a new invention in ideals—after the fashion of a religious conversion nor by the incursion of a hitherto alien element into the current scheme of life, but rather by force of a gradual and unintended, scarcely perceptible, shifting of emphasis between the several cultural factors that conjointly go to make up the working scheme of things.

Along with this shifting of matter-of-fact knowledge into the foreground among the ideals of civilized life, there has also gone on a similarly unpremeditated change in the attitude of those persons and establishments that have to do with this learning, as well as in the rating accorded them by the community at large. Again it is a matter of institutional growth, of self-wrought changes in the scheme of use and wont; and here as in other cases of institutional growth and displacement, the changes have gone forward for the most part blindly, by impulse, without much foreknowledge of any ulterior consequences to which such a sequence of change might be said to tend. It is only after the new growth of use and wont has taken effect in an altered range of principles and standards, that its direction and ulterior consequences can be appreciated with any degree of confidence. But this development that has thrown up matter-of-fact knowledge into its place of paramount value for modern culture has in a peculiar degree been unintended and unforeseen; the like applies to the case of the schools and the personnel involved; and in a peculiar degree the drift and bearing of these changes have also not been appreciated while they have been going forward, doubtless because it has all been a peculiarly unprecedented phenomenon and a wholly undesigned drift of habituation. History records nothing that is fairly comparable. No era in the historic past has set a pattern for guidance in this matter, and the experience of none of the peoples of history affords a clue by which to have judged beforehand of the probable course and outcome of this specifically modern and occidental phase of culture.

Some slight beginnings and excursions in the way of a cultivation of matter-of-fact learning there may have been, now and again, among the many shifting systems of esoteric lore that have claimed attention here and there, early and late; and these need by no means be accounted negligible. But they have on the whole come to nothing much better than broken excursions, as seen from the point of view of the latterday higher learning, and they have brought into bearing nothing appreciable in the way of establishments designed without afterthought to further the advance of disinterested knowledge. Anything like a cultural era that avowedly takes such a quest of knowledge as its chief and distinctive characteristic is not known to history. From this isolated state of the case it follows, unfortunately, that this modern phase is to be studied only in its own light; and since the sequence of development has hitherto reached no secure consummation or conclusion, there is also much room for conflicting opinions as to its presumptive or legitimate outcome, or even as to its present drift.

II

But notorious facts make this much plain, that civilized mankind looks to this quest of matter-of-fact knowledge as its most substantial asset and its most valued achievement,—in so far as any consensus of appreciation or of aspirations is to be found among civilized mankind; and there is no similar consensus bearing on any other feature of that scheme of life that characterizes modern civilization. It is similarly beyond dispute that men look to the modern system of schools and related establishments of learning for the furtherance and conservation of this intellectual enterprise. And among the various items of this equipment the modern university is, by tradition, more closely identified with the quest of knowledge than any other. It stands in a unique and peculiarly intimate relation to this intellectual enterprise. At least such is the current apprehension of the university's work. The university is the only accepted institution of the modern culture on which the quest of knowledge unquestionably devolves; and the visible drift of circumstances as well as of public sentiment runs also to making this the only unquestioned duty incumbent on the university.

It is true, many other lines of work, and of endeavor that may not fairly be called work, are undertaken by schools of university grade; and also, many other schools that call themselves "universities" will have substantially nothing to do with the higher learning. But each and several of these other lines of endeavor, into which the universities allow themselves to be drawn, are open to question. Their legitimacy remains an open question in spite of the interested arguments of their spokesmen, who advocate the partial submergence of the university in such enterprises as professional training, undergraduate instruction, supervision and guidance of the secondary school system, edification of the unlearned by "university extension" and similar excursions into the field of public amusement, training of secondary school teachers, encouragement of amateurs by "correspondence," etc. What and how much of these extraneous activities the university should allow itself is a matter on which there is no general agreement even among those whose inclinations go far in that direction; but what is taken for granted throughout all this advocacy of outlying detail is the secure premise that the university is in the first place a seminary of the higher learning, and that no school can make good its pretensions to university standing except by proving its fitness in this respect.[4]

The conservation and advancement of the higher learning involves two lines of work, distinct but closely bound together: (a) scientific and scholarly inquiry, and (b) the instruction of students.[5] The former of these is primary and indispensable. It is this work of intellectual enterprise that gives its character to the university and marks it off from the lower schools. The work of teaching properly belongs in the university only because and in so far as it incites and facilitates the university man's work of inquiry,—and the extent to which such teaching furthers the work of inquiry is scarcely to be appreciated without a somewhat extended experience. By and large, there are but few and inconsequential exceptions to the rule that teaching, as a concomitant of investigation, is distinctly advantageous to the investigator; particularly in so far as his work is of the nature of theoretical inquiry. The instruction necessarily involved in university work, therefore, is only such as can readily be combined with the work of inquiry, at the same time that

---

4 The essential function of the university is to bring together, for the transmission of experience and impulse, the sages of the passing and the picked youths of the coming generation. By the extent and fulness with which they establish these social contacts, and thus transmit the wave of cumulative experience and idealist impulse—the real sources of moral and intellectual progress—the universities are to be judged.—Victor Branford, Interpretations and Forecasts, ch. VI. "The Present as a Transition." p 288.

5 Cf., Geo. T. Ladd, University Control, p. 349.

it goes directly to further the higher learning in that it trains the incoming generation of scholars and scientists for the further pursuit of knowledge. Training for other purposes is necessarily of a different kind and is best done elsewhere; and it does not become university work by calling it so and imposing its burden on the men and equipment whose only concern should be the higher learning.

University teaching, having a particular and special purpose—the pursuit of knowledge—it has also a particular and special character, such as to differentiate it from other teaching and at the same time leave it relatively ineffective for other purposes. Its aim is to equip the student for the work of inquiry, not to give him facility in that conduct of affairs that turns such knowledge to "practical account." Hence the instruction that falls legitimately under the hand of the university man is necessarily subsidiary and incidental to the work of inquiry, and it can effectually be carried on only by such a teacher as is himself occupied with the scrutiny of what knowledge is already in hand and with pushing the inquiry to further gains. And it can be carried on by such a teacher only by drawing his students into his own work of inquiry. The student's relation to his teacher necessarily becomes that of an apprentice to his master, rather than that of a pupil to his schoolmaster.

A university is a body of mature scholars and scientists, the "faculty,"—with whatever plant and other equipment may incidentally serve as appliances for their work in any given case. The necessary material equipment may under modern conditions be very considerable, as may also the number of care-takers, assistants, etc.; but all that is not the university, but merely its equipment. And the university man's work is the pursuit of knowledge, together with whatever advisory surveillance and guidance he may consistently afford such students as are entering on the career of learning at a point where his outlook and methods of work may be of effect for them. No man whose energies are not habitually bent on increasing and proving up the domain of learning belongs legitimately on the university staff. The university man is, properly, a student, not a schoolmaster. Such is the unmistakable drift of sentiment and professed endeavour, in so far as it is guided by the cultural aspirations of civilized mankind rather than by the emulative strategy of individuals seeking their own preferment.[6]

---

6 Cf., e.g., J. McKeen Cattell, University Control, Part III, ch. V., "Concerning the American University." "The university is those who teach and those who learn and the work they do." "The university is its men and their work. But certain externals are necessary or at least usual—buildings and equipment, a president and trustees."

The papers by other writers associated with Mr Cattell in this volume run to the same effect whenever they touch the same topic; and, indeed, it would be difficult to find a deliberate expression to the contrary among men entitled to speak in these premises.

All this, of course, implies no undervaluing of the work of those men who aim to prepare the youth for citizenship and a practical career. It is only a question of distinguishing between things that belong apart. The scientist and the scholar on the one hand, and the schoolmaster on the other hand, both belong within the later growth of civilization; but a differentiation of the two classes, and a division of their work, is indispensable if they are to do their work as it should be done, and as the modern community thoughtfully intends that it should be done. And while such a division of labour has hitherto not been carried through with any degree of consistency, it is at least under way, and there is nothing but the presumption of outworn usage that continues to hold the two lines of work together, to the detriment of both; backed, it is true, by ambitions of self-aggrandizement on the part of many schools and many of their directorates.

The schoolmaster and his work may be equally, or more, valuable to the community at large—presumably more rather than less—but in so far as his chief interest is of the pedagogical sort his place is not in the university. Exposition, instruction and drill belong in and professional schools. The consistent aim there is, and should be, to instruct, to inculcate a knowledge of results, and to give the pupil a working facility in applying it. On the university level such information and training is (should be) incidental to the work of research. The university man is almost unavoidably a teacher, by precept and example, but he can not without detriment to his work as scientist or scholar serve as a taskmaster or a vehicle of indoctrination. The student who comes up to the university for the pursuit of knowledge is expected to know what he wants and to want it, without compulsion. If he falls short in these respects, if he has not the requisite interest and initiative, it is his own misfortune, not the fault of his teacher. What he has a legitimate claim to is an opportunity for such personal contact and guidance as will give him familiarity with the ways and means of the higher learning,—any information imparted to him being incidental to this main work of habituation. He gets a chance to make himself a scholar, and what he will do with his opportunities in this way lies in his own discretion.

The difference between the modern university and the lower and professional schools is broad and simple; not so much a difference of degree as of kind. There is no difficulty about apprehending or appreciating this difference; the dispute turns not on the practicability of distinguishing between the two, but on the desirability of letting such a distinction go into effect. It is a controversy between those who

It may be in place to add here that the volume referred to, on University Control, has been had in mind throughout the following analysis and has served as ground and material for much of the argument.

wish to hold fast that which once was good and those who look to make use of the means in hand for new ends and meet new exigencies.

The lower schools (including the professional schools) are, in the ideal scheme, designed to fit the incoming generation for civil life; they are therefore occupied with instilling such knowledge and habits as will make their pupils fit citizens of the world in whatever position in the fabric of workday life they may fall. The university on the other hand is specialized to fit men for a life of science and scholarship; and it is accordingly concerned, with such discipline only as will give efficiency in the pursuit of knowledge and fit its students for the increase and diffusion of learning. It follows that while the lower schools necessarily take over the surveillance of their pupils' everyday life, and exercise a large measure of authority and responsible interference in that behalf, the university assumes (or should assume) no responsibility for its students' fortunes in the moral, religious, pecuniary, domestic, or hygienic respect.

Doubtless the larger and more serious responsibility in the educational system belongs not to the university but to the lower and professional schools. Citizenship is a larger and more substantial category than scholarship; and the furtherance of civilized life is a larger and more serious interest than the pursuit of knowledge for its own idle sake. But the proportions which the quest of knowledge is latterly assuming in scheme of civilized life require that the establishments the to which this interest is committed should not be charged with extraneous duties; particularly not with extraneous matters themselves of such grave consequence as this training for citizenship and practical affairs. These are too serious a range of duties to be taken care of as a side-issue, by a seminary of learning, the members of whose faculty, if they are fit for their own special work, are not men of affairs or adepts in worldly wisdom.

III

In point of historical pedigree the American universities are of another derivation than their European counterpart; although the difference in this respect is not so sharp a matter of contrast as might be assumed at first sight. The European (Continental) universities appear to have been founded, originally, to meet the needs of professional training, more particularly theological (and philosophical) training in the earlier times. The American universities are, historically, an outgrowth of the American college; and the latter was installed, in its beginnings, largely as a means of professional training; chiefly training for Divinity, secondarily for the calling of the schoolmaster. But in neither case, neither in that of the European university nor in that of the American College, was this early vocational aim of the schools allowed to decide their character in the long run, nor to circumscribe the lines of their later growth. In both cases, somewhat alike, the two groups of schools came to their mature development, in the nineteenth century, as establishments occupied with disinterested learning, given over to the pursuit of intellectual enterprise, rather than as seminaries for training of a vocational kind. They still had a vocational value, no doubt, and the vocational needs of their students need not have been absent from the considerations that guided their directorates. It would particularly be found that the (clerical) directorates of the American colleges had more than half an eye to the needs of Divinity even at so late a date as when, in the third quarter of the century, the complexion of the American college situation began seriously to change. It is from this period—from the era of the Civil War and the Reconstruction—that the changes set in which have reshaped the academic situation in America.

At this era, some half a century ago, the American college was, or was at least pressed to be, given over to disinterested instruction, not specialized with a vocational, or even a denominational, bias. It was coming to take its place as the superior or crowning member, a sort of capstone, of the system of public instruction. The life history of any one of the state universities whose early period of growth runs across this era will readily show the effectual guidance of such an ideal of a college, as a superior and definitive member in a school system designed to afford an extended course of instruction looking to an unbiased increase and diffusion of knowledge. Other interests, of a professional or vocational kind, were also entrusted to the keeping of these new-found schools; but with a conclusive generality the rule holds that in these academic creations a college establishment of a disinterested, non-vocational character is counted in as the indispensable nucleus,—that much was at that time a matter of course.

The further development shows two marked features: The American university has come into bearing; and the college has become an intermediate rather than a terminal link in the conventional scheme of education. Under the names "undergraduate" and "graduate," the college and the university are still commonly coupled together as subdivisions of a complex whole; but this holding together of the two disparate schools is at the best a freak of aimless survival. At the worst, and more commonly, it is the result of a gross ambition for magnitude on the part of the joint directorate. Whether the college lives by itself as an independent establishment on a foundation of its own, or is in point of legal formality a subdivision of the university establishment, it takes its place in the educational scheme as senior member of the secondary school system, and it bears no peculiarly close relation to the university as a seat of learning. At the closest it stands to the university in the relation of a fitting school; more commonly its relations are closer with the ordinary professional and vocational schools; and for the most part it stands in no relation, beyond that of juxtaposition, with the one or the other.

The attempt to hold the college and the no means together in bonds of ostensible Solidarity is by university an advisedly concerted adjustment to the needs of scholarship as they run today. By historical accident the older American universities have grown into bearing on the ground of an underlying college, and the external connection so inherited has not usually been severed; and by ill-advised, or perhaps unadvised, imitation the younger universities have blundered into encumbering themselves with an undergraduate department to simulate this presumptively honourable pedigree, to the detriment both of the university and of the college so bound up with it. By this arrangement the college—undergraduate department—falls into the position of an appendage, a side issue, to be taken care of by afterthought on the part of a body of men whose chief legitimate interest runs—should run—on other things than the efficient management of such an undergraduate training-school,—provided always that they are a bona fide university faculty, and not a body of secondary-school teachers masquerading under the assumed name of a university.

The motive to this inclusion of an undergraduate department in the newer universities appears commonly to have been a headlong eagerness on the part of the corporate authorities to show a complete establishment of the conventionally accepted pattern, and to enroll as many students as possible.

Whatever may have been true for the earlier time, when the American college first grew up and flourished, it is beyond question that the undergraduate department which takes the place of the college today can not be rated as an institution of the higher learning. At the best it is now a school for preliminary training, preparatory to entering on the career of learning, or in preparation for the further training required for the professions; but it is also, and chiefly, an establishment designed to give the concluding touches to the education of young men who have no designs on learning, beyond the close of the college curriculum. It aims to afford a rounded discipline to those whose goal is the life of fashion or of affairs. How well, or how ill, the college may combine these two unrelated purposes is a question that does not immediately concern the present inquiry. It is touched on here only to point the contrast between the American college and the university.

It follows from the character of their work that while the university should offer no set curriculum, the college has, properly, nothing else to offer. But the retention or inclusion of the college and its aims within the university corporation has necessarily led to the retention of college standards and methods of control even in what is or purports to be university work; so that it is by no means unusual to find university (graduate) work scheduled in the form of a curriculum, with all that boarding-school circumstance and apparatus that is so unavoidable an evil in all undergraduate training. In effect, the outcome of these short-sighted attempts to take care of the higher learning by the means and method of the boys' school, commonly is to eliminate the higher learning from the case and substitute the aims and results of a boys' training-school.

Undergraduate work being task work, it is possible, without fatal effect, to reduce it to standard units of time and volume, and so control and enforce it by a system of accountancy and surveillance; the methods of control, accountancy and coercion that so come to be worked out have all that convincing appearance of tangible efficiency that belongs to any mechanically defined and statistically accountable routine, such as will always commend itself to the spirit of the schoolmaster; the temptation to apply such methods of standardized routine wherever it is at all feasible is always present, and it is cogently spoken for by all those to whom drill is a more intelligible conception than scholarship. The work of learning, which distinctively belongs in the university, on the other hand, is a matter of personal contact and co-operation between teacher and student, and is not measurable in statistical units or amenable to mechanical tests; the men engaged in this work can accordingly offer nothing of the same definite character in place of the rigid routine and accountancy advocated by the schoolmasters; and the outcome in nearly all cases where the control of both departments vests in one composite corporate body, as it usually does, is the gradual insinuation of undergraduate methods and standards in the graduate school; until what is nominally university work settles down, in effect, into nothing more than an extension of the undergraduate curriculum. This effect is had partly by reducing such of the graduate courses as are found amenable to the formalities of the undergraduate routine, and partly by dispensing with such graduate work as will not lend itself, even ostensibly, to the schoolmaster's methods.

What has been said of the college in this connection holds true in the main also of the professional and technical schools. In their aims, methods and achievements these schools are, in the nature of the case, foreign to the higher learning. This is, of course, not said in disparagement of their work; rather the contrary. As is the case with the college, so these schools also are often included in the university corporation by ties of an external and factitious kind, frequently by terms of the charter. But this formal inclusion of them under the corporate charter does not set aside the substantial discrepancy between their purpose, work and animus and those of the university proper. It can only serve to trouble the single-mindedness of both. It leaves both the pursuit of learning and the work of preparation for the professions somewhat at loose ends, confused with the bootless illusion that they are, in some recondite way, parallel variants of a single line of work.

In aim and animus the technical and professional schools are "practical," in the most thorough going manner; while the pursuit of knowledge that occupies the scientists and scholars is not "practical" in the slightest degree. The divergent lines of interest to be taken care of by the professional schools and the university, respectively, are as widely out of touch as may well be within the general field of human knowledge. The one is animated wholly by considerations of material expediency, and the range of its interest and efforts is strictly limited by consideration of the useful effect to which the proficiency that it gives is to be turned; the other knows nothing of expediency, and is influenced by no consideration of utility or disutility, in its appreciation of the knowledge to be sought. The animus of the one is worldly wisdom; of the other, idle curiosity. The two are incommensurably at variance so far as regards their purpose, and in great measure also as regards their methods of work, and necessarily so.

But with all this divergence of purpose and animus there is after all a broad and very substantial bond of community between the technical schools, on the one hand, and the proper work of the university, on the other hand, in that the two are, in great measure, occupied with the same general range of materials and employ somewhat the same logical methods in handling these materials. But the relation that results from this community of material is almost wholly external and mechanical. Nor does it set up any presumption that the two should expediently be included in the same corporate establishment, or even that they need be near neighbors or need maintain peculiarly close relations of personnel. The technical schools, and in a less degree the professional schools not properly classed as technical, depend in large measure on results worked out by the scientists, who properly belong in the universities. But the material so made use of for technical ends are taken over and turned to account without afterthought. The technologist's work is related to that of the scientists very much as the work of the designer is related to that of the inventor. To a considerable extent the scientists similarly depend on the work of the technical men for information, and for correction and verification of their own theoretical work. But there is, on this account, nothing to gain by associating any given technical school with any given university establishment; incorporation in any given university does not in any degree facilitate the utilization of the results of the sciences by the technical men; nor is it found in practice to further the work of the sciences. The schools in question do not in any peculiar degree draw on the work of the scientists attached to their particular university, nor do these scientists, on the other hand, have any special use for the work of their associated technical schools. In either case the source drawn on is the general literature of the subject, the body of materials available at large, not the work of particular men attached to particular schools. The generalizations of science are indispensable to the technical men; but what they draw on is the body of science at large, regardless of what any given university establishment may have had to do with the work out of which the particular items of scientific information have emerged. Nor is this scientific material useful to the technologists for the further pursuit of science; to them the scientific results are data, raw material to be turned to practical use, not means by which to carry scientific inquiry out to further results.

Similarly, the professions and the technical schools afford valuable data for the use of the professed scholars and scientists, information that serves as material of Investigation, or that will at least be useful as a means of extending correcting, verifying and correlating lines of inquiry on which they are engaged. But the further bearing of these facts upon the affairs of life, their expediency or futility, is of no interest or consequence. The affairs of life, except the affairs of learning, do not touch the interest of the university man as a scholar or scientist. What is of importance to him in all these matters with which the professions and technologists are busy is their bearing on those matters of fact into which his scientific interest leads him to inquire. The tests and experiments carried out at these technical schools, as well as the experience gathered by the members of their staff, will occasionally afford him material for further inquiry or means whereby to check results already arrived at; but for such material he does not by preference resort to any one of the technical schools as contrasted with any other, and it is quite an idle question whether the source of any such serviceable information is a school attached to his own university. The investigator finds his material where he can; which comes to saying that he draws on the general body of technical knowledge, with no afterthought as to what particular technical school may have stood in some relation or other to the information which he finds useful.

Neither to the man engaged in university work nor to the technical schools that may serve him as occasional sources of material is there any advantage to be derived from their inclusion in the university establishment. Indeed, it is a detriment to both parties, as has already been remarked, but more decidedly to the university men. By including the technical and professional schools in the university corporation the technologists and professional men attached to these schools are necessarily included among the academic staff, and so they come to take their part in the direction of academic affairs at large. In what they so do toward shaping the academic policy they will not only count for all they are worth, but they are likely to count for something more than their due share in this respect; for they are to some extent trained to the conduct of affairs, and so come in for something of that deference that is currently paid to men of affairs, at the same time that this practical training gives them an advantage over their purely academic colleagues, in the greater assurance and adroitness with which they are able to present their contentions. By virtue of this same training, as well as by force of current practical interest, the technologist and the professional man are, like other men of affairs, necessarily and habitually impatient of any scientific or scholarly work that does not obviously lend itself to some practical use. The technologist appreciates what is mechanically serviceable; the professional man, as, for instance, the lawyer, appreciates what promises pecuniary gain; and the two unite with the business-man at large in repudiating whatever does not look directly to such a utilitarian outcome. So that as members of the academic staff these men are likely to count at their full weight toward the diversion of the university's forces from disinterested science and scholarship to such palpably utilitarian ends.

But the active measures so taken by the academic authorities at the instance of the schoolmasters and "practical" men are by no means the only line along which their presence in the academic corporation affects the case. Intimate association with these "utilitarians" unavoidably has its corrupting effect on the scientists and scholars, and induces in them also something of the same bias toward "practical" results in their work; so that they no longer pursue the higher learning with undivided interest, but with more or less of an eye to the utilitarian main chance; whereby the advantages of specialization, which are the reason for these schools, are lost, and the pride of the modern community is wounded in its most sensitive spot—the efficiency of its specialists.

So also, on the other hand, the formal incorporation of these technological and professional men in the academic body, with its professedly single-minded interest in learning, has its effect on their frame of mind. They are, without intending it, placed in a false position, which unavoidably leads them to court a specious appearance of scholarship, and so to invest their technological discipline with a degree of pedantry and sophistication; whereby it is hoped to give these schools and their work some scientific and scholarly prestige, and so lift it to that dignity that is pressed to attach to a non-utilitarian pursuit of learning. Doubtless this pursuit of scholarly prestige is commonly successful, to the extent that it produces the desired conviction of awe in the vulgar, who do not know the difference; but all this make-believe scholarship, however successfully staged, is not what these schools are designed for; or at least it is not what is expected of them, nor is it what they can do best and most efficiently.

To the substantial gain of both parties, though with some lesion of the vanity of both, the separation between the university and the professional and technical schools should be carried through and made absolute. Only on such conditions can either the one or the other do its own work in a workmanlike manner. Within the university precincts any aim or interest other than those of irresponsible science and scholarship—pursuit of matter-of-fact knowledge—are to be rated as interlopers.

CHAPTER TWENTY-TWO

The Idea of a Modern University

From *Universities: American, English, German* (1930)

J. ABRAHAM FLEXNER

This selection is an excerpt from *Universities: American, English, German*, Abraham Flexner, 1930, published by Oxford University Press, London, United Kingdom.

Editors' Note

Abraham Flexner was an educationalist and reformer who specialized in medical and higher education. In 1890, he founded a highly successful preparatory school in Louisville, Kentucky, and remained director for fifteen years. He published *The American College: A Criticism* (1908) in which he argues that the college lacks a clear view of a liberal education. Flexner's assessment caught the eye of the Henry Pritchett, President of the Carnegie Foundation who commissioned him to write a survey of the quality of medical colleges in the US and Canada. His 1910 report had an instantaneous effect and led to the reform of medical colleges including the closure of rural and Black colleges. *Universities: American, English, German* appeared in 1930 that extended his argument concerning the humanist purpose of the university and its appropriate focus of serious learning as opposed to job training. Flexner helped shape and became the first director of the Institute of Advanced Studies, located in Princeton. The volume is an expansion of three lectures he gave at Oxford in May 1928. He begins by paying homage to Newman's Idea of the University and inserting the word 'modern' to indicate that the university is 'an expression of the age' and to focus in turn on American, English and German Universities.

MP

Recommended Reading

Flexner, Abraham (1908). *The American College: A Criticism.* New York, Century. Institute of Advanced Studies, Abraham Flexner. Retrieved from https://www.ias.edu/people/flexner

* * * * *

I

Seventy-five years ago, an eminent Oxonian, Cardinal Newman, published a book entitled *The Idea of a University*. I have adopted in a modified form the title of that volume. I am undertaking in this chapter to discuss the idea of a *modern* university. In inserting the word "modern" I am endeavouring to indicate in the most explicit fashion that a university, like all other human institutions—like the church, like governments, like philanthropic organizations—is not outside, but inside the general social fabric of a given era. It is not something apart, something historic, something that yields as little as possible to forces and influences that are more or less new. It is, on the contrary—so I shall assume—an expression of the age, as well as an influence operating upon both present and future. I propose to elaborate this point of view and, as I proceed, to ask myself to what extent and in what ways universities in America, in England, and in Germany have made themselves part of the modern world, where they have failed to do so, where they have made hurtful concessions, and where they are wholesome and creative influences in shaping society towards rational ends.

Quite obviously I am assuming that to some extent, however slight, we are masters of our fate. The modern world is developing under the pressure of forces that reason cannot readily control. Pitted against these forces, our abilities may for the moment seem feeble and ineffectual. But the existence of universities implies there is something, perhaps much, in the past for which it is worthwhile to fight to which it is worthwhile to cling; and that there is something—no one knows how much—which we may ourselves do to mould to our liking the civilization of the future. Man, as Professor Woodbridge has admirably said, "is not content to take nature as he finds her. He insists on making her over."[1] But the modern world—no matter how new we think it to be—is rooted in a past, which is the soil out of which we grow a past during which poets and scientists and thinker; and peoples have accumulated treasures of truth beauty, and knowledge, experience, social, political; and other, which only a wastrel would ignore. On the other hand, science, democracy, and other forces steadily increasing in intensity are creating a different world of which universities must take account.

II

Universities differ in different countries' if as Lord Haldane says, "it is in universities that ... the soul of a people mirrors itself,"[2] then it would be absurd to expect them to conform to a single pattern. Moreover, as a matter of history, they have changed profoundly—and commonly in the direction of the social evolution of which they are part. The Paris of 1900 has little in common with the Paris of 1700; the Oxford of the twentieth century, externally so largely the same, is nevertheless a very different thing from the Oxford of the eighteenth century; Althoff's Berlin is not Wilhelm von Humboldt's, though they are separated by hardly a hundred years; very different indeed is the Harvard, of which Mr. Eliot became president in 1869, from the Harvard which he left on his retirement in 1909. Historians have traced certain aspects of this evolution in detail; and nothing in their stories is more striking than the adjustments—sometimes slow and unconscious, sometimes deliberate and violent—made in the course of centuries by institutions usually regarded as conservative, frequently even as the stronghold of reaction: I say then that universities have in most countries changed; but have they latterly changed profoundly enough, or have they been so intelligently modified as to be the effective and formative agencies which are needed in a society that is driven it knows not whither by forces of unprecedented strength and violence? An American sociologist has invented the term "social lag." Institutions as such tend for quite obvious reasons to lag behind the life which they express and further. To what extent are the universities of America, England, and Germany hampered by "social lag"?

---

1 Frederick, J. E. Woodbridge, *Contrasts in Education* (New York 1929), p. 17.

2 Viscount Haldane, *Universities and National Life* (London, 1912), p. 29.

III

There is danger at precisely the opposite end of the line. I have spoken of the intelligent modification of universities—of their modification in the light of needs, facts, and ideals. But a university should not be a weather vane, responsive to every variation of popular whim. Universities must at times give society, not what society wants, but what it needs. Inertia and resistance have their uses, provided they be based on reasonable analysis, on a sense of values, not on mere habit. In response to the criticism that universities lag, instances in plenty can—and will—be given by way of showing that universities are up to date or even ahead of the times. But the two characteristics are not mutually exclusive. Universities are complex and organic institutions: their arms may be sound, while both legs may be broken. They may lag fundamentally, even while superficially catering to whim or fashion; they may lag fundamentally at the very moment when at this or that point they are as expert as newspapers and politicians in catching the current breeze. A proper amount of critical resistance, based on a sense of values, would—as we shall see—save them from absurd, almost disastrous blunders.

IV

Of all this, more hereafter. In the present chapter, I shall not discuss universities, but merely the idea of a university, and I am going to procure a free field for speculation by assuming the impossible and, indeed, the undesirable; suppose we could smash our existing universities to bits, suppose we could remake them to conform to our heart's desire, what sort of institution should we set up? We should not form them all alike—English, French, American, German. But, whatever allowances we might make for national tradition or temperament, we should see to it somehow that in appropriate ways scholars and scientists would be conscious of four major concerns: the conservation of knowledge and ideas; the interpretation of knowledge and ideas; the search for truth; the training of students who will practise and "carryon." I say, to repeat, "the major concerns" of scholar and scientist. Of course, education has other and important concerns. But I wish to make it plain at the outset that the university is only one of many educational enterprises. It has, in the general educational scheme, certain specific functions. Other agencies discharge or should discharge other functions. We shall see whether universities now discern and discharge their special functions or whether they meddle with functions which do not constitute their proper business.

The conservation of knowledge and ideas is and has always been recognized as the business of universities, sometimes, perhaps, as almost their only business, occasionally, even today, as too largely their business. In any event, universities have always taken this to be one of their functions; and however universities may change, no reconstruction will or should deprive them of it. But one should add this: conservation and interpretation are one thing in institutions that are .concerned with merely or chiefly that; they are a different thing in a university where fresh streams of thought are constantly playing upon the preserved treasures of mankind.

Original thinkers and investigators do not therefore represent the only type of university professor. They will always be the distinguished figures; theirs will usually be the most profound and far-reaching influence. But even universities, modern universities, need and use men of different stamp—teachers whose own contributions to learning are of less importance than their influence in stimulating students or their resourcefulness in bringing together the researches of others. Michael Foster was not the less a great university professor, though he was not himself a great original thinker: in subtle ways that defy expression, he created the great Cambridge school of physiology. So, too Paulsen was not the less a great university professor' though he was not himself a great original thinker, but rather a broad and profound scholar of sound judgment and beautiful spirit who helped hundreds, struggling with the perplexities of life and thought, to find themselves. But, be it noted, both did this not for boys, but for mature students, under conditions that threw upon them responsibility for efforts and results. And this is a university criterion of first-rate importance. The university professor has an entirely objective responsibility—a responsibility to learning, to his subject, and not a psychological or parenta1 responsibility for his students. No fear that he will in consequence be dehumanized. What could be more charming, more intimate, more personal, more cooperative than the relations between the great continental masters and their disciples during the best part of the nineteenth century?

It is however creative activity, productive and critical inquiry—all in a sense without practical responsibility—that must bulk ever larger and larger in the modern university. Conservation continues to be not only important, but essential alike to education and to research; but, as other educational agencies improve and as our difficulties thicken, it is destined, I think to become incidental to the extension of knowledge, to training at a high level, and to a critical attempt to set a value upon the doings of men.

Of the overwhelming and increasing importance of the study and solution of problems or the advancement of knowledge—they are interchangeable phrases—one can readily convince one's self, no matter where one looks. Let us consider for a moment the social and political situation within which we live, and I take this realm first, because it is the realm in which universities are doing least, the realm which is most difficult and dangerous to approach, the realm which is for these reasons perhaps the most important to master. Democracy has dragged in its wake social, economic, educational, and political problems infinitely more perplexing than the relatively simple problems which its credulous crusaders undertook to solve. Society cannot retreat; whatever may happen sporadically or temporarily in Italy or Spain, we shall in the end probably fare better, if the adaptations and inventions requisite to making a success of democracy are facilitated. But adaptations in what ways? Statesmen must invent—not statesmen, fumbling in the dark or living on phrases, but statesmen equipped by disinterested students of society with the knowledge needed for courageous and intelligent action. Now the postulates, ideas, terminology, phraseology, which started the modern world on new paths, have become more or less obsolete, partly through their own success, partly through changes due to science and the industrial revolution. To be sure, men" have always acted blindly, ignorantly; but for the time being at least, the chasm between action, on the one hand, and knowledge, on the other, is widening rather than contracting. Practice cannot be slowed down or halted; intelligence must, however, be accelerated.

This contention could be equally well illustrated by Germany, France, England, or the United States. What has happened in the United States? There was between 1776 and 1790 a revolution based upon a simple philosophy. Time, even a brief century, brought changes; but the philosophy had meanwhile crystallized. A thin rural population living on the seaboard had increased beyond a hundred millions spread over an empire; steam and electricity had transferred importance from agriculture to industry; huge cities had grown up; enormous discrepancies of wealth had been created. But the documentary basis of government and society remains essentially the same. We find ourselves therefore now enmeshed in a phraseology that is discordant with the facts. The phraseology tends to hold things fixed; but readjustments have somehow to be effected. Publicists and jurists have therefore been forced to make inherited formulae mean something that they do not mean and could not have meant. The easy and effective reconceiving and rewording of theory and ideas are thus gravely hampered. Somewhere, away from the hurly-burly of practical responsibility and action, the social and political problems involved in these discords must be exposed. The "great society" must and wants to understand itself—partly as a matter of sheer curiosity, partly because human beings are in a muddle and cannot get out unless they know more than they now know. Towards fundamental knowing the newspaper cannot help much; men of action—politicians and business men—help but slightly. They themselves know too little; they are not disinterestedly concerned with finding out; they have usually their own axes to grind. Almost the only available agency is the university. The university must shelter and develop thinkers, experimenters, inventors, teachers, and students, who, without responsibility for action, will explore the phenomena of social life and endeavour to understand them.

I do not mean to say that this is altogether a novelty. Great scholars have in all countries in fragments of time snatched from routine duties made important contributions to political and economic thought: "in fragments of time snatched from routine duties"—from administrative burdens, from secondary instruction, from distracting tasks undertaken to piece out a livelihood. But though individuals differ in their requirements, no university in any country has made really adequate provision or offered really adequate opportunity and encouragement. I have not in mind the training of practical men, who, faced with responsibility for action, will do the best they can. That is not the task of the university. Between the student of political and social problems and the journalist, industrialist, merchant, viceroy, member of Parliament or Congress, there is a gap which the university cannot fill, which society must fill in some other way. Perhaps no outright educational institution should be expected to fill it; educated men can be allowed to do some things for themselves though, at the moment, we appear to be under a different impression.

One may go further: a study of mediaeval charters, of the financing of the Napoleonic Wars, of the rise of Prussia, of the origins of local government in the American Colonies, of the ideas of Plato, Aristotle, or Hobbes—these topics—just slightly musty—would be generally regarded as appropriately academic, for they may be investigated in a library. But is it equally good form—academically speaking—to study Mr. Keynes rather than Ricardo, the war debts with which successive commissions have wrestled rather than the repudiated state debts which most Americans quite wrongly prefer to regard as possessing merely historic interests, the present-day consequences of the industrial revolution rather than its early evolution? A field expedition to unearth an Assyrian palace is admittedly a proper undertaking for university professors; but should coal strikes, Indian unrest, rubber, oil, and American lynchings be for the present mainly left to journalists, travellers, and politicians? Do they become proper subjects of academic interest only when they approach the post-mortem stage? Quite the contrary: with all the difficulties arising from contemporaneousness, the task of the scientist, dealing with present social phenomena, is probably easier than that of the Hellenist or mediaevalist, intent upon reconstructing the past. "Think of the happiness of the scholar if he could see a Greek republic or a Roman colony actually living under his own eyes—granted that he recover from the havoc of some of his best established delusions!"[3]

3 Salvador de Madariaga, *Aims and Methods of a Chair of Spanish Studies* (Clarendon Press, Oxford, 1928), p. 12.

I have said that data of one kind or another are not so difficult to obtain. But generalization is another matter. The social scientist may resent the premature generalizations of his predecessors. He will himself not get very far unless he himself tentatively generalizes; unless, in a word, he has ideas as well as data. Essays and investigations may be piled mountain high; they will never by themselves constitute a science or a philosophy of economics, psychology, or society. The two processes—the making of hypotheses and the gathering of data—must go on together, reacting upon each other. For in the social sciences as elsewhere generalization is at once a test of and a stimulus to minute and realistic research. The generalizations will not endure; why should they? They have not endured in mathematics, physics, and chemistry. But, then, neither have the data. Science, social or other, is a structure: "a series of judgments, revised without ceasing, goes to make up the incontestable progress of science. We must believe in this progress, but we must never accord more than a limited amount of confidence to the forms in which it is successively vested."[4]

The task, then, of finding a basis and providing a methodology for the social sciences, is today more pressing than it has ever been because of the accelerated rate of social change and the relatively more rapid progress in the physical and biological sciences: "The events of 1914–1918, to quote a single example, showed that the statesmen, the social scientists, the moral and religious teachers of Europe, to whom belonged, as their main duty, the preservation of peace, failed utterly; the directors and inventors of the physical sciences had assigned to them as their main duty the killing of as many of the national enemies as possible, and they succeeded magnificently. Twenty years hence the same situation may recur; and unless the two disciplines concerned can meanwhile come to an understanding, half the population and all the accumulated wealth of Europe may be destroyed with even more complete efficiency."[5]

As long as evolution proceeded slowly over centuries, men could feel their way and make adjustments imperceptibly on an empirical basis. But the restraints which for centuries slowed down or limited adjustments have been largely removed. Societies have to act—intelligently, if possible—if not, then unintelligently, blindly, selfishly, impulsively. The weight and prestige of the university must be thrown on the side of intelligence. If the university does not accept this challenge, what other institution can or will? In this present-day world, compounded of tradition, good

---

4 Duclaux, *Pasleur—The History of a Mind* (translated by Smith and Hedges, Philadelphia and London, 1920), p. 111.

5 Graham Wallas, *Physical and Social Science* (Huxley Memorial Lecture 1930, London), p. 1. The quotation is slightly paraphrased.

and bad, racial mixtures, nationalistic and internationalistic strivings, business interests, physical forces of incredible power for good or ill, emancipated workers and peasants, restless Orientals, noisy cities, conflicting philosophies—in this world rocking beneath and around us, where is theory to be worked out, where are social and economic problems to be analysed, where are theory and facts to be 'brought face to face, where is the truth, welcome or unwelcome, to be told, where are men to be trained to ascertain and to tell it, where, in whatever measure it is possible, is conscious, deliberate, and irresponsible thought to be given to the task of reshaping this world of ours to our own liking, unless, first and foremost, in the university? The wit of man has thus far contrived no other comparable agency.

The urgency of the need is not, as I have said, without its dangers. The history of the more manageable sciences contains a warning which the social scientist will do well to heed. Chemistry made no progress as long as men were concerned immediately to convert base metal into gold; it advanced when, for the time being, it ignored use and practice. Today chemical theory and chemical practice are continuously fertilizing each other. So, again, medicine stood almost still until the pre-clinical sciences were differentiated and set free—free to develop without regard to use and practice. The same situation has more recently developed on the clinical side; disease is most likely to be understood—and ultimately combatted—if it is approached as a phenomenon, and patients and problems must be selected on the basis of the clinician's interest, in so far as he is engaged in investigation. The social sciences have not yet developed far enough to win assured scientific status. A sympathetic onlooker is fearful lest the frail theoretic or scientific structure is being subjected to a practical strain that it is not competent to bear. To be sure, the social scientist must find his material in the thick of events; but quâ scientist, he must select and approach and frame his problems, from the viewpoint of science, without incurring responsibility for policies. In the social as in the physical sciences, the university is, in so far as scientific effort to understand phenomena is concerned, indifferent to the effect and use of truth. Perhaps, in due course, use and theory may in the social sciences also prove mutually helpful; perhaps social experimentation, involving application, may prove the only laboratory. But even so, it is one thing to incur responsibility for policies, and quite another to set up an experiment primarily in the interest of ascertaining truth or testing theory. The modern university must neither fear the world nor make itself responsible for its conduct.

I have been urging that universities maintain contacts with the actual world and at the same time continue to be irresponsible. Are the two attitudes incompatible? Can they really take an objective position in reference to social, political, and economic phenomena? Can they study phenomena without wanting to tell legislatures, communities, municipal authorities, and chambers of commerce what they ought to do at any particular moment about some particular thing? I think they must and can. It is a question of ideals and organization.[6] For experimental purposes they may, without sacrifice of intellectual integrity, make suggestions and watch results; but this is different from running a city government or a political party, involving, as such responsibilities do, compromises of principle that are fatal to fearless thinking. The analogy of the medical clinic, already mentioned, is not complete, but it is suggestive. The professor of medicine needs patients, just as the social scientist needs his environment. The professor of medicine ought to be thoroughly humane, realizing fully that he is dealing with, and in that sense responsible for, human life. But the professor of medicine is primarily a student of problems and a trainer of men. He has not the slightest obligation to look after as many sick people as he can; on the contrary, the moment he regards his task as that of caring for more and more of the sick, he will cease to discharge his duty to the university—his duty to study problems, to keep abreast of literature, to make his own contributions to science, to train men who can "carry on." The greatest and most productive of American surgical thinkers lived his entire scientific life in this fashion: he was considerate and humane in the care of his patients; he trained a group of remarkably competent surgeons; but his central thought and activity never swerved from the study of problems; one problem after another yielded its mystery to him; but having solved a problem, he ceased to occupy himself actively with it; other persons could do that, while he pushed on to something new, important, unknown. "We are still, as you know, groping more or less in the dark," he once wrote, "and always shall be, I trust; for otherwise there would be no game in medicine. There are, however, light spots back of us, where before there was darkness."[7] In those words the university professor spoke—the professor of surgery, of medicine, of law, of economics, of all subjects whatsoever.

Industry has found ways of utilizing the sheerest scientific research—it does not require that of the university; medicine is groping about for a similar connecting link—the medical faculty would be ruined if it served in both capacities. The social sciences must be detached from the conduct of business, the conduct of politics, the reform of this.' that, and the other, if they are to develop as sciences, even though they continuously need contact with the phenomena of business, the phenomena of politics, the phenomena of social experimentation.

---

6 The present British Government has set up an Economic Advisory Council, an academic group which discusses, from the academic or theoretic point of view, economic and political questions. The Council does not decide policies: that is left to the Government.

7 Extract from a letter written by Dr. William S. Halsted, Professor of Surgery, Johns Hopkins Medical School, 1889–1922.

V

The situation is not essentially different in respect to the so-called "exact sciences," though universities have in the more vigorous western countries become more hospitable to their cultivation for their own sake. These sciences—mathematics, physics, chemistry, and biology—have made greater progress in the last century than in many preceding centuries. Even so, they are still in their infancy. In what is usually called their "pure" form—I mean their cultivation without reference to application—they have now so securely established themselves, theoretically at least, that I need not emphasize their importance. It is, however, not so generally realized that science, pure or applied, creates more problems than it solves. First, on the theoretic or philosophic side: we have become increasingly and painfully aware of our abysmal ignorance. No scientist, fifty years ago, could have realized that he was as ignorant as all first-rate scientists now know themselves to be. It was but recently that we believed that Newton had arrived at rock-bottom! It is a disquieting change from that complacent state of mind to the attitude of Charles Peirce, who described the laws of nature as habits or customs; or to the attitude of Gilbert Lewis who asks: "Can we not see that exact laws, like all the other ultimates and absolutes, are as fabulous as the crock of gold at the rainbow's end?"[8] The theoretic consequences of scientific discovery may thus be very disconcerting; for the scientist, bent perhaps merely upon the gratification of his own curiosity, periodically and episodically destroys the foundations upon which both science and society have just become used to reclining comfortably. We listen nowadays not to one Copernicus—a voice crying in the wilderness—but to many, and their voices are magnified and transmitted through the entire social and intellectual structure. Physics and chemistry, viewed as merely intellectual passions, will not stay "put"; they have an elusive way of slipping through the fingers of the investigator.

I have spoken of the theoretic consequences of scientific progress and of the need of a place in which calm, philosophic reflection can be brought to bear upon them. Consider now the practical consequences of scientific advance, the problems thus created, and the need of opportunities for their consideration and solution. Medicine offers an obvious example. Whether out of humanitarian or sheer scientific interest, men study the phenomena of disease. What happens? A problem is solved—the problem of this or that infection or contagion. Quite unexpected consequences ensue. One problem is solved; other problems are created. Life is lengthened. Thereupon we are confronted by a new crop of diseases, almost negligible as long as the infancy death rate was high and the expectation of life limited to the

8 G. N. Lewis, *The Anatomy of Science* (Yale University Press, 1926), p. 154.

thirties; thus has medical science increased, not diminished, its own burden. But this is not all: men live longer and more safely; they live more healthily and contentedly in huge cities than in small villages or in the open country. At once, serious social problems, involving education, government, law, custom, morality, arise from the congestion of population following improved sanitation. Nor is this all. There are more people—many more. They must be fed and clothed. Raw materials are needed; the excess of manufactured products must be marketed. Competition becomes more and more intense—for raw materials, for colonies, for markets. War is no longer a solution—it merely creates additional problems. Thus science, in the very act of solving problems, creates more of them. Such are the consequences of progress in a portion of the physical and biological sciences in a small corner of the western world. Inevitably, the sciences will be more thoroughly and more widely cultivated. What new problems will be thereby created, we are powerless to conceive. But so much at least is clear: while pure science is revolutionizing human thought, applied science is destined to revolutionize human life. We are at the beginning, not at the end, of an epoch. Problems therefore abound and press upon us—problems due to ignorance, problems created by knowledge. They must be studied before intelligent action can be taken. Hand-to-mouth contrivance does not suffice. Who is going to study them? Who and where? There will be, of course, from time to time a lonely Mendel or a lonely Darwin, who may do epoch making things. But more and more the worker needs co-workers and facilities such as the individual is not likely to possess; he needs, also, soil in which to grow. However deeply the flash of genius may penetrate, the bulk of the world's work in research and teaching will be done in universities -if universities are what they ought to be.

VI

Our world is not, however, merely a matter of democracy and science. Indeed, if some sort of cultural equilibrium is to be attained, the humanistic disciplines, in which philosophy is included, necessarily become of greater rather than less importance; and by humanistic disciplines I refer not only to the humanities as such, but to the human values inherent in a deep knowledge of science itself. With the quick march of science, philosophy and humanism have gone under a cloud; when they assert themselves, they are prone to do so apologetically, on the ground that they too are, or can be, scientific. To be sure, they are and can; I shall in a moment have a word to say on that point. But quite aside from their pursuit in a scientific spirit, the world has not lost, and, unless it is to lose its savour, will never lose the pure, appreciative, humanistic spirit -the love of beauty, the concern for ends established by ideals that dare to command rather than to obey. Now science, while widening our vision, increasing our satisfactions, and solving our problems, brings with it dangers peculiarly its own. We can become so infatuated with progress in knowledge and control—both of which I have unstintedly emphasized—that we lose our perspective, lose our historic sense, lose a philosophic outlook, lose sight of relative cultural values. Something like this has happened to many, perhaps to most, of the enthusiastic, clear-headed, forward-looking, perhaps too exclusively forward-looking, and highly specialized young votaries of science. They are, culturally, too often thin and metallic; their training appears technological rather than broadly and deeply scientific. I have urged that science, qua science, is indifferent to use and effect. Taste and reason do not intervene to stop the scientist prosecuting his search for truth; they do sit in judgment on the uses to which society puts the forces which the scientist has set free. I say, our younger scientists not infrequently appear to have been dehumanized; so also do some humanists. In the modern university, therefore, the more vigorously science is prosecuted, the more acute the need that society be held accountable for the purposes to which larger knowledge and experience are turned. Philosophers and critics, therefore, gain in importance as science makes life more complex—more rational in some ways, more irrational in others.

But there are other senses in which humanism must be promoted by modern universities. For humanism is not merely a thing of values—it has, like science, consequences. At first sight, what can be more innocent than the resurrection of a dead language? But every time a dead language is exhumed, a new nationality may be created. The humanists, not merely the Turks or the politicians or the newspapers, are at least partly responsible for the Balkanization of Eastern Europe and for the recrudescence of Celtic feeling. Like the scientist, the humanist creates as well as solves problems; he helps to free the Serbs and the Greeks from Turkish rule; he helps both to create and to solve the Home Rule problem in Great Britain—irresponsibly in either instance; he assists powerfully in stimulating self-consciousness in India, in Egypt, in China, and among the American Negroes; he finds himself one of the causes of an exacerbation of nationalism and racialism which no one has yet learned to mollify or cure. He has, I repeat, no practical responsibility for" the trouble he makes; it is his business and duty to preserve his independence and irresponsibility. But he must go on thinking; in that realm his responsibility is of the gravest. And, perhaps, in the fullness of time, the very licence of his thought may, without intention or forethought on his part, suggest inventions or profoundly influence solutions, as it has done heretofore.

I cannot presume, even if I had space, to enumerate all the reasons for desiring a vigorous renascence of humanistic studies. But I must touch on one more point. During the last century, palaeontologist and historian have shown us how little we know of the story and import of man's career on this planet. A tremendous gap remains to be filled by archaeologists, philologists, and palaeographers—by Greek and Latin scholars working in libraries and in the field, by Orientalists, digging at Megiddo, in the Nile Valley, at Dura, and elsewhere. The story of the Athenian Empire will have to be rewritten in the light of recent readings of the pieced-together fragments of a few Greek tablets; who knows what will happen when the Agora discloses its secrets? And were the Hittite, Sumerian, and Malay languages and remains properly cultivated, we might arrive at very different conceptions than are now accepted as to the origin, development, and spread of culture. I need not labour the point by dwelling on the importance of a humanistic development covering mediaeval and modern times. Suffice it to say that further study of mediaeval and modern art, literature, music, and history will inevitably revise notions formed on the basis of the defective data which have hitherto controlled our thinking.

Intensive study of phenomena under the most favourable possible conditions—the phenomena of the physical world, of the social world, of the aesthetic world, and the ceaseless struggle to see things in relation—these I conceive to be the most important functions of the modern university. We shall get further with the physical world than with the social world or the aesthetic world; but the difference is only one of degree—all are important, all are worthwhile—worthwhile in themselves, worthwhile because they have bearings, implications, uses. But the university will not exhaust its function when it piles up its heaps of knowledge. Within the same institution that is busy in ascertaining facts, intelligence will be at work piecing facts together, inferring, speculating. There will be a Rutherford, breaking up the atom, and a Whitehead or Eddington, trying to make out what it all means; a Virchow demonstrating cellular pathology, and a Banting bringing from the four corners of the earth the various bits that, fitted together, produce insulin. When the late Jacques Loeb was asked whether he was a chemist or physiologist, he is reported to have replied, "I am a student of problems." It is fashionable to rail at specialization; but the truth is that specialization has brought us to the point we have reached, and more highly specialized intelligence will alone carry us further. But, of course, specialization alone does not suffice; there must somehow be drawn into the university also minds that can both specialize and generalize. The philosophic intelligence must be at work, trying new patterns, trying, however vainly, to see things in the large, as new material is accumulated. And this process should go on in the university more effectively than anywhere else, just because the university is the active centre of investigation and reflection and because it brings together within its framework every type of fundamental intelligence.

VII

A modern university would then address itself whole-heartedly and unreservedly to the advancement of knowledge, the study of problems, from whatever source they come, and the training of men—all at the highest level of possible effort. The constitution of the stars, the constitution of the atom, the constitutions of Oklahoma, Danzig, or Kenya, what is happening in the stars, in the atom, in Oklahoma, what social and political consequences flow from the fact that the politician is becoming more and more obsolescent while the business man and the idealist are playing a larger part in determining the development of society—all these are important objects to know about. It is not the business of the university to do anything about any of them. The university cannot regulate the weather in Mars, it cannot run business, it cannot directly influence what happens at Westminster or Washington. But neither can it hold itself aloof.

There are dangers to be encountered in modernizing universities, in the sense in which I have used the term. Quite obviously, such a modern university has more things to think about than a mediaeval institution given to expounding Aristotle, the Fathers, and the classic philosophers. But precisely because modern universities have many interests, they must be extremely critical of every claimant. Now, men—especially mediocre men—do not always distinguish the serious from the trivial, the significant from the insignificant. A university, seeking to be modern, seeking to evolve theory, seeking to solve problems, may thus readily find itself complicating its task and dissipating energy and funds by doing a host of inconsequential things.

There is a second danger. The moment a real idea has been let loose, the moment technique has been developed, mediocrity is jubilant; the manufacture of make-believe science flourishes. Learning has never been free from pedantry or from superficiality. But the modern world, what with its abundant facilities for publication and its ridiculous fondness for "learned" degrees, groans under a tropical growth of make-believe. Now, as against this tendency, against the tendency towards specialization of a mechanical or technological kind, we need to remember that universities depend on ideas, on great men. One Virchow, one Pasteur, one Willard Gibbs can change the entire intellectual order in his respective sphere. But great men are individuals; and individuals and organizations are in everlasting conflict. The university is an institution. It cannot, on the one hand, be amorphous or chaotic. Neither, on the other, can it flourish unless it is elastic enough to supply the different conditions that different productive individuals find congenial. It may well turn out that these conditions are just as favourable to somnolence as to productivity. It does not much matter that some persons go to sleep, provided only enough others are wide awake and fertile at the maximum of their powers. The important thing is not that a few persons doze or loaf or are ineffectual; the important thing is that a Hertz, a Maxwell, a Mommsen, and a Gildersleeve find within the university the conditions that suit them as individuals—conditions favourable to their own development and to the development of a varied group of co-workers.

VIII

I do not wish now to anticipate what I shall have to say of American, English, and German universities. But it must be obvious already that my criticism will cover two points, viz., what universities do not now touch, what they have no business to touch. The program which I have sketched is surely not lacking in extent or difficulty; its successful execution would call for more talent and more money than any university now possesses. Moreover, the kind of work that such universities should do requires proper conditions—books, laboratories, of course, but also quiet, dignity, freedom from petty cares, intercourse at a high social and intellectual level, a full and vaned life nicely adjusted to individual idiosyncrasies. We sh;11 have occasion in subsequent chapters to consider with how much intelligence universities nowadays draw the line in these matters. Let me concede, for the purpose of argument (and for that only), that all the things that universities do are in themselves worth doing—a very large concession. Does it follow that universities *should* do them? Does it follow that universities *can* do them? I answer both questions in the negative. If universities are charged with the high functions that I have enumerated, they will do well to discharge them effectively—do well to assemble the men to gather the money, to provide the facilities that are requisite to their performance. I think it can be shown that universities do not yet discharge these functions well; that they assume obligations that are irrelevant and unworthy. If the functions, against which I should draw the line, are really worth discharging, society must find other ways of discharging them. Of course there is nothing sacrosanct about the three or four traditional faculties or the traditional subjects. As the world has changed, new faculties have been needed; new subjects have from time to time been created. But even in the most modern university a clear case must be made out, if for no better reason than the fact that expansion means increase of professors and students—the former difficult to obtain, the latter likely through sheer size to destroy the organic character of the institution. And the case, as I see it, must rest on the inherent and intellectual value of the proposed faculty or the proposed subject. Practical importance is not a sufficient title to academic recognition: if that is the best that can be said, it is an excellent reason for exclusion. A university is therefore not a dumping ground. Universities that are held to their appropriate tasks will be unfit to do other tasks. A far-reaching educational reconstruction may thus become necessary. In no two countries is it going to be brought about in identical fashion. Indeed, it need not be uniformly accomplished in anyone country. But, however this may be, the reorganization of universities, in order that they may do supremely well what they almost alone can do, may accomplish much by forcing the reorganization of the rest of the educational system.

IX

On the basis which I have discussed, the pursuit of science and scholarship belongs to the university. What else belongs there? Assuredly neither secondary, technical, vocational, nor popular education. Of course, these are important; of course, society must create appropriate agencies to deal with them; but they must not be permitted to distract the university.

With merely technical, merely vocational, or merely popular education we shall encounter no difficulty in dealing; but the term "secondary education" is so vague and so variously used that I must explain the sense in which I shall use it throughout these pages. To my mind, the difference between secondary and university education is the difference between immaturity and maturity. Secondary education involves responsibility of an intimate kind for the student, for the subject-matter that he studies, even for the way in which he works, lives, and conducts himself—for his manners, his morals, and his mind. The university has no such complicated concern. At the university the student must take chances—with himself, with his studies, with the way in which he works. The freedom of the university does not mean either that the professor is indifferent or that at the very outset the student should attack a piece of research independently: on the contrary, he has, while free, to work through a difficult apprenticeship before he attains independence. In the same way, the entire texture of secondary education need not be uniform. Freedom and responsibility may be increased, as adolescence advances; in one way or another, the peculiar character of the secondary school may taper off, as the university approaches. But in any event, there will be a break, a jolt, a crisis, precisely as there is a break when a grown boy or girl leaves home. It is not the business of education to avoid every break, every jolt, every crisis. On the contrary, the boy having become a man, a jolt tests his mettle; unless he survives and gains in moral and intellectual strength, the university is no place for him, for the university should not be even partly a secondary school.[9]

9 It is clear, for example, that, as I employ the term, the American high school is not co-extensive with secondary education: on the contrary, in the United States, «secondary

Of the professional faculties, a clear case can, I think, be made out for law and medicine;[10] not for denominational religion, which involves a bias, hardly perhaps for education, certainly not at all for business, journalism, domestic "science," or library "science," to which I shall return in detail later.[11] It is true that most physicians and most lawyers are mere craftsmen; it is even true that their training largely occupies itself with teaching them how to do things. I should go further: I should add that an unproductive faculty of law or medicine is no whit the better for being attached to a university; it has no business there; it would do as well by society and by its students if it were an independent vocational school.

How are we to distinguish professions that belong to universities from vocations that do not belong to them? The criteria are not difficult to discern. Professions are, as a matter of history—and very rightly—"learned professions"; there are no unlearned professions. Unlearned professions—a contradiction in terms—would be vocations, callings, or occupations. Professions are learned, because they have their roots deep in cultural and idealistic soil. Moreover, professions derive their essential character from intelligence. Of course, the surgeon uses his hands; the physician uses a stethoscope; the lawyer uses a clerk and an accountant. But these are the accidents of activity. The essence of the two professions resides in the application of free, resourceful, unhampered intelligence to the comprehension of problems—the problems of disease, the problems of social life, bequeathed to us by history and complicated by evolution. Unless legal and medical faculties live in the atmosphere of ideals and research, they are simply not university faculties at all.

Professions may be further distinguished by their attitude towards results. The scientist or the scholar who takes shape in the physician or the jurist has objects to accomplish. The achievement of these objects incidentally brings in a livelihood; but the livelihood is, theoretically at least (and for many centuries practically too), of secondary or incidental, even though to the individual, of essential, importance. Professions have primarily objective, intellectual, and altruistic purposes. A profession is therefore an order, a caste, not always in fact free from selfish aims, but in its ideals at least devoted to the promotion of larger and nobler ends than the satisfaction of individual ambitions. It has a code of honour—sometimes, like the Hippocratic oath, historically impressive.

---

education» would swallow not only the high school, but much, perhaps most of the college. See p. 53.

10 I do not in this volume discuss schools of law or schools of technology, for the simple reason that I have never studied them. The omission implies no opinion of any kind.

11 See pp. 158–91, 172.

It will become clear, as we go on, that, compared with present theory and practice, the conception of the university which I have outlined is severe. Have I lost sight of the importance of "training"—training college teachers or educational administrators or candidates for governmental posts? I think not. I have merely assumed that persons who have had a genuine university education will emerge with disciplined minds, well stored with knowledge, possessing a critical, not a pedantic edge, and that such persons may thereafter for the most part be safely left to their own devices. I suspect, if I must tell the whole truth, that persons who sacrifice broad and deep university experience in order to learn administrative tricks will in the long run find themselves intellectually and vocationally disadvantaged. From the standpoint of practical need, society requires of its leaders not so much specifically trained competency at the moment as the mastery of experience, an interest in problems, dexterity in finding one's way, disciplined capacity to put forth effort. Lower or special schools or experience itself will furnish technique, if that is what students desire.

X

The emphasis which I have placed upon thinking and research may create the impression that I am really discussing institutes of research rather than universities. Such is not the case. Institutes of research, as we know them, differ in certain respects from universities as I am trying to conceive them. In the first place, the research institute stands or falls by its success in research, whereas, in projecting the modern university, I have been careful to associate training with research. The history of research institutes throws light upon this point. The modern research institute was first set up in Paris for Pasteur, because within the French university of Pasteur's time one could not procure the conditions requisite to scientific research. The movement broadened in Germany under the influence of Friedrich Althoff, the forceful and fertile administrator who from 1882 to 1907 was the guiding spirit of the Prussian *Cultus Ministerium*. A jurist and a bureaucrat, Althoff was especially interested in medicine; and to some extent at least, his general program was governed by his ideals of medical education and research. He strove with tireless energy and splendid success to equip all the faculties of the Prussian universities, so that they might, under modern conditions, realize and develop the conception of training and research which had been embodied in the University of Berlin at its origin. Althoff perceived, however, that even under ideal university conditions a small number of rare geniuses might squander in teaching or administration rare abilities that ought to be concentrated upon research. He was thus led to plan a series of institutes in which the most fertile minds might be devoted to research in fields in which fundamental progress had already been made—fields, in which the basic sciences had already attained definiteness and solidity, in which problems, theoretic as well as substantive, could be clearly formulated, in which personnel of high quality had already been trained. The feasibility of the research institute was thus pretty narrowly circumscribed. It does not follow that, because the research institute is feasible and timely in physics, chemistry, or medicine, it is either feasible or timely in less well developed fields of interest, however urgent the need.

The points just mentioned suggest at once the strength and the weakness of the research institute. The research institute is a sort of flying column, that can be directed hither or yon, wherever results seem attainable, wherever personnel of exceptional character is available. But so specific is the research institute that its particular activities depend on an individual or a small group. Whatever the institute be called, its energies centre about a person. The important things are not subjects, but persons; when the person goes, the subject goes. If a university chair is vacated, it must usually be filled—with a productive scholar and teacher if possible, with a scholar, at any rate, if a productive scholar is not obtainable. Not so, the research institute. In 1911, an institute of experimental therapeutics was set up at Dahlem for Wassermann; when Wassermann died in 1920, there was no successor, or the situation had changed. His institute was turned over to Professor Neuberg as an institute of bio-chemistry. What happened was not that one institute was abolished and another created; what really happened was that Wassermann died, and that Neuberg was enabled to carry on his own work. The research institute does not have to include all subjects within a definite field; it can demobilize as readily as mobilize. The university may have to employ makeshifts temporarily; the research institute, never.

From the standpoint of progress under favourable conditions, these are great advantages. But there are disadvantages. Forecasting in *The New Atlantis* a foundation aiming to obtain "the knowledge of causes," Bacon conceived an institution equipped with the paraphernalia of what we term research including fellows and "novices and apprentices that the succession do not fail." The university has at hand a student body from which "novices and apprentices may be drawn by professors who have had opportunity to ascertain their merits. The research institute, lacking a student body of its own, must seek out young men, possessed of ability and training. If financially strong, it can take the risk; but its" novices and apprentices" are rarely known at first hand, as they may easily be within the university.

Again, in the complexity of modern science there is no telling from what source the magic conception will come. The very breadth of the university increases greatly its potential fertility. The research institute may therefore be hampered by limitations consequent upon intense concentration. Too highly specialized institutes, especially if somewhat practically minded, are likely to be fruitless. Althoff foresaw this danger. "If," says his recent biographer,[12] "the research institute is detached from the university and made directly accountable to the ministry, this idea must not be too narrowly interpreted. All these institutions serve the purposes of the university, namely, teaching and investigation. Indeed, the Prussian educational authorities are so strongly convinced of the soundness of the universities that all the most recent organizations are in some way or other more or less intimately connected with the universities." Thus a research institute, set up within or in connection with a modern university, might escape some of the limitations to which the isolated institute is exposed.

There is a further point on which I must touch. The research institute enjoys, I have said, the advantages of concentration and mobility. Yet Althoff was right in opposing a narrow conception. Too definite a conception or formulation may eliminate the element of surprise—important to both teaching and research. Both research institute and university laboratory are engaged in solving problems; both are engaged in training men. Is the head of a research division only seeking knowledge? By no means. He has about him a group of assistants—younger men whom he sifts and trains, precisely as does the university professor. His students are simply more advanced, more highly selected. Thus the research institute might be described as a specialized and advanced university laboratory, enjoying certain marked advantages and not free from possible disadvantages. Successful research institutes are no substitute for universities. Indeed, they cannot succeed, unless universities furnish them a highly trained personnel—a debt, I hasten to add, which they repay as they give further training to men and women, many of whom become university teachers. Far more hopeful, in my opinion, than the rapid multiplication of research institutes at this moment would be the freeing of existing universities from inhibitions and encumbrances, and their development into the instruments competent to perform well their proper functions.

XI

So much in general. I began by saying that in this chapter I should discuss the idea of a university that would answer the intellectual needs of this modern age. It is the idea, not the organization that I have been speaking of. To organization excessive importance is likely to be attributed. Nevertheless, organization or lack of organization is not entirely immaterial. We shall see in subsequent chapters how in one country excessive organization and in another poor organization obstruct

12 Arnold Sachse, *Friedrich Althoff und Sein Werk* (Berlin, 1928), p. 294.

the realization of the idea of a university. In all countries university reform is now the subject of earnest discussion. In all countries, history, traditions, vested interests hamper reconstruction. Obstacles are not always bad: a rich and beautiful past may interfere with reconstruction, while at the same time offering considerable compensation. When therefore the moment for action arises, one needs to view existing realities against the background of a clearly defined general principle. We shall find both conditions and possibilities highly varied—absurdities that may easily be eliminated, sharp corners that need to be cautiously turned, preconceptions that need to be vigorously combatted, historic values that must not be sacrificed, practical commitments that can only be gradually shifted to other agencies. In the end, when reconstruction has been achieved, we shall find ourselves not with a standardized, but with a very varied result—in no two countries alike, and total uniformity in not even one. Our chances of meeting the needs of modern life will be better, if we are content to accept anomalies and irregularities, though there are also anomalies and irregularities which are intolerable. The line is not easy to draw; different countries, different individuals may draw it in different places; but the precise point at which it is drawn is of relatively little importance, as long as the main function of the modernized university stands out with sufficient prominence.

CHAPTER TWENTY-THREE

The Dilemmas of the Higher Learning

From *The Higher Learning in America* (1940)

ROBERT MAYNARD HUTCHINS

This selection is taken from *The Higher Learning in America*, 1940, from The Storrs Lectures series, published by Yale University Press, New Haven, CT.

Editors' Note

Robert Maynard Hutchins (1899–1977) was an American educational philosopher and university leader. Principally associated with the University of Chicago—where he was successively President (1929–1945) and Chancellor (1945–1951)—he was earlier Dean of Yale Law School, in which role he pioneered interdisciplinary approaches to the study of law.

Appointed to be President at Chicago at the age of 30, the youngest ever president of a leading university, Hutchins set about reforming the university and simultaneously developing his educational ideas in a long series of texts. In particular, he developed a concern for what it was to be educated in a time of change and turmoil. (The First World War was not long behind and both the USA and Europe at least were in turbulent and unsettled situations.) Subsequently, after Chicago, Hutchins became Head of the Ford Foundation, in which capacity he established the Fund for the Advancement of Education and the Fund for Adult Education: for Hutchins, university education was but a preparation for lifelong learning. He then, after leaving the Ford Foundation, founded the Center for the Study of Democratic Institutions, insisting again on an interdisciplinary approach to such study.

His educational philosophy was driven by a sense that universities were failing their students, who were in his view receiving an impoverished experience. It was doubly impoverished, being overly narrow and unduly focused on practical matters. It arose from a 'service-station conception' of the university. (*The Higher Learning in America*, p. 6) As a result, students were intellectually malnourished and ill-fitted to become citizens. Hutchins central solution lay in a 'general education' built around 'great books' (p. 81). This would constitute a 'higher learning', in imparting a higher-order vantage point and engagement with the general culture of society. Although Hutchins recognizes that difficulties attach to implementing such a programme, not least that 'not all [professors] have read all the books they would have to teach', Hutchins did what he could to institute the necessary reforms while he was at Chicago, instituting a two-year generalist bachelor's programme, reserving study in depth to the Master's stage (although subsequently these changes were overturned).

RB

*****

There is a conflict between one aim of the university, the pursuit of truth for its own sake, and another which it professes too, the preparation of men and women for their life work. This is not a conflict between education and research. It is a conflict between two kinds of education. Both kinds are found in all parts of a university. As I shall show in a moment, professional training is given in almost every department, and the pursuit of truth for its own sake may occasionally be met with even in a professional school.

I need not tell you which of these two aims of the modern university has lately been more popular. A mere recital of the new schools, avowedly professional in purpose, that have appeared in the past thirty-five years will convince you that we have seen a dramatic shift in the composition of our universities. Since the beginning of the century the following units designed to fit students for specific occupations have appeared and have become respectable: schools of journalism, business, librarianship, social service, education, dentistry, nursing, forestry, diplomacy, pharmacy, veterinary surgery, and public administration. There are many others that have appeared, but have not yet become respectable. I have confined myself to what might be called the standard subjects.

These new schools, of course, consume a very large portion of the attention of students, faculty, and administrators. New developments in older professional disciplines are having the same effect. The growth of university medicine since 1910 has been phenomenal. The total assets contributing to medical education and research at the University of Chicago are more than forty million dollars, and medicine now consumes 25 per cent of the University's annual budget. Full-time faculties in law and engineering lead, of course, to greater expense than we were formerly put to; for part-time professors ordinarily carried away little or nothing as direct salary. In engineering the equipment becomes more elaborate as technology advances, and no end to the process is in sight. The modest requirements of a classics group of ten professors pale into insignificance beside the demands of the same number of engineers.

Emphasis on professionalism is further promoted by the increasing practice of pointing work from the junior year onward toward some professional school. The modern university is full of prelaw, prebusiness, predentistry, preëngineering, and premedical students whose course of study is determined by their professional ambitions. In some institutions the professional schools themselves begin with the junior year. This, as I shall show later, would be a sound organization under certain circumstances. Unfortunately those circumstances do not obtain today.

We find, moreover, that outside professional schools and in departments of arts, literature, and science the atmosphere in which the student labors is highly professional. Students do graduate work in organic chemistry because industry engages a large number of Ph.D.'s in this field every year. Students study for the M.A. because it is becoming necessary for positions in secondary schools. In the Middle West 45 per cent of the graduates of colleges of liberal arts go into teaching. In some colleges this proportion rises to 90 per cent. These colleges have been forced to offer the Master's degree so that their students may teach in secondary schools. They must also offer professional courses in education because state laws and accrediting agencies require such training for the prospective teacher at all levels of the public schools. In the universities students study for the Ph.D. because it is almost impossible to secure a college or university post without it. Seventy-five per cent of them have no interest in research; at least, that percentage never does any more after the exertions of the dissertation. It is hardly an exaggeration to say that university departments exist to train people to teach in university departments.

The pursuit of knowledge for its own sake is being rapidly obscured in universities and may soon be extinguished. Every group in the community that is well enough organized to have an audible voice wants the university to spare it the necessity of training its own recruits. They want to get from the university a product as nearly finished as possible, which can make as large and as inexpensive a contribution as possible from the moment of graduation. This is a pardonable, perhaps even a laudable, desire. But the effect of it on the universities will be that soon everybody in a university will be there for the purpose of being trained for something.

You may ask, what of it? You may suggest, and with reason, that the surroundings of a university are better than those in which the young practitioner might otherwise learn to practice. You may point out that a desirable uniformity may be obtained by insisting on educational requirements through which all neophytes must pass. You may say that the legal profession, for example, is not to be trusted with the education of the young lawyer; and if you do, you will, I am afraid, be right. My answer is that the burdens imposed upon the universities by this arrangement are bad for them and bad for the professions, and that the hope of doing a better job of training young people in the practices of a profession by having the universities do it is quite illusory.

It is plain enough, I suppose, that it is bad for the universities to vocationalize them. I do not deny that the professional atmosphere has an electrical effect on some students. I have seen Big Men at Yale, football heroes and social luminaries, wake up in the Law School under the stimulus of the incentives and competition of professional work. The close connection between law-school grades and law-office jobs and the fact that it is the fashion to work in law school accomplish a good many miracles of this variety. Undergraduate study can make no such appeal: it has no apparent connection with anything and the fashion of working at it would be difficult to start.

On the other hand, the vocational atmosphere is ruinous to attempts to lead the student to understand the subject. By hypothesis he is learning to practice the profession. You must, therefore, make clear to him at every step that the questions you are discussing have a direct bearing on his future experiences and on his success in meeting them. You must give him practical advice. A friend of mine recently took an hour to explain to his law-school class the economic and social background of the fellow-servant rule. At the end of the discussion one student inquired, "What's this got to do with the law?" There is a good deal to be said for the boy's position; he had come to the university under the impression that it would prepare him for the bar examinations and teach him the rules of the game. He felt that he was being cheated. Under these circumstances the temptation is irresistible to tell your students stirring anecdotes of your own days at the bar, to let them in on the tricks of the trade, and to avoid confusing their minds by requiring them to think about anything except what the courts will do.

The curriculum of such a school is what you might expect it to be. It is confined to those subjects which experience, tradition, or the state examinations have sanctified. The emphasis of the school is determined by vocational pressures: if, for example, big business is the thing, the course of study will revolve around commercial law. It is conceivable that public law may take the place of commercial law if the public service as an occupation continues to be a popular topic of conversation. Criminal law, a subject of the greatest practical and theoretical importance, is required in law schools because nobody would study it otherwise: there is in general no money in it. Jurisprudence, which should be central in any law curriculum, is studied by few and like legal history is regarded as a peripheral or ornamental subject.

If you set out to prepare a boy for a trade there are and can be no limits to the triviality to which you will descend except those imposed by the limitations on the time at your disposal. You can justify almost anything on the ground that it may be helpful to the young man in his profession. And if you take the view that a university may properly prepare boys for trades, there is no limit to the number of trades you can train them for except those imposed by the limitations on your resources. Since you can usually' make a school pay if you make it vocational enough, there are really no limits at all. Any occupation that wishes to be dignified will say that it is a profession and suggest that the university cooperate by offering a curriculum preparing young people for it. This is a free country, which in my business means that anybody is free to make suggestions to a university and demand that they be carried out.

It follows that the professors in a university so conceived and so dedicated will be selected not because of their intellectual capacity, but because of the length, breadth, and depth of their practical experience. An ability to think and interest in thinking about the subject might be a handicap to a member of the staff. Although the salary scale in law schools is higher than in nonprofessional departments, the standard of scholarship is lower. In few other fields can a considerable reputation be grounded on the production of textbooks, manuals, or teaching materials. Moreover, a law teacher is supposed to be a good teacher first of all, which in professional schools is likely to mean a popular teacher. Sins of omission in scholarship are forgiven him if the boys agree that he knows the law. I have watched non-lawyers come into law schools as professors and observed that the first thing they feel called on to do is to act as though they had had brilliant careers at the bar. In some cases they have thus defeated the object of their appointment, which was to diminish rather than increase the amount of vocational instruction.

These attitudes of students and teachers have resulted in the isolation of professional schools from the less frankly vocational elements in a university. Whether other departments are actually pursuing the truth for its own sake or not, they usually pretend that they are. The result is that there is hardly a law school in the United States that is really part of the university to which it nominally belongs. The Yale Law School, indeed, has gone so far as to get attached to the Harvard Business School and to cooperate with it in a way in which it would never think of doing with any Yale department, and in which the Harvard Law School would never think of doing with the Harvard Business School.

The Institute of Human Relations at Yale was an attempt to unify certain professional and nonprofessional disciplines. The centrifugal forces at work were so strong, however, that some elements were blown out of the Institute at an early date; and in spite of large resources and an elaborate plant the rest of the organization has been held together with some difficulty.

Superficially, at least, the law is connected with economics, ethics, politics, history, and psychology. Even in universities which have good departments in these fields the law school has little to do with them, and they have little to do with it. The engineering schools are notorious for their particularistic views of the natural sciences upon which engineering depends, and even of English composition, which, we are told, is something quite different in engineering from what it is in any other walk of life. Even in medical schools, which because of their organization into the clinical and preclinical years have a clearer notion of the relation of the sciences and the arts, you are likely to hear that a scientist outside the medical school can contribute little to medical progress and still less to medical education. If we assume that the professional disciplines have something that the rest of the university should know about and that the rest of the university might possibly shed some light on the professional disciplines, we must agree that isolation is bad for everybody. Indeed we can hardly make a case for including professional schools in universities at all except on the ground that mutual interchange with nonprofessional departments will give them something they could not otherwise get.

Vocationalism leads, then, to triviality and isolation; it debases the course of study and the staff. It deprives the university of its only excuse for existence, which is to provide a haven where the search for truth may go on unhampered by utility or pressure for "results." I do not need to tell you how hard it is in these times and in this country to keep this characteristic activity of a university alive. There is, as a matter of fact, no discernible enthusiasm for it in the United States. Think where research in any meaning of the word would be if it had not been for the Rockefeller, Carnegie, and Harkness fortunes. The spirit of the age is not congenial to long-term, quiet investigations of matters which seem remote from daily life; nor is it in fact congenial to the impartial, detached study of subjects that touch daily life more nearly. Everybody wants the university to advance his special brand of propaganda, to join his private pressure group. He cannot imagine that the university is not interested in pressure or propaganda. He assumes that if it is not with him it must be against him. We have come to the point where the pursuit of truth for its own sake is actually regarded as dangerous by nervous newspaper publishers and worried business men.

Under these circumstances, we cannot cheerfully see the essential activity of a university submerged by wave after wave of vocationalism. But I suggest that vocationalism is not merely bad for the universities; it is bad also for the professions.

I beg to lay down this fundamental proposition that every profession requires for its continuous development the existence of centers of creative thought. To the extent to which universities and professional schools abandon creative thought and degenerate into trade schools the profession must degenerate into a trade. I attribute the decline of the church in this country to the decline of the theological schools, the plight of the law to the plight of the law schools, the condition of engineering to the condition of the engineering schools, and the comparative excellence of medicine to the comparative excellence of the medical schools developed since 1910.

If we examine those medical schools we see that they were made part of universities in order to secure for them the benefit of any thinking that might be going on in them. The professors were to be in the main men who could think about medicine. Hence it was provided that they must have time to do it. The number of students was to be small enough to give the faculty opportunity to encourage and direct the thinking of students. The emphasis was not on hospital beds or on classroom facilities: it was on laboratories. A connection was sought not with large hospitals but with strong departments in the basic sciences. Throughout all the modifications which these schools have undergone, where close association with the basic sciences has been preserved, their excellence has been maintained. Where those departments have been' weak or have become the slaves of a professional group, the medical school has deteriorated. It is not too much to say that an intimate relationship with strong scientific departments is the indispensable requirement for a strong medical school. Such a school may become strong temporarily through assembling a distinguished group of clinicians and through the excellence of its supply of clinical material. The pressure of clinical work is such, however, that it becomes routine and the school becomes routine if it is cut off from a center of creative thought.

It is for this reason that the location of professional schools is of more significance than at first appears. Putting law schools near the courts and medical schools near the hospitals may have some advantages; they are nothing compared to the disadvantages of removing them from the university. Emphasis on the practical is not an emphasis that professional schools need. The demands of the profession are pressed upon them constantly. Only by a close association with a university can these demands be minimized and the emphasis placed where it needs to be, on the intellectual problems of the profession.

But location is not enough. Why is it that the clergy do not command the respect that we should all like to feel for them? I think you will find the answer by looking at the catalogue of any divinity school. It is now made up of subjects which, it is assumed, will assist the pastor in coping with his first charge. He learns about building management, and community singing, and church socials, and what is called religious education. Theology, which deals with the intellectual problems of his profession, has almost disappeared from the curriculum. Why is it that American engineers do not in general rise to such commanding positions outside engineering practice as do the members of the profession in England? The answer is the relatively narrow vocational course of study which the American engineer must pursue. And if there are regrettable differences between the standards of the British bar and those of the American bar, is it not possible that one reason for them is that the American law school emphasizes training for the practice and the English universities emphasize understanding the law?

Turning professional schools into vocational schools degrades the universities and does not elevate the professions. I should also contend that it cannot accomplish the only purpose it can have, namely, the preparation of the student for the practice of his life work. It is, in short, bad for the student as well as for the universities and the professions.

My contention is that the tricks of the trade cannot be learned in a university, and that if they can be they should not be. They cannot be learned in a university because they get out of date and new tricks take their place, because the teachers get out of date and cannot keep up with current tricks, and because tricks can be learned only in the actual situation in which they can be employed.

I pass over the sad circumstance that a student who spends his university career in specific vocational preparation and then does not go into the vocation has wasted his university career. Since 50 per cent of engineering graduates do not become engineers, the engineering schools should try to give them an education useful in any occupation instead of teaching them tricks that are useful, if at all, only in engineering.

All that can be learned in a university is the general principles, the fundamental propositions, the theory of any discipline. The practices of the profession change so rapidly that an attempt to inculcate them may merely succeed in teaching the student habits "that will be a disservice to him when he graduates. Efforts to keep up with the current events usually result in keeping up with the event before last, so that I should not be surprised to learn that law schools are just beginning to teach their students how to proceed under N. R. A. The case method in schools of business leads to the study of cases which occurred during a boom, a year or so after a depression has set in. The practices of the practical world are changing from day to day and even from hour to hour. It is hard for the practitioner to keep up with them, to say nothing of the professor removed from the practical world. But suppose he can keep up with them; he has no guarantee that they will still be in vogue when his students seek to apply them. In fact he knows that the chances are that they will have disappeared and others which he failed to mention will have taken their place. Consider the feelings of a professor who drilled his students in the manipulation of the rules of common-law practice in Illinois, only to see them radically altered by the Practice Act.

What should he have taught them? He should have tried to see to it that they understood the principles, if any, of pleading. If they did they could have worked out for themselves the rationale of the rules of any jurisdiction; they might even understand the Illinois Practice Act.

You may say that the university medical school shows that both the principles and the practice of a profession may be learned in a university. The example of medicine is misleading. To make the example apposite to any other profession you would have to have two things which medicine has: first, a well-developed group of preclinical sciences in close association with the professional school, and second the actual conditions of practice on the university campus. The first of these some professional disciplines have, though they usually fail to make use of them. Engineering, for example, can find the physical sciences on the campus if it is willing to associate with them. Other professional branches, like the law, have nowhere to turn, for even if we assume that the social sciences are the sciences preclinical to the law, we cannot pretend that they are well worked out. They are, in fact, so badly worked out that at present it may be better for the law schools to stick to the law than to confuse themselves further by association with the social sciences.

The second of the requirements for achieving the results in training for practice that the medical school achieves is not enjoyed by any other professional unit. Only in medicine do we find the actual conditions of practice on the university campus. In the university medical school the professors are practicing medicine; their patients are suffering from diseases just as real as those which appear in any doctor's office. The student learns to practice in the only way in which anybody can learn to practice anything, by practicing. In law, engineering, journalism, business, and other real and imitation professional schools, the conditions of practice do not exist, and hence the student cannot learn to practice. If we were to attempt to get in law the same results that the medical school gets in medicine, we should have to organize the law school like a law office, with the professors practicing their profession, for a suitable fee, and the students learning as their assistants. Under the present system attempts to teach law students the art of practicing law will not succeed; they will, moreover, do positive harm, for they will divert the law student from what he might learn in law school, which is the theory, the fundamental propositions, the general principles of the law.

It is for this reason that "practical" work should not be attempted in professional schools even if it were possible to succeed with it: it interferes with the education of the student. It seems reasonably clear that a member of a learned profession should be educated. An educated man knows what he is doing and why. It is possible, I suppose, to be a very good cook without knowing any chemistry. At least the cookbooks confine themselves to telling you what to do under certain circumstances. It is not yours to reason why; you follow the instructions. It is perhaps for this reason that cooking has never been regarded as one of the learned professions. A man can be a good automobile driver, or bricklayer, or ditch digger on the same terms. All he needs to know is the rules of the trade. He does not need to understand them. But a profession cannot be truly learned unless its members understand the subject matter with which it deals.

The subject matter of a learned profession is intellectual. Though the rules of the trade may be learned in the practice, and indeed can only be learned there, the intellectual content of the profession can generally be mastered only in a university; at least a university should be the ideal place for such study. To the extent to which the attention of the student is directed to vocational interests and away from the intellectual content of the discipline the university fails to do the only thing it might do and attempts something in which it is bound to fail.

Yet we live in a world that is not merely unintellectual but anti-intellectual as well. Even the universities are anti-intellectual. The college, we say, is for social adaptation; the university is for vocational adjustment. Nowhere does insistence on intellectual problems as the only problems worthy of a university's consideration meet such opposition as in the universities themselves. We try to adjust students to life by giving them information about it, though we know the information will be archaic when they graduate. We try to adjust students to their life work by telling them how a professional man operates; we seldom bother to tell them why. The result is a course of study which is anti-intellectual from beginning to end.

A student may, then, enter a professional school without ever having been compelled to think, without, in short, being educated. In the same innocent condition he may enter a learned profession. We cannot wonder that the learned professions are no more learned than they are. If the student has not learned to think and if the technical procedures that have been taught him are of little value, what has he acquired in the professional school that could not be better learned elsewhere? As we saw at the beginning, he has learned to work. It is too bad that he has not been put to work on something worthwhile. If he had been, he might have been just as successful in the practice of his profession; for paradoxically enough a grasp of theory might enable him to meet practical situations which were overlooked or not foreseen by his instructors.

From this inspection of the universities we can see what our dilemmas are. The first is the dilemma of professionalism. We do not feel safe in turning over education for the professions to the members of them. Universities are corporations not for profit, and can perhaps be trusted somewhat further. Many activities, such as public administration, are very important to the public. We see no way of preparing men to engage in them. The universities should be able to do something about this, too. Yet we know that a professional emphasis at present means a vocational emphasis and that such an emphasis is bad for the universities, bad for the professions, and bad for the students.[1]

Professionalism produces our second dilemma, which is the dilemma of isolation. To the extent to which professors are concerned with preparation for a specific trade they are isolated from professors interested in another specific trade, and both groups are isolated from those who are not interested in any trade at all but are attempting to pursue the truth for its own sake. On the other hand, all university departments with few exceptions are now engaged in the recent observation of professional training of some kind. The advantages of association with them are therefore highly dubious. University departments and professional schools now have no common frame of reference; it is possible that cooperation might increase confusion. An isolated vocational school can at least be certain that it is engaged in trying to prepare students for the vocation.

The third dilemma is that of anti-intellectualism. We are afflicted here again by the circularity of education and the national life. The professions and the public demand people trained according to their idea of what that training should be. How can their ideas be changed? Only by an education which they can get only in a university. Can a university train men for a profession in ways which the profession does not approve? Can a university make a profession learned in spite of itself? One of the chief concerns of a university department and *a fortiori* of a professional school is that its graduates shall get jobs. These departments and schools are not likely to break into a type of education with which the profession is unacquainted and of which it will be suspicious.

These dilemmas can, I think, be resolved; but it will take another chapter to do it. I will say here by way of suggestion and summary that the dilemma of professionalism can be met in part by a thoroughgoing revision of our notions of what a profession is. From the university standpoint, at least, a professional discipline to be a professional discipline must have intellectual content, and have it in its own right. All there is to journalism can be learned through a good education and newspaper work. All there is to teaching can be learned through a good education and being a teacher. All there is to public administration can be discovered by getting a good education and being a public servant. As Aristotle said in the

1 Cf. Dean C. H. Wilkinson. Worcester College, Oxford. "Specialism has largely taken the place of education and, with its twin brother professionalism, is spreading like a blight over the land."

Politics, "The same education and the same habits will be found to make a good man and a good statesman and king." If the universities can revert to a condition where the number of professional schools and courses is limited to those that have intellectual content in their own right, they will have gone some distance toward disposing of the dilemma of professionalism.

They will go still farther toward disposing of it if they can insist that the professional schools and departments that remain deal with their subject matters in the true university spirit, that is, in the spirit of studying them for their own sake. Every learned profession has a great intellectual heritage, and it is this which should be the prime object of the attention of professional schools. I believe that these schools will find that their students will be "better prepared for practice if they are trained to think in the subject matter of the professional discipline than if they have been taught by the cookbook method."

Studying professional subject matters in this spirit will produce better practitioners. It will also help to meet the dilemma of isolation. Subject to a qualification that I shall introduce later, the unifying principle of a university is the pursuit of truth for its own sake. So far as professional departments adopt this principle as their own they take their place in the university's community of scholars. If the number of professional groups can be limited to those that have intellectual content; if they and all other departments can conduct their work in the same spirit; if we can develop general education so that all advanced study will rest on a common body of knowledge, we may succeed in making our universities true communities and communities of true scholars.

Only by this route can we resolve the dilemma of anti-intellectualism. If the leading universities can develop ideals which are intelligible to them; if they can adhere to them even if for a time they lose students and money, it may be that they can sometime make themselves and their ideals intelligible to our people. The justification for the privileges of universities is not to be found in their capacity to take the sons of the rich and render them harmless to society or to take the sons of the poor and teach them how to make money. It is to be found in the enduring value of having constantly before our eyes institutions that represent an abiding faith in the highest powers of mankind. The whole world needs this symbol now as never before. It is this symbol that I hope the American universities may become.

CHAPTER TWENTY-FOUR

The Idea of a Multiversity

From *The Uses of the University* (1963)

CLARK KERR

This selection by Clark Kerr (then President of the University of California) is taken from *The Uses of the University* (1963). Published by Harvard University Press Cambridge, MA, and Presented as an annual Godkin Lecture under the auspices of the Harvard Graduate School of Public Administration. The Godkin Lectures on the Essentials of Free Government and the Duties of the Citizen were established at Harvard University in 1903 in memory of Edwin Lawrence Godkin (1831–1902).

Editors' Note

Clark Kerr's early career was as an industrial sociologist, but it was as a university leader, administrator and analyst for which he is most remembered. Yet, even as an industrial sociologist, he took the broadest view, situating his work against a horizon of 'the logic of industrialization' (Kerr et al., 1960). Appointed in 1952 as the first Chancellor of the University of California, Berkeley, Kerr was subsequently invited in 1958 to lead the entire University of California system, a position he held until 1967, when he was dismissed by Governor Ronald Reagan. Through his years as a university leader, Kerr was in the thick of national academic debates, especially over free speech, to which he was resolutely wedded, and the

Vietnam War. While President of the University of California, Kerr was pivotal in the development of the California Master Plan for Higher Education, which saw the establishment of an inter-connected system that included world-leading institutions (such as Berkeley) in which the different kinds of tertiary institution were granted their own position and responsibilities, providing ladders of opportunity for all students (Kerr, 2001).

The Uses of the University arose out of the Godkin lectures that Kerr was invited to give at Harvard University (a signal honour in itself, especially that a Berkeley administrator should be so recognized). The book not merely analyses the character of the great research university but does so at a level that continues to resonate over the following decades. The central idea of the university as a 'multiversity', having 'fuzzy' edges, could be said to anticipate much later applications of postmodernism, complexity theory, and rhizomatic talk of 'multiplicities, in their collective sense of a lack of a centre and the presence of an ineradicable instability. A multiversity was so not in the sense of being distributed across many campuses but rather in the sense of being a 'pluralistic' institution; and Kerry explicitly sets off this conception as against a monistic university (cf. Minogue). 'The multiversity is based more on conflict and on interaction; the monistic university more on unity and integration' (ibid., p. 106). Such an institution raised large matters of governance: 'a community should have a soul, a single animating principle; the multiversity has several … held together by a common grievance over parking'.

RB

Recommended Reading

Kerr, C. (2001). *The Gold and the Blue: a Personal Memoir of the University of California 1949–1967. Volume One.* Berkeley and London: University of California.

Kerr, C., Dunlop, J. T., Harbison, F., and Myers, C. A. (1960). *Industrialism and Industrial Man.* London: Pelican.

* * * * *

The university started as a single community—a community of masters and students. It may even be said to have had a soul in the sense of a central animating principle. Today the large American university is, rather, a whole series of communities and activities held together by a common name, a common governing board, and related purposes. This great transformation is regretted by some, accepted by many, gloried in, as yet, by few. But it should be understood by all.

The university of today can perhaps be understood, in part, by comparing it with what it once was—with the academic cloister of Cardinal Newman, with the research organism of Abraham Flexner. Those are the ideal types from which it has derived, ideal types which still constitute the illusions of some of its inhabitants. The modern American university, however, is not Oxford nor is it Berlin; it is a new type of institution in the world. As a new type of institution, it is not really private and it is not really public; it is neither entirely of the world nor entirely apart from it. It is unique.

"The Idea of a University" was, perhaps, never so well expressed as by Cardinal Newman when engaged in founding the University of Dublin a little over a century ago.[1] His views reflected the Oxford of his day whence he had come. A university, wrote Cardinal Newman, is "the high protecting power of all knowledge and science, of fact and principle, of inquiry and discovery, of experiment and speculation; it maps out the territory of the intellect, and sees that ... there is neither encroachment nor surrender on any side." He favored "liberal knowledge," and said that "useful knowledge" was a "deal of trash."

Newman was particularly fighting the ghost of Bacon who some 250 years before had condemned "a kind of adoration of the mind ... by means whereof men have withdrawn themselves too much from the contemplation of nature, and the observations of experience, and have tumbled up and down in their own reason and conceits." Bacon believed that knowledge should be for the benefit and use of men, that it should "not be as a courtesan, for pleasure and vanity only, or as a bond-woman, to acquire and gain to her master's use; but as a spouse, for generation, fruit and comfort."[2]

To this Newman ... replied that "Knowledge is capable of being its own end. Such is the constitution of the human mind, that any kind of knowledge, if it really be such, is its own reward." And in a sharp jab at Bacon he said: "The Philosophy of Utility, you will say, Gentlemen, has at least done its work; and I grant it—it aimed low, but it has fulfilled its aim." Newman felt that other institutions should carry on research, for "If its object were scientific and philosophical discovery, I do not see why a University should have any students"—an observation sardonically echoed by today's students who often think their professors are not interested in them at all but only in research. A University training, said Newman, "aims at raising the intellectual tone of society, at cultivating the public mind, at purifying the

1 John Henry Cardinal Newman, *The Idea of a University* (New York: Longmans Green and Co., 1947). The quotations used here are from pp. 129, 91, xxvii, 157.

2 Francis Bacon, "The Advancement of Learning," *Essays, Advance of Learning New Atlantic and Other Places* (New York: Odyssey Press, Inc., 1937), pp. 214–215.

national taste, at supplying true principles to popular enthusiasm and fixed aims to popular aspirations, at giving enlargement and sobriety to the ideas of the age, at facilitating the exercise of political powers, and refining the intercourse of private life." It prepares a man "to fill any post with credit, and to master any subject with facility."

This beautiful world was being shattered forever even as it was being so beautifully portrayed. By 1852, when Newman wrote, the German universities were becoming the new model. The democratic and industrial and scientific revolutions were all well underway in the western world. The gentleman "at home in any society" was soon to be at home in none. Science was beginning to take the place of moral philosophy, research the place of teaching. "The Idea of a Modern University," to use Flexner's phrase,[3] was already being born. "A University," said Flexner in 1930, "is not outside, but inside the general social fabric of a given era. ... It is not something apart, something historic, something that yields as little as possible to forces and influences that are more or less new. It is on the contrary ... an expression of the age, as well as an influence operating upon both present and future."

It was clear by 1930 that "Universities have changed profoundly—and commonly in the direction of the social evolution of which they are part." This evolution had brought departments into universities and still new departments; institutes and ever more institutes; created vast research libraries; turned the philosopher on his log into a researcher in his laboratory or the library stacks; taken medicine out of the hands of the profession and put it into the hands of the scientists; and much more. Instead of the individual student, there were the needs of society; instead of Newman's eternal "truths in the natural order," there was discovery of the new; instead of the generalist, there was the specialist. The university became, in the words of Flexner, "an institution consciously devoted to the pursuit of knowledge, the solution of problems, the critical appreciation of achievement and the training of men at a really high level." No longer could a single individual "master any subject"—Newman's universal liberal man was gone forever.

But as Flexner was writing of the "Modern University," it, in turn, was ceasing to exist. The Berlin of Humboldt was being violated just as Berlin had violated the soul of Oxford. The universities were becoming too many things. Flexner himself complained that they were "secondary schools, vocational schools, teacher-training schools, research centers, 'uplift' agencies, businesses-these and

---

3 Abraham Flexner, *Universities: American English German* (New York, Oxford University Press, 1930). The quotations are from pp. 3, 4, 42, 179, 132, 25, 44–45, 197, 193, 231, 235, 197 (again), 178–179.

other things simultaneously." They engaged in "incredible absurdities," "a host of inconsequential things." They "needlessly cheapened, vulgarized and mechanized themselves." Worst of all, they became "'service stations' for the general public."

Even Harvard. "It is clear," calculated Flexner, "that of Harvard's total expenditures not more than one-eighth is devoted to the *central* university disciplines at the level at which a university ought to be conducted." He wondered: "Who has forced Harvard into this false path? No one. It does as it pleases; and this sort of thing pleases." It obviously did not please Flexner. He wanted Harvard to disown the Graduate School of Business and let it become, if it had to survive it all, the "Boston School of Business." He would also have banished all Schools of Journalism and Home Economics, football, correspondence courses, and much else.

It was not only Harvard and other American universities, but also London, Flexner asked "in what sense the University of London is a university at all." It was only "a federation."

By 1930, American universities had moved a long way from Flexner's "Modern University" where "The heart of a university is a graduate school of arts and sciences, the solidly professional schools (mainly, in America, medicine and law) and certain" research institutes." They were becoming less and less like a "genuine university," by which Flexner meant "an organism, characterized by highness and definiteness of aim, unity of spirit and purpose." The "Modern University" was as nearly dead in 1930 when Flexner wrote about it, as the old Oxford was in 1852 when Newman idealized it. History moves faster than the observer's pen. Neither the ancient classics and theology nor the German philosophers and scientists could set the tone for the really modern university—the multiversity.

"The Idea of a Multiversity" has no bard to sing its praises; no prophet to proclaim its vision; no guardian to protect its sanctity. It has its critics, its detractors, its transgressors. It also has its barkers selling its wares to all who will listen—and many do. But it also has its reality rooted in the logic of history. It is an imperative rather than a reasoned choice among elegant alternatives.

President Nathan Pusey wrote in his latest annual report to the members of the Harvard Board of Overseers that the average date of graduation of the present Board members was 1924; and much has happened to Harvard since 1924. Half of the buildings are new. The faculty has grown five-fold, the budget nearly fifteen-fold. "One can find almost anywhere one looks similar examples of the effect wrought in the curriculum and in the nature of the contemporary university by widening international awareness, advancing knowledge, and increasingly sophisticated methods of research. ... Asia and Africa, radio telescopes, masers and lasers and devices for interplanetary exploration unimagined in 1924—these and other developments have effected such enormous changes in the intellectual orientation and aspiration of the contemporary university as to have made the university we knew as students now seem a strangely underdeveloped, indeed a very simple and an almost unconcerned kind of institution. And the pace of change continues."[4]

Not only at Harvard. The University of California last year had operating expenditures from all sources of nearly half a billion dollars, with almost another 100 million for construction; a total employment of over 40,000 people, more than IBM-and in a far greater variety of endeavors; operations in over a hundred locations, counting campuses, experiment stations, agricultural and urban extension, centers, and projects abroad involving more than fifty countries; nearly 10,000 courses in its catalogues; some form of contact with nearly every industry, nearly every level of government, nearly every person in its region. Vast amounts of expensive equipment were serviced and maintained. Over 4,000 babies were born in its hospitals. It is the world's largest purveyor of white mice. It will soon have the world's largest primate colony. It will soon also have 100,000 students—30,000 of them at the graduate level; yet much less than one third of its expenditures are directly related to teaching. It already has nearly 200,000 students in extension courses-including one out of every three lawyers and one out of every six doctors in the state. And Harvard and California are illustrative of many more.

Newman's. "Idea of a University" still has its devotees—chiefly the humanists and the generalists and the undergraduates. Flexner's "Idea of a Modern University" still has its supporters—chiefly the scientists and the specialists and the graduate students. "The Idea of a Multiversity" has its practitioners—chiefly the administrators, who now number many of the faculty among them, and the leadership groups in society at large. The controversies are still around in the faculty clubs and the student coffee houses; and the models of Oxford and Berlin and modern Harvard all animate segments of what was once a "community of masters and students" with a single vision of its nature and purpose. These several competing visions of true purpose, each relating to a different layer of history, a different web of forces, cause much of the malaise in the university communities of today. The university is so many things to so many different people that it must, of necessity, be partially at war with itself.

How did the multiversity happen? No man created it; in fact, no man visualized it. It has been a long time coming about and it has a long way to go. What is its history? How is it governed? What is life like within it? What is its justification? Does it have a future?

---

4 Harvard University, *The President's Report, 1961–62,* p. 3.

The Strands of History

The multiversity draws on many strands of history. To the extent that its origins can be identified, they can be traced to the Greeks. But there were several traditions even then. Plato had his Academy devoted to truth largely for its own sake, but also truth for the philosophers who were to be kings. The Sophists, whom Plato detested so much that he gave them an evil aura persisting to this day, had their schools too. These schools taught rhetoric and other useful skills—they were more interested in attainable success in life than they were in the unattainable truth. The Pythagoreans were concerned, among other things, with mathematics and astronomy. The modern academician likes to trace his intellectual forebears to the groves of Academe; but the modern university with its professional schools and scientific institutes might look equally to the Sophists and the Pythagoreans. The humanists, the professionals, and the scientists all have their roots in ancient times. The "Two Cultures" or the "Three Cultures" are almost as old as culture itself.

Despite its Greek precursors, however, the university is, as Hastings Rashdall wrote, "a distinctly medieval institution."[5] In the Middle Ages it developed many of the features that prevail today—a name and a central location, masters with a degree of autonomy, students, a system of lectures, a procedure for examinations and degrees, and even an administrative structure with its "faculties." Salerno in medicine, Bologna in law, and Paris in theology and philosophy were the great pacesetters. The university came to be a center for the professions, for the study of the classics, for theological and philosophical disputes. Oxford and Cambridge, growing out of Paris, developed in their distinctive ways with their particular emphasis on the residential college instead of the separate faculties as the primary unit.

By the end of the eighteenth century the European universities had long since become oligarchies in their subject matter, centers of reaction in their societies—opposed, in large part, to the Reformation, unsympathetic to the spirit of creativity of the Renaissance, antagonistic to the new science. There was something almost splendid in their disdain for contemporary events. They stood like castles without windows, profoundly introverted. But the tides of change can cut very deep. In France the universities were swept away by the Revolution, as they almost had been in England at the time of Cromwell.

It was in Germany that the rebirth of the university took place. Halle had dropped teaching exclusively in Latin in 1693; Göttingen had started the teaching of history in 1736; but it was the establishment of Berlin by Wilhelm von

5 Hastings Rashdall, *The Universities of Europe in the Middle Ages* (3 vols., 1895, ed. F. M. Powicke and A. B. Emden, Oxford: Clarendon Press, 1936), III, 358.

Humboldt in 1809 from his vantage point in the Prussian Ministry that was the dramatic event. The emphasis was on philosophy and science, on research, on graduate instruction, on the freedom of professors and students (*Lehrfreiheit* and *Lernfreiheit*). The department was created, and the institute. The professor was established as a great figure within and without the university. The Berlin plan spread rapidly throughout Germany, which was then entering a period of industrialization and intense nationalism following the shock of the defeat at the hands of Napoleon. The university carried with it two great new forces: science and nationalism. It is true that the German university system later bogged down through its uncritical reliance on the great professorial figure who ruled for life over his department and institute, and that it could be subverted by Hitler because of its total dependence on the state. But this does not vitiate the fact that the German university in the nineteenth century was one of the vigorous new institutions in the world.

In 1809 when Berlin was founded, the United States already had a number of colleges developed on the model of the colleges at Oxford and Cambridge. They concentrated on Calvinism for the would-be preacher and classics for the young gentleman. Benjamin Franklin had had other ideas for the University of Pennsylvania, then the College of Philadelphia, in the 1750's.[6] Reflecting Locke, he wanted "a *more useful* culture of young minds." He was interested in training people for agriculture and commerce; in exploring science. Education should "serve mankind." These ideas were not to take root for another century. Drawing on the French Enlightenment, Jefferson started the University of Virginia with a broad curriculum including mathematics and science, and with the electives that Eliot was to make so famous at Harvard half a century later. He put great emphasis on a library—an almost revolutionary idea at the time. Again the application of the ideas was to be long delayed.

The real line of development for the modern American university began with Professor George Ticknor at Harvard in 1825. He tried to reform Harvard on the model of Göttingen where he had studied, and found that reforming Harvard must wait for an Eliot with forty years and the powers of the presidency at his disposal. Yale at the time was the great center of reaction—its famous faculty report of 1828 was a ringing proclamation to do nothing, or at least nothing that had not always been done at Yale or by God.'[7] Francis Wayland at Brown in the 1850's

6 Benjamin Franklin, *Proposals Relating to the Education of Youth in Pensilvania* (Philadelphia, 1749).

7 *Reports of the Course of Instruction in Yale College by a Committee of the Corporation and the Academical Faculty* (New Haven, Conn.: Hezekiah Howe, 1828).

made a great fight for the German system, including a program of electives, as did Henry Tappan at Michigan—both without success.

Then the breakthrough came. Daniel Coit Gilman, disenchanted with the then grim prospects at California, became the first president of the new university of Johns Hopkins in 1876. The institution began as a graduate school with an emphasis on research. For Flexner, Gilman was the great hero-figure—and Johns Hopkins "the most stimulating influence that higher education in America had ever known." Charles W. Eliot at Harvard followed the Gilman breakthrough and Harvard during his period (1869 to 1909) placed great emphasis on the graduate school, the professional school, and research-it became a university. But Eliot made his own particular contribution by establishing the elective system permitting students to choose their own courses of study. Others quickly followed-Andrew Dickson White at Cornell, James B. Angell at Michigan, Frederick Barnard at Columbia, William W. Folwell at Minnesota, David Starr Jordan at Stanford, William Rainey Harper at Chicago, Charles K. Adams at Wisconsin, Benjamin Ide Wheeler at California. The state universities, just then expanding, followed the Hopkins idea. Yale and Princeton trailed behind.

The Hopkins idea brought with it the graduate school with exceptionally high academic standards in what was still a rather new and raw civilization; the renovation of professional education, particularly in medicine; the establishment of the preeminent influence of the department; the creation of research institutes and centers, of university presses and learned journals and the "academic ladder"; and also the great proliferation of courses. If students were to be free to choose their courses (one aspect of the Lernfreiheit of the early nineteenth century German university), then professors were free to offer their wares (as Lehrfreiheit, the other great slogan of the developing German universities of a century and a half ago, essentially assured). The elective system however, came more to serve the professors than the students for whom it was first intended, for it meant that the curriculum was no longer controlled by educational policy as the Yale faculty in 1828 had insisted that it should be. Each professor had his own interests, each professor wanted the status of having his own special course, each professor got his own course—and university catalogues came to include 3,000 or more of them. There was, of course, as a result of the new research, more knowledge to spread over the 3,000 courses; otherwise the situation would have been impossible. In any event, freedom for the student to choose became freedom for the professor to invent; and the professor's love of specialization has become students' hate of fragmentation. A kind of bizarre version of academic laissez-faire has emerged. The student, unlike Adam Smith's idealized buyer, must consume-usually at the rate of fifteen hours a week. The modern university was born. Along with the Hopkins experiment came the land grant movement-and these two influences -turned out to be more compatible than might at first appear. The one was Prussian, the other American; one elitist, the other democratic; one academically pure, the other sullied by contact with the soil and the machine. The one looked to Kant and Hegel, the other to Franklin, Jefferson, and Lincoln. But they both served an industrializing nation and they both did it through research and the training of technical competence. Two strands of history were woven together in the modern American university. Michigan became a German-style university and Harvard a land grant type of institution, without the land.

The land grant movement brought schools of agriculture and engineering (in Germany relegated to the *Technische Hochschulen*), of home economics and business administration; opened the doors of universities to the children of farmers and workers, as well as of the middle and upper classes; introduced agricultural experiment stations and service bureaus. Allan Nevins in commenting on the Morrill Act of 1862 said: "The law annexed wide neglected the areas to the domain of instruction. Widening the gates of opportunity, it made democracy freer, more adaptable and more kinetic."[8]

A major new departure in the land grant movement came before World War I when the land grant universities extended their activities beyond their campus boundaries. "The Wisconsin Idea" came to flower under the progressivism of the first Roosevelt and the first La Follette. The University of Wisconsin, particularly during the presidency of Charles Van Hise (1903 to 1918), entered the legislative halls in Madison with reform programs, supported the trade union movement through John R. Commons, developed agricultural and urban extension as never before. The university served the whole state. Other state universities did likewise. Even private universities, like Chicago and Columbia, developed important extension programs.

New contacts with the community were created. University athletics became, particularly in the 1920's, a form of public entertainment, which is not unknown even in the 1960's, even in the Ivy League. Once started, university spectator sports could not be killed even by the worst of teams or the best of de-emphasis; and few universities seriously sought after either.

A counterrevolution against these developments was occasionally waged. A. Lawrence Lowell at Harvard (1909 to 1934) emphasized the under-graduate houses and concentration of course work,) as against the graduate work and electives of Eliot. It is a commentary not just on Harvard but also on the modern American university that Eliot and Lowell could look in opposite directions and

8 Allan Nevins, *The State Universities and Democracy* (Urbana: University of Illinois Press, 1962), p. vi.

the same institution could follow them both and glory in it. Universities have a unique capacity for riding off in all directions and still staying in the same place, as Harvard has so decisively demonstrated. At Chicago, long after Lowell, Robert M. Hutchins tried to take the university back to Cardinal Newman, to Thomas Aquinas, and to Plato and Aristotle. He succeeded in reviving the philosophic dialogue he loves so well and practices so expertly; but Chicago went on being a modern American university.

Out of the counterreformation, however, came a great new emphasis on student life—particularly undergraduate. Earnest attempts were made to create American counterparts of Oxford and Cambridge; residence halls, student unions, intramural playfields, undergraduate libraries, counselling centers sprang up in many places during the thirties, forties, and fifties. This was a long way from the pure German model, which had provided the student with only the professor and the classroom, and which had led Tappan to abolish dormitories at Michigan. British influence was back, as it was also with the introduction of honors programs, tutorials, independent study.

Out of all these fragments, experiments, and conflicts a kind of unlikely consensus has been reached. Undergraduate life seeks to follow the British, who have done the best with it, and an historical line that goes back to Plato; the humanists often find their sympathies here. Graduate life and research follow the Germans, who once did best with them, and an historical line that goes back to Pythagoras; the scientists lend their support to all this. The "lesser" professions (lesser than law and. medicine) and the service activities follow the American pattern since the Americans have been best at them, and an historical line that goes back to the Sophists; the social scientists are most likely to be sympathetic. Lowell found his greatest interest in the first, Eliot in the second, and James Bryant Conant (1934 to 1954) in the third line of development and in the synthesis. The resulting combination does not seem plausible but it has given America a remarkably effective educational institution. A university anywhere can aim no higher than to be as British as possible for the sake of the undergraduates, as German as possible for the sake of the graduates and the research personnel, as American as possible for the sake of the public at large—and as confused as possible for the sake of the preservation of the whole uneasy balance.

The Governance of the Multiversity

The multiversity is an inconsistent institution. It is not one community but several—the community of the undergraduate and the community of the graduate; the community of the humanist, the community of the social scientist, and the community of the scientist; the communities of the professional schools; the community of all the nonacademic personnel; the community of the administrators. Its edges are fuzzy—it reaches out to alumni, legislators, farmers, businessmen, who are all related to one or more of these internal communities. As an institution, it looks far into the past and far into the future, and is often at odds with the present. It serves society almost slavishly—a society it also criticizes, sometimes unmercifully. Devoted to equality of opportunity, it is itself a class society. A community, like the medieval communities of masters and students, should have common interests; in the multiversity, they are quite varied, even conflicting. A community should have a soul, a single animating principle; the multiversity has several—some of them quite good, although there is much debate on which souls really deserve salvation.

The multiversity is a name. This means a great deal more than it sounds as though it might. The name of the institution stands for a certain standard of performance, a certain degree of respect, a certain historical legacy, a characteristic quality of spirit. This is of the utmost importance to faculty and to students, to the government agencies and the industries with which the institution deals. Protection and enhancement of the prestige of the name are central to the multiversity. How good is its reputation, what John J. Corson calls its "institutional character"?[9]

Flexner thought of a university as an "organism." In- an organism, the parts and the whole are inextricably bound together. Not so the multiversity many parts can be added and subtracted with little effect on the whole or even little notice taken or any blood spilled. It is more a mechanism—a series of processes producing a series of results—a mechanism held together by administrative rules and powered by money.

Hutchins once described the modern university as a series of separate schools and departments held together by a central heating system. In an area where heating is less important and the automobile more, I have sometimes thought of it as a series of individual faculty entrepreneurs held together by a common grievance over parking.

It is, also, a system of government like a city, or a city state: the city state of the multiversity. It may be inconsistent but it must be governed—not as the guild it once was, but as a complex entity with greatly fractionalized power. There are several competitors for this power.

The students. The students had all the power once; that was in Bologna. Their guilds ran the university and dominated the masters. And the students were

---

9 John J. Corson, *Governance of Colleges and Universities* (New York: McGraw-Hill, 1960), pp. 175–179.

tougher on the masters than the masters have ever been on the students. The Bologna pattern had an impact on Salamanca and Spain generally and then in Latin America, where students to this day are usually found in the top governing councils. Their impact is generally more to lower than to raise academic standards although there are exceptions such as Buenos Aires after Peron under the leader ship of Risieri Frondizi. Students also involve the university as an institution in the national political controversies of the moment.

Jefferson tried a system of student self-government in the 1820'S but quickly abandoned it when all the professors tendered their resignations. He favored self-government by both students and faculty, but never discovered how both could have it at the same time-nor has anybody else. Although José Ortega y Gassett, in addressing the student federation at the University of Madrid, was willing to turn over the entire "mission of the university" to the students, he neglected to comment on faculty reaction.[10]

As part of the "Wisconsin idea" before World War I, there was quite a wave of creation of student governments. They found their power in the area of extracurricular activities, where it has remained. Their extracurricular programs helped broaden student life in such diverse fields as debating, theatrical productions, literary magazines.

Students do have considerable strictly academic influence, however, quite beyond that with which they are usually credited. The system of electives gives them a chance to help determine in which areas and disciplines a university will grow. Their choices, as consumers, guide university expansion and contraction, and this process is far superior to a more rigid guild system of producer determination as in medicine where quotas are traditional. Also students, by their patronage, designate the university teachers. The faculty may, in fact, appoint the faculty, but within this faculty group the students choose the real teachers. In a large university a quarter of the faculty may be selected by the students to do half or more of the actual teaching; the students also "select" ten percent or more to do almost none at all.

The faculty. The guilds of masters organized and ran the University of Paris, and later they did the same at Oxford and Cambridge. Faculty control at Oxford and Cambridge, through the colleges, has remained stronger than anywhere else over the centuries, but even there it has been greatly diminished in recent times.

In the United States, the first great grant of power to the faculty of a major university was at Yale when Jeremiah Day was president (1817 to 1846). It was (hiring the Day regime that the Yale faculty report of 1828 was issued. Harvard

10 José Ortega y Gassett, *The Mission of the University* (London: Kegan Paul, Trench, Trubner and Co., Ltd., 1946), p. 56.

has had, by contrast, as McGeorge Bundy has said in his inimitable style, "a tradition of quite high-handed and centralized executive behaviour—and it has not suffered, in balance, as a consequence."[11]

Faculties generally in the United States and the British Commonwealth, some earlier and some later, have achieved authority over admissions, approval of courses, examinations, and granting of degrees—all handled in a rather routine fashion from the point of view of the faculty as a whole. They have also achieved considerable influence over faculty appointments and academic freedom, which are not handled routinely. Faculty control and influence in these areas are essential to the proper conduct of academic life. Once the elective system was established, educational policy became less important to the faculty, although, as at Harvard under Lowell, the elective system was modified to call for general rules on concentration and distribution of work. Since Harvard adopted its program for general education in 1945[12] and Hutchins left Chicago, there has been remarkably little faculty discussion of general educational policy. By contrast, there has been a great deal in England, particularly in the "new universities," where faculty discussion of educational policy has been very lively, and faculty influence, as a consequence, substantial.

Organized faculty control or influence over the general direction of growth of the American multiversity has been quite small, as illustrated by the development of the federal grant university. Individual faculty influence, however, has been quite substantial, even determinative, in the expanding areas of institutes and research grants. Still it is a long way from Paris at the time of Abelard.

Public authority. "Public" authority is a very mixed entity of emperors and popes, ministers of education, grants committees, trustees, and Royal Commissions. But almost everywhere, regardless of the origin of the system, there has come to be a public authority. Even in the Middle Ages, emperors and popes, dukes, cardinals, and city councils came to authorize or establish the universities to make them legitimate—the guild alone was not enough. When Henry VIII had trouble about a wife it shook Oxford and Cambridge to the core.

In modern times, Napoleon was the first to seize control of a university system. He completely reorganized it and made it part of the nationally administered educational system of France, as it remains to this day. He separated off research activities and special training institutions for teachers, engineers, and so forth. The

---

11 McGeorge Bundy, "Of Winds and Windmills: Free Universities and Public Policy," in Charles G. Dobbins, ed., *Higher Education and the Federal Government, Programs and Problems* (Washington, D.G: American Council on Education, 1963), p. 93.

12 *General Education in a Free Society,* Report of the Harvard Committee with an Introduction by James Bryant Conant (Cambridge, Mass.: Harvard University Press, 1945).

universities became a series of loosely related professional schools. Not until the 1890's were the universities brought back together as meaningful entities and a measure of faculty control restored. Soviet Russia has followed the French pattern with even greater state control.

In Germany, the state governments traditionally have controlled the 'universities in great detail. So also has the government in Italy. In Latin America a degree of formal autonomy from the government has either been retained or attained, although informal reality usually contradicts the theory.

Even in Great Britain, the "public" has moved in on the faculties. Royal Commissions have helped modernize Oxford and Cambridge. The Redbrick and Scottish universities and London either have had from the beginning or acquired governing boards of a mixed nature, including lay members representative of public authority. Since 1919, and particularly since World War II, the University Grants Committee has made its influence felt in a less and less gentle and more and more effective way.

The lay board has been the distinctive American device for "public" authority in connection with' universities, although the device was used in Holland in the late sixteenth century. Beyond the lay board in the state universities are the state department of finance and the governor and the legislature with a tendency toward increasingly detailed review.

Richard Hofstadter has made the interesting observation that the first lay board and the first effective concept of academic freedom developed in Holland at the same time; and that academic freedom has never been inherited from some Golden Age of the past but has instead been imported from the institutions of the surrounding society.[13]

Through all these devices, public influences have been asserted in university affairs. Public influence has increased as much in Paris as student influence has declined in Bologna. Everywhere, with the decreasing exception of Oxford and Cambridge, the ultimate authority lies in the "public" domain; everywhere, with a few exceptions, it is fortunately not exercised in an ultimate fashion. We have, however, come a long way from the guilds of masters, the guilds of students, the guilds of masters and students. The location of power has generally moved from inside to outside the original community of masters and students. The nature of the multiversity makes it inevitable that this historical transfer will not be reversed in any significant fashion, although the multiversity does permit the growth of subcultures which can be relatively autonomous and can have an impact on the totality.

---

13 Richard Hofstadter and Walter P. Metzger, *The Development of Academic Freedom in the United States* (New York: Columbia University Press, 1955), pp. 71, 61.

The distribution of power is of great importance. In Germany it came to be lodged too completely in the figure of the full professor at one end and the minister of education at the other; in Oxford and Cambridge, at one time, in an oligarchy of professors; in the United States, during a substantial period, almost exclusively in the president; in Latin America, too often, in the students within and the politicians without.

Influences—external and semi-external. Beyond the formal structure of power, as lodged in students, faculty, administration, or "public" instrumentalities, lie the sources of informal influence. The American system is particularly sensitive to the pressures of its many particular publics. Continental and British universities are less intertwined with their surrounding societies than the American and thus more inward-looking and self-contained. When "the borders of the campus are the boundaries of our state," the lines dividing what is internal from what is external become quite blurred; taking the campus to the state brings the state to the campus. In the so-called "private" universities, alumni, donors, foundations, the federal agencies, the professional and business communities bulk large among the semi-external influences; and in the so-called "public" universities, the agricultural, trade union, and public school communities are likely to be added to the list, and also a more searching press. The multiversity has many "publics" with many interests; and by the very nature of the multiversity many of these interests are quite legitimate and others are quite frivolous.

The administration. The original medieval universities had at the start nothing that could be identified as a separate administration, but one quickly developed. The guild of masters or students selected a rector; and later there were deans of the faculties. At Oxford and Cambridge, there came to be the masters of the colleges. In more modern times in France, Germany, and Italy, the rector has come to stand between the faculty and the minister of education, closer to the minister of education in France and closer to the faculty in Germany; internally he has served principally as chairman of the council of deans where deans still retain substantial authority as in France and Italy. In Germany the full professor, chairman of his department, director of his institute, is a figure of commanding authority.

Even in England, even in Oxford and Cambridge, the central administration is attaining more influence—the vice chancellorship can no longer be rotated casually among the masters. The vice chancellor now must deal with the university grants committee and the vice chancellors of the other universities. The university itself is a much more important unit with its research laboratories, central library, its lecturers in specialized subjects; the college is much less self-contained than it was. All of this has created something of a crisis in the administration of Oxford and Cambridge where administrators once were not to be seen or heard and the work was accomplished by a handful of clerks working in a Dickensian office. Oxbridge is becoming more like the Redbricks. London is *sui generis.*

The general rule is that the administration everywhere becomes, by force of circumstances if not by choice, a more prominent feature of the university. As the institution becomes larger, administration becomes more formalized and separated as a distinct function; as the institution becomes more complex, the role of administration becomes more central in integrating it; as it becomes more related to the once external world, the administration assumes the burdens of these relationships. The managerial revolution has been going on also in the university.

Multiversity President, Giant or Mediator-Initiator?

It is sometimes said that the American multiversity president is a two-faced character. This is not so. If he were, he could not survive. He is a many faced character, in the sense that he must face in many directions at once while contriving to turn his back on no important group. In this he is different in degree from his counterparts of rectors and vice chancellors, since they face in fewer directions because their institutions have fewer doors and windows to the outside world. The difference, however, is not one of kind. And intensities of relationships vary greatly; the rector of a Latin American university, from this point of view, may well have the most trying task of all, though he is less intertwined in a range of relationships than the North American university president.

The university president in the United States is expected to be a friend of the students, a colleague of the faculty, and a good fellow with the alumni, a sound administrator with the trustees, a good speaker with the public, an astute bargainer with the foundations and the federal agencies, a politician with the state legislature, it friend of industry, labor, and agriculture, a persuasive diplomat with donors, a champion of education generally, a supporter of the professions (particularly law and medicine), a spokesman to the press, a scholar in his own right, a public servant at the state and national levels, a devotee of opera and football equally, a decent human being, a good husband and father, an active member of a church. Above all he must enjoy traveling in airplanes, eating his meals in public, and attending public ceremonies. No one can be all of these things. Some succeed at being none.

He should be firm, yet gentle; sensitive to others, insensitive to himself; look to the past and the future, yet be firmly planted in the present; both visionary and sound; affable, yet reflective; know the value of a dollar and realize that ideas cannot be bought; inspiring in his visions yet cautious in what he does; a man of principle yet able to make a deal; a man with broad perspective who will follow the details conscientiously; a good American but ready to criticize the status quo fearlessly; a seeker of truth where the truth may not hurt too much; a source of public policy pronouncements when they do not reflect on his own institution. He should sound like a mouse at home and look like a lion abroad. He is one of the marginal men in a democratic society of whom there are many others-on the margin of many groups, many ideas, many endeavors, many characteristics. He is a marginal man but at the very center of the total process.

Who is he really?

To Flexner, he was a hero-figure, "a daring pioneer" who filled an "impossible post" yet some of his accomplishments were "little short of miraculous"; thus the "forceful president"—the Gilman, the Eliot, the Harper. The necessary revolutions came from on high. There should be Giants in the Groves. To Thorstein Veblen he was a "Captain of Erudition,"[14] and Veblen did not think well of captains. To Upton Sinclair, the university president was "the most universal faker and most variegated prevaricator that has yet appeared in the civilized world."[15]

To the faculty, he is usually not a hero-figure. Hutchins observed that the faculty really "prefer anarchy to any form of government"[16] particularly the presidential form. The issue is whether the president should be "leader" or "officeholder," as Hutchins phrased it; "educator" or "caretaker," as Harold W. Dodds[17] stated it; "creator" or "inheritor," as Frederick Rudolph[18] saw it; "initiator" as viewed by James L. Morrill[19] or consensus-seeker as viewed by John D. Millett;[20] the wielder

14 Thorstein Veblen, *The Higher Learning in America* (Stanford Calif.: Academic Reprints, 1954), p. 85.

15 Upton Sinclair, *The Goose-Step: A Study of American Education* (Pasadena: John Regan & Co., 1923), pp. 382–384.

16 Robert Maynard Hutchins, *Freedom, Education and The Fund: Essays and Addresses, 1946–1956* (New York: Meridian Books, 1956), pp. 167–196

17 Harold W. Dodds, *The Academic President-Educator or Caretaker?* (New York: McGraw-Hill, 1962).

18 Frederick Rudolph, *The American College and University: A History* (New York: Alfred A. Knopf, 19b2), p. 492.

19 James Lewis Morrill, *The Ongoing State University* (Minneapolis: University of Minnesota Press, 1960), p. 48.

20 John D. Millett, *The Academic Community: An Essay on Organization* (New York: McGraw-Hill, 1962), p. 259.

of power or the persuader, as visualized by Henry M. Wriston;[21] "pump" or "bottleneck" as categorized by Eric Ashby.[22]

The case for leadership has been strongly put by Hutchins. A university needs a purpose, "a vision of the end." If it is to have a "vision," the president must identify it; and, without vision, there is "aimlessness" and the "vast chaos of the American university." "The administrator must accept a special responsibility for the discussion, clarification, definition and proclamation of this end." He must be a "troublemaker, for every change in education is a change in the habits of some members of the faculty." For all this he needs the great "moral virtues" of "courage," "fortitude," "justice," and "prudence." In looking for administrators who really thought and wrote about the "end" of their institution, Hutchins particularly identified Marcus Aurelius as the great prototype.[23] Lowell, too, believed a president should have a "plan" and that although the faculty was "entitled to propose changes," the plan should not basically be subject to interference. He also had the rather quaint idea that the president should "never feel hurried" or "work … under pressure."[24]

There were such leaders in higher education. Hutchins was one. Lowell was another; and so was Eliot. When Eliot was asked by a faculty member of the medical school how it could be after eighty years of managing its own affairs the faculty had to accommodate to so many changes, he could answer, "There is a new president."[25] Even in Oxford, of all places, as it belatedly adapted to the new world of scholarship, Benjamin Jowett as Master of Balliol could set as his rule: "Never retract, never explain. Get it done and let them howl."[26] Lord Bryce could comment in his *American Commonwealth* on the great authority of the president in the American university, on his "almost monarchical position."[27]

But the day of the monarchs has passed—the day when Benjamin Ide Wheeler could ride his white horse across the Berkeley campus or Nicholas Murray Butler rule from Morningside Heights. Flexner rather sadly recorded that "the day of the excessively autocratic president is … over. He has done a great service …" Paul Lazarsfeld 'could observe the "academic power vacuum" that resulted—leadership

21 Henry M. Wriston, *Academic Procession: Reflections of a College President* (New York: Columbia University Press, 1959), p. 172.

22 Eric Ashby, "The Administrator: Bottleneck or Pump?" *Daedalus*, Spring 1962, pp. 264–278.

23 Hutchins, pp. 177, 16g.

24 A. Lawrence Lowell, *What a University President Has Learned* (New York: Macmillan, Ig38), pp. 12, 19.

25 Rudolph, p. 291.

26 James Morris, "Is Oxford Out of This World?" *Horiton,* January 1963, p. 86.

27 James Bryce, *The American Commonwealth,* new edition (New York: Macmillan, 1914), II, 718–719.

no longer taken by the president nor assumed by the faculty, with the result of little "institutional development."[28] Hutchins was the last of the giants in the sense that he was the last of the university presidents who really tried to change his institution and higher education in any fundamental way. Instead of the not always so agreeable autocracy, there is now the usually benevolent bureaucracy, as in so much of the rest of the world. Instead of the Captain of Erudition or even David Riesman's "staff sergeant," there is the Captain of the Bureaucracy who is sometimes a galley slave on his own ship; and "no great revolutionary figure is likely to appear."[29]

The role of giant was never a happy one. Hutchins concluded that the administrator has many ways to lose, and no way to win, and came to acknowledge that patience, which he once called a "delusion and a snare," was also a virtue. "It is one thing to get things done. It is another to make them last." The experience of Tappan at Michigan was typical of many, as Angell later saw it: "Tappan was the largest figure of a man that ever appeared in the Michigan campus. And he was stung to death by gnats."[30]

The giant was seldom popular with the faculty and was often bitterly opposed, as in the "revolution" against Wheeler at California. And faculty government gained strength as faculties gained distinction. The experiences of Tappan, Wheeler, Hutchins, even Thomas Jefferson, are part of the lore of the university presidency. So are those of Wayland, who resigned from Brown in frustration after vainly trying something new, Woodrow Wilson with all his battles over innovations at Princeton, and many others.

Moreover the university has changed; it has become bigger and more complex, more tensed with checks and balances. As Rudolph saw it, there came to be "a delicate balance of interests, a polite tug of war, a blending of emphases." The presidency was "an office fraught with so many perils, shot through with so many ambiguities, an office that was many things to many men."[31] There are more elements to conciliate, fewer in a position to be led. The university has become the multiversity and the nature of the presidency has followed this change.

Also the times have changed. The giants were innovators during a wave of innovation, to use the terms of Joseph Schumpeter drawn from another context. The American university required vast renovation to meet the needs of the changing and growing nation. As Eliot said in his inaugural address, "The University

---

28 Paul F. Lazarsfeld, "The Sociology of Empirical Social Research," *American Sociological Review*, December 1962, pp. 75 1–767.

29 David Riesman, *Constraint and Variety in American Education* (Garden City, N.Y.: Doubleday, 1958), pp. 30–32.

30 Ernest Earnest, *Academic Procession* (Indianapolis: Bobbs-Merrill, 1953), p. 74.

31 Rudolph, p. 423.

must accommodate itself promptly to significant changes in the character of the people for whom it exists." The title of Wilson's inaugural address was, "Princeton for the Nation's Service." They and others helped take what had been denominational colleges and turn them into modern national universities. They were not inventors—the Germans did the inventing—but they came along at a stage in history when massive innovation was the order of the day. The giants today, when found at all, are more likely to be in a few of the old Latin American universities undergoing modernization or the new British universities in the midst of an intense discussion of educational policy.

The giants had performed "a great service," but gentler hands were needed. University administration reverted to the more standard British model of "government by consent and after consultation."[32] There is a "kind of lawlessness"[33] in any large university with many separate sources of initiative and power; and the task is to keep this lawlessness within reasonable bounds. The president must seek "consensus" in a situation when there is a "struggle for power" among groups that share it.[34] "The president must use power economically, and persuasion to the fullest extent."[35] As Allan Nevins sees it, "The sharpest strain on growth lies not in finding the teachers, but expert administrators," and the new type of president required by the large universities "will be a coordinator rather than a creative leader … an expert executive, a tactful moderator. …"[36]

Academic government has taken the form of the Guild, as in the colleges of Oxford and Cambridge until recent times; of the Manor, as in Columbia under Butler; and of the United Nations, as in the modern multiversity. There are several "nations" of students, of faculty, of alumni, of trustees, of public groups. Each has its territory, its jurisdiction, its form of government. Each can declare war on the others; some have the power of veto. Each can settle its own problems by a majority vote, but altogether they form no single constituency. It is a pluralistic society with multiple cultures. Coexistence is more likely than unity. Peace is one priority item, progress another.

The president in the multiversity is leader, educator, creator, initiator, wielder of power, pump; he is *also* officeholder, caretaker, inheritor, consensus seeker, persuader, bottleneck. But he is mostly a mediator.

---

32 Eric Ashby, "Self-Government in Modern British Universities," *Science and Freedom*, December 1956, p. 10.

33 Theodore Caplow and Reece J. McGee, *The Academic Marketplace* (New York: Basic Books, 1958), p. 206.

34 Millett, p. 224.

35 Wriston, p. 172.

36 Nevins, pp. 118–119.

The first task of the mediator is peace—how he may "the Two-and-Seventy jarring Sects confute." Peace within the student body, the faculty, the trustees; and peace between and among them. Peace between the "Two Cultures" and the "Three Cultures" and their subcultures; among all the ideas competing for support. Peace between the internal environment of the academic community and the external society that surrounds and sometimes almost engulfs it. But peace has its attributes. There is the "workable compromise" of the day that resolves the current problem. Beyond this lies the effective solution that enhances the long-run distinction and character of the institution. In seeking it, there are some things that should not be compromised, like freedom and quality—then the mediator needs to become the gladiator. The dividing lines between these two roles may not be as clear as crystal, but they are at least as fragile.

The second task is progress; institutional and personal survival are not enough. A multiversity is inherently a conservative institution but with radical functions. There are so many groups with a legitimate interest in the status quo, so many veto groups; yet the university must serve a knowledge explosion and a population explosion simultaneously. The president becomes the central mediator among the values of the past, the prospects for the future, and the realities of the present. He is the mediator among groups and institutions moving at different rates of speed and sometimes in different directions; a carrier of change—as infectious and sometimes as feared as a "Typhoid Mary." He is not an innovator for the sake of innovation, but he must be sensitive to the fruitful innovation. He has no new and bold "vision of the end." He is driven more by necessity than by voices in the air. "Innovation" may be the historical "measurement of success," the great characterizing feature of the "giants of the past";[37] but innovations sometimes succeed best when they have no obvious author. Lowell once observed that a president "cannot both do things and get credit for them"—that he should not "cackle like a hen that laid an egg."

The ends are already given—the preservation of the eternal truths, the creation of new knowledge, the improvement of service wherever truth and knowledge of high order may serve the needs of man. The ends are there; the means must be ever improved in a competitive dynamic environment. There is no single "end" to be discovered; there are several ends and many groups to be served.

The quality of the mediation is subject to judgment on two grounds, the keeping of the peace and the furthering of progress—the resolution of interpersonal and inter-group warfare, and the reconciliation of the tug of the anchor to the past with the pull of the Holy Grail of the future. Unfortunately peace and progress are more frequently enemies than friends; and since, in the long run, progress is more

37 Dodds, p. 43.

important than peace to a university, the effective mediator must, at times, sacrifice peace to progress. The ultimate test is whether the mediation permits progress to be made fast enough and in the right directions, whether the needed innovations take precedence over the conservatism of the institution. Mediators, though less dramatic than giants, are not a homogenized group; they only look that way.

They also appear to some people to be doing very little of consequence. Yet their role is absolutely essential if carried out constructively. They serve something of the function of the clerk of the meeting for the Quakers—the person who keeps the business moving, draws forth ideas, seeks the "sense of the meeting." David Riesman has suggested the term "evocator." The techniques must be those of the mediator; but to the techniques may also be added the goals of the innovator. The essence of the role, when adequately performed, is perhaps best conveyed by the term "mediator-initiator."

Power is not necessary to the task, though there must be a consciousness of power. The president must police its use by the constituent groups, so that none will have too much or too little or use it too unwisely. To make the multiversity work really effectively, the moderates need to be in control of each power center and there needs to be an attitude of tolerance between and among the power centers, with few territorial ambitions. When the extremists get in control of the students, the faculty, or the trustees with class warfare concepts, then the "delicate balance of interests" becomes an actual war.

The usual axiom is that power should be commensurate with responsibility, but, for the president, the *opportunity to persuade* should be commensurate with the responsibility. He must have ready access to each center of power, a fair chance in each forum of opinion, a chance to paint reality in place of illusion and to argue the cause of reason as he sees it.

Not all presidents seek to be constructive mediators amid their complexities. One famous president of a New York university succeeded in being at home only five months in five years. Some find it more pleasant to attend meetings, visit projects abroad, even give lectures at other universities; and at home they attend ceremonial functions, go to the local clubs, and allow the winds of controversy to swirl past them. Others look for "visions." But most presidents are in the control tower helping the real pilots make their landings without crashes, even in the fog.

Hutchins wrote of the four moral virtues for a university president. I should like to suggest a slightly different three—judgment, courage, and fortitude—but the greatest of these is fortitude since others have so little charity. The mediator, whether in government or industry or labor relations or domestic quarrels, is always subject to some abuse. Re wins few clear-cut victories; he must aim more at avoiding the worst than seizing the best. He must find satisfaction in being *equally* distasteful to each of his constituencies; he must reconcile himself to the harsh reality that successes are shrouded in silence while failures are spotlighted in notoriety. The president of the multiversity must be content to hold its constituent elements loosely together and to move the whole enterprise another foot ahead in what often seems an unequal race with history.

Life in the Multiversity

The "Idea of a University" was a village with its priests. The "Idea of a Modern University" was a town—a one-industry town—with its intellectual oligarchy. "The Idea of a Multiversity" is a city of infinite variety. Some get lost in the city; some rise to the top within it; most fashion their lives within one of its many subcultures. There is less sense of community than in the village but also less sense of confinement. There is less sense of purpose than within the town but there are more ways to excel. There are also more refuges of anonymity—both for the creative person and the drifter. As against the village and the town, the "city" is more like the totality of civilization as it has evolved and more an integral part of it; and movement to and from the surrounding society has been greatly accelerated. As in a city, there are many separate endeavors under a single rule of law.

The students in the "city" are older, more likely to be married, more vocationally oriented, more drawn from all classes and races than the students in the village;[38] and they find themselves in a most intensely competitive atmosphere. They identify less with the total community and more with its subgroups. Burton R. Clark and Martin Trow have a particularly interesting typology of these subcultures: the "collegiate" of the fraternities and sororities and the athletes and activities majors; the "academic" of the serious students; the "vocational" of the students seeking training for specific jobs; and the "nonconformist" of the political activists, the aggressive intellectuals, and the bohemians.[39] These subcultures are not mutually exclusive, and some of the fascinating pageantry of the multiversity is found in their interaction one on another.

The multiversity is a confusing place for the student. He has problems of establishing his identity and sense of security within it. But it offers him a vast range of choices, enough literally to stagger the mind. In this range of choices he encounters the opportunities and the dilemmas of freedom. The casualty rate

38 W. Max Wise, *They Come For the Best of Reasons—College Students Today* (Washington, D.C.: American Council on Education, 1958).

39 Burton R. Clark and Martin Trow, *Determinants of College Student Subculture*, unpublished manuscript, Center for the Study of Higher Education, University of California, Berkeley, Ig63.

is high. The walking wounded are many. *Lernfreiheit*—the freedom of the student to pick and choose, to stay or to move on—is triumphant.

Life has changed also for the faculty member. The multiversity is in the main stream of events. To the teacher and the researcher have been added the consultant and the administrator. Teaching is less central than it once was for most faculty members; research has become more important. This has given rise to what has been called the "non teacher"[40]—"the higher a man's standing the less he has to do with students"—and to a threefold class structure of what used to be "the faculty": those who only do research, those who only teach (and they are largely in an auxiliary role), and those who still do some of both. In one university I know, the proportions at the Ph.D. level or its equivalent are roughly one researcher to two teachers to four who do both.

Consulting work and other sources of additional income have given rise to what is called the "affluent professor," a category that does include some but by no means all of the faculty. Additionally, many faculty members, with their research assistants and teaching assistants, their departments and institutes, have become administrators. A professor's life has become, it is said, "a rat race of business and activity, managing contracts and projects, guiding teams and assistants, bossing crews of technicians, making numerous trips, sitting on committees for government agencies, and engaging in other distractions necessary to keep the whole frenetic business from collapse."[41]

The intellectual world has been fractionalized as interests have become much more diverse; and there are fewer common topics of conversation at the faculty clubs. Faculty government has become more cumbersome, more the avocation of active minorities; and there are real questions whether it can work effectively on a large scale, whether it can agree on more than preservation of the status quo. Faculty members are less members of the particular university and more colleagues within their national academic discipline groups.

But there are many compensations. "The American professoriate" is no longer, as Flexner once called it, "a proletariat." Salaries and status have risen considerably. The faculty member is more a fully participating member of society, rather than a creature on the periphery; some are at the very center of national and world events. Research opportunities have been enormously increased. The faculty member within the big mechanism and with all his opportunities has a new sense of independence from the domination of the administration or his colleagues; much administration has been effectively decentralized to the level of the

---

40 Robert Bendiner, "The Non-Teacher," *Horiton*, September 1962, p. 14.

41 Merle A. Tuve, "Is Science Too Big for the Scientist?" *Saturday Review*, June 6, 1959, p. 49.

individual professor. In particular, he has a choice of roles and mixtures of roles to suit his taste as never before. He need not leave the Groves for the Acropolis unless he wishes; but he can, if he wishes. He may even become, as some have, essentially a professional man with his home office and basic retainer on the campus of the multiversity but with his clients scattered from coast to coast. He can also even remain the professor of old, as many do. There are several patterns of life from which to choose. So the professor too has greater freedom. *Lehrfreiheit*, in the old German sense of the freedom of the professor to do as he pleases, also is triumphant.

What is the justification of the modern American multiversity? History is one answer. Consistency with the surrounding society is another. Beyond that, it has few peers in the preservation and dissemination and examination of the eternal truths; no living peers in the search for new knowledge; and no peers in all history among institutions of higher learning in serving so many of the segments of an advancing civilization. Inconsistent internally, as an institution, it is consistently productive. Torn by change, it has the stability of freedom. Though it has not a single soul to call its own, its members pay their devotions to truth.

The multiversity in America is perhaps best seen at work; adapting and growing, as it responded to the massive impact of federal programs beginning with World" War II. A vast transformation has taken place without a revolution, for a time almost without notice being taken. The multiversity has demonstrated how adaptive it can be to new opportunities for creativity; how responsive to money; how eagerly it can play a new and useful role; how fast it can change while pretending that nothing has happened at all; how fast it can neglect some of its ancient virtues. What are the current realities of the federal grant university?

CHAPTER TWENTY-FIVE

The Problem of University Transformation

From *Creating Entrepreneurial Universities: Organizational Pathways of Transformation* (1998)

BURTON R. CLARK

The Problem of University Transformation is a selection taken from *Creating Entrepreneurial Universities: Organizational Pathways of Transformation* by Burton R. Clark, a text published in the IAU Press Issues in Higher Education series. The IAU Press Issues in Higher Education series is introduced by Guy Neave, International Association of Universities, Paris. Published for IAU Press, by Pergamon, Oxford, United Kingdom.

Editors' Note

Burton R. Clark was a major scholar of higher education, which he researched for fifty years while on the faculty of several of America's most prestigious universities (Harvard, Yale, Stanford, Berkeley). His work helped to inaugurate the sociology of higher education, leading to major works such as 'The Academic Life', 'The Higher Education System' and (for our extract here) 'Creating Entrepreneurial Universities'.

In his work, Clark tackled large themes and did so on the widest canvas, often drawing on data that he—with his teams—collected from across the world. In the process, he played a signal part in the process of founding the comparative study of higher education. The disciplines and their relationships, the changing connections between universities and their wider worlds, academic organizations as communities, the dramatic changes in the spaces occupied by the university in the second half of the twentieth century as its knowledge creating function became evermore important, and the consequent implications for internal governance and shape of universities: these were just some of the themes that Clark pursued, offering insights and schemas that remain potent today.

The identification of the 'cooling out' function of the community colleges, the schema of a 'triangle of coordination' (with different countries occupying contrasting positions in the triangular space marked out by the academy, the state and the market) and the sighting of newly emerging 'entrepreneurial university' were among his scholarly legacies. It is the last of these ideas that justifies his presence here, an idea that also had its basis in extensive comparative work across continents.

It is worth observing that Clark never pressed unduly the claims of sociology: for him, it was but one perspective in the larger study of higher education. In a volume that he edited (with contributions from most of the then foremost scholars from across the world), he brought out the value of the study of higher education being understood as a multi-perspectival endeavour. He was also co-editor of a mega scholarly project, a four-volume encyclopedia of higher education. Being able critically to place the sociology of higher education in this way, while being a participant within it, imparted an unusually wide canvas to his own work.

RB

Recommended Reading

Clark, B. R. (1983). *The Higher Education System: Academic Organization in Cross-National Perspective.* Berkeley and Los Angeles: University of California.

Clark, B. R. (ed.) (1984). *Perspectives on Higher Education: Eight Disciplinary and Comparative Views.* Berkeley: University of California.

Clark, B. R. (1987). *The Academic Life: Small Worlds, Different Worlds.* Princeton.

Clark, B. R. and Neave, G. R. (editors-in-chief) (1992). *The Encyclopedia of Higher Education.* Four Volumes. Oxford: Pergamon.

* * * * *

We have seen five European universities in action, each transforming itself over a period of ten to 15 years by vigorous effort that can be characterized as entrepreneurial. Each university's development is itself a complex institutional story, one best told when embedded in contextual peculiarities and unique features of organizational character. When thus portrayed, the universities offer different histories, settings, and profiles. We then know Warwick in the English Midlands as a major research university only three decades old that faced down hard times in the 1980s and positioned itself to compete with the best universities in its own country and the world. We know Joensuu in rural Finland as a minor comprehensive university formed out of humble beginnings in the late 1960s that had to take risks and push hard 15 years later simply to achieve a sustainable niche in its own national system. As a completely technological university located on the west coast of Sweden we see Chalmers as a place that has retained a specialized form even as it asserts innovative strength across a spectrum of fields in engineering and applied science and assumes a special status in the Swedish university system. Twente, hard by the German border in The Netherlands, stands as a technological university of somewhat broader character, with a growing second focus in applied social science and its own set of distinctive campus features. Glasgow's Strathclyde, defined in the British system as Scotland's historic technological university, has taken on an even more semicomprehensive form where three of its five faculties (business, education, and the arts) are concentrated in research, teaching, and service outside science and technology. Five universities, five distinct places, conditioned by national and local contexts, different origins and developmental trajectories, and the commitment and effort of particular individuals.

But we have also seen that the institutional stories can be framed in a common conceptual structure. Formed largely from research observations, five identified elements become generalized pathways of a type of university transformation which builds upon inquiry and moves an institution aggressively into increasingly competitive orbits of science and learning. The abstracted pathways serve analytically as middle-range categories. They rise up from the realities of particular institutions to highlight features shared across a set of universities, but at the same time they still allow for local variation. Operating at only a first level of generality, the elements avoid the mists of vagueness encountered in the rarified atmosphere of unanalyzed academic abstractions and commencement-day rhetorics that clog academic and public images of how universities operate and change. My conceptual framework also shuns sweeping expressions of leadership and mission, reengineering and empowerment, strategy and stakeholding, the bromides and platitudes of the dominant management literature of the 1980s and 1990s. (Micklethwait and Wooldridge, 1996) I have stayed close to the special features of *academic* organization and have sought concreteness in the organized tools of this particular sector of society. Four elements are highly structural: w' observe them in tangible offices, budgets, outreach centers, and departments. Only the more ephemeral element of institutional idea, floating in the intangible realm of intention, belief, and culture, is hard to pin down. Emphasizing manifest structures helps greatly in explaining the development of organized social systems. Without doubt, organizational change is sustained when it acquires specific carrying vehicles. Significant change in universities has definite organizational footing.

With the five-element framework in hand, pinpointing developmental pathways, we can confront a prior question: is there a generalizable need to transform lurking in these five cases that may also be deepening in other universities? Ambition to do more than currently could be done certainly played a major role in the examined institutions. Thoughtful administrators and faculty saw that their institution could not become all that it could be if it remained in its 1970s form; a revised posture less hobbled by imbedded constraints was required. In sensing that significant transformation was compelling, the five universities chosen for study were surely not alone. A few other institutions in Europe have similarly embarked on a transforming journey; still others around the world have had cause to contemplate major change. Confidence in the traditional ways of organizing and operating academia has been eroding.

In this concluding chapter I want to explore the reasons why other universities will find themselves treading the entrepreneurial path, or will ignore the need to undergo significant transformation at considerable peril. I argue that widespread features of a rapidly changing university world pressure individual institutions in many nations to become more enterprising. If multitudes of universities need to engage in the hard work of entrepreneurially led change, then the interrelated elements brought forward in our five-case analysis may be seen as answers to a global problem of growing university insufficiency.

Modern universities develop a disturbing imbalance with their environments. They face an overload of demands; they are equipped with an undersupply of response capabilities. In a demand-response equation of environment-university relationships they may be seen as falling so badly out of balance that if they remain in traditional form they move into a nearly permanent stage of disequilibrium. A tolerable balance requires a better alignment. Transforming pathways are then a means of controlling demand and enhancing response capability. To orchestrate the elements, institutional focus takes center stage.

The concept of the focused university, on which I conclude, points to a type of organizational character that growing classes of universities will need for sustainable development. In evermore turbulent settings, universities can become robust as they develop problem-solving capabilities built around a flexible focus. But to do so they must become uncommonly mindful of their characterological development. Facing complexity and uncertainty, they will have to assert themselves in new ways at the environment-university interface. But they will still have to be universities, dominated as ever by educational values rooted in the activities of research, teaching, and study.

The Demand-Response Imbalance

I remarked in the introduction to this study that national systems of higher education can neither count on returning to any earlier steady state nor of achieving a new stage of equilibrium. As principal actors within those systems, public and private universities have entered an age of turmoil for which there is no end in sight. Disjuncture is rooted in a simple fact: *demands on universities outrun their capacity to respond*. From all sides inescapable broad streams of demands rain upon the higher education system and derivatively upon specific universities within it:

- More students, and more different types of students, seek and obtain access. Ever more accessible higher education means endless "clienteles" entitled to various types of education in their lifetimes. The general trend of elite to mass to universal higher education is well-known. But its effects in creating endless demands have not been well understood. This channel of demand in itself, if left unanswered—as in the case of open-door universities on the European continent—badly overloads the response capabilities of individual institutions. And as an "environmental" demand, the clamor for inclusion is organizationally penetrating: it flows into, through, and out of universities as applicants become participants for two, four, six or eight years, and more, only to again negotiate passage as adult students in continuing education.
- More segments of the labor force demand university graduates trained for highly specialized occupations. At different degree levels, graduating students expect qualification in diverse specialties. Graduates also need retraining throughout their professional careers. Thus the training requirements for the labor force also become virtually endless. This channel of demand in itself can badly overload universities when answers have not been found to control demand and bolster response capabilities. Again, a seemingly "environmental" demand does not merely knock at the door. Rather, future careers are expressed in a vast array of training tracks and specialized student careers within the academy. "Output" boundaries are increasingly permeable.
- Patrons old and new expect more of higher education. Those in government expect more to be done at lower unit cost. It has become a virtual iron law internationally that national and regional governments will not support mass higher education at the same unit-cost level as they did for prior elite arrangements. As other patrons, particularly industry, invest in universities, their diverse expectations become pressing. Patronage shades off into a growing chorus of interest groups repeatedly expressing their voices. "Accountability" extends in many directions. This stream of demand also becomes virtually endless. And the viewpoints of the many patrons also

readily cross old university boundaries as group representatives take "their" allotted places on university boards, committees, and advisory groups.

- Most important of all, *knowledge outruns resources.* No university, and no national system of universities, can control knowledge growth. With expanding knowledge in mind, science experts have long spoken of "endless frontiers." Flowing from the research imperative built into modern disciplines and interdisciplinary fields of study, knowledge expansion *and* specialization, *and* reconfiguration are self-propelling phenomena.

The unbelievable scale and scope of just the contemporary knowledge base can be readily illustrated. As of the early-to-mid 1990s, the field of chemistry produced worldwide a million research articles in less than two years. Mathematics generated more than a hundred thousand new theorems a year. The biological sciences fragmented and recombined as well as produced new knowledge at a rate that required curricular revision of teaching materials every two to three years. Economists have turned their logics to every sector of society, rapidly creating subfields that concentrate on such topics as the economics of the family, crime, and social welfare.

Psychology has become 20 and more specialties, some so large that they break away in national and international associations of their own. Historians recently produced more literature in two decades than they did in all previous periods: by proliferating such specialties as the history of science in nineteenth-century Japan, they endlessly divide attention by societal activity, historical time, and country. Throughout the humanities new points 'If view that contest traditional understandings have emerged in a confusing jumble, causing some humanists to see the university as an institution that has lost its soul. And the knowledge produced and circulated in universities is now greatly extended by the growing array of knowledge producers located in other sectors of society. Business schools in universities are only partly responsible for the vast outpouring of books about business management which had risen in the mid-1990s to over 2,000 a year, more than five a day.

The point is inescapable: internationally, no one controls the production, reformulation, and distribution of knowledge. Fields of knowledge are the ultimate uncontrollable force that can readily leave universities running a losing race. Just by itself, the faculty of a university, department by department, expresses an inexhaustible appetite for expansion in funding, personnel, students, and space. Rampaging knowledge is a particularly penetrating demand, rooted in the building blocks of the system: it shapes basic-unit orientation, organization, and practice. Since it has no stopping place, it never ceases. As one field of knowledge after another stretches across national boundaries and brings more parts of universities into a truly international world of science and education, growth in knowledge specialties also becomes the ultimate internationalizing force for the higher education sector of society.

These four broad streams of endless demand converge to create enormous *demand overload*. Universities are caught in a cross-fire of expectations. And all the channels of demand exhibit a high rate of change.

In the face of the increasing overload, universities find themselves limited in response capability. Traditional funding sources limit their provision of university finance: governments indicate they can pay only a decreasing share of present and future costs. "Underfunding" becomes a constant. Traditional university infrastructure becomes even more of a constraint on the possibilities of response. If left in customary form, central direction ranges between soft and soggy. Elaborated collegial authority leads to sluggish decision-making: 50 to 100 and more central committees have the power to study, delay, and veto. The senate becomes more of a bottleneck than the administration. Evermore complex and specialized, elaborated basic units—faculties, schools, and departments—tend to become separate entities with individual privileges, shaping the university into a federation in which major and minor parts barely relate to one another. Even when new departments can be added to underpin substantive growth and program changes, the extreme difficulty of terminating established academic tribes or recombining their territories insures that rigidity will dominate. Resources go to maintenance rather than to the inducement and support of change.

As demands race on, and response capability lags, institutional insufficiency results. A deprivation of capability develops to the point where timely and continuous reform becomes exceedingly difficult. Systemic crisis sets in.

How are universities near the end of the twentieth century sometimes made sufficient unto their changing environments? How are demand and response brought into reasonable balance? Adaptive responses that ease the strain take place at both system and institutional levels. System solutions set the broad context for university pathways of adaptive action.

The Search for System Solutions

National and provincial systems of higher education primarily cope with the growing demand-response imbalance by differentiation. Through both planned schemes and unplanned adjustments, systems sort out gross bundles of tasks to different types of universities, colleges, and research establishments. (Clark, 1983; Teichler, 1988; Neave, 1996; Meek et al, 1996) Formal sectors are built: in Europe, universities and polytechnics have often been set apart; in the United States, universities, four-and-five-year colleges, and two-year community colleges are commonly separated into a tripartite division of labor. Additionally, where private institutions exist, they develop individual niches in the overall national system. Access is thereby differentiated, labor market relations segmented, and different patrons provide different types and levels of support and expect different results. Beyond such broad sector separation further differentiation often occurs among universities: specialized and comprehensive universities are common in European systems.

But formal differentiation is often strongly opposed. Recently in European countries, a political tug-of-war has taken place between political parties and interest groups who want to maintain or construct an integrated, even homogeneous, single national system and those who stress the advantages of a formal division of labor. A combination of nominal integration and operational differentiation has become a useful compromise. While such institutions as polytechnics and teacher training colleges are blessed with the university title and brought into an all-encompassing single system, the differentiation of institutions, programs, and degree levels continues. The university label is stretched to give it multiple meanings and usages.

The American system offers an extreme case of the creation of different types of universities. Private institutions quite freely anoint themselves as universities; public colleges, state by state, lobby themselves into the university title. The growing aggregation of 400 or more places called universities has stretched into a half-dozen major categories: some grant many doctorates and do much research; some grant a few doctorates and do a little research; and some neither grant doctorates nor do hardly any research. (Carnegie Foundation for the Advancement of Teaching, 1994) Crossover types readily appear; e.g., some universities and colleges that are not permitted by state authorities to award doctorates proceed on their own to develop a research culture, secure more research funds than some institutions that do doctoral work, and link up with other institutions to give a joint doctorate. In Britain, after the government collapsed the old binary line and allowed polytechnics to become known as universities, the stretch in meaning of the term became much greater. A differentiation in resources and teaching and research commitments that previously took place between two main types of institutions became greater differentiation within a single formal type.

A "democratization" of titles does not bring full operational convergence: institutions become known more by what they do rather than by what they are called. Hence in national systems and on the worldwide stage we find some universities heavily concentrated on research and some that hardly do any at all; those that give many advanced degrees and others that concentrate almost completely on the first major degree; those oriented to knowledge for its own sake and those centered on useful knowledge; some that take up national roles and others situated as regional places; and on and on.

Internationally, in the 1980s and 1990s, differential effective access to sources of income rapidly became the favorite way to differentiate university systems.

We have seen this national tool operate in Britain, Holland, Sweden, and Finland. Governmental mainline support with its standardizing effects is deliberately reduced or allowed to fall as a share of university costs. The system overall must turn to what we have categorized as second and third streams of support; each has largely differentiating effects. In research-grant competition, standardization gives way to winners and losers; research niches occupied by different universities offer comparative advantage. In exploiting numerous third-stream sources, universities have different possibilities set by location and historic capacity. Then as they individually maneuver, struggling to gain more resources, they widen the differences in specific configurations of external linkages. System evolution toward diversified income promotes a dynamic of institutional diversity and competition. Universities are potentially more individualized. Patrons are then all the more inclined to think they should treat unequal things unequally.

In overcoming response inadequacies, national systems of higher education can go beyond the broadbrush of the differentiation response; they can explore the utility of reforms by engaging in deliberate institutional experimentation. In Finnish higher education the process is known as "learning by experimenting" (Välimaa, 1994). There, recent experiments included the block-grant budgetary arrangement at Joensuu, the flexible workload scheme piloted at Jyväskylä, and several changes explored in other institutions in quality assessment and in the development of a new polytechnic sector. The Finns have learned that pilot experimentation is relatively easy to initiate: everyone can readily agree to have an experiment get underway "because it is meant to be only a trial and it might fail." The critical moment of "learning by experimenting," for the system at large, comes "when the supporters of the experiment want to expand it system-wide." (p. 153) Then others can coalesce in opposition around their doubts and in support of interests that might be weakened: academic labor unions have resisted in Finland when they anticipated a reduction in bargaining power and less equity in staff rewards.

One large advantage of experimentation in the search for solutions is that small-scale efforts at the outset avoid the large mistakes made when central officials mandate reforms across the entire system without preliminary testing. Since there is no way by means of prior reasoning that central planners can know enough about all local contexts and constraints, the Large Plan (or Big Bang) approach maximizes the scale and scope of unanticipated and undesired consequences. Centralized governments are biased in favor of this road to failure.

Systems of higher education are blunt instruments for reform. (For case studies that reveal bluntness in system efforts to "restructure" higher education in five American states, see MacTaggart and Associates, 1996) Using the differentiation response, systems can indeed establish broad divisions of labor, implicitly if not explicitly, that serve somewhat to limit demands made upon; particular universities and colleges. Ministries and coordinating bodies can point institutions toward different combinations of programs and degrees; they can encourage different segments to adopt different doctrines supporting particular tasks. But systems acting from above have great difficulty in activating local initiatives. In western Europe the reverse has happened: system organization traditionally has worked to induce institutional passivity and weak local leadership. The national or state ministry provided administrative services and lumped together the staff of the university sector in system-wide categories of rank and salary; in effect, it created membership in a national civil service. Within the universities senior professors had commanding authority in their separate departments and institutes. This "continental mode" of state bureaucracy and faculty guild left a weak middle -the elected short-term rector assisted by only a small central staff and surrounded by congregations of powerful professors. (Clark, 1983, pp. 125–129) The "British mode" of authority structure was just a half-step away, with only modest authority located in vice-chancellorships (compared to that of American university presidents) and a web of faculty committees in and around an academic senate very involved in the consideration of change. Weak institutional steering became the norm. With some strengthening of rectorial authority and the enlarging and professionalizing of central staff, this pattern changed somewhat in many European universities in the 1970s, 1980s, and early 1990s, but not enough to constitute a sturdy response capability with which to face mounting and fast-moving demands. The weak center has severely limited the university capacity to change. Thus, the bluntness of system initiatives amidst the growing scale and complexity of the university sector has coexisted with a *structured* lack of initiative at the institutional level.

Weak capacity to balance demand and response, we should note, varies somewhat between one-faculty and multifaculty universities. Although they do not escape the problem of deepening imbalance, specialized universities are better positioned than the comprehensive institutions to control demand around their subject specialization and, with a more integrated character, to pursue an entrepreneurial response. Their subject concentration helps measurably to solve the growing problem of institutional focus. It is no mystery why in Europe or America, or elsewhere, specialized universities can more readily move toward entrepreneurial postures than comprehensive ones, particularly if their specialty is technology or business. When I sought nominations of universities for this study, it was no accident that the institutions named by knowledgeable European colleagues, including ones not chosen for study, turned out often to be specialized places, for example, the technologically oriented University of Compiegne in France, the business-administration oriented University of St. Gallen in Switzerland.

In contrast, the imbalance thesis applies strongly to comprehensive public universities. Organized around a wide array of subjects that stretches from classics to medicine, these institutions virtually promise higher officials, legislators, and the general public they will be all things for all demands. Martin Trow (1970, pp. 184–185) noted a quarter-century ago in an analysis of "elite" and "popular" functions of modern higher education that responding to external needs and demands was even then fast becoming an endless task:

> If one popular function is the provision of mass higher education to nearly everybody who applies for it, the second is the provision of useful knowledge and service to nearly every group and institution that wants it … the demand on the universities for such service is increasing all the time. This in part reflects the growth of the knowledge-base created by the scientific explosion of the past few decades. Not only is much of this new knowledge of potential applied value to industry, agriculture, the military, the health professions. etc., but also new areas of national life are coming to be seen as users of knowledge created in the university.

The implicit commitment of universities to embrace all of the expanding knowledge core of modern society deepened the commitment both to extend access and to service the interests of outside groups with diverse bundles of relevant knowledge and useful training. System management has been unable to control this explosion in commitments: overloaded universities have simply become more overloaded.

Other observers have also taken early note of the increasing imbalance. Based on a study of 17 universities and colleges then under stress, David Riesman warned in the 1970s against the danger of institutions overextending their resources in order to be all things to all people. (Riesman, 1973, p. 445) Two decades later, in the 1990s, the tendency to overextend resources has become more marked and the results more painful. Based on site visits and interviews in the mid-1990s at 13 colleges and universities in the American system, Leslie and Fretwell found there "was broad recognition that missions had become too loose, that too many different programs were being offered, and that scarce resources were being spread too thin across too many activities." (Leslie & Fretwell, 1996, p. xiv) Administrators and faculty "reported (and lamented) that they had made too few hard decisions" during the previous two decades. Their lament "was frequently punctuated with one phrase: 'we have tried too hard to be all things to all people,' with the unspoken trailer [that] 'we have become too diffuse to use our scarce resources well'." (p. 22) These American observers concluded that "a theme … ran throughout our site visits: being distinctive and purposeful is better than being all things to all people." (p. 16) And institutional strain this time, in the 1990s, was seen by participants as systemically different from periods of stress in the past: "It is a common refrain among those with whom we have consulted to suggest that things are not going to be the same this time, or ever again." (p. xii)

The differentiation response, it seems, finally comes down to the individual university. Each university has always had unique features that stem from geographic location, genetic imprints, student backgrounds, idiosyncratic historical developments, faculty strengths and weaknesses, and the play of particular personalities. Now, particularly as knowledge outruns resources, a university's basic departments are under ever greater pressure to commit to specialties that differentiate them from their peer-discipline departments at other universities, whether in physics or psychology or history. And what happens among departments and faculties radiates upward to intensify the need for entire universities to differentiate themselves in niches of knowledge, clientele, and labor market linkage. Such differentiation can be left to drift, and hence to occur slowly; but with accelerating change, the costs of drift and delay rise—the demand-response imbalance only deepens. Institutional action then has to be set in motion.

System organizers can help to clear the way by reducing state mandates and manipulating broad incentives, but only universities themselves can take the essential actions. The point was made in striking fashion by Clark Kerr in 1993 (p. 33, emphasis added) when he stressed that

> For the first time, a really international world of learning, highly competitive, is emerging. If you want to get into that orbit, you have to do so on merit. You cannot rely on politics or anything else. You have to give a good deal of autonomy to institutions for them to be dynamic and to move fast in international competition. *You have to develop entrepreneurial leadership to go along with institutional autonomy.*

Enter the growing necessity of what we can now call "the entrepreneurial response."

The Entrepreneurial Response

If the state and other external patrons cannot exercise the required initiative, how can universities shift from a passive to an active mode? As historically constituted, their internal faculties and departments cannot separately do the job. Oversight of their particular fields and protection of their own material interests has been their customary mandate. Only an overall organizational realignment, constructed in a first approximation by the elements captured in this study, can set into motion a new highly active mode. The five cases and certain relevant studies can help to place those elements in the broader framework of the imbalance thesis.

The strengthened steering core

Warwick, Twente, Strathclyde, Chalmers, Joensuu—all exhibited in 1995 a greater systematic capacity to steer themselves than they had possessed 15 years earlier. That ability did not take anyone form. It could be relatively centralized or decentralized, generally appearing in practice as a locally unique combination of the two—a "centralized decentralization." (Henkel, 1997, p. 137) At a given time this evolving steering capability appeared in different institutions at different stages of development and in degree. It could have been initiated by strong-minded change agents, figures drawn to leadership positions from within or without who wished to break the cake of custom. But in the sustained work of implementation such personal leadership commonly gave way to collegial groups. Stronger line authority also appeared: rector's office to dean to department head, or, in flat structures that bypass deans, from center to department head. Individuals and groups were held accountable.

Most important, the administrative backbone fused new managerial values with traditional academic ones. Management points of view, including the notion of entrepreneurship, were carried from center to academic heartland, while faculty values infiltrated the managerial space. The blending of perspectives worked best when academics who were trusted by peers served in central councils and took up responsibility for the entire institution. Since the underlying traditional academic culture cannot be ignored, cannot be pushed aside, it must be put to work and thereby adapted. Central faculty involvement became a crucial step in avoiding what the academic staff would otherwise see as hard managerialism, too much top-down command. In the hard work of transformation in these cases and elsewhere, much depends on how well managerial and faculty values become intertwined and then expressed in daily operating procedures.

Whatever its shape, the strengthened managerial core consists of agents who work to find resources for the institution as a whole. They seek other patrons instead of waiting passively for the government to return to full funding. They work to diversify income and thereby enlarge the pool of discretionary money. They seek out new infrastructure units that reach across old university boundaries to link up more readily than traditional departments with outside establishments, especially industrial firms. The core gives the institution a greater collective ability to make hard choices among fields of knowledge, backing some to the disadvantage of others; this in turn shapes access possibilities and job-market connections. The strengthened steering mechanism is necessary for the task of cross-subsidizing among the university's many fields and degree levels, taxing rich programs to aid less-fortunate ones that otherwise would be relegated to the corner or even dropped from the enterprise because they cannot pay their way. Agents of the core thereby not only seek to subsidize new activities but also try to enhance old valuable programs in the academic heartland. As much manoeuvring among contradictory demands becomes necessary, the agents of the constructed core become institutionally responsible for doing so.

A strengthened administrative core, then, is a mandatory feature of a heightened capability to confront the root imbalance of modern universities.

The enhanced development periphery

The new peripheries that enterprising universities construct also take quite different specific forms. They variously consist of outreach administrative units that promote contract research, contract education, and consultancy. They include a varied array of research centers that are generally, but not always, multi-or transdisciplinary. The new units and centers may be closely or loosely linked to the steering core and the heartland departments. Like science parks that become autonomous, some peripheral units may have the name and sponsorship of the university but then operate much like mediating institutions situated between the university and outside organizations. Again, there is no one way, no one model to emulate.

But the developmental peripheries we have observed have a valuable common outcome: they move a university toward a dual structure of basic units in which traditional departments are supplemented by centers linked to the outside world. The matrix-like structure becomes a tool for handling the inevitable growth of the service role of universities. Department-based "specialist groups" are complemented by "project groups" that admit external definitions of research problems and needed training. The new groups cross old lines of authority; they promote environmental linkages in their daily practice. We noted at Chalmers that they can even effect reciprocal knowledge transfer; the university learns from outside firms as the companies learn from the university. The matrix structure allows for more temporary units, thereby introducing flexibility amidst stability. With tenured staff mainly based in the departments and nontenured and part-time staff often predominating in the outreach centers, the more temporary units of the periphery are more readily disbanded.

Since units of a developmental periphery extend, cross, and blur boundaries, they can decisively shape the long-run character of a university. They can develop new competencies close to useful problem solving. They can generate income that helps to diversify funding. They answer the call for interdisciplinary efforts. But if not judged by academic values as well as managerial and budgetary interests for their appropriateness in a university, they can move an institution toward the character of a shopping mall. A connected and somewhat focused construction of the periphery requires a collective institutional capacity to make choices based on educational values. New outward-looking units can make the problem of overall institutional focus all the more difficult: research centers contend with old departments, transdisciplinary perspectives with disciplinary orientations, the useful with the basic, the outward-looking with the inward-oriented. But when carefully monitored, the periphery becomes a second virtually essential element with which to lessen the imbalance between environmental demands and response capacity. Traditional departments alone cannot effect all the needed linkages: in themselves, they cannot add up to an effective focus. The new periphery is necessary, even if it adds to the organized complexity of the university.

As a halfway house to the outside world, the developmental periphery becomes an organized location within a university for the entry and absorption of whole new modes of thinking. In ideal typical terms formulated by an international study group in the mid-1990s, their designated "Mode 1" refers to the traditional way of handling knowledge in disciplinary frameworks. A newly emerging "Mode 2," transdisciplinary and problem-oriented, was seen by the study group as located largely outside universities in a host of knowledge-centered enterprises that stretch from major industrial laboratories to policy think tanks to management consultancies to new small and medium-sized enterprises. (Gibbons et al., 1994; see also Ziman, 1994) Between the ideal types there lies a lengthy continuum of different practical combinations. The peripheries of universities we observed in this study incorporate much Mode 2. Their units are established precisely to go beyond disciplinary definitions; they extend university boundaries to bring in the perspectives of outside problem-solving groups; they are prepared to take their leads from the outside and to work close to application. They are often strongly committed to the straight-on production of useful knowledge.

An enhanced developmental periphery plays many roles in enterprising universities, not the least in bringing new modes of thinking and problem solving within newly stretched boundaries. Organizationally, in Peter Scott's terms, it helps to stretch the "core" university into the "distributed" university, where knowledge, the primary commodity, is more "applications-generated." (Scott, 1997, pp. 11–14)

The discretionary funding base

Demand overload hits hard at the core support of universities. Student growth and knowledge growth together increase enormously the costs of systems of higher education and individual universities. Higher costs then change the relationship of universities to their principal patrons, especially funding ministries.

If higher education in earlier days had been a minor charge in governmental budgets, it now becomes a major expenditure. As a big-ticket item, university support moves up the agenda of governmental concerns and is thrown into direct competition with other major interests. Politicians pay attention. They put universities on their personal and party agendas. The sheer happenstance of where university support is decided in the state bureaucratic and legislative structure can even become critical, variously contending with the major sums sought by schools, welfare agencies, health departments, prisons, agricultural interests, and the military. Even in good times of rising state income and outlay, governments then seek to control higher education costs. In bad times of general retrenchment they insist on major cuts. They issue dire warnings in statements that echo internationally that the future will bring even more constraint. Government becomes an uneven patron, often acting like a sometime purchaser of university services; it can hardly be depended on in the long term. Its own changing agenda will at times give overwhelming priority to coping with depression, national debt, and international entanglements.

Traditional universities come to a fork in the financial road. They can passively fall in line and undergo parallel financial increases and decreases—as the government goes, so they go—with the governmental stimulus determining university response; or they can actively intervene by deciding to develop additional lines of income from pursued patrons. University ambition encourages the second choice, competition virtually demands it. Such budgetary activity is a crucial step in university entrepreneurship. Active cost containment is also then given a high priority by the institution itself, from central staff to the many departments and units in the academic heartland and the developmental periphery.

To build a diversified funding base in a university is to construct a portfolio of patrons to share rising costs. As new patrons contribute, their expectations of what they should get in return readily intrude to become new constraints. Universities then need greater self-consciousness on where they draw the line between what they are willing to do and not do to meet those demands. The collective will, located in the steering core, then comes into play to define new limits around greatly expanded boundaries; heartland departments also have to test their own edges of legitimacy.

But whatever the relations with specific patrons, a diversified funding base enhances university discretion. The enlarged portfolio of income streams increases total resources. It allows a university to "roll with the punches"; a loss here is replaced by a gain there. It allows a university to build reserves (and to borrow monies) and then to take innovative steps, as Warwick did when it used accumulated surpluses from its earned income to fund a new, striking research fellowship scheme. Diversity in financing, it now appears, "can be regarded as a prerequisite for adaptability." (Hölttä, 1995, p. 56) The multistream financial base enhances the evermore important capacity to crosssubsidize internally: top-slicing and redistribution of funds by central committees tap the monies brought in by some fields and activities to aid others judged to be necessary and needy. Cross-subsidy becomes the financial heart of university integration. (Massy, 1994; Williams, 1995)

The internal disposition of funds raised through diversified sources is always contentious and never permanently solved. Professors and departments active in bringing in money do not like to see some of it passed off to others who are not, especially if the other departments appear to be lost in mists of conceptual ambiguity, even bogged down in self-imposed disarray. The greater the internal dispersion of fields and interests, the greater the need to have the haves help the have-nots. *And* the more contentious the issue of internal redistribution becomes. Comprehensive universities have great difficulty in moving money across the gulf between, for example, physics and classics as specific fields or more broadly between engineering and the humanities. Cross-subsidization may flow from teaching to research, or in some cases in the reverse direction. It may flow across levels of education, from undergraduate to graduate, or the other way around. Certainly a primary issue in diversified funding, it is central to the making of choices leading to better focused universities.

The stimulated heartland

Since universities consist of widely divergent fields in their traditional departments, enterprising action typically spreads unevenly in the old heartland. Science and technology departments commonly become entrepreneurial first and most fully. Social science departments, aside from economics and business, find the shift more difficult and commonly lag behind. Humanities departments have good reason to be resisting laggards: new money does not readily flow their way from either governmental or nongovernmental patrons. Deliberate effort on their part to go out and raise funds by offering new services may seem particularly out of place, even demeaning. Since departmental adoption of an entrepreneurial attitude will normally vary, a university that has partially transformed itself to be more enterprising might largely exist in a schizophrenic state, entrepreneurial on one side and traditional on the other. Administrators and faculty at the five universities studied rejected this option. Schizophrenic character did not appeal to them: it suggested a split that would mean endless, bitter contention. If that were to be the outcome, then the move into entrepreneurial action might well be more trouble than it was worth: doubters in other universities would be right.

Overall scale and scope are perhaps decisive here. Small to middle size universities—6,000 to approximately 13,000 in our five cases—are still positioned to seek a unified character, even if they stretch from microbiology to folklore. An integrated identity has much to offer: perceivable gains outweigh apparent losses. But large universities of 20,000, 30,000, 50,000 and more, particularly when organized in large stand-alone faculties or schools—the dominant form in Europe and in much of the world—might well find that entrepreneurial habits do not spread well across their major parts. They might then be forced to operate with an entrepreneurial/traditional split in character, with minimal interaction and little or no cross-subsidy across major components. The entrepreneurial side could depend on diversified income and look to new forms of outreach and knowledge production. The traditional side could depend on mainline allocation based on student enrolment and degree output as the foundation for the future.

Impressive in the universities studied was the extent to which the heartland departments had bought into entrepreneurial change. Their changeover has not been easy, not even in the specialized institutions most fully based on science and technology. Even in science departments professors may be committed to knowledge for its own sake in a way that excludes applied interests. But the distinction between basic and applied has steadily blurred and science departments can typically find foci that combine the two. In the social sciences and humanities, as we have seen, departments also find new ways to be educationally useful as they relate to new demands with, for example, policy analysis and multimedia explorations. One traditional department after another finds educational as well as economic value in becoming a more enterprising basic unit.

Stimulated academic departments must find ways to fuse their new administrative capability and outreach mentality with traditional outlooks in their fields. Academic norms operate close to the surface: they define whether changes are "up-market" or "down-market." Departmental entrepreneurship that leads to shoddy goods, as defined by other academics, can readily set in motion a vicious circle of declining reputation and less selective recruitment of staff and students. Departments have to make clear that they are not willing to respond to all demands that swirl around them in their respective fields of activities—from potential students, young and old, industrial firms and professional associations, local, regional, national, and international governmental departments. They have to select and thereby to focus. When carried out effectively, a widespread embodiment of entrepreneurship in a university strengthens *selective* substantive growth in its basic units.

The entrepreneurial belief

The most difficult part of this study's analysis was to grasp organizational Ideas and beliefs and relate them to structures that Support processes of change. A long-standing popular misconception places a Great Person with a Large Idea at the front end of change. A modern derivative of this view depicts a chief executi.ve officer or management team formulating at the outset a global strategic plan. Idea becomes purpose, a mission statement soon follows, and all else becomes means to a prechosen end. But the reality of change in complex organizations, especially in universities, is different. New, institutionally defining ideas are typically tender and problematic at the outset of an important change. They must be tested, worked out, and reformulated. If they turn out to be utopian, they are soon seen as counterproductive wishful thinking. If found to be excessively opportunistic they provide no guidance: any adjustment will do. Ideas become realistic and capable of some steering as they reflect organizational capability and tested environmental possibilities. New organizational ideas are but symbolic experiments in the art of the possible.

An institutional *idea* that makes headway in a university has to spread among many participants and link up with other ideas. As the related ideas become expressed in numerous structures and processes, and thereby endure, we may see them as institutional *beliefs* that stress distinctive ways. Successful entrepreneurial beliefs, stressing a will to change, can in time spread to embrace much and even all of an institution, becoming a new *culture*. What may have started out as a simple or naive idea becomes a self-asserting shared view of the world offering a unifying *identity*. A transformed culture that contains a sense of historical struggle can in time even become a *saga*, an embellished story of successful accomplishment. Our five universities have moved along this ideational road.

Such cultural transformation at Warwick started out in the early 1980s with the tender idea that it would "earn" its way. With growing success, the earned income approach became a sturdy belief that here was an unusual British university aggressively developing new sources of income, new patterns of organization, and new productive relationships with the outside world. True believers dominated the steering core and became more numerous in a campus-wide culture. Outsiders took special note. By its twenty-fifth year, the university was uncommonly well-equipped symbolically to celebrate itself with an enriched story of "the Warwick way." An organizational saga was emerging.

Twente started its move in the early 1980s with an almost defiant assertion that it was "*the* entrepreneurial university," hardly knowing what that would mean in practice. It turned out to mean that Twente would develop a strengthened managerial core and a newly devised developmental periphery and the other operational elements this study has identified. Spreading out in the academic heartland, the initial simply stated idea became an embedded belief, then a widespread culture. By the mid-1990s this small place claimed a rugged identity formed around a recent history of largely successful struggle: a saga was on its way. Twente came to believe in itself to the point of making vigorous efforts to spread its particular attitudes and special operational forms to others: it took up leadership in an emerging small circle of European self-defined "innovative universities."

The leading idea at Strathclyde in the early 1980s was not sharply formulated. A new vice-chancellor felt strongly that the place had to become more managerial, more businesslike, more able to stand on its own feet. If it were to prosper it had to be run differently. In time, the initial managerial idea, expressed in a distinctive central steering group, a productive periphery, and an entrepreneurial "spirit" in some heartland departments became folded into a generalized belief system of "useful learning." This doctrine embraced two hundred years of development while it asserted a will to work with industry and government to solve current problems. The Strathclyde doctrine of useful learning only needed to be slightly embellished and romanticized, as exemplified in the bicentennial celebration I described, in order to become an organizational saga.

Chalmers self-consciously began to assert in the early 1980s a commitment to "innovation." As the idea and related practices were worked out a sense of difference grew. A long-standing Chalmers "spirit" was intensified to become an embracing culture that helped predispose the institution to take up in 1994 the highly unusual status of a foundation university, an institutional definition that nearly all other Swedish universities were unable or unwilling to consider. The sense of distinctiveness was thereby further extended, intensifying overall identity. In this ideational part of the quest, deeply rooted cultural features have become parts of a Chalmers saga in which past developments, current intentions, and future character are depicted as closely linked. Chalmers enthusiasts could readily say in the mid-1990s that their place was something different in the state of Sweden. They also had confident reason to believe that a similar entrepreneurial culture will increasingly appear in other Swedish universities.

Joensuu in the mid-1980s took to an idea of becoming a pilot institution that would experiment with an important basic change for the entire Finnish national system of universities. In its national setting the idea of doubly decentralizing budget-based control all the way down to the department level was a radical one. Joensuu effected the idea to the point of departmental dominance. Early acceptance of a second idea, piloted at another university, that of flexible workloads, helped to make the institution significantly different from those operating in traditional

Finnish style. As the "piloting" ideas worked their way into the fabric of the institution, Joensuu has grown up symbolically as well as physically, strengthening its sense of self and its place in the world.

* * *

We have noted repeatedly throughout this study that the five elements of transformation become just that by means of their interaction. Each by itself can hardly make a significant difference. Those who see universities from the top-down might readily assume that the strengthened steering core is the leading element. But a newly constituted management group, for example, is soon without teeth if discretionary funds are not available, new units in the periphery cannot be constructed, heartland departments fall into opposition, and the group's idea of a transformed institution gains no footing. The interaction of transforming elements also largely takes place incrementally over a number of years. Our results accord strongly with an incrementalist view of organizational change. (Lindblom, 1959, 1979; Redner, ed., 1993) Particularly for universities, we stress *interactive instrumentalism*. Transformation requires a structured change capability and development of an overall internal climate receptive to change. As we have seen by reviewing development over ten to 15 year periods, the building of structural capability and cultural climate takes time and is incrementally fashioned. Action taken at the center requires faculty involvement and approval. Change in new and old units in the periphery and in the heartland is piecemeal, experimental, and adaptive. The operational units, departments and research centers, remain the sites where research, teaching, and service are performed: what they do and do not do becomes finally central. As put sharply by David W. Leslie (1996, p. 110) in arguing against linear-rational views of strategic planning: "change in colleges and universities comes when it happens in the trenches; what faculty and students do is what the institution becomes. It does not happen because a committee or a president asserts a new idea."

Even in the business world, we may note, careful analysts who trace organizational change over many years observe that successful firms essentially engage in "cumulative incrementalism": they inch forward by making rapid partial changes. Firms choose to "spread and minimize risks by initiating many different projects," rather than try to engage in large-scale strategic change. (Stopford & Baden-Fuller, 1994, p. 523) They engage in "concentric entrepreneurialism." Even in business, leadership is depicted as a diffused phenomenon: "Leadership is acutely context sensitive ... The need may be for more than one leader over time if performance is to be maintained. Equally important may be the creation of collective leadership at a senior level ... which may then be supported by the development of a sense of complementary leadership at lower levels. Leading change involves action by people at every level of the business." (Pettigrew & Whipp, 1991, pp. 280–281) And from a third careful business analyst: "Capabilities grow through the actions of the members of the firm—through the behaviors of employees at all organizational levels" (Leonard-Barton, 1995, p. 28).

Such findings from sustained analysis of business firms over years of development concur with developmental studies of universities: leadership can be an attribute of groups; entrepreneurship is a phenomenon of total organizations and their many collective parts. "The entrepreneurial response" on which we have concentrated is an all-university capability.

The Focused University

The entrepreneurial response to the growing imbalance in the environment-university relationship gives universities a better chance to control their own destinies. The response may be seen as a way to recover the autonomy lost, particularly in public universities, when mounting demands began to dominate the capacity of universities to respond. The new autonomy is different from the old. In an earlier day autonomous public universities could be given full state support and largely left alone to educate a few students, engage in limited basic research, and prepare professionals for several fields of work. When only one young person in 20 sought university training, most people most of the time did not think about what the university was doing and what it could do for them. Fields of research were simpler, knowledge growth, while moving at a striking pace, could still be grasped. As the end of the twentieth century approaches, however, the demand side of the environment-university relationship has spun out of control and institutional response has become increasingly insufficient. Now when virtually everyone can demand some involvement or relationship, loosely coupled universities have offered ad hoc, diffuse responses.

Universities are caught up in grand contradictions: with less money, do more and more; maintain as always the expanding cultural heritage, the best of the past, but quickly and flexibly develop new fields of study and modes of thought; relate to everyone's demand because all are "stakeholders." An American university president crisply formulated in the mid-1990s that the modern research university (public *and* private) has become "overextended. underfocused; overstressed, underfunded." (Vest, 1995) Alert rectors and vice-chancellors in Europe could readily agree, recognizing that not only can the condition of underfunded lead to a sense of being overstressed, but that "underfocused" and "overextended" may be virtually two sides of the same institutional posture.

The entrepreneurial response offers a formula for institutional development that puts autonomy on a self-defined basis: diversify income to increase financial resources, provide discretionary money, *and* reduce governmental dependency; develop new units outside traditional departments to introduce new environmental relationships and new modes of thought and training; convince heartland departments that they too can look out for themselves, raise money, actively choose among specialties, and otherwise take on an entrepreneurial outlook; evolve a set of overarching beliefs that guide and rationalize the structural changes that provide a stronger response capability; and build a central steering capacity to make large choices that help focus the institution. The entrepreneurial response in all its fullness gives universities better means for redefining their reach—to include more useful knowledge, to move more flexibly over time from one program emphasis to another, and finally to build an organizational identity and focus. Warwick, Twente, Strathclyde, Chalmers, and Joensuu have all in somewhat different specific ways shown us how to focus university reach.

Universities need foci that help them solve the problem of severe imbalance and to define anew their societal usefulness. They need to find sustainable niches in the ecology of a knowledge industry that becomes more international and more dispersed among institutions outside formal higher education. The difficulties are huge. Comprehensive universities, those of wide scope, in Europe, America, and elsewhere will remain under great popular and governmental pressure to cover the broadest possible range of subjects and interests. Scattering their promises, and in many cases unable to cap their size, they will continue to tend to spread in a virtually uncontrolled fashion. They take on even more tasks and expectations, undercutting the possibilities of building a critical mass of resources, faculty, and students in different basic units. To contain unbridled comprehensiveness, choices have to be made about the relative magnitude of beginning and advanced levels of study, different services to clienteles and occupations, and especially about fields of knowledge to highlight and downplay. And within every field choices have to be made to pursue certain specialties while ignoring others. If such choices are not made, then all units and subunits simply receive fair shares on the downslope of limited resources and hardened structures. Steering is left to the mercy of sunk costs.

As active university postures come to the fore, we find they can have positive effects on university character that are not anticipated in traditional thought. The entrepreneurial pathways tend to build coherence. A university becomes more willing to assert to the outside world that it is different, even distinctive. The whole institution can legitimately claim that it has its act together and is thereby better prepared to cope with the confusing complexity and rising uncertainty characteristic of modern higher education. A reputation of coherent competence provides a symbolic bridge to the environment for a favorable gathering of money, staff, and students.

As entrepreneurial responses multiply, universities become more individualized. To make the point in striking fashion, that higher education is not one thing and it has no one future, the Carnegie Council of the 1970s entitled their last report on the U.S. system *Three Thousand Futures*. (Carnegie Council, 1980) Actively forming their own character in different specific contexts, and developing different specific strengths and weaknesses, entrepreneurial universities, anywhere in the world, similarly develop their own distinctive futures. Rather than praising homogeneity, they put their trust in diversified capability—a posture appropriate for an evermore complex and competitive domain.

An entrepreneurial achievement of distinctiveness serves internally to unify an identity and thereby, ironically, to rebuild a sense of community. "Entrepreneur" may continue to be a negative term in the minds of traditional academics, all the more so after they have seen hard managerialism in action. They may go on thinking of entrepreneurship as raw individualistic striving that is socially divisive. They may continue to fear that a traditional academic community, assumed to exist, will be fragmented if entrepreneurial behavior takes over. However, diffuse in structure and fragmented in intent, traditional European universities, and many others around the world, have had little or no common symbolic and material integration. What integration they have had is steadily eroded by increasing scale and scope. Collective entrepreneurship overcomes their scattered character, leading toward a more integrated self. When entire departments and faculties are assertive, and especially when a whole university takes on an entrepreneurial character, the old understandings are turned upside down. Academic groups, small and large, then see themselves in common situations with common problems, common allies, and common enemies, and in need of common action. A common culture grows, an identity is shared.

Collegiality is then put to work in a different way. Bernard J. Shapiro (President, McGill University) and Harold T. Shapiro (President, Princeton University) have cogently argued that collegiality is normally "biased in favor of the status quo -not to mention the status quo ante." The challenge is "to redefine our understandings and commitment so that, in empirical terms, collegiality and difficult choices are not mutually exclusive." (1995, p. 10) The collective forms of entrepreneurship captured in this study change the equation. They put collegiality to work in the service of hard choices. Collegiality then looks to the future. It becomes biased in favor of change.

Self-defining, self-regulating universities have much to offer. Not least is their capacity in difficult circumstances to recreate an academic community. Toward such universities, the entrepreneurial response leads the way.

References

Carnegie Council on Policy Studies in Higher Education (1980). *Three Thousand Futures*. San Francisco: Jossey-Bass.

Carnegie Foundation for the Advancement of Teaching (1994). *A Classification of Institutions of Higher Education: 1994 Edition*. Princeton, New Jersey.

Clark, B. R. (1983). *The Higher Education System: Academic Organization in Cross-National Perspective*. Berkeley and Los Angeles: University of California Press.

Gibbons, M., Limoges, C., Nowotny, H., Schwartzman, S., Scott, P. and Trow, M. (1994). *The New Production of Knowledge: The Dynamics of Science and Research in Contemporary Societies*. London: Sage Publications.

Henkel, M. (1997). Academic values and the university as corporate enterprise. *Higher Educ. Q.* 51(2): 134–143.

Hölttä, S. (1995). *Towards the Self-Regulative University*. (Publications in Social Sciences No. 23). Joensuu, Finland: University of Joensuu.

Kerr, C. (1993). Universal issues in the development of higher education. In: J. B. Balderston and F. E. Balderston (eds.) *Higher Education in Indonesia: Evolution and Reform*. Berkeley: Center for Studies in Higher Education, University of California, pp. 19–35.

Leonard-Barton, D. (1995). *Wellsprings of Knowledge: Building and Sustaining the Sources of Innovation*. Boston: Harvard Business School Press.

Leslie, D. W. (1996). 'Strategic governance:' the wrong questions? *The Review of Higher Education* 20(1): 101–112.

Leslie, D.W and Fretwell, Jr. E. K. (1996). *Wise Moves in Hard Times: Creating & Managing Resilient Colleges & Universities*. San Francisco: Jossey-Bass.

Lindblom, C. E. (1959). The science of 'muddling-through.' *Public Admin. Review* 19(2): 78–88. (1979). Still muddling, not yet through. *Public Admin. Review* 39 Nov.–Dec.: 517–526.

MacTaggart, T. J. and Associates (1996). *Restructuring Higher Education: What Works and What Doesn't in Reorganizing Governing Systems*. San Francisco: Jossey-Bass.

Massy, W. F. (1994). *Resource Allocation Reform in the United States*. Washington, D.C.: National Association of College and University Business Officers.

Meek, V. L., Goedegebuure, L., Kivinen, O. and Rinne, R. (eds). (1996). *The Mockers and Mocked: Comparative Perspectives on Differentiation, Convergence and Diversity in Higher Education*. Oxford: International Association of Universities Press and Pergamon-Elsevier Science.

Micklethwait, J. and Wooldridge, A. (1996). *The Witch Doctors: Making Sense of the Management Gurus*. New York: Random House (Times Books).

Neave, G. (1996). Homogenization, integration and convergence: the cheshire cat of higher education analysis. In: V. L. Meek, L. Goedegebuure, O. Kivinen, and R. Rinne (eds.) *The Mockers and Mocked: Comparative Perspectives on Differentiation, Convergence and Diversity in Higher Education*. Oxford: International Association of Universities Press and Pergamon-Elsevier Science, pp. 26–4 1.

Pettigrew, A. and Whipp, R. (1991). *Managing Change/or Competitive Success*. Oxford: Blackwell Publishers.

Redner, H. (ed.) (1993). *All Heretical Heir of the Enlightenment: Politics, Policy & Science in the Work of Charles E. Lindblom*. Boulder, Colorado: Westview Press.

Riesman, D. (1973). Commentary and epilogue. In: D. Riesman and V. A. Stadtman (eds.) *Academic Transformation: Seventeen Institutions Under Pressure*. New York: McGraw-Hill.

Scott, P. (1997). The changing role of the university in the production of new knowledge. *Tertiary Education and Management*, 3(1): 5–14.

Shapiro, B. J. and Shapiro, H. T. (1995). Universities in *Higher Education*: *Some Problems* and *Challenges* in a *Changing World*. Quebec: McGill University (Office of the President, unpublished paper).

Stopford, J. M. and Baden-Fuller, C.W.F. (1994). Creating corporate entrepreneurship. *Strategic Management Journal* 15(7): 521–536.

Teichler, U. (1988). *Changing Patterns of the Higher Education System: The Experience of Three Decades*. London: Jessica Kingsley.

Trow, M. A. (1970). Elite and popular functions in American higher education. In: W. R. Niblett (ed.) *Higher Education: Demand & Response*. San Francisco: Jossey-Bass, pp. 181–201.

Viilimaa, J. (1994). A trying game: experiments and reforms in Finnish higher education. *European J. of Educ.* 29(2): 149–163.

Vest, C. M. (1995). Research universities: overextended, underfocused; overstressed, underfunded. Paper presented at the Cornell Symposium on the American University, May 22, 1995. Boston: Massachusetts Institute of Technology (President's Office, unpublished paper).

Williams, G. L. (1995). The 'marketization' of higher education: reforms and potential reforms in higher education finance. In: D. D. Dill and B. Sporn (cds.) *Emerging Patterns of Social Demand and University Reform: Through a Glass Darkly*. Oxford: International Association of Universities and Pergamon-Elsevier Science, pp. 170–193.

Ziman, J. (1994). *Prometheus Bound: Science in a Dynamic Steady State*. Cambridge: Cambridge University Press.

CHAPTER TWENTY-SIX

The Roots of Commercialization

From *Universities in the Marketplace: The Commercialization of Higher Education* (2003)

DEREK BOK

This selection is taken from *Universities in the Marketplace*, by Derek Bok, 2003. Princeton University Press, New Jersey, NJ.

Editors' Note

Derek Bok not only served for twenty years as President of Harvard University but was called back in 2006 to serve as an Interim President. Unusually among leaders of research-intensive universities, Bok has long taken a particular interest in students and their learning, and his book *Higher Learning*, was written during his first incumbency as President. In that book, Bok evinced a concern with the state of undergraduate education in America and showed a willingness to critique the system of which he was part. The (poor) level of students' critical thinking abilities, the (undue) freedom given to students to choose their own selection of modules in forming their programme of study, the extent to which students had to work their way through college (not least to meet their tuition fees) all came in for his critical gaze. On his view, 'liberal education' was in jeopardy; and he set out a programme of reform 'aimed at improving student learning'.

His book, *Universities in the Marketplace: The Commercialization of Higher Education*, demonstrates still further Bok's ability to take a penetrating look from within at what has elsewhere been termed 'academic capitalism'. While, *prima facie*, it offers an even-handed assessment of 'the benefits and costs of commercialization', in fact it is the costs that mostly attracts Bok's attention. And the costs in question are those that impair 'academic values'. Bok explains how it is that American universities at least have come to be so focused on income generation—the 'chronic condition of American universities', increasing competition, 'the spirit of private enterprise' and the sheer opportunities for money-making. The costs, though, are considerable: 'a sacrifice in normal admissions standards' and an 'undermining' of academic standards more broadly, a shift in academic culture away so as to impair the student experience, challenges even to 'the basic canons of scholarly and scientific inquiry' and, thereby, risks to the reputation of the university itself. Furthermore, 'one ... perceives a persistent tendency to exaggerate the benefits and overlook or underestimate the dangers'.

MP

Recommended Reading

Bok, D. (1986). *Higher Learning*. Cambridge, MA and London: Harvard University.

Slaughter, S. and Rhoades, G. (2009). *Academic Capitalism and the New Economy: Markets, States and Higher Education*. Baltimore, MD: Johns Hopkins University.

* * * * *

> It is one of the unwritten, and commonly unspoken commonplaces lying at the root of modern academic policy that the various universities are competitors for the traffic of merchantable instruction in much the same fashion as rival establishments in the retail trade compete for custom.
>
> (Thorstein Veblen, *The higher learning in America: A memorandum on the conduct of universities by businessmen*, 1918)

Toward the end of the twentieth century, American universities—with their stately buildings, tree-lined quadrangles, and slightly disheveled, often-preoccupied professors—found themselves in an enviable position. No longer quiet enclaves removed from the busy world, they had emerged as the nation's chief source for the three ingredients most essential to continued growth and prosperity: highly trained specialists, expert knowledge, and scientific advances others could transform into valuable new products or life-saving treatments and cures.

This newfound importance brought growing interest from the media, increased funding from government agencies and foundations, and closer scrutiny from public officials. It also brought abundant new opportunities to make money. Universities learned that they could sell the right to use their scientific discoveries to industry and find corporations willing to pay a tidy sum to sponsor courses delivered by Internet or cable television. Apparel firms offered money to have colleges place the corporate logo on their athletic uniforms or, conversely, to put the university's name on caps and sweatshirts sold to the public. Faculty members began to bear such titles as Yahoo Professor of Computer Science or K-Mart Professor of Marketing. The University of Tennessee, in a coup of sorts, reportedly sold its school color to a paint company hoping to find customers wishing to share in the magic of the college's football team by daubing their homes with "Tennessee Orange." One enterprising university even succeeded in finding advertisers willing to pay for the right to place their signs above the urinals in its men's rooms.

Commercial practices may have become more obvious, but they are hardly a new phenomenon in American higher education. By the early 1900s, the University of Chicago was already advertising regularly to attract students, and the University of Pennsylvania had established a "Bureau of Publicity" to increase its visibility. In 1905, Harvard was concerned enough about its profitable football team to hire a 26-year-old coach at a salary equal to that of its president and twice the amount paid to its full professors. As President Andrew Draper of the University of Illinois observed, the university "is a business concern as well as a moral and intellectual instrumentality, and if business methods are not applied to its management, it will break down."[1]

What is new about today's commercial practices is not their existence but their unprecedented size and scope. Before 1970, university presidents may have sounded like hucksters on occasion and resorted at times to advertising and other methods borrowed from the world of business. Nevertheless, commercialization in the strict sense of the term—that is, efforts to sell the work of universities for a profit—was largely confined to the periphery of campus life: to athletic programs and, in a few institutions, to correspondence schools and extension programs.[2] Today, opportunities to make money from intellectual work are pursued

1 "The University Presidency," Atlantic Monthly 97 (1906), p. 36.

2 Some writers speak expansively of commercialization to include a wide range of behaviors and trends, notably (1) the influence of economic forces on universities (e.g., the growth of computer science majors and departments); (2) the influence of the surrounding corporate culture (e.g., the increased use on campuses of terms such as CEO, bottom line, or brand name); (3) the influence of student career interests on the curriculum (e.g., more vocational courses); (4) efforts to economize in university expenditures (hiring more adjunct teachers) or to use administrative methods adapted from business; or (5) attempts to quantify matters within the university that are not truly quantifiable, such as trying to express matters of

throughout the university by professors of computer science, biochemistry, corporate finance, and numerous other departments. Entrepreneurship is no longer the exclusive province of athletics departments and development offices; it has taken hold in science faculties, business schools, continuing education divisions, and other academic units across the campus.

What accounts for the growth of commercial activity in institutions dedicated to higher learning? To Veblen, the obvious culprits were university presidents and their entourage of bureaucratic helpers. Intent upon accumulating money to expand the size and reputation of the institution, campus administrators were forever forcing the methods of the marketplace on a reluctant community of scholars. In Veblen's view, the remedy for the disease was as obvious as its cause: "The academic executive and all his works are an anathema and should be discontinued by the simple expedient of wiping him off the slate."[3]

If Veblen harbored any doubts about the reasons for commercialization, he did not acknowledge them. Even in his day, however, it should have been plain that the roots of the problem went beyond the academic bureaucracy. More than a few university presidents protested the growth of football programs, only to be overcome by the tidal force of enthusiastic students and alumni. Today, it is even more apparent that the recent surge in money-making activity on campus stems from causes far deeper than policies emanating from the president. University officials have surely initiated entrepreneurial ventures. But they often have little or nothing to do with the efforts of prominent professors to found their own companies, sell their services as teachers to corporations, or allow private companies to market their lectures through the Internet, tape, or videocassette. Nor is there any doubt that the greatest obstacles to reforming intercollegiate athletics continue to lie, not in the president's office, but among the alumni supporters, boosters, legislators, and others who insist on fielding winning teams.

If Veblen was wrong in heaping so much blame on university presidents, what else helps account for the recent burst of commercial activity on campus? Part of the explanation lies in the growing influence of the market throughout our society.

---

value in monetary terms rather than qualitatively. Often, words such as commercialization, corporatization, or commodification are employed for rhetorical purposes to capitalize on the widespread distrust of business and business methods in academic circles. In view of the several meanings of commercialization and the motives with which the term is often used, it is especially important to be clear about one's own definition at the outset. To repeat, therefore, in this book commercialization is used to refer to efforts within the university to make a profit from teaching, research, and other campus activities.

3 The Higher Learning in America: A Memorandum on the Conduct of Universities by Businessmen (reprint ed., 1957), p. 209.

Commercialization has plainly taken root, not only in higher education, but also in many other areas of American life and culture: health care, museums, public schools, even religion.[4] Entrepreneurial initiative, high executive salaries, and aggressive marketing techniques are all spreading to fields of endeavor quite outside the realm of business. Such practices set examples that legitimate the use of similar methods in universities. Nevertheless, merely noting the existence of a trend does not explain why it came about, let alone account for its sudden and deep penetration into an academic culture long considered an "ivory tower" set apart from the marketplace.

Several scholars have attributed the recent growth of money-making activity to a lack of purpose in the university.[5] Having lost sight of any clear mission beyond a vague commitment to "excellence," our sprawling multiversities are charged with creating a vacuum into which material pursuits have rushed in unimpeded. Explanations of this kind almost invariably come from philosophers, literary scholars, and other humanists. Although they talk expansively about the university, their background is chiefly in the humanities. Since these are the fields of study most widely accused of having lost their intellectual moorings, it is not surprising that their professors see a similar aimlessness as the cause of other ills that have overtaken the academy.

If one looks more broadly at the university, however, one quickly finds that many faculties and departments are quite clear about their purposes and that these are the very parts of the institution in which commercialization is most rampant. Within the traditional disciplines, no faculty members feel a stronger sense of mission than the scientists, yet it is there—not in the humanities—that commercialization has taken hold most firmly. Among the several faculties, none has a clearer sense of purpose than schools of business and medicine, yet it is their professors—not their colleagues in literature and philosophy—who are most deeply involved in lucrative consulting and entrepreneurial activity.

If there is an intellectual confusion in the academy that encourages commercialization, it is a confusion over means rather than ends. To keep profit-seeking within reasonable bounds, a university must have a clear sense of the values needed to pursue its goals with a high degree of quality and integrity. When the values

---

4 For a critical account of these developments, see, for example, Robert Kuttner, Everything for Sale: The Virtues and Limits of Markets (1996).

5 See Allen Bloom, *The Closing of the American Mind: How Higher Education Has Failed Democracy and Impoverished the Souls of Today's Students* (1987); Bill Readings, *The University in Ruins* (1996); Stanley Aronowitz, *The Knowledge Factory: Dismantling the Corporate University and Creating the Higher Learning* (2000). (Mr. Aronowitz is a sociologist.) This is not a new complaint; the same charge was made around 1900. See Laurence R. Veysey, *The Emergence of the Modern University* (1965), p. 346.

become blurred and begin to lose their hold, the urge to make money quickly spreads throughout the institution. Just what these values are and how they are threatened by commercial pursuits are subjects discussed in subsequent chapters. For the moment, it is enough to say that loss of *purpose* is not a useful explanation for the recent growth of money-making ventures in the university.

Critics from the left have a different theory to explain the burgeoning commercial activity on campus. To them, such behavior is simply another illustration of the attempts by the businessmen and lawyers who sit on boards of trustees to "commodify" education and research, reduce the faculty to the status of employees, and ultimately, make the university serve the interests of corporate America.[6]

The influence of the private economy on the university is undeniable. Wealthy donors clearly alter the shape of the institution through the power of their benefactions. Anyone harboring doubts on this score need only contrast the opulence of business schools with the shabbiness of most schools of education and social work. The world of commerce and industry affects the curriculum in even more striking ways through the jobs it provides and the salaries it offers; witness the growth of undergraduate business majors, the rise of computer science departments, and the generous compensation offered to professors of management and economics, compared to that paid to colleagues in literature and philosophy.

It is one thing, however, to note the effects of the economy on academic institutions and quite another to imagine a plot on the part of business leaders to bend universities to their corporate purposes. It is true that toward the end of the nineteenth century, as American colleges transformed themselves into large research institutions, clergymen began to give way to business executives and lawyers on most university boards. Still, ascribing this trend to some sort of national corporate plot seems rather farfetched; there is a more benign explanation. As institutions of higher learning grew larger and more complicated, they needed trustees who could help them raise money and develop better methods of administration. Clergymen were poorly equipped for these tasks and were increasingly out of step, in any case, with faculties that were steadily becoming more secular and professional. Business executives and corporate lawyers simply seemed better suited to the changing needs of the university.

In the early years, some business-oriented trustees did try to impose their views on the institution, even to the point of firing faculty members with radical

---

6 See, for example, Wesley Shumar, *College for Sale: A Critique of the Commodification of Higher Education* (1997). For a history of the evolution of boards of trustees and one author's view of its significance, see Clyde W. Barrow, *Universities and the Capitalist State: Corporate Liberalism and the Reconstruction of American Higher Education*, 1894–1928 (1990).

opinions. But professors soon organized to protest such interference. Eventually, board members had to modify their behavior and defer to scholarly judgments in academic matters or risk doing harm to the reputation of their university. Long before the recent wave of commercialization, therefore, trustees of major universities had become far less intrusive. By the 1960s, they were serving, as they do now, largely out of loyalty to their alma mater or from a sense of civic duty, rarely interfering with academic decisions except where necessary to guard the financial health of the institution. Today, if trustees encourage commercial ventures, they are far more likely to do so in order to find resources for the university's needs rather than to promote the selfish interests of American business.

Professors of higher education offer a different explanation for the growth of commercial activity on campus. In their view, the recent wave of entrepreneurial behavior is a response to the reductions in government support for higher education that began in the 1970s.[7] As the economy slowed after the energy crisis of 1973, Congress could no longer sustain the rapid increases in research funding that occurred during the 1950s and 1960s. State legislatures, burdened by the mounting costs of prisons, welfare, and health care for the indigent, followed suit and cut their appropriations for higher education, especially in the 1980s and 1990s. The result, according to this theory, was to force university officials and faculty members to look for new sources of funding. Eventually, enterprising presidents and entrepreneurial professors found ways to market their specialized knowledge and scientific discoveries in return for the cash they needed to make up for declining state support.

Government cutbacks may well be the precipitating cause that has led a number of universities in Britain, Australia, Scandinavia, and Holland to become more entrepreneurial.[8] In the United States, however, funding cuts are not the whole story. After all, the past two decades are hardly the first time that American higher education has experienced financial difficulties. Government funding slowed or declined in the early 1970s, not to mention the 1930s, yet universities did not respond with a burst of profit-seeking ventures.

Moreover, private universities in America have been no less entrepreneurial than their public counterparts even though few of them have had much state funding to lose, and most have seen their endowments surge during the heady stock market booms of the 1980s and 1990s. Basic biomedical scientists have been among the more enterprising in the academy, notwithstanding continued real increases in research support from the National Institutes of Health. Business

---

7 See Sheila Slaughter and Larry L. Leslie, *Academic Capitalism: Politics, Policies and the Entrepreneurial University* (1997).

8 Ibid. describes the process in Australia.

schools and their faculties have pursued new money-making ventures with notable zeal despite having suffered few, if any, of the financial cutbacks that have beset other parts of the university. In short, declining appropriations may have played a part, but something more is surely required to explain the rise of entrepreneurial activity on American campuses during the last twenty years.

Universities share one characteristic with compulsive gamblers and exiled royalty: there is never enough money to satisfy their desires. Faculty and students are forever developing new interests and ambitions, most of which cost money. The prices of books and journals rise relentlessly. Better and more costly technology and scientific apparatus constantly appear and must be acquired to stay at the cutting edge. Presidents and deans are anxious to satisfy as many of these needs as they can, for their reputation depends on pleasing the faculty, preserving the standing of the institution, and building a legacy through the development of new programs.

The need for money, therefore, does not merely occur now and then in the wake of some ill-considered decision on the part of state officials to cut university budgets. It is a chronic condition of American universities, a condition inherent in the very nature of an institution forever competing for the best students and faculty. Such talented, ambitious people are constantly asking for more programs, more books, more equipment, more of everything required to satisfy their desire to pursue new interests and opportunities. In this sense, the recent surge of commercial activity is best understood as only the latest in a series of steps to acquire more resources, beginning with the use of aggressive marketing to attract tuition-paying students in the early twentieth century, and moving on to the determined search for government and foundation funding after World War II, and the increasingly sophisticated and intensive effort over the last fifty years to coax gifts from well-to-do alumni and other potential donors.[9]

What made commercialization so much more prevalent in American universities after 1980 was the rapid growth of opportunities to supply education, expert advice, and scientific knowledge in return for handsome sums of money. During the first half of the twentieth century, the chances to profit from such activities were not nearly so abundant. Executive education for business had not yet generated much interest. With very few exceptions (such as Harry Steenbock of the University of Wisconsin, who discovered how to enrich milk with vitamin D),

9 Each of these efforts has elicited its own corresponding criticism. Seeking out students produced charges of "consumerism." Soliciting government grants led to complaints in the late 1960s that universities were complicit in unsavory policies of the CIA and Defense Department. The launching of larger and larger capital drives has provoked concerns that university presidents are now being chosen primarily for their fund-raising abilities.

academic scientists did not produce much research that had immediate commercial value. Outside of a few fields, such as chemistry and certain branches of engineering, corporations did not perceive much need to seek professorial advice.

The outlook for remunerative activity began to change after World War II. The contributions of science to the war effort convinced Washington policymakers to invest heavily in research, both in the natural sciences and, with the development of the National Institutes of Health, in medicine, as well. From 1948 to 1968, federal support for basic scientific research rose 25-fold in real dollars to reach almost $3 billion per year. The results exceeded expectations. Academic scientists helped develop the hydrogen bomb, launch satellites into space, and put a man on the moon. Advances in electrical engineering gave rise to civilian applications, most notably through the growth of electronics and the rise of the computer industry. The discovery of DNA and the development of gene-splicing techniques produced a revolution in medicine that helped launch a new biotechnology industry.

After three decades of large-scale federal support, priorities for basic science began to change. In the late 1970s, the slowdown in economic growth and the challenge of strong industrial competitors in Europe and Japan caused Congress to search for new ways to stimulate economic growth. As the Cold War waned, the emphasis of science policy in Washington shifted to place less weight on maintaining military superiority and more on ensuring America's competitiveness in the world economy.

This change in priorities led the government to consider new ways of linking university research to the needs of business. In 1980, Congress passed the Bayh-Dole Act, which made it much easier for universities to own and license patents on discoveries made through research paid for with public funds. Federal and state legislation offered subsidies for a variety of university-business cooperative ventures to help translate the fruits of academic science into new products and processes. Tax breaks encouraged industry to invest more in university-based science.

By all accounts, these initiatives achieved their purpose. Within a decade, two hundred universities had established offices to seek out commercially promising discoveries and patent them for licensing to companies. By the year 2000, universities had increased the volume of their patenting more than 10-fold and were earning more than $1 billion per year in royalties and license fees. Some twelve thousand academic scientists were participating in more than one thousand collaborative arrangements with local companies.[10] Many campuses had created

10 See, for example, Richard Florida, "The Role of the University: Leveraging Talent, not Technology," Issues in Science and Technology 15 (1999), p. 67; Raymond Smilor, Glenn

centers to give technical assistance to small businesses or developed incubators offering seed money and advice to help entrepreneurs launch new enterprises. Several institutions formed special venture capital units to invest in companies founded by their professors.

Meanwhile, advances in genetics had suddenly made academic research commercially important to industry. Investors were willing to invest millions of dollars on the promise of a new idea without waiting for an actual product, let alone a healthy profit margin. New companies could be founded on the strength of a discovery in a university laboratory. Quickly, corporations doubled and redoubled their share of total academic research support, increasing it from 2.3 percent in the early 1970s to almost 8 percent by the year 2000.

Opportunities for profit also emerged after World War II in the field of adult education, as professionals in many fields felt the need to acquire new knowledge and to master new skills in order to prosper in an increasingly complex society. Extension schools attracted more students seeking to upgrade their vocational skills. Continuing education for doctors expanded greatly, as physicians scrambled to keep up with the rapid advances in medical science. Executive programs for business became increasingly popular, while corporate training of all kinds blossomed into a multibillion dollar per year activity.

The growth of money-making possibilities extended well beyond universities as institutions. Individual faculty members, especially in the best universities, found new ways to supplement their incomes with lucrative activities on the side. As biotechnology boomed, life scientists not only started to seek patents on their discoveries and take attractive consulting assignments; they also began to receive stock from new firms eager for their help and even to found new companies based on their own discoveries. Outside the sciences, business school professors traveled to corporations willing to pay substantial sums for days spent consulting or teaching their executives. Legal scholars began to collect large fees for advising law firms or their corporate clients. Economists, political scientists, psychologists, and many others discovered that their counsel was worth a tidy sum to companies, consulting firms, and other private organizations.

Even university administrators saw new possibilities for earning money outside the familiar realm of teaching and research. Alumni offices began organizing cruises, complete with lectures, to carry graduates to exotic places. Business offices started to license the use of the university's name on sweatshirts, mugs, and

---

B. Dietrich, and David V. Gibson, "The Entrepreneurial University: The Role of Higher Education in the United States in Commercialization and Economic Development," International Social Studies Journal (UNESCO) (1993), p. 1.

other paraphernalia. University museums built attractive shops to sell related bits of merchandise, and college bookstores moved off campus to downtown locations in search of greater profits.

Within a few short decades, therefore, a brave new world had emerged filled with attractive possibilities for turning specialized knowledge into money. University presidents, enterprising professors, and even administrative staff were all busy exploiting these opportunities.

Adding impetus to the search for money was a mounting competition among the nation's research universities. Institutional rivalry has always marked American higher education to a greater extent than in other countries. But several factors helped to intensify this tendency over the latter half of the twentieth century. Increases in the college-going population and a vast growth in federal funding and philanthropic aid helped to support a larger number of institutions with legitimate ambitions to become research universities of the first rank. Better transportation and increased financial aid permitted more students to consider a much wider range of institutions in deciding where to pursue their education. Meanwhile, state legislatures began to give more help to science and technology at their leading universities, hoping to boost their local economies by emulating the success achieved by Silicon Valley and Route 128 in Massachusetts. Even the advent of annual rankings by publications such as *U.S. News and World Report* may have played a part. Although every college president can recite the many weaknesses of these ratings, they do provide a highly visible index of success, and competition is always quickened by such measures, especially among institutions like universities whose work is too intangible to permit more reliable means of evaluation.

Increased competition in turn produced greater effort to find resources, because almost anything a university did to try to lift its reputation cost money: recruiting outstanding new professors, financing the merit scholarships to attract better students, and providing the salaries and facilities needed to keep respected faculty members from leaving for more welcoming venues. Increasingly, therefore, success in university administration came to mean being more resourceful than one's competitors in finding the funds to achieve new goals. Enterprising leaders seeking to improve their institution felt impelled to take full advantage of any legitimate opportunities that the commercial world had to offer.

Summing up, then, commercialization turns out to have multiple causes. Financial cutbacks undoubtedly acted as a spur to profit-seeking for some universities and some departments. The spirit of private enterprise and entrepreneurship that became so prominent in the 1980s helped encourage and legitimate such initiatives. A lack of clarity about academic values opened the door even wider. Keener competition gave still further impetus. But none of these stimuli would have borne such abundant fruit had it not been for the rapid growth of money-making opportunities provided by a more technologically sophisticated, knowledge-based economy.

What should one make of all the entrepreneurial activity that has ensued? Public officials intent on economic growth are undoubtedly pleased with the vigor universities have shown in placing their discoveries and expertise at the service of private industry. By all accounts, corporate investments in academic science have yielded a handsome return in new products and improved technology.[11] As a result, companies have increased their support, relieving the government of some of the burden of funding university research. Meanwhile, programs of continuing education have sprung up on campuses everywhere to satisfy the growing needs of professionals for further schooling at later points in their careers.

The new opportunities for earning money have clearly helped make universities more attentive to public needs. In Europe as well as America, students of higher education have credited market forces with causing universities to become less stodgy and elitist and more vigorous in their efforts to aid economic growth.[12] Many people doubtless applaud this result and feel that universities are doing more to justify the large sums of public money governments spend on their behalf.

At the same time, the rise of entrepreneurial universities has not met with universal enthusiasm. Professors on the left complain about the "commodification" of higher education, claiming that universities have turned into "knowledge factories" where academic ideals are routinely compromised for the sake of money. According to sociologist Stanley Aronowitz, "the learning enterprise has become subject to the growing power of administration, which more and more responds not to faculty and students, except at the margins, but to political and market forces that claim sovereignty over higher education."[13] To cultural anthropologist Wesley Shumar, learning and research have "come to be valued in terms of their ability to be translated into cash or merchandise and not in any other ways, such as aesthetic or recreational pleasure. Eventually, the idea that there are other kinds of value is lost."[14]

Most critics do not paint the current situation in quite such bleak colors. But many are afraid that commercially oriented activities will come to overshadow

11 Wesley M. Cohen, Richard Florida, Lucien Randazzese, and John Walsh, "Industry and the Academy: Uneasy Partners in the Cause of Technological Advance," in Roger G. Noll, ed., Challenges to Research Universities (1998), pp. 171, 172–82.

12 See, for example, Burton Clark, *Creating Entrepreneurial Universities: Organizational Pathways of Transition* (1998).

13 Stanley Aronowitz, *The Knowledge Factory*, p. 164.

14 Wesley Shumar, *College for Sale*, p. 5.

other intellectual values and that university programs will be judged primarily by the money they bring in and not by their intrinsic intellectual quality. They view with dismay how the surrounding economy draws more and more students into vocational fields of study, elevates the salaries of computer scientists, business school professors, and others whose work relates to business, and attracts ever greater sums of outside money for subjects of commercial relevance to the neglect of other worthy, but less practical, fields of study. Even those who support the university's efforts to aid economic growth worry about the side effects of profit-seeking and the unseemliness of institutions of learning hawking everything from sweatshirts to adult education.

These concerns are linked to a broader disquiet over the encroachments of the marketplace on the work of hospitals, cultural institutions, and other areas of society that have traditionally been thought to serve other values. Almost everyone concedes that competitive markets are effective in mobilizing the energies of participants to satisfy common desires. And yet the apprehensions remain. However hard it is to explain these fears, they persist as a mute reminder that something of irreplaceable value may get lost in the relentless growth of commercialization.

CHAPTER TWENTY-SEVEN

Digital Diploma Mills

The Automation of Higher Education (1998)

DAVID F. NOBLE

This selection by David Noble was published in *First Monday* Volume 3, Number 1, January 5, 1998. Retrieved from http://firstmonday.org/ojs/index.php/fm/article/view/569/490[1]

Editors' Note

David Noble was a critical historian of technology and science and well-known for his work *Forces of Production: A Social History of Industrial Automation* (1984) that provided a social history of tool automation in the U.S. and the management practices designed to discipline the unions. In his last writings he focused on universities co-founding the National Coalition for Universities in the Public Interest (with Ralph Nader and Leonard Minsky), defending the concept of academic freedom and the academics as public servants against the corporatorization on universities. In his paper 'Digital Diploma Mills' (Noble 1998) he argued that

1 Disclaimer: Although the editors and publisher made every effort to locate the copyright holders of David F. Noble's Digital Diploma Mills: The Automation of Higher Education (1998), no copyright holder was found, in which case this article has been treated as if it were in the public domain.

universities were undergoing a technical transformation which screened the ways in which new technologies is often used to regulate and control of work of academics and to appropriate intellectual property at the expense of genuine improvements in teaching and learning. As he explains the 'the distribution of digitized course material online, without the participation of professors who develop such material—is often justified as an inevitable part of the new "knowledge-based" society.' He goes on to argue 'It is not a progressive trend towards a new era at all, but a regressive trend, towards the rather old era of mass-production, standardization and purely commercial interests.' The book is an expansion of the original essay that more widely investigates the meaning of the Internet for the future of higher education.

MP

Recommended Reading

Noble, David (1984). *Forces of Production: A Social History of Industrial Automation*. New York: Knopf.

Noble, David (1998). Digital Diploma Mills: The Automation of Higher Education, First Monday, 3 (1–5), http://www.firstmonday.org/ojs/index.php/fm/issue/view/88

* * * * *

Abstract

In recent years changes in universities, especially in North America, show that we have entered a new era in higher education, one which is rapidly drawing the halls of academe into the age of automation. Automation—the distribution of digitized course material online, without the participation of professors who develop such material—is often justified as an inevitable part of the new 'knowledge-based' society. It is assumed to improve learning and increase wider access. In practice, however, such automation is often coercive in nature—being forced upon professors as well as students—with commercial interests in mind. This paper argues that the trend towards automation of higher education as implemented in North American universities today is a battle between students and professors on one side, and university administrations and companies with 'educational products' to sell on the other. It is not a progressive trend towards a new era at all, but a regressive trend, towards the rather old era of mass production, standardization and purely commercial interests.

Introduction

Recent events at two large North-American universities signal dramatically that we have entered a new era in higher education, one which is rapidly drawing the halls of academe into the age of automation. In mid-summer the UCLA administration launched its historic "Instructional Enhancement Initiative" requiring computer Web sites for all of its arts and sciences courses by the start of the Fall term, the first time that a major university has made mandatory the use of computer telecommunications technology in the delivery of higher education. In partnership with several private corporations (including the Times Mirror Company, parent of the Los Angeles Times), moreover, UCLA has spawned its own for-profit company, headed by a former UCLA vice chancellor, to peddle online education (the Home Education Network).

This past spring in Toronto, meanwhile, the full-time faculty of York University, Canada's third largest, ended an historic two-month strike having secured for the first time anywhere formal contractual protection against precisely the kind of administrative action being taken by UCLA. The unprecedented faculty job action, the longest university strike in English Canadian history, was taken partly in response to unilateral administrative initiatives in the implementation of instructional technology, the most egregious example of which was an official solicitation to private corporations inviting them to permanently place their logo on a university online course in return for a $10,000 contribution to courseware development. As at UCLA, the York University administration has spawned its own subsidiary (Cultech), directed by the vice president for research and several deans and dedicated, in collaboration with a consortium of private sector firms, to the commercial development and exploitation of online education.

Significantly, at both UCLA and York, the presumably cyber-happy students have given clear indication that they are not exactly enthusiastic about the prospect of a high-tech academic future, recommending against the Initiative at UCLA and at York lending their support to striking faculty and launching their own independent investigation of the commercial, pedagogical, and ethical implications of online educational technology. This Fall the student handbook distributed annually to all students by the York Federation of Students contained a warning about the dangers of online education.

The classroom vs. the boardroom

Thus, at the very outset of this new age of higher education, the lines have already been drawn in the struggle which will ultimately determine its shape. On the one side university administrators and their myriad commercial partners, on the other those who constitute the core relation of education: students and teachers. (The chief slogan of the York faculty during the strike was "the classroom vs. the boardroom"). It is no accident, then, that the high-tech transformation of higher education is being initiated and implemented from the top down, either without any student and faculty involvement in the decision-making or despite it. At UCLA the administration launched their Initiative during the summer when many faculty are away and there was little possibility of faculty oversight or governance; faculty were thus left out of the loop and kept in the dark about the new Web requirement until the last moment.

And UCLA administrators also went ahead with its Initiative, which is funded by a new compulsory student fee, despite the formal student recommendation against it. Similarly the initiatives of the York administration in the deployment of computer technology in education were taken without faculty oversight and deliberation much less student involvement. What is driving this headlong rush to implement new technology with so little regard for deliberation of the pedagogical and economic costs and at the risk of student and faculty alienation and opposition? A short answer might be the fear of getting left behind, the incessant pressures of 'progress'. But there is more to it. For the universities are not simply undergoing a technological transformation. Beneath that change, and camouflaged by it, lies another: the commercialization of higher education.

For here as elsewhere technology is but a vehicle and a disarming disguise.

The major change to befall the universities over the last two decades has been the identification of the campus as a significant site of capital accumulation, a change in social perception which has resulted in the systematic conversion of intellectual activity into intellectual capital and, hence, intellectual property. There have been two general phases of this transformation. The first, which began twenty years ago and is still underway, entailed the commoditization of the research function of the university, transforming scientific and engineering knowledge into commercially viable proprietary products that could be owned and bought and sold in the market. The second, which we are now witnessing, entails the commoditization of the educational function of the university, transforming courses into courseware, the activity of instruction itself into commercially viable proprietary products that can be owned and bought and sold in the market. In the first phase the universities became the site of production and sale of patents and exclusive licenses. In the second, they are becoming the site of production of—as well as the chief market for—copyrighted videos, courseware, CD-ROMs, and Web sites.

The first phase began in the mid-1970s when, in the wake of the oil crisis and intensifying international competition, corporate and political leaders of the major industrialized countries of the world recognized that they were losing their monopoly over the world's heavy industries and that, in the future, their supremacy would depend upon their monopoly over the knowledge which had become the lifeblood of the new so-called 'knowledge-based' industries (space, electronics, computers, materials, telecommunications, and bioengineering). This focus upon 'intellectual capital' turned their attention to the universities as its chief source, implicating the universities as never before in the economic machinery. In the view of capital, the universities had become too important to be left to the universities. Within a decade there was a proliferation of industrial partnerships and new proprietary arrangements, as industrialists and their campus counterparts invented ways to socialize the risks and costs of creating this knowledge while privatizing the benefits. This unprecedented collaboration gave rise to an elaborate web of interlocking directorates between corporate and academic boardrooms and the foundation of joint lobbying efforts epitomized by the work of the Business-Higher Education Forum. The chief accomplishment of the combined effort, in addition to a relaxation of anti-trust regulations and greater tax incentives for corporate funding of university research, was the 1980 reform of the patent law which for the first time gave the universities automatic ownership of patents resulting from federal government grants. Laboratory knowledge now became patents, that is, intellectual capital and intellectual property. As patent holding companies, the universities set about at once to codify their intellectual property policies, develop the infrastructure for the conduct of commercially viable research, cultivate their corporate ties, and create the mechanisms for marketing their new commodity, exclusive licenses to their patents. The result of this first phase of university commoditization was a wholesale reallocation of university resources toward its research function at the expense of its educational function.

Class sizes swelled, teaching staffs and instructional resources were reduced, salaries were frozen, and curricular offerings were cut to the bone. At the same time, tuition soared to subsidize the creation and maintenance of the commercial infrastructure (and correspondingly bloated administration) that has never really paid off. In the end students were paying more for their education and getting less, and the campuses were in crisis[2].

The second phase of the commercialization of academia, the commoditization of instruction, is touted as the solution to the crisis engendered by the first.

2 Tuition began to outpace inflation in the early 1980s, at precisely the moment when changes in the patent system enabled the universities to become major vendors of patent licenses. According to data compiled by the National Center for Educational Statistics, between 1976 and 1994 expenditures on research increased 21.7 percent at public research universities while expenditure on instruction decreased 9.5 percent. Faculty salaries, which had peaked in 1972, fell precipitously during the next decade and have since recovered only half the loss.

Ignoring the true sources of the financial debacle—an expensive and low-yielding commercial infrastructure and greatly expanded administrative costs—the champions of computer-based instruction focus their attention rather upon increasing the efficiencies of already overextended teachers. And they ignore as well the fact that their high-tech remedies are bound only to compound the problem, increasing further, rather than reducing, the costs of higher education. (Experience to date demonstrates clearly that computer-based teaching, with its limitless demands upon instructor time and vastly expanded overhead requirements—equipment, upgrades, maintenance, and technical and administrative support staff—costs more not less than traditional education, whatever the reductions in direct labor, hence the need for outside funding and student technology fees). Little wonder, then, that teachers and students are reluctant to embrace this new panacea. Their hesitation reflects not fear but wisdom[3].

The birth of educational maintenance organizations

But this second transformation of higher education is not the work of teachers or students, the presumed beneficiaries of improved education, because it is not really about education at all. That's just the name of the market. The foremost promoters of this transformation are rather the vendors of the network hardware, software, and "content"—Apple, IBM, Bell, the cable companies, Microsoft, and the edutainment and publishing companies Disney, Simon and Schuster, Prentice-Hall, et al.—who view education as a market for their wares, a market estimated by the Lehman Brothers investment firm potentially to be worth several hundred billion dollars. 'Investment opportunity in the education industry has never been better,' one of their reports proclaimed, indicating that this will be

---

3 Recent surveys of the instructional use of information technology in higher education clearly indicate that there have been no significant gains in either productivity improvement or pedagogical enhancement. Kenneth C. Green, Director of the Campus Computing Project, which conducts annual surveys of information technology use in higher education, noted that "the campus experience over the past decade reveals that the dollars can be daunting, the return on investment highly uncertain." "We have yet to hear of an instance where the total costs (including all realistically amortized capital investments and development expenses, plus reasonable estimates for faculty and support staff time) associated with teaching some unit to some group of students actually decline while maintaining the quality of learning," Green wrote. On the matter of pedagogical effectiveness, Green noted that "the research literature offers, at best, a mixed review of often inconclusive results, at least when searching for traditional measures of statistical significance in learning outcomes."

'the focus industry' for lucrative investment in the future, replacing the health care industry. (The report also forecasts that the educational market will eventually become dominated by EMOs—education maintenance organizations—just like HMOs in the health care market). It is important to emphasize that, for all the democratic rhetoric about extending educational access to those unable to get to the campus, the campus remains the real market for these products, where students outnumber their distance learning counterparts six-to-one.

In addition to the vendors, corporate training advocates view online education as yet another way of bringing their problem-solving, information processing, 'just-in-time' educated employees up to profit-making speed. Beyond their ambitious in-house training programs, which have incorporated computer-based instructional methods pioneered by the military, they envision the transformation of the delivery of higher education as a means of supplying their properly prepared personnel at public expense.

The third major promoters of this transformation are the university administrators, who see it as a way of giving their institutions a fashionably forward-looking image. More importantly, they view computer-based instruction as a means of reducing their direct labor and plant maintenance costs—fewer teachers and classrooms—while at the same time undermining the autonomy and independence of faculty. At the same time, they are hoping to get a piece of the commercial action for their institutions or themselves, as vendors in their own right of software and content. University administrators are supported in this enterprise by a number of private foundations, trade associations, and academic-corporate consortia which are promoting the use of the new technologies with increasing intensity. Among these are the Sloan, Mellon, Pew, and Culpeper Foundations, the American Council on Education, and, above all, Educom, a consortium representing the management of 600 colleges and universities and a hundred private corporations.

Last but not least, behind this effort are the ubiquitous technozealots who simply view computers as the panacea for everything, because they like to play with them. With the avid encouragement of their private sector and university patrons, they forge ahead, without support for their pedagogical claims about the alleged enhancement of education, without any real evidence of productivity improvement, and without any effective demand from either students or teachers.

In addition to York and UCLA, universities throughout North America are rapidly being overtaken by this second phase of commercialization. There are the stand-alone virtual institutions like the University of Phoenix, wired private institutions like the New School for Social Research, campuses of state universities like the University of Maryland and the new Gulf Coast campus of the University of Florida (which boasts no tenure). On the state level, the states of Arizona and

California have initiated their own state-wide virtual university projects, while a consortia of western "Smart States" have launched their own ambitious effort to wire all of their campuses into an online educational network. In Canada, a national effort has been undertaken, spearheaded by the Telelearning Research Network centered at Simon Fraser University in Vancouver, to bring most of the nation's higher education institutions into a "Virtual U" network.

The overriding commercial intent and market orientation behind these initiatives is explicit, as is illustrated by the most ambitious U. S. effort to date, the Western Governors' Virtual University Project, whose stated goals are to "expand the marketplace for instructional materials, courseware, and programs utilizing advanced technology," "expand the marketplace for demonstrated competence," and "identify and remove barriers to the free functioning of these markets, particularly barriers posed by statutes, policies, and administrative rules and regulations."

'In the future,' Utah governor Mike Leavitt proclaimed, "an institution of higher education will become a little like a local television station." Start up funds for the project come from the private sector, specifically from Educational Management Group, the educational arm of the world's largest educational publisher Simon and Schuster and the proprietary impulse behind their largesse is made clear by Simon and Schuster CEO Jonathan Newcomb: "The use of interactive technology is causing a fundamental shift away from the physical classroom toward anytime, anywhere learning—the model for post secondary education in the twenty-first century." This transformation is being made possible by 'advances in digital technology, coupled with the protection of copyright in cyberspace.'

Similarly, the national effort to develop the 'Virtual U' customized educational software platform in Canada is directed by an industrial consortium which includes Kodak, IBM, Microsoft, McGraw-Hill, Prentice-Hall, Rogers Cablesystems, Unitel, Novasys, Nortel, Bell Canada, and MPR Teltech, a research subsidiary of GTE. The commercial thrust behind the project is explicit here too. Predicting a potential fifty billion dollar Canadian market, the project proposal emphasizes the adoption of "an intellectual property policy that will encourage researchers and industry to commercialize their innovations" and anticipates the development of 'a number of commercially marketable hardware and software products and services,' including 'courseware and other learning products.' The two directors of the project, Simon Fraser University professors, have formed their own company to peddle these products in collaboration with the university. At the same time, the nearby University of British Columbia has recently spun off the private WEB-CT company to peddle its own educational Web site software, WEB-CT, the software designed by one of its computer science professors and now being used by UCLA. In recent months, WEB-CT has entered into production and distribution relationships with Silicon Graphics and Prentice-Hall and is fast becoming a major player in the American as well as Canadian higher education market. As of the beginning of the Fall term, WEB-CT licensees now include, in addition to UCLA and California State University, the Universities of Georgia, Minnesota, Illinois, North Carolina, and Indiana, as well as such private institutions as Syracuse, Brandeis, and Duquesne.

Education as a commodity

The implications of the commoditization of university instruction are two-fold in nature, those relating to the university as a site of the production of the commodities and those relating to the university as a market for them. The first raises for the faculty traditional labor issues about the introduction of new technologies of production. The second raises for students major questions about costs, coercion, privacy, equity, and the quality of education.

With the commoditization of instruction, teachers as labor are drawn into a production process designed for the efficient creation of instructional commodities, and hence become subject to all the pressures that have befallen production workers in other industries undergoing rapid technological transformation from above. In this context faculty have much more in common with the historic plight of other skilled workers than they care to acknowledge. Like these others, their activity is being restructured, via the technology, in order to reduce their autonomy, independence, and control over their work and to place workplace knowledge and control as much as possible into the hands of the administration. As in other industries, the technology is being deployed by management primarily to discipline, de-skill, and displace labor.

Once faculty and courses go online, administrators gain much greater direct control over faculty performance and course content than ever before and the potential for administrative scrutiny, supervision, regimentation, discipline and even censorship increase dramatically. At the same time, the use of the technology entails an inevitable extension of working time and an intensification of work as faculty struggle at all hours of the day and night to stay on top of the technology and respond, via chat rooms, virtual office hours, and e-mail, to both students and administrators to whom they have now become instantly and continuously accessible. The technology also allows for much more careful administrative monitoring of faculty availability, activities, and responsiveness.

Once faculty put their course material online, moreover, the knowledge and course design skill embodied in that material is taken out of their possession, transferred to the machinery and placed in the hands of the administration. The administration is now in a position to hire less skilled, and hence cheaper, workers to deliver the technologically prepackaged course. It also allows the administration, which claims ownership of this commodity, to peddle the course elsewhere without the original designer's involvement or even knowledge, much less financial interest. The buyers of this packaged commodity, meanwhile, other academic institutions, are able thereby to contract out, and hence outsource, the work of their own employees and thus reduce their reliance upon their in-house teaching staff.

Redundant faculty in the virtual university

Most important, once the faculty converts its courses to courseware, their services are in the long run no longer required. They become redundant, and when they leave, their work remains behind. In Kurt Vonnegut's classic novel Player Piano the ace machinist Rudy Hertz is flattered by the automation engineers who tell him his genius will be immortalized. They buy him a beer. They capture his skills on tape. Then they fire him. Today faculty are falling for the same tired line, that their brilliance will be broadcast online to millions. Perhaps, but without their further participation. Some skeptical faculty insist that what they do cannot possibly be automated, and they are right. But it will be automated anyway, whatever the loss in educational quality. Because education, again, is not what all this is about; it's about making money. In short, the new technology of education, like the automation of other industries, robs faculty of their knowledge and skills, their control over their working lives, the product of their labor, and, ultimately, their means of livelihood.

None of this is speculation. This Fall the UCLA faculty, at administration request, have dutifully or grudgingly (it doesn't really matter which) placed their course work—ranging from just syllabi and assignments to the entire body of course lectures and notes—at the disposal of their administration, to be used online, without asking who will own it much less how it will eventually be used and with what consequences. At York University, untenured faculty have been required to put their courses on video, CD-ROM or the Internet or lose their job. They have then been hired to teach their own now automated course at a fraction of their former compensation. The New School in New York now routinely hires outside contractors from around the country, mostly unemployed PhDs, to design online courses. The designers are not hired as employees but are simply paid a modest flat fee and are required to surrender to the university all rights to their course. The New School then offers the course without having to employ anyone. And this is just the beginning.

Educom, the academic-corporate consortium, has recently established their Learning Infrastructure Initiative which includes the detailed study of what professors do, breaking the faculty job down in classic Tayloristic fashion into discrete tasks, and determining what parts can be automated or outsourced. Educom believes that course design, lectures, and even evaluation can all be standardized, mechanized, and consigned to outside commercial vendors. 'Today you're looking at a highly personal human-mediated environment,' Educom president Robert Heterich observed. 'The potential to remove the human mediation in some areas and replace it with automation—smart, computer-based, network-based systems—is tremendous. It's gotta happen.'

Toward this end, university administrators are coercing or enticing faculty into compliance, placing the greatest pressures on the most vulnerable—untenured and part-time faculty, and entry-level and prospective employees. They are using the academic incentive and promotion structure to reward cooperation and discourage dissent. At the same time they are mounting an intensifying propaganda campaign to portray faculty as incompetent, hide-bound, recalcitrant, inefficient, ineffective, and expensive—in short, in need of improvement or replacement through instructional technologies. Faculty are portrayed above all as obstructionist, as standing in the way of progress and forestalling the panacea of virtual education allegedly demanded by students, their parents, and the public.

The York University faculty had heard it all. Yet still they fought vigorously and ultimately successfully to preserve quality education and protect themselves from administrative assault. During their long strike they countered such administration propaganda with the truth about what was happening to higher education and eventually won the support of students, the media, and the public. Most important, they secured a new contract containing unique and unprecedented provisions which, if effectively enforced, give faculty members direct and unambiguous control over all decisions relating to the automation of instruction, including veto power. According to the contract, all decisions regarding the use of technology as a supplement to classroom instruction or as a means of alternative delivery (including the use of video, CD-ROMs, Internet Web sites, computer-mediated conferencing, etc.) 'shall be consistent with the pedagogic and academic judgments and principles of the faculty member employee as to the appropriateness of the use of technology in the circumstances.' The contract also guarantees that 'a faculty member will not be required to convert a course without his or her agreement.' Thus, the York faculty will be able to ensure that the new technology, if and when used, will contribute to a genuine enhancement rather than a degradation of the quality of education, while at the same time preserving their positions, their autonomy, and their academic freedom. The battle is far from won, but it is a start.

Student reactions

The second set of implications stemming from the commoditization of instruction involve the transformation of the university into a market for the commodities being produced. Administrative propaganda routinely alludes to an alleged student demand for the new instructional products. At UCLA officials are betting that their high-tech agenda will be 'student driven', as students insist that faculty make fuller use of the Web site technology in their courses. To date, however, there has been no such demand on the part of students, no serious study of it, and no evidence for it. Indeed, the few times students have been given a voice, they have rejected the initiatives hands down, especially when they were required to pay for it (the definition of effective demand, i.e., a market).

At UCLA, students recommended against the Instructional Enhancement Initiative. At the University of British Columbia, home of the WEB-CT software being used at UCLA, students voted in a referendum four-to-one against a similar initiative, despite a lengthy administration campaign promising them a more secure place in the high-tech future. Administrators at both institutions have tended to dismiss, ignore, or explain away these negative student decisions, but there is a message here: students want the genuine face-to-face education they paid for not a cyber-counterfeit. Nevertheless, administrators at both UCLA and UBC decided to proceed with their agenda anyway, desperate to create a market and secure some return on their investment in the information technology infrastructure. Thus, they are creating a market by fiat, compelling students (and faculty) to become users and hence consumers of the hardware, software, and content products as a condition of getting an education, whatever their interest or ability to pay. Can all students equally afford this capital-intensive education?

Another key ethical issue relates to the use of student online activities. Few students realize that their computer-based courses are often thinly-veiled field trials for product and market development, that while they are studying their courses, their courses are studying them. In Canada, for example, universities have been given royalty-free licenses to Virtual U software in return for providing data on its use to the vendors. Thus, all online activity including communications between students and professors and among students are monitored, automatically logged and archived by the system for use by the vendor. Students enrolled in courses using Virtual U software are in fact formally designated 'experimental subjects.' Because federal monies were used to develop the software and underwrite the field trials, vendors were compelled to comply with ethical guidelines on the experimental use of human subjects. Thus, all students once enrolled are required to sign forms releasing ownership and control of their online activities to the vendors.

The form states 'as a student using Virtual U in a course, I give my permission to have the computer-generated usage data, conference transcript data, and virtual artifacts data collected by the Virtual U software … used for research, development, and demonstration purposes.'

According to UCLA's Home Education Network president John Korbara, all of their distance learning courses are likewise monitored and archived for use by company officials. On the UCLA campus, according to Harlan Lebo of the Provost's office, student use of the course Web sites will be routinely audited and evaluated by the administration. Marvin Goldberg, designer of the UCLA WEB-CT software, acknowledges that the system allows for "lurking" and automatic storage and retrieval of all online activities. How this capability will be used and by whom is not altogether clear, especially since Web sites are typically being constructed by people other than the instructors. What third parties (besides students and faculty in the course) will have access to the students' communications? Who will own student online contributions? What rights, if any, do students have to privacy and proprietary control of their work? Are they given prior notification as to the ultimate status of their online activities, so that they might be in a position to give, or withhold, their informed consent? If students are taking courses which are just experiments, and hence of unproven pedagogical value, should students be paying full tuition for them? And if students are being used as guinea pigs in product trials masquerading as courses, should they be paying for these courses or be paid to take them? More to the point, should students be content with a degraded, shadow cyber-education? In Canada student organizations have begun to confront these issues head on, and there are some signs of similar student concern emerging also in the U. S.

Conclusion

In his classic 1959 study of diploma mills for the American Council on Education, Robert Reid described the typical diploma mill as having the following characteristics: 'no classrooms,' 'faculties are often untrained or nonexistent,' and 'the officers are unethical self-seekers whose qualifications are no better than their offerings.' It is an apt description of the digital diploma mills now in the making. Quality higher education will not disappear entirely, but it will soon become the exclusive preserve of the privileged, available only to children of the rich and the powerful. For the rest of us a dismal new era of higher education has dawned. In ten years, we will look upon the wired remains of our once great democratic higher education system and wonder how we let it happen. That is, unless we decide now not to let it happen.

PART FOUR

Other Contributions to the Discourse

CHAPTER TWENTY-EIGHT

The Fundamental Question

From *Mission of the University* (1930)

JOSÉ ORTEGA Y GASSET

Translated with Introduction by Howard Lee Nostrand, this selection is taken from *Mission of the University*, by José Ortega y Gasset, 1946, Edited by Dr. Karl Mannheim. Published for the International Library of Sociology and Social Reconstruction, by Kegan Paul, Trench, Trubner & Co., Ltd.

Editors' Note

Ortega y Gasset became the Professor of Metaphysics at the University of Madrid in 1911, a post he occupied for some twenty-five years. He was, however, much more than this, being 'at once a teacher, an essayist, a publisher-editor, a philosopher, and a statesman' (Lee Nostrand, Introduction to *Mission of the University*, p. 3). He was, therefore, a person who engaged in several spheres of life and tended to see matters against the largest horizons. Life, civilization, the prospects for humanity and the role of all of the branches of knowledge were themes that occupied his scholarly attentions. Synthesis—of understanding, of approaches, of the different forms of knowledge—was an abiding concern of his.

Mission of the University was born against the background of the Spanish Civil War and was reborn as a translation in English in 1946, and quickly then became part of the post-second World War literature that sought to find new foundations for the university. (The texts by Jaspers, Moberly and Leavis were also part of this genre, Ortega's text having a definite influence on Moberly at least.) Subsequently, *Mission of the University* has fallen back in its position in the literature on the idea of the university, a fact partly attributable to the rhetorical and—doubtless for some—florid language in which Ortega develops his argument.

Perhaps the key concept for Ortega is that of 'culture', culture being understood as 'the vital system of ideas of a period'. So far as the university is concerned, it has 'developed the mere seed of professional instruction into an enormous activity' and 'it has added the function of research'. In so doing, 'it has abandoned almost entirely the teaching or transmission of culture'. And Ortega felt that this change 'has been pernicious', the whole of Europe having become 'uncultured'. Accordingly, 'the transmission of culture' should be understood as the first function of the university, ahead both of the teaching of the professions and scientific research. On what basis is the selection to be made so as to enable the student properly to develop in this way? 'We must pick out that which appears as strictly necessary for the life of the ... student', and then identify 'what the student can really learn with thoroughness and understanding'. This is Ortega's 'principle of economy in education', that 'only so much must be taught as can truly be learned'.

RB

Recommended Reading

Jose Ortega y Gasset: *Mission of the University*—"An Uplifting Principle in the History of the Western World", Chapter 3 in J. Wyatt (1990). Commitment to Higher Education. Buckingham: Society for Research into Higher Education and Open University Press.

* * * * *

The reform of higher education cannot be limited, nor can even its main features be limited, to the correction of abuses.[1] Reform is always the creation of new usages. Abuses are always of minor importance. For either they are abuses in the most natural sense of the word, namely, isolated, infrequent cases of departure from usage; or else they are so frequent and customary, so persistent and so generally tolerated, that they are no longer to be called abuses. In the first case, they will presumably be corrected automatically; in the second case, it would be futile to correct them, for their frequency and acceptance indicate that they are not

1 EDITOR'S NOTE: The first three paragraphs of Chapter II have here been omitted. In them, Ortega recapitulates Chapter 1, and complains of the hall in which he had read that chapter. This is the only omission made in the present translation.

exceptions to a rule, but manifestations of usages which are bad. It is something in the usage, the policy, and not the breach of it, which needs our attention.

Any reform movement which is limited to correcting slovenly or slipshod abuses in our university will lead inevitably to a reform which is equally slovenly.

What matters is usage. I can go further: a clear symptom that the usages constituting an institution are sound is the ability to withstand a good dose of abuses without serious harm, as a healthy man bears up under stress that would break a weakling. But an institution cannot be built of wholesome usage, until its precise mission has been determined. An institution is a machine in that its whole structure and functioning must be devised in view of the service it is expected to perform". In other words, the root of university reform is a complete formulation of its purpose. Any alteration, or touching up, or adjustment about this house of ours, unless it starts by reviewing the problem of its mission—clearly, decisively, truthfully—will be love's labour lost.

Through their failure to do this, all the improvements attempted hitherto, motivated in some cases by excellent intentions, including the projects worked out some years ago by the university faculty itself, have inevitably come to nought. They will never achieve the one thing which is both sufficient and requisite for any being—individual or collective—to live to the full of its powers: namely, that its life be the true, authentic fulfilment of its powers, and not some falsification of this inexorable destiny, imposed upon it by our stubborn and arbitrary preferences. The best attempts of the last fifteen years—not to speak of the worst—instead of putting the question squarely, "What is a university for, and what must it consequently be?" have done the thing that was easiest and most sterile. They have looked about to see what is done in the universities of other peoples.

I do not criticize our informing ourselves by observing an exemplary neighbour; on the contrary, that is necessary. But such observation cannot excuse us from the labour of determining our destiny for ourselves. By this I do not mean any quest after "racial purity" and all that nonsense. Even if we were all—men or nations—identical with one another, imitation would still be fatal. For in imitating, we evade that creative exertion of labouring at a problem, from which we can learn the real nature, including the limits and the defects, of the solution we borrow. There is no question here of "racial purity", which is, in Spain anyway, as common as hayseeds. It is immaterial whether we come to the same conclusions and the same forms as other countries; what matters is that we arrive by our own legs, after a personal combat with the fundamental question at issue.

The reasoning of our best attempts so far has been fallacious: British life has been, and is, a marvel; *therefore* the British secondary schools must be exemplary, *since* out of them British life has grown. German science is prodigious; *therefore* the German university is a model institution, *because* it engendered the prodigy. So let us imitate the British secondary schools and the German higher education.

The error stems directly from the nineteenth century as a whole. The English rout Napoleon I: "The battle of Waterloo was won on the playing fields of Eton." Bismarck crushes Napoleon III: "The war of 1870 is the victory of the Prussian schoolmaster and the German professor."

These clichés rest upon a fundamental error which we shall simply have to get out of our heads. It consists in supposing that nations are great *because* their schools are good—elementary, secondary, or higher. It is the residue of a pious "idealism" of the past century. It ascribes to the school a force which it neither has nor can have. That century, in order to feel enthusiasm for a thing, or even just to esteem it especially, found it necessary to exaggerate the thing to heroic proportions. Certainly *when* a nation is great, so will be its schools. There is no great nation without great schools. But the same holds for its religion, its statesmanship, its economy, and a thousand other things. A nation's greatness is the integration of many elements. If a people is bad politically, it is vain to expect anything at all of the most perfect school system. In such a case schools are for the few, who live apart and estranged from the rest of the country. Perhaps someday these educated few may influence the collective life of their country, and succeed in improving the whole national school system.

Principle of education: the school, when it is truly a functional organ of the nation, depends far more on the atmosphere of national culture in which it is immersed than it does on the pedagogical atmosphere created artificially within it. A condition of equilibrium between this inward and outward pressure is essential to produce a good school.

Consequence: even granting that English secondary education and German higher education are perfect, they would not be transferable, for the institutions are only a part of a larger entity. Their being, in its totality, is nothing less than the whole nation which created and maintains them.

Furthermore, the short-circuited reasoning I have described prevented ifs victims from looking squarely at these model schools and seeing what they are within themselves, purely as institutional structures. The framework was confused with the ambient air of English life, or German thought. Now in as much as neither English life nor German thought can be transported here but, at best, only the disengaged institutional structures, it is quite important that we see what these actually are, apart from those virtues which enveloped and pervaded them in their native countries.

Then one sees that the German university is, as an institution, a rather deplorable object. If German science had been dependent for its nourishment on the forces of the university, as an institution, that science would be of very small account. Fortunately an atmosphere of free inquiry has combined with the German's natural talent and disposition for science to outweigh the glaring imperfections of the German university. I am not well acquainted with English secondary education; but what I can discern of it leads me to think that there too the institutional structure is very defective.

But there is no need of my personal opinions. It is a fact, that secondary education in England and the university in Germany are undergoing a crisis. Fundamental criticism of the latter by the first Prussian Minister of Education since the founding of the Republic: Becker. The discussion which has ensued.[2]

Because they have been willing to imitate and to evade thinking through the questions for themselves, our best professors live in all respects in a spirit fifteen or twenty years behind the times, except that they are up to date in the details of their fields. And this is the tragic lag behindhand, which is the fate of people who try to save themselves the effort of being authentic and forming their own convictions. The number of years comprising this lag is not a matter of chance. All the creation of history—in science, in politics—arises out of a certain pervading state of mind, or "spirit of the times". This state of mind changes at rhythmic intervals: the interval of the generation.[3] Out of the spirit of a generation come ideas, evaluations, and so on. The person who imitates these must wait until they have been formulated; or in other words, until the preceding generation has finished its work. Then he adopts its principles, at the time when they are beginning to decline, and a new generation is already making its reform, inaugurating the regime of a new spirit. Each generation struggles for fifteen years to establish itself, and its synthesis holds together another fifteen years—inevitable anachronism of an imitative, unauthentic people.

Let us look abroad for information. But not for a model.

There is no evading the fundamental question, then: What is the mission of the university?

---

2 EDITOR'S NOTE: See p. 49 and note. For the explanation of Ortega's unfinished sentences see his dedication, p. 26 and the Introduction, page 8.

3 EDITOR'S NOTE: Ortega has elaborated "The Concept of the Generation" in *The Modern Theme*, Chapter I and ff. For the background of the concept, see the résumé and brief bibliography in Christian Sénéchal, *Les grands courants de la littérature française contemporaine*, Paris: Malfère (1933), pp. 419–21; the introduction of Bopp and Paulhan to Albert Thibaudet, *Histoire de la littérature française de 1789 à nos jours*, Paris: Stock (1937); and also Sainte-Beuve's observation. concerning individual literary production, in *Nouveaux Lundis*, III, art. "Chateaubriand", part II (1862): "Quinze ans d'ordinaire font une carrier; il est donné à quelques-uns de la doubler, d'en recommencer ou même d'en remplir une seconde."

To determine what the mission of the university is, let us try first to define what the university actually means to-day, in Spain and elsewhere. Whatever may be the differences in status, all the universities of Europe have some general characteristics in common.[4]

We meet the fact, first of all, that the university is the institution in which higher education is imparted to almost all those who receive any. "Almost," because there are also the specialized schools, whose separate existence gives rise to a problem likewise separate. Having made this exception, we may lay it aside and work with the practical generalization, that the people who receive higher education receive it in the university. But then we find ourselves face to face with another

---

4 AUTHOR'S NOTE: It is usual, for example, to exaggerate the differences between the English and continental universities, neglecting the fact that the greatest differences are to be laid not to the universities themselves, but to the very extraordinary English character. What should be compared between countries is the tendencies which mark the evolution of their universities—not the degree, naturally variable, in which the tendencies have progressed. Thus, the conservatism of the English has caused them to maintain appearances, in their higher institutions, which they themselves recognize to be relevant, and which, they indeed, value as mere fictions quite incidental to the vital reality of British university life. It would seem ridiculous for someone to presume to limit the free will of the Englishman and censure him for indulging, if he could and wanted to, in the luxury of consciously perpetuating these fictions. But it would be just as näive to take these figments seriously, and suppose that the Englishman deludes himself about their fictitious character. The studies I have read on the English university fall invariably into the subtle snare of English irony. They fail to notice if England preserves the non-professional aspect of the university, like the wig of the magistrate, it is not through any obstinate belief that these are actualities, but precisely because they are antiquated and superfluous. Otherwise they could not provide the luxury, the diversion the occasion for awe and other values which the Englishman seeks in these mere appearances. Beneath the quaint peruke, the injustice is modern to the minute; and beneath its nonprofessional aspect, the English university has become, in the last forty years, as professionalized as any other.

It is likewise not of the slightest importance for our central theme-the mission of the university—that the English universities are not institutions of the state. While this fact is of great importance for the life and history of the English people it does not prevent their universities from functioning essentially in the same way as the state-maintained universities of the continent. In the last analysis it would turn out that even in England the universities are institutions of the state; only the Englishman has an entirely different conception of the state from the continental idea of it. To sum up the point I wish to make: first, the enormous differences which exist between the universities of the various nations are not so much concerned with the universities proper as with the nations themselves; and second, the most striking fact in the last forty years is a convergent movement of all the universities of Europe that is tending to make them all homogeneous.

limitation more important than that of the specialized schools. All those who receive higher education are not all those who could and should receive it; they are only the children of the well-to-do classes. The university represents a privilege difficult to justify or defend. Theme: the working class in the university—a theme as yet intact. For two reasons. First, if one believes it is right, as I do, to offer the knowledge of the university to the working man, it is because one considers this knowledge valuable and desirable. The problem of universalizing the university rests upon the previous determination of what the higher learning and instruction are to be. And second, the process of making the university accessible to the working man is only in small part the concern of the university; it is almost wholly the business of the state. Only a great reform of our state will make our university effective. Failure of all the attempts made so far, such as "university extension", etc.[5]

The important thing at this point is to bear well in mind that all the people who receive higher education receive it in the university. If a greater number should receive it tomorrow than at present, so much the better for the force of the argument which follows.

Of what does this higher instruction consist, which is offered in the university to the vast legion of youth? It consists of two things:

(A) The teaching of the learned professions.
(B) Scientific research and the preparation of future investigators.

The university teaches people to be doctors, pharmacists, lawyers, judges, economists, public servants, teachers of the sciences and the humanities in secondary schools, and so on.

In the second place, science itself is cultivated in the university, through research and the transmission of its methods. In Spain, this function of creative science, and of creating scientists, is at a minimum; not by reason of any defect of the university, nor because the university considers that such activities are not its mission, but on account of the notorious lack of scientific callings and aptitude

---

5 EDITOR'S NOTE: It should be noted that after half a century of growth, university extension in the United States has become an important agency for the training of people who must meanwhile earn their living. The cultural education of the working man is still admittedly deficient; but this is due rather to our poor understanding of the objective than to a lack of well-intentioned agencies. Organizations and institutions interested in the education of the working man are too numerous to need mention. Among the oldest are the British "Workers' Educational Association" and Ruskin College in Oxford (founded 1899). For the explanation of Ortega's unfinished sentences see his dedication, p. 26 and the Introduction, page 8.

for research which marks our race. No doubt if science were abundantly carried on in Spain, it would be in the university by preference, as is more or less the case in the other countries. Let this point serve as an example, and save us the repetition of the same principle at every step: the obstinate backwardness of Spain in intellectual activity entails the result that we find here in a state of germination or mere tendency what appears elsewhere in its full development. For the purpose of stating the university problem in its basic form, these differences of degree are immaterial. It is sufficient that all the reforms of recent years clearly evince the intention to increase the research activities of our universities and the training of scientists: in short, to orient the entire institution in this direction. Common place and deceptive objections may be advanced on the other side. It is, however, notorious that our best professors, those who have the most influence in the course of the attempted reforms, believe that our university should vie with the foreign universities. And that is enough.

The higher education consists, then, of professionalism and research. Without attacking the subject now, let us note in passing that it is surprising to find two such disparate tasks joined, fused together. For there can be no doubt about this: to be a lawyer, a judge, a doctor, a druggist, a teacher of Latin or history in a secondary school, is very different from being a jurist, a physiologist, a biochemist, a philologist, etc. The former are engaged in practical professions; the latter in purely scientific occupations. Furthermore, society needs many doctors, pharmacists, teachers; but it needs only a restricted number of scientists.[6] If we really needed many of these it would be a catastrophe, since a true calling for science is extremely rare. It is surprising, then, to find mixed together the professional instruction which is for all, and research which is for a very few. But let us put this matter aside for a few moments. Is the higher education nothing more than professionalism and research? At first sight we discover nothing else. But if we scrutinize the programmes of instruction more closely, we discover that the student is nearly always required, apart from his professional apprenticeship and his research, to take some courses of a general character—philosophy, history.

It takes no great acumen to recognize in this requirement the last, miserable residue of something more imposing and more meaningful. The symptom that something is a residue—whether in biology or in history—is that we do not perceive why it is with us. In its present form, it serves no end at all; one must trace it back to some other age of its evolution in order to find whole and active what

6 AUTHOR'S NOTE: This number needs to be greater than has been attained at present; but even so, incomparably smaller than the number in the other professions.

exists today only as a residual stump.[7] The justification which is advanced today, in support of that ancient precept of higher education, is rather vague. The student ought, it is said, to receive something of "general culture".

"General culture." The absurdity of the term, its Philistinism, betrays its insincerity. Culture," referring to the human mind and not to stock or crops, cannot be anything else but general. There is no being "cultured" in physics or mathematics. That would mean simply to be *learned* in a particular subject. The usage of the expression "general culture" shows an underlying notion that the student ought to be given some ornamental knowledge, which in some way is to educate his moral character or his intellect. For so vague a purpose, one discipline is as good as another, among those that are more or less indefinite and not so technical—like philosophy, or history" or sociology!

But the fact is that if we go back to the medieval epoch in which the university was created, we see clearly that the relic before us is the humble remains of what then constituted higher education, proper and entire.

The medieval university does no research.[8] It is very little concerned with professions. All is "*general culture*"—theology, philosophy, "arts."[9]

But what is called "general culture" to-day was something very different for the Middle Ages. It was not an ornament for the mind or a training of the character. It was, on the contrary, the system of ideas, concerning the world and humanity, which the man of that time possessed. It was, consequently, the repertory of convictions which became the effective guide of his existence.

Life is a chaos, a tangled and confused jungle in which man is lost. But his mind reacts against the sensation of bewilderment: he labours to find "roads", "ways" through the woods,[10] in the form of clear, firm ideas concerning the

---

7 AUTHOR'S NOTE: Imagine for a moment the conditions of primitive life. One of its constant characteristics is the lack of personal security. It is perilous for two persons to approach each other, for everyone goes about armed. Hence this act has to be safeguarded by customs and ceremonies which give assurance that weapons have been left behind, and that the hand is not going to reach suddenly for one that is hidden. For this purpose, the best procedure is for each man, upon approaching, to grasp the hand of the other-the killing hand, which is normally the right hand. Such is the origin and purpose of our salute by shaking hands, which in the present times, remote from that type of life, is an incomprehensible relic.

8 AUTHOR'S NOTE: Which does not mean that no research was done in the Middle Ages.

9 EDITOR'S NOTE: The exaggeration here does not essentially damage Sr. Ortega's thesis that the modern university should teach a kind of "culture" which this reference to the Middle Ages helps to describe.

10 AUTHOR'S NOTE: Whence there arises at the beginning of all cultures a term expressing "road" in this sense: the *hodos* and *methodos* of the Greeks, the *tao* and *te* of the Chinese, the *path* and *vehicle* of India.

universe, positive convictions about the nature of things. The ensemble, or system, of these ideas, is culture in the true sense of the term; it is precisely the opposite of external ornament. Culture is what saves human life from being a mere disaster; it is what enables man to live a life which is something above meaningless tragedy or inward disgrace.

We cannot live on the human level without ideas. Upon them depends what we do. Living is nothing more or less than doing one thing instead of another. Hence the oldest book of India: "Our acts follow our thoughts as the wheel of the cart follows the hoof of the ox." In this sense—which by itself implies no intellectualistic doctrine[11]—we are our ideas.

Gideon, in this case exceptionally profound, would make it clear that man is always born into a specific period. That is, he is called to live his life at some definite stage in the unfolding of human destinies. A man belongs to a generation; he is of one substance with it. And each generation takes its place not in some chance location, but directly and squarely upon the preceding one. This comes to mean that man lives, perforce, at *the level of his time*,[12] and more particularly, *at the level of the ideas of his time.*

Culture is the *vital* system of ideas of a period. It makes 1not a particle of difference whether these ideas, or convictions, lie partly or wholly in the province of science. Culture is not science. It is characteristic of our present culture that a great part of its content proceeds out of science; but in other cultures this has not been the case, nor is it decreed anywhere that in ours it will always be so to the same degree as at present.

Compared with the medieval university, the contemporary university has developed the mere seed of professional instruction into an enormous activity; it has added the function of research; and it has abandoned almost entirely the teaching or transmission of culture.

It is evident that the change has been pernicious. Europe today is taking its sinister consequences. The convulsive situation in Europe at the present moment is due to the fact that the average Englishman, the average Frenchman, the average German are *uncultured*: they are ignorant of the essential system of ideas concerning the world and man, which belong to our time. This average person is the new barbarian, a laggard behind the contemporary civilization, archaic and primitive in

---

11 AUTHOR's NOTE: Our ideas or convictions may well be unintellectualistic, as mine are, and in general, the ideas of our age.

12 AUTHOR'S NOTE: For the concept of "the height of the times", see *The Revolt of the Masses.*

contrast with his problems, which are grimly, relentlessly modern.[13] This new barbarian is above all the professional man, more learned than ever before, but at the same time more uncultured—the engineer, the physician, the lawyer, the scientist.

The blame for this unpredicted barbarity, this radical and tragic anachronism, rests primarily with the pretentious nineteenth-century university of all countries. If this institution should by chance be torn to bits in the frenzy of a barbarous revolution, it would not have the feeblest reason to complain. When one has examined the matter, he must needs come to the conclusion that the guilt of the universities is not compensated for by the prodigious and brilliant' service which they have undeniably rendered to science. Let us not be the dupes of science. For if science is the grandest creation of man, it is made possible, after all, by human life. A crime perpetrated against the fundamental conditions of human life cannot be atoned for through science.

The harm is so ingrained that I shall barely be understood by the generation anterior to the one I am addressing.

In the book of a Chinese thinker who lived in the fourth century B.C., Chuang-tsu, certain symbolic characters are conversing together, and one of them, called the God of the Northern Sea, asks, "How shall I talk of the sea to the frog, if he has never left his pond? How shall I talk of the frost to the bird of the summer land, if it has never left the land of its birth? How shall I talk of life with the sage, if he is the prisoner of his doctrine?"

Society needs good professional men—judges, doctors, engineers—and therefore the university is prepared to furnish professional training. But society needs before this, and more than this, to be assured that the capacity is developed for another kind of profession, the profession of governing. In every society someone governs, whether a group or a class, few people or many. By "governing" I mean not so much the legal exercise of authority as a diffuse pressure, or influence, exerted upon the body politic. Today, the societies in Europe are governed by the bourgeois classes, the majority of whom are composed of professional men. It is of the first importance to these societies, therefore, that these professional people, aside from their several professions, possess the power to make their lives a vital influence, in harmony with the height of their times. Hence it is imperative to set up once more, in the university, the teaching of the culture, the system of vital ideas, which the age has attained. This is the basic function of the university. This is what the university must be, above all else.

---

13 AUTHOR'S NOTE: The analysis of this serious situation is presented in *The Revolt of the Masses.*

If the working man should become the governing man tomorrow, the problem remains the same: he must govern in accordance with the height of the times—otherwise his regime will be supplanted.[14]

When one considers that the European countries have deemed it admissible to grant professional titles and prestige to magistrates and doctors without making sure that these men have a clear idea, for example, of the physical conception we now have of the world, and an equally Clear idea of the character and limitations of the marvellous science by which that concept had been attained—we need not be surprised that affairs have come to such a pass in Europe. At a juncture like this, let us not bandy about fine phrases. The vague desire for a vague culture, I repeat, will lead us nowhere. Physics, and its method, is one of the great essential instruments of the modern mind. Into that science have gone four centuries of intellectual discipline, and its doctrine is intimately connected with the cultured man's concept of God and society, of matter and that which is not matter, together with all the other essentials for an enlightened life. Of course, one can do without that science and be neither disgraced nor condemned—in certain situations: if one is a humble shepherd in the hills, or a serf attached to the soil, or a manual labourer enslaved to the machine. But the gentleman who professes to be a doctor, or magistrate, or general, or philologist, or bishop-that is, a person who belongs to the directive class of society—if he is ignorant of what the physical cosmos is to-day for the European man, is a perfect barbarian, however well he may know his laws, or his medicines, or his Holy Fathers. And I should say the same of the person who has not a decently coherent picture of the great movements of history which have brought Humanity to its present parting of the ways (for ours is a day of crucial situations). And I should say the same again of the person who has no definite idea of how speculative philosophy conceives to-day its perpetual essay to formulate a plan of the universe; or how biology endeavours to interpret the fundamental facts of organic life.

For the moment, let us not obscure this simple, evident proposition, by raising the question of how a lawyer, without preparation in higher mathematics, can understand the idea of twentieth-century physics. We shall deal with that question later. For now, let us simply admit into our minds, as we must, the light which proceeds from this observation. The man who does not possess the concept of physics (not the science of physics proper, but the vital idea of the world which it has created), and the concept afforded by history and by biology, and the scheme of speculative philosophy, is not an educated man. Unless he should happen to be

14 AUTHOR'S NOTE: Since in actual practice the working man does govern, sharing that function with the middle class, it is urgent that the university education be extended to him.

endowed with exceptional qualities, it is extremely unlikely that such a man will be, in the fullest sense, a good doctor, a good judge, or a good technical expert. But it is certain that all the other things he does in life, including parts of his profession itself which transcend its proper academic boundaries, will turn out unfortunately. His political ideas and actions will be inept; his affairs of the heart, beginning with the type of woman he will prefer, will be crude and ridiculous; he will bring to his family life an atmosphere of unreality and cramped narrowness, which will warp the upbringing of his children; and outside, with his friends, he will emit thoughts that are monstrosities, and opinions that are a torrent of drivel and bluff.

There is no other way: to move with assurance in the tangle of life, one must be cultivated, one must know the topography—the "ways" and "methods". One must have an idea of the time and place in which he lives: in a word, the "culture" of the age. Now then, this culture is either received, or else it is invented. He who exposes himself to the labour of inventing it for himself, accomplishing alone what thirty centuries of humanity have already accomplished, is the only man who has the right to deny the proposition that the university must undertake to impart culture. But the unfortunate truth is that this lone person, who could oppose my thesis, would have to be a madman!

Civilization has had to await the beginning of the twentieth century, to see the astounding spectacle of how brutal, how stupid, and yet how aggressive is the man learned in one thing and fundamentally ignorant of all else.[15] Professionalism and specialism, through insufficient counterbalancing, have smashed the European man in pieces; and he is consequently missing at all the points where he claims to be, and is badly needed. The engineer possesses engineering; but that is just one piece, one dimension of the European man: the whole man is not to be found in this fragment called "engineer". And so in the rest of the cases. When one says that "Europe is broken in pieces", thinking to use a baroque and exaggerated expression, he says more truth than he suspects. Indeed, the crumbling away of Europe which we are witnessing is the result of the invisible fragmentation that the European man has progressively undergone.[16]

The great task immediately before us is something like a jigsaw puzzle: we have to reassemble out of scattered pieces—*disiecta membra*—a complete living organism, the European man. What we must achieve is that every individual, or (not to

---

15 AUTHOR'S NOTE: See the chapter entitled "The barbarism of specialization" in *The Revolt of the Masses.*

16 AUTHOR'S NOTE: The statement is true to such a point that it cannot only be made thus vaguely, but it can be developed by enumerating the precise phases of the progressive fragmentation, in the three generations of the past century and the first generation of the twentieth.

be Utopian) many individuals, should each succeed in constituting the type of the whole man in its entirety. What force can bring this about, if it is not the university?

Then there are no two ways about it. The university must add this other function, huge as it is, to the list of those it already attempts to accomplish.

For that matter, outside Spain a movement is making itself felt with great vigour, to orient higher education towards the teaching of culture, or the transmission to the newer generation of the system of ideas concerning the world and man which has reached its maturity with the passing generation.

We come to the conclusion therefore that the university's teaching comprises these three functions:

I. The transmission of culture
II. The teaching of the professions
III. Scientific research and the training of new scientists

Have we thus answered our question, What is the mission of the university? By no means! we have only massed together what the university of to-day believes to be its business, and a work which, in our judgment, it is not doing but must do. We have prepared the question; no more than that.

It seems to me unnecessary, or at least incidental, to debate as did the philosopher Scheler and the Minister of Education Becker, a few years ago, over the question whether these functions are to be performed by a single institution or by various institutions.[17] It is vain because in the end all these functions would unite in the person of the student: they would all eventually come to gravitate around his adolescent years, as a common centre.

The question is different. It is this: Even when instruction is limited, as at present, to professional matters and the methods of science, the result is a fabulous profusion of studies. It is impossible even for the better than ordinary student to come anywhere near real success in learning what the university professes to teach him. But institutions exist—they are necessary and they have meaning—because the ordinary man exists. If there were none but extraordinary creatures, it is very probable that there would be no institutions, either educational or political.[18] It is

17 EDITOR'S NOTE: See especially Carl Heinrich Becker (by error "Beeker" in the Spanish editions), *Gedanken zur Hochschulreform*, Leipzig: Quelle u. Meyer, 1919; and Max Scheler, "*Innere Widersprüche der deutschen Universitäten*," Westdeutsche Wochenschrift I, 32: 493–5; 33: 511–12; 34: 524–7; 35: 539–41; 36: 551–3.

18 AUTHOR's NOTE: Anarchy is logical when it declares all institutions to be useless and thus pernicious, for it starts with the postulate that every man is extraordinary by birth—i.e. good, prudent, intelligent, and just.

therefore necessary to consider any institution with reference to the man of ordinary endowment. For him it is made, and he must be its unit of measure.

Let us suppose for a moment that in the university, as it is, we find nothing which deserves to be called an abuse. Everything is running smoothly and properly according to what the university professes itself to be. Very well: even then I should say the university of today is an abuse in itself, because it is, in itself, a falsehood.

It is so thoroughly impossible for the ordinary student to master what the university tries to teach him, that it has become I a part of university life to accept the failure. In other words, it is taken for granted, as a regular thing, that what the university attempts to be is a delusion. We accept the falsity of the university's inward life—its very essence is composed of its own falsification. This is the root of the whole trouble (as it always is in life, individual or collective). The original sin stems from the pretension to be other than one's true self. It is our privilege to *try* to be whatever we wish; but it is vicious to pretend to be what we are not, and to delude ourselves by growing habituated to a radically false idea of what we are. When the habitual behaviour of a man or an institution is false, the next step is complete demoralization. And thence to degeneracy, for it is not possible for anyone to submit to the falsification of his nature without losing his self-respect.

That is why Leonardo da Vinci said: "Chi non può quel che vuol, quel che può voglia"—"Who cannot what he will, let him will what he can."

This maxim of Leonardo's must guide from the beginning any real reform of the university. Only a firm resolution to be genuine will bear fruit. And not only the life of the university, but the whole new life must be fashioned by artisans whose first thought is *authenticity*. (Note this, Younger Generation. Otherwise, you are lost. In fact you show signs of being lost already.)

An institution, then, which feigns to give and to require what it cannot, is false and demoralized. Yet this principle of deceit is to be found throughout the whole plan and structure of the present university.

The conclusion seems to me inescapable, that we must turn the present university upside down, so to speak, and stand it upon precisely the opposite principle. Instead of teaching what *ought* to be taught, according to some Utopian desire, we must teach only what *can* be taught; that is, *what can be learned*.

I shall attempt to develop the implications of this formula.

> The problem extends in reality quite beyond the subject of higher education. It involves the capital question of education at all levels.

What has been the great historic advance in pedagogy? Beyond doubt, the turn it has taken under the inspiration of Rousseau, Pestalozzi, Froebel, and German idealism, amounting to a revolutionary avowal of the obvious. In education there are three elemental factors: what is taught (knowledge, wisdom), and the teacher and the learner. Yet with peculiar blindness, education had centred about knowledge and the teacher. The learner was no factor in pedagogy. The innovation of Rousseau and his successors was simply to shift the centre of gravity of the science from knowledge and the teacher to the learner, recognizing that it is the learner and his characteristics which alone can guide us in our effort to make something organic of education. Knowledge and research have their own structure, which is not applicable to that other activity proposing to impart knowledge. The principle of pedagogy is entirely different from that on. which culture and science are built.

But we must go a step further. Rather than lose ourselves in a minute study of the learner's characteristics as a child, as a youth, etc., we are constrained to limit the subject for our present purpose, and consider the child and the youth from a more modest point of view, which is more precise: namely, as a student and apprentice. Then we strike upon the fact that it is not the child as a child, or the youth because of his youth, that obliges us to ply this special profession we call "teaching". It is something far less complicated, and in fact, very definite and simple.

Let me explain.

The Principle of Economy in Education

From *Mission of the University* (1930)

Translated with Introduction by Howard Lee Nostrand, this selection is taken from *Mission of the University*, by José Ortega y Gasset, 1946, Edited by Dr. Karl Mannheim. Published for the International Library of Sociology and Social Reconstruction, by Kegan Paul, Trench, Trubner & Co., Ltd.

* * * * *

The science of political economy emerged from the war in much the same shattered state as did the economies of the belligerent nations. There was nothing to do but set about reconstructing this whole body of knowledge from the ground up. Such adventures are as a rule beneficial in the life of a science, for they force it to seek a more solid basis than has been in use, a more general and fundamental principle. And in fact at the present time, political economy is arising from its ruins, for a reason so obvious that it is embarrassing to mention. To wit: that economic *science* necessarily responds to the fundamental principle underlying the economic *activity* of man. Why is it that mankind engages in economic occupations, producing, managing, bartering, saving, appraising, etc.? For one astonishing reason, and that alone: because many of the things man desires and requires are not to be had in unlimited abundance. If all we need existed in plenty and to spare it would never have occurred to men to fatigue themselves with economic exertion.

Air, for example, does not usually give rise to activity we could call economic. Yet as soon as air becomes scarce in some way or other, it immediately occasions economic activity. For example children in a schoolroom need a certain amount of air. If the room is small there is a scarcity of air; hence an economic problem, ending in an enlarged school which is accordingly more expensive.

Again, even though our planet is rolling in air, so to speak, its air is not all of the same quality. "Pure air" is to be had only at certain places, at certain altitudes, under specific conditions of climate. "Pure air" is scarce. And that simple fact provokes an intense economic activity among the Swiss—hotels, sanatoriums—converting this scarce raw material into health, at so much per day.

This is all astonishingly simple, I repeat; but it is undeniably true. Scarcity is the basis of economic activity, and indeed the Swedish economist Cassel, some years ago, revised the science of economics by taking as a point of departure the *principle of scarcity*.[19] Einstein has remarked many times that "if perpetual motion existed, there would be no such thing as physics". Similarly, we may be sure that in Elysium there is no economic activity, and consequently no science of economics.

I am persuaded that an analogous situation has its effect in education. Why does pedagogical activity exist at all? Why is it an occupation and a preoccupation of man? To these questions the romantics gave most brilliant, moving, and transcendental answers, in which they drew upon all things human and a good portion of the divine. For their taste, it was always necessary to obscure the bare nature of things with festoons of ornamental foliage, and a touch of melodrama. We, on the contrary—am I not right, young people?—we are content to accept things for what they are (at least for the time being), and nothing more. We like their bareness. We do not mind cold and inclemency. We know that life is hard, and will be hard. We accept the rigour of it; we do not try to sophisticate destiny. Because life is hard, it does not seem to us any the less magnificent. On the contrary, if it is hard it is also solid and sturdy. Above all, it is free of any hypocrisy. We value openness in our dealings with things. We like to strip things bare, and when they are thus denuded, to wash them clean as we examine them, and see what they are in *puris naturalibus*.

Man is occupied and preoccupied with education for a reason which is simple, bald, and devoid of glamour: in order to live with assurance and freedom and efficiency, it is necessary to know an enormous number of things, and the child or youth has an extremely limited capacity for learning. That is the reason. If

---

19 AUTHOR'S NOTE: See Gustav Cassel, *Theoretische Sozialökonomie*, 1921, pp. 3 ff. In part this amounts to a return to some positions of classic economics, as opposed to the economics of the last sixty years.

childhood and youth lasted a century apiece, or if the child and the adolescent possessed intelligence and the power of attention practically without limit, the teaching activity would never exist. Even if those appealing, transcendental reasons had never operated at all, mankind would have had to develop that variety of the species known as the teacher.

Scarcity of the capacity to learn is the cardinal principle of education. It is necessary to provide for teaching precisely in proportion as the learner is unable to learn.

Is it not a too striking coincidence that the ferment in education erupted towards the middle of the eighteenth century, and has continued to increase up to the present? Why did this not happen sooner? The explanation is simple: it was precisely at that time that the first great flowering of modern culture ripened for harvest. In a short time, the treasure of active human knowledge became enlarged by a tremendous increment. Life was entering into the full swing of the new capitalism, which recent inventions had made possible: life was consequently assuming a new and appalling complexity, and it was exacting a greater and greater equipment of technics. Accordingly, along with the necessity for learning a quantity of things quite beyond the capacity to learn, pedagogy was promptly intensified and expanded to meet the need.

In primitive epochs, on the other hand, there is scarcely such a thing as education.[20] Why should there be, if there is scarcely any need for it—if the capacity to learn is far ahead of the material to be assimilated? The capacity is in excess. There are but a few branches of knowledge, certain magic formulas and rituals for fabricating the most difficult instruments, like the canoe, or for curing illness and casting out devils. This is all the subject matter there is. Since it is so scant, anyone could learn it without applying himself with any special effort. Hence there arises a peculiar situation, which corroborates my thesis in the most unexpected fashion. The fact is that education appears among primitive peoples in an inverted form: the vocation of teaching is actually one of concealing. The sacred formulas are conserved as secrets, and passed on esoterically to a chosen few. Outsiders would learn them all too readily. Whence the universal phenomenon of secret rites.

The phenomenon is so persistent that it reappears at any level of civilization, when there arises a particularly novel variety of knowledge, superior in kind to all

20 EDITOR'S NOTE: The primitive cultures we are able to observe do of course transmit to their youth, considerable knowledge of zoology and anatomy, botany, social usage and even philosophy of the differences in tribal cultures. But the point remains valid, that primitive cultures are not confronted with our problem of an unmanageable quantity of important knowledge.

that has been previously known. Since the new and enviable knowledge exists at first only in small quantity, it is a valuable kind of property, to be imparted only in jealous secrecy. Thus it happened with the Pythagorean school's philosophy of precision, and even with so enlightened a philosopher as Plato. For we have his famous seventh epistle, written with the purpose of protesting against the accusation that he had taught his philosophy to Dionysius of Syracuse, as if that were a heinous crime. All primitive education in which there is little to teach, is esoteric and secretive; in that respect it is the antithesis of education as we conceive it in our day.

Education comes into being, then, when the knowledge which has to be acquired is out of proportion to the capacity to learn. Today, more than ever before, the profusion of cultural and technical possessions is such that it threatens to bring a catastrophe upon mankind, in as much as every generation is finding it more nearly impossible to assimilate it.

It is urgent therefore for us to base our science of teaching, its methods and institutions, upon the plain, humble principle that the child or the youth who is to be the learner cannot learn all we should like him to know—the principle of economy in education.

Since it could not be otherwise, this rule has always been in operation where there has been pedagogical activity; but only because it could not be helped, and hence in a restricted degree. It has never been set up as a principle, perhaps because at first sight it is not dramatic—it does not talk of imposing transcendentals.

The university of today, outside Spain even more than within, is a tropical underbrush of subject matters. If to this 'we add what we have deemed imperative—the teaching of culture—the verdure threatens to hide the horizon altogether: the horizon of youth which needs to be clear and open, in order that it may expose to view the beckoning glow afar off. There is no remedy but to rise up against this turgid overgrowth and use the principle of economy like a hatchet. First of all, a thorough pruning.

The principle of economy not only implies that it is necessary to economize in the subject matter to be offered. It has a further implication: that the organization of higher education, the construction of the university, must be based upon the student, and not upon the professor or upon knowledge. The university must be the projection of the student to the scale of an institution. And his two dimensions are, first, what he is—a being of limited learning capacity—and second, what he needs to know in order to live his life.

(The present student movement comprises many ingredients. Out of the conventional ten parts, seven are made up of pure buffoonery. But the other three are absolutely reasonable and more than justify the whole student agitation. One is the political unrest of the country: the soul of the nation is perturbed. The second is a series of real though incredible abuses on the part of a few professors. And the third, which is the most important and decisive, influences the students without their realizing it. It is the fact that neither they nor anybody in particular, but the times themselves, the present circumstances in education throughout the world, are forcing the university to centre itself once more on the student—to *be* the student, and not the professor, as it was in the heyday of its greatness.[21] The tendencies of the times press on inevitably, though mankind, impelled as it is by them, may be unaware of their presence, and quite unable to define them or give them a name. The students should eliminate the discreditable parts of their activity and emphasize these three, especially the last, for in these they are entirely right.[22])

We must begin, therefore, with the ordinary student, and take 1 as a nucleus of the institution, as its central and basic portion, *exclusively* the subject matters which can be required with absolute stringency i.e., those a good ordinary student can really learn.

This, I repeat, is what the university should be, at its very base. Presently we shall see that the university must be, in addition, several other things which are no less important. But what is important at this point is not to confuse things: it is to separate carefully from one another the various functions and organs of that imposing institution, the university.

How are we to determine the body of subjects which are to constitute the torso or *minimum* of the curriculum? By submitting the present conglomeration to two tests:

I. We must pick out that which appears as strictly necessary for the life of the man who is now a student. Life, with its inexorable requirements, is the criterion that should guide this first stroke of the pruning knife.

---

21 EDITOR'S NOTE: This is true of both the Parisian and the Bolognese families of the medieval university. While Paris is said to have had a "magisterial constitution", as opposed to the "student constitution" of the other family, yet even at Paris the students, through their organization in "nations", had a responsible part in the maintenance of discipline and morale.

22 AUTHOR's NOTE: The concept that the university is the student is to be carried out even to the point of affecting its material organization. It is absurd to consider the university, as it has been considered hitherto, the professor's house in which he receives pupils. Rather the contrary: put the students in charge of the house, and let the student body constitute the torso of the institution, complemented by the faculties of professors. The maintenance of discipline through beadles gives rise to shameful squabbles, and organizes the students into a rebellious horde. The students are not to blame, but the institution, which is badly planned. The students themselves, properly organized for the purpose, should direct the internal ordering of the university, determine the decorum of usages and manners, impose disciplinary measures, and feel responsible for the morale.

II. What remains, having been judged strictly necessary, must be further reduced to what the student can really learn with thoroughness and understanding.

It is not enough that this or that is necessary. When we least expect, the necessary suddenly passes beyond the capabilities of the student. It would be fantastic on our part to rant and rave that it is necessary. Only so much must be taught as can truly be learned. On this point we must be unshakable, though the line of action which issues from it is drastic.

CHAPTER TWENTY-NINE

Introduction; The Field: Knowledge in Computerized Societies; The Problem: Legitimation; The Method: Language Games

From *The Postmodern Condition: A Report on Knowledge* (1984)

JEAN-FRANCOIS LYOTARD

Translated by Geoff Bennington and Brian Massumi, these excerpts *The Postmodern Condition: A Report on Knowledge*, by Jean François Lyotard, 1984, From the Theory and History of Literature series, Volume 10, with Foreword by Fredric Jameson. Published by University of Minnesota Press, Minneapolis, MN. Originally published in 1979.

Editors' Note

Jean-Francois Lyotard (1924–1998) was a French philosopher and cultural critic who was intimately involved in the development of philosophical thought in the second half of the twentieth century. 'The sublime', 'differend', the decline of 'meta-narratives', the 'inhuman', 'libidinal economy', 'parologies', 'performativity' and the very idea of 'the postmodern condition' were concepts that Lyotard either originated or creatively drove forward in his extensive writings. His book, *The Postmodern Condition: A Report on Knowledge*, was perhaps the signal publication in inaugurating the term 'postmodernism', and so stimulating that whole school of thought. In it is contained the famous assertion that 'Simplifying to the extreme, I define postmodern as incredulity towards metanarratives' (p. xxiv).

Why include Lyotard and extracts from The Postmodern Condition in this reader? The answer is hinted at in the book's sub-title, which tightly links considerations of the emerging postmodern condition to (Lyotard's reflections on) the emerging character of knowledge: the two states of affairs were intimately linked. The book was originally commissioned by the Council of Universities in Québec so as to offer a kind of consultancy report on the changes befalling knowledge. However, the Council must have received much more than it had bargained for since, as implied, Lyotard used the opportunity to develop from on high—as it were—an analysis at once philosophical and social-theoretical on knowledge, modernity, and societal self-understanding. For Lyotard, a new era was forming, characterised by a number of inter-related phenomena: a collapse of large ideas—of progress, reason, and enlightenment; conflicts between readings of the world; and new technologies that were shifting what it was to know and were adding to world instability. This was the dawning of an age of mutually incoherent language games (an idea taken from Wittgenstein) and of a multiplicity of 'parologies'.

In such an age, for Lyotard, it would be wrong to suggest that knowledge had lost all legitimacy. Rather, knowledge was finding a new source of legitimation in 'performativity'. Insightfully, even in the late 1970s, Lyotard observed (*The Postmodern Condition*, p. 51), that 'The question (overt or implied) now asked by the professionalist student, the State, or institutions of higher education is no longer "Is it true?" but "What use is it?" … this is … equivalent to "Is it saleable? … and "Is it efficient?"'

RB

Recommended Reading

Lyotard, J.-F. (1993). *The Inhuman*. Cambridge: Polity.

Lyotard, J.-F. (1994). *Lessons on the Analytic of the Sublime*. Stanford: University of Stanford.

Lyotard, J.-F. (2002). *The Postmodern Explained to Children: Correspondence 1982–1985*. London: Turnaround.

Lyotard, J.-F. (2004). *Libidinal Economy*. London and New York: Continuum.

Peters, M. A. (1995). (Ed.) *Education and the Postmodern Condition*. Foreword by J-F Lyotard. (Critical Studies in Education & Culture). New York: Praeger.

*****

Introduction

The object of this study is the condition of knowledge in the most highly developed societies. I have decided to use the word *postmodern* to describe that condition. The word is in current use on the American continent among sociologists and critics; it designates the state of our culture following the transformations which, since the end of the nineteenth century, have altered the game rules for science, literature, and the arts. The present study will place these transformations in the context of the crisis of narratives.

Science has always been in conflict with narratives. Judged by the yardstick of science, the majority of them prove to be fables. But to the extent that science does not restrict itself to stating useful regularities and seeks the truth, it is obliged to legitimate the rules of its own game. It then produces a discourse of legitimation with respect to its own status, a discourse called philosophy. I will use the term *modern* to designate any science that legitimates itself with reference to a metadiscourse of this kind making an explicit appeal to some grand narrative, such as the dialectics of Spirit, the hermeneutics of meaning, the emancipation of the rational or working subject, or the creation of wealth. For example, the rule of consensus between the sender and addressee of a statement with truth-value is deemed acceptable if it is cast in terms of a possible unanimity between rational minds: this is the Enlightenment narrative, in which the hero of knowledge works toward a good ethico-political end—universal peace. As can be seen from this example, if a metanarrative implying a philosophy of history is used to legitimate knowledge, questions are raised concerning the validity of the institutions governing the social bond: these must be legitimated as well. Thus justice is consigned to the grand narrative in the same way as truth.

Simplifying to the extreme, I define *postmodern* as incredulity toward metanarratives. This incredulity is undoubtedly a product of progress in the sciences: but that progress in turn presupposes it. To the obsolescence of the metanarrative apparatus of legitimation corresponds, most notably, the crisis of metaphysical philosophy and of the university institution which in the past relied on it. The narrative function is losing its functors, its great hero, its great dangers, its great voyages, its great goal. It is being dispersed in clouds of narrative language elements—narrative, but also denotative, prescriptive, descriptive, and so on. Conveyed within each cloud are pragmatic valencies specific to its kind. Each of us lives at the intersection of many of these. However, we do not necessarily establish stable language combinations, and the properties of the ones we do establish are not necessarily communicable.

Thus the society of the future falls less within the province of a Newtonian anthropology (such as stucturalism or systems theory) than a pragmatics of language particles. There are many different language games—a heterogeneity of elements. They only give rise to institutions in patches—local determinism.

The decision makers, however, attempt to manage these clouds of sociality according to input/output matrices, following a logic which implies that their elements are commensurable and that the whole is determinable. They allocate our lives for the growth of power. In matters of social justice and of scientific truth alike, the legitimation of that power is based on its optimizing the system's performance efficiency. The application of this criterion to all of our games necessarily entails a certain level of terror, whether soft or hard: be operational (that is, commensurable) or disappear.

The logic of maximum performance is no doubt inconsistent in many ways, particularly with respect to contradiction in the socioeconomic field: it demands both less work (to lower production costs) and more (to lessen the social burden of the idle population). But our incredulity is now such that we no longer expect salvation to rise from these inconsistencies, as did Marx.

Still, the postmodern condition is as much a stranger to disenchantment as it is to the blind positivity of delegitimation. Where, after the metanarratives, can legitimacy reside? The operativity criterion is technological; it has no relevance for judging what is true or just. Is legitimacy to be found in consensus obtained through discussion, as Jürgen Habermas thinks? Such consensus does violence to the heterogeneity of language games. And invention is always born of dissension. Postmodern knowledge is not simply a tool of the authorities; it refines our sensitivity to differences and reinforces our ability to tolerate the incommensurable. Its principle is not the expert's homology, but the inventor's paralogy.

Here is the question: is a legitimation of the social bond, a just society, feasible in terms of a paradox analogous to that of scientific activity? What would such a paradox be?

The text that follows is an occasional one. It is a report on knowledge in the most highly developed societies and was presented to the Conseil des Universities of the government of Québec at the request of its president. I would like to thank him for his kindness in allowing its publication.

It remains to be said that the author of the report is a philosopher, not an expert. The latter knows what he knows and what he does not know: the former does not. One concludes, the other questions -two very different language games. I combine them here with the result that neither quite succeeds.

The philosopher at least can console himself with the thought that the formal and pragmatic analysis of certain philosophical and ethico-political discourses of legitimation, which underlies the report, will subsequently see the light of day. The report will have served to introduce that analysis from a somewhat sociologizing slant, one that truncates but at the same time situates it.

Such as it is, I dedicate this report to the Institut Polytechnique de Philosophie of the Université de Paris VIII (Vincennes)—at this very postmodern moment that finds the University nearing what may be its end, while the Institute may just be beginning.

The Postmodern Condition

1. The Field: Knowledge in Computerized Societies

Our working hypothesis is that the status of knowledge is altered as societies enter what is known as the postindustrial age and cultures enter what is known as the postmodern age.[1] This transition has been under way since at least the end of the 1950s, which for Europe marks the completion of reconstruction. The pace is faster or slower depending on the country, and within countries it varies according to the sector of activity: the general situation is one of temporal disjunction which makes sketching an overview difficult.[2] A portion of the description would necessarily be conjectural. At any rate, we know that it is unwise to put too much faith in futurology.[3]

Rather than painting a picture that would inevitably remain incomplete, I will take as my point of departure a single feature, one that immediately defines our object of study. Scientific knowledge is a kind of discourse. And it is fair to say that for the last forty years the "leading" sciences and technologies have had to do with language: phonology and theories of linguistics,[4] problems of communication

---

1 Alain Touraine, *La Société postindustrielle* (Paris: Denoël, 1969) [Eng. trans. Leonard Mayhew, *The Post-Industrial Society* (London: Wildwood House, 1974)]; Daniel Bell, *The Coming of Post-Industrial Society* (New York: Basic Books, 1973); Ihab Hassan, *The Dismemberment of Orpheus: Toward a Post Modern Literature* (New York: Oxford University Press, 1971); Michel Benamou and Charles Caramello, eds., *Performance in Postmodern Culture* (Wisconsin: Center for Twentieth Century Studies & Coda Press, 1977); M. Köhler, "Postmodernismus: ein begriffgeschichtlicher Überblick," *Amerikastudien* 22, 1 (1977).

2 An already classic literary expression of this is provided in Michel Butor, *Mobile: Etude pour une représentation des Etats-Unis* (Paris: Gallimard, 1962).

3 Jib Fowles, ed., *Handbook of Futures Research* (Westport. Conn.: Greenwood Press, 1978).

4 Nikolai S. Trubetskoi, *Grundzüge der Phonologie* (Prague: Travaux du cercle linguistique de Prague, vol. 7, 1939) [Eng. trans. Christiane Baltaxe, *Principles of Phonology* (Berkeley: University of California Press, 1969)].

and cybernetics,[5] modern theories of algebra and informatics,[6] computers and their languages,[7] problems of translation and the search for areas of compatibility among computer languages,[8] problems of information storage and data banks,[9] telematics and the perfection of intelligent terminals,[10] paradoxology.[11] The facts speak for themselves (and this list is not exhaustive).

These technological transformations can be expected to have a considerable impact on knowledge. Its two principal functions research and the transmission of acquired learning—are already feeling the effect, or will in the future. With respect to the first function, genetics provides an example that is accessible to the layman: it owes its theoretical paradigm to cybernetics. Many other examples could be cited. As for the second function, it is common knowledge that the miniaturization and commercialization of machines is already changing the way in which learning is acquired, classified, made available, and exploited.[12] It is reasonable to suppose that the proliferation of information-processing machines is having,

---

5 Norbert Wiener, *Cyberbetics and Society: The Human Use of Human Beings* (Boston: Houghton Mifflin, 1949); William Ross Ashby, *An Introduction to Cyberbetics* (London: Chapman & Hall, 1956).

6 See the work of Johannes von Neumann (1903–57).

7 S. Bellert, "La Formalisation des systèmes cybernétiques," in *Le Concept d'information dans la science contemporaine* (Paris: Minuit, 1965).

8 Georges Mounin, *Les Problèmes théoriques de la traduction* (Paris: Gallimard, 1963). The computer revolution dates from 1965, with the new generation of IBM 3605: R. Moch, "Le Tournant informatique," *Documents contributifs*, Annex 4, *L'lnformatisation de la société* (Paris: La Documentation française, 1978); R. M. Ashby, "La Seconde Génération de la micro-électronique," *La Recherche* 2 (June 1970): 127ff.

9 C. L. Gaudfernan and A. Taïb. "Glossaire," in P. Nora and A. Mine, *L'lnformatisation de la société* (Paris: La Documentation française, 1978); R. Beca, "Les Banques de données," *Nouvelle informatique et nouvelle croissance*, Annex 1, *L'lnformatisation de la société.*

10 L. Joyeux, "Les Applications avancées de l'informarique," *Documents contributifs*. Home terminals (Integrated Video Terminals) will be commercialized before 1984 and will cost about $1,400, according to a report of the International Resource Development: *The Home Terminal* (Conn.: I.R.D. Press, 1979).

11 Paul Watzlawick, Janet Helmick-Beavin, Don D. Jackson, *Pragmatics of Human Communication: A Study of Interactional Patterns, Pathologies, and Paradoxes* (New York: Norton, 1967).

12 J. M. Treille, of the Groupe d'analyse et de prospective des systèmes économiques et technologiques (GAPSET), states that, "Not enough has been said about the new possibilities for disseminating stored information, in particular, using semiconductor and laser technology. ... Soon everyone will be able to store information cheaply wherever he wishes, and, further, will be able to process it autonomously" (*La Semaine media* 16, 16 February 1979). According to a study by the National Science Foundation, more than one high school

and will continue to have, as much of an effect on the circulation of learning as did advancements in human circulation (transportation systems) and later, in the circulation of sounds and visual images (the media).[13]

The nature of knowledge cannot survive unchanged within this context of general transformation. It can fit into the new channels, and become operational, only if learning is translated into quantities of information.[14] We can predict that anything in the constituted body of knowledge that is not translatable in this way will be abandoned and that the direction of new research will be dictated by the possibility of its eventual results being translatable into computer language. The "producers" and users of knowledge must now, and will have to, possess the means of translating into these languages whatever they want to invent or learn. Research on translating machines is already well advanced.[15] Along with the hegemony of computers comes a certain logic, and therefore a certain set of prescriptions determining which statements are accepted as "knowledge" statements.

---

student in two has ready access to the services of a computer, and all schools will have one in the early 1980s (*La Semaine media* 13, 25 January 1979).

13 L. Brunel, *Des Machines et des hommes* (Montreal: Québec Science, 1978): Jean-Louis Missika and Dominique Wolton, *Les réseaux pensants* (Librairie technique et documentaire, 1978). The use of videoconferences between the province of Quebéc and France is becoming routine: in November and December 1978 the fourth series of videoconferences (relayed by the satellite "Symphonie") took place between Quebéc and Montreal on the one hand, and Paris (Université Paris Nord and the Beaubourg Center) on the other (*La Semaine media* 5, 30 November 1978). Another example is provided by electronic journalism. The three big American networks (ABC, NBC, and CBS) have increased the number of production studios around the world to the extent that almost all the events that occur can now be processed electronically and transmitted to the United States by satellite. Only the Moscow offices still work on film, which is sent to Frankfurt for satellite transmission. London has become the great "packing point" (*La Semaine media* 20, 15 March 1979). [TRANS: For Lyotard's usage of the words *learning and knowledge*, see sec. 6 of this text and note 65.]

14 The unit of information is the bit. For these definitions see Gaudfernan and Taïb, "Glossaire." This is discussed in René Thorn, "Un protée de la sémantique: l'information" (1973), in *Modèdes mathématiques de la morphogenèse* (Paris: *Union Générale d'Edition*, 1974). In particular, the transcription of messages into code allows ambiguities to be eliminated: see Watzlawick et al., *Pragmatics of Human Communication*, p. 98.

15 The firms Craig and Lexicon have announced the commercial production of pocket translators: four modules for four different languages with simultaneous reception, each containing 1,500 words, with memory. Weidner Communication Systems Inc. produces a Multilingual Word Processor that allows the capacity of an average translator to be increased from 600 to 2,400 words per hour. It includes a triple memory: bilingual dictionary, dictionary of synonyms, grammatical index (*La Semaine media* 6, 6 December 1978, 5).

We may thus expect a thorough exteriorization of knowledge with respect to the "knower," at whatever point he or she may occupy in the knowledge process. The old principle that the acquisition of knowledge is indissociable from the training (*Bildung*) of minds, or even of individuals, is becoming obsolete and will become ever more so. The relationship of the suppliers and users of knowledge to the knowledge they supply and use is now tending, and will increasingly tend, to assume the form already taken by the relationship of commodity producers and consumers to the commodities they produce and consume—that is, the form of value. Knowledge is and will be produced in order to be sold, it is and will be consumed in order to be valorized in a new production: in both cases, the goal is exchange. Knowledge ceases to be an end in itself, it loses its "use-value."[16]

It is widely accepted that knowledge has become the principle force of production over the last few decades;[17] this has already had a noticeable effect on the composition of the work force of the most highly developed countries[18] and constitutes the major bottleneck for the developing countries. In the postindustrial and postmodern age, science will maintain and no doubt strengthen its preeminence in the arsenal of productive capacities of the nation-states. Indeed, this situation is

---

16 Jürgen Habermas, *Erkenntnis und Interesse* (Frankfurt: Suhrkamp, 1968) [Eng. trans. Jeremy Shapiro, *Knowledge and Human Interests* (Boston: Beacon, 1971)].

17 "Man's understanding of nature and his mastery over it by virtue of his presence as a social body ... appears as the great foundation-stone *[Grundpfeiler]* of production and of wealth," so that "general social knowledge becomes a direct force of production," writes Marx in the *Grundrisse* (1857–58) [(Berlin: Dietz Verlag, 1953), p. 593; Eng. trans. Martin Nicolaus (New York: Vintage, 1973), p. 705]. However, Marx concedes that it is not "only in the form of knowledge, but also as immediate organs of social practice" that learning becomes force, in other words, as machines: machines are "*organs of the human brain created by the human hand*; the power of knowledge, objectified" [p. 706]. See Paul Mattick, *Marx and Keynes*: *The Limits of the Mixed Economy* (Boston: Extending Horizons Books, 1969). This point is discussed in Lyotard, "La place de l'aliénation dans le retournement marxiste" (1969), in *Dèrive à partir de Marx et Freud* (Paris: Union Générale d'Edition 1973), pp. 78–166.

18 The composition of the labor force in the United States changed as follows over a twenty-year period (1950–71):

	1950	1971
Factory, service sector, or agricultural workers	62.5%	51.4%
Professionals and technicians	7.5	14.2

White-collar 30.0 34.0 (Statistical Abstracts, 1971)

one of the reasons leading to the conclusion that the gap between developed and developing countries will grow ever wider in the future.[19]

But this aspect of the problem should not be allowed to overshadow the other, which is complementary to it. Knowledge in the form of an informational commodity indispensable to productive power is already, and will continue to be, a major—perhaps *the* major—stake in the worldwide competition for power. It is conceivable that the nation-states will one day fight for control of information, just as they battled in the past for control over territory, and afterwards for control of access to and exploitation of raw materials and cheap labor. A new field is opened for industrial and commercial strategies on the one hand, and political and military strategies on the other.[20]

However, the perspective I have outlined above is not as simple as I have made it appear. For the mercantilization of knowledge is bound to affect the privilege the nation-states have enjoyed, and still enjoy, with respect to the production and distribution of learning. The notion that learning falls within the purview of the State, as the brain or mind of society, will become more and more outdated with the increasing strength of the opposing principle, according to which society exists and progresses only if the messages circulating within it are rich in information and easy to decode. The ideology of communicational "transparency," which goes hand in hand with the commercialization of knowledge, will begin to perceive the State as a factor of opacity and "noise." It is from this point of view that the problem of the relationship between economic and State powers threatens to arise with a new urgency.

Already in the last few decades, economic powers have reached the point of imperiling the stability of the State through new forms of the circulation of capital that go by the generic name of *multinational corporations*. These new forms of circulation imply that investment decisions have, at least in part, passed beyond the control of the nation-states.[21] The question threatens to become even

---

19 Because of the time required for the "fabrication" of a high-level technician or the average scientist in comparison to the time needed to extract raw materials and transfer money-capital. At the end of the 1960s, Mattick estimated the net rate of investment in underdeveloped countries at 3–5% of the GNP and at 10–15% in the developed countries [*Marx and Keynes*, p. 248.]

20 Nora and Mine, *L'Informatisation de la société*, especially pt. 1, "Les défis;" Y. Stourdzé, "Les Etats-Unis et la guerre des communications," *Le Monde*, 13–15 December 1978. In 1979, the value of the world market of telecommunications devices was $30 billion; it is estimated that in ten years it will reach $68 billion (*La Semaine media* 19, 8 March 1979).

21 F. De Combret, "Le redéploiement industriel," *Le Monde*, April 1978; M. Lepage, *Demain le capitalisme* (Paris: Le Livre de Poche, 1978); Alain Cotta, *La France et l'impératif mondial* (Paris: Presses Universitaires de France, 1978).

more thorny with the development of computer technology and telematics. Suppose, for example, that a firm such as IBM is authorized to occupy a belt in the earth's orbital field and launch communications satellites or satellites housing data banks. Who will have access to them? Who will determine which channels or data are forbidden? The State? Or will the State simply be one user among others? New legal issues will be raised, and with them the question: "who will know?"

Transformation in the nature of knowledge, then, could well have repercussions on the existing public powers, forcing them to reconsider their relations (both de jure and de facto) with the large corporations and, more generally, with civil society. The reopening of the world market, a return to vigorous economic competition, the breakdown of the hegemony of American capitalism, the decline of the socialist alternative, a probable opening of the Chinese market these and many other factors are already, at the end of the 1970s, preparing States for a serious reappraisal of the role they have been accustomed to playing since the 1930s: that of guiding, or even directing investments.[22] In this light, the new technologies can only increase the urgency of such a reexamination, since they make the information used in decision making (and therefore the means of control) even more mobile and subject to piracy.

It is not hard to visualize learning circulating along the same lines as money, instead of for its "educational" value or political (administrative, diplomatic, military) importance; the pertinent distinction would no longer be between knowledge and ignorance, but rather, as is the case with money, between "payment knowledge" and "investment knowledge"—in other words, between units of knowledge exchanged in a daily maintenance framework (the reconstitution of the work force, "survival") versus funds of knowledge dedicated to optimizing the performance of a project.

If this were the case, communicational transparency would be similar to liberalism. Liberalism does not preclude an organization of the flow of money in which some channels are used in decision making while others are only good for the payment of debts. One could similarly imagine flows of knowledge travelling along identical channels of identical nature, some of which would be reserved for the "decision makers," while the others would be used to repay each person's perpetual debt with respect to the social bond.

---

22 It is a matter of "weakening the administration," of reaching the "minimal state." This is the decline of the Welfare State, which is accompanying the "crisis" that began in 1974.

2. The Problem: Legitimation

That is the working hypothesis defining the field within which I intend to consider the question of the status of knowledge. This scenario, akin to the one that goes by the name "the computerization of society" (although ours is advanced in an entirely different spirit), makes no claims of being original, or even true. What is required of a working hypothesis is a fine capacity for discrimination. The scenario of the computerization of the most highly developed societies allows us to spotlight (though with the risk of excessive magnification) certain aspects of the transformation of knowledge and Its effects on public power and civil institutions-effects it would be difficult to perceive from other points of view. Our hypothesis, therefore, should not be accorded predictive value in relation to reality, but strategic value in relation to the question raised.

Nevertheless, it has strong credibility, and in that sense our choice of this hypothesis is not arbitrary. It has been described extensively by the experts[23] and is already guiding certain decisions by the governmental agencies and private firms most directly concerned, such as those managing the telecommunications industry. To some extent, then, it is already a part of observable reality. Finally, barring economic stagnation or a general recession (resulting, for example, from a continued failure to solve the world's energy problems), there IS a good chance that this scenario will come to pass: it is hard to see what other direction contemporary technology could take as an alternative to the computerization of society.

This is as much as to say that the hypothesis is banal. But only to the extent that it fails to challenge the general paradigm of progress in science and technology, to which economic growth and the expansion of sociopolitical power seem to be natural complements. That scientific and technical knowledge is cumulative is never questioned. At most, what is debated is the form that accumulation takes—some picture it as regular, continuous, and unanimous, others as periodic, discontinuous, and conflictual.[24]

But these truisms are fallacious. In the first place, scientific knowledge does not represent the totality of knowledge; it has always existed In addition to, and

---

23 "La Nouvelle Informatique et ses utilisateurs," Annex 3, L 'Informatisation de la société (note 8).

24 B. P. Lécuyer, "Bilan et perspectives de la sociologie des sciences dans les pays occidentaux," *Archives européennes de sociologie* 19 (1978): 257–336 (bibliography). Good information on English and American currents: the hegemony of Merton's school until the beginning of the 1970s and the current dispersion, especially under the influence of Kuhn; not much information on German sociology of science.

in competition and conflict with, another kind of knowledge, which I will call narrative in the interests of simplicity (its characteristics will be described later). I do not mean to say that narrative knowledge can prevail over science, but its model is related to ideas of internal equilibrium and conviviality[25] next to which contemporary scientific knowledge cuts a poor figure, especially if It IS to undergo an exteriorization with respect to the "knower" and an alienation from its user even greater than has previously been the case. The resulting demoralization of researchers and teachers is far from negligible; it is well known that during the 1960s, In all of the most highly developed societies, it reached such explosive dimensions among those preparing to practice these professions—the students—that there was noticeable decrease in productivity at laboratories and universities unable to protect themselves from its contamination.[26] Expecting this, with hope or fear, to lead to a revolution (as was then often the case) is out of the question: it will not change the order of things in postindustrial society overnight. But this doubt on the part of scientists must be taken into account as a major factor in evaluating the present and future status of scientific knowledge.

It is all the more necessary to take it into consideration since -and this is the second point -the scientists' demoralization has an impact on the central problem of legitimation. I use the word in a broader sense than do contemporary German theorists in their discussions of the question of authority.[27] Take any civil law as an example: It states that a given category of citizens must perform a specific kind of action. Legitimation is the process by which a legislator is authorized to promulgate such a law as a norm. Now take the example of a scientific statement: it is subject to the rule that a statement must fulfil a given set of conditions in order to be accepted as scientific. In this case, legitimation is the process by which a "legislator" dealing with scientific discourse is authorized to prescribe the stated conditions (in general, conditions of internal consistency and experimental verification) determining whether a statement is to be included in that discourse for consideration by the scientific community.

The parallel may appear forced. But as we will see, it is not. The question of the legitimacy of science has been indissociably linked to that of the legitimation of the legislator since the time of Plato. From this point of view, the right to decide what is true is not independent of the right to decide what is just, even if the

---

25 The term has been given weight by Ivan Illich, *Tools for Conviviality* (New York: Harper & Row, 1973).

26 On this "demoralization", see A. Jaubert and J.-M. Lévy-Leblond, eds., (Auto) *critique de la science* (Paris: Seuil, 1973), pt.1.

27 Jürgen Habermas, *Legitimationsprobleme im Spätkapitalismus* (Frankfurt: Suhrkamp, 1973) [Eng. trans. Thomas McCarthy, *Legitimation Crisis* (Boston: Beacon Press, 1975)].

statements consigned to these two authorities differ in nature. The point is that there is a strict interlinkage between the kind of language called science and the kind called ethics and politics: they both stem from the same perspective, the same "choice" if you will—the choice called the Occident.

When we examine the current status of scientific knowledge—at a time when science seems more completely subordinated to the prevailing powers than ever before and, along with the new technologies, is in danger of becoming a major stake in their conflicts—the question of double legitimation, far from receding into the background, necessarily comes to the fore. For it appears in its most complete form, that of reversion, revealing that knowledge and power are simply two sides of the same question: who decides what knowledge is, and who knows what needs to be decided? In the computer age, the question of knowledge is now more than ever a question of government.

3. The Method: Language Games

The reader will already have noticed that in analyzing this problem within the framework set forth I have favored a certain procedure: emphasizing facts of language and in particular their pragmatic aspect.[28] To help clarify what follows it would be useful to summarize, however briefly, what is meant here by the term pragmatic.

A denotative utterance[29] such as "The university is sick," made in the context of a conversation or an interview, positions its sender (the person who utters the statement), its addressee (the person who receives it), and its referent (what

---

28 In the wake of Peirce's semiotics, the distinction of the syntactic, semantic, and pragmatic domains is made by Charles W. Morris, "Foundations of the Theory of Signs," in Otto Neurath, Rudolph Catnap, and Charles Morris, eds., *International Encyclopedia of Unified Science*, vol. 1, pt. 2 (1938): 77–137. For the use of this term I refer especially to: Ludwig Wittgenstein, *Philosophical Investigations* [trans. G. E. M. Anscombe (New York: Macmillan, 1953)]; J. L. Austin, *How to Do Things with Words* (Oxford: Oxford University Press, 1962); J. R. Searle, *Speech Acts* (Cambridge: Cambridge University Press, 1969); Jürgen Habermas, "Unbereitende Bermerkungen zu einer Theorie der kommunikativen Kompetens," in Habermas and Luhmann, *Theorie der gesellschaft oder Sozialtechnologie* (Stuttgart: Suhrkamp, 1971); Oswald Ducrot, *Dire et ne pas dire* (Paris: Hermann, 1972); J. Poulain, "Vers une pragmatique nucléaire de la communication" (typescript, Université de Montréal, 1977). See too Watzlawick et al. *Pragmatics of Human Communication* (note 11).

29 "Denotation" corresponds here to "description" in the classical usage of logicians. Quine replaces "denotation" by "true of"; see W. V. Quine, *Word and Object* (Cambridge, Mass.: MIT Press, 1960). J. L. Austin, *How to Do Things with Words*, p. 39. prefers "constative" to "descriptive."

the statement deals with) in a specific way: the utterance places (and exposes) the sender in the position of "knower" (he knows what the situation is with the university), the addressee is put in the position of having to give or refuse his assent, and the referent itself is handled in a way unique to denotatives, as something that demands to be correctly identified and expressed by the statement that refers to it.

If we consider a declaration such as "The university is open," pronounced by a dean or rector at convocation, it is clear that the previous specifications no longer apply. Of course, the meaning of the utterance has to be understood, but that is a general condition of communication and does not aid us in distinguishing the different kinds of utterances or their specific effects. The distinctive feature of this second, "performative,"[30] utterance is that its effect upon the referent coincides with its enunciation. The university is open because it has been declared open in the above-mentioned circumstances. That this is so is not subject to discussion or verification on the part of the addressee, who is immediately placed within the new context created by the utterance. As for the sender, he must be invested with the authority to make such a statement. Actually, we could say it the other way around: the sender is dean or rector—that is, he is invested with the authority to make this kind of statement—only insofar as he can directly affect both the referent, (the university) and the addressee (the university staff) in the manner I have indicated.

A different case involves utterances of the type, "Give money to the university"; these are prescriptions. They can be modulated as orders, commands, instructions, recommendations, requests, prayers, pleas, etc. Here, the sender is clearly placed in a position of authority, using the term broadly (including the authority of a sinner over a god who claims to be merciful): that is, he expects the addressee to perform the action referred to. The pragmatics of prescription entail concomitant changes in the posts of addressee and referent.[31]

Of a different order again is the efficiency of a question, a promise, a literary description, a narration, etc. I am summarizing. Wittgenstein, taking up the study of language again from scratch, focuses his attention on the effects of different modes of discourse; he calls the various types of utterances he identifies along the

---

30 The term *performative* has taken on a precise meaning in language theory since Austin. Later in this book, the concept will reappear in association with the term performativity (in particular, of a system) in the new current sense of efficiency measured according to an input/output ratio. The two meanings are not far apart. Austin's performative realizes the optimal performance.

31 A recent analysis of these categories is to be found in Habermas, "Unbereitende Bemerkungen," and is discussed by J. Poulain, "Vers une pragmatique nucléaire."

way (a few of which I have listed) *language games*.[32] What he means by this term is that each of the various categories of utterance can be defined in terms of rules specifying their properties and the uses to which they can be put-in exactly the same way as the game of chess is defined by a set of rules determining the properties of each of the pieces, in other words, the proper way to move them.

It is useful to make the following three observations about language games. The first is that their rules do not carry within themselves their own legitimation, but are the object of a contract, explicit or not, between players (which is not to say that the players invent the rules). The second is that if there are no rules, there is no game,[33] that even an infinitesimal modification of one rule alters the nature of the game, that a "move" or utterance that does not satisfy the rules does not belong to the game they define. The third remark is suggested by what has just been said: every utterance should be thought of as a "move" in a game.

This last observation brings us to the first principle underlying our method as a whole: to speak is to fight, in the sense of playing, and speech acts[34] fall within the domain of a general agonistics.[35] This does not necessarily mean that one plays in order to win. A move can be made for the sheer pleasure of its invention: what else is involved in that labor of language harassment undertaken by popular speech and by literature? Great joy is had in the endless invention of turns of phrase, of words and meanings, the process behind the evolution of language on the level of *parole*. But undoubtedly even this pleasure depends on a feeling of success won at the expense of an adversary—at least one adversary, and a formidable one: the accepted language, or connotation.[36]

---

32 *Philosophical investigations*, sec. 23.

33 John Von Neumann and Oskar Morgenstern, *Theory of Games and Economic Behavior* (Princeton University Press, 1944), p. 49: "The *game* is simply the totality of the rules which describe it." This formulation is foreign to the spirit of Wittgenstein, for whom the concept of the game cannot be mastered by a definition, since definition is already a language game (*Philosophical Investigations*, especially secs. 65–84).

34 The term comes from Searle: "Speech acts ... are the basic or minimal units of linguistic communication" [*Speech Acts*, p. 16]. I place them within the domain of the *agon* (the joust) rather than that of communication.

35 Agonistics is the basis of Heraclitus's ontology and of the Sophists' dialectic, not to mention the early tragedians. A good part of Aristotle's reflections in the *Topics* and the *Sophistici Elenchi* is devoted to it. See F. Nietzsche, "Homer's Contest" [trans. Maximilian A. Mügge, in *Complete Works*, vol. 2 (London: T. N. Fowlis, 1911; reprint, New York: Gordon Press, 1974)].

36 In the sense established by Louis Hjelmslev, in *Prolegomena to a Theory of Language* (Madison: University of Wisconsin Press, 1963), and taken up by Roland Barthes, *Elements de*

This idea of an agonistics of language should not make us lose sight of the second principle, which stands as a complement to it and governs our analysis: that the observable social bond is composed of language "moves." An elucidation of this proposition will take us to the heart of the matter at hand.

---

sémiologie (1964) (Paris: Seuil. 1966). 4:1 [Eng. trans. Annette Lavers and Colin Smith, *Elements of Semiology* (New York: Hill and Wang, 1968)].

CHAPTER THIRTY

The Very Idea of a University

Aristotle, Newman and Us* (2010)

ALASDAIR MACINTYRE

This selection by Alastair MacIntyre (2009) was published by Wiley Online Library in *New Blackfriars, 91*(1031), 4–19. DOI: 10.1111/j.1741-2005.2009.01333.x

Editors' Note

Alasdair MacIntyre (1929–) is a Scottish philosopher born in Glasgow who has worked in the US since 1970 and become well known for his works of moral and political philosophy, especially *After Virtue* (1981) that shows how modern liberal individualist moral language has been turned into a tool of social control and proposes the Aristotelian practical philosophy of learning in small communities to renew moral agency. His later works (MacIntyre, 1990; MacIntyre & Knight, 1988,) seek to develop justices and rationalities without leading to cultural relativism after diagnosing the disorder of modern academic moral philosophy as one of the impossibilities of critical dialogue between rival schools. In the piece selected

---

* The John Henry Newman Annual Lecture 9 June 2009, organized by the Catholic Halls of Oxford University: Blackfriars, Campion Hall and St Benet's, with the generous support of The Catholic Herald. First published in *The British Journal of Educational Studies* December, 2009.

for this volume 'The Very Idea of a University' MacIntyre picks up the claims of Readings and others that Newman's notion of the university curriculum reflected a kind of literary culture is no longer relevant and suggests three lines of thought derived from Aristotle that demonstrates Newman's continued moral application and importance today in being able to think about ends, especially the ends of the university.

MP

Recommended Reading

MacIntyre, A. (1990). *Three Rival Versions of Moral Enquiry: Encyclopaedia, Genealogy, and Tradition* (Gifford Lectures). Notre Dame, Ind.: University of Notre Dame Press.

MacIntyre, A. and Knight, K. (1988). *The MacIntyre Reader*. Notre Dame, Ind.: University of Notre Dame Press.

*****

I

The case that hostile critics have urged against Newman's *The Idea of a University* is impressive. J. M. Roberts wrote nearly twenty years ago that "it is no longer possible to write a book with such a title ... no general doctrine of universities is possible" ("*The Idea of a University* revisited" in *Newman after a Hundred Years*, ed. Ian Ker and Alan G. Hill, Oxford: Clarendon Press, 1990, p. 222). And Bill Readings later argued that Newman's conception of the university curriculum reflected a kind of literary culture that "held together diverse specialties in a unity", a type of culture that no longer exists and that it is impossible to recreate (*The University in Ruins*, Cambridge, Mass.: Harvard University Press, 1996, p. 167). Those two critics could not have been more at odds with each other, Roberts a distinguished member of the British University establishment, yet the two of them in agreement on Newman's irrelevance.

What is held to make Newman irrelevant to the concerns of those now at work in universities are three of his central affirmations, each entailing the denial of a conviction central to the functioning of contemporary universities. So why does that make Newman's claims irrelevant rather than just false? It is because, on the view taken by his critics, it is not only that Newman's idea of a university fails to hold true of contemporary universities, but that anyone who thought that it might hold true would have grossly misunderstood the nature and functioning of the contemporary university. To criticize contemporary universities from Newman's standpoint would be, on their view, like blaming a jet engine for not having the excellences of a windmill.

What then are the three matters on which what Newman says is taken to be at once false and irrelevant? The first is his conception of the unity of knowledge, or more accurately of the unity of understanding, of how each academic discipline contributes the knowledge of some particular aspect or part of the universe, so that in the search for understanding we need not only to study a number of different disciplines—physics, physiology, history, literature, mathematics, psychology—but also how each of these bears on the others, what the relationships between them are (*The Idea of a University*, ed. Martin J. Svaglic, Notre Dame, Indiana: University of Notre Dame Press, 1982, Discourse III, pp. 33–5 and Discourse VI, p. 103). Newman was careful to emphasize that it is not just the study of a number of disciplines that educates (Discourse VI, p. 98). What educates is knowledge of several disciplines, such that one comes to understand both the indispensability of each for an overall understanding of the order of things and the limitations of each. The superficial generalist is as much the product of a defective education as the narrow specialist.

It is a commonplace that Newman in 1852 not only did not foresee the rise of the modem research university, first in Germany, then in the United States, but took it for granted that research was a task for institutions other than universities. What puts Newman in opposition to the research university however is not just this, but, above all his claim that intensive specialization and narrowness of intellectual focus deform the mind, that the qualities characteristic of the minds of successful researchers are qualities incompatible with those of an educated mind. This claim follows from Newman's affirmation of his conception of the unity of knowledge, of the unity of understanding, together with his view of the effects of the academic division of labor. "There can be no doubt," Newman wrote, "that every art is improved by confining the professor of it to that single study. But, *although the art itself is advanced by this concentration of mind in its service, the individual who is confined to it goes back*" (Discourse VII, p. 127).

That you may tend to injure and deform your mind by developing a narrowness of vision and a onesidedness in judgment, if you devote yourself wholeheartedly to a life of scholarly research, is a thought that the protagonists of the twenty first century prestigious research university are scarcely capable of entertaining. We might exaggerate somewhat, if we formulated Newman's view in contemporary terms by saying that the possession of a Ph. D. or a D. Phil. is too often the mark of a miseducated mind, but we would come close enough to it to make it clear why Newman must seem not just irrelevant, but offensive to such protagonists.

Consider now a second way in which Newman is held to have disqualified himself from participation in our debates. He insists not only that theology is among the disciplines that must be taught in any university worthy of the name, but that it is the key discipline, that unless theology is given its due place in the curriculum, the relationships between disciplines will be distorted and misunderstood. Since nobody in the twenty-first century thinks that an institution from which theology is absent cannot legitimately call itself a university, and since, even in universities where theology is taught, it is treated as simply one more specialized discipline among others, Newman's claims must sound eccentric to contemporary ears. We might be tempted to say that, for the vast majority of our academic contemporaries, it is their belief that universities are secular institutions that leads them to reject Newman's thesis about the place of theology in the curriculum. Yet Newman too held that universities are secular institutions. His claim is that it is *qua* secular institution that the university needs what he takes to be the secular discipline of theology. So what can this need be? Newman's answer returns us to his conception of the unity of understanding.

Without a recognition of theology as the key discipline the university curriculum, so Newman argued, will disintegrate into a fragmented multiplicity of disciplines, each self-defining, each claiming autonomy in its own sphere. Some disciplines will of course continue to draw on each other, as physics does on mathematics, geology on chemistry. But there will be no conception of a whole to which each discipline contributes as a part. And of course this is just how it has become in the contemporary university, a condition one of whose symptoms is the great difficulty that university teachers generally have nowadays in arriving at agreement on what, if any, general education requirements should be imposed on undergraduates. University teachers are no longer members of an educated public constituted by agreements on what books every educated person needs to have read and what skills every educated person needs to possess. For now there is no such public inside or outside the university, as Bill Readings rightly insisted. I am not suggesting that the principal cause of this condition is the absence of theology from the curriculum or its treatment as just one more specialized discipline. But it would have been Newman's view that the fragmentation of our curriculum is a condition that needs to be remedied and that only an acknowledgment of theology as the key unifying discipline can adequately remedy it.

Newman therefore with his judgments that the knowledge of God is a part of our secular knowledge and that such knowledge is the key to understanding affronts the secularized thinkers of our time, just as he affronted the secularizing thinkers of his own. Part of what affronts them is that Newman was well aware that belief that God exists is contestable and that there are no knockdown arguments, equally compelling to every intelligent person, for the existence of God. But it is characteristic of contemporary unbelievers to believe that, only if they were offered some knockdown argument whereby belief in God would be incontestable, would they be rationally entitled to believe that God exists. To which the theist has to respond that any being whose existence was thus justified would not be God. It is not that there are not arguments sufficient to justify the theist's assertion of the existence of God, but that the soundness of those arguments will always be open to contestation, just because of the nature of God and of His relation to His creation.

Newman's idea of a university is then taken to be irrelevant to the contemporary university not only because of the overwhelmingly dominant place that the acquisition of specialized knowledge through research has in the contemporary university, and not only because no discipline could be accorded the place that theology has in Newman's scheme, but also because the claim that the knowledge of God is at once contestable and yet genuine and indispensable secular knowledge is at odds with the present day secular university's understanding of the secular.

A third respect in which it seems to many that Newman's views cannot be brought to bear on the contemporary university concerns how a university education is to be justified, both to those who are invited to become its students and to those whom it invites to sustain it financially, whether private and corporate donors or governments. Universities today would not survive, let alone flourish, if they were not able credibly to promise to their students a gateway to superior career possibilities and to donors and governments both a supply of appropriately skilled manpower and research that contributes to economic growth. Universities, that is to say, promise to be cost-effective enterprises. For Newman by contrast the activities that contribute to the teaching and learning of a university have goods internal to them that make those activities worthwhile in themselves. It may of course be the case that incidentally universities do contribute to career success and economic growth. But, on Newman's view, a university can succeed in both these respects and yet fail as a university. So there are three major issues that put Newman at odds with the contemporary research university's understanding of its mission: its pursuit of highly specialized knowledge, the secular university's understanding of what it is to be secular, and the university's self-justification by appeal to considerations of social utility. If we recognize that, given these three characteristics, no contemporary university could exemplify anything like Newman's idea of a university, should we simply agree with Roberts and Readings in taking Newman's claims to be not only false, but also irrelevant?

II

I want to suggest three lines of thought which separately and jointly give us reason to take Newman's central claims seriously. Each of them begins from asking a set of Aristotelian questions and ends with an answer drawn from Newman. And about this we should not be surprised. For it was Newman who declared that "while we are men, we cannot help, to a great extent, being Aristotelian" and that "In many subject-matters to think correctly is to think like Aristotle" (*Discourse V*, p. 83). To think *like* Aristotle, for the questions from which I begin are perhaps not Aristotle's own, but they are questions which, if one presses an Aristotelian enquiry beyond a certain point, one is bound to ask. They are also—and Newman's remark on why he is an Aristotelian is very much to the point—questions that are inescapable for any sufficiently reflective human being, so that, even if Newman had never written *The Idea of a University*, we should have been compelled to raise them.

The first is this: What is it that we need to understand, if on some occasion the outcome of our practical deliberations has been perhaps disastrous, or at least very different from what we had expected? What are the different ways in which we may have gone astray? If our conception of practical reasoning is in general Aristotelian, there are several ways in which our deliberations may have been defective. Consider for example the kind of decision that will alter the course of someone's life, perhaps too the lives of others close to her or him, such choices as that to emigrate or not to emigrate *or* to change the land use of one's farm in some drastic way *or* the choice between participating in rebuilding one's town after some natural disaster and starting anew somewhere else.

Bad decisions may result from some failure to identify or rank order correctly the goods at stake in choosing this rather than that. And such failure may in turn derive from some misconception of what the agent's final good *qua* human being is. Or they may result from a failure to identify correctly the actions that in these particular circumstances would have to be undertaken to achieve the relevant goods. These two kinds of error will have been made in the course of formulating the premises of the agent's practical syllogisms. But they are not the only types of error of which we need to beware. For all such practical reasoning, whether successful or not, presupposes two sets of background assumptions about the natural and social contexts in which the reasoning and the actions that flow from that reasoning take place. Each of these types of assumption can also be a source of practical failure. What are they?

There are first of all assumptions about the present and future stability or otherwise of different aspects of our natural or social environments. So we all of us make assumptions, generally tacit, about the probability or improbability of the occurrence of earthquakes, volcanic eruptions, droughts, floods, disruptions in food supplies, famines, breakdowns in transportation, changes in the crime rate, breakdowns in tribal or family life, the strength or weakness of social and moral traditions, the functioning of the stock market and of the economy more generally—the list goes on and on. A second set of assumptions are about how others in the present or future will be likely to respond to our actions, so as either to further or to frustrate our intentions. Those—also generally tacit—assumptions concern not just the nature of their decision-making, but also the significance that our actions may have for their decision-making, among them their assumptions about our assumptions about them.

I have noticed in both cases that such assumptions are generally not spelled out. What is of crucial importance for the soundness of our practical reasoning is that we should be able to recognize when some of our assumptions do need to be made explicit and put in question and which type of assumption it is that we need to examine on this or that particular occasion. What would it be to be able to do this and to do it well? It would involve knowing both how to draw on the relevant findings of a range of disciplines and how to evaluate the reliability of those findings. So what kind of education would someone have to have received in order to do this? What kind of mind would such a one have?

It is in trying to answer these questions that we find ourselves returned to Newman's text. For the education of such a one will have to have included a more than superficial engagement with several disciplines, each with its own subject-matter and its own ways of viewing that subject-matter, as, for example, in understanding human beings and their activities we need to treat of them, says Newman, "as physiologists, or as moral philosophers, or as writers of economics or of politics, or as theologians" (Discourse III, 3, p. 36). But Newman adds that, in evaluating each of these disciplinary contributions, "the mind never views any part ... without recollecting that it is but a part" (Discourse VI, 6, p. 103), a part contributing to the understanding of a whole. If the mind fails to do this, it will be apt "to give undue prominence to one" or more disciplines and "to unsettle the boundary lines between science and science" (Discourse V, 1, p. 75), so that for example, it may attempt to understand the distribution of wealth in different parts of a city in purely economic terms, neglecting other social and moral dimensions, or it may treat some psychological disorder that involves lack of self-knowledge as though it were only a biochemical phenomenon.

Such confusions too often mark the public discourse of our present day culture. They make too many of us victims of the expertise of those trained to see things only in the narrow focus of their own discipline. Newman took it that what he called the constrained and contracted mind of the specialist characteristically expressed itself in opinionated and boring conversation (Discourse VI, 6, p. 104). And so it still does. But such minds have now become more dangerous because more apt to set on foot large-scale consequences. And the range of disciplines that we may need in order to achieve the kind and degree of understanding that issue in sound practical reasoning has increased. Sometimes we need to correct what economists tell us by appealing to the historians, and sometimes of course vice versa. Sometimes we need to correct what neurophysiologists tell us by appealing to psychologists, and sometimes vice versa, and sometimes we may need as well or instead to go to novelists or dramatists. Note too that in many cases no evaluation of the claims made for this or that finding of specialized enquiry will be possible for those innocent of the relevant mathematics. We all of us therefore need to be schooled in a number of disciplines, just because each has its own methods, insights, and standards. To be educated is, on this view, not only to know how to bring each discipline to bear in appropriate ways, but also how to respond to the unjustified claims made in the name of each. And for this we need not the contracted mind of the specialist, but a different sort of mind.

From this perspective Newman's enterprise begins to look somewhat different and the accusation that his conception of a university is irrelevant to universities as they now are misses the point. For perhaps the principal question that Newman was posing was not, as he supposed, "What is a university?", but "What is an educated mind?", a question which he answers in Aristotelian fashion by saying that everything has its own specific perfection, that there is a specific perfection of the intellect (Discourse V, 9, p. 92), and that the end of education is the achievement of that perfection, that "true enlargement of mind which is the power of viewing many things as one whole, of referring them severally to their place in the universal system, of understanding their respective values, and determining their mutual dependence" (Discourse VI, 6, p. 107). To develop highly specialized knowledge only in one particular sphere, to focus one's mind on only one subject-matter, may certainly be valuable, but it will not enable the mind to achieve its specific perfection and is apt to prevent the mind from doing so.

The irrelevance to the contemporary university of Newman's prescriptions is thus cast in a new light. It is an indictment not of Newman, but of the contemporary university. For, if this irrelevance is as great as his critics claim, then whatever universities are achieving, they are not producing educated minds or, to put matters more justly, they are doing so only incidentally and accidentally. And, if they were to be able to rebut this accusation, it could only be because they had drastically revised their undergraduate curriculum, so that every student was introduced and somewhat more than introduced to, say, the calculus and the mathematics of probability, to historical and literary studies, to some parts of physics, certainly to thermodynamics, to the elements of biochemistry, and to ecological and evolutionary biology. Yet whatever disciplines we name in this catalogue, there always has to be something more, namely the communication of an understanding of the various ways in which the findings of those disciplines bear upon each other and so contribute to a larger understanding than any of them by themselves can provide. We should notice too that the teaching of this kind of curriculum will require a corresponding kind of education for teachers, since we shall need teachers of literature who are well informed about biochemistry and teachers of physics who are able to think historically, all of them being at home with the relevant mathematics.

III

To this proposal there will of course be a number of objections, of which here I consider only one, merely, that whether or not this is an account of what education is or should be, it is not or not yet Newman's account, and this in two different ways. First, in elucidating Newman's conception of understanding I began by considering some features of practical reasoning. But, it may be said, Newman's conception is of understanding as achieved by theoretical enquiry. So that I may seem to have started in the wrong place. What matters however is that the conception of understanding at which we have arrived, although presupposed by successful practical reasoning, is itself a conception of the mind's theoretical grasp of the relations of parts and aspects to the whole. What this involves can be brought out by noting how questions that Newman takes to be central to theoretical understanding go characteristically unasked in the fragmented curriculum of the present day.

Consider Newman's suggestive discussion (Discourse III, 2, pp. 35–6) of how the different disciplines enable us to understand ourselves. We are, according to physics, composed of particles interacting with each other and with our environment. Chemistry tells us that we are sites of a variety of reactions, biology, as Newman was shortly to learn from Darwin, that we are in key part what we are because of the evolution of species. Sociology and economics characterize the structure of our roles and relationships, history informs us that we are what our past has made us and what we have made of our past. And theology views all these same features from a very different perspective. The crucial questions are: In what then does the unity of a human being consist? And what is it about human beings that enables them to ask this question about themselves? But these are questions, in Newman's idiom philosophical questions, which can only be asked by students who have a more than superficial grasp both of the relevant disciplines and of how they relate to each other. And they are questions that go unasked in the contemporary curriculum.

One respect in which this account of Newman's conception of multidisciplinary understanding does indeed fall short is the absence so far of any discussion of Newman's thesis that, if the curriculum is to have the unity that it needs to have, if it is to disclose the unity of the order of things, then the discipline of theology is indispensable. For it is theology that provides the curriculum with its unity and we will not understand the bearing of the other disciplines on each other adequately, if we do not understand theology's bearing on them and theirs on theology.

The theology of which Newman spoke was not specifically Catholic theology, but a theology shared with all theists, with all those for whom, as Newman put it, the word 'God' "contains … a theology in itself" (p. 27). God, as understood by theists is "an Individual, Self-Dependent, All-perfect, Unchangeable Being; intelligent, living, personal and present … who created and upholds the universe … who is sovereign over, operative amidst, independent of, the appointments which He has made; One in whose hands are all things, who has a purpose in every event and a standard for every deed, and thus has relations of His own towards the subject-matter of each particular science which the book of knowledge unfolds, who has … implicated Himself in all the history of creation, the constitution of nature, the course of the world, the origin of society, the fortunes of nations, the action of the human mind; and who thereby necessarily becomes the subject-matter of a science …" (Discourse II, 7, p. 27).

This surely states a doctrine unacceptable to the contemporary secular academic mind, although perhaps what that mind rejects in taking itself to reject this doctrine is not in fact this doctrine. Whether that is so or not is a question that I shall approach indirectly by developing a second line of thought about what it is to understand. When we bring one or more of the particular disciplines to bear upon some event or state of affairs that we need to understand, say, the explanation of the incidence of bubonic plague in medieval Europe, and the part that it played in shaping social and economic life, or the varying causes of climate change during the earth's history, or the phenomena of neutron oscillation, the explanations at which we arrive are always partial and incomplete in that they always direct our attention to something more, to something needing further enquiry. Sometimes this is because certain questions are still left open, sometimes because that to which the explanation refers us as cause or causes itself stands in need of explanation, and sometimes because there is an appeal to principles or laws that have application in this particular sphere, but we do not as yet understand why those principles or laws must take the form that they do.

Moreover, as our enquiries proceed, we move towards unifying our various explanations, both those which lie wholly within one particular discipline and those which have a bearing on explanations in other disciplines. And this enables us to understand increasingly the place of this or that occurrence or state of affairs in the overall order of things. Yet our explanations are always imperfectly unified, just as they always remain in some respects incomplete, and so our enquiries never terminate, are never final. What they presuppose is twofold: first, that we are indeed directed towards a final, if unattainable end, that we do have a conception of what it would be to have achieved a kind of understanding that is perfected and completed—for it is only by contrast with this conception that we characterize our present explanations as partial, imperfect and incomplete—and secondly, and correspondingly, that the order of things, although indefinitely complex, has an intelligible unity that is gradually and increasingly disclosed by our enquiry and that will continue to be disclosed by those enquiries, no matter how far we carry them.

What is involved in having such a conception of the order of things as an intelligible unity, a conception that medieval Aristotelians, at least, would have confidently ascribed to Aristotle? It is to take it for granted that the further that we carry our enquiries the nearer we come to understanding every part and aspect of the universe in relation to every other, just because of an indefinitely sustained underlying ordered unity. To move towards understanding on this view is to move towards achieving what scornful and sceptical critics have sometimes spoken of as a God's eye view of things, thinking thereby to discredit this conception of the achievement of understanding. But by so doing such critics have revealed an insightful grasp of what is at stake in accepting or rejecting this conception of understanding and indeed in accepting or rejecting the counterpart conception of an ordering power that is not itself a part or aspect of the finite order of things, but one without which the universe could not present itself to our minds as an intelligible unity, an ordering power that has the defining characteristics of the God of theism.

What this line of thought suggests is that about one thing at least Newman is right, namely that, if theology were not to be granted the place in the curriculum that he assigns to it, then the secular disciplines could not stand in the relationships to each other that he assigns to them. His defence of theology is integral to his conception of the unity of the order of things and to the unity of the curriculum. They stand or fall together. Take away theology and the curriculum will be fragmented into a series of specialized disciplines, leaving at best the possibility of some kind of factitious unity imposed by social agreement. It turns out therefore that from Newman's point of view his attack upon specialization in the curriculum and his attack on the removal of theology from the curriculum are one and the same attack.

That there is an impressive philosophical case to be made *against* the theological conception of understanding that I am ascribing to Newman no one at work in a contemporary university is likely to be unaware. But the philosophical case *for* that conception has its own interest and it is important to distinguish the line of argument that leads to it from three other lines of argument with which it may easily be confused. First, it is not only different from, but incompatible with the so-called argument for or from intelligent design, whether in Archdeacon Paley's eighteenth century version or in more recent versions. For that bad argument begins from an attempt to identify examples of natural phenomena whose complexity is such that, so it is alleged, they cannot be explained by the natural sciences. By contrast the line of thought that I have sketched begins not from contentions about the limits or failures of scientific enquiries, but rather from the continuing success of such enquiries and the justified confidence of those engaged in them. Newman's early reading of Hume had led him to be suspicious of the claims advanced by eighteenth century proponents of intelligent design. I do not think that he would be any more sympathetic to their unfortunate contemporary heirs.

A second contrast is between R. G. Collingwood's account of the metaphysical presuppositions of scientific theorizing and the account that I am defending, although I am certainly indebted to Collingwood. Collingwood understood that in different periods the intelligible unity of the order of nature had been conceived in different and incompatible ways, the post-Aristotelian and Ptolemaic conceptions of the late middle ages giving way to Galilean and Newtonian conceptions, and these in turn to quantum mechanical and relativistic conceptions, each of which had, so Collingwood contended, its own distinctive metaphysical presuppositions and commitments. But on the view that I am taking the underlying presupposition of scientific enquiry is that, even although each of these particular attempts to characterize the intelligible unity of nature has either already failed or may at some point in the future fail, there is at a deeper level a unity yet to be discovered and an understanding yet to be achieved, so that we are committed to presupposing belief in an ordering power without which the concept of a continuing intelligible and unified order would be empty.

A third contrast is with the positions taken by Nicholas Maxwell in his *The Comprehensibility of the Universe* (Oxford: Clarendon Press, 1998). Maxwell treats the intelligibility and unity of the physical universe as something to which our commitment is inescapable, once we have understood the theoretical aims of physical enquiry (see especially pp. 180–1). And I am also indebted to his discussion of these issues. Moreover he provides impressive reasons for holding that the best conjecture as to why the physical universe has the intelligible unity that it has would be that God exists, if only the concept of an all good and all powerful God were not, on Maxwell's view, rendered wholly implausible by the facts of human and natural evil. The two crucial differences between my—and Newman's—line of thought on the one hand and Maxwell's on the other are: first, that Newman, like other theists, did not find the objection to theism posed by the problem of evil insuperable, and, secondly, that for Newman, like other theists, belief in God *cannot* be a conjecture and is in relation to scientific enquiry, we might be tempted to say, an inescapable presupposition.

Inescapable? That must surely not be so. Newman himself noted of natural science that a "vast multitude of its teachers ... have been either unbelievers or skeptics" (Discourse IX, p. 167) and periodic surveys of members of the American Academy of Science during the twentieth century have shown that the numbers of believers in God among them, never large, steadily dwindled to about five percent. But what then is the antitheist's alternative to Newman's position? It is that there is some noncircular inductivist justification for inferring from the characteristics of the universe to date to the unity and continuing intelligibility of the universe. That scientific enquirers who are antitheists badly need just such a justification, if their claims are to be sustained, is clear. That such a justification can be provided remains far from clear. And the onus for providing it is on the antitheist.

IV

I turn now to the third area of contention between Newman and the protagonists of the contemporary university. The contemporary university, as I noted earlier, boasts that it is socially useful and often justifies itself by citing as an example of its usefulness the provision of skilled manpower. By contrast Newman's view was that what matters about an educated individual is not primarily any set of useful skills that she or he may happen to possess, but her or his capacity for judgment, judgment both in putting these skills to work and in acting "as a friend, as a companion, as a citizen", and in domestic life and in the pursuits of leisure (Discourse VII, 8, p. 129). Newman is quoting from the argument advanced by John Davison—one of the reforming Fellows of Oriel in the early nineteenth century—in defense of a curriculum that introduces the student to "religion (in its evidence and interpretation), ethics, history, eloquence, poetry, theories of general speculation, the fine arts, and works of wit", studies which, so Davison had claimed, are "such as give a direct play and exercise to the faculty of judgment" and thus educate "the active and inventive powers" (Discourse VII, 9, p. 132). The question that readers will want to put to Davison and Newman is: What then are the marks of judgment? What is it to possess or to fail to possess it? And of course in putting this question to Davison and Newman, we are close to asking of Aristotle, "What is *phronesis*?" and of Aquinas "What is *prudentia*?" Let me consider then just one aspect of judgment, one that throws additional light on Newman's proposed curriculum, and suggests that without something like that curriculum we will not only be defective practical reasoners, but will even be apt not to know what we are doing.

Human action always has several dimensions. "What are you doing?" we ask. "Solving an equation; predicting next week's stock prices; pleasing my employer; working late in the office; absenting myself from dinner with my family; alienating my oldest child." Or perhaps "Digging a hole; building a condominium tower; constructing a new competitor for scarce water resources; ignoring some of the relevant geological facts; endangering lives in twenty years' time." Even examples as sketchy as these bring out some salient features of action: first, that what we are not doing or are failing to do by doing what we do may be as important as what we do; secondly, that ignorance of relevant facts from a variety of disciplines may make us unable to recognize aspects of what we are doing; and thirdly that, by focusing on particular aspects of what we are doing we may conceal from ourselves other aspects. There always may of course be aspects of our actions of which we remain unaware through no fault or defect of our own and some of them may be such that we have no need to be aware of them. But the range of facts of which we may at some point badly need to be aware, if we are to know what we are doing, is clearly wide and requires, as we have already emphasized, some knowledge of a number of disciplines.

Evidently of course such academic knowledge, although necessary, is insufficient for an agent to be able to answer the question "What are you doing?" She or he needs also to know how to deploy that knowledge when and as it is required and this ability can be developed only through engagement in a range of practices. Yet, lacking an education that has introduced agents to a sufficient number of disciplines, they will be unlikely to develop that ability. And they will also need another characteristic that cannot be acquired through academic study, that of valuing the quality of knowing what they are doing and of valuing that quality in others. One can of course know what one is doing and nonetheless do the wrong thing. But even to begin to say what is involved in judging and acting rightly would be to open up questions too large for this occasion. What has already been said is sufficient to establish the connection between Newman's account of the curriculum and his conviction that what it is to have an educated mind is one thing, what it is to have professional skills something else, even if it is important for the exercise of professional skills that those who exercise them have educated minds.

If we are to take this line of argument further, we must do so in two directions, one of which involves us in rejecting an assumption of Newman's, an assumption shared with most, if not quite all of his educated contemporaries. It is that the type of university education that he commends is suitable only for a small and privileged minority. Yet, if in fact in the contemporary world this kind of education is needed in order to know what one is doing, then everyone needs it and not only the makers of large-scale social and economic decisions. Indeed it is crucial for plain persons that they should have this type of education, so that they can begin to recognize when those who exercise power over their lives no longer know what they are doing. But the question of how such an education might be made widely available is yet another that I put on one side. I do so in order to make a claim whose truth or falsity is of crucial significance in the debate between the followers of Newman and the protagonists of the contemporary research university.

V

That claim is that a surprising number of the major disorders of the latter part of the twentieth century and of the first decade of the twenty first century have been brought about by some of the most distinguished graduates of some of the most distinguished universities in the world and this as the result of an inadequate general education, at both graduate and especially undergraduate levels, that has made it possible for those graduates to act decisively and deliberately without knowing what they were doing. Examples of such disasters include: the Vietnam War, the policies of the United States towards Iran for more than half a century, and the present world economic crisis. Of course I cannot here argue adequately for such a contentious claim. But I can illustrate it by considering some salient features of the genesis of the present economic crisis.

Too many people have already forgotten the great forerunner of this crisis, the collapse of the hedge fund, Long-Term Capital Management, in 1997, a collapse so massive that for a short time it threatened the entire financial system. Long-Term Capital Management had on their board two Nobel Prize winning economists, who made use for the first time of certain complex mathematical models that, so they confidently believed, enabled them to enter into large-scale derivative contracts with measurable risk and without significant danger. And so far as both the mathematics and the economic theory was concerned they knew very well what they were doing (see Roger Loewenstein, *When Genius Failed: The Rise and Fall of Long-Term Capital Management*, New York: Random House, 2000). What they lacked was historical knowledge of two different kinds of contingency: knowledge in depth of the histories of risk-taking firms and of the vicissitudes encountered in those histories and knowledge of the politics of the different cultures within which markets operate, so that, most notably, they misinterpreted events in Russia and were taken wholly by surprise when the Russian "government simply decided it would rather use its rubles to pay Russian workers than Western bondholders" (Loewenstein p. 144).

The collapse of Long-Term Capital Management had about it something of the character of a farce, of a story of experts ludicrously victimized by their own expertise. Its successor, our present crisis, has instead some of the characteristics of a tragedy, a tale of characters who self-confidently take themselves to be farsighted walking, as if blindly, over a cliff, and in their *hubris* taking all too many others with them. For it was cohorts drawn from the most highly educated among us who trusted in sophisticated mathematics whose applications the vast majority of them did not understand, who relied upon conceptions of risk that they had never adequately analyzed, who went down historically well-marked roads not knowing that those roads had been already travelled more than once, and who lacked the dramatic imagination that could have told them just what kind of a play it was in which they had allotted themselves roles. They lacked, that is, just what Davison's—and Newman's—curriculum might have given them. It is small wonder then that they were also oblivious to what they might have learned from Newman's Aristotelian contemporary, Karl Marx.

VI

What we have to learn then from Newman is first of all that undergraduate education has its own distinctive ends, that it should never be regarded as a prologue to or a preparation for graduate or professional education, and that its ends must not be subordinated to the ends of the necessarily specialized activities of the researcher. But it is not just that undergraduate education has its own ends. It is also that undergraduate education, when well conducted, is in key part an education in how to think about the ends of a variety of human activities and, that is to say, in how to evaluate, among others, such activities as those of the specialist and the researcher, the activities of those dedicated to the ends which the contemporary research university serves. The danger is therefore that in research universities the ability to think about ends, including the ends of the university, will be lost and with it the ability to engage in radical self-criticism, so that the leadership of those universities will become complacent in their wrongheadedness. How unsurprising it is then that so often from their point of view Newman's lectures should now appear not only false, but irrelevant.

CHAPTER THIRTY-ONE

The Principle of Reason

The University in the Eyes of Its Pupils (1983)

JACQUES DERRIDA

This abridged version of Derrida's article was published in *Diacritics*, translated by Catherine Porter and Edward P. Morris, Vol. 13, No. 3 (Autumn, 1983), pp. 2–20 Retrieved from http://www.jstor.org/stable/464997

Editor's Note

Jacques Derrida was a French philosopher born in Algeria and world renown for his deconstructionist poststructuralism that sought to question the logocentrism of the Western philosophical tradition and the institutions of Western culture. His work cut a swathe across the humanities and social sciences. Derrida supported many different political causes and his work generated a great deal of negative criticism in particular from Marxists and analytical philosophers. Derrida was a founding member of the Research Group on the Teaching of Philosophy. 'The Principle of Reason: The University in the Eyes of Its Pupils' is an essay belonging to the collection *The Eyes of the University* (Derrida 2004) that records his struggle to preserve the teaching of philosophy and to clarify its rationale and reason for being. He criticises the way in which the university is formed increasingly around 'end-oriented research' and calls for 'a new university Enlightenment' that acknowledges if the university has a reason for being it is reason itself.

MP

Recommended Reading

Derrida, Jacques (2004). *Eyes of the University: Right to Philosophy* 2, trans. Jan Plug and others. Stanford: Stanford University Press. *Du droit* à *la philosophie,* 1990.

* * * * *

Today, how can we not speak of the university?

I put my question in the negative, for two reasons. On the one hand, as we all know, it is impossible, now more than ever, to dissociate the work we do, within one discipline or several, from a reflection on the political and institutional conditions of that work. Such a reflection is unavoidable. It is no longer an *external* complement to teaching and research; it must make its way through the very objects we work with, shaping them as it goes, along with our norms, procedures, and aims. We cannot not speak of such things. On the other hand, the question "how can we not" gives notice of the *negative*, or perhaps we should say preventive, complexion of the preliminary reflections I should like to put to you. Indeed, since I am seeking to initiate discussion, I shall content myself with saying how one should not speak of the university. Some of the typical risks to be avoided, it seems to me, take the form of a bottomless pit, while others take the form of a protectionist barrier.

Does the university, today, have what is called a *raison d'être*? I have chosen to put my question in a phrase—*raison d'être*, literally, "reason to be"—which is quite idiomatically French. In two or three words, that phrase names everything I shall be talking about: reason and being, of course, and the essence of the University in its connections to reason and being; but also the cause, purpose, direction, necessity, justification, meaning and mission of the University; in a word, its destination. To have a *raison d'être*, a reason for being, is to have a justification for existence, to have a meaning, an intended purpose, a destination; but also, to have a cause, to be explainable according to the "principle of reason" or the "law of sufficient reason," as it is sometimes called—in terms of a reason which is also a cause (a ground, *ein Grund*), that is to say also a footing and a foundation, ground to stand on. In the phrase *raison d'être*, that idea of causality takes on above all the sense of final cause, in the wake of Leibniz, the author of the formulation—and it was much more than a formulation—"the Principle of Reason." To ask whether the University has a reason for being is to wonder why there is a University, but the question "why" verges on "with a view to what?" The University *with a view to what*? What is the University's view? What are its views? Or again: what do we see from the University, whether for instance, we are simply in it, on board; or whether, puzzling over destinations, we look out from it while in port or, as French has it, "*au large*," on the open sea, "at large"? As you may have noticed, in asking "what is the view from the University?" I was echoing the title of the impeccable parable James Siegel published in *Diacritics* two years ago: "Academic Work: The View from Cornell" [Spring, 1981]. Today, indeed, I shall do no more than decipher that parable in my own way. More precisely, I shall be transcribing in a different code what I read in that article—the dramatic, exemplary nature of the topology and politics of this university, in terms of its views and its site: the topolitics of the Cornellian point of view.

Starting with its first words, Metaphysics associates sight with knowledge, and knowledge with knowing how to learn and knowing how to teach. I am referring of course to Aristotle's *Metaphysics*. I shall return presently to the political import of its opening lines; for the moment, let us look at the very first sentence: "All men, by nature, have the desire to know." Aristotle thinks he sees a sign of this in the fact that sensations give pleasure, "even apart from their usefulness." The pleasure of useless sensations explains the desire to know for the sake of knowing, the desire for knowledge with no practical purpose. And this is more true of sight than of the other senses. We give preference to sensing "through the eyes" not only for taking action, but even when we have no praxis in view. This one sense, naturally theoretical and contemplative, goes beyond practical usefulness and provides us with more to know than any other; indeed, it unveils countless differences. We give preference to sight just as we give preference to the uncovering of difference.

But is sight enough? For learning and teaching, does it suffice to know how to unveil differences? In certain animals, sensation engenders memory, and that makes them more intelligent and more capable of learning. But for knowing how to learn, and learning how to know, sight, intelligence and memory are not enough. We must also know how to hear, and to listen. I might suggest somewhat playfully that we have to know how to shut our eyes in order to be better listeners. Bees know many things, since they can see; but they cannot learn, since they are among the animals that lack the faculty of hearing. Thus, despite appearances to the contrary, the University, the place where people know how to learn and learn how to know, can never be a kind of hive. Aristotle, let us note in passing, has ushered in a long tradition of frivolous remarks on the philosophical commonplace of the bee, the sense and senses of the bee, and the bee's reason for being. Marx was doubtless not the last to have overworked that topos, when he insisted on distinguishing human industry from animal industry, as exemplified in bee society. Seeking such nectar as may be gathered from the vast anthology of philosophical bees, I find a remark of Schelling's, in his *Lessons on the Method of Academic Studies*,[1] more to my taste. An allusion to the sex

1 In regard to this "naturalism" (a frequent, but not general phenomenon that Kant, for example, eludes at the beginning of the *Conflict of the Faculties*), and also to the classic motif of

of bees often comes to the aid of the rhetoric of naturalism, organicism, or vitalism as it plays upon the theme of the complete and interdisciplinary unity of knowledge, the theme of the university as an organic social system. This is in the most classic tradition of interdisciplinary studies. I quote Schelling:

> The aptitude for doing thoughtful work in the specialized sciences, the capacity to work in conformity with that higher inspiration which is called scientific genius, depends upon the ability to see each thing, including specialized knowledge, in its cohesion with what is originary and unified. Any thought which has not been formed in this spirit of unity and totality [*der Ein- und Allheit*] is empty in itself, and must be challenged; whatever is incapable of fitting harmoniously within that bud-ding, living totality is a dead shoot which sooner or later will be eliminated by organic laws; doubtless there also exist, within the realm of science, numerous sex-less bees [*geschlechtlose Bienen*] who, since they have not been granted the capacity to create, multiply in inorganic shoots the outward signs of their own witlessness [*ihre eigne Geistlosigkeit*]. [*Philosophies de I'universite*, p. 49]

(I don't know what bees, not only deaf but sexless, Schelling had in mind at the time. But I am sure that even today such rhetorical weapons would find many an eager buyer. One professor has recently written that a certain theoretical movement was mostly sup-ported, within the university, by homosexuals and feminists-a fact which seemed very significant to him, and doubtless a sign of asexuality.)

Opening the eyes to know, closing them—or at least listening—in order to know how to learn and to learn how to know: here we have a first sketch of the rational animal. If the University is an institution for science and teaching, does it have to go beyond memory and sight? In what rhythm? To hear better and learn better, must it close its eyes or narrow its outlook? In cadence? What cadence? Shutting off sight in order to learn is of course only a figurative manner of speak-ing. No one will take it literally, and I am not proposing to cultivate an art of blink-ing. And I am resolutely in favor of a new university Enlightenment [*Aufklarung*]. Still, I shall run the risk of extending my figuration a little farther, in Aristotle's company. In his *De anima* (421 b) he distinguishes between man and those animals that have hard, dry eyes [*tôn sklerophtalmôn*], the animals lacking eyelids, that sort of sheath or tegumental membrane [*phragma*] which serves to protect the eye and permits it, at regular intervals, to close itself off in the darkness of inward thought

---

interdisciplinarity as an effect of the architectonic totality, see, for example, Schleiermacher's 1808 essay "Gelegentliche Gedanken Ober Universititen in deutschem Sinn, nebst einem Anhang Ober ein neu zu errichtende." A French translation of this text appears in a noteworthy collection, Philosophies de I'université, l'idéalisme allemand et a question de l'Université, ed. Ferry, Pesron, Renault [Paris: Payot, 1979].

or sleep. What is terrifying about an animal with hard eyes and a dry glance is that it always sees. Man can lower the sheath, adjust the diaphragm, narrow his sight, the better to listen, remember, and learn. What might the University's diaphragm be? The University must not be a sclerophthalmic animal, a hard-eyed animal; when I asked, a moment ago, how it should set its sights and adjust its views, that was another way of asking about its reasons for being and its essence. What American English calls "the faculty," those who teach, is in French le corps enseignant, the teaching corps (just as we say "the diplomatic corps") or teaching body. What can the University's body see or not see of its own destination, of that in view of which it stands its ground? Is the University the master of its own diaphragm?

Now that I have opened up this perspective, allow me to close it off quick as a wink and, in the twinkling of an eye, let me confide in you, to make what in French I could call a *confidence* but in English must call a confession.

Before preparing the text of a lecture, I find I must prepare myself for the scene I shall encounter as I speak. That is always a painful experience, an occasion for silent, paralytic deliberation. I feel like a hunted animal, looking in darkness for a way out where none is to be found. Every exit is blocked. In the present case, the task seemed triply impossible.

In the first place, this was not to be just a lecture like any other; rather, it had to be something like an inaugural address. Of course, Cornell University has welcomed me generously many times since I first came to speak here in 1975. I have many friends here, and Cornell is in fact the first American university I ever taught for. That was in Paris, in 1967–68, as David Grossvogel will undoubtedly remember: he was in charge of a program that had also been directed by Paul de Man. But today, for the first time, I am taking the floor to speak as an Andrew Dickson White Professor-at-Large. In French, "Au large" is the expression a great ship uses to hail a small craft about to cross her course: "Wear off. Give way." In this case, the title with which your university has honored me at once brings me closer to you and adds to the anguish of the cornered animal. Was this inaugural lecture a well-chosen moment to ask whether the University has a reason for being? Wasn't I about to act with all the unseemliness of a stranger who in return for noble hospitality plays prophet of doom with his hosts, or at best eschatological harbinger, like Elijah denouncing the power of kings or announcing the end of the realm?

A second cause for worry is that I find myself involved already, quite imprudently, that is, blindly and without foresight, in an act of dramaturgy, writing out the play of that view in which Cornell, from its beginnings, has felt so much to be at stake. The question of the view has informed the writing-out of the institutional scene, the landscape of your university, the alternatives of expansion and enclosure, life and death. From the first it was considered vital not to close off the view. This was recognized by Andrew Dickson White, Cornell's first president:

may I pay him this homage? At a moment when the trustees wanted to locate the university closer to town, Ezra Cornell took them to the top of East Hill to show them the sights, and the site, he had in mind. "We viewed the landscape," writes Andrew Dickson White. "It was a beautiful day and the panorama was magnificent. Mr. Cornell urged reasons on behalf of the upper site, the main one being that there was so much more room for expansion."[2] Ezra Cornell gave good reasons, and since the Board of Trustees, reasonably enough, concurred with them, reason won out. But in this case was reason quite simply on the side of life? Drawing on K. C. Parsons' account of the planning of the Cornell campus, James Siegel observes (and I quote) that

> for Ezra Cornell the association of the view with the university had something to do with death. Indeed Cornell's plan seems to have been shaped by the thematics of the Romantic sublime, which practically guaranteed that a cultivated man in the presence of certain landscapes would find his thoughts drifting metonymically through a series of topics—solitude, ambition, melancholy, death, spirituality, "classical inspiration"—which could lead, by an easy extension, to questions of culture and pedagogy. [p. 69]

A matter of life and death. The question arose once again in 1977, when the university administration proposed to erect protective railings on the Collegetown bridge and the Fall Creek suspension bridge to check thoughts of suicide inspired by the view of the gorge. "Barriers" was the term used; we could say "diaphragm," borrowing a word which in Greek literally means "partitioning fence." Beneath the bridges linking the university to its surroundings, connecting its inside to its outside, lies the abyss. In testimony before the Campus Council, one member of the faculty did not hesitate to express his opposition to the barriers, those diaphragmatic eyelids, on the grounds that blocking the view would mean, to use his words, "destroying the essence of the university." What did he mean? What *is* the essence of the university?

Perhaps now you can better imagine with what shudders of awe I prepared myself to speak to you on the subject-quite properly sublime - of the essence of the University. Sublime in the Kantian sense of the term: in the *Conflict of the Faculties*, Kant averred that the University should be governed by "an idea of reason," the idea of the whole field of what is presently teachable [*das ganze gegenwirtige Feld der Gelehrsamkeit*]. As it happens, no experience in the present allows for an adequate grasp of that present, presentable totality of doctrine, of teachable theory.

---

2 James Siegel, "Academic Work: The View from Cornell," Diacritics 11:1 [Spring 1981], 68–83; the quotation, on page 69, is taken from Kermit Parsons, The Cornell Campus: A History of Its Planning and Development [Ithaca: Cornell University Press, 1968].

But the crushing sense of that inadequacy is the exalting, desperate sense of the sublime, suspended between life and death.

Kant says, too, that the approach of the sublime is first heralded by an inhibition. There was a third reason for the inhibition I myself felt as I thought about speaking to you today. I was resolved of course to limit myself to preliminary, preventive remarks—propedeutical remarks, to use the word German took over from Greek to designate the teaching that comes before teaching. I would speak only of the risks to be avoided, the abyss, and bridges, and boundaries as one struggles with such fearful questions. But that would still be too much, because I wouldn't know how to pick and choose. In my teaching in Paris I have devoted a year-long seminar to the question of the University. Furthermore, I was recently asked by the French government to write a proposal for the establishment of an International College of Philosophy, a proposal which for literally hundreds of pages considers all of the difficulties involved. To speak of such things in an hour would be more than just a challenge. As I sought to encourage myself, daydreaming a bit, it occurred to me that I didn't know how many meanings were conveyed by the phrase "at large," as in "professor at large." I wondered whether a professor at large, not belonging to any department, nor even to the university, wasn't rather like the person who in the old days was called *un ubiquiste*, a "ubiquitist," if you will, in the University of Paris. A ubiquitist was a doctor of theology not attached to any particular college. Outside that context, in French, an *ubiquiste* is someone who travels a lot and travels fast, giving the illusion of being everywhere at once. Perhaps a professor at large, while not exactly a ubiquitist, is also someone who, having spent a long time on the high seas, "au large," occasionally comes ashore, after an absence which has cut him off from everything. He is unaware of the context, the proper rituals, and the changed environment. He is given leave to consider matters loftily, from afar. People indulgently close their eyes to the schematic, drastically selective views he has to express in the rhetoric proper to an academic lecture about the academy. But they may be sorry that he spends so much time in a prolonged and awkward attempt to capture the benevolence of his listeners.

As far as I know, nobody has ever founded a university against reason. So we may reasonably suppose that the University's reason for being has always been reason itself, and some essential connection of reason to being. But what is called the principle of reason is not simply reason. We cannot for now plunge into the history of reason, its words and concepts, into the puzzling scene of translation which has shifted logos to ratio to raison, reason, *Grund*, ground, *Vernunft*, and so on. What for three centuries now has been called the principle of reason was thought out and formulated, several times, by Leibniz. His most often quoted statement holds that "Nothing is without reason, no effect is without cause." According to Heidegger, though, the only formulation Leibniz himself considered authentic, authoritative, and rigorous is found in a late essay, *Specimen inventorum*: "There are two first principles in all reasoning, the principle of non-contradiction, of course ... and the principle of rendering reason." The second principle says that for any truth—for any true proposition, that is—a reasoned account is possible. "*Omnis veritatis reddi ratio potest.*" Or, to translate more literally, for any true proposition, reason can be rendered.[3]

Beyond all those big philosophical words—reason, truth, principle—that generally command attention, the principle of reason also holds that reason must be rendered. (In French the expression corresponding to Leibniz's *reddere rationem* is *rendre raison de quel-que chose*; it means to explain or account for something.) But what does "render" mean with respect to reason? Could reason be something that gives rise to exchange, circulation, borrowing, debt, donation, restitution? But in

---

3 Translator's Note. About national idioms and idioms which, like Latin, aspire to greater catholicity: Leibniz's *rationem reddere*—a phrase by no means his exclusive property, but common to philosophy at large- is easily carried over into ordinary French as *rendre raison, rendre raison de quelque chose*; but in English, today, "render reason" sounds outlandish. The Oxford dictionary shows that English had the idiom at one time; setting aside a willfully archaic and dialectical sentence from Walter Scott, the most recent example adduced is from An Exposition of the Creed, by John Pearson, bishop of Chester, published in London in 1659, and it is an example not Without interest for our purposes. "Thus," says Pearson as he expounds Article IX, "the Church of Christ in it's [sic] primary institution was made to be of a diffusive nature, to spread and extend itself from the City of Jerusalem, where it first began, to all the parts and corners of the earth. This reason did the ancient fathers render why the Church was called Catholick." [An Exposition ..., (Ann Arbor, Michigan: University Microfilms, 1968), p. 697]. He then goes on to say that for a second reason the church is called catholic because it teaches everything, or at least everything necessary to Christian faith. Apparently, there was a whole teaching of diffusion and dissemination well before our own time. To judge from the quotations given by OED, to render reason (to give it back, as it were) worked in exchange and concert with to yield reason and to give reason; any one of the three could mean to give grounds for one's thoughts and assertions, but also, to give an account of one's acts or conduct, when summoned to do so: to be held accountable and to speak accordingly. In 1690, writing not of reason but only of understanding, Locke argued that we rank things under distinct names "according to complex ideas in us," as he says, "and not according to precise, distinct, real essences in them." We cannot denominate things by their real essences, as Locke puts the matter, for the good reason that "we know them not." Even the familiar objects of our everyday world are composed we know not how; they must have their reason, but we cannot give it back to them. Thus, for all his practical bent, Locke is drawn to say, and I quote him once again, "When we come to examine the stones we tread on, or the iron we daily handle, we presently find that we know not their make, and can give no reason of the different qualities we find in them" [*An Essay concerning Human Understanding*, 111, vi, 8–9]. In English, as in French or Latin, at one time people could give reason, or render it, or not be able to render it.—E.P.M.

that case, who would be responsible for that debt or duty, and to whom? In the phrase *reddere rationem*, "ratio" is not the name of a faculty or power (*Logos, Ratio, Reason, Vernunft*) that is generally attributed by metaphysics to man, zoon logon ekon, the rational animal. If we had more time, we could follow out Leibniz's interpretation of the semantic shift which leads from the ratio of the principium *reddendae rationis*, the principle of rendering reason, to reason as the rational faculty—and in the end, to Kant's definition of reason as the faculty of principles. In any case, if "reason" in the principle of reason is not the rational faculty or power, that does not mean it is a thing, encountered somewhere among the beings and the objects in the world, which must be rendered up, given back. The question of this reason cannot be separated from a question about the modal verb "must" and the phrase "must be rendered." The "must" seems to cover the essence of our relationship to principle, it seems to mark out for us requirement, debt, duty, request, command, obligation, law, the imperative. Whenever reason can be rendered (*reddi potest*), it must. Can we, without further precautions, call this a moral imperative, in the Kantian sense of pure practical reason? It is not clear that the sense of "practical," as it is determined by a critique of pure practical reason, gets to the bottom of the "must," or reveals its origin, although such a critique has to presuppose such a "must." It could be shown, I think, that the critique of practical reason continually calls on the principle of reason, on its "must" which, although it is certainly not of a theoretical order, is nonetheless not simply "practical" or "ethical" in the Kantian sense.

A responsibility is involved here, however. We have to respond to the call of the principle of reason. In *Der Satz vom Grund* [*The Principle of Reason*], Heidegger names that call Anspruch: requirement, claim, request, demand, command, convocation; it always entails a certain addressing of speech. The word is not seen, it has to be heard and listened to, this apostrophe that enjoins us to respond to the principle of reason.

A question of responsibility, to be sure. But is answering to the principle of reason the same act as answering for the principle of reason? Is the scene the same? Is the landscape the same? And where is the university located within this space?

To respond to the call of the principle of reason is to "render reason," to explain effects through their causes, rationally; it is also to ground, to justify, to account for on the basis of principles or roots. Keeping in mind that Leibnizian moment whose originality should not be underestimated, the response to the call of the principle of reason is thus a response to the Aristotelian requirements, those of metaphysics, of primary philosophy, of the search for "roots," "principles," and "causes." At this point, scientific and technoscientific requirements lead back to a common origin. And one of the most insistent questions in Heidegger's meditation is indeed that of the long "incubation" time that separated this origin from the emergence of the principle of reason in the seventeenth century. Not only does that principle constitute the verbal formulation of a requirement present since the dawn of Western science and philosophy, it provides the impetus for a new era of purportedly "modern" reason, metaphysics and technoscience. And one cannot think the possibility of the modern university, the one that is re-structured in the nineteenth century in all the Western countries, without inquiring into that event, that institution of the principle of reason.

But to answer for the principle of reason (and thus for the university), to answer for this call, to raise questions about the origin or ground of this principle of foundation (*Der Satz vom Grund*), is not simply to obey it or to respond in the face of this principle. We do not listen in the same way when we are responding to a summons as when we are questioning its meaning, its origin, its possibility, its goal, its limits. Are we obeying the principle of reason when we ask what grounds this principle which is itself a principle of grounding? We are not—which does not mean that we are disobeying it, either. Are we dealing here with a circle or with an abyss? The circle would consist in seeking to account for reason by reason, to render reason to the principle of reason, in appealing to the principle in order to make it speak of itself at the very point where, according to Heidegger, the principle of reason says nothing about reason itself. The abyss, the hole, the *Abgrund*, the empty "gorge" would be the impossibility for a principle of grounding to ground itself. This very grounding, then, like the university, would have to hold itself suspended above a most peculiar void. Are we to use reason to account for the principle of reason? Is the reason for reason rational? Is it rational to worry about reason and its principle? Not *simply*; but it would be over-hasty to seek to disqualify this concern and to refer those who experience it back to their own irrationalism, their obscurantism, their nihilism. Who is more faithful to reason's call, who hears it with a keener ear, who better sees the difference, the one who offers questions in return and tries to think through the possibility of that summons, or the one who does not want to hear any question about the reason of reason? This is all played out, along the path of the Heideggerian question, in a subtle difference of tone or stress, according to the particular words emphasized in the formula *nihil est sine ratione*. This statement has two different implications according to whether "*nihil*" and "*sine*" are stressed, or "*est*" and "*ratione*." I shall not attempt here, given the limits of this talk, to pursue all of the reckonings involved in this shift of emphasis. Nor shall I attempt—among other things, and for the same reasons—to reconstitute a dialogue between Heidegger and for example Charles Sanders Peirce. A strange and necessary dialogue on the compound theme, indeed, of the university and the principle of reason. In a remarkable essay on "The limits of Professionalism," Samuel Weber quotes Peirce who, in 1900, "in the context of a discussion on the role of higher education" in the United States, concludes as follows:

> Only recently have we seen an American man of science and of weight discuss the purpose of education, without once alluding to the only motive that animates the genuine scientific investigator. I am not guiltless in this matter myself, for in my youth I wrote some articles to uphold a doctrine called pragmatism, namely, that the meaning and essence of every conception lies in the application that is to be made of it. That is all very well, when properly understood. I do not intend to recant it. But the question arises, what is the ultimate application; and at that time I seem to have been inclined to subordinate the conception to the act, knowing to doing. Subsequent experience of life has taught me that the only thing that is really desirable without a reason for being so, is to render ideas and things reasonable. One cannot well demand a reason for reasonableness itself.[4]

To bring about such a dialogue between Peirce and Heidegger, we would have to go beyond the conceptual opposition between "conception" and "act," between "conception" and "application," theoretical view and praxis, theory and technique. This passage beyond is sketched out briefly by Peirce in the very movement of his dissatisfaction: what might the ultimate application be? What Peirce only outlines is the path where Heidegger feels the most to be at stake, especially in *Der Satz vom Grund*. Being unable to follow this path myself here in the way I have attempted to follow it elsewhere, I shall merely draw from it two assertions, at the risk of oversimplifying.

1. The modern dominance of the principle of reason had to go hand in hand with the interpretation of the essence of beings as objects, an object present as representation [*Vorstellung*], an object placed and positioned before a subject. This latter, a man who says "*il*," an ego certain of itself, thus ensures his own technical mastery over the totality of what is. The "re-" of *repraesentatio* also expresses the movement that accounts for—"renders reason to"—a thing whose presence is encountered by rendering it present, by bringing it to the subject of representation, to the knowing self. This would be the place, if we only had the time, to consider the way Heidegger makes the language do its work (the interaction between *begegnen, entgegen, Gegenstand, Gegenwart* on the one hand, *Stellen, Vorstellen, Zustellen* on the other hand).[5] This relation of representation—which in its whole extension is

---

4 In this quotation from Peirce's Values in a Universe of Chance [(Stanford, Ca.: Stanford University Press, 1958), p. 332], in addition to the last sentence, I have italicized the allusion to desire in order to echo the opening words of Aristotle's Metaphysics. Weber's article appeared in a double issue of *The Oxford Literary Review* 5:1–2 (1982), pp. 59–79.

5 Here is but one example: *"Rationem reddere heisst: den Grund zurückgeben. Weshal zurück und wohin zurück? Weil es sich in den Bewisgingen, allgemein gesprochen im Erkennen um das*

not merely a relation of knowing—has to be grounded, ensured, protected: that is what we are told by the principle of reason, the *Satz vom Grund.* A dominance is thus assured for representation, for *Vorstellen*, for the relation to the object, that is, to the being that is located before a subject that says "I" and assures itself of its own present existence. But this dominance of the "being-before" does not reduce to that of sight or of *theoria*, nor even to that of a metaphor of the optical (or indeed *sklerophthalmic*) dimension. It is in *Der Satz vom Grund* that Heidegger states all his reservations on the very presuppositions of such rhetoricizing interpretations. It is not a matter of distinguishing here between sight and non-sight, but rather between two ways of thinking of sight and of light, as well as between two conceptions of listening and voice. But it is true that a caricature of representational man, in the Heideggerian sense, would readily endow him with hard eyes permanently open to a nature that he is to dominate, to rape if necessary, by fixing it in front of himself, or by swooping down on it like a bird of prey. The principle of reason installs its empire only to the extent that the abyssal question of the being that is hiding within it remains hidden, and with it the question of the grounding of the ground itself, of grounding as grunden (to ground, to give or take ground: *Boden-nehmen*), as *begrunden* (to motivate, justify, authorize) or especially as stiften (to erect or institute, a meaning to which Heidegger accords a certain pre-eminence).[6]

2. Now that institution of modern technoscience that is the university Stiftung is built both on the principle of reason and on what remains hidden in that principle. As if in passing, but in two passages that are important to us, Heidegger asserts that the modern university is "grounded" [*gegrundet*], "built" [*gebaut*] on the principle of reason, it "rests" [*ruht*] on this principle.[7]

Vorstellen der Gegenstinde handelt, kommt dieses zurück ins Spiel. Die lateinische Sprache der Philosophie sagt es deutlicher: das Vorstellen ist repraesentatio. Das Begegnende wird auf das vorstellende Ich zu, auf es zurbck und ihm entgegen praesentiert, in eine Gegenwart gestellt. Gemass dem principium reddendae rationis muss das Vorstellen, wenn es ein erkennendes sein soil, den Grund des Gegegnenden auf das Vorstellen zu und .h. ihm zurückgeben (reddere). Im erkennenden Vorstellen wird dem erkennenden Ich der Grund zu gestellt. Dies Verlangt das principium rationis. Des Satz vom Grund is darum für Leibniz der Grundsatz des zuzustellenden Grundes" [*Der Satz vom Grund* (Pfullingen: G. Neske, 1957), p. 45].

6 In "*Vom Wesen des Grundes*," Wegmarken [Frankfurt am Main: Klostermann, 1976], pp. 60–61.

7 "And yet, without this all powerful principle there would be no modern science, and without such a science there would be no university today. The latter rests upon the principle of reason [*Diese grundet auf dem Satz vom Grund*]. How should we represent that to ourselves

> But if today's university, locus of modern science, "is grounded on the principle of grounding," that is, on reason [*grundet auf dem Satz vom Grund*], nowhere do we encounter within it the principle of reason itself, nowhere is this principle thought through, scrutinized, interrogated as to its origin. Nowhere, within the university as such, is anyone wondering from where that call [*Anspruch*] of reason is voiced, nowhere is anyone inquiring into the origin of that demand for grounds, for reason that is to be provided, rendered, delivered: "*Woher spricht dieser Anspruch des Grundes aus seine Zustellung*?" And this dissimulation of its origin within what remains unthought is not harmful, quite the contrary, to the development of the modern university; indeed, Heidegger in passing makes certain laudatory remarks about that university: progress in the sciences, its militant interdisciplinarity, its discursive zeal, and so on. But all this is elaborated above an abyss, suspended over a "gorge"—by which we mean on grounds whose own grounding remains invisible and unthought.

Having reached this point in my reading, instead of involving you in a micrological study of Heidegger's *Der Satz vom Grund* or of his earlier texts on the University (in particular his inaugural lesson of 1929, *Was ist Metaphysik*, or the Rector's Speech of 1933, *Die Selbstbehauptung der deutschen Universität*)—a study which I am attempting elsewhere, in Paris, and to which we shall doubtless refer in the discussions that come after this talk—instead of meditating at the edge of the abyss—even if on a bridge protected by "barriers"—I prefer to return to a certain concrete actuality in the problems that assail us in the university.

The framework of grounding, or foundation, and the dimension of the fundamental impose themselves on several counts in the space of the university, whether we are considering the question of its reason for being in general, or its specific missions, or the politics of teaching and research. Each time, what is at stake is the principle of reason as principle of grounding, foundation or institution. A major debate is under way today on the subject of the politics of research and teaching, and on the role that the university may play in this arena: whether this role is central or marginal, progressive or decadent, collaborative with or independent of that of other research institutions sometimes considered better suited to certain ends. The terms of this debate tend to be analogous—I am not saying they are identical—in all the highly industrialized countries, whatever their political

---

[*Wie sollen wir uns dies vorstellen*], the university founded *gegründet* on a sentence (a primary proposition: *auf einen Satz*)? Can we risk such an assertion [*Drüfen wir eine solche Behauptung wagen*]?" [*Der Satz vom Grund, Dritte Stunde*, p. 49].

regime, whatever role the State traditionally plays in this arena (and, as we all know, even the Western democracies vary considerably in this respect). In the so-called "developing countries," the problem takes shape according to models that are certainly different but in all events inseparable from the preceding ones.

Such a problematics cannot always—cannot any longer—be reduced to a problematics centered on the nation-state; it is now centered instead on multinational military-industrial complexes or techno-economic networks, or rather international technomilitary networks that are apparently multi- or trans-national in form. In France, for some time, this debate has been organized around what is called the "orientation" [finalisation] of research. "Oriented" research is research that is programmed, focused, organized in an authoritarian fashion in view of its utilization (in view of "*ta khreia*," Aristotle would say), whether we are talking about technology, economy, medicine, psychosociology, or military power—and in fact we are talking about all of these at once. There is doubtless greater sensitivity to this problem in countries where the politics of research depend closely upon state-managed or "nationalized" structures, but I believe that conditions are becoming more and more homogeneous among all the technologically advanced industrialized societies. We speak of "oriented" research where, not so long ago, we spoke—as Peirce did—of "application." For it is growing more and more obvious that, without being immediately applied or applicable, research may "pay off," be usable, "end-oriented," in more or less deferred ways. And what is at stake is not merely what sometimes used to be called the techno-economic, medical, or military "by-products" of pure research. The detours, delays and relays of "orientation," its random aspects as well, are more disconcerting than ever. Hence the attempt, by every possible means, to take them into account, to integrate them to the rational calculus of programmed research. A term like "orient" is preferred to "apply," in addition, because the word is less "utilitarian," it leaves open the possibility that noble aims may be written into the program.

You may wonder what is being advocated, in France, in opposition to this concept of oriented research. The answer is basic, "fundamental" research, disinterested research with aims that would not be pledged in advance to some utilitarian purpose. Once upon a time it was possible to believe that pure mathematics, theoretical physics, philosophy (and, within philosophy, especially metaphysics and ontology) were basic disciplines shielded from power, inaccessible to programming by the pressures of the State or, under cover of the State, by civil society or capital interests. The sole concern of such basic research would be knowledge, truth, the disinterested exercise of reason, under the sole authority of the principle of reason.

And yet we know better than ever before what must have been true for all time, that this opposition between the basic and the end-oriented is of real but limited relevance. It is difficult to maintain this opposition with thoroughgoing conceptual as well as practical rigor, especially in the modern fields of the formal sciences, theoretical physics, astrophysics (consider the remarkable example of the science of astronomy, which is becoming useful after having been for so long the paradigm of disinterested contemplation), chemistry, molecular biology, and so forth. Within each of these fields—and they are more interrelated than ever—the so-called basic philosophical questions no longer simply take the form of abstract, sometimes epistemological questions raised after the fact; they arise at the very heart of scientific research in the widest variety of ways. One can no longer distinguish between technology on the one hand and theory, science and rationality on the other. The term techno-science has to be accepted, and its acceptance confirms the fact that an essential affinity ties together objective knowledge, the principle of reason, and a certain meta-physical determination of the relation to truth. We can no longer—and this is finally what Heidegger recalls and calls on us to think through—we can no longer dissociate the principle of reason from the very idea of technology in the realm of their modernity. One can no longer maintain the boundary that Kant, for example, sought to establish between the schema that he called "technical" and the one he called "architectonic" in the systematic organization of knowledge-which was also to ground a systematic organization of the university. The architectonic is the art of systems. "Under the government of reason, our knowledge in general," Kant says, "should not form a rhapsody, but it must form a system in which alone it can support and favor the essential aims of reason." To that pure rational unity of the architectonic, Kant opposes the scheme of the merely technical unity that is empirically oriented, according to views and ends that are incidental, not essential. It is thus a limit between two aims that Kant seeks to define, the essential and noble ends of reason that give rise to a fundamental science versus the incidental and empirical ends which can be systematized only in terms of technical schemas and necessities.

Today, in the orientation or "finalization" of research—forgive me for presuming to recall such obvious points—it is impossible to distinguish between these two sets of aims. It is impossible, for example, to distinguish programs that one would like to consider "worthy," or even technically profitable for humanity, from other programs that would be destructive. This is not new; but never before has so-called basic scientific research been so deeply committed to aims that are at the same time military aims. The very essence of the military, the limits of military technology and even the limits of its accountability are no longer definable. When we hear that two million dollars a minute are being spent in the world today for armaments, we may assume that this figure represents simply the cost of weapons manufacture. But military investments do not stop at that. For military power, even police power, and more generally speaking the entire defensive and offensive security establishment benefits from more than just the "by products" of basic research. In the advanced technological societies, this establishment programs, orients, orders, and finances, directly or indirectly, through the State or otherwise, the front-line research that is apparently the least "end-oriented" of all. This is all too obvious in such areas as physics, biology, medicine, biotechnology, bioprogramming, data processing and telecommunications. We have only to mention telecommunications and data processing to assess the extent of the phenomenon: the "orientation" of research is limitless, everything in these areas proceeds "in view" of technical and instrumental security. At the service of war, of national and international security, research programs have to encompass the entire field of information, the stockpiling of knowledge, the workings and thus also the essence of language and of all semiotic systems, translation, coding and decoding, the play of presence and absence, hermeneutics, semantics, structural and generative linguistics, pragmatics, rhetoric. I am accumulating all these disciplines in a haphazard way, on purpose, but I shall end with literature, poetry, the arts and fiction in general: the theory that has these disciplines as its object may be just as useful in ideological warfare as it is in experimentation with variables in all-too-familiar perversions of the referential function. Such a theory may always be put to work in communications strategy, the theory of commands, the most refined military pragmatics of jussive utterances (by what token, for example, will it be clear that an utterance is to be taken as a command in the new technology of telecommunications? How are the new resources of simulation and simulacrum to be controlled? And so on ...). One can just as easily seek to use the theoretical formulations of sociology, psychology, even psychoanalysis in order to refine what was called in France during the Indochinese or Algerian wars the powers of "psychological action"—alternating with torture. From now on, so long as it has the means, a military budget can invest in anything at all, in view of deferred profits: "basic" scientific theory, the humanities, literary theory and philosophy. The compartment of philosophy which covered all this, and which Kant thought ought to be kept unavailable to any utilitarian purpose and to the orders of any power whatsoever in its search for truth, can no longer lay claim to such autonomy. What is produced in this field can always be used. And even if it should remain useless in its results, in its productions, it can always serve to keep the masters of discourse busy: the experts, professionals of rhetoric, logic or philosophy who might otherwise be applying their energy elsewhere. Or again, it may in certain situations secure an ideological bonus of luxury and gratuitousness for a society that can afford it, within certain limits. Furthermore, when certain random consequences of research are taken into account, it is always possible to have in view some eventual benefit that may ensue from an apparently useless research project (in philosophy or the humanities, for example). The history of the sciences encourages researchers to integrate that margin of randomness into their centralized calculation. They then proceed to adjust the means at their disposal, the available financial support, and the distribution of credits. A State power or the forces that it represents no longer need to prohibit research or to censor discourse, especially in the West. It is enough that they can limit the means, can regulate support for production, transmission, and diffusion. The machinery for this new "censorship" in the broad sense is much more complex and omnipresent than in Kant's day, for example, when the entire problematics and the entire topology of the university were organized around the exercise of royal censorship. Today, in the Western democracies, that form of censorship has almost entirely disappeared. The prohibiting limitations function through multiple channels that are decentralized, difficult to bring together into a system. The unacceptability of a discourse, the non certification of a research project, the illegitimacy of a course offering are declared by evaluative actions: studying such evaluations is, it seems to me, one of the tasks most indispensable to the exercise of academic responsibility, most urgent for the maintenance of its dignity. Within the university itself, forces that are apparently external to it (presses, foundations, the mass media) are intervening in an ever more decisive way. University presses play a mediating role that entails the most serious responsibilities, since scientific criteria, in principle represented by the members of the university corporation, have to come to terms with many other aims. When the margin of randomness has to be narrowed, restrictions on support affect the disciplines that are the least profitable in the short run. And that provokes, within the professions, all kinds of effects, certain ones of which seem to have lost any direct relation to that causality—which is itself still largely over determined. The shifting determination of the margin of randomness always depends upon the techno-economic situation of a society in its relation to the entire world arena. In the United States, for example (and it is not just one example among others), without even mentioning the economic regulation that allows certain surplus values-through the channel of private foundations among others-to sustain research or creative projects that are not immediately or apparently profitable, we also know that military programs, especially those of the Navy, can very rationally subsidize linguistic, semiotic or anthropological investigations. These in turn are related to history, literature, hermeneutics, law, political science, psychoanalysis, and so forth.

The concept of information or informatization is the most general operator here. It integrates the basic to the oriented, the purely rational to the technical, thus bearing witness to that original intermingling of the metaphysical and the technical. The value of "form" is not foreign to it; but let us drop this difficult point for now. In *Der Satz vom Grund*, Heidegger locates this concept of "information" (understood and pronounced as in English, he says at the time when he is putting America and Russia side by side like two symmetrical and homogeneous continents of metaphysics as technique) in a dependence upon the principle of reason, as a principle of integral calculability. Even the principle of uncertainty (and he would have said the same thing of a certain interpretation of undecidability) continues to operate within the problematics of representation and of the subject-object relation. Thus he calls this the atomic era and quotes a book of popularization entitled "We shall live thanks to atoms" with prefaces both by Otto Hahn, Nobel prize-winner and "fundamentalist" physicist, and Franz Joseph Strauss, then minister of national defence. Information ensures the insurance of calculation and the calculation of insurance. In this we recognize the period of the principle of reason. Leibniz, as Heidegger recalls, is considered to have been the inventor of life insurance. In the form of information [*in der Gestalt der Information*], Heidegger says, the principle of reason dominates our entire representation [*Vorstellen*] and delineates a period for which everything depends upon the delivery of atomic energy. Delivery in German is *Zustellung*, a word that also applies, as Heidegger points out, to the delivery of mail. It belongs to the chain of *Gestell*, from the *Stellen* group [*Vorstellen, Nachstellen, Zustellen, Sicherstellen*] that characterizes technological modernity. "Information" in this sense is the most economic, the most rapid and the clearest (univocal, *eindeutig*) stockpiling, recording and communication of news. It must instruct men about the safeguarding [*Sicherstellung*] of what will meet their needs, *ta khreia*. Computer technology, data banks, artificial intelligences, translating machines, and so forth, all these are constructed on the basis of that instrumental determination of a calculable language. Information does not inform merely by delivering an information content, it gives form, "*in-formiert,*" "*formiertz ugleich.*" It installs man in a form that permits him to ensure his mastery on earth and beyond. All this has to be pondered as the effect of the principle of reason, or, put more rigorously, has to be analyzed as the effect of a dominant interpretation of that principle, of a certain emphasis in the way we heed its summons. But I have said that I cannot deal with the question of such stress here; it lies outside the scope of my topic.

* * * * *

What, then, is my topic? What do I have in view that has led me to present things as I have done so far? I have been thinking especially of the necessity to awaken or to resituate a responsibility, in the university or in face of the university, whether one belongs to it or not.

Those analysts who study the informative and instrumental value of language today are necessarily led to the very confines of the principle of reason thus interpreted. This can happen in any number of disciplines. But if the analysts end up for example working on the structures of the simulacrum or of literary fiction, on a poetic rather than an informative value of language, on the effects of undecidability, and so on, by that very token they are interested in possibilities that arise at the outer limits of the authority and the power of the principle of reason. On that basis, they may attempt to define new responsibilities in the face of the university's total subjection to the technologies of informatization. Not so as to refuse them; not so as to counter with some obscurantist irrationalism (and irrationalism, like nihilism, is a posture that is completely symmetrical to, thus dependent upon, the principle of reason). The theme of extravagance as an irrationalism-there is very clear evidence for this-dates from the period when the principle of reason was being formulated. Leibniz denounced it in his *New Essays on Human Understanding*. To raise these new questions may sometimes protect an aspect of philosophy and the humanities that has always resisted the influx of knowledge; it may also preserve the memory of what is much more deeply buried and ancient than the principle of reason. But the approach I am advocating here is often felt by certain guardians of the "humanities" or of the positive sciences as a threat. It is interpreted as such by those who most often have never sought to understand the history and the system of norms specific to their own institution, the deontology of their own profession. They do not wish to know how their discipline has been constituted, particularly in its modern professional form, since the beginning of the nineteenth century and under the watchful vigilance of the principle of reason. For the principle of reason may have obscurantist and nihilist effects. They can be seen more or less everywhere, in Europe and in America among those who believe they are defending philosophy, literature and the humanities against these new modes of questioning that are also a new relation to language and tradition, a new affirmation, and new ways of taking responsibility. We can easily see on which side obscurantism and nihilism are lurking when on occasion great professors or representatives of prestigious institutions lose all sense of proportion and control; on such occasions they forget the principles that they claim to defend in their work and suddenly begin to heap insults, to say whatever comes into their heads on the subject of texts that they obviously have never opened or that they have encountered through a mediocre journalism that in other circumstances they would pretend to scorn.[8]

---

8 Among many possible examples, I shall mention only two recent articles. They have at least one trait in common: their authors are highly placed representatives of two institutions whose power and influence hardly need to be recalled. I refer to "The Crisis in English Studies" by Walter Jackson Bate, Kingsley Porter University Professor at Harvard [Harvard Magazine, Sept./Oct. 1982], and to "The Shattered Humanities" by Willis J. Bennett,

It is possible to speak of this new responsibility that I have invoked only by sounding a call to practice it. It would be the responsibility of a community of thought for which the frontier between basic and oriented research would no longer be secured, or in any event not under the same conditions as before. I call it a community of thought in the broad sense—"at large"—rather than a community of research, of science or philosophy, since these values are most often subjected to the unquestioned authority of a principle of reason. Now reason is only one species of thought—which does not mean that thought is "irrational." Such a community would interrogate the essence of reason and of the principle of reason, the values of the basic, of the principal, of radicality, of the *arkhe* in general, and it would attempt to draw out all the possible consequences of this questioning. It is not certain that such thinking can bring together a community or found an institution in the traditional sense of these words. What is meant by community and institution must be rethought. This thinking must also unmask—an infinite task—all the ruses of end-orienting reason, the paths by which apparently disinterested research can find itself indirectly reappropriated, reinvested by programs of all sorts. That does not mean that "orientation" is bad in itself and that it must be combatted, far from it. Rather, I am defining the necessity for a new way of educating students that will prepare them to undertake new analyses in order to evaluate these ends and to choose, when possible, among them all.

As I mentioned earlier, along with some colleagues I was asked last year by the French government to prepare a report in view of the creation of an International College of Philosophy. I insisted, in that report, on stressing the dimension that in this context I am calling "thought"—a dimension that is not reducible to technique, nor to science, nor to philosophy. This International College would not only be a College of Philosophy but also a place where philosophy itself would be questioned. It would be open to types of research that are not perceived as legitimate today, or that are insufficiently developed in French or foreign institutions,

---

Chairman of the National Endowment for the Humanities [Wall Street Journal, Dec. 31, 1982]. The latter of these articles carries ignorance and irrationality so far as to write the following: "A popular movement in literary criticism called 'Deconstruction' denies that there are any texts at all. If there are no texts, there are no great texts, and no argument for reading." The former makes remarks about deconstruction—and this is not by chance—that are, we might say, just as unnerved. As Paul de Man notes in an admirable short essay ["The Return to Philology," Times Literary Supplement, December 10, 1982], Professor Bate "has this time confined his sources of information to Newsweek magazine. ... What is left is a matter of law - enforcement rather than a critical debate. One must be feeling very threatened indeed to become so aggressively defensive."

including some research that could be called "basic"; but it would not stop there. We would go one step further, providing a place to work on the value and meaning of the basic, the fundamental, on its opposition to goal-orientation, on the ruses of orientation in all its domains. As in the seminar that I mentioned earlier, the report confronts the political, ethical, and juridical consequences of such an undertaking. I cannot go into more detail here without keeping you much too long.

These new responsibilities cannot be purely academic. If they remain extremely difficult to assume, extremely precarious and threatened, it is because they must at once keep alive the memory of a tradition and make an opening beyond any program, that is, toward what is called the future. And the discourse, the works, or the position-taking that these responsibilities inspire, as to the institution of science and research, no longer stem solely from the sociology of knowledge, from sociology or politology. These disciplines are doubtless more necessary than ever; I would be the last to want to disqualify them. But whatever conceptual apparatus they may have, whatever axiomatics, whatever methodology (Marxist or neo-Marxist, Weberian or neo-Weberian, Mannheimian, some combination of these or something else entirely), they never touch upon that which, in themselves, continues to be based on the principle of reason and thus on the essential foundation of the modern university. They never question scientific normativity, beginning with the value of objectivity or of objectivation, which governs and authorizes their discourse. Whatever may be their scientific value—and it may be considerable—these sociologies of the institution remain in this sense internal to the university, intra-institutional, controlled by the deepseated standards, even the programs, of the space that they claim to analyze. This can be observed, among other things, in the rhetoric, the rites, the modes of presentation and demonstration that they continue to respect. Thus I shall go so far as to say that the discourse of Marxism and psychoanalysis, including those of Marx and Freud, *inasmuch* as they are standardized by a project of scientific practice and by the principle of reason, are intra-institutional, in any event homogeneous with the discourse that dominates the university in the last analysis. And the fact that this discourse is occasionally proffered by people who are not professional academics changes nothing essential. It simply explains, to a certain extent, the fact that even when it claims to be revolutionary, this discourse does not always trouble the most conservative forces of the university. Whether it is understood or not, it is enough that it does not threaten the fundamental axiomatics and deontology of the institution, its rhetoric, its rites and procedures. The academic landscape easily accommodates such types of discourse more easily within its economy and its ecology; however, when it does not simply exclude those who raise questions at the level of the foundation or non-foundation of the foundation of the university, it reacts much more fearfully to those that address sometimes the same questions to Marxism, to psychoanalysis, to the sciences, to philosophy and the humanities. It is not a matter simply of questions that one formulates while submitting oneself, as I am doing here, to the principle of reason, but also of preparing oneself thereby to transform the modes of writing, approaches to pedagogy, the procedures of academic exchange, the relation to languages, to other disciplines, to the institution in general, to its inside and its out-side. Those who venture forth along this path, it seems to me, need not set themselves up in opposition to the principle of reason, nor need they give way to "irrationalism." They may continue to assume within the university, along with its memory and tradition, the imperative of professional rigor and competence. There is a double gesture here, a double postulation: to ensure professional competence and the most serious tradition of the university even while going as far as possible, theoretically and practically, in the most directly underground thinking about the abyss beneath the university, to think at one and the same time the entire "Cornellian" landscape—the campus on the heights, the bridges, and if necessary the barriers above the abyss—and the abyss itself. It is this double gesture that appears unsituatable and thus unbearable to certain university professionals in every country who join ranks to foreclose or to censure it by all available means, simultaneously denouncing the "professionalism" and the "antiprofessionalism" of those who are calling others to these new responsibilities.

I shall not venture here to deal with the debate on "professionalism" that is developing in your country. Its features are, to a certain extent at least, specific to the history of the American university. But I shall conclude on this general theme of "professions." At the risk of contradicting what I have been urging here, I should like to caution against another kind of precipitous reaction. For the responsibility that I am trying to situate cannot be simple. It implies multiple sites, a stratified terrain, postulations that are undergoing continual displacement, a sort of strategic rhythm. I said earlier that I would be speaking only of a certain rhythm, for example that of the blinking of an eye, and that I would only be playing one risk off against another, the barrier against the abyss, the abyss against the barrier, the one with the other and the one under the other.

Beyond technical goal-orientation, even beyond the opposition between technical goal-orientation and the principle of sufficient reason, beyond the affinity between technology and metaphysics, what I have here called "thought" risks in its turn (but I believe this risk is unavoidable—it is the risk of the future itself) being reappropriated by socio-political forces that could find it in their own interest in certain situations. Such a "thought" indeed cannot be produced outside of certain historical, techno-economic, politico-institutional and linguistic conditions. A strategic analysis that is to be as vigilant as possible must thus with its eyes wide open attempt to ward off such reappropriations. (I should have liked to situate at this point certain questions about the "politics" of Heideggerian thought, especially as elaborated prior to *Der Satz vom Grund*, for example in the two inaugural discourses of 1929 and 1933.)

I shall limit myself, however, to the double question of "professions." First: does the university have as its essential mission that of producing professional competencies, which may sometimes be external to the university? Second: is the task of the university to ensure within itself—and under what conditions—the reproduction of professional competence by preparing professors for pedagogy and for research who have respect for a certain code? One may answer the second question in the affirmative without having done so for the first, and seek to keep professional forms and values internal to the university outside the market place while keeping the goal-orientation of social work outside of the university. The new responsibility of the "thought" of which we are speaking cannot fail to be accompanied at least by a movement of suspicion, even of rejection with respect to the professionalization of the university in these two senses, and especially in the first, which regulates university life according to the supply and demand of the marketplace and according to a purely technical ideal of competence. To this extent at least, such "thought" may, at a minimum, result in reproducing a highly traditional politics of knowledge. And the effects may be those that belong to a social hierarchy in the exercise of technopolitical power. I am not saying that this "thought" is identical with that politics, and that it is therefore necessary to abstain from it; I am saying that under certain conditions it can serve that politics, and that everything thus comes down to the analysis of those conditions. In modern times, Kant, Nietzsche, Heidegger and numerous others have all said as much, quite unmistakably: the essential feature of academic responsibility must not be professional education (and the pure core of academic autonomy, the essence of the university, is located in the philosophy department, according to Kant). Does this affirmation not repeat the profound and hierarchizing political evaluation of Metaphysics, I mean of Aristotle's *Metaphysics*? Shortly after the passage that I read at the beginning (981b and following), one sees a theoretico-political hierarchy being put into place. At the top, there is theoretical knowledge. It is not sought after in view of its utility; and the holder of this knowledge, which is always a knowledge of causes and of principles, is the leader or *arkhitekton* of a society at work, is positioned above the manual laborer [*kheiroteknes*] who acts without knowing, just as a fire burns. Now this theoretician leader, this knower of causes who has no need of "practical" sk ill, is in essence a teacher. Beyond the fact of knowing causes and of possessing reason [*to logon ekhein*], he bears another mark [*semeion*] of recognition: the "capacity to teach" [*to dunasthai didaskein*]. To teach, then, and at the same time to direct, steer, organize the empirical work of the laborers. The theoretician-teacher or "architect" is a leader because he is on the side of the arkhe, of beginning and commanding. He commands—he is the premier or the prince—because he knows causes and principles, the "whys" and thus also the "wherefores" of things. Before the fact, and before anyone else, he answers to the principle of reason which is the first principle, the principle of principles. And that is why he takes orders from no one; it is he, on the contrary, who orders, prescribes, lays down the law (982a 18). And it is normal that this superior science, with the power that it confers by virtue of its very lack of utility, is developed in places [*topoi*], in regions where leisure is possible. Thus Aristotle points out that the mathematical arts were developed in Egypt owing to the leisure time enjoyed by the priestly caste [*to ton iereon ethnos*], the priestly folk.

Kant, Nietzsche and Heidegger, speaking of the university, premodern or modern, do not say exactly what Aristotle said, nor do all three of them say exactly the same thing. But they also do say the same thing. Even though he admits the industrial model of the division of labor into the university, Kant places the so-called "lower" faculty, the faculty of philosophy-a place of pure rational knowledge, a place where truth has to be spoken without controls and without concern for "utility," a place where the very meaning and the autonomy of the university meet—Kant places this faculty above and outside professional education: the architectonic schema of pure reason is above and outside the technical schema. In his *Lectures on the Future of our Educational Establishments*, Nietzsche condemns the division of labor in the sciences, condemns utilitarian and journalistic culture in the service of the State, condemns the professional ends of the University. The more one does [tut] in the area of training, the more one has to think [*denken*]. And, still in the first Lecture: "*Man muss nicht nur Standpunkte, sondern auch Gedanken haben!*"; one must not have viewpoints alone, but also thoughts! As for Heidegger, in 1929, in his inaugural lesson entitled "*What is Metaphysics*," he deplores the henceforth technical organization of the university and its compartmentalizing specialization. And even in his Rector's Speech, at the very point where he makes an appeal on behalf of the three services (*Arbeitsdienst, Wehrdienst, Wissensdienst*, the service of work, the military, and knowledge), at the very point where he is recalling that these services are of equal rank and equally original (he had recalled earlier that for the Greeks *theoria* was only the highest form of praxis and the mode, par excellence, of *energeia*), Heidegger nevertheless violently condemns disciplinary compartmentalization and "exterior training in view of a profession," as "an idle and inauthentic thing" [*Das Mussige und Unechte ausserlicher Berufsabrichtung* ...].

Desiring to remove the university from "useful" programs and from professional ends, one may always, willingly or not, find oneself serving unrecognized ends, reconstituting powers of caste, class, or corporation. We are in an implacable political topography: one step further in view of greater profundity or radicalization, even going beyond the "profound" and the "radical," the principial, the *arkhe*, one step further toward a sort of original anarchy risks producing or reproducing the hierarchy. "Thought" requires both the principle of reason and what is beyond the principle of reason, the *arkhe* and anarchy. Between the two, the difference of a breath or an accent, only the enactment of this "thought" can decide. That decision is always risky, it always risks the worst. To claim to eliminate that risk by an institutional program is quite simply to erect a barricade against a future. The decision of thought cannot be an intra-institutional event, an academic moment.

All this does not define a politics, nor even a responsibility. Only, at best, some negative conditions, a "negative wisdom," as the Kant of *The Conflict of the Faculties* would say: preliminary cautions, protocols of vigilance for a new *Aufklirung*, what must be seen and kept in sight in a modern re-elaboration of that old problematics. Beware of the abysses and the gorges, but also of the bridges and the barriers. Beware of what opens the university to the outside and the bottomless, but also of what, closing it in on itself, would create only an illusion of closure, would make the university available to any sort of interest, or else render it perfectly useless. Beware of ends; but what would a university be without ends?

Neither in its medieval nor in its modern form has the university disposed freely of its own absolute autonomy and of the rigorous conditions of its own unity. During more than eight centuries, "university" has been the name given by a society to a sort of supplementary body that at one and the same time it wanted to project outside itself and to keep jealously to itself, to emancipate and to control. On this double basis, the university was supposed to represent society. And in a certain way it has done so: it has reproduced society's scenography, its views, conflicts, contradictions, its play and its differences, and also its desire for organic union in a total body. Organicist language is always associated with "techno-industrial" language in "modern" discourse on the university. But with the relative autonomy of a technical apparatus, indeed that of a machine and of a prosthetic body, this artifact that is the university has reflected society only in giving it the chance for *reflection*, that is, also, for *dissociation*. The time for reflection, here, signifies not only that the internal rhythm of the university apparatus is relatively independent of social time and relaxes the urgency of command, ensures for it a great and precious freedom of play. An empty place for chance: the invagination of an inside pocket. The time for reflection is also the chance for turning back on the very conditions of reflection, in all the senses of that word, as if with the help of a new optical device one could finally see sight, could not only view the natural land-scape, the city, the bridge and the abyss, but could view viewing. As if through an acoustical device one could hear hearing, in other words, seize the inaudible in a sort of poetic telephony. Then the time of reflection is also an other time, it is heterogeneous with what it reflects and perhaps gives time for what calls for and is called thought. It is the chance for an event about which one does not know whether or not, presenting itself within the university, it belongs to the history of the university. It may also be brief and paradoxical, it may tear up time, like the instant invoked by Kierkegaard, one of those thinkers who are foreign, even hostile to the university, who give us more to think about, with respect to the essence of the university, than academic reflections themselves. The chance for this event is the chance of an instant, an Augenblick, a "wink" or a "blink," it takes place "in the twinkling of an eye," I would say, rather, "in the twilight of an eye," for it is in the most crepuscular, the most westerly situations of the Western university that the chances of this "twinkling" of thought are multiplied. In a period of "crisis," as we say, a period of decadence and renewal, when the institution is "on the blink," provocation to think brings together in the same instant the desire for memory and exposure to the future, the fidelity of a guardian faithful enough to want to keep even the chance of a future, in other words the singular responsibility of what he does not have and of what is not yet. Neither in his keeping nor in his purview. Keep the memory and keep the chance—is this possible? And chance—can it be kept? Is it not, as its name indicates, the risk or the advent of the fall, even of decadence, the falling-due that befalls you at the bottom of the "gorge"? I don't know. I don't know if it is possible to keep both memory and chance. I am tempted to think, rather, that the one cannot be kept without the other, without keeping the other and being kept from the other. Differently. That double guard will be assigned, as its responsibility, to the strange destiny of the university. To its law, to its reason for being and to its truth. Let us risk one more etymological wink: truth is what keeps, that is, both preserves and is preserved. I am thinking here of *Wahrheit*, of the *Wahren* of *Wahrheit* and of *veritas*—whose name figures on the coat of arms of so many American universities. It institutes guardians and calls upon them to watch faithfully—truthfully—over itself.

Let me recall my incipit and the single question that I raised at the outset: how can we not speak, today, of the university? Have I said it, or done it? Have I said how one must not speak, today, of the university? Or have I rather spoken as one should not do today, within the University? Only others can answer. Beginning with you.

CHAPTER THIRTY-TWO

Preface to the English Edition

From *Homo Academicus* (1984)

PIERRE BOURDIEU

Translated by Peter Collier, the 'Preface to the English Edition' is an excerpt taken from *Homo Academicus*, by Pierre Bourdieu, 1988, published by Polity Press, Cambridge, United Kingdom. The original text, except for the Preface and Postscript was first published by Les Editions de Minuit, Paris, France, 1984.

Editors' Note

Pierre Bourdieu was a French sociologist with strong philosophical orientation who pursued the question of power and its social dynamics and cultural reproduction in maintaining political order. He emphasised an anthropological concept of practice influenced strongly by Durkheim, Marx, Wittgenstein, and structuralist thinkers to build research frameworks and theories that investigated the forms of capital—cultural, social and symbolic forms as opposed traditional economic forms (Bourdieu, 1986). Bourdieu demonstrated the ways in which capital are based on social networks to create and reproduce inequality. His distinctive concepts of *habitus*, *field* and *symbolic violence* as an indispensable part of his theory of practice enabled him to the distinctive nature of investigate social classes in post-industrial society. *Homo Academicus* precisely reflects Bourdieu's method as he analyses the types and forms of academic, scientific and intellectual power and turns to the study of the historical conditions of the production of the university. The extended Preface to the English Edition provides the opportunity for Bourdieu to engage with the tradition of poststructuralist thought with a heavy focus on May '68, before turning to matters of sociological method and 'The Conflict of the Faculties.' This is an embedded and powerful form of analysis that is also for Bourdieu a form of self-analysis.

MP

Recommended Reading

Bourdieu, P. (1986). The forms of capital. In J. Richardson (Ed.) *Handbook of Theory and Research for the Sociology of Education*. New York, Greenwood, pp. 241–258. At https://www.marxists.org/reference/subject/philosophy/works/fr/bourdieu-forms-capital.htm

* * * * *

It is history which is the true unconscious.
Emile Durkheim, *The evolution of educational thought*

This analysis of the academic world is the end product of the critical reflection on scientific practice which I have never ceased to conduct as part of the very process of my research, since the time when, as a young ethnologist, I took my own native region as the object of my ethnological observation.[1] Thus my sociological analysis of the academic world aims to trap *Homo Academicus,* supreme classifier among classifiers, in the net of his own classifications. It is a comic scenario, that of Don Juan deceived or The Miser robbed, and there are those who, hoping to feel endangered or to make others feel threatened, prefer to treat it in tragic terms. I for my part think that the experience whose results this book presents is perhaps not so different from that attributed by David Garnett to the hero of his short story *A Man in the Zoo,* where the young man, as the result of a quarrel with his girlfriend, writes in despair to the director of the zoo to offer him a mammal missing from his collection, that is, himself, so that he is placed in a cage, next to the chimpanzee, with a notice saying: 'Homo sapiens. This specimen is the gift of John Cromantie, Esquire. Visitors are requested not to tease the man with personal remarks.'

The sociologist who chooses to study his own world in its nearest and most familiar aspects should not, as the ethnologist would, domesticate the exotic, but,

---

1 P. Bourdieu, 'Celibat et condition paysanne', Etudes rurales, April-September 1962, pp. 32–136.

if I may venture the expression, exoticize the domestic, through a break with his initial relation of intimacy with modes of life and thought which remain opaque to him because they are too familiar. In fact the movement towards the originary, and the ordinary, world should be the culmination of a movement towards alien and extraordinary worlds. But it hardly ever is: in Durkheim as in Lévi-Strauss, there is no prospect of subjecting to analysis the 'forms of classification' employed by the scholar, and seeking in the social structures of the academic world (which Durkheim had none the less analysed superbly in his *The Evolution of Educational Thought*) the sources of the categories of professorial understanding. And yet, social science may expect to derive its most decisive progress from a constant effort to undertake a sociological critique of sociological reasoning—that is, to establish the social derivation not only of the categories of thought which it consciously or unconsciously deploys, such as those pairs of antithetical terms which so often inform the scientific construction of the social world, but also of the concepts which it uses, and which are often no more than commonsense notions introduced uncritically into scholarly discourse (like the notion of 'profession', which is tacitly repudiated in this study),[2] or of the problems which it elects to study, which not infrequently are nothing but more or less skilfully disguised versions of the latest 'social problems' ('poverty' or 'hooliganism', 'under-achievement in school' or 'the senior citizen', etc.).

One cannot avoid having to objectify the objectifying subject. It is by turning to study the historical conditions of his own production, rather than by some form or other of transcendental reflection, that the scientific subject can gain a theoretical control over his own structures and inclinations as well as over the determinants whose products they are, and can thereby gain the concrete means of reinforcing his capacity for objectification. Only a sociological self -analysis of this kind, which owes and concedes nothing to self -indulgent narcissism, can really help to place the scholar in a position where he is able to bring to bear on his familiar world the detached scrutiny which, with no special vigilance, the ethnologist brings to bear on any world to which he is not linked by the inherent complicity of being involved in its social game, its *illusio,* which creates the very value of the objectives of the game, as it does the value of the game itself.

In making a scientific analysis of the academic world, one takes as one's object an institution which has been socially licensed as entitled to operate an objectification which lays claim to objectivity and universality. Far from leading to a nihilistic attack on science, like certain so-called 'postmodern' analyses, which do no more than *Preface* to *the English Edition* add the flavour of the month dressed with a

2 The repudiation is of the Chicago school type of sociology of professions. [Tr.]

soupçon of 'French radical chic' to the age-old irrationalist rejection of science, and more especially of social science, under the aegis of a denunciation of 'positivism' and 'scientism', this sort of sociological experimentation applied to sociological study itself aims to demonstrate that sociology *can* escape from the vicious circle of historicism or sociologism, and that in pursuit of this end it need only make use of the knowledge which it provides of the social world in which science is produced, in order to try to gain control over the effects of the social determinisms which affect both this world, and, unless extreme caution is exercised, scientific discourse itself. In other words, far from destroying its own foundations when it brings to light the social determinants which the logic of the fields of production brings to bear on all cultural productions, sociology claims an epistemological privilege: that conferred by the fact of being able to reinvest in scientific practice its own scientific gains, in the form of a sociological increase in epistemological vigilance.

What scientific profit can there be in attempting to discover what is entailed by the fact of belonging to the academic field, that site of permanent rivalry for the truth of the social world and of the academic world itself, and by the fact of occupying a determined position within it, defined by a certain number of properties, an education and training, qualifications and status, with all their concomitant forms of solidarity or membership? Firstly, it provides an opportunity for conscious neutralization of the probabilities of error which are inherent in a position) understood as a point of view implying a certain angle of vision, hence a particular form of insight and blindness. But above all it reveals the social foundations of the propensity to theorize or to intellectualize, which is inherent in the very posture of the scholar feeling free to withdraw from the game in order to conceptualize it, and assuming the objective, which attracts social recognition as being scientific, of arriving at a sweeping overview of the world, drafted from an external and superior point of view. There is patent bad faith in refusing to credit science, when it encroaches on the world of the scholar, with the qualities readily granted to structuralist objectivism when it handles the 'savage mind', assumed to be inaccessible to itself; none the less, this should not prevent us from asking if the will to know is not surreptitiously motivated in the present case by a special kind of will to power, which is displayed in the fact of attempting to adopt towards rivals, reduced to the state of objects, a point of view which they are unable or unwilling to adopt towards themselves. But in the event the declared intention of the enterprise is hardly relevant, since the enterprise functions as a mechanism generating 'problem situations' as Popper would say. The tendency to forget to programme into the complete theory of the world analysed the gap between the theoretical and the practical experience of this world is compensated for by the inevitably reflexive view imposed by the sociological analysis of the social conditions of sociological analysis: the objective analysis, or even the objectivist or structuralist analysis, of the structures of a world in which the scientist responsible for the work of objectification is himself ensconced, and of which he has an initial representation which is capable of surviving objective analysis, will then reveal its own limits in its turn by calling attention, for instance, to its own individual or collective defence mechanisms, which often take the form of an operation of negation, and through which the agents aim to maintain in being, for themselves and for others, representations of the social world which clash with the representation constructed by science through a totalization which ordinary existence precludes, in spirit and in letter. Objective analysis obliges us to realize that the two approaches, structuralist and constructivist (by which I mean a kind of phenomenology of one's initial experience of the social world and of the contribution which this experience makes towards one's construction of that world), are two complementary stages of the same procedure. If the agents do indeed contribute to the construction of these structures, they do so at every stage within the limits of the structural constraints which affect their acts of construction both from without, through determinants connected with their position in the objective structures, and from within, through the mental structures—the categories of professorial understanding—which organize their perception and appreciation of the social world. In other words, although they are never more than particular angles of vision, taken from points of view which the objectivist *analysis situs* constitutes as such, the partial and partisan views of the agents engaged in the game, and the individual or collective struggles through which they aim to impose these views, are part of the objective truth of this game, playing an active part in sustaining or transforming it, within the limits set by the objective constraints.

It is understandable that a book aiming to account for this sort of initiatory itinerary orientated towards that reappropriation of the self which, paradoxically, is only accessible through objectification of the familiar world, is bound to be read differently by readers who are part of this world as opposed to those who are outsiders. And this is so despite the fact that this text, given its object, has the singularity of providing its own context—contrary to what usually happens, in the international (and also the intergenerational) circulation of ideas, where texts are transmitted without the context of their production and use, and count on receiving a so-called 'internal' reading which universalizes and eternalizes them while derealizing them by constantly relating them to the sole context of their reception.[3]

3 Because of this, the authors find themselves reduced (more or less completely, depending on the readers' information) to the works bearing their name and are stripped of all the social properties associated with their position in their field of origin, that is, the most institutionalized dimension of their authority and their symbolic capital (although prefaces written by authors placed within the field may serve, if necessary, to effect the transfer

It could be supposed that, contrary to the native reader who understands only too well in one sense, but who may be inclined to resist objectification, the foreign reader, because (at least at first sight) he has no direct stake in the game which is described, will be less inclined to offer resistance to the analysis. All the more so since, as it happens in the theatre that one may laugh unwittingly at the portrait of one's own foibles, the foreign reader can always elude the challenges implicit in situations or relations which he *does* find familiar, by isolating only the most blatantly exotic, but perhaps also the least significant, characteristics of academic traditions thus dismissed as archaisms, thereby managing all the better to keep his distance.[4] In fact, *mutatis mutandis*, the foreign reader finds himself faced with the same alternative as the native reader (and the sociologist himself): he can use the objectification of a world in which he participates at least by analogy (as witness the international solidarity between holders of equivalent positions in the different national fields) in order to reinforce the defence mechanisms of his bad faith, by accentuating the differences which particularize the species *homo academicus gallicus*; or, alternatively, he may use it to lay the foundations of a self-analysis, either by concentrating on the invariants of the genus *homo academicus*, or, better still, by educating himself with what he may discover about himself through

---

necessary to restore their endangered symbolic capital ...). The freedom which is thus left to the reader's judgement is quite relative because of the fact that the effects of authority can continue to operate through the medium of the solidarity obtaining between holders of homologous positions in different national scientific fields, and in particular between the dominant, who can profit from the power which they exercise over the circulation of translations and the agencies of consecration in order to operate international transfers of academic power and also to control the access to the national market of products liable to threaten their own production. On the other hand, this relative freedom has as its counterpart the danger of misunderstanding and allodoxia which is entailed by ignorance of the context: thus it is, for instance, that some essayists come to eclipse the stars of the first magnitude from whom they borrow the very source of their radiance.

4 There is no lack of sociologists, historians or anthropologists who, unable to adopt towards their own world the detached scrutiny of the foreigner, will find in this book, which is the product of a methodical effort to achieve this scrutiny without losing the benefits of familiarity, an opportunity to reinforce their native confidence in their own world—as expressed in all naivety in certain studies of France and its universities by foreign authors. The paradigm of this sociology which enthrones ethnocentrism as method (and which can be the product of emigres needing to justify, in their own eyes, the fact that they have emigrated) is a work by Terry Clark which measures the French university against a set of arbitrary criteria which are no more than the idealized traits of the American university (D. T. Clark, *Prophets and Patrons: The French University and the Emergence of the Social Science*, Cambridge, Mass., Harvard University Press, 1973).

the objectification, however harsh at first sight, of one of the positions of *homo academicus gallicus* which is homologous to his own position in his own field. In order to foster the second kind of reading, the only one, I believe, which reflects the epistemological intentions of this book, one would need either to offer a constructed set of transformational rules enabling systematic transfers to be made from one historical tradition to another,[5] or at least, more modestly, to suggest starting points for the transposition of the analyses, those, for instance, which concern the rhetorical strategies of teachers' judgements, the pairs of adjectives which structure professorial understanding, or the objective and subjective bases of that management of one's own and other people's time which ensures the maintenance of the hierarchy of power, that is, if I may make a slight modification to Leibniz's famous definition of time, 'the order of successions' on which depends the perpetuation in time of the social order.[6]

The scientific virtue (and perhaps also the ethical value) of the notion of the field resides no doubt in the fact that this notion tends to exclude those partial and unilateral objectifications of the unconscious of other people, whether rivals or opponents, which characterize the 'sociology of intellectuals', and which differ from the folk-sociology of intellectual gossip only in their claims to the 'ethical neutrality' of science, which render them guilty of a veritable abuse of symbolic power. Thus for instance when in *The Opium of the Intellectuals* (a classic of the genre) Raymond Aron undertakes to lay bare the reasons behind the arguments of his opponents of the day, and describes the social determinants of the ethical or political stances of those he calls intellectuals (excluding himself, of course, from the stigmatized class), that is, Jean-Paul Sartre, Simone de Beauvoir and the other 'left-wing intellectuals', Aron makes no attempt to ask himself from what point of view he operates this sovereign objectification (no more than does Simone de Beauvoir herself in the diametrically opposite article which she, devotes, at roughly the same time and with the same lack of moral hesitation, to 'right-wing thought')[7]: trapped within the lights of his self-interest, he is entirely blind, as

5 At each point of the analysis, as regards, for instance, the distance between the academic field and political or economic power —which, it would seem, is (or at least was) for historical reasons greater than in any other country—one ought to examine what is variable and what is invariant and try to discover in the variations of the parameters used for the model the sources of the variations observed in reality.

6 I think that the strategy adopted on this point by the translator, to give carefully chosen English or American equivalents for the words designating specific institutions, while retaining the French words in parentheses, should render this work of transposition easier.

7 Simone de Beauvoir, 'La Pensee de droite aujourd'hui', Les Temps modernes, nos 112–13 and 114–15, 1985, pp. 1539–75 and 2219–61. [Tr.]

blind as those whose blindness he denounces, to the since within which he is situated, yet within which may be defined the objective relation which connects him to them, and which is the source both of his insights and of his I oversights.

The construction of the field of production, substituting for a polemic where prejudice is disguised as analysis a polemic where scientific reason challenges itself, that is, challenges its own limits, implies a break with naive and self-indulgent objectifications unaware of their sources. It can only be an unjustifiable abstraction (which could fairly be called reductive) to seek the source of the understanding of cultural productions in these productions themselves, taken in isolation and divorced from the conditions of their production and utilization, as would be the wish of *discourse analysis*, which, situated on the border between sociology and linguistics, has nowadays relapsed into indefensible forms of internal analysis. Scientific analysis must work to relate to each other two sets of relations, the space of works or discourses taken as differential stances, and the space of the positions held by those who produce them. This means for instance that anyone particular work produced by an academic on the subject of the events of May 1968 only yields its significance if, using the principle of intertextuality, it is set in the space of the works dealing with this subject, within which its symbolically pertinent properties are defined, and if this space is related to the homologous space of the positions held by their authors in the academic field. Any reader familiar with this literature will be able to verify, if they refer to the diagram, how this functions as an instrument of analysis: the differences observed in the distribution of power and prestige among the authors correspond to the differences, intentional or not, which they display not only in their overall judgement of the events but also in their way of expressing them. The hypothesis that there is an almost perfect homology between the space of the stances (conceived as a space of forms, styles and modes of expression as much as of contents expressed) and the space of the positions held by their authors in the field of production finds its most remarkable confirmation in the fact, which will be blindingly obvious to all observers familiar with the details of what happened in the universities in 1968, that the distribution in the academic field—constructed by considering *exclusively* the most typically academic characteristics of the different professors (the institution they belong to, their academic qualifications, etc.)—corresponds very closely to the distribution in terms of political positions or trade-union affiliations and even Stances adopted during the events of May 1968. Thus it is that the Director of the Ecole Normale Supérieure, Robert Flacelière, who made a very firm stand against the student movement, is surrounded on the diagram by the names of the professors who signed motions in support of his action, whereas those who took up positions favourable to the movement are all situated in the opposite area. This means that it is not, as is usually thought, political stances which determine people's stances on things academic, but their positions in the academic field which inform the stances that they adopt on political issues in general as well as on academic problems. The margin of autonomy which ultimately devolves to the specifically political sources of the production of opinions then varies according to the degree to which the interests directly associated with their position in the academic field are directly concerned or, in the case of the dominant agents, threatened.

But one could go further and reintroduce into the model not only the political stance but also the works themselves, considered in their most visibly social properties, like their genre or their place of publication, and in their topic as well as their form: thus we see, for instance, that the distribution of works according to their degree of conformity to academic norms corresponds to the distribution of their authors according to their possession of specifically academic power. And to give a more concrete idea of this relation I need only mention the astonishment of a certain young American visitor, at the beginning of the seventies, to whom I had to explain that all his intellectual heroes, like Althusser, Barthes, Deleuze, Derrida and Foucault, not to mention the minor prophets of the moment, held marginal positions in the university system which often disqualified them from officially directing research (in several cases, they had not themselves written a thesis, at least not in canonical form, and were therefore not allowed to direct one).

If we linger a while over the case of these philosophers, who are the most likely to be familiar to Anglo-Saxon readers, we see that! knowing the structure of the overall space in which they are situated enables us to put ourselves so to speak *in their place* in the social space, through a genuinely 'participant objectification' which has I nothing reductively polemical about it, and to reconstruct the point of, view from which their intellectual project was defined. As may be seen from the diagram, they were caught in a dual relation with the worlds of philosophy and the social sciences. Their relation to the temporally dominant pole of institutionalized philosophy, which, frozen in the motionless time of lectures informed by the eternal recurrence of the topics set for competitive examinations, is personified by the university professors who control the organs of reproduction of the corps, agencies entrusted with the selection of teachers for secondary education, such as the *agrégation* competitive examination, or for higher education, such as the Comité Consultatif des Universités, the Universities Consultative Committee. In their relation with the philosophical high priests of the Sorbonne, who, like most of them, are products of the 'great lay seminary', the Ecole Normale Supérieure, which is the apex of the whole academic hierarchy, they appear like religious heretics, Of, in other words, rather like freelance intellectuals installed within the university system itself, or at least, to venture a Derridean pun, encamped on the margins or in the marginalia of an academic empire threatened on all sides by barbarian invasions (that is, of course, as seen by the dominant fraction). More or less totally deprived of, or liberated from, the powers and privileges but also the tasks and the responsibilities of the ordinary professor (examining the entrance examinations, supervising theses, etc.) they have strong connections with the intellectual world, and especially with the avant-garde reviews (*Critique*, *Tel Quel*, etc.) and with journalism (especially the *Nouvel Observateur*): Michel Foucault is no doubt the most representative of this position, since, until the end of his life, and even when he became professor at the Collège de France (after this enquiry was completed), he remained almost entirely bereft of specifically academic and even scientific powers, and therefore of the clientele which these powers afford, even if because of his fame he wielded considerable power over the press and, through it, over the whole field of cultural production. The marginal nature of this position, even more striking in the cases of Althusser or Derrida, who held minor posts (tutor or *caïman*—'alligator', in Ecole Normale slang—at the Ecole Normale Supérieure), is obviously not unconnected with the fact that all these heretics with a vocation to become heresiarchs, beyond the differences, the divergencies, and sometimes the conflicts which separate them, share a sort of *anti-institutional mood* homologous in its form to that of a considerable fraction of students: they are inclined to react impatiently to the discrepancy between their already considerable fame in the outside world, that is, outside the university and also outside France, and the subaltern status which is accorded them inside the French university world, in collusion with their contempt and their rejection, by an institution which, when they were adolescents, had attracted and even consecrated them.[8]

If it was necessary to start by considering the case of the most obscure pole, it is because that is the one most likely to escape the foreign observer or the superficial analyst (not to mention the polemicist whose home ground it is), although it no doubt played a decisive part—and not just as a foil, but also as the opponent who had to be constantly fought in order to assert the right to exist or at least to subsist—in the same way that the old Sorbonne did, when faced with the *Annales* team, in the constitution or the reinforcement of the ethical or political dispositions which will define the general trend of the works. It remains the case that it is above all in relation to the other pole, that of the all-conquering social sciences, which are incarnated by Lévi-Strauss, who rehabilitates these disciplines

8 The University of Vincennes, created after 1968, crystallized the new intellectual lifestyle and established within the university itself, thereby greatly scandalizing the defenders of the old university, a version of intellectual life which in other times would have been relegated to intellectual reviews or bohemian cafes.

traditionally despised by the philosophy teachers from the Ecole Normale, and who establishes them as the paragon of intellectual achievement, under the heading of *anthropologie*, that it is necessary to redefine these philosophical projects which had initially been constituted between 1945 and 1955, both with reference to the phenomenological and existential tradition and the figure of the philosopher as endowed by Sartre with exemplary stature, and also, and above all, against it. The adoption, instead of the banal and restrictive term 'ethnology', of the term 'anthropology', which, borrowed from the Anglo-Saxon tradition, is also laden with all the prestige of a great philosophical past (it is in this period that Foucault translates and publishes Kant's *Anthropoiogy*), symbolizes the formidable challenge that the social sciences, through their most eminent representatives, offer to philosophy, which previously was all-powerful. This challenge comes out into the open in the confrontation between Lévi-Strauss and Sartre, in the first real protest against its undivided rule over the whole intellectual field for a quarter of a century. Indeed, although Sartre and Merleau-Ponty also had to take the social sciences into account during the preceding generation, they were in an incomparably easier situation, since, because of the extreme decadence of the Durkheimian school and the very inferior status of an empirical sociology still in its infancy I and 'compromised', in those highly politized times, by its American origins, they were confronted with only a 'scientistic' psychology (albeit with the exception of Piaget) and a psychoanalysis with no influence (despite the presence at the Sorbonne of Lagache, a fellow student of Sartre and Merleau-Ponty at the Ecole Normale).

Henceforth, as the final diagram clearly shows,[9] it is the social sciences as a whole or even as a mutually supportive autonomous bloc (the arts faculties become faculties of the arts and social sciences) which hold the symbolically dominant position, confronting the representatives of philosophy, threatened with an entirely new situation not only in its position of dominant discipline but also in its intellectual identity and its research programmes: this is the case in linguistics, a truly dominant discipline, with Benveniste and the virtual presence of Jakobson (living abroad but consecrated by Lévi-Strauss), and, albeit less importantly, Martinet; in

9 Since I am conscious that the analysis of the academic field which is presented in this book would lose a great deal of the interest which it can offer all those who are interested in the cultural production of France over the last twenty years if they were unable to make out the space of the works and the tendencies whose shadows loom behind the space of the positions, I have decided to spell out the names of the academics studied instead of leaving them in the semi-anonymity of their initials as I had done in the French edition in order to avoid the effects of denunciation or of over-interpretation which, with the passage of time (twenty years after the study) and the distance gained by the foreign observer, should today be attenuated.

'anthropology', with Lévi-Strauss, backed up by Dumézil; in history, with Braudel, long since consecrated by the long discussion that Sartre had devoted to his *Méditerranée,* working to lay the institutional foundations of a renovated and integrated social science, with the 6th section of the Ecole Pratique des Hautes Etudes, its prestigious scientific council (including Lévi-Strauss, Aron, Le Bras, Friedmann), its research centres in full development, its reviews (including *Les Annales,* inherited from Marc Bloch and Lucien Febvre, and *L'Homme,* founded by Lévi-Strauss, which supplants the ageing *Temps modernes,* relegated to the status of purveyor of partisan, Parisian literary essays), and, soon, its Parisian stronghold, the Maison des Sciences de I'Homme; in psychoanalysis with Lacan, who, socially and symbolically allied to Lévi-Strauss and to Merleau-Ponty, has great importance in the field (although he was not included in the correspondence analysis, and therefore not in the diagram, because he did not hold an official position in the university—the refusal to permit him to lecture at the Ecole Normale Superieure had been at the root of the revolt against Flacelière); in sociology itself which, although relegated to the bottom division of the major new intellectual powers, manages, through Raymond Aron and his polemics with Sartre or the new philosophical currents *(D'une sainte famille à l'autre),* to command the respect of a generation of philosophers who had still been brought up to write essays on the themes launched, between the two wars, by the *Introduction to the Philosophy of History.*

One might also pause for a moment to consider the case of Roland Barthes, which shows us more clearly than others the relation of twofold difference which is characteristic of the avant-garde of the seventies: not being one of the institutional elite (he is neither *normalien* nor *agrégé,* nor a 'philosopher'), and, doubtless moved by the obscure sentiment of revenge felt by the outsider, he is able to engage with the ordinary professors (represented in this instance by Picard) in public controversy which their feelings of statutory dignity prohibit in the more consecrated of the young heresiarchs; and he can also display towards the great masters, who accumulate both ordinary and extraordinary claims to his gratitude, an unambiguous reverence, which others grant only in much more subtle or perverse forms. Condensing in his social being the tensions or contradictions inherent in the awkward position of the marginal academic institutions (like the Ecole des Hautes Etudes 'après Braudel' or, at other times, Nanterre or Vincennes), which try to convert a twofold opposition, often linked to a double privation, into a willed transcendence, and which, as places of transit for some and as terminus for others, cause divergent trajectories to meet momentarily, Roland Barthes represents the peak of the class of essayists, who, having nothing to oppose to the forces of the field, are condemned, in order to exist, or subsist, to float with the tides of the external or internal forces which wrack the milieu, notably through journalism. He calls to mind the image of a Theophile Gautier whom a contemporary described as 'a spirit floating on every breeze, quivering at every touch, able to absorb every impression and to retransmit it in turn, but needing to be set in motion by a neighbouring spirit, always eager to borrow a watchword, which so many others would then come to seek from him': like the good Théo, who was accused of lacking 'character' by his friend Flaubert who failed to see that his very inconsistency was the source of his importance, and who inspired someone else to remark that he adopted in turns the Chinese, the Greek, the Spanish, the medieval, the sixteenth-century, the Louis XIII, the Louis XIV, the rococo and the romantic styles, Roland Barthes gives instantaneous expression to all the changes in the forces of the field while appearing to anticipate them, and in this respect it is sufficient to follow his itinerary, and his successive enthusiasms, to discover all the tensions which were applied to the point of least resistance of the field, where what is called fashion continually flowers.

It is clear that the relation of twofold opposition would inevitably be experienced very differently according to the position occupied in the field and the previous trajectory, as we have just seen in the case of Roland Barthes, and according to the specifically philosophical capital which could be invested in the effort to overcome the tension it engendered. Those who, like Althusser and above all Foucault, had been led by their rejection of what has been called the 'philosophy of the subject', and of the 'humanism' associated with existentialist ideas, towards a tradition of epistemology and of history of science represented by Gaston Bachelard, Georges Canguilhem and Alexandre Koyré (among others), were predisposed, with that touch of ostentatious extravagance needed to signal their distance from the 'positivism' of the scholars ('Man is dead ...'),[10] to identify with the 'subjectless philosophy', which Lévi-Strauss, loyal in this to the Durkheimian tradition, had just reaffirmed, giving it a modernist air by referring to a notion of the unconscious which reconciled Freud revised by Lacan, Saussure summarized by Jakobson, and, if not the old Durkheim, still excluded from the very closed circle of distinguished philosophers, at least Marcel Mauss, easier to adapt at the cost of some bold reinterpretations to the new intellectual regime (Merleau-Ponty, who played an important part in the transition between the two intellectual generations because of his particularly open and comprehensive attitude towards the social sciences, notably biology, psychology and linguistics, had written an article entitled 'From Mauss to Lévi-Strauss'). Thus through a strange ruse of intellectual reason it happened that the Durkheimian philosophy of man became rehabilitated, with the more acceptable face of an anthropology legitimated by linguistics, in opposition

10 'L'Homme est mort' was a phrase of Foucault's in *Les Mots et les choses*, Paris, 1966 (*The Order of Things*, London, 1970). [Tr.]

to the 'philosophy of the subject' that an earlier generation of *normaliens*, that of Sartre, Aron and Nizan, had set up in the thirties in opposition to this 'totalitarian' philosophy of the Durkheimians, among others.

But, let there be no mistake about it, the acknowledgement of the social sciences implies no unconditional surrender. Although each philosopher in his own way betrays his deference to or dependence on the social sciences—if only, like Derrida, by choosing them as the target of his criticism, or by borrowing their themes (for instance the criticism of the use of pairs of adjectives in literary criticism)—the philosophers constantly mark (and not least in their style, as with Foucault, who indulges in set-pieces of rhetorical elegance, or with Derrida who imports into the philosophical field the procedures and effects which are used in *Tel Quel* circles) their statutory distance from the ordinary practitioners of the 'so-called social sciences', as Althusser liked to put it (and thus, not surprisingly, they elicit quite a different reaction from those who read them and expect to find in their reading a demonstration of the dignity which they invest in their writing). And they deploy all the resources of their culture in order to transfigure, perhaps above all in their own eyes, the 'historicist' philosophy which they borrow from social science along with many of its themes, its problems and its mode of thought. Thus it is that Foucault finds in Nietzsche an acceptable philosophical sponsor for the socially improbable combination of artistic transgression and scientific invention that he achieves and for the screen-concepts which, like that of genealogy, help to provide a cover for an ambitious enterprise in social history or genetic sociology. Similarly, as I have shown in the case of the analysis which he devoted to the *Critique of Judgement*, Derrida knows how to suspend (deconstruction' just in time to prevent it tipping over into a sociological analysis bound to be perceived as a vulgar 'sociologistic reduction', and thus avoids deconstructing himself *qua* philosopher.[11]

In addition to all this argument, which cannot take the place of genuine genetic sociology of the works themselves, perceived from the particular points of view (specified by the secondary social, religious or sexual characteristics of the different producers) in which they were elaborated, we could not understand the critical liberty which gives these works a family resemblance and which makes them much more than variously successful reconversions of the philosophical enterprise, if we failed to see that this critical liberty is rooted in the especially intense experience of an especially dramatic crisis. The previously dominant disciplines, philology, literary history and even philosophy, whose intellectual foundations are threatened by their new rivals, disciplines like linguistics, semiology, anthropology,

---

11 Cf. P. Bourdieu, *Distinction: A Social Critique of the Judgement of Taste*, trans. R. Nice, Cambridge, Mass., Harvard University Press, 1984, pp. 494ff.

or even sociology, find that the social foundations of their academic existence are also under siege from the criticisms welling up on all sides, usually in the name of the social sciences and on the initiative of teachers from these disciplines, against the archaic nature of their contents and their pedagogical structures. This double criticism frequently awakens touching reactions of traditionalist conservatism in those professors who did not have the instinct and the boldness to recycle themselves in time, and in particular among those whom I call the 'oblates'[12] and who, consigned from childhood to the school institution (they are often children of the lower or middle classes or sons of teachers), are totally dedicated to it. These reactions are bound to exacerbate the revolt of those who are by their capital and dispositions led to break simultaneously with institutionalized philosophy and the philosophical institution. The break, which sometimes takes on the aspect of a civil war, is accomplished in fact, well before 1968, between the professors who remained attached to the traditional definition of their discipline and the social foundations of its existence in terms of a social body (like the *agrégation*), and the members of the new avant-garde who managed to find in the resources Inherent In membership of a prestigious discipline the means necessary to operate a successful reconversion and who are perceived as traitors or renegades by the guardians of orthodoxy—who, like themselves, are products of the 'great seminary'. All the more so because these modernists, despite being called by a precocious and often dramatic consecration to fulfil the highest academic destinies, found that they were relegated, often with their own connivance, to awkward positions which predispose them to feel and express, whether in direct or in transposed forms, a crisis of the academic institution of which their very position in the institution is proof enough. A crisis affecting an institution which has the function of inculcating and imposing forms of thought must weaken or ruin the social foundations of thought, bringing in its wake a crisis of faith, a veritable, practical *epoche* of doxa, which encourages and facilitates the appearance of a reflexive awareness of these foundations. If the experience and the expression of this crisis took a more radical form in France than elsewhere, it is because, owing to the particularly archaic nature of an educational system hypnotized by illusory images of its grandeur, those consecrated by a bankrupt institution were obliged, if they were to be worthy of the ambitions which it had inculcated in them, to break with the derisory and henceforth untenable roles which it assigned to them, and were led to invent new ways of playing the part of the teacher (all based on adopting a reflexive distance from practice and from the ordinary definition of their functions), by lending him

12 'Oblates': see note 31 to chapter 2. [Tr.]

the strange features of an intellectual master of reflection who reflects on himself and in so doing, helps to destroy himself qua master.[13]

Because of their self-critical dispositions and their impatience with authority, and especially with the power wielded in the name of science, these self-destructive masters were prepared to harmonize their rhythms with the movements which pulsated through the ethical and political avant-garde of the student world. The students of bourgeois origins who have become academically downclassed, and who populate the arts faculties, especially in the new disciplines, are victims of verdicts which, like those of the school, appeal to reason and science in order to block off the paths leading (back) to power. They are spontaneously inclined to denounce science, power, the power of science, and above all perhaps a power which, like the triumphant technocracy of the moment, appeals to science in order to legitimate itself. Moreover, the new 'student life' which is created in the faculties suddenly invaded by an incomparably more numerous and more diversified clientele than in the past, in terms both of social origins and of gender (it is around 1970 that girls become as numerous as boys in the arts faculties) forms a social experiment through which, as in bohemian circles in the nineteenth century, a new bourgeois 'life-style' developed, making room for values excluded from the old, pre-war, neo-Kantian university and still not admitted in the disciplines professed by the boarding schools leading to the 'schools, for the elite'—that is, desire, pleasure and 'anti-repressive' dispositions, All these are themes which will be strongly orchestrated by all the philosophical avant-garde,[14] from Deleuze to Foucault via Derrida and even Althusser (with his 'ideological state apparatuses'), not to mention the minor heresiarchs, more closely 'tuned in' to the new vulgate.[15]

I have made no concessions in writing this book, but I trust that it bears no malice, for it comprises, as the reader will have guessed, a considerable proportion of self-analysis by proxy, as well as a distance, no doubt encouraged by sociology but first affirmed in the fact of abandoning philosophy for the social sciences—and that obviously, at a time when, thanks to Lévi-Strauss's rehabilitation of ethnology,

13 It is a singularity absolutely analogous to that of the nineteenth-century academic institution entrusted with training and consecrating painters, and, particularly, the extraordinary concentration in the hands of the great dignitaries of the Academy of the power of consecration and, thereby, access to the market, which goes a long way towards explaining why the revolution which gave birth to modern painting, with Manet and impressionism, appeared in France earlier than elsewhere.

14 One tends to forget that the student revolt of May 1968 was triggered by a clash between students and the academic authorities over freedom of access to female students' accommodation.

15 These 'minor heresiarchs' are Jean Baudrillard, Jean-François Lyotard, among others. [Tr.]

it became possible to do so without stooping too low ... And the special place held in my work by a somewhat singular sociology of the university institution is no doubt explained by the peculiar force with which I felt the need to gain rational control over the disappointment felt by an 'oblate' faced with the annihilation of the truths and values to which he was destined and dedicated, rather than take refuge in feelings of self-destructive resentment.

CHAPTER THIRTY-THREE

On the University

From *Edward Said and Critical Decolonization* (2007)

EDWARD W. SAID

This selection by Edward E. Said is taken from *Edward Said and Critical Decolonization*, 2007, Edited by Feril J. Ghazoul. Published by The American University in Cairo Press. Cairo, Egypt.

Editors' Note

Edward Said was a literary theorist born in Palestine who established postcolonial criticism through his book *Orientalism* (1979) that drawing on the work of Foucault and others studied how the Western world inaccurately represents the East as the Orient and initiated an analysis of the politics of the discourse that serves to maintain colonial and postcolonial orders. *Orientalism* analysed the different forms that a persistent Eurocentrism falsely depicts and distorts the Arab and Islamic cultures as oil suppliers and terrorists, and sometimes in terms of exotic and romantic representations that focuses on sexuality and brutality. This Said argues is a form of cultural imperialism. Much of his work revolves around questions of nationalism, colonialism and literature, representations of intellectuals, decolonization and forms of democratic criticism. He argued 'humanism is not a way of consolidating and affirming what "we" have always known and felt, but rather a means of questioning, upsetting, and reformulating so much of what is presented to us as commodified, packaged, uncontroversial, and uncritically codified certainties' (Said, 2004, p. 28). 'On the University' was first given at the American University in Cairo's Seventy-Sixth Annual Commencement where he argues: 'To assume that the ends of education are best advanced by focusing principally on our own separateness, or what accords with our own ethnic identity, culture, and traditions ironically places us where, as inferior or lesser races, we had been placed by nineteenth-century racial theory, unable to share in the general riches of human culture.'

MP

Recommended Reading

Said, Edward (1979). *Orientalism.* New York, Vintage.
Said, Edward (2004). *Humanism and Democratic Criticism.* New York, Columbia University Press.

* * * * *

Mr. President, Senator Hatfield, members of the AUC Board of Trustees, members of the AUC faculty and administrative staff, members of the graduating class, distinguished guests, parents, relatives and friends, ladies and gentlemen:

I don't mind admitting to you as a sign of my almost biblical age, that I grew up in Cairo fifty years ago during the 1940s, and that the American University in Cairo was the first university I had anything to do with. Two of my Jerusalem cousins were students here, my father was a close friend of John Badeau, AUC's president then, later John Kennedy's Ambassador to Egypt, and, finally, Ewart Hall was Cairo's main concert hall, where the rudiments of my musical education were formed. I was also gradually aware of AUC's great national counterparts, Cairo University, and al-Azhar, each of them, like AUC, doing something very valuable for generations of Egyptian, Arab, and Muslim students. I am also proud to say that in 1994 my son Wadie perfected his quite extraordinary command of Arabic at CASA here, a major achievement for a New York City kid who, as a matter of solidarity with his Arab origin, made himself remarkably fluent in the language and culture of his heritage, at a time when both were objects of cultural hostility in the United States, the land of his birth and upbringing.

I am honored and pleased to be here today, first, as an Arab Palestinian and a child of Egypt's immense and unparalleled cultural history, and, second, as an American. The combination of these two different strains in AUC, and of course in you, the class of 1999, the last class of the century, is both highly challenging and even enriching, but it is also quite problematic. Anyone who knows both societies knows what kinds of differences exist between American and Egyptian societies, so I won't dwell here on what is obvious. What is worth noting is that in institutions like AUC, and its counterpart AUB, the idea of a secular liberal education, pioneered in the nineteenth and twentieth centuries by the great colleges of the United States, was implanted with very positive results in mostly Islamic, Arab, and, in terms of sheer longevity, extremely old societies in the process of renewing and liberating themselves after long periods of outside domination.

Whatever the results of this bold mixture, they are neither simple nor entirely predictable. Each of you, teachers and students alike, must have your own assessment based on your years of interacting with dizzyingly different ideas, different personal experiences, expectations, frustrations, and fulfillments, but I can't imagine that anyone of you would say that the results were anything less than interesting, rich, and, yes, unsettling. The main thing, though, is that this collective, mixed experience of yours has taken place, and for future students and teachers will continue to take place, in a very special location, namely, a university. As someone who has spent all his adult life working in, and for, the university, let me assure you, as one of my own teachers once said it, it's certainly a lot more fun than working. Many of you, graduates with real jobs in the real world, will certainly discover that.

But that isn't my main point, which is that in every known society—from the ancient Near East, the Arab world to China, India, Greece, and elsewhere—the academy, as Plato called it, was a protected, almost utopian place. Only there could collective learning and the development of knowledge occur and, as in recent years we have discovered, it could occur only if academic freedom from non-academic authority was somehow guaranteed and could prevail. It is an extraordinary thing to discover via George Makdisi's remarkable book The Rise of Humanism in Classical Islam and the Christian West that the origins of the modern system of knowledge that we call humanism did not originate, as Jakob Burkhardt and many others believed it did, in Italy during the fifteenth- and sixteenth-century Renaissance, but, rather, in the Arab colleges, madrasas, mosques, and courts of Iraq, Sicily, Egypt, Andalusia, from the eighth century on. And in those places were formed the traditions and the curricula of legal, theological, as well as secular, learning—the so-called studia adabiya—from which European humanists, like Pico della Mirandola, Ficino, Aretino, and Thomas Moore, derived many of their ideas, not only about learning itself, but also about the environment of learning, where disputation, dissent, and argument were the order of the day.

For those of us who are of Arab origin, and who in the modern period have gotten used to the notion that Europe and the West gave rise to modes of study, notions of academic discipline, and the whole idea of what in Arabic we call ijtihad, or the central role of individual effort in study and interpretation, it is salutary indeed to realize that our Arab-Islamic culture contributed substantially to what later was to become the whole system of education, which today we call modern, liberal, and Western. I have very little patience with ethnocentrism of the kind trumpeted by Samuel Huntington, and others like him who claim that all ideas of democracy, freedom, and enlightenment are Western ideas, since the facts of history are, as we now know with reference to education, very mixed, very various, very much a matter of the contribution made by all humankind, all peoples, all cultures. There isn't a single source for anything: All peoples share in the making of history, all peoples make history. So let us agree, then, that whether we look to the time of Ibn 'Abbad or Ibn 'Arabi, or that of John Dewey in the twentieth century, we will find serious thinkers suggesting more or less the same thing, that the place of education is a special province within the society, a place where freedom of inquiry and thought occur and are protected, and where—it must be said—the social and political context plays an important role, by defining the limits and expectations of the learning process. The American University in Cairo is in Cairo, therefore, not in New York or London. That is obvious. Cairo is a specific environment with its own history, laws, language, and norms: Not to take account of all of that is plain wrong.

Yet, the status of university or school, as well as what goes along with them intellectually and socially, is special, is different from other sites in society, like the government bureaucracy, the workplace, or the home. The fact is, I believe, that all societies today assign a special privilege to the academy that, whether it exempts it from intercourse with the everyday world or whether it involves it directly in that world, says that unique conditions do, indeed ought to, prevail in it. To say that someone is educated, or an educator, is to say something having to do with the mind, with intellectual and moral values, with a particular process of inquiry, discussion, and exchange, none of which is as regularly encountered outside as they are inside the academy. The idea is that academies form the mind of the young, prepare them for life, just as—to look at things from the point of view of the teacher to teach is to be engaged in a vocation or calling having principally to do, not with financial gain, but with the unending search for truth.

These are very high and important matters, and for those of us who have made education our life, they testify to the genuine aura surrounding the academic and intellectual enterprise. There is something hallowed and consecrated about the academy: There is a sense of violated sanctity, experienced by us when the university or school is subjected to crude political pressures. Yet, I believe, to be convinced of these genuinely powerful truths is not entirely to be freed of the circumstances—some would call them encumbrances—that impinge on education today, influence our thinking about it, shape our efforts in the academy. The point

I want to make is that, as we consider these situational or contextual matters, the search for academic freedom, to which such occasions as this are so manifestly dedicated, becomes more important, more urgent, more requiring of careful and reflective analysis. So whereas it is universally true that contemporary societies treat the academy with seriousness and respect, each community of academics, intellectuals, and students must wrestle with the problem of what academic freedom in that society at that time actually is, and should be.

The best definition of a university that I know is by John Henry Cardinal Newman, who in 1854 came from England to Ireland to establish what has since become University College, Dublin. Here is what he said on the occasion:

A university has this object and this mission; it contemplates neither moral impression nor mechanical production; it professes to exercise the mind neither in art nor in duty; its function is intellectual culture; here it may leave its scholars, and it has done its work when it has done as much as this. It educates the intellect to reason well in all matters, to reach out towards truth and to grasp it.

Perhaps you young graduates don't feel that you had this experience, or perhaps you feel that, now that you have finished your course of study, you need no longer be concerned with the university, except as an alumnus. That would be a mistake. You are not only graduates and former students, you are citizens, and citizenship requires resolute attention to what is most important about the life of your society. And surely there can be nothing more important in the long run of Egypt's life than education, and the life of the mind, especially here in our part of the world, where, alas, we lag behind in democracy, the freedoms of expression, opinion, and the press, and full participation in societies so long dominated by national security concerns, and not the intellectual and civic health of the people. So the freedom of the university is a lifelong concern, and it requires your sustained support and concern.

But to return to Newman. Note the care with which he selects his words for what actions take place in the pursuit of knowledge: words like exercise, educates, reach out, and grasp. In none of these words is there anything to suggest coercion, or direct utility, or immediate advantage or dominance. "Knowledge," Newman says in another place, is "something intellectual, something which grasps what it perceives through the senses; something which takes a view of things; which sees more than the senses convey; which reasons upon what it sees, and while it sees; which invests it with an idea." Then he adds: "not to know the relative disposition of things is the state of slaves or children; to have mapped out the universe is the boast, or at least the ambition, of philosophy," which Newman defines as the highest state of knowledge.

These are incomparably eloquent statements, and they can only be a little deflated when we remind ourselves that Newman was speaking to, and about,

English men, not women, and then also about the education of young Catholics, not of Egyptians or Arabs. Nonetheless, the profound truth in what Newman says is, I believe, designed to undercut any partial, or somehow narrow, view of education whose aim might seem only to re-affirm one particularly attractive and dominant identity, religion, and authority, that which is the resident power or authority of the moment. Perhaps, like many of his Victorian contemporaries, Newman was arguing earnestly for a type of education that placed the highest premium on English, European, or Christian values in knowledge. But sometimes, even though we may mean to say something, another thought at odds with what we say insinuates itself into our rhetoric, and in effect criticizes it, delivers a different and less assertive idea than on the surface we might have intended. This happens when we read Newman. Suddenly we realize that, although he is obviously extolling what is an overridingly Western conception of the world, with little explicit allowance made for what is African, or Arab, or Latin American, or Indian, we realize that he says that education should map out the universe, thus letting slip the notion that even an English or Western identity wasn't enough, wasn't at bottom, or at best, what education and freedom were all about, which are about "the universe."

Certainly, it is difficult to find in Newman anything like a license, either for blinkered specialization or for gentlemanly aestheticism. What he expects of the academy is, he says, "the power of viewing many things at once as one whole, of referring them severally to their true place in the universal system, of understanding their respective values, and determining their mutual dependence." This synthetic wholeness has a special relevance to the fraught political situations of conflict, the unresolved tension, and social as well as moral disparities that are constitutive to the world of today's academy. He proposes a large and generous view of human diversity. To link the practice of education and, by extension, of freedom in the academy directly to the settling of political scores, or to an equally unmodulated reflection of real national and religious conflict, is neither to pursue knowledge nor, in the end, to educate ourselves and our students, which is an everlasting effort at understanding. But what happens when we take Newman's prescriptions about viewing many things as one whole, or referring them to their true place in the universal system, and we transpose these notions to today's world of embattled national identities, cultural conflicts, and power relations? Is there any possibility of bridging the gap between the ivory tower of contemplative rationality, ostensibly advocated by Newman, and our own urgent need as Arabs for self-realization and self-assertion with its background in a history of repression and denial? Can the university survive as a real university if its governance and teaching mission become the objects of scrutiny and direct interference, not of its teachers, but of powers outside the university?

I think not. I will go further and say that it is precisely the role of the contemporary academy to keep open the gap between itself and society, since society itself is too directly ruled by politics to serve so general and so finally intellectual and moral a role as the university plainly must. We must first, I think, accept that nationalism or religion resurgent, or even nationalism and religion militant, whether it is the nationalism of the victim or of the victor, such a nationalism has its limits. Nationalism and religion are the philosophy of identity made into a collectively organized passion. For those of us just emerging from marginality and persecution, our traditions constitute a necessary thing: A long deferred and denied identity needs to come out into the open and take its place among other human identities. But that is only the first step. To make all, or even most of, education subservient to this goal is to limit human horizons, without either intellectual or, I would argue, political warrant. To assume that the ends of education are best advanced by focusing principally on our own separateness, or what accords with our own ethnic identity, culture, and traditions ironically places us where, as inferior or lesser races, we had been placed by nineteenth-century racial theory, unable to share in the general riches of human culture. To say that women should read mainly an approved women's literature, Muslims should study and perfect only approved Muslim techniques of understanding and interpretation, that Arabs should return to a set of acceptable works for all knowledge and wisdom, that they should in a university read only what is considered safe and orthodox, is in fact to keep us back, to prevent us from participating in the march of humanity. There is room for all at the rendezvous of victory, said Aime Cesaire; no race has a monopoly on beauty or intelligence.

A single over-mastering identity guided by a religious or secular authority outside the academy at the core of the academic enterprise, whether that identity be Western, African, Islamic, Arab, or Asian, is a confinement, a deprivation. The world we live in is made up of numerous identities, numerous ideas, lives, philosophies interacting, sometimes harmoniously, sometimes antithetically. Not to deal with that whole—which is in fact a contemporary version of the whole referred to by Newman as a true enlargement of mind—is not to have academic freedom. We cannot make our claim as seekers after justice, if we advocate knowledge only of and about ourselves, knowledge only that is approved by a team of referees who decide what can and cannot be read. Who then will referee the referees? Now, one of the innovations of an American University in Egypt is precisely that it encourages its students to experience not only their culture and traditions, but another set as well. This, I believe, is deeply enriching, perhaps unsettling, and the very opposite of homogenizing learning into only one approved form. But it is being challenged, and it must resist attempts at book banning or prohibiting ideas.

Our model for academic freedom should therefore be the migrant or traveler: For if, in the real world outside the academy, we must needs be ourselves and only ourselves, inside the academy, like this one, we should be able to discover and travel among other selves, other identities, other varieties of the human adventure. But, most essentially, in this joint discovery of self and other, it is the role of the academy to transform what might be conflict, or contest, or assertion into reconciliation, mutuality, recognition, creative interaction. But, rather than viewing the search for knowledge in the academy as the search for coercion and control over others, we should regard knowledge as something for which risks must be taken, and we should think of academic freedom as an invitation to explore knowledge, in the hope of understanding, and perhaps even assuming, more than one kind. We must always view the academy as a place to voyage in, owning none of it, but at home everywhere in it. There can be no forbidden knowledge if the modern university is to maintain its place, its mission, its power to educate.

An altogether different challenge to the concept of academic freedom is found in national universities in much of the contemporary Arab world. I speak here, generally, of most of the large public universities in countries all through the area. Most of these countries are, in fact, run by secular governments. What is important to understand, however, is that, with few exceptions, Arab universities are not only nationalist universities, but are also political institutions, for perfectly understandable reasons. In Palestine, Bir Zeit and al-Najah, for instance, have resisted Israeli occupation and preserved Palestinian identity admirably. Elsewhere, the Arab world which had been dominated, either by Ottoman or by European colonialism, became independent after World War II. National independence, for countries like Egypt and Syria, meant that young people at last could be educated fully in the traditions, histories, languages, and cultures of their own particular Arab countries. In my own case, for instance, I was educated entirely in British colonial schools, in Palestine and Egypt, where everything was focused on the history of British society, its literature, and values. Much the same was true in the main British and French colonies, such as India and Algeria, where it was assumed that native elites would be taught the rudiments of intellectual culture, in idioms and methods designed, in effect, to keep those native elites basically subservient to colonial rule, the superiority of European learning, and so forth. Until I was about sixteen, I knew a great deal more about the eighteenth-century enclosure system in England than I did about how the Islamic waqf operated in my own part of the world, and to me—irony of ironies—colonial proconsuls, like Cromer and Kitchener, were more familiar to me than Haroun al-Rashid or Khalid ibn al-Walid.

So that when independence was achieved, as a result of anticolonial struggles, one of the first things to be changed was education. I recall, for instance, that after the Revolution of 1952 in Egypt, a great deal of emphasis was placed on the Arabization of the curriculum, of intellectual norms, of values to be inculcated in schools and universities. The same was true of Algeria after 1962, where an entire generation of Muslims were, for the first time, entitled and enjoined to study Arabic, which had been forbidden except as a language in mosques, while Algeria was considered and ruled as a department of France. It is important to understand, therefore, the justified passion that went into reclaiming the educational territory, for so long dominated by foreign rulers in the Arab world, and it is equally important to understand the tremendous spiritual wound felt by many of us, because of the sustained presence in our midst of domineering foreigners who taught us to respect distant norms and values more than our own. Our culture was felt to be of a lower grade, perhaps even congenitally inferior, and something to be ashamed of.

Now it would be both wrong, and even absurd, to suggest that a national education based on Arabic norms is, and of itself, either trivial or impoverished. Of course not. Yet, it is also true to say that in the newly independent countries of the Arab world, the national universities were often re-conceived, I believe, as (rightly or wrongly) extensions of the newly established national security state. Once again, it is clear that all societies accord a remarkable privilege to the university and school, as crucibles for the shaping of national identity. This is true everywhere, at sometimes too high a price. In the US there was a great deal of pressure on universities to benefit the defense department, especially during the Cold War and the Vietnam War.

Yet, all too often in the Arab world, true education has been short-circuited, so to speak. Whereas in the past young Arabs fell prey to the intervention of foreign ideas and norms, now they were to be remade in the image of the ruling party, which, given the Cold War, and the Arab-Israeli struggle, became also the party of national security, and, in some countries, the only party. Thus adding to the vastly increased pressure on universities to open their doors to everyone in the new society—an extremely admirable policy pioneered in Egypt—universities also became the proving ground for earnest patriots. This was also true during the McCarthy period in the US, when anyone suspected of left-wing ideas was persecuted. Professorial appointments were, as they are in many places in the world today, the equivalent of civil service appointments. Yet, alas, political conformity, rather than intellectual excellence, was often made to serve as a criterion for promotion and appointment, with the general result that timidity, a studious lack of imagination, careful conservatism came to rule intellectual practice. This is a danger everywhere—in the US, Europe, the Third World, etc. Often the atmosphere of the university has changed from freedom to accommodation, from brilliance and daring to caution and fear, from the advancement of knowledge to self-preservation.

Not only did many brilliant and gifted people leave the Arab world in a massive brain drain, but I would say that the whole notion of academic freedom underwent a significant downgrading during the past three decades. It became possible for one to be free in the university only if one completely avoided anything that might attract unwelcome attention or suspicion. I do not want to make of this occasion a long, anguished recital of how badly demoralized and discouraged a place the Arab world, in most of its contemporary aspects, has become, but I do think it is important to link its depressed situation with the lack of democratic rights, the absence of a free press, and of an atmosphere bereft of well-being and confidence in the society. No one can say that these things are not connected to each other, because they so obviously are. Political repression has never been good for academic freedom, and, perhaps more importantly, it has been disastrous for academic and intellectual excellence when such things as book banning and censorship are practiced. My assessment, as I said, is that too high a price has been paid where political or religious passions, and an ideology of conformity, are allowed to dominate, and perhaps even to swallow up, civil institutions, such as the university. To make the practice of intellectual discourse dependent upon conformity to a pre-determined political or religious ideology is to nullify intellect altogether.

It comes, finally, to two images for inhabiting the academic and cultural space provided by the university. On the one hand, authority is there in order to reign and hold sway. Here, in such a conception of academic space, the academic professional and the public authority is the sultan and potentate. In that form, teaching teaches students not to question, but to follow authority, not to be sceptical—which is to continue searching—but to cling to dogma. The other model is considerably more mobile, more playful, although no less serious. The image of traveler depends not on power, but on motion, on a willingness to go into different worlds, use different idioms, understand a variety of disguises, masks, rhetorics, and be free to do so, and to be critical, to think for oneself. Travelers must suspend the claim of customary routine, in order to live in new rhythms and rituals. Most of all, and most unlike the sultan who must guard only one place and defend its frontiers, the traveler crosses over, traverses territory, abandons fixed positions, all the time. To do this with dedication and love, as well as a realistic sense of the terrain, is, I believe, academic freedom at its highest, since one of its main features is that you can leave authority and dogma to the sultan. Academic freedom is risk and danger. It means allowing oneself a few years where the conventions of society are suspended, so that the search for knowledge can go on for the love of knowledge alone. To be a life-long member in the academic world, as you new graduates and your teachers are, is therefore to enter a ceaseless quest for principles and knowledge, liberation, and finally justice.

CHAPTER THIRTY-FOUR

The Idea of Excellence

From *The University of Ruins* (1996)

BILL READINGS

This selection is taken from *The University in Ruins*, by Bill Readings, 1996. Published by Harvard, University Press, Cambridge, MA.

Editors' Note

The University in Ruins—from which both of the extracts here are taken—is one of the foremost reflective books on the university that appeared in the second half of the twentieth century. Readings goes back to the Germanic origins of the modern university and sees the modern university as successively reflecting three ideas: 'the Kantian concept of reason, the Humboldtian idea of culture, and now the techno-bureaucratic notion of excellence' (p. 14). En route, the university moves from being an intellectual space to being 'an ideological apparatus of the nation state to being a relatively independent bureaucratic system'. And Readings charts this stage-by-stage evolution in some detail and also forensically pursues particular issues.

One of those issues is that of 'excellence' and, given the way in which the very term 'excellence' has become so ubiquitous, Readings' analysis is one of exceptional foresight. In brief, Readings argues that the idea of excellence is empty. To say of a university that it is 'excellent' tells us nothing. Indeed, 'the appeal to excellence marks the fact that there is no longer any idea of the University, or rather that the idea has now lost all content' (p. 39). The use of the term 'excellence' is a linguistic and tactical vehicle that allows for diversity in a market system of higher education. It is not even an ideological term for the university is now an 'autonomous bureaucratic corporation'.

Against this analysis, 'We have to recognize that the University is a ruined institution, while thinking what it means to dwell in those ruins without recourse to romantic nostalgia' (p. 169). Readings offers two gambits, first that 'the loosening of disciplinary structures has to be made the opportunity for the installation of disciplinarity as a permanent question' (p. 177). Second, the idea of community has to be rethought and—in a chapter not included here—Readings considers that 'we need to think about a community in which communication is not transparent' (p. 185) and urges a conception of community not based on a striving for consensus but situated against a 'horizon of dissensus' (p. 187). This is a community in which 'we do not know in advance the nature of our obligations to others' (p. 188). This is no less than a 'posthistorical university' (p. 192).

RB

* * * * *

The significance of making a distinction between the modern University as ideological arm of the nation-state and the contemporary University as bureaucratic corporation is that it allows one to observe an important phenomenon. "Excellence" is rapidly becoming the watchword of the University, and to understand the University as a contemporary institution requires some reflection on what the appeal to excellence may, or may not, mean.

A few months after I first gave a talk on the significance of the concept of excellence, Canada's principal weekly news magazine, *Maclean's*, brought out its third annual special issue on the Canadian universities, parallel to the kind of ranking produced by *U.S. News and World Report*. The November 15, 1993, issue of *Maclean's*, which purported to rank all the universities in Canada according to various criteria, was entitled, to my surprise, *A Measure of Excellence*.[1] Now what this suggests to me is that excellence is not simply the equivalent of "total quality management" (TQM). It is not just something imported into the University from business in the attempt to run the University *as if* it were a business. Such importations assume, after all, that the University is not really a business, is only like a business in some respects.

When Ford Motors enters into a "partnership" with The Ohio State University to develop "total quality management in all areas of life on campus," this partnership is based on the assumption that "the mission[s] of the university and the

---

1 *Maclean's*, 106, no. 46 (November 15, 1993).

corporation are not that different," as Janet Pichette, vice-president for business and administration at Ohio State, phrases it.[2] Not "that different" perhaps, but not identical either. The University is on the way to becoming a corporation, but it has yet to apply TQM to all aspects of its experience, although the capacity of Ohio State's president E. Gordon Gee to refer to "the university and the customers it serves" is a sign that Ohio State is well on the way. The invocation of "quality" is the means of that transformation, since "quality" can apply to "all areas of life on campus" indifferently, and can tie them together on a single evaluative scale. As the campus newspaper, the *Ohio State Lantern*, reports it: "Quality is the ultimate issue for the university and the customers it serves, Gee said, referring to faculty, students, their parents, and alumni."[3] The need felt by the author of this article to clarify the question of to whom the president was referring in speaking of the University's "customers" is a touching sign of an almost archaic vision of education, one that imagines that some confusion might still arise on the issue.

Hence we might suggest a clarification for President Gee: quality is not the ultimate issue, but excellence soon will be, because it is the recognition that the University is not just *like* a corporation; it *is* a corporation. Students in the University of Excellence are not *like* customers; they *are* customers. For excellence implies a quantum leap: the notion of excellence develops *within* the University, as the idea around which the University centers itself and through which it becomes comprehensible to the outside world (in the case of *Maclean's*, the middle and upper classes of Canada).

Generally, we hear a lot of talk from University administrators about excellence, because it has become the unifying principle of the contemporary University. C. P. Snow's "Two Cultures" have become "Two Excellences," the humanistic and the scientific.[4] As an integrating principle, excellence has the singular advantage of being entirely meaningless, or to put it more precisely, non-referential. Here is one example of the way in which excellence undermines linguistic reference, in a letter to faculty and staff from a dean of engineering (William Sirignano) complaining about his dismissal by the chancellor of the University of California at Irvine (Laurel Wilkening), reported in the campus newspaper:

> "The Office of the President and the central administration at the VCI campus are too embroiled in crisis management, self-service and controversy to be a great force for

---

2 Quoted in Aruna Jagtiani, "Ford Lends Support to Ohio State," *Ohio State Lantern*, July 14, 1994, p. 1.

3 Ibid.

4 See C. P. Snow, *Two Cultures and A Second Look* (Cambridge: Cambridge University Press, 1969).

> *excellence* in academic programs," Sirignano wrote in the Mar. 22 memo. He encouraged the new dean, department chairs and faculty to "create those pressures for *excellence* for the school" ... The transition in leadership "will be a challenge to the pursuit of *excellence* and upward mobility for the School of Engineering," he said. "It's not going to be easy to recruit an *excellent* dean in this time of fiscal crisis."[5]

In a situation of extreme stress, and in order to oppose the University president, the dean appeals to the language of excellence with a regularity that is the more remarkable in that it goes unremarked by the staff writer covering the incident.[6] Indeed, the staff writer has selected those phrases that include the word "excellence" as being those that most precisely sum up what the letter is about. Excellence appears here as uncontestable ground, the rhetorical arm most likely to gain general assent. To return to the example of the Ford-Ohio State partnership, a significant number of academics, I would guess, could see through the imposition from the outside of "total quality management," could resist the ideology implicit in the notion of quality and argue that the University was not as analogous to a business as Ford claimed. But Sirignano is an academic, writing to an academic, for an audience of academics. And his appeal to excellence is not hedged or mitigated, is not felt to require explanation. Quite the contrary. The need for excellence is what we all agree on. And we all agree upon it because it is not an ideology, in the sense that it has no external referent or internal content.

Today, all departments of the University can be urged to strive for excellence, since the general applicability of the notion is in direct relation to its emptiness. Thus, for instance, the Office of Research and University Graduate Studies at Indiana University at Bloomington explains that in its Summer Faculty Fellowship program "Excellence of the proposed scholarship is the major criterion employed in the evaluation procedure."[7] This statement is, of course, entirely meaningless, yet the assumption is that the invocation of excellence overcomes the problem of the question of value across disciplines, since excellence is the common denominator of good research in all fields. Even if this were so, it would mean that excellence could not be invoked as a "criterion," because excellence is not a fixed standard of

---

5 Phat X. Chern, "Dean of Engineering Forced Out," New University (University of California at Irvine), April 4, 1994, my italics.

6 Some sense of the distance we have travelled is apparent in the historical irony of the fact that this is a letter written to criticize the University on March 22, the very date recalled in the naming of the revolutionary movement in French universities in 1968 as "The Movement of March 22." *Sic transit.*

7 "Summer Faculty Fellowships: Information and Guidelines," Indiana University, Bloomington Campus, May 1994.

judgment but a qualifier whose meaning is fixed in relation to something else. An excellent boat is not excellent by the same *criteria* as an excellent plane. So to say that excellence is a criterion is to say absolutely nothing other than that the committee will not reveal the criteria used to judge applications.

Nor is the employment of the term "excellence" limited to academic disciplines within the University. For instance, Jonathan Culler has informed me that the Cornell University Parking Services recently received an award for "excellence in parking." What this meant was that they had achieved a remarkable level of efficiency in *restricting* motor vehicle access. As he pointed out, excellence could just as well have meant making people's lives easier by increasing the number of parking spaces available to faculty. The issue here is not the merits of either option but the fact that excellence can function equally well as an evaluative criterion on either side of the issue of what constitutes "excellence in parking," because excellence has no content to call its own. Whether it is a matter of increasing the number of cars on campus (in the interests of employee efficiency—fewer minutes wasted in walking) or decreasing the number of cars (in the interests of the environment) is indifferent; the efforts of parking officials can be described in terms of excellence in both instances.[8] Its very lack of reference allows excellence to function as a principle of translatability between radically different idioms: parking services and research grants can each be excellent, and their excellence is not dependent on any specific qualities or effects that they share.

This is clearly what is going on in the case of the *Maclean's* article, where excellence is the common currency of ranking. Categories as diverse as the make-up of the student body, class size, finances, and library holdings can all be brought together on a single scale of excellence. Such rankings are not entered into blindly or cavalierly. With a scrupulousness of which the academic community could be proud, the magazine devotes two whole pages to discussing how it produced its ratings. Thus, the student body is measured in terms of incoming grades (the higher the better), grade point average during study (the higher the better), the number of "out of province" students (more is better), and graduation rates within standard time limits (achieving normalization is a good thing). Class size and quality are measured in terms of the student-teacher ratio (which should be low) and the ratio of tenured faculty to part-timers or graduate teaching assistants (which should be high). Faculty are evaluated in terms of the number with Ph.D.'s, the number of award winners, and the number and quantity of federal grants obtained, all of which are taken to be signs of merit. The category "finances" judges the fiscal

8 As a purely internal unit of value, excellence shares with Machiavelli's *virtù* the advantage of permitting calculation to be engaged in on a homogeneous scale. On *virtù*, see Machiavelli, *The Prince*, ed. and tr. Robert M. Adams (New York: Norton, 1977).

health of a University in terms of the proportions of the operating budget available for current expenses, student services, and scholarships. Library holdings are analyzed in terms of volumes per student and the percentage of the university budget devoted to the library, as well as the percentage of the library budget dedicated to new acquisitions. A final category, "reputation," combines the number of alumni who give to the University with the results of a "survey of senior university officials and chief executive officers of major corporations across Canada" (p. 40). The result is a "measure of excellence" arrived at by combining the figures at a ratio of 20 percent for students, 18 percent for class size, 20 percent for faculty, 10 percent for finances, 12 percent for libraries, and 20 percent for "reputation."

A number of things are obvious about this exercise, most immediately the arbitrary quality of the weighting of factors and the dubiousness of such quantitative indicators of quality. Along with questioning the relative weight accorded to each of the categories, we can ask a number of fundamental questions about what constitutes "quality" in education. Are grades the only measure of student achievement? Why is efficiency privileged, so that it is automatically assumed that graduating "on time" is a good thing? How long does it take to become "educated"? The survey assumes that the best teacher is one who possesses the highest university degree and the most grants, the teacher who is the most faithful reproduction of the system. But what says that makes a good professor? Is the best University necessarily the richest one? What is the relation to knowledge implied by focusing on the library as the place where it is stocked? Is quantity the best measure of the significance of library holdings? Is knowledge simply to be reproduced from the warehouse, or is it something to be produced in teaching? Why should senior university officials and the CEOs of major corporations be the best judges of "reputation"? What do they have in common, and isn't this compatibility worrying? Does not the category of "reputation" raise prejudice to the level of an index of value? How were individuals chosen? Why is the "reputational survey" included in ranking designed to establish reputation?

Most of these questions are philosophical, in that they are systemically incapable of producing cognitive certainty or definitive answers. Such questions will necessarily give rise to further debate, for they are radically at odds with the logic of quantification. Criticism of the categories used (and the way upon which they are decided) has indeed been levelled at *Maclean's*, as it has at the *U.S. News and World Report's* equivalent survey. This is perhaps why *Maclean's* includes a further three-page article entitled "The Battle for the Facts," which portrays the heroic struggle of the journalists to find the truth despite the attempts of some universities to hide it. This essay also details the reservations expressed by a number of universities, for example the complaint of the president of Manitoba's Brandon University that "Many of the individual strengths of universities are not picked up in this ranking by *Maclean's*" (p. 46). Once again, the president argues only with the particular criteria, not with the logic of excellence and the ranking that it permits. And when the authors of the article remark that "The debate sheds a telling light on the deep unease over accountability," they do not refer to a critique of the logic of accounting. Far from it. Any questioning of such performance indicators is positioned as a resistance to public accountability, a refusal to be questioned according to the logic of contemporary capitalism, which requires "clear measures to establish university performance" (p. 48).

Given this situation, to question criteria is necessary, yet a more general point needs to be made concerning the general compliance of universities with the logic of accounting. The University and *Maclean's* appear to speak the same language, as it were: the language of excellence. Yet the question of what it means to "speak the same language" is a tricky one in Canada. This survey is going on in a country that is bilingual, where the different universities quite literally speak different languages. And behind the fact that the criteria are heavily biased in favor of anglophone institutions lies the fundamental assumption that there is a single standard, a measure of excellence, in terms of which universities can be judged. And it is excellence that allows the combination on a single scale of such utterly heterogeneous features as finances and the make-up of the student body. A measure of the flexibility of excellence is that it allows the inclusion of reputation as one category among others in a ranking which is in fact definitive of reputation. The metalepsis that allows reputation to be 20 percent of itself is permitted by the intense flexibility of excellence; it allows a category mistake to masquerade as scientific objectivity.

Most of all, excellence serves as the unit of currency within a closed field. The survey allows the a priori exclusion of all referential issues, that is, any questions about what excellence in the University might *be*, what the term might *mean*. Excellence is, and the survey is quite explicit about this, a means of relative ranking among the elements of an *entirely closed system*: "For the universities, meanwhile, the survey affords an opportunity for each to clarify its own vision—and to measure itself against its peers" (p. 40). Excellence is clearly a purely internal unit of value that effectively brackets all questions of reference or function, thus creating an internal market. Henceforth, the question of the University is only the question of relative value-for-money, the question posed to a student who is situated entirely as a *consumer*, rather than as someone who wants to think. (I shall return to the question of what it means to "think" later in this book.)

The image of students browsing through catalogues, with the world all before them, there to choose, is a remarkably widespread one that has attracted little comment. While I would not want to imply that students should not get the chance to choose, I do think it is worth reflecting on what this image assumes. Most obviously, it assumes the ability to pay. The question of access to tertiary education is bracketed. Tertiary education is perceived simply as another consumer durable, so that affordability or value-for-money becomes one category among others influencing an individual choice. Think of magazine consumer reports about which car to buy. Price is one factor among others, and the effect of the integration of heterogeneous categories of ranking into a single "excellence quotient" becomes apparent. Choosing a particular university over another is presented as not all that much different from weighing the costs and benefits of a Honda Civic against those of a Lincoln Continental in a given year or period.

In its October 3, 1994, issue, *U.S. News and World Report* even takes advantage of this potential parallel between the car industry and the University.[9] An article straightforwardly entitled "How to Pay for College" is followed by a series of tables that rate the "most efficient schools" and the "best values," comparing "sticker prices" (advertised tuition) to "discount tuition" (actual tuition once scholarships and grants are factored in). Student and parent consumers are reminded that just as when they buy a car, especially in the years of the U.S. auto industry's scramble for customers, the first price quoted is not what they are expected to pay. *U.S. News and World Report* reminds its readers that there are similar hidden discounts in university education, and that wise consumers—who now span all the income brackets (the logic of consumerism no longer only influences the "less-well-off")—should pay attention to value-for-money. Fuel efficiency, whether calculated in miles per gallon or spending per student, is a growing concern when measuring excellence.[10]

---

9 "News You Can Use," *U.S. News and World Report*, 117, no. 13 (October 3, 1994), pp. 70–91. U.S. News and World Report has not limited its focus simply to undergraduate education, as this particular issue might seem to suggest. Earlier in the same year, it published a special "info-magazine" issue devoted Notes to Pages 28–29 entirely to "America's Best Graduate Schools." That the issue was sponsored by a car company—specifically, a car: the "Neon" from Plymouth and Dodge—is an irony that should not be lost here.

10 That the link between consumerism and the rhetoric of excellence appeals to a wide audience is certainly a fact that these magazines count on, not only to sell copies of individual issues but also to keep readers coming back for more information and more magazines in the future. Interestingly enough, the measures of excellence and value-for-money in universities seem to change on a yearly basis, not unlike those in the car industry. To keep up with these trends, each year the wise consumer should allegedly pick up *Maclean's* and/or *U.S. News and World Report* to have the most up to date information possible. For instance, while McGill held first place in *Maclean's* "Medical/Doctoral" category in 1993, by 1994 it had dropped to a less impressive third overall: *Maclean's*, 107, no. 46, (November 14, 1994).

However much such a vision might scare us, or however much some of us might think we can resist the logic of consumerism when it comes to tertiary education, everyone still seems to be for excellence.[11] It functions not merely as the standard of external evaluation but also as the unit of value in terms of which the University describes itself to itself, in terms of which the University achieves the self-consciousness that is supposed to guarantee intellectual autonomy in modernity. Given that, who could be against excellence? Thus, for example, the Faculty of Graduate Studies of the Université de Montréal describes itself as follows:

> Created in 1972, the Faculty of Graduate Studies [*Faculté des études supérieures*] has been entrusted with the mission of maintaining and promoting standards of excellence at the level of master's and doctoral studies; of coordinating teaching and standardizing [*normalisation*] programmes of graduate study; of stimulating the development and coordination of research in liaison with the research departments of the University; of favoring the creation of interdisciplinary or multidisciplinary programs.[12]

Likewise, the reader who would like to be fully informed about the criteria *U.S. News and World Report* used to calculate the "Most Efficient" and "Best Value" universities must also buy the previous issue of the magazine, because, as we are told in the article that accompanies the tables, "Only schools that finished in the top half of our rankings of national universities and national liberal arts colleges, *published last week*, were considered as potential best values" (October 3, 1994, p. 75, my italics). Being fully informed is presumably a two-issue affair for *U.S. News and World Report*.

11 Obviously, not all universities welcome the implication that they resemble car sales. As Edwin Below, director of financial aid at Wesleyan University, puts it: "I am much more likely to see if we overlooked something [in the financial aid offer] when families are honest about their financial concerns than if they treat the process like they were buying a used car" (quoted in *U.S. News and World Report*, October 3, 1994, p. 72). However, not all University officials seem to mind similarities, even if they are not willing to draw the exact parallel themselves. According to the same issue of *U.S. News and World Report*, "a growing number of schools, such as Carnegie Mellon University III Pittsburgh, are letting families know that they welcome [financial aid] appeals. In letters sent this spring to all prospective students offered aid, the university's message was clear: 'Send us a copy of your other offers-we want to be competitive'" (p. 72).

12 Publicity brochure, October 1, 1992, published by the Direction des Communications, Université de Montréal, my translation. The original reads as follows: "Créée en 1972, la Faculte des études supérieures a pour mission de maintenir et de promouvoir des standards d'excellence au niveau des études de maîtrise et de doctorat; de coordonner l'enseignement et la normalisation des programmes d'études supérieures; de stimuler Ie développement et la coordination de la recherche en liaison avec les unités de recherche de l'Université; de favoriser la création de programmes interdisciplinaires ou multidisciplinaires."

Note here the intersection of excellence with "integration and standardization" and the appeal to the "interdisciplinary." The French "normalisation" gives a strong sense of what is at stake in "standardization"—especially to those familiar with the work of Michel Foucault. Is it surprising that corporations resemble Universities, health-care facilities, and international organizations, which all resemble corporations? Foucault's *Discipline and Punish* explores the eighteenth- and nineteenth-century reorganization of the mechanisms of state power, especially the judicial system, around the surveillance and normalization of delinquents in place of their exemplary punishment by torture and execution. Criminals are treated rather than destroyed, but this apparent liberalization is also a mode of domination that is the more terrible in that it leaves no room whatsoever for transgression. Crime is no longer an act of freedom, a remainder that society cannot handle but must expel. Rather, crime comes to be considered as a pathological deviation from social norms that must be cured. Foucault's chapter on "Panopticism" ends with ringing rhetorical questions:

> The practice of placing individuals under "observation" is a natural extension of a justice imbued with disciplinary methods and examination procedures. Is it surprising that the cellular prison, with its regular chronologies, forced labour, its authorities of surveillance and registration, its experts in normality, who continue and multiply the functions of the judge, should have become the modern instrument of penalty? Is it surprising that prisons resemble factories, schools, barracks, hospitals, which all resemble prisons?[13]

The notion of excellence, functioning less to permit visual observation than to permit exhaustive accounting, works to tie the University into a similar net of bureaucratic institutions. "Excellence," that is, functions to allow the University to understand itself solely in terms of the structure of corporate administration. Hence, as I mentioned briefly in Chapter 1, Alfonso Borrero Cabal, writing the report *The University as an Institution Today* for UNESCO, consciously structures his vision of the University in terms of administration: "Part I—the Introduction—deals with administration in terms of the internal institutional organization and the external or outward-projecting idea of service ... Part II deals with the first meaning of administration: the organization and internal functioning of the university ... Part III deals with the external sense of administration, that of service

13 Michel Foucault, *Discipline and Punish*, tr. Alan Sheridan (New York: Vintage, 1979), pp. 227–228.

to society."[14] This primarily administrative approach is explicitly situated as a result of the University's need to "become part of the international scene" (p. 19). Globalization requires that "greater attention is given to administration" in order to permit the integration of the market in knowledge, which Borrero Cabal situates directly in relation to the need for "development." With the end of the Cold War, as Marco Antonio Rodrigues Dias remarks in his preface, "the main problem in the world is 'underdevelopment'" (p. xv). What this actually means is that the language in which global discussions are to be conducted is not that of cultural conflict but of economic management. And the language of economic management structures Borrero Cabal's analysis of the university around the globe. Hence for example he argues: "Planning, execution, evaluation: the natural actions of responsible persons and institutions. They make up the three important stages that complete the cycle of the administrative process. In logical order, planning precedes execution and evaluation, but all planning has to start with evaluation" (p. 192).

The idea that the sequential processes of business management are the "natural actions" of "responsible persons" may come as a surprise to some of us. What kind of "responsibility" is this? Clearly not that of a parent to a child, for example. The only responsibility at stake here is the responsibility to provide managerial accounts for large corporations, something that becomes clearer when Borrero Cabal begins to flesh out what he means by planning: "Since 'strategic planning,' … 'administration by objectives,' … and systems of 'total quality' are frequently discussed, it is natural to adopt these means of planning, which are as old as humanity even though they were not formalized until the end of the 18th century" (p. 197).

Once again, the "natural" is invoked. Borrero Cabal cites a number of authorities in order to suggest that early hunter-gatherers were, in fact, engaged in reflection on total quality management, an argument that reminds one of the fine scorn Marx pours upon Ricardo:

> Even Ricardo has his Robinson Crusoe Stories. Ricardo makes his primitive fisherman and primitive hunter into owners of commodities who immediately exchange their fish and game in proportion to the labourtime which is materialized in these exchange-values. On this occasion he slips into the anachronism of allowing the primitive fisherman and hunter to calculate the value of their implements in accordance with the annuity tables used on the London Stock Exchange in 1817."[15]

---

14 Alfonso Borrero Cabal, *The University as an Institution Today* (Paris and Ottawa: UNESCO and IDRC, 1993) p. xxiv, my italics.

15 Karl Marx, *Capital: A Critique of Political Economy*, vol 1, tr. Ben Fowkes (Harmondsworth: Penguin, 1976), p. 169, n. 31.

Borrero Cabal's recourse to anachronism is, of course, the product of a desire to make the exclusive rule of business management not seem discontinuous with the prior role of the University. Although he does admit that economic criteria and cultural development are at odds, he simply notes the fact and then passes on to give more outlines for the management of University administration by analogy with a large corporation. Hence he admits that he has omitted "the all-essential ingredient of culture" from his analysis of the relation between "the university and the work world," saying that: "Consequently it is often felt that economic criteria take precedence over the cultural development of people and nations. This reduces professional work to quantitative purposes: the profession is not conceived of as 'the cultural and moral elevation of people and nations' (Garcia Corrido 1992), but reduced to what is necessary but not sufficient, that is, tangible output and per capita income" (p. 161).

Having acknowledged the conflict between a strictly economic rationale and the traditional cultural mission, Borrero Cabal goes on to provide a strictly economic description of the functioning of the University in terms of cost and benefit. He does make occasional remarks that we should not forget about culture but seems unsure where it should fit in. Hence, and not surprisingly, he is more at ease with the invocation of excellence. He approvingly quotes the Director General of UNESCO: "Federico Mayor (1991) gives the following qualifying terms: It is impossible to guarantee the quality of education without having the aim of excellence resting on the domain of research, teaching, preparation, and learning. … The search for excellence reaffirms its pertinence and closely links it to quality" (p. 212). The aim of excellence serves to synthesize research, teaching, preparation, and learning, all the activities of the University, if we add administration (and one of Borrero Cabal's only concrete recommendations is that university administration should be made a program of study). What is remarkable is how Borrero Cabal could suggest that these are "qualifying terms" in order to understand what "institutional quality" in the University might be. Excellence is invoked here, as always, to say precisely nothing at all: it deflects attention from the questions of what quality and pertinence might be, who actually are the judges of a relevant or a good University, and by what authority they become those judges.

What Borrero Cabal suggests for the University is a process of constant self-evaluation, in relation to "performance indicators," which allow us to judge "quality, excellence, effectiveness and pertinence" (p. 212). All of these terms are, he acknowledges, "taken from economic jargon" (p. 213), and permit the University's self-evaluation to be a matter of accounting, both internally and externally. In short, for Borrero Cabal, accountability is strictly a matter of accounting: "In synthesis, if the concept of accountability is accepted as part of the academic lexicon, it is equivalent to the capacity that the university has for accounting for its roles, mission, and functions to itself, and for accounting to society how they are translated into efficient service" (p. 213). Note the use of "translation" in this passage; although "accounting" may exceed bookkeeping in the sense that it is not merely a matter of money, it is the principle of cost and benefit that acts as a principle of translation. Cost-benefit analysis structures not only the University's internal bookkeeping but also its academic performance (in terms of goal achievement) and the social bond with the University at large. The social responsibility of the University, its accountability to society, is solely a matter of services rendered for a fee. Accountability is a synonym for accounting in "the academic lexicon."

In this context, excellence responds very well to the needs of technological capitalism in the production and processing of information, in that it allows for the increasing integration of all activities into a generalized market, while permitting a large degree of flexibility and innovation at the local level. Excellence is thus the integrating principle that allows "diversity" (the other watchword of the University prospectus) to be tolerated without threatening the unity of the system.

The point is not that no one knows what excellence is but that *everyone* has his or her own idea of what it is. And once excellence has been generally accepted as an organizing principle, there is no need to argue about differing definitions. Everyone is excellent, in their own way, and everyone has more of a stake in being left alone to be excellent than in intervening in the administrative process. There is a clear parallel here to the condition of the political subject under contemporary capitalism. Excellence draws only one boundary: the boundary that protects the unrestricted power of the bureaucracy. And if a particular department's kind of excellence fails to conform, then that department can be eliminated without apparent risk to the system. This has been, for example, the fate of many classics departments. It is beginning to happen to philosophy.

The reasons for the decline of classics are of course complex, but they seem to me to have to do with the fact that the study of classics traditionally presupposes a subject of culture: the subject that links the Greeks to nineteenth-century Germany, and legitimates the nation-'state as the modern, rational, reconstruction of the transparent communicational community of the ancient *polis*. That fiction of communicational transparency is apparent from the erroneous assumptions of nineteenth-century historians (still apparent in mass-cultural representations) that ancient Greece was a world of total whiteness (dazzling marble buildings, statues, and people), a pure and transparent origin. That the ideological role of this subject is no longer pertinent is itself a primary symptom of the decline of culture as the regulatory idea of the nation-state. Hence classical texts will continue to be read, but the assumptions that necessitated a department of classics for this purpose (the need to prove that Pericles and Bismarck were the same kind of men) no longer hold, so there is no longer a need to employ a massive institutional apparatus designed to make ancient Greeks into ideal Etonians or Young Americans *avant la lettre.*[16]

This disciplinary shift is most evident in the United States, where the University has always had an ambiguous relation to the state. This is because American civil society is structured by the trope of the promise or contract rather than on the basis of a single national ethnicity. Hence where Fichte's university project, as we shall see, offers to realize the essence of a *Volk* by revealing its hidden nature in the form of the nation-state, the American University offers to deliver on the promise of a rational civil society—as in the visionary conclusion to T. H. Huxley's address on the inauguration of John Hopkins University. It is worth quoting at some length the extended opposition between past and future, between essence and promise, that characterizes Huxley's account of the specificity of American society and the American University, in order to see exactly how he can speak of America as a yet-to-be-fulfilled promise even on the hundredth anniversary of the Declaration of Independence:

> I constantly hear Americans speak of the charm which our old mother country has for them ... But anticipation has no less charm than retrospect, and to an Englishman landing on your shores for the first time, travelling for hundreds of miles through strings of great and well-ordered cities, seeing your enormous actual, and almost infinite potential, wealth in all commodities, and in the energy and ability which turn wealth to account, there is something sublime in the vista of the future. Do not suppose that I am pandering to what is commonly understood by national pride. ... Size is not grandeur, and territory does not make a nation. The great issue, about which hangs a true sublimity, and the terror of overhanging fate, is what are you going to do with all of these things? What is to be the end to which these are to be the means? You are making a novel experiment in politics on the greatest scale which the world has yet seen.[17]

---

16 Hence ancient texts can now be read in considerably stranger ways, ways that recognize historical discontinuity without immediately recuperating it in terms of a Fall narrative as "the glory we have lost." One of the more striking examples of this is the contemporary recognition by thinkers such as Lyotard that Aristotle's notions of the "golden mean" and of *phronesis* have nothing to do with the assumptions of democratic centrism—producing a much more politically radical account of Aristotle's call for prudent judgment on a case-by-case basis. The point Aristotle makes in the *Nichomachean Ethics* is that the mean is refractory with regard to the individual and that no rule of calculation will allow the judge to arrive at it, since what constitutes prudent behavior radically differs from case to case. I have discussed the political implications of this "revolutionary prudence" in "PseudoEthica Epidemica: How Pagans Talk to the Gods," *Philosophy Today*, 36, no. 4 (Winter 1992).

17 "1876 Address on University Education (Delivered at the opening of the Johns Hopkins University, Baltimore)," in T. H. Huxley, 'Science and Education', vol. 3 of *Collected Essays* (London: Macmillan, 1902), pp. 259–260.

Huxley himself, as Rector of Aberdeen, played an important role in the development of the Scottish University in the later nineteenth century, its independence from the Oxbridge model being marked by an openness to the natural sciences and medicine as disciplines and by the fact that it was not controlled by the Anglican church. These two features make the Scottish University more clearly "modern," which is to say, closer to the American model.[18] And Huxley's speech picks out the crucial feature that will define the modernity of johns Hopkins: the fact that the United States as a nation has no intrinsic cultural *content*. That is to say, the American national idea is understood by Huxley as a promise, a scientific experiment. And the role of the American University is not to bring to light the content of its culture, to realize a national meaning; it is rather to deliver on a national *promise*, a contract.[19] As I shall explain later on, this promissory structure is what makes

18 As Giner de los Rios puts it, the Scottish University shares with the American a greater influence of the German research University: "The British type is seen in its pure form in Oxford and Cambridge, or modified more towards the Latin or German type in Scotland or Ireland, in new universities, and in the United States." *La universidad espanola: obras completas de Francisco Giner de los Rios*, vol. 2 (Madrid: University of Madrid, 1916), p. 108; quoted in Borrero Cabal, The University as an Institution Today, p. 30.

19 Ronald Judy, in the short history of the American University with which he prefaces his *(Dis)Forming the American Canon: African-Arabic Slave Narratives and the Vernacular* (Minneapolis: University of Minnesota Press, 1993), also situates the foundation of Johns Hopkins as a crucial turning point that defines the specificity of the American University: "These movements towards academic professionalization and instrumental knowledge reached their culmination with the incorporation of Johns Hopkins University in 1870, or more precisely with the appointment of Daniel Coit Gilman as its president in 1876. Gilman made Johns Hopkins a model research institution where the human and physical sciences (*Naturwissenschaften*) flourished as disciplined methodologies" (15). Judy's account differs slightly from mine in that he associates with the founding of Johns Hopkins the very bureaucratic ideology of methodological specificity that undermines the possibility of general culture-the displacement of culture by bureaucratically managed knowledge that I locate as the distinguishing trait of the contemporary University of Excellence. Hence he argues that the disciplinary specificity of the humanities curriculum arises in the late nineteenth century, "at precisely that moment when the humanities were no longer required to respond to the demand for relevance." pointing to David S. Jordan's institution of the first English degree at Indiana University in 1885 (16). Judy calls this "the professionalization of the human sciences" and links it to the development of an overarching "culture of bureaucracy" that unites the human and the natural sciences under a general rubric of professionalization (17).

Judy is thus telling a story quite comparable to my own concerning the replacement of the general idea of culture by a generalized bureaucracy, except that he locates it in the latter half of the nineteenth century rather than in the latter part of the twentieth. This

the canon debate a particularly American phenomenon, since the establishment of cultural content is not the realization of an immanent cultural essence but an act of republican will: the paradoxical contractual *choice* of a tradition. Thus the *form* of the European idea of culture is preserved in the humanities in the United States, but the cultural form has no inherent content. The content of the canon is grounded upon the moment of a social contract rather than the continuity of a historical tradition, and therefore is always open to revision.

This contractual vision of society is what allows Harvard to offer itself "in the service of the nation" or New York University to call itself a "private university in the public service." What such service might mean is not singularly determined by a unitary cultural center. The idea of the nation is always already an abstraction in America, resting on promise rather than on tradition. Excellence can thus most easily gain ground in the United States; it is more open to the futurity of the promise than is "culture," and the question of cultural content was already bracketed in the American University in the late nineteenth century, as Ronald Judy points out. The contemporary advent of excellence may therefore be understood to represent the abandonment of the vestigial appeal to the *form* of culture as the mode of self-realization of a republican people who are citizens of a nation-state-the relinquishing of the University's role as a model of even the contractual social bond in favor of the structure of an autonomous bureaucratic corporation.

Along the same lines, one can understand the point that I have already made concerning the status of "globalization" as a kind of "Americanization." Global "Americanization" today (unlike during the period of the Cold War, Korea, and Vietnam) does not mean American national predominance but a global realization of the contentlessness of the American national idea, which shares the emptiness of the cash'-nexus and of excellence. Despite the enormous energy expended in attempts to isolate and define an "Americanness" in American Studies programs, one might read these efforts as nothing more than an attempt to mask the fundamental anxiety that it in some sense *means nothing* to be American, that "American culture" is becoming increasingly a structural oxymoron. I take it as significant of such a trend that an institution as prestigious and as central to an idea of American culture as the University of Pennsylvania should have recently decided to disband its American Studies program. That universities in the United States have been the quickest to abandon the trappings of justification by reference to national

---

disagreement is, I think, less historical than cartographical. I am concerned to introduce a transitional step into the passage from the modern German University of national culture to the bureaucratic University of Excellence, one which positions the American University as the University of a national culture that is contentless.

culture should hardly be surprising in a nation defined by a suspicion of state intervention in symbolic life, as expressed in the separation of church and state.

The United States, however, is by no means alone in this movement. The British turn to "performance indicators" should also be understood as a step on the road toward the discourse of excellence that is replacing the appeal to culture in the North American University.[20] The performance indicator is, of course) a measure of excellence, an invented standard that claims to be capable of rating all departments in all British universities on a five-point scale. The rating can then be used to determine the size of the central government grant allocated to the department in question. Since this process is designed to introduce a competitive market into the academic world, investment follows success, so the government intervenes to accentuate differentials in perceived quality rather than to reduce them. Thus more money is given to the high-scoring university departments, while the poor ones, rather than being developed, are starved of cash (under the Thatcher regime, this was of course understood as an encouragement to such departments to pull themselves up by their bootstraps). The long-term trend is to permit the concentration of resources in centers of high performance and to encourage the disappearance of departments, and even perhaps of universities, perceived as "weaker."

Hence, for instance, the University of Oxford has been moved to envision the construction of a Humanities Research Center, despite traditional local suspicion of the very notion of the research project as something that only Germans and Americans could think of applying to the humanities. Benjamin Jowett is supposed to have remarked of research, "There will be none of *that* in my college." Such changes are hailed by conservatives as "exposure to market forces," whereas what is occurring is actually the highly artificial creation of a fictional market that presumes exclusive governmental control of funding. However, the very artificiality of the process by which a version of the capitalist marketplace is mimed throws into relief the preliminary necessity of a unified and virtual accounting mechanism. This is coupled with the structural introduction of the threat of crisis to the functioning of the institution. And the result is nothing less than the double logic of excellence at work in its finest hour.

Indeed, a crisis in the University seems to be a defining feature of the "West," as is evidenced in the Italian students' movement of 1993, or the repeated French attempts at "modernization." Of course, it was the Faure plan for the modernization of the University that produced the events of 1968 in France (which I shall

---

20 For an account of the debate over "performance indicators" see Michael Peters, "Performance and Accountability in 'Post Industrial Society': The Crisis of British Universities," *Studies in Higher Education*, 17, no. 2 (1992).

discuss in Chapter 9). However, such attempts at modernization have continued, and the arguments presented recently by Claude Allègre in *L'Âge des Savoirs: Pour une Renaissance de l'Université* display a striking consonance with the developments I have discussed in the United States, Canada, and Britain. Allegre was the special counselor to Lionel Jospin at the Ministry of Education from 1988 to 1992, and his book is essentially an expose of the arguments guiding the reform of the French University, perceived as a locus of stagnation and resistance to change (an argument with which few could disagree). Interestingly, he argues that this drive to reform is "above all a resurgence of the aspirations of 68 … but a discreet and calm resurgence."[21] Just to whose aspirations he is referring is never spelled out, but it turns out that what 1968 meant above all was openness. And the twin characteristics of this new opening are, the reader will hardly be surprised to learn, integration and excellence:

> We tried to develop [reforms] by opening up a University that was folded in on itself and bringing it closer to the City.
>
> Opening up the University to the City: this is its adaptation to professional needs.
>
> Opening up the University to knowledges: this is the effort to renew research and to recognize *excellence*.
>
> Integration of the University in its City: this is the University 2000 at the heart of urban planning, it is the policy of partnership with local groups.
>
> Integration of the French University in a European ensemble: this is the meaning of European evaluation.[22]

The internal policy of the University is to be resolved in France by the appeal to excellence, which serves as the term that regroups and integrates all knowledge-related activities. This, in turn, permits the wider integration of the University as one corporate bureaucracy among others, both in the direction of the city and of the European Community. The city is no longer the "streets," nor even a vision of civic life (the Renaissance city-state that Allègre's title might lead us to expect). Rather, it is an agglomerate of professional-bureaucratic capitalist corporations whose needs are primarily centered upon the supply of a managerial-technical class. The city gives the University its commercial form of expression. And the European Community supplants the nation-state as the figure of the entity that provides the University with its political form of expression, an expression which is explicitly tied to the question of evaluation. The University will produce excellence

21 Claude Allegre, *L'Âge des savoirs: pour une renaissance de l'Université* (Paris: Gallimard, 1993), p. 232, my translation.

22 Ibid., p. 232, my italics.

in knowledges, and as such will link into the circuits of global capital and transnational politics without difficulty. This is because there is no cultural content to the notion of excellence, nothing specifically "French," for example, except insofar as "Frenchness" is a commodity on the global market.

Excellence exposes the pre-modern traditions of the University to the force of market capitalism. Barriers to free trade are swept away. An interesting example of this is the British government's decision to allow the polytechnics to rename themselves as universities. Oxford Polytechnic becomes Brookes University, and so on. This classic freemarket maneuver guarantees that the only criterion of excellence is performativity in an expanded market. It would be an error to think that this was an *ideological* move on the part of the Conservative government, however. The decision was not primarily motivated by concern for the content of what is taught in the universities or polytechnics. Even if the tendency of polytechnics to form links with business in the interests of incorporating practical training into degrees might seem to fuel the strand of petty-bourgeois anti-intellectualism in the British Conservative party, it is also true that it was in the polytechnics that the work of the Birmingham school of Cultural Studies had had its greatest impact. Hence the sudden redenomination of polytechnics as universities is best understood as an *administrative* move: the breaking down of a barrier to circulation and to market expansion, analogous to the repeal of sumptuary laws that permitted the capitalization of the textile trade in Early Modern England.

One form of such market expansion is the development of interdisciplinary programs, which often appear as the point around which radicals and conservatives can make common cause in University reform. This is partly because interdisciplinarity has no inherent political orientation, as the example of the Chicago School shows.[23] It is also because the increased flexibility they offer is often attractive to administrators as a way of overcoming entrenched practices of demarcation, ancient privileges, and fiefdoms in the structure of universities. The benefits of interdisciplinary openness are numerous—as someone who works in an interdisci-

---

23 This statement may sound too relativistic. Of course, if it is true that, as Julie Thompson Klein contends in *Interdisciplinarity* (Detroit: Wayne State University Press, 1990), p. 11, "all interdisciplinary activities are rooted in the ideas of unity and synthesis, evoking a common epistemology of convergence," such an idea could be supported by the left and the right, who would merely disagree as to where the point of convergence should lie. In fact, the account of the interdisciplinary that Klein gives is a convincing argument for some suspicion of the implicit harmonic convergence in interdisciplinary work. One of my major aims in this book is to suggest that in thinking about the University we should lay aside the automatic privileging of unity and synthesis, without however simply making disharmony and conflict into a negative goal.

plinary department I am particularly aware of them—but they should not blind us to the institutional stakes that they involve. At present interdisciplinary programs tend to supplement existing disciplines; the time is not far off when they will be installed in order to replace clusters of disciplines.

Indeed, this is a reason to be cautious in approaching the institutional claim to interdisciplinarity staked by Cultural Studies when it replaces the old order of disciplines in the humanities with a more general field that combines history, art history, literature, media studies, sociology, and so on. In saying this, I want to join Rey Chow in questioning, from a sympathetic point of view, the unqualified acceptance both of interdisciplinary activity and of Cultural Studies that has been fairly common among academic radicals.[24] We can be interdisciplinary in the name of excellence, because excellence only preserves pre-existing disciplinary boundaries insofar as they make no larger claim on the entirety of the system and pose no obstacle to its growth and integration.

To put this another way, the appeal to excellence marks the fact that there is no longer any idea of the University, or rather that the idea has now lost all content. As a non-referential unit of value entirely internal to the system, excellence marks nothing more than the moment of technology's self-reflection. All that the system requires is for activity to take place, and the empty notion of excellence refers to nothing other than the optimal input/output ratio in matters of information.[25] This is perhaps a less heroic role than we are accustomed to claim for the University, although it does resolve the question of parasitism. The University

---

24 Rey Chow, in "The Politics and Pedagogy of Asian Literatures in American Universities," *differences*, 2, no. 3 (1990), has provided some useful reminders of how the turn to Cultural Studies in the teaching of Asian literature can function as a conservative strategy: "When scholars are departmentalized simply because they are all 'doing' 'China,' 'Japan,' or 'India' what actually happens is the predication of so-called 'interdisciplinarity' on the model of the colonial territory and the nation state" (40).
Chow makes a convincing argument that the consideration of Asian literatures in terms of general culture is a marginalizing gesture that locates the Asian "only in the universalist language of 'interdisciplinarity,' 'cross-cultural plurality,' etc., in which it becomes a localized embellishment of the general narrative" (36). Like myself, Chow is not simply dismissing interdisciplinarity or Cultural Studies; what she does is provide a strong example of how the organization of the humanities is part of a process that she calls, following Edward Said, "informationalization."

25 On the informationalization of cultural knowledge, see Edward Said, "Opponents, Audiences, Constituencies and Community" in Hal Poster, *The Anti-Aesthetic: Essays on Postmodern Culture* (Port Townsend: Bay Press, 1983), and Jean-François Lyotard, "New Technologies" in *Political Writings*, tr. Bill Readings and Kevin-Paul Geiman (Minneapolis: University of Minnesota Press, 1993).

is now no more of a parasitical drain on resources than the stock exchange or the insurance companies are a drain on industrial production. Like the stock exchange, the University is a point of capital's self-knowledge, of capital's ability not just to manage risk or diversity but to extract a surplus value from that management. In the case of the University this extraction occurs as a result of speculation on differentials in information.

The implication of this shift in function is that the analysis of the University as an Ideological State Apparatus, in Althusser's terms, is no longer appropriate, since the University is no longer primarily an ideological arm of the nation-state but an autonomous bureaucratic corporation. To take another, perhaps less weighted, example we can compare the University to the National Basketball Association. Both are bureaucratic systems that govern an area of activity whose systemic functioning and external effects are not dependent on an external reference. The game of basketball has its rules, and those rules allow differences to arise that are objects of speculation. And while Philadelphia 76ers' victories have effects on their fans, and fans have effects on 76ers' victories (both as supporters and as financiers), those victories or defeats are not directly linked to the essential meaning of the city of Philadelphia. Results are not meaningless, but they arise within the system of basketball rather than in relation to an external referent.

For the University to become such a system involves a major change in the way in which it has been understood to produce institutional meaning. As I shall show later on, Schiller positioned the University of Culture as the quasi-church appropriate to the rational state, by claiming that the University would perform the same services for the state as the Church had for the feudal or absolutist monarch. However, the contemporary University of Excellence should now be understood as a bureaucratic system whose internal regulation is entirely self-interested without regard to wider ideological imperatives. Hence the stock market seeks maximum volatility in the interest of intensifying the profits attendant on the flux of capital rather than the stability of exchange that might defend strictly national interests.

The corollary of this is that we must analyze the University as a *bureaucratic system* rather than as the ideological apparatus that the left has traditionally considered it. As an autonomous system rather than an ideological instrument, the University should no longer be thought of as a tool that the left will be able to use for other purposes than those of the capitalist state. This explains the ease with which former West Germans have colonized the Universities of what was once the German Democratic Republic (GDR) since reunification. The Universities of the old GDR have been purged of those considered to be political apparatchiks of the Honecker regime. No parallel purges, however, have occurred in the Universities of the former Bundesrepublik, despite the fact that reunification was not supposed to be the conquest of the East by the West. The conflict, that is, is not presented as that between two ideologies (which would have necessitated purges on both sides), but as a conflict between the East, where the University used to be under ideological control, and the West, where the University was supposed to be non-ideological.

Of course, the Western universities had a massive ideological role to play during the Cold War, and much can be said about individual cases. But overall one is struck by the silence and speed of this replacement, by the fact that the counter-arguments that could be mounted in favor of the intellectual project of the former East Germany simply *cannot be heard* any longer. This is because the fall of the Wall means that the University is no longer primarily an ideological institution, and those from the West are better positioned to play the new roles required. If the posts of the purged have in many cases gone to young academics from the former West, this is not because they are primarily agents of a competing ideology, but because of bureaucratic efficiency. The young former West Germans are not necessarily more intelligent or more learned than those they replace; they are simply "cleaner," which is to say, less easily identifiable as ideological agents of their state. This is a primary symptom of the decline of the nation-state as the counter-signatory to the contract by which the modern University, the University of Culture, was founded. As my remarks on Allègre's invocation of the European Community have already suggested, the emergence of the University of Excellence in place of the University of Culture can only be understood against the backdrop of the decline of the nation-state.

The demand for "clean hands," be it in German universities or in Italian politics, may be presented as a desire to renew the state apparatus, but I think it is better understood as the product of a general uncertainty concerning the role of the state, a call for "hands off." Complex and often contradictory, such a desire may result, as in Italy, in such paradoxical alliances as that of integrationist Fascists (the MSI) with separatists (the Northern League). Notably, this alliance occurred under the umbrella of Berlusconi's oddly transparent organization, Forza Italia, whose nationalism is the evocation of a football chant, and whose claim to govern is based on a rather dubious assertion of "business success." If I may offer a rather strange diagnosis of this apparent paradox, it is that the alliance in Italy is between those who wish for the question of community in Italy no longer to be posed: either because the Duce may return to provide an answer about "being Italian" and impose it with brutal violence (the Lega will tell people to "be regional") or because Berlusconi will reassure us that it is not a question, that the answer is as transparent and obvious as the light blue haze emanating from a television screen, or the light blue shirt on a footballer's back. Berlusconi does not offer a renewed nationalism (as his alliance with the MSI might lead us to fear) but a sanitized nationalist nostalgia that blankets and suppresses all questions concerning the nature of community.

Instead of the question of community, which was once posed both within and against the terms of nationalism, we get a generalized but meaningless nationalism that pushes aside questions. The national question, that is, is simply accepted as a generalized matter of nostalgia, be it for the evils of Fascism (Fini, the current leader of the MSI, is not a Duce, even in his dreams), or for the light blue colors of the royal house of Savoy. And the government is to get on with the matter of running the state as a business.

The nation understands itself as its own theme park, and that resolves the question of what it means to live in Italy: it is to have been Italian once. Meanwhile, the state is merely a large corporation to be entrusted to businessmen, a corporation that increasingly serves as the hand-maiden to the penetration of transnational capital. The governmental structure of the nation-state is no longer the organizing center of the common existence of peoples across the planet, and the University of Excellence serves nothing other than itself, another corporation in a world of transnationally exchanged capital.

Dwelling in the Ruins

From *The University in Ruins* (1996)

This selection is taken from *The University in Ruins*, by Bill Readings, 1996. Published by Harvard, University Press, Cambridge, MA.

* * * * *

Up to this point, my description of the current situation may seem to have rather dire consequences for the University in general and for the humanities in particular. However, such is by no means the case. A certain amount of crystal-ball gazing might lead us to want to say things such as: the humanities will in twenty years' time no longer be centered in the study of national literatures. And these predictions might prove more or less correct. However, my argument is less concerned with the precise disciplinary shape that the University of the twenty-first century will assume than with what that shape will *mean*, which is to say, how it will be given meaning as an institutional system. This is why my analysis thus far has tended to ignore the uneven and combined development that is the actual form of the appearance of the tendencies that I have sought to isolate. And it is also the reason for my own habit of privileging self-description (such as prospectuses) over empirical study in the analysis of how universities work. I will cheerfully admit that in all probability far less will have changed in the daily life of professors and students than one might expect. Significant shifts, though, are taking place in the way in which everyday practices are organized and ascribed meaning. These shifts are even taking place at a remarkably intense rhythm (rhythm rather than speed, since these shifts are not linear but interruptive). For purely heuristic purposes, I subsume these shifts under the name "dereferentialization," which marks a decline in the ideological function of the University that is intimately linked to the symptomatic rise of ideology-critique as a methodology inside the University.

This process of dereferentialization, though, is not a historical necessity for Thought. That is to say, I do not invoke dereferentialization as an alibi for retirement from the University. Instead, it seems to me that an engagement with and transvaluation of this shift can allow innovative and creative thinking to occur. But for any such innovation to occur, we must address two issues: the place of the University in society at large, and the internal shape of the University as an institution. Within modernity, the University held a central place in the formation of subjects for the nation-state, along with the production of the ideology that handled the issue of their belonging to that nationstate (culture). Its internal organization as a community was meant to reflect that structure of belonging or community in which a general culture of conversation held together diverse specialties in a unity that was either organic (Fichte), societal (Newman), or transactional (Habermas).

In all of these accounts, the University held the promise of being a microcosm of the nation-state. In my final two chapters, I want to ask what can be done with and in a University that, along with the nation-state, is no longer central to the question of common life. This involves two questions: that of the institution's function as an institution, and that of the community that the institution may harbor. I shall not argue, though, for either a new institution or a new community, but rather for a rethinking of both terms. If my preference is for a thought of dissensus over that of consensus—as I shall argue in the next chapter—it is because dissensus cannot be institutionalized. The precondition for such institutionalization would be a second-order consensus that dissensus is a good thing, something, indeed, with which Habermas would be in accord. A version of this tendency is persuasively argued for in Gerald Graff's *Beyond the Culture Wars: How Teaching the Conflicts Can Revitalize American Education.*[1]

For my part, I will propose a certain pragmatism, a pragmatism that does not simply accept the institution's lack of external reference and glory in it (as does Stanley Fish in *There's No Such Thing as Free Speech*), but that tries to make dereferentialization the occasion for *détournements* and radical lateral shifts.[2] Such moves

1 Gerald Graff, *Beyond the Culture Wars: How Teaching the Conflicts Can Revitalize American Education* (New York and London: Norton, 1992).

2 Stanley Fish, *There's No Such Thing as Free Speech: And It's a Good Thing Too* (Oxford: Oxford University Press, 1994). I think in particular of Fish's essay on the Milton Society

may be critical, but they will not appeal to a transcendent self-knowing subject capable of standing outside his or her own behavior and critiquing it. To refer back to another term I have already introduced, such an institutional pragmatics will be without *alibis*, without "elsewheres," a truth whose name might be invoked to save us from responsibility for our actions. Here lies another of my differences with Fish and Rorty: this is a pragmatism that does not believe that it adds up to its own alibi, or that its denial of the grand narratives is not itself a project. To put this another way, being a good pragmatist is not in itself a guarantee that one will always be right. It may be pragmatic to abandon pragmatism, so pragmatism cannot function as a project in the modernist sense. Hence institutional practices—even in an institution stripped of Platonic illusions—cannot be their own reward. If I have certain principles (more accurately, certain habits or tics of thought), they are not grounded in anything more foundational than my capacity to make them seem interesting to others, which is not the same thing as convincing other people of their "rightness."

Institutional pragmatism thus means, for me, recognizing the University today for what it is: an institution that is losing its need to make transcendental claims for its function. The University is no longer simply modern, insofar as it no longer needs a grand narrative of culture in order to work. As a bureaucratic institution of excellence, it can incorporate a very high degree of internal variety without requiring its multiplicity of diverse idioms to be unified into an ideological whole. Their unification is no longer a matter of ideology but of their exchange-value within an expanded market. Administering conflict thus does not mean resolving it, as one might take the example of the Cold War to have demonstrated. The non-ideological role of the University deprives disruption of any claim to automatic radicalism, just as it renders radical claims for a new unity susceptible to being swallowed up by the empty unity of excellence.

Those of us who, like me, have found the University a place where the critical function has in the past been possible, have to face up to the fact that our current gains in critical freedom (unimaginable shifts in the institutional face of new programs, etc.) are being achieved in direct proportion to the reduction in their general social significance. This is not in itself any reason to abandon projects for change or innovation. Far from it. But what is required is that we do not delude ourselves as to their significance, that we do not satisfy ourselves with rebuilding a ghost town. Energies directed exclusively toward University reform risk blinding

---

of America, in which he argues that "institutional life is more durable than the vocabulary of either dissolution or revolution suggests" (271). Thus, all novelty and difference are accommodated by the self-adjusting tradition, which rests on nothing other than its own history of self'-adjustments.

us to the dimensions of the task that faces us—in the humanities, the social sciences, and the natural sciences—the task of rethinking the categories that have governed intellectual life for over two hundred years.[3]

We have to recognize that the University is a *ruined institution*, while thinking what it means to dwell in those ruins without recourse to romantic nostalgia. The trope of ruins has a long history in intellectual life. The campus of the State University of New York at Buffalo is decorated by some artificial concrete ruins that allude to Greco-Roman temple architecture, something that might seem incongruous in North America were it not that it coincides with a history that I have already sketched. This history is that of modernity's encounter with culture, where culture is positioned as the mediating resynthesis of knowledges, returning us to the primordial unity and immediacy of a lost origin—be it the total sunlight and dazzling whiteness of an artificial Antiquity or the earthy social unity of the Shakespearean Globe.[4] This story has been with us since at least the Renaissance, which actually took place in the nineteenth century as the nostalgia of Burckhardt, Pater, and Michelet for an originary moment of cultural reunification; and I have discussed its incarnations elsewhere.[5]

Du Bellay's sonnet cycle "The Ruins of Rome" claims to be the first illustration of the Renaissance of France as a linguistically unified nation-state, the Renaissance for which he calls in his *Défense et illustration de la langue française*. The claim to new origin and national specificity is somewhat vitiated in that his arguments are largely a pirate translation from an Italian dialogue by Speroni. France, says du Bellay, can arise as a modern nation-state by giving a new life and critical dignity to the national language, a task he undertakes on the ground plan offered by the ruins of Rome. A lost splendor will endow the building of a renewed vernacular, much as the stones of Roman monuments were taken and used for building Renaissance palaces.

Where du Bellay saw in the ruins of Rome the foundations of modernity, the Romantics appreciated ruins as ruins, even constructing artificial ones in the grounds of stately homes, just as the monster in Mary Shelley's *Frankenstein*

---

3 One simple example: for a consideration of the way in which the internet threatens to delegitimize the structure of scholarly publishing, see my "Caught in the Net: Notes from the Electronic Underground," *Surfaces*, 4, no. 104 (1994), available via gopher from the Université de Montréal gopher site.

4 The University of California also has some piled ruins, which are known locally as "Stonehenge," an equally incongruous cultural reference.

5 See my "When Did the Renaissance Begin?" in *Rethinking the Henrician Era*, ed. Peter Herman (Chicago: University of Illinois Press, 1993) for a more developed account of the invention of the Renaissance and the question of the visibility of history.

constructs his subjectivity in part from overhearing the reading of Volney's *Ruins of Empires*. According to this romantic story, the fragmented subject (the monster, himself pieced together by technology from bits of past bodies that have lost their organic life) aesthetically appropriates the scattered shards of a now broken and lifeless tradition. That which he cannot live he apprehends aesthetically, thus performing a secondary synthesis both of the tradition (as object of aesthetic appreciation) and of his own subjectivity (as subject of that act of appreciation). Art redeems a fractured and merely technical life; a unified life that can no longer be lived is resynthesized as art.

The Romantics, appreciating ruins as ruins rather than as traces of a renascent past, recuperate tradition as aesthetic sensation through a subjective attitude of nostalgia. The Buffalo simulacrum of Greco-Roman culture as the foundation of the North American State University seems to propose an uneasy mixture of the two: a grounding of both the arts and the sciences in a particular tradition (and certainly not a Native American one). The simulation of ruins has to do with the Romantic aesthetic appreciation of the past, and their positioning beside the concrete buildings of the new University is indebted to a hermeneutic claim for knowledge as an interactive encounter with tradition. In either case, ruins are the objects of subjective appropriation and mastery, whether epistemological or aesthetic.

Freud's point in comparing the unconscious to the ruins of Rome was that the present did not ever achieve the modernist task of being simply present, of condemning the past either to become present (be reborn) or to enter utter oblivion.[6] Hence, in *Civilization and its Discontents*, he revises the allusion to insist upon its limitations: the figure of the building constructed from ruins is inadequate, he says, because it fails to convey the sense that, in the unconscious, two buildings from heterogeneous historical periods are impossibly co-present.[7] The past is not erased but haunts the present. Thus, the traumatic return of repressed memory is a constant threat. To inhabit the ruins of the University must be to practice an institutional pragmatism that recognizes this threat, rather than to seek to redeem epistemological uncertainty by recourse to the plenitude of aesthetic sensation (nostalgia) or

6 Freud tells us in *The Interpretation of Dreams*, ed. and tr. James Strachey (New York: Avon Books, 1965), p. 530: "If we examine the … structure [of dreams and daytime phantasies], we shall perceive the way in which the wishful purpose that is at work in their production has mixed up the material of which they are built, has re-arranged it and has formed it into a new whole. They stand in much the same relation to the childhood memories from which they are derived as do some of the Baroque palaces of Rome to the ancient ruins whose pavements and columns have provided the material for the more recent structures."

7 Sigmund Freud, *Civilization and its Discontents*, tr., James Strachey (New York and London: Norton, 1961), pp. 16–17.

epistemological mastery (knowledge as progress). The ruins of culture's institution are simply there, where we are, and we have to negotiate among them.

This is a different way to think about our relation to tradition than that proposed by the German Idealists (in which hermeneutic reworking returned the tradition to a new unity and vitality, a renaissance).[8] We should not attempt to bring about a rebirth or renaissance of the University, but think its ruins as the sedimentation of historical differences that remind us that Thought cannot be present to itself. We live in an institution, and we live outside it. We work there, and we work with what we have at hand. The University is not going to save the world by making the world more true, nor is the world going to save the University by making the University more real. The question of the University is not that of how to achieve a stable or perfect relation between inside and outside, between the ivory tower and the streets. So, let us treat the University as we treat institutions. After all, I do not need to believe a story about Man (universal subject of history) creating power by taming nature and bending it to his will in order to switch on the light, nor does my incredulity mean that the light will go off. Nor does continuing to believe this story keep the light on if I cannot afford to pay my electricity bill. Enlightenment has its costs.

Although this may seem to make light of institutions, it actually involves a political recognition that institutions have a weight that exceeds the beliefs of their clientele. What I mean by dwelling in ruins is not despair or cynicism; it is simply the abandonment of the religious attitude toward political action, including the pious postponement or renunciation of action. Remember Leonard Cohen's dictum: "they sentenced me to twenty years of boredom, for trying to change the

8 It implies an institutional pragmatism, what Samuel Weber calls "deconstructive pragmatics." See *Institution and Interpretation* (Minneapolis: University of Minnesota Press, 1989), esp. ch, 2, "The Limits of Professionalism." Where Stanley Fish and Richard Rorty tend to celebrate the historical fact of institutional existence in their insistence on the status of actual practices, Weber sketches the contours of an argument against disciplinary autonomy and the concomitant ideology of professional mastery. He does so by recourse to Peirce's notion of "conditional possibility" in order to refuse the fixity of disciplinary boundaries. Such a transgression of disciplinary limits exposes the phobic exclusions upon which professional authority and competence are based. As Weber points out, "the modern university was the institutional means by which the professional claim to a monopoly of competence could be established and maintained" (32). Against this he proposes not a holistic refusal of abstraction and limit but a "deconstructive pragmatics" that "would work from the 'inside' of the various disciplines, in order to demonstrate concretely, in each case, how the exclusion of limits from the field organizes the practice it makes possible" (32), This seems to me an exemplary instance of the critique of institutions without recourse to alibis: neither the alibi of the perfect institution nor the alibi of the potential absence of all institutions.

system from within."[9] Change comes neither from within nor from without, but from the difficult space—neither inside nor outside—where one is. To say that we cannot redeem or rebuild the University is not to argue for powerlessness; it is to insist that academics must work without alibis, which is what the best of them have tended to do.

To return to my analogy of the Italian city, this means neither razing the old to build a rational city on a grid, nor believing that we can make the old city live again by returning to the lost origin. Structurally, each of these options presupposes that the city is not where we live, that we are somehow out in the suburbs, wondering what to do with uninhabited ruins. The city is where we dwell. The ruins are continuously inhabited, although they are also from another time whose functionality has been lost. Even if the University is legible to us only as the remains of the idea of culture, that does not mean that we have left its precincts, that we view it from the outside. The question that is raised by the analogy is how we can do something other than offer ourselves up for tourism: the humanities as cultural manicure, the social sciences as travelogue, the natural sciences as the frisson of real knowledge and large toys. If the process of consumerization seems more advanced in the humanities, this may only be a matter of a funding-induced perspective. How much does our vision of what science education achieves owe to Disney? Our idea of the natural sciences is already deeply structured by the mass media, through organizations such as NASA and the Epcot Center, in a way that makes the production of scientific knowledge deeply entrenched in the reproductive systems of mass culture.[10]

The cancellation of the Superconducting Super Collider suggests that the end of the Cold War does not simply have effects on the readiness of states to fund national competition in the realm of humanistic culture. Indeed, there is an increasing problem with what education in the natural sciences might consist of, what kind of subject it might be directed to. Information technology combines with the drying up of funds to suggest that there may no longer be an open market for graduate students educated in the pure sciences, while vocational engineering schools seem more adapted to the market. Hence, the question of to whom an education in physics or chemistry may be directed has no obvious answer. American physics departments in particular may have as much reason as the humanities to fear trial by "marginal utility" or "market forces" in funding battles, once there is no longer a quasi-inexhaustible defense budget. Incidentally, the highest percentage of post-graduate unemployment in Canada is not in the humanities but among

9 Leonard Cohen, "First We Take Manhattan," from I'm Your Man (CBS Records, 1988).

10 This is the sort of point that Andrew Ross makes in *Strange Weather* (London: Verso, 1991), although he rather exaggerates its delegitimating effect on scientific practices and norms.

physics majors. All of which suggests that the dualist split between humanities and natural sciences that has been the most apparent structural reality of the University in the twentieth century is no longer the practical certainty it once was. Not that it has ever really been so. English was initially perceived in the United States as a practical and businesslike alternative to the classics.[11] Of course, as Graff points out, the study of English literature was soon professionalized under the German model of *Geisteswissenschaht* as an autonomous field of research in order that its teaching might accede to the dignity of a "science," a field of knowledge.[12]

Earlier in this book, I dropped dark hints about the fate of departments of philosophy, which seem to be heading down the path already followed by classics, once the sumptuary laws that made a University without a strong philosophy department unthinkable have been dropped in favor of market imperatives. This may not be a bad thing, since it does not necessarily mean that a set of questions about the nature and limits of thinking, about the good life, etc., which were once asked under the heading of "philosophy," have ceased or will cease to be asked. It simply means that nothing in contemporary society makes it evident that individuals should be trained to ask such questions. Instead, philosophy departments are spinning off into applied fields in which experts provide *answers* rather than refining questions—medical ethics being the most obvious example, not least because the boom in medical ethics is the product of the interaction between biomedical technology and the economics of the U.S. medical insurance "system."

Instead, responsibility for questioning seems to have devolved onto literature departments insofar as those departments are themselves increasingly abandoning the research project of national literature. "English and Comparative Literature" tends to function in the United States as a catch-all term for a general humanities department and is likely for that reason to be gradually replaced by the less weighted title "Cultural Studies." It is worth thinking about why Cultural Studies should win out over the traditional designations of "History of Ideas" or "Intellectual History." This has to do both with their relationship with the existing research project of the history department and also with the extent to which the term "studies" acknowledges that the professionalization of the academy today is no longer structured by research into a central idea. To put this another way, as my argument in Chapter 7 has demonstrated, the idea of culture in Cultural Studies is not really an idea in the

---

11 See Gerald Graff, *Professing Literature* (Chicago: University of Chicago Press. 1987), pp. 19–36.

12 As Graff reminds us, "in literary studies, as everyone knows, the advance guard of professionalization was a German-trained cadre of scholarly 'investigators,' who promoted the idea of scientific research and the philological study of modern languages" (*Professing Literature*, p. 55).

strong sense proposed by the modern University. Cultural Studies, that is, does not propose culture as a regulatory ideal for research and teaching so much as recognize the inability of culture to function as such an idea any longer.

I am frankly not equipped to trace the parallel processes that may emerge in the natural sciences and social sciences, but the apparent horizon in arts and letters for the North American University can be roughly sketched as the development of an increasingly interdisciplinary general humanities department amid a cluster of vocational schools, which will themselves include devolved areas of expertise traditionally centered in the humanities, such as media and communications. Such vocational schools will tend to increase the social science component in traditionally humanistic fields of inquiry, a process in which the designation of Cultural Studies as a disciplinary endeavor that straddles the humanities (critique of aesthetic objects) and the social sciences (sociology, communications) will doubtless play a part. This is a historical irony, since such a prospect has striking similarities to the original plan of many land-grant universities, before most of them bought into the research University model as the way to acquire increased prestige and concomitant funding. Such a horizon of expectation is already being marketed to us under the slogan of the "Liberal Arts College within the University of Excellence." Needless to say, the liberal arts college is invoked here less in terms of its pedagogical tradition than in terms of its potential attraction to consumers.

Such is the role that the humanities are called upon to play in the University of Excellence, one that wavers between consumer service (the sense of individual attention for paying students) and cultural manicure. And the claims for scientific research in the humanities, for a *Geisteswissenschaft*, that have through the history of the modern University assured a dignity to the humanities, no longer find themselves reflected in and guaranteed by a guiding idea of culture for the University as a whole. Hence it is not the research model, I fear, that will save the humanities (or indeed the natural sciences), since the organization of the humanities as a field structured by a project of research no longer appears self-evident (with the decline of the nation-state as the instance that served as origin and telos for such organization). In a general economy of excellence, the practice of research is of value only as an exchange-value within the market; it no longer has intrinsic use-value for the nation-state.

The question remains of how Thought, in the sense in which I have described it in Chapter 10, may be addressed within the University. We should be clear about one thing: nothing in the nature of the institution will enshrine Thought or protect it from economic imperatives. Such a protection would actually be highly undesirable and damaging to Thought. But at the same time, thinking, if it is to remain open to the possibility of Thought, to take itself as a question, must not seek to be economic. It belongs rather to an economy of waste than to a restricted economy of calculation.[13] Thought is non-productive labor, and hence does not show up as such on balance sheets except as waste. The question posed to the University is thus not how to turn the institution into a haven for Thought but how to think in an institution whose development tends to make Thought more and more difficult, less and less necessary. If we are not to make the situation of the professor into an analogy for the waning power of the priesthood—faced by unbelief on the one hand and television evangelism on the other—this requires us to be very clear about our relation to the institution, to give up being priests altogether. In other words, the ruins of the University must not be, for students and professors, the ruins of a Greco-Roman temple within which we practice our rites as if oblivious to their role in animating tourist activities and lining the pockets of the unscrupulous administrators of the site.

In attempting to sketch how one might dwell in the ruins of the University without belief but with a commitment to Thought, I want to return to what I said about the problem of evaluation. The challenge that faces those who wish to preserve the task of thinking as a question is a difficult one that does not admit of easy answers. It is not a matter of coming to terms with the market, establishing a ratio of marginal utility that will provide a sanctuary. Such a policy will only produce the persistent shrinking of that sanctuary, as in the case of old-growth timber in the United States. How many philosophers, or redwoods, are required for purposes of museification? If the grand project of research and the minimal argument of species-preservation are likely to prove unsuccessful, it is necessary that our argument for certain practices of Thought and pedagogy measure up to the situation and accept that the existing disciplinary model of the humanities is on the road to extinction.

Within this context, a certain opportunism seems prescribed. To dwell in the ruins of the University is to try to do what we can, while leaving space for what we cannot envisage to emerge. For example, the argument has to be made to administrators that resources liberated by the opening up of disciplinary space, be it under the rubric of the humanities or of Cultural Studies, should be channelled into supporting short-term collaborative projects of both teaching and research (to speak in familiar terms) which would be disbanded after a certain period, whatever their success. I say "whatever their success" because of my belief that such collaborations have a certain half-life, after which they sink back into becoming quasi-departments with budgets to protect and little empires to build. Or to put it another way, they become modes of unthinking participation in institutional-bureaucratic life.

What I am calling for, then, is not a generalized interdisciplinary space but a certain rhythm of disciplinary attachment and detachment, which is designed so

13 See Georges Bataille, "La notion de dépense" in *La part maudite* (Paris: Minuit, 1949), for the origins of this distinction.

as not to let the question of disciplinarity disappear, sink into routine. Rather, disciplinary structures would be forced to answer to the name of Thought, to imagine what kinds of thinking they make possible, and what kinds of thinking they exclude. It is perhaps a lesson of structuralism that, when faced with a disciplinary project, a crucial way of situating that project is by considering what it is not, what it excludes. Thus a concentration in European philosophy, for example, would be obliged—by the nature of the interruptive pattern that I propose—to address both non-European philosophy and European non-philosophy.

The intellectual advantages of such an organizational structure reside in the fact that it can draw on the energy of the North American tendency toward "free electives," while detaching the terms of such choice from consumerism. The system of course-choice that Charles Eliot introduced at Harvard had two problems, both consequent upon making the student the sole locus of elective choice: it presumed a student capable of informed choice as to how to become informed, and it presumed that knowledge had an organic structure through which the student could navigate. Indeed, Eliot's opponents were quick to remark upon the need for a core curriculum or a distribution requirement, in order to limit student choice and to preserve the structure of knowledge from simple market conditions.[14] The result was a compromise, so that the tension between choice and distribution requirements has continued to agitate debates on curriculum in U.S. universities.

My argument is that the market structure of the posthistorical University makes the figure of the student as consumer more and more a reality, and that the disciplinary structure is cracking under the pressure of market imperatives. The means by which the question of the structure of knowledge can be preserved as a *question* in such a situation, the means by which knowledge can be something other than marketed information, are not the reassertion of a fixed disciplinary structure by dictatorial fiat. What makes the William Bennetts of this world so angry is that such a solution is no longer competitive. Hence I suggest that we make the market in courses a matter of Thought and discussion by situating it on the side of the faculty and administration, rather than by leaving it as solely a matter for student desire—which the faculty seeks to satisfy and the bureaucracy seeks to manage.

Thus I propose an abandonment of disciplinary grounding but an abandonment that retains as structurally essential the *question of the disciplinary form that can be given to knowledges*. This is why the University should not exchange the rigid and outmoded disciplines for a simply amorphous interdisciplinary space in the humanities (as if we could still organize knowledge around the figure of "Man").

---

14 See W. B. Carnochan, *The Battleground of the Curriculum: Liberal Education and American Experience* (Stanford: Stanford University Press, 1993), for a brief and illuminating account of this debate.

Rather, the loosening of disciplinary structures has to be made the opportunity for the installation of disciplinarity as a *permanent question*. The short-term projects I suggest are designed to keep open the question of what it means to group knowledges in certain ways, and what it has meant that they have been so grouped in the past. This keeps open the question of disciplinarity at the heart of any proposal for the grouping of knowledges in a constellation such as "Modern Art History" or "African-American Literature." Only by being constrained periodically to reinvent themselves can such groupings remain attentive to the terms of their production and reproduction. However, before we commit ourselves to loosening the disciplinary structures of the University, it would first be necessary to make some very firm deal about hiring prospects on the basis of an overall ratio of tenured faculty to students rather than, as now, on the rather specious basis of "disciplinary coverage." It is remarkable how few departments of English, for example, actually turned out to "need" so many medievalists.[15]

I have a certain diffidence about such plans as this, though, which always smack of bad utopianism, since there is no general model, no *the* University of the Future, merely a series of specific local circumstances. I supply these suggestions merely in the interest of attempting to find possibilities that work in the service of Thought in the current (and, I think, implacable) bourgeois economic revolution in the University. It is essential to understand that this is not a move of "big politics," not an attempt to divert the process toward another result, a different end. Rather, it seems to me, recognizing the University as ruined means abandoning such teleologies and attempting to make things happen within a system without claiming that such events are the true, real, meaning of the system. The system as a whole will probably remain inimical to Thought, but on the other hand, the process of dereferentialization is one that opens up new spaces and breaks down

---

15 My remarks about coverage are no slur to medievalists in particular. I think that the twilight of modernity makes the pre-modern a crucial site for understanding what a non-Enlightenment structure of thought might look like. My point is rather that the relative weakness of arguments for disciplinary coverage proceeds from the fact that such arguments presume the University to be primarily an ideological institution, when actually this is not the case. I will go further and say that my suggestion is a crucial means for preserving classical and medieval texts from the extinction that currently threatens them. I also do not have space here to get into an argument about tenure, so I merely presume its continuation in the short term. However, I think that the increasing proletarianization of the professoriat suggests that tenure may not *necessarily*—I italicize, to remind readers that I only wish to consider a possibility 'be the most effective defence of faculty interests in the future. Finally, note that the notion of faculty-student ratio is an economic rationale that I believe can be sold to administrators with potentially interesting results.

existing structures of defense against Thought, even as it seeks to submit Thought to the exclusive rule of exchange-value (like all bourgeois revolutions). Exploiting such possibilities is not a messianic task, and since such efforts are not structured by a redemptive metanarrative, they require of us the utmost vigilance, flexibility, and wit.

Given the prospect of such a generalized disciplinary regroupment, it seems to me necessary that we engage in a consideration of how the University might function as a place where a community of thinkers dwell, with the proviso that we rethink critically the notion of community, so as to detach it from both the organicist tradition and the feudal corporation. On this basis, it may become possible to provide some hints as to the kinds of institutional politics that might be pursued in order to transvalue the process of dereferentialization, to make the destruction of existing cultural forms by the encroachment of the open market into an opportunity for Thought rather than an occasion for denunciation or mourning.

Name Index

A

B

C

D

E

F

G

H

J

K

L

M

N

O

P

Q

R

S

T

U

V

W

Subject Index

A

B

C

D

E

V

W

Y

GLOBAL STUDIES IN EDUCATION

A.C. (Tina) Besley, Michael A. Peters,
Cameron McCarthy, Fazal Rizvi
General Editors

Global Studies in Education is a book series that addresses the implications of the powerful dynamics associated with globalization for re-conceptualizing educational theory, policy and practice. The general orientation of the series is interdisciplinary. It welcomes conceptual, empirical and critical studies that explore the dynamics of the rapidly changing global processes, connectivities and imagination, and how these are reshaping issues of knowledge creation and management and economic and political institutions, leading to new social identities and cultural formations associated with education.

We are particularly interested in manuscripts that offer: a) new theoretical, and methodological, approaches to the study of globalization and its impact on education; b) ethnographic case studies or textual/discourse based analyses that examine the cultural identity experiences of youth and educators inside and outside of educational institutions; c) studies of education policy processes that address the impact and operation of global agencies and networks; d) analyses of the nature and scope of transnational flows of capital, people and ideas and how these are affecting educational processes; e) studies of shifts in knowledge and media formations, and how these point to new conceptions of educational processes; f) exploration of global economic, social and educational inequalities and social movements promoting ethical renewal.

For additional information about this series or for the submission of manuscripts, please contact one of the series editors:

A.C. (Tina) Besley: t.besley@waikato.ac.nz
Cameron McCarthy: cmccart1@illinois.edu
Michael A. Peters: mpeters@waikato.ac.nz
Fazal Rizvi: frizvi@unimelb.edu.au

www.ingramcontent.com/pod-product-compliance
Ingram Content Group UK Ltd.
Pitfield, Milton Keynes, MK11 3LW, UK
UKHW021853100926
8556IPUK00020B/1211

9 781433 121906